THE THEOLOGY OF MARTIN LUTHER

THE THEOLOGY OF MARTIN LUTHER

A Critical Assessment

Hans-Martin Barth

Fortress Press

Minneapolis

THE THEOLOGY OF MARTIN LUTHER
A Critical Assessment

English translation copyright © 2013 Fortress Press. All rights reserved. Except for brief quotations in critical articles or reviews, no part of this book may be reproduced in any manner without prior written permission from the publisher. Visit http://www.augsburgfortress.org/copyrights or write to Permissions, Augsburg Fortress, Box 1209, Minneapolis, MN 55440.

First publication: *Die Theologie Martin Luthers. eine Kritische Würdigung*

Original copyright © 2009 Gütersloher Verlagshaus, Gütersloh, part of the Random House GmbH, Munich.

The translation of this work was supported by a grant from the Goethe-Institut which is funded by the German Ministry of Foreign Affairs.

Cover art: Luther Memorial, Germany. Copyright © imagebroker.net/SuperStock
Cover design: Laurie Ingram
Print ISBN: 978-0-8006-9875-1
eBook ISBN: 978-1-4514-2435-5

Library of Congress Cataloging-in-Publication Data
Barth, Hans-Martin.
[Theologie Martin Luthers. English]
The theology of Martin Luther / Hans-Martin Barth ; translated by Linda M. Maloney.
p. cm.
Includes bibliographical references (p.   ) and indexes.
ISBN 978-0-8006-9875-1 (alk. paper)
1. Luther, Martin, 1483-1546. 2. Theology, Doctrinal—History—16th century I. Title.
BR333.3.B3713 2013
230'.41092—dc23   2012022761

The paper used in this publication meets the minimum requirements of American National Standard for Information Sciences—Permanence of Paper for Printed Library Materials, ANSI Z329.48-1984.

The translation of this work was supported by a grant from the Goethe-Institut, which is funded by the German Ministry of Foreign Affairs.

Contents

Preface

According to Luther, theology should be about "the kernel of the nut, the interior of the wheat, the marrow in the bones." He wanted to find out what matters in life and death and to distinguish the essential from what is inessential or even hurtful. As regards his own time, he may well have been largely successful. But in the meantime half a millennium has passed, and the question arises whether from today's point of view he was able to separate the chaff from the wheat, whether he succeeded in getting to the marrow of the bones, and whether the heart of the nut he cracked is still tasty today and will continue to nourish in time to come.

It is nearly impossible to get a complete overview of the literature on Luther; his own works, in their various editions, represent a challenge to anyone studying them. Where is the core, the marrow, the innermost part of the wheat to be found? What is strong and nourishing here, what is digestible? There is need for a critical examination in view of a radically altered socio-cultural situation and the theological questions that require an answer today. The present book seeks to make its contribution in this context.

I myself am thus returning to my theological beginnings, though Luther has accompanied me throughout my entire life. I always especially enjoyed giving lectures on his theology in Marburg, and they were not devoid of laughter. At the end of a summer semester we got together to eat "Luther bread" I had brought from Wittenberg. Every lecture was introduced with a word from Luther, followed by a "minute of silence."

Having grown up in a Lutheran state church, I was later able to get to know worldwide Lutheranism, in Lutheran centers for theological study in Hungary, Japan, and India. I gave guest lectures on topics in Lutheran theology in Gettysburg, Pennsylvania, and in Saõ Leopoldo, Rio Grande do Sul. Ecumenical communication of Luther was the subject of lecture series at the Istituto di Studi Ecumenici, first in Verona and then in Venice and at the Waldensian seminary in Rome. I was even able to introduce Luther into the interreligious dialogue at the Buddhist Otani University in Kyoto. All this lent me a plethora of insights, experiences, and materials to which I can now have recourse. This book summarizes my decades of engagement with the Reformer, which became more and more critical over time.

My companion in study, Prof. Dr. Bernhard Brons of Nuremberg, reviewed the manuscript with great theological-historical and systematic-theological skill. Quite a few of his objections and comments would be worth a separate publication. I am grateful to my former doctoral student, Prof. Dr. Gernot Schulze-Wegener of Rauschenberg, for help in correcting the text and for a number of suggestions, and likewise—as with all my previous publications—to my wife, who in our many conversations about Luther has done great honor to her middle name, Käthe. Frau Inge Radparvar has again been brilliant in overcoming the technical problems of producing the manuscript. Diedrich Steen, lector and program director at Gütersloh, has earned my gratitude by his attention not only to overlooked typos but also to the appealing presentation and composition of the book. I regret that in this book once again I have not succeeded in making meaningful use of inclusive language.

Retired Landesbischof Prof. Dr. Gerhard Müller has read some of the chapters, and I am grateful to my Marburg colleague, Prof. Dr. Hans Schneider, for some helpful suggestions. Not all my conversation partners agreed with all my theses. Some of them pointed out that those who did not share my decisions would express criticism. Meanwhile, someone else has warned me that I should "not be too critical." The frame of reference for my critique has been my understanding of Christian faith as I expressed it in my work on dogmatics (in its third edition of 2008). Every reader will have to work out a further critical examination of Luther's theology for herself or himself. The numerous footnotes are primarily for specialists.

While I was working on my dissertation (on Luther) I made a reference card with a quotation from Luther that I had found by accident (WA 17/1, 81, 30-31): *Utut mecum sit, tamen Deus est Deus*: whatever may become of me, God is still God. For me, that is the "kernel of the nut."

Marburg, Reformation Day 2008
Hans-Martin Barth

PART I

Approach: Points of Entry and Difficulties of Access

1

Luther: Objectively and/or Subjectively

LUTHER AT FIRST GLANCE

In our part of the world Martin Luther is one of those historical entities everyone has heard about, but only a few people can say anything more precisely. That is certainly true for the bulk of our society; probably it is equally true of the situation within the churches themselves, at least the Lutheran church. In Catholic theology and the Catholic Church the Reformer is occasionally perceived as an authentic witness to Christian existence despite the remaining dogmatic reservations in his regard, but within our own ranks he is often approached with a certain bewilderment.

Evidently there are difficulties in gaining access to Luther, and also a certain suspicion that it might not be worthwhile. Important authors have played their part in spreading a negative cliché about the Reformer. In his famous Washington speech of 1945, Thomas Mann asserted that "Martin Luther, a gigantic incarnation of the German spirit, was exceptionally musical. I frankly confess that I do not love him. Germanism in its unalloyed state, the Separatist, Anti-Roman, Anti-European shocks me and frightens me, even when it appears in the guise of evangelical freedom and spiritual emancipation; and the specifically Lutheran, the choleric coarseness, the invective, the fuming and raging, the extravagant rudeness coupled with tender depth of feeling and with the most clumsy superstition and belief in incubi, and changelings, arouses my instinctive antipathy. I should not have liked to be Luther's dinner guest. . . ."[1]

Is Martin Luther really a medieval German lout who has no place in today's civilized Europe, with its absence of internal boundaries and its lively economic and intellectual exchanges? It could seem that way. Karl Barth, the Swiss theologian, found at the beginning of World War II that the German people suffered "from the heritage of a paganism that is mystical and that is in consequence unrestrained, unwise and illusory. And it suffers, too, from the heritage of the greatest Christian of Germany, from Martin Luther's error on the relation between Law and Gospel, between the temporal and the spiritual order and power. This error has established, confirmed and idealized the natural paganism of the German people, instead of limiting and restraining it. . . . Hitlerism is the present evil dream of the German pagan who first became Christianized in a Lutheran form. . . ."[2] Are these the words of the disappointed theologian and professor who experienced the beginnings of National Socialism and as a result lost his professorship, or is this an indictment of a genuinely false development in Protestant theology?

At the beginning of the twenty-first century negative judgments like those expressed by Thomas Mann or Karl Barth are scarcely comprehensible—for lack of a comparable state of knowledge. Luther has become an unknown. Even fifty years ago someone could speak about "fear of Luther."[3] Nowadays if there is any fear, it is fear about Luther: is he a disgrace to Protestantism? What remains true, in any case, is that he either attracts or repels those who occupy themselves with him. Anyone who takes him seriously must adopt a position; you can't just shrug your shoulders at Luther or you haven't really encountered him.

The uneasiness many feel toward the Reformer may also be rooted in the fact that he is so hard to classify. Obviously he is not a saint like Francis of Assisi, who is able to win the hearts even of modern people with his sympathetic naïveté; Francis is lovable, undemanding, not a figure subject to aesthetic or spiritual approval or disapproval! Just compare the cheerful atmosphere of Assisi, which today still manages to glow with the spirit of the Poverello, with the grey everydayness of the northern German provincial city of Wittenberg. The tourist business, no matter how hard it tries, can't make much business out of Luther! His life and work are connected with an atmosphere of struggle and resistance: "I was born to go to war and give battle to sects and devils and to fall in the field"; hence, he says, his books are stormy and bellicose. "I must root out the stumps and trunks, hew away the thorns and briars . . ."; he was the one, he said, who had to "pioneer and hew a path."[4] It is not always evident that a cheerful, ironic humor underlies such pithy words: "I eat like a Bohemian and drink like a German, thanks be to God for this. Amen."[5] In saying this Luther wanted to reassure his worried wife Katherine that he was really in good health. Often such boorish language is actually used for a theological purpose that can turn your stomach. Characteristic of Luther is "the decisive alternative, the exclusive either–or."[6] We will have to deal with that later. "There is no middle kingdom between the Kingdom of God and the kingdom of Satan."[7] Are these the words of a reflective theologian or of an incurable fundamentalist? Luther is not a saint, but he is also not a broad thinker like Thomas Aquinas or Descartes, who offered models for interpreting the world and mastering the problem of being that were subject to discussion. Why should we bother with him? The crisis of dealing with Luther in some sense reflects the crisis of

Protestantism: it is not a pious movement intended to improve the world through meditation and ascetic forms of life, nor is it a secular ideology providing ideological perspectives and advice for political action. There is no path from Reformation piety to esoterica, and the secular and secularizing elements of Protestantism do not gain it the sympathy of intellectuals, not anymore at least. Protestantism represents a "third way" whose dangers and opportunities become clear especially in dealing with Luther.

Objective Observations

In the public imagination Luther stands behind a portentous development in Western history that probably would have happened without him but is ineradicably connected with his name: the division of Christianity, the collapse of the unity of a socio-economically shaped culture and religious determination of meaning, pluralism, individualization, the rise of a modernity whose blessings appear highly dubious to us today. Certainly 1517 by no means marked the first division within Christianity; in the year 1054 the Latin church had separated from the East, and the paths between Chalcedonian and non-Chalcedonian Christianity had already diverged as a result of the Council of Chalcedon in 451. There never was a unity of the church like that dreamed of by romantic ecumenists today; we only need to think of the abundance of competing and mutually combative movements in the ancient church or the multiple voices in the New Testament. Nevertheless, Luther's name is connected to the awareness that the unity of Europe is broken. Even if one should be inclined to minimize his role in this development, there remains the notion that (though without really intending it) he "founded" a Christian confession. He is thus regarded as the instigator of a confessionalism we today find offensive and in need of overcoming, involved and involving itself in political entanglements. Even within Protestantism itself it was difficult for a long time to convey that the Protestant church did not have its beginning in 1517, but in the New Testament! Likewise, the political position of the Reformer is designated, with very little regard for subtlety, in terms of the labels "Peasants' War" and "servant of princes."

It is true that Luther's statements on the Jews are a horrible strain. Julius Streicher, the Gauleiter of Franken and one of the worst anti-Semites of the Third Reich, said during the Nuremberg trials that if Luther were alive he would be taking Streicher's place in the dock. Hans Asmussen asked in 1947: "Does Luther have to go to Nuremberg?"[8] Of course, none of the anti-Semitic Nazis read Luther to find out how to behave toward the Jews. To that extent we can only speak in a very indirect sense of the influence of Luther's anti-Jewish sayings in history. But it is bad enough that anti-Semites could appeal to applicable sayings of Luther at a time when he was still regarded as an authority in Germany!

All the difficulties we have listed as standing in the way of a positive relationship to Luther probably weigh little in face of the fact that no self-reflective person focused on his or her own self-realization is able to be fully open to the fundamental concern of Luther's theology: the idea of the grace of God as the basis of all things and controlling all things. The eschatological horizon that was taken for granted by Luther and most of his contemporaries, which oppressed them on the one hand and consoled them on the other, has vanished. What we regard as important is not what may happen after death but what happens before it. The idea of a last judgment, hell, and eternal damnation seems medieval and passé. What we are looking for is help with living, not "forgiveness of sins." "That free will is nothing" (from the German translation of Luther's *De servo arbitrio*), that human fate could itself be "nothingness," is an idea those unconcerned with religion as well as our ecclesially socialized contemporaries set entirely aside, and yet in fact it calls for discussion.

SUBJECTIVE EXPERIENCES

What might still make us want to concern ourselves with Luther? Why is it that he has repeatedly accompanied people throughout their lives, in person so to speak, and that even I have wrestled with his thought for decades and am now writing a book about him? Luther's theology, and still more intensely Luther's faith, were impressed on me as things that would strengthen and deepen my own faith, and for that reason I seem to have a need to communicate both to others. Occupying myself with Luther has always somehow done me good. I have been increasingly disturbed by the detritus that has to be removed in order to get to the source, and yet I constantly find it is worth it.

I probably met Luther first in my father's study. A reproduction of the famous painting by Lucas Cranach, showing Luther in the pulpit of the church at Wittenberg, hung there: in the center the crucifix, on one side Luther in the pulpit with his arm outstretched and pointing to Christ, and on the other side the sermon's audience. Luther was certainly not the primary subject, but he was part of it. As a university student in my fourth semester I heard Paul Althaus's lectures on Luther's theology that became his book on the subject.[9] That was the only lecture series I carefully studied during my university years. I went to the library and looked up the passages in the Weimar edition of Luther's works that Althaus had cited. That gave me not only intellectual but in a sense physical contact with Luther's works. Besides that, it was during these years that I met someone who, as I sensed, lived wholly in the spirit of Lutheran devotion: the elderly Frankish dean, Friedrich

Graf, in Thalmässing. Luther's Small Catechism was his book of devotions; every day, from Monday to Saturday, he meditated on one of the major parts, from the Ten Commandments to the "Table of Duties." He took Sundays off because on those days he preached. I was uncomfortable when he asked me about particular passages in the catechism and saw that I did not know them correctly. But I know he didn't want to expose me; he wanted to call my attention to something that for him was the bread and elixir of life. In the end he gave me the hundred-volume Erlangen edition of Luther with commentary, which he greatly preferred to the Weimar edition because one could take its handy little volumes to bed, something that was impossible with the mighty Weimar volumes. His love for Luther was probably the impulse that caused me ultimately to write my dissertation on Luther's theology.[10] I would criticize that book in many respects today, for at that time I did not possess sufficient distance from the subject. That has changed. I find Luther's statements about the Jews simply unbearable, in spite of all the well-known theological and historical attempts at explanation. Luther's views on women and their roles in the church, as progressive as they may have been at the time, are obviously altogether inadequate today. But above all the utter fixation on sin and forgiveness, the radical Christocentrism that in Luther's time had a legitimate and necessary function, today represents a reductionism that must be reintegrated in the whole of trinitarian faith; that is something I learned in the course of my ecumenical work.[11] I have discovered yet another new context through my encounter with the world religions, and yet there also Martin Luther remained for me a guiding presence and source of orientation.[12]

In most depictions of Luther the Reformation is presented as a great theological conflict, a struggle for the truth that was about life and death. That, of course, is not wrong. But I would like to put the accent somewhere else. In my view the Reformation was primarily a pastoral movement. The struggle was not about correctness but about the truth that makes free and sustains freedom. Hence Luther's theology has to be presented, considered, critiqued, and communicated from a pastoral-therapeutic perspective.

Anyone who has worked with Luther's theology has entered into the innermost heart of Christian faith. Much of what the Reformer has to say is "edifying" in the best sense of the word. It is an impulse to spiritual growth and an aid in personal crises. In that sense, for example, Luther's writings belong not on the desk but on the nightstand. Those who occupy themselves with Luther arrive unexpectedly at the center of the Christian church and have no chance of busying themselves in the niche of a "Lutheran sect." In Luther we encounter a person who had no fear for the church and therefore was ready to criticize it radically. Luther knew that "we are not the ones who can preserve the church, nor were our forefathers able to do so. Nor will our successors have this power. No, it was, is, and will be he who says, 'I am with you always, to the close of the age.'"[13] Luther would not bother to conduct constant polling and study the affinity profiles of the church members, as the Lutheran Church in Germany has, in its anxiety, repeatedly attempted. Nor was Luther satisfied with the results of the Reformation he had set in motion. But he knew that he had to surrender himself to God's project. "God's word and grace" was, in his experience, "a passing shower of rain which does not return where it has once been."[14] The Reformer was realistic in his view of the church without being gloomy.

Those who occupy themselves with Luther get to the center of Christian theology. From here one can understand and unlock the whole; here, as in a kaleidoscope, the most important problems are brought together. Erwin Mülhaupt has written a book called *Predigten mit Luthers Hilfe*;[15] I can also imagine a book called *Dogmatik mit Luthers Hilfe*.[16] Anyone who has understood Luther has, at any rate, "broken through" to a place, has found a lead by which to orient herself or himself in life. Certainly the crucial break in European intellectual history was completed not with the Renaissance and Reformation, but in the Enlightenment. This naturally raises the question of the extent to which Luther's theology can still be relevant to modern Protestantism, which is clearly shaped by that rupture. One can critique Luther from the point of view of modern Protestantism, but in turn one can also put modern Protestantism under a critical microscope from Luther's point of view. Both procedures make sense, and they are mutually productive.

But in spite of every precaution, any author who presents a version of "Luther's theology" is also in some way presenting "his" or "her" Luther.[17] Love for Luther may excuse this in individual cases. Still, there are enough different interpretations of Luther to make a mutual questioning and correction possible.

NOTES

[1] Quoted from Glaser/Stahl 1983, 286. English: Don Heinrich Tolzmann, ed., *Thomas Mann's Addresses Delivered at the Library of Congress, 1942–1949* (Oxford and New York: Peter Lang, 2003), "Germany and the Germans," 45–66, at 52.

[2] Quoted from Glaser/Stahl 1983, 262–63. Cf. Gerhard Ebeling, "Über die Reformation hinaus? Zur Luther-Kritik Karl Barths," 33–75 in Joachim Heubach, ed., *Luther und Barth* (Erlangen: Martin-Luther-Verlag, 1989). English: Karl Barth, *A Letter to Great Britain from Switzerland* (London: The Sheldon Press, 1941), 36–37, as cited in Charles E. Ford, "Dietrich Bonhoeffer, the Resistance, and the Two Kingdoms," *Lutheran Forum Reformation* (1993): 28–34.

[3] Kurt Ihlenfeld, *Angst vor Luther?* (Witten and Berlin: Eckart-Verlag, 1967).

[4] WA 30/2, 68, 12-16; cf. WA 30/2, 650, 16-17. Published English translations vary.

[5] Martin Luther to his wife Katherine, 2 July 1540, LW 50, 208 (WA.Br 9, 168, 5-6).

[6] Jörg Baur, "Extreme Theologie," in idem, *Luther und seine klassischen Erben* (Tübingen: Mohr [Siebeck], 1993), 8.

[7] LW 33, 227 (WA 18, 743, 33-34).

[8] Quoted in Glaser/Stahl 1983, 8.

[9] Althaus 1962 (1981).

[10] Barth, Hans-Martin 1967a.

[11] Cf. Hans-Martin Barth, *Begegnung wagen—Gemeinschaft suchen* (Göttingen: Vandenhoeck & Ruprecht, 2000).

[12] Barth, Hans-Martin 2008a.

[13] LW 47, 118 (WA 50, 476, 31-35).

[14] LW 45, 352 (WA 15, 32, 7-8).

[15] Erwin Mülhaupt, *Evangelisch leben! Predigten mit Luthers Hilfe* (Göttingen: Vandenhoeck & Ruprecht, 1958).

[16] Respectively (and somewhat loosely) "Luther Helps you Preach" and "Luther Helps you with Dogmatics."—Trans.

[17] Cf. Nikos Kazantzakis, *God's Pauper: St. Francis of Assisi: A Novel*, trans. P. A. Bien (London and Boston: Faber & Faber, 1975).

2

Methodological Problems

How should we present Luther's theology? There are essentially two possible approaches: historical-genetic or systematic-theological. But we need to clarify the guiding perspective we are following and at what point its flagrant theological falsities should be treated.

HISTORICAL-GENETIC PRESENTATION

In attempting a historical-genetic presentation one will first try to clarify the preconditions for Luther's theology: his psychological problems with his parents, late medieval piety, scholastic theology with its two currents, the Thomistic-oriented *via antiqua* and the *via moderna* derived from Duns Scotus and William of Ockham, principal currents in Augustinian theology,[1] humanism, and the new technological opportunities such as printing and leaflets.

Then it will be necessary to trace the development of Luther's theology. The first question to arise will be when the reforming shift should be seen to begin, as early as 1514 or only in 1518; probably this represents a process of maturation. One must then make clear how Luther's theology acquired specific accents in the course of its various confrontations: with Rome, with the enthusiasts, in the Peasants' War, and ultimately in the consolidation phase of the Reformation churches.[2] Did Luther experience a midlife crisis (1527/1528)? Was there for him some sort of aging crisis, senility, eleventh-hour panic? What about the relationship between the "young" and the "old" Luther? If we assume this kind of contrast, when was the transition phase or turning point? It is striking how comparatively little interest scholars have evinced in the aged Luther.[3]

Finally one should ask about what in Luther's theology survived and whether there are revocations, self-corrections, and self-critique in his work. One could also start at the end of Luther's development and look back from there to the beginnings.

Systematic-Theological Presentation

Luther did not compose a major systematic-theological work like Calvin's *Institutes*. Melancthon's *Loci communes*, which is regarded as the first work of Lutheran dogmatics, is no substitute. Luther was an occasional author whose writings were evoked by particular situations. This confronts us with the question whether it is even possible to present Luther in systematic-theological terms.[4] Whoever attempts such a thing must take care not to clothe Luther's thought with her or his own system and possibly make use of Luther to legitimate his or her own opinion. In some sense this accusation applies, among others, to Paul Althaus's version of Luther.[5]

How might we organize the work? Without adopting the outlines of classical dogmatics in detail we could consider the structure of Luther's theology in terms of the three articles of the creed. But that would scarcely give expression to the specific profile of Luther's theology. Albrecht Peters attempted to develop Luther's theology in terms of the principal articles of the catechism.[6] While that is very revealing in detail, it does not offer a clear overview. Finally, we could consider commenting on a basic writing such as *De servo arbitrio* or the Smalcald Articles. Gerhard Ebeling developed a comprehensive Lutheran theology by examining and commenting on the theses of the 1536 *Disputatio de homine*.[7]

However, the particular profile of Luther's theology appears in the fact that he thinks on the one hand in alternatives and on the other in complementarities. Philosophy is contrasted with theology, human or church tradition with the word of God, a theology of self-determination and self-development with the theology of the cross: these are some of the alternatives. Complementary, though not symmetrical, are Law and Gospel, God's rule with the "right" and "left" hands, action and contemplation, God in hiddenness and revealedness— or is this last a contradictory opposition? Positions are developed against negations, and therefore from time to time positive and negative correspond. Luther's theology moves between *assertio* and *damnatio*, between Yes and No!

If we link the leading concepts in Luther's theology with "and"—"Law and Gospel," "both justified and sinner"—we must from time to time attempt to convey the specific content of this "and." That may be difficult in some cases, but it is the best way to make clear the dynamics of Luther's theology in its clarity and its complexity.

The present book attempts to make this dynamic clear in the individual chapter titles. To avoid the impression that the Reformer fell victim to a dualistic principle throughout his work we will begin each chapter with a key concept, followed by the alternatives and complementarities, in order to indicate the particular character of the individual polarities. While the confrontation between theology and philosophy, scripture and tradition, true and false church is a matter of conflict, rivalry, and struggle, the relationship between Law and Gospel, freedom and righteousness, word and sacrament is one of tension, dialectic, and genuine complementarity. Again, speaking of God in divine hiddenness and revealedness, of human existence in sin and righteousness, and of the two divine governments is a matter of breakthrough, identity, and division of labor. In turn, action and contemplation in daily life, as well as time and eternity in God's salvific and integrative action, exist together without tension.

How should Luther's theology be located and evaluated today? I see it as a stage in the history of Christianity at which the message of human justification was more deeply grasped than ever before. Luther's comprehensive conception of faith reveals anew the dignity of the human being and at the same time motivates and liberates to the acceptance of responsibility. Finally, the model of church emerging from his initiative, namely one of mutuality, community, and freedom grounded in the Gospel, has never yet been realized in the Lutheran churches. Luther's theology acts, without making headlines, as yeast for all Christianity. I also regard the Reformer's theological approach as supportive in the midst of the present social and cultural chaos. The more opaque the situation, the more depends on the spiritual groundedness of one's own existence. The fundamental idea of conciliarity, derived from the thesis of the universal, mutual, and common priesthood of the faithful, is the only conceivable model for the future church and for society as well. In that sense some basic ideas in Luther's theology may still have their greatest impact in the future, even though not in institutional form.

THE PLACE OF THEOLOGICAL MISJUDGMENTS

In many accounts of Luther's theology the Reformer's wrong judgments are given no place, or at any rate not an adequate one. The matter of witchcraft, which had a shocking subsequent history especially in regions that were confessionally attached to the Reformation, is usually left out. Jörg Haustein's monograph on the subject was simply ignored.[8] The problem of the Turks is not discussed at all in the comprehensive works or, if it is mentioned, it is considered within its historical circumstances and is not regarded as a systematic-theological theme.[9] Luther's dreadful statements about the Jews are dismissed in a few sentences. Here, in any event, "little can be explained, scarcely anything understood, and nothing excused."[10] In Bernhard Lohse's theology of Luther the attitude of the Reformer toward the Jews appears as an excursus at the end of the book.[11] The effect is to compromise everything that has been said before about Luther's theological achievement, for the question of course arises whether Luther's writings on the Jews were a theological deviation or whether these inexcusable attacks do not disqualify Luther's theological approach altogether.

The problem of the Turks and the Jews is frequently treated in connection with Luther's eschatology, but the texts themselves show that this is too narrow. We must pursue the question of how Luther's statements on these topics relate to his theology of justification, the cross, and faith. Since the writings on the Jews in particular, but also those against the Turks, and ultimately also belief in the devil and witches are a severe burden on Luther's theology from our contemporary perspective, these murky points will be treated at the beginning of the present book. The subsequent presentation will then have to show whether Luther's theology can stand in the face of these objections raised at the outset.

QUESTIONS AND GUIDING PERSPECTIVES

The works on Luther's theology currently on the market make an effort to clarify the historical situation and to understand Luther within that system. They find support in a multitude of special studies.[12] Gerhard Ebeling's acute analysis has set some standards for this. His concern was "to liberate Luther and his work in multiple ways from the alienations of the history of his influence, e.g., those of national, confessional, Enlightenment, and political images of Luther."[13] The *Luther Handbuch* (2005) attempts to offer an overview and to bring together the results of previous research; no guiding perspective can be discerned. The internal Protestant quarrel over Luther was shaped in particular by Karl Barth's invective against the Reformer. Catholic research on Luther, which seems to have slackened in recent years, had its own questions and was sometimes aimed at "bringing Luther back home."[14] Orthodox voices are beginning to be heard, but they are few in number and cautious in their opinions.[15] The issue for Marxist interpretation was, in any event, not a more acute understanding of Luther's theology.

Is there such a thing as a central question, a guiding theme in Luther's theology? It is a popular assumption that Luther's primary concern was with the question: "How can I find a gracious God?" In this light Luther's theology appears to be psychologically conditioned, oriented to an egoistic notion of salvation that is no longer conceivable today, and thus completely out of date. Theodosius Harnack placed the doctrine of reconciliation and redemption at the center of his presentation of Luther. In the context of liberal Protestant theology in the second half of the nineteenth century, that was a courageous and demanding task. The American Methodist theologian Philipp S. Watson sees Luther's theology from the point of view "let God be God!" and views the Reformer as having been concerned with God's divinity. It is certainly just as appropriate to begin with Luther's "theologia crucis" (Walther von Loewenich, differently also Klaus Schwarzwäller) or to make the "victory of faith" the guiding thread (Lennart Pinomaa). Gerhard Ebeling understands Luther's theology as a "language event" resulting from a hermeneutics of the word of God and likewise aiming toward such a hermeneutics.

In my view Luther's theology points toward something that is twofold and at the same time singular, namely the glory of God and the salvation of human beings. According to Luther, evangelical doctrine is "directed to God's glory and human salvation," something that, however, as Luther bitterly avows, does not interest people.[16] The glory of God consists in this: that God is our benefactor.[17] Here Luther is connecting with a guiding thread from the ancient church as expressed by Irenaeus of Lyons in his phrase "gloria Dei vivens homo"—"the glory of God is the human being fully alive."[18] It is not that every individual theme in Luther's theology can be derived from this phrase, but it does constitute a scarlet thread throughout his altogether pastoral theology. It is in service of liberation from sin, death, and the devil and is meant to encourage toward life, action, and the joy of living: "ubi Christus, ibi gaudium est."[19] The Reformation was a pastoral movement!

Luther's works still serve as a treasure trove of "lovely" citations. Paul Althaus, and also Oswald Bayer, may have had an unspoken desire to make them available and not allow them to become things of the past. But that is by no means enough any more. It is no longer adequate to place oneself, in thought and language, within the sixteenth century and there rejoice in Luther's pithy expressions. The Enlightenment, the technological revolution, and globalization have all too obviously inserted themselves between Luther and the people of today. It is therefore striking that—apart from some confessional shadow-boxing—there has still never been a real theological confrontation with Luther. Walther von Loewenich was probably the last to warn impressively against treating Luther uncritically. The challenges he articulated in his broadly conceived work, *Luther und der Neuprotestantismus*,[20] have by no means been laid to rest. It is also inadequate to do theology "as a follower of Luther" without really confronting him in the first place.[21] Whereas the concern of Luther scholarship in the twentieth century was to liberate Luther from the encrustations acquired in the history of his influence and to arrive at the genuine Luther of the sixteenth century, the task of today's work on Luther must be to bring the Reformer into contact with the present confessional, religious, and cultural situation.[22] That is impossible apart from the critical question of what in Luther's thought can still be usable, still be acceptable, and where theology, even a theology consciously rooted in Luther, must distance or even separate itself from him. It is a matter of questioning the "quasi-normative authority accorded [Luther] in Protestantism, for which we can scarcely name any comparable parallels in other Christian confessions,"[23] and possibly of rejecting it. For that reason the individual chapters in this book will be framed, at the beginning by an attempt at placing the particular problem complex in the context of current theological discussion, and at the end by a critical evaluation. The questions posed at the beginning may arouse curiosity about how Luther attacked the problem complex at issue. In the course of the exposition of his views, however, other questions may emerge. The critical evaluation will look back again at Luther from the perspective of current perceptions and test those places where his position can be defended and where it must be corrected or augmented.

NOTES

[1] Cf. Hamm 1982. Recently Johann von Staupitz has emerged more prominently in research; on him see Berndt Hamm, "Johann von Staupitz (ca. 1468–1524)—spätmittelalterlicher Reformer und 'Vater' der Reformation," *ARG* 92 (2001): 6–42, and Leppin 2006, esp. 72–76; 78–88; 97–100.

[2] On this see especially Leppin 2006, who sees the Reformer as moving more and more toward the margins of the Reformation process after 1525.

[3] But cf. Junghans 1983.

[4] Cf. Lohse 1995; Bayer 2003; Korsch 2007 (2006); Suda 2006.

[5] Compare Paul Althaus, *Die christliche Wahrheit. Lehrbuch der Dogmatik* (Gütersloh: Mohn, 51957) with Althaus 1962.

[6] Peters 1990, 1991, 1992, 1993, 1994.

[7] Ebeling 1989.

[8] Haustein 1990. It is not even mentioned in the Luther Handbook edited by Albrecht Beutel (*Handbuch* 2005).

[9] Cf. Lohse 1995, 355.

[10] Bayer 2003, 303. Bayer devotes three lines to this problem on p. 4 and ten lines on p. 303.

[11] Lohse 1995, 356–67.

[12] Cf. the annual Luther bibliography in the *Lutherjahrbuch*!

[13] Karl-Heinz zur Mühlen, in *Handbuch* 2005, 483.

[14] Cf. Jos E. Vercruysse, "Luther in der römisch-katholischen Theologie und Kirche," *LuJ* 63 (1996): 103–28.

[15] Cf., e.g., *Luther et la Réforme Allemande dans une Perspective oecumenique*. Les Études Théologiques de Chambésy 3 (Chambésy: Editions du Centre orthodoxe du Patriarcat oecuménique, 1983), as well as Marios Begzos, "Luther im Licht der Orthodoxen Theologie," *EEΘΣΠΑ (EETHSPA)* 37 (2002): 467–79.

[16] WA 47, 483, 22: ". . . doctrina nunc ist gerichtet ad gloriam Dei et salutem hominum."

[17] LW 25, 516 (WA 56, 520, 20): ". . . gloria eius est, Quod beneficus in nos est."

[18] *Adv. Haer.* IV, 7. Quite appropriately, in Luther's sense, the *Protestatio* of the evangelical Estates in Speyer formulates: this is about "matters touching God's glory and the salvation and beatitude of our souls. . . ." Quoted from Bayer 2003, 301.

[19] WA 20, 365, 13-14: "where Christ is, there is joy."

[20] von Loewenich 1963.

[21] Cf. Dietrich Korsch, *Dogmatik im Grundriss. Eine Einführung in die christliche Deutung menschlichen Lebens mit Gott* (Tübingen: Mohr Siebeck, 2000), 5–6; but cf. Korsch 2007!

[22] Korsch 2007, 4, wants to see his interpretation understood as a "touchstone for the possibility of a productive relating of Protestantism to the current culture of conflict."

[23] Kaufmann 2005, 484.

3

Entry Points

We can imagine the widest variety of points of entry into Luther's theology: by way of biography, the history of influence, the various interpretations of Luther, the attempt to locate Luther within the history of theology, and finally even by way of a reflection on Luther's philosophical abilities. All these approaches have their specific advantages and disadvantages.

LUTHER'S BIOGRAPHY

If anyone wants to get acquainted with a difficult intellectual *oeuvre*, an approach by way of the author's biography has much to recommend it. Especially in the context of Christian faith, theology and biography should have a lot to do with one another. In many cases the correspondence is impressive and revealing: consider Dietrich Bonhoeffer or Karl Barth, but equally Augustine or Paul. It is true that this approach remains ambivalent: looking at biography can also obscure a theological approach or muffle a theological statement; in any case it remains subordinate to the analysis of a theoretical approach. Truth is incarnate in biography but also transcends it. This basic consideration alone can give a preacher the courage to enter the pulpit. The Reformation is not founded on Luther's biography! This is not the place to go into detail,[1] but we may be permitted a few remarks:

We can turn to Luther's image and ask: what does this face say? New portraits emerged again and again in the course of Luther's life: in 1520 the ascetic monk, in 1521 the innocent Junker Jörg, in 1523 the scholar with the doctor's hat surrounded by a halo, and finally the elderly Luther, portly and wearing a fur collar. How do these pictures relate to his writings?

We can leaf through Luther's table talk and letters. In contrast to Thomas Mann, I would very much like to have been Luther's dinner guest. I am not surprised that in the course of years a good deal of this table talk was written down and ultimately published. It conveys a vivid portrait of the Reformer, who was less discreet in weighing his words at home than he was in his public appearances.[2]

An approach to Luther through his letters also recommends itself, especially the last letters to his wife, the "dear wife, Katherine von Bora, preacher, brewer, gardener, and whatsoever else she may be."[3] It makes sense, of course, to look for theologically oriented biographies of the Reformer, that is, depictions that attempt to blend biographical and theological development.[4] In the process one may encounter psychological discussions: what was Luther's relationship to his parents? Is his concept of God explained by a father-complex? How should we interpret his anxiety neuroses and depressions? Was Luther's theology the "ideological systematizing of the emotions" of a man subject to melancholy?[5] Is it the result of an identity crisis that did not reach a proper resolution?[6] Quite certainly the basic forms of a theology have to do with the "basic forms of fear" in the one who proposes it. The fundamental connections are undeniable. No faith and no theology comes to be without psychological implications. The question, of course, is whether it remains mired in fixations or arrives at a fruitful crisis, whether there are indications of irreversible destructive movements or signs of an intellectual and spiritual process of growth. The psychological approach, in isolation at least, can offer only limited progress toward the goal. At the same time, the psychological approach is helpful when inquiring about the present-day relevance of Luther's individual theological statements.

Another possible way of approaching Luther's theology by way of his biography would be to search for his understanding of himself.[7] How did he see himself; what was his estimation of himself? Apparently he experienced his mission as a task given him by God. He calls himself "the prophet of the Germans."[8] But he also asks himself: "Do you suppose that all previous teachers were ignorant? Are our forefathers all fools in your eyes? Are you the one latter-day nest egg of the Holy Spirit?"[9] He had to deal with the fact that people took him as their reference, but he finds that they "believe not in Luther but in Christ himself. The word has them, and they have the word. They pay no heed to Luther, whether he be a knave or a saint. God can speak through Balaam as well as Isaiah, through Caiaphas as well as through Peter, yes, even through an ass. I subscribe to their opinion. I myself do not know Luther either, nor do I want to know him, nor do I preach anything about him, but about Christ."[10] I myself do not know Luther: try plugging your own name in there if you want to be clear about what that statement means!

HISTORY OF INFLUENCE

Access to Luther's theology by way of the history of its influence is difficult to the extent that it has been variously interpreted and evaluated depending on one's standpoint: compare only the evaluation of Luther in the former German Democratic Republic with that in the Federal Republic; it is also different in western and southern Europe from what it is in Germany. It is true that many Protestant churches throughout the world celebrate Reformation Day and sing "A Mighty Fortress" in translation, but in the Protestant world (numbering about 380 million members in 2008) Luther has a much lower standing than the Lutheran churches (some 60 million members) imagine. Besides, the history of influence is hard to grasp and to judge according to well-defined criteria.

Of course, it is easiest to perceive the effects of Luther's theology in the spheres of church history and the history of theology, but the consequences in the politico-social sphere should not be overlooked either. His understanding of the universal, mutual, and common priesthood of the faithful is unquestionably part of the early history of modern democracy. His active engagement on behalf of schools and education as well as for an organized diaconal service was not without consequences. His new valuing of one's work or profession as a "calling" contributed, over the centuries, to an understanding of professional work as not primarily a job in which one engages in order to support oneself, but as fulfillment. In view of the current situation of the labor market, however, and the demands for mobility and flexibility, here also new theological paths must be opened. In the realm of intellectual history Luther's significance for the German language and respect for the word in general can scarcely be overestimated.[11] In the field of music as well, especially church music, Luther has left his traces. The Lutheran hymnal contains more than thirty songs that are traced to him in whole or in part, in text and/or melody: new versions of psalms, hymns, liturgical pieces, and free poetic compositions.

Here let me add a few of the more technical difficulties that impede a further history of influence. Essential parts of Luther's *oeuvre* are in Latin, and a knowledge of Latin is something almost no one possesses any longer. But even "Luther-German" presents a problem today: what was once noted as a strength of the Reformer, his way of working with language, now appears as a handicap, as evidenced even in reactions to the revised Luther Bible. The ability to read early modern high German texts in the original must be deliberately revived and practiced. Apart from that, however, the world of language itself has changed; Luther's images and comparisons no longer have the same impact they once did. The agrarian-patriarchal culture of a small provincial Saxon town with, at the time, about two thousand inhabitants is most certainly not our own. Luther is hard to take! While he could still be regarded as "modern" in the nineteenth century, he appears today as "premodern" or even "anti-modern." We will have to see how and to what extent he could come to be regarded as "postmodern."[12]

Luther's theology cannot be understood solely in terms of the history of its influence, but that history does place it in a critical light. We certainly cannot make Luther responsible for everything that came of the Reformation. Nevertheless, we must examine the connections that may be there.

INTERPRETATIONS OF LUTHER

INTERPRETATIONS WITHIN PROTESTANTISM

In the course of time, socio-cultural developments, and trends in fashion, interpretations of Luther have obviously changed as well, though in every age they depend on the particular point of view. Within Protestantism people have repeatedly appealed to Luther to legitimate themselves, support their own opinions, or advance them as critique of others. For Lutheran orthodoxy, Luther represented the guarantee of correct teaching: "God's word and Luther's teaching will never fade away or vanish!" But there was serious theological inquiry about Luther's place in salvation history. Orthodox dogmatics was familiar with a piece on Luther's calling: "De vocatione beati Lutheri."[13] Reference was made to the "angel" in Revelation (Rev 14:6) "with an eternal gospel to proclaim to those who live on the earth—to every nation and tribe and language and people." Sermons on this text were common on Reformation Sunday. A song composed in southern Germany (but no longer included in the Lutheran hymnal) rejoiced that "out of midnight came an evangelical man who took up the Scriptures, let human teaching fail and revealed the plans of God's word; salvation illumines us all and none can turn it aside."[14] This was written during Luther's own lifetime.

Pietism was ambivalent with regard to Luther: on the one hand he was seen as an example of an enlightened human being, on the other as a reformer whose work still required completion. Philipp Jakob Spener, in his reforming program "Pia desideria" and in his writings on the spiritual priesthood, referred specifically to Luther; Gottfried Arnold, in contrast, turned Luther's critique of Rome against the Lutheran church of his own time. For him Luther was by no means an unassailable authority. At least since the rise of Pietism there has been no fixed interpretation of Luther even within Lutheranism.

The Enlightenment exalted Luther as one who prepared the way for reason and freedom of conscience, someone who led humanity out of the Middle Ages! But some Enlightenment figures desired to continue Luther's work. Frederick the Great found that in any case the secularization of church property had done good things for the public treasury. Only with the beginnings of research on Luther in the nineteenth century came the first efforts at an objective picture of Luther's person and theology. Of course, an essential precondition for that was the work, beginning in 1883, on a critical edition of Luther's works, the "Weimarana." Theodosius Harnack made the first major attempt to understand the uniqueness of Luther's theology in a two-volume work in which he developed the tension between Law and Gospel and recalled Luther's words about the hidden God, something that until that time had been almost forgotten.[15]

The so-called "Luther Renaissance," which tried to understand Luther's theology apart from its embeddedness in the history of theology, is associated with the name of Karl Holl. Holl himself interpreted Luther's faith with a strongly ethical accent, as "a religion of conscience." This view survived well into the time between the two World Wars, preparing the way at the same time for the Nazi alienation of Luther by means of the "German Christians." There was a search for a species-specific German religion and a pride in the fact that the Germans did not need to derive their religion from Palestine because they had their Luther. His theology was located between German mysticism and German idealism and augmented with misty statements about belief in fate and the primeval sentiments of Nordic humanity.[16] The church historian Hans Preuss, subjectively pious but politically naïve, who played a prominent role in the burning of books in the palace square at Erlangen on the orders of the Nazis, wrote a book entitled *Martin Luther, der Deutsche*.[17] After the war the Marxists in East Germany set about reconstructing their Luther. First he was seen as a servant of princes whose emancipatory significance was far inferior to that of Thomas Müntzer. But the more the DDR was stabilized, the more intensely was Luther claimed as the pioneer of the "early bourgeois revolution" and an opponent of established relationships, until finally he was prized as a source of foreign exchange.[18]

Current interpretations of Luther within Lutheranism strive for a historically objective picture. There seems to be no overarching theological perspective, probably because at the moment there are no ideological positions anyone hopes could be sustained by reference to Luther, or because Luther is no longer suitable for such a campaign.

The conclusion: in dealing with Luther's theology one must be on guard against oneself so as not to impose models of interpretation that may, without one's noticing it, import one's own prejudices or preferences. Obviously, particular caution is required in the case of those who claim Luther's support for their own positions. Ultimately Luther's theology demands not imitation but transposition and further development.

ECUMENICAL PERSPECTIVES

In the nature of things, Roman Catholic interpretation of Luther took a different course. For centuries the polemic of Johannes Cochlaeus governed the Catholic image of Luther, and at the end of the twentieth century there were still those who appealed to it.[19] After Luther's death it was said that he committed suicide; a wound he caused accidentally with his dagger during his days as a student of jurisprudence was said to have resulted from a duel and even a murder. At the beginning of the twentieth century the Dominican Heinrich Denifle interpreted Luther's break with church authority pansexually: according to Denifle the Reformation served the purpose of moral and especially sexual liberation. He saw in Luther a preponderance of the three great passions of lust, anger, and pride; Luther's gospel "proved at first to be a school, a seminar of sins and vices."[20] Hartmann Grisar, also a Dominican, did not reproach Luther on moral grounds but attributed his theology to psychosomatic suffering, morbid fantasies, and an exceptional degree of self-absorption. With Joseph Lortz began a Catholic interpretation of Luther that can be taken seriously. He interpreted Luther as the victim of truly regrettable conditions in the church of his time but reproached him for not having fully listened to Sacred Scripture. In a certain sense Otto Hermann Pesch still followed this line of thinking when he saw Luther as the victim of an isolated philosophical tradition and regretted that the Reformer was not a Thomist.[21] Ultimately there were advocates of the thesis that Vatican II would have been Luther's council. Peter Manns was able to praise him as a spiritual figure and Pope John Paul II affirmed Luther's deep piety, "driven by his burning passion for the question of eternal salvation."[22]

What has been Luther's reception in the Orthodox churches? First, it is striking that Luther's works are not accessible in Greek or Russian. The Reformation is regarded as a Western phenomenon, a heresy that arose out of a schism. It characterizes the crisis of the West and represents a reaction to the institutionalization of the church; from that point of view it is history's revenge for the separation of the Roman church from Byzantium. It can be positively interpreted when regarded as a development made necessary by the schism of 1054. Orthodox opinions on Luther should be evaluated against the background of the fact that Orthodoxy, from many points of view, has become a battleground between Roman Catholicism and Protestantism, with both sides seeking to win converts there. A synod in Constantinople in 1836 called Luther a "heresiarch," an arch-heretic. It seems natural to Orthodox theologians to accuse the Reformation of having introduced an unneeded new principle into theology and not having paid attention to the criteria of the ancient church. The results have been an overvaluation of the individual, subjectivism, and ultimately rationalism. What is seen as positive in Luther is his critique of the Roman system, his appeal to Sacred Scripture, and his emphasis on the position and value of theology.[23] Of course, from an Orthodox perspective the question remains: Did Luther bring to light the true Gospel and simultaneously lose sight of the church?

It is obvious that today Luther has to be encountered and responded to in an ecumenical context. Precisely the critical questions directed at Luther from non-Protestant churches lead us farther. They are concentrated in four areas:

- Gospel without church?
- Christ at the expense of trinitarian faith?
- The human being without a proper God-given potential?
- Faith without love?

But Luther must, in turn, be brought into the ecumenical context. He is not Protestant property![24]

Within Protestantism it is necessary to ask again about Luther's position in salvation history. The Reformation, contrary to its intention, did not encompass all Christianity; it did not fully succeed. Lutheran theology—despite being exported to the United States—seems to remain in some sense tied to central and northern Europe, and indeed to German-speaking regions. This raises again the question of the meaning of the Reformation, the present function of Protestantism, and the task of the Protestant diaspora. Finally, I find it to be a theological and spiritual challenge that the de-Christianization of Europe has advanced most rapidly in the core territories of the Reformation.

Luther as Theologian

Anyone who wants to understand Luther's theology must of course locate it within the history of theology, in the context in which it arose.

Traditions

As an Augustinian monk, Luther from the outset had a particular affinity for Augustine, whom he understood more as a theologian than as a philosopher. He was aided in this by a special interest in Augustine in Erfurt at the time. What is especially interesting today in theological disputes and discussions is his relationship to Thomas Aquinas. We now know that Luther did study Thomas, but the man from Aquino was not the center of his theological interest. Thus, for example, he did not write a tractate "contra Thomam," and we must suppose that he had Thomists more than Thomas in mind when he called Thomas the "source and wellspring of all error and heresy on earth" and the destruction of "godly doctrine."[25]

It is true that in the Reformer's time Thomas did not hold the dominant position in theology that would be accorded him later: it was only after Luther's death, namely in 1567, that he was named a "Doctor of the Church," and in 1923 that he was called "the Universal Doctor"; since 1879 his work has been considered the guideline for teaching Catholic theology. The new Code of Canon Law of 1983 still says that those studying theology are to "learn to penetrate more intimately the mysteries of salvation, especially with St. Thomas as a teacher."[26] In some sense the intensive adoption of Thomas in the Roman Catholic Church is a reaction to Luther's theology!

Three points of view are especially significant with regard to Luther's dependence on nominalism, or particularly on William of Ockham. According to Ockham knowledge begins with the analysis of the individual object; this puts a strong accent on experience. Then Ockham emphasized the authority of revelation, since we can have no immediate experience of the transcendent world. His idea of God is ultimately connected with this: he attributed to God a *potentia absoluta*, namely, a freedom with respect to everything outside God that borders on caprice, and at the same time a *potentia ordinata* by which God limits God's own self. We cannot deny that there are points of contact here with Luther's theology; the extent to which there is direct dependence is a matter of discussion. On the whole it seems that Catholic research on Luther has overestimated the influence of nominalism on him. Ockham himself, indeed, criticized the court conditions of his time, the papacy and its involvement in political power games, something that may again suggest we should see in Luther a certain degree of affinity with Ockham.[27]

Luther's relationship to neo-Platonism and mysticism is disputed. All those who desire in some sense to claim Luther for esotericism try to find some appropriate positive material here,[28] while those authors who share the traditional Protestant prejudice against all mysticism and enthusiasm try to make counter-arguments. As regards the historical Luther, we can mention three primary strands of mysticism:

The young Luther took account of Dionysius the Areopagite and praised him, though with some reservations: mystical theology is not garrulous, but is aware of the spirit's leisure and of silence, being drawn into ecstasy, and this creates "the true theologian."[29] In his early years he had a special admiration for Johannes Tauler.[30] But he was already skeptical about mystical speculations on the inner obscurity of God; Luther considered Christ's sufferings much more important. Ultimately he warned against a mystical theology that was more inclined to follow Plato than Christ. It is very revealing to compare Luther's words about the hidden God with those of Nicholas of Cusa.

FIELDS OF WORK

Luther was not a specialized dogmatist, church historian, or practical theologian; it was only in the seventeenth century that the various theological disciplines were separated. Luther saw himself as an interpreter of Scripture and a theologian in a broad sense. He is an exegete who concerned himself with translation from the original languages, seeking to discover the literal meaning of a scriptural passage and interpret it with a clear purpose: his interest was in the glory of God and the salvation of humans. This is expressed most clearly in his sermons and in his catechisms, which grew in part from his preaching. As a systematic theologian he drew his insights from Sacred Scripture, while as a scriptural interpreter and translator he was guided by his systematic-theological insights. The result was an astonishing coherence in his thought, even though throughout his life he remained averse to closed theological systems. For him Scripture and its interpretation were at the service of proclamation and pastoral care; his objective was an applied theology. His theological "method" consisted of a back-and-forth of listening to Sacred Scripture and systematic reflection on it in the service of human beings. Especially in the present situation, when theology is drifting apart into numerous theological disciplines, he can serve as an example for a theology that acts as a single whole.

SUGGESTIONS FOR READING

Which of Luther's writings are the best points of entry into his theology? One need not immediately set out to read the hundred-volume Weimar edition; nowadays the Insel editions prepared by Karin Bornkamm and Gerhard Ebeling are quite helpful. These contain the most important writings of Luther in a German that has been smoothed out. Especially to be recommended are "Das Magnificat verdeutscht und ausgelegt" (1521),[31] "Eine einfältige Weise zu beten, für einen guten Freund" (1535),[32] "Acht Sermone, von ihm gepredigt zu Wittenberg in der Fastenzeit" (1522; the so-called "invocative sermons"),[33] and the "Bekenntnis" (1528).[34] Especially useful for discussion is the "Disputation über den Menschen" (1536).[35] Anyone who wants to follow through the year with Luther texts can find a thematically arranged breviary.[36] I see it as a good opportunity to get to know Luther if one were to take a single Luther quotation that appeals to one and place it on one's desk or pin it on the wall and live with it for awhile. It is worthwhile acquiring a collection of classic quotations from Luther.

Luther the Philosopher

Luther the philosopher has scarcely been discovered; most histories of philosophy pass over him in silence or give him only a brief treatment. Luther often polemicized against philosophy, but it was a polemic with its own serious philosophical implications. In three respects Luther certainly emerged as a philosopher. For one thing, he was a disputant at the highest level, as we can see from the series of theses he prepared for theological dissertations in his faculty. Again, he was a skilled dialectician with a joy in paradox, though he did not use it merely for purposes of rhetorical style. In a sense dialectic constitutes the constructive principle of his theology, which developed in a polar tension between alternatives and complementarities. Finally, from our present point of view Luther may be seen in some sense as an existentialist, as indicated among other things by his eloquence. The category of the individual was constitutive for his thinking: "it is about your neck, it is about your life"[37]—the individual is irreplaceable and there can be no substitute. Luther took the mortal destiny of individual persons seriously. In his first invocative sermon he says: "The summons of death comes to us all, and no one can die for another. Every one must fight his own battle with death by himself, alone. We can shout into another's ears, but every one must himself be prepared for the time of death, for I will not be with you then, nor you with me."[38] Martin Heidegger's phrase, "being toward death," was probably inspired by this passage.

Notes

[1] Cf., e.g., Brecht 1983, 1986, 1987; Beutel 1991; Leppin 2006; Kaufmann 2006; Lexutt 2008.

[2] Cf., e.g., *Luther im Gespräch. Aufzeichnungen seiner Freunde und Tischgenossen. Nach den Urtexten der Tischreden übertragen und herausgegeben von Reinhard Buchwald* (Frankfurt: Insel, 1983).

[3] Insel edition VI; quoted is VI, 262. "In domestic affairs I defer to Käthe. Otherwise I am led by the Holy Ghost" (anecdotal: see Manfred Wolf, *Thesen und andere Anschläge: Anekdoten, Essays, Episoden und Martin Luther* [Leipzig: Evangelische Verlagsanstalt, 2005]).

[4] Ebeling 1983; Oberman 1981a; von Loewenich 1982; Kaufmann 2006; Leppin 2006.

[5] Cf. Paul J. Reiter, *Martin Luthers Umwelt, Charakter und Psychose sowie die Bedeutung dieser Faktoren für seine Entwicklung und Lehre*, 2 vols. (Copenhagen: Levin & Munksgaard, 1937–1941); the quotation is from 2: 295.

[6] Cf. Erik H. Erikson, *Young Man Luther: A Study in Psychoanalysis and History* (New York: W. W. Norton, 1993), 225.

[7] Leppin 2006 presents Luther's statements about himself, I think wrongly, as the expression of a morally dubious "self-stylization." On this cf. my review in *MdKI* 59 (2008): 43–44. Likewise, Korsch 2007 is unjust to the Reformer when he tries to understand Luther's theology as primarily and consistently the result of a "transposition of his own self-interpretation"; ibid., 40, and cf. 46 (cf. also: breach "in the form of religious self-interpretation," 20; "religious self-interpretation" proves "simply valid," 56; "reorientation of his own self-interpretation on the basis of his awareness of standing before God," 148, and see also 16, 43, 53, 134, 153, 157; meanwhile he

also speaks of Jesus' "self-interpretation before God," 64. Faith and the theology that reflects on it are certainly about more than "self-interpretation."

[8]LW 47, 29 (WA 30/3, 290, 28): "(for this haughty title I will henceforth have to assign to myself, to please and oblige my papists and asses)" (printed in parentheses).

[9]LW 43, 160 (WA 23, 421, 26-28).

[10]LW 43, 68 (WA 10/2, 58, 30-35).

[11]Cf. Herbert Wolf, *Martin Luther. Eine Einführung in germanistische Lutherstudien* (Stuttgart: Metzler, 1980), and idem, *Germanistische Luther-Biographie* (Heidelberg: C. Winter, 1985; 1996), as well as Stolt 2000.

[12]Hans-Martin Barth, "Martin Lutero all'origine della società moderna," *Protestantesimo* 52 (1997): 21–31.

[13]E.g., Johann Gerhard, *Loci theologici*, tomus V, locus XXIII, sectio VIII.

[14]*EKG* 202, 2.

[15]Theodosius Harnack, *Luthers Theologie mit besonderer Beziehung auf seine Versöhnungs- und Erlösungslehre* (Erlangen: T. Blaesing, 1862–1886; repr. Amsterdam: Editions Rodopi, 1969).

[16]Cf. the texts in Glaser/Stahl 1983, 209–26 ("Luther: northernized").

[17]Hans Preuss, *Martin Luther, der Deutsche* (Gütersloh: Bertelsmann, 1934).

[18]Lohse 1981, 209–43, offers a thorough presentation of the history of interpretations of Luther. Cf. also Jan Hermann Brinks, "Einige Überlegungen zur politischen Instrumentalisierung Martin Luthers durch die deutsche Historiographie im neunzehnten und zwanzigsten Jahrhundert," *Zeitgeschichte* 22 (1995): 233–48.

[19]Cf. Vercryusse, "Luther in der römisch-katholischen Theologie und Kirche," with reference to the works of Dietrich Emme (nn. 99-101).

[20]Quoted in Werner Beyna, *Das moderne katholische Lutherbild* (Essen: Ludgerus-Verlag, 1969), 43.

[21]It should be acknowledged that Otto Hermann Pesch has offered some pathbreaking studies on Luther's theology that have been highly respected in Lutheran circles as well; cf. especially *Die Theologie der Rechtfertigung bei Martin Luther und Thomas von Aquin. Versuch eines systematisch-theologischen Dialogs* (Mainz: Matthias-Grünewald, 1967), and Pesch 1982 (1983).

[22]Quoted in Vercryusse, "Luther in der römisch-katholischen Theologie und Kirche," 123.

[23]Cf. *Luther et la réforme allemande* (1983), as well as Damaskinos Papandreou, "Martin Luther in orthodoxer Sicht," *KD* 30 (1984): 100–15.

[24]Cf. Hans-Martin Barth, "Die Theologie Martin Luthers im globalen Kontext. Lutherforschung auf dem Weg zum Jahr 2017," *MdKI* 59 (2008): 3–8.

[25]Cf. LW 36, 204; 32, 258 (WA 15, 184, 32-33); cf. Denis R. Janz, *Luther on Thomas Aquinas. The Angelic Doctor in the Thought of the Reformer* (Stuttgart: Steiner, 1989), 75.

[26]*CIC* can. 252, §3.

[27]Cf. Volker Leppin, *Geglaubte Wahrheit. Das Theologieverständnis Wilhelms von Ockham* (Göttingen: Vandenhoeck & Ruprecht, 1995), and idem, *Wilhelm von Ockham. Gelehrter, Streiter, Bettelmönch* (Darmstadt: Primus, 2003).

[28]Cf. Wehr 1999; Berndt Hamm and Volker Leppin, eds., with Heidrun Munzert, *Gottes Nähe unmittelbar erfahren. Mystik im Mittelalter und bei Luther* (Tübingen: Mohr Siebeck, 2006).

[29]". . . hec in disputatione et multiloquio tractari non potest, sed in summo mentis ocio et silentio, velut in raptu et extasi. Et hec facit verum theologum." WA 3, 372, 23-25.

[30]Cf. Leppin 2006, 83–88.

[31]"The Magnificat," LW 21, 295–358 (WA 7, 544–604). See also *The Magnificat; Luther's Commentary*, trans. A. T. W. Steinhaeuser (Minneapolis: Augsburg, 1967).

[32]"A Simple Way to Pray," LW 43, 187–211 (WA 38, 358–75); cf. Barth, Hans-Martin 1989a, and *A Simple Way to Pray*, with a foreword by Marjorie J. Thompson (Louisville: Westminster John Knox, 2000), excerpted from LW.

[33]"Eight Sermons at Wittenberg," LW 51, 70–100 (WA 10/3, 1–64); see also Timothy F. Lull, *Martin Luther's Basic Theological Writings* (Minneapolis: Fortress Press, 22005), 282–306.

[34]"Confession Concerning Christ's Supper," LW 37, 360–72 (WA 26, 499–509).

35"The Disputation Concerning Man," LW 34, 133–44 (WA 39/1, 175–80); here, though, the Latin version should be used (LDStA 664–68). Luther's *Small Catechism* is also good for discussion.

36Suzanne Tilton, *Through the Year with Martin Luther* (Peabody MA: Hendrickson, 2007).

37Councils may decide what they will, "you cannot place confidence in them or satisfy your conscience; you must decide for yourself; it is about your neck, it is about your life," WA 10/1/2, 335, 17-19.

38LW 51, 70 (WA 10/3, 1,7–2,1).

4

Difficulties in Approaching Luther

Antisemitism? Luther and the Jews

Contemporary questions

Today, especially as a Protestant Christian and theologian in Germany, one cannot reflect on Luther's attitude toward Judaism in his time without thinking of Auschwitz. The Nazis and the so-called "German Christians" appealed explicitly to Luther for their attitude toward Jews. The publications of the Nazi "Luther scholar" Theodor Pauls played an especially ominous role.[1] The minister for church affairs at that time, Hans Kerrl, had a group of state churches subscribe to a document declaring that "in regard to the faith there is no clearer opposition" than that "between the message of Jesus Christ and the Jewish religion of legalism and expectation of a political messiah." The signers affirmed the statement that "the life of the people demands a serious and responsible racial policy."[2] The Nazi officialdom did not, of course, appeal directly to Luther's utterances for their degrading treatment of Jewish people and ultimately their murder in the concentration camps, even though—alas!—it would have been possible. For his writings on the Jews contained an ideological basis for their persecution in Luther's Germany. Peter von der Osten-Sacken has pointed to an especially tragic case: Rabbi Reinhold Lewin wrote a dissertation on "Luther's attitude toward the Jews" that, because of its superior quality, won the annual prize of the Lutheran theological faculty at the University of Breslau. In 1942 (or 1943?) he, his wife, and their two children were deported to Auschwitz or Theresienstadt, where all trace of him is lost.[3]

Thus it is inadequate for a presentation of Luther's theology to say with Oswald Bayer that "Luther's terrible mistake in his late writings on the Jews in identifying them as enemies of the word of God—with fatal effect—is a source of painful alienation."[4] Let me say in passing that, unfortunately, it is not merely a matter of "late" writings. It is equally unsatisfactory that the *Handbuch Luther*, published in 2005, while soberly attesting that the compulsory measures recommended by Luther went "far beyond the restrictive rules of canon law," does not seek to explain this, and certainly does not inquire how it accords with Luther's theology.[5] The section of the *Handbuch* on "controversial writings," authored by Hellmut Zschoch, does not even mention the writings on the Jews.[6]

The most obvious question to be directed to Luther the Christian theologian today would be where love fits into his words on this subject. Luther would perhaps reply that his concern is with the faith: "Love does not curse or take vengeance, but faith does. To understand this, you must distinguish between God and man, between persons and issues."[7] In Luther's thinking, certainly, this signifies the primacy of the "cause" of faith before human beings—certainly an unfortunate alternative in a Christian sense (cf. Eph 4:15). Where, in his anti-Jewish attacks, is the connection between faith and love that Luther postulates elsewhere? Why did he not appeal to his Jewish contemporaries by pointing to the justification of the ungodly? Why is his faith not expressed in good works toward Jews as well, as the Reformer otherwise expects and often declares? If there is no answer to these theological questions, how is it that Luther, the lover of Hebrew and the Old Testament, reacted with such prejudice, and indeed hatred, to the living tradents of the Hebrew language and Bible? Is there anything to be learned from his argumentation, or is any part of it acceptable in any sense?

STAGES

For a long time there was an attempt to see a cordial attitude toward the Jews in the young Reformer and then the severity of the late writings on the Jews as coming from the aging Luther. This view has not been confirmed. Luther's basic attitude seems to have remained the same, even though his concrete recommendations changed. We need not describe in detail the development of Luther's attitude.[8] Nor is it the case, as one might think after reading a monograph that erases the "rest of" Luther, that the Reformer thought about the Jews night and day and had nothing else in his head. But recent studies have shown that even his first lectures on the Psalms, the *Dictata super Psalterium* (1513–1515), contained quite a few anti-Jewish remarks that could in no way have been theologically motivated. The Jews, Luther says, crucified Christ in their own way in many forms and would be happy to tear Christians into pieces; in rejecting faith in Christ, says he, they became wild beasts. They said horrible things about Christ and Christians, "things that no one hears, and the more boldly they speak and curse us, the less the Christians hear [about it]. If they heard it, they would altogether destroy them [the Jews]."[9] This reference to machinations that are never made public of course threw open the door to the wildest speculations. More important than such isolated remarks, however, is the fact that Luther tried to employ biblical arguments. He strove for a hermeneutics combining the literal meaning with a christological interpretation. The "enemies" in the Psalms could thus be identified as enemies of Christ and so especially as the Jews. In this way the Psalter became a "Christian textbook of enmity toward the Jews."[10]

Some very different tones, also making themselves heard in the years after 1514, can be found in the 1523 writing "Dass Jesus Christus ein geborener Jude sei" (That Jesus Christ was Born a Jew).[11] Luther had been accused of denying the virginity of Mary, the Mother of God, and saying that Jesus was "the seed of Abraham," that is, only a human being, thus coming close to Judaism. He took this occasion to present his view of the Jewish problem as he had come to perceive it. It is possible that in the meantime he had personally encountered Jews who had converted to the Christian faith.[12] Now he wanted to appeal to the members of the people Israel and himself contribute to their return to the faith of their ancestors, their own true faith.[13] He criticized the way people had treated them heretofore, namely "as if they were dogs rather than human beings."[14] Violence was completely out of place here. He suggests opening middle-class professions to Jews so that they would no longer be forced to practice usury. "If we really want to help them, we must be guided in our dealings with them not by papal law but by the law of Christian love. We must receive them cordially, and permit them to trade and work with us, that they may have occasion and opportunity to associate with us, hear our Christian teaching, and witness our Christian life. If some of them should prove stiff-necked, what of it? After all, we ourselves are not all good Christians either."[15] What Luther imagines here is apparently "a general social integration of the Jews, with a missionary purpose," though conversion is not to be made a condition for it.[16] At any rate, with this comparatively open attitude Luther found followers among other Reformers such as Justus Jonas, Andreas Osiander, and Urbanus Rhegius.[17]

It certainly should not be overlooked that in this 1523 writing Luther also engaged in critical confrontation with the Jews. It is true that the heart's blood of his theology is evident when he boasts to them of how Christ governs consciences with the holy Gospel, "a most gracious preachment of God's loving-kindness, the forgiveness of sins, and redemption from death and hell, by which all who from the heart believe it will be comforted, joyous, and, as it were, drowned in God with the overwhelming comfort of his mercy."[18] But in order to understand this Jews must first accept that the Messiah is not to be expected in the future, but has already come. Luther sought—to put it in modern terms—to conduct the debate exegetically. He welcomes the fact that the Jews, in contrast to the babble of the papists, rightly refer to the Bible[19] (like himself, so to speak). If he were a Jew, he said in a table discussion in 1533, "I would rather be broken on the wheel ten times" than believe the pope; the papacy had caused the worst outrages for the Jews.[20] But he also knew that they had their own hermeneutics, which he considered utterly false: with their "grammar" they distort and tatter Sacred Scripture, and every rabbi thinks he is better at it than the next.[21] The rabbis work with their own commentary, with equivocations and false interpretations;[22] they think "we need to learn the Bible from them,"[23] and their only purpose in doing so is to lure us away from the New Testament; therefore anyone who wants to study Hebrew should be steered toward the New Testament![24] It would be better to ignore rabbinic exegesis; it is "all too prone to stick to us of itself," and without our knowing it the Jewish interpretation will worm its way in, "as every translator without exception has experienced. I, too, was not exempt from it."[25] Jews may understand Hebrew better, but "we Christians have the meaning and import of the Bible because we have the New Testament, that is, Jesus Christ," who was promised in the Old Testament and brought a correct understanding of Scripture with him.[26] Luther complains, for example, with regard to Daniel 9:24-27: "God help us! This passage has been dealt with so variously by both Jews and Christians that one might doubt whether anything certain can be derived from it!"[27] When, in interpreting Isaiah 7:14, the Jews point out that the text does not speak here of a *bethulah*, that is, a virgin, but of an *almah*, a "young woman," Luther has to deal with this ponderously and at length. In his 1523 writing he is still laboring for a balance and avoids using the word "virgin" in translating Isaiah 7:14, "to please the Jews," replacing it with the German word "Magd" (maiden), which he thinks is more accurate. Later he also contends with Jewish exegetes over the correct understanding of individual Hebrew concepts. Sometimes there is no clear argumentation at all; he interprets "the last words of David" according to "my own views." He adds: "May God grant that our theologians boldly apply themselves to the study of Hebrew and retrieve the Bible for us from those rascally thieves."[28] One should "diligently seek and find the Lord Jesus in the Hebrew Old Testament."[29] The Reformer expects that a better knowledge of Hebrew will strengthen his christocentrically-aimed hermeneutics. He seldom refers to the living scripture written in the hearts of believers; the Jews in any case, like the pope, have as little idea of it as does a sow of playing the harp.[30] He is convinced that they are basically aware that they are wrong; they have "felt" it for a long time and now they are seeking escape routes and defending themselves with "all manner of preposterous glosses."[31] If he finds the wording of a biblical passage inadequate, Luther calls on the course of history: it is not without reason that the Jews, since the appearance of Christ, have endured a terrible past of nearly 1,500 years, which can only be explained as God's punishment.[32] "Scripture and history" agree "perfectly."[33]

The Reformer cannot understand that the Jews are not enlightened by what he learned in direct conversation with Jewish interlocutors, apparently a few years later. The Jews do not join the reform movement; in fact, there are rumors that—very much to the contrary—Christians are converting to Judaism. After a phase of increasing aversion and distancing, the radical stance of Luther's later years took shape in him.

Reading the 1543 writing "Von den Juden und ihren Lügen" (On the Jews and their Lies)[34] must always have been a challenge to every Christian; after the Holocaust it is positively unbearable. According to this, "next to the devil" a Christian has "no more bitter, venomous, and vehement foe" than a Jew.[35] One seeing one, the Christian should think: "Alas, that mouth which I there behold has cursed and execrated and maligned every Saturday my dear Lord Jesus Christ, who has redeemed me with his precious blood; in addition, it prayed and pleaded before God" that I and all Christians might perish miserably.[36] A great many pages are expended in describing how the Jews falsify and twist what is meant by Abraham's descendants, circumcision, and the law of Moses. Luther engages at length and ponderously with "their interpretation"[37] of the Bible, with sayings Luther says give him also "very great joy and comfort that we have such strong testimony also in the Old Testament."[38] He accompanies his polemic against Jewish interpretation of Scripture with a warning against students of Hebrew such as the Basel scholar Sebastian Münster, who in his opinion "Judaize" and make themselves too dependent on rabbinic interpretations instead of understanding the Old Testament christologically.[39] Thus he says in one of the recorded table conversations that Münster and his source, the orientalist Sanctes (Sante Pagnini, d. 1541), are very diligent, but "he [Münster] makes too many concessions to the rabbis."[40] The Jews call Jesus a sorcerer and the son of a whore: "What shall we Christians do with this rejected and condemned people, the Jews? . . . With prayer and the fear of God we must practice a sharp mercy to see whether we might save at least a few from the glowing flames"; of course, one should not avenge oneself.[41] So he continues: "I shall give you my sincere advice." What follows, indeed, is a series of suggestions that had been made even before Luther: "First, to set fire to their synagogues or schools and to bury and cover with dirt whatever will not burn, so that no man will ever again see a stone or cinder of them." The theological foundation for this is dreadful: "This is to be done in honor of our Lord and of Christendom, so that God might see that we are Christians . . . ." The New Testament has been forgotten; without any hermeneutical reflection, for example, he recalls the Old Testament instruction in Deuteronomy 13:16, ripped from its context, about the imposition of the ban.[42] "Second," Luther advises "that their houses also be razed and destroyed. For they pursue in them the same aims as in their synagogues. Instead they might be lodged under a roof or in a barn, like the gypsies. . . . Third, I advise that all their prayer books and Talmudic writings, in which such idolatry, lies, cursing, and blasphemy are taught, be taken from them. Fourth, I advise that their rabbis be forbidden to teach henceforth on pain of loss of life and limb. . . . Fifth, I advise that safe-conduct on the highways be abolished completely for the Jews. . . . Sixth, I advise that usury be prohibited to them, and that all cash and treasure of silver and gold be taken from them and put aside for safekeeping" because "they have stolen and robbed from us all they possess. . . ."[43] "Seventh, I recommend putting a flail, an ax, a hoe, a spade, a distaff, or a spindle into the hands of young, strong Jews and Jewesses and letting them earn their bread in the sweat of their brow, as was imposed on the children of Adam (Gen. 3[:19])."[44] The authorities should drive the Jews from their territories and tell them "to return to their land and their possessions in Jerusalem, where they may lie, curse, blaspheme, defame, murder, steal, rob. . . ."[45]

Three days before his death Luther thought it necessary to release an "admonition against the Jews" in Eisleben. He repeats his well-known accusations, but still contends that even so "we want to exercise Christian love toward them and pray for them, that they may convert. . . ."[46] Apparently during his journey there an elemental aversion to the Jews had once again seized him, for he writes to his wife that while passing through a village in which many Jews were living "such a cold wind blew from behind into the carriage and on my head through the beret," which may have been the cause of his dizziness.[47]

We cannot say, of course, that Luther, in his attacks on the Jews, "denies their humanity."[48] But it is bad enough that he finds the Jews to be "a heavy burden to us, like a plague, pestilence, and vain misfortune in our land."[49] That certainly sounds like the Nazi motto, originally formulated by Heinrich von Treitschke, "The Jews are our misfortune." Late in life he no longer rejected the evil accusations about poisoning wells and ritual murders. The only subject that vanishes is desecration of the Host, probably because of the Reformation's altered doctrine of the Eucharist. The Reformer accuses the Jews of blaspheming God; to the extent this is not public, he says, it is happening in secret. He takes up the defamation of Jewish physicians. He says Jews are arrogant and greedy for money. In light of many of these elements Peter von der Osten-Sacken concludes that they have "simply nothing more to do with religious anti-Judaism, even when they serve that purpose for Luther. We cannot avoid describing them as elements of a proto-antisemitism within the overall phenomenon of Luther's antipathy to the Jews. . . ."[50] One must speak of "a structural affinity between the Reformer's anti-Judaism and the anti-Semitism that became established in the nineteenth and twentieth centuries."[51] He shares the opinion of the Jewish historian Marianna Awerbuch: "He [Luther] preached hatred and the destruction of human dignity. This we must acknowledge, and we must learn to live with this fact."[52]

ATTEMPTS AT EXPLANATION

Anyone who loves Luther and owes something to him, be it only for his translation of the Bible, will feel the need to find a plausible explanation for Luther's unbearable expressions about the Jews, because they obviously do not represent mere "slips of the tongue" or signs of senility,[53] nor can they be explained as testimony to the general boorishness of the sixteenth century. Reservation or aggressivity toward the Jews were present, with varying degrees of intensity—apart from the brief phase in 1523—throughout Luther's adult life. Cheap apologetics are thus certainly out of place, but we must make some attempt to discover how the Reformer could have been drawn into that channel. The attempts at explanation presented to date refer to historical conditions or are partly psychological and partly theological in nature.

Of course, one is regularly tempted to argue psychologically. Was Luther disappointed that the Jews, who saw themselves trapped in the canonical restrictions of the Roman church and thus had to feel, so to speak, that they were confederates of the Reformation, did not join it? Was it the relative lack of success of the Reformation as a whole that caused him, at the end of his life, to react once more with such aggression against Jews, Turks, and the Pope? In that case the late writings on the Jews should be understood primarily as an "act of revision" on the part of the "aging prophet" over against his expressions in 1523.[54] Was it, in fact, a paradoxical "envy" of the Jews as the "firstborn of the people of God" that moved him?[55] Was Luther fighting, in the form of the Jews, something within himself, his own tendency to be proud[56] and opinionated?

There has been a tendency to point to the "spirit of the times";[57] ultimately Luther's remarks, when compared with those of his contemporaries, are not essentially out of line. In the wake of brutal pogroms against the Jews, sometimes after a plague epidemic, a century and a half before Luther space was cleared for Marian churches by burning down synagogues, for example in Nuremberg, Regensburg, and Würzburg. The canonical regulations for dealing with the Jews were highly restrictive. Even a humanist like Johannes Reuchlin demanded "improvement or expulsion" of the Jews,[58] and Erasmus of Rotterdam himself saw "limits to tolerance,"[59] to say nothing of Luther's opponent Johann Eck[60] and still others. There is no question that the "spirit of the times" exercised a strong influence on Luther as well. But how, then, did he arrive at his comparatively open attitude in the document of 1523? Why did he not continue in that vein, and why were others, such as Justus Jonas or Osiander, able to pursue the path he opened in that 1523 writing? Does this represent a retreat to the Middle Ages on Luther's part? If so, how did that happen?

Luther was, of course, dependent on particular literary sources.[61] But how was it that he, otherwise so adept at freeing himself from existing authorities, did not judge these sources critically? Recently scholarship has focused especially on a book by Anton Margaritha, *Der gantz Jüdisch glaub* (The Whole Jewish Faith), as Luther's source.[62] Margaritha was a convert to Christianity and spoke from the one-sided perspective often found in converts about the faith he had abandoned. Luther was ordinarily quite skeptical toward Jewish converts; why did he, in this case, abandon all caution, especially since Margaritha had adopted not the Reformation faith but the ancient one? Did the book fit all too well within his long-established view of the matter?

An attempt has been made to relativize at least the worst of Luther's anti-Jewish counsels by opining that they were not meant seriously; Luther by no means expected that they would actually be applied. His nasty proposal was simply meant to move the authorities to drive the Jews out of the Protestant lands.[63] From the outset the Reformer's concern was for a "Christian homogenization"[64] of those territories. If that interpretation is accurate it would in any case describe a thoroughly unchristian and inhumane strategy. A reference to the conditions of the times can, if at all, only minimally excuse the Reformer.

What about the theological arguments? It is striking that Luther often speaks of the Jews together with other people who did not believe, or did so only in a limited way, including pagans, Turks, or superficial and hypocritical Christians. Can we take this, with Wilhelm Maurer, as a reason to see here the Reformer's knowledge of the "solidarity of guilt?"[65] In that case "the Jew" would only be a type of sinful humanity, a paradigm of how it is with everyone. "For until today Christ is in ourselves spat upon, killed, scourged, crucified." Lying in wait for the soul are "without interruption the flesh with its senses, the world with its desires, and the devil with his whisperings (and temptations), just as the Jews did for Christ in the flesh."[66] But that cannot mean that Luther, in speaking of the Jews, did not have quite concrete Jewish people in mind. Besides, it of course in no way excuses what he said about them in his late writings.

The Catholic theologian Johannes Brosseder attempted a rescue of Luther developed from the very center of Reformation theology.[67] He assigns Luther's counsel to exercise a "sharp mercy" toward the Jews to the function of the "Law." According to Luther the Law had the task of convincing human beings of their guilt and so bringing them on the path to the Gospel. Luther's statements about the Jews, says Brosseder, should be understood in the context of a "universalizing" of the doctrine of justification. In fact, one could consider Paul, who sees handing a sinner over to Satan as for his soul's salvation (1 Cor 5:5)—a procedure that is already problematic in regard to Paul. Luther's understanding contradicts this attempted solution to the degree that, according to his conviction elsewhere expressed, the Law's *usus theologicus* may not be confused with its *usus politicus*.[68]

It is repeatedly pointed out that Luther's late anti-Jewish writings must be read together with those against the Turks and the Pope. They "are parts of an indissoluble genre of end-time prophecy."[69] They are "an expression of Luther's verdict on the state of the church at the end of history."[70] When one makes the state of the world at the time responsible for Luther's apocalyptic,[71] saying that the Reformer himself was subject to it but it is passé in our present day, his attacks on the Jews (and others) appear to lose their weight.

Recently Michael Beyer has proposed the thesis that Luther's "aggressive attitude" toward the Jews, however much it "more than alienates," could be regarded as "social engagement." This would be explained by the "potential danger Luther associated with the Jews as regards the functioning class order." According to Beyer, the Reformer felt that usury and missionary work among Christians were factors that could destabilize the existing order.[72] This may be accurate from Luther's point of view, but to the present-day observer it represents a horrid perversion of the concept of "social engagement," similar in that respect to the Inquisition or the persecutions of Jews by the "Third Reich," which would have to be explained also as a form of "social engagement" on the part of the persecutors.

All these arguments seem to have a relative and thus limited validity. But the crucial reason could be something quite different. It is obvious that Luther was disturbed by Jewish interpretation of their Bible, his Old Testament. He made efforts to show that the Old Testament had to be interpreted through the New: "and in this manner I should like to free the whole Hebrew Bible for the Jews from their shameful and blasphemous commentaries . . . ." Knowledge of Hebrew was to be used for the same purpose.[73] Of course the Reformer was convinced of the truth of his own position. But in the Jews he encountered people who appealed to the Bible, at least its Old Testament part, with the same exclusivity he claimed for himself and like no others among his opponents. He could undermine the traditions of the old believers with the aid of the Bible; he could accuse the Spiritualists and the Anabaptists of stubborn fantasy by referring to Sacred Scripture. But the Jews themselves appealed to the Bible and came to conclusions altogether different from his. He asserts that they themselves "feel" that they are in the wrong. But could it be that Luther had within himself just such a "feeling," an inner uncertainty that he sought to hold in check with his polemics?

CRITICAL EVALUATION

We should not try to excuse Luther by means of psychological arguments drawn from history, or by theological arguments either, however much these need to be detailed. There remain only regret and lament that such a tragic thing could happen. Probably the Holocaust would have been carried out without Luther's anti-Jewish writings. But that those writings are part of the pre-history of the Shoah is a fact that must not be covered up.[74] That Luther called for violence against things, but not against human beings in the sense of death-dealing, existence-extinguishing measures, is no consolation. Nevertheless, distinctions are called for. Luther's anti-Judaism was only marginally related to the biologically-grounded race hatred of the Nazi criminals. He always recognized the possibility that the Jews could convert. But one cannot convert from one's "race"; everyone is mercilessly subject to a persecution based on "race." Moreover, anti-Judaism is not identical with anti-Semitism. Hans-Martin Kirn rightly insists that "the question of the epoch-spanning connections between late medieval and Reformation anti-Judaism and (proto)anti-Semitism on the one hand and modern racist anti-Semitism directed at extirpation on the other has not yet been adequately explored."[75] If Luther's anti-Judaism was essentially religious in its foundation, of course, we are presented with the problem of the ability of Christian, and especially Reformation, theology, and in fact of religion as such, to create and maintain peace.

Luther's conflict with Judaism took place largely in the medium of scriptural interpretation. This challenges us to test his hermeneutics. We are inclined to suspect that he may have adopted the anti-Jewish tones that appear already in the New Testament and uncritically strengthened them. Then we should ask how his guiding principles, *solus Christus* and *sola scriptura*, were related to one another in this context. The formal principle *sola scriptura* could then have become independent of the material principles.[76] But the real problem is of course concentrated in the Old Testament, the Hebrew Bible. It would shed some light if one were to compare the biblical passages treated by Luther in his arguments with rabbinic or kabbalistic interpretation and evaluate them in light of today's exegetical knowledge. This, certainly, puts up for renewed discussion the legitimacy of a Christian interpretation of the Hebrew Bible. The wrong Luther did to Judaism must entail an obligation for Lutheran churches to engage with Jewish theology as thoroughly as possible and to eliminate wrong attitudes and misunderstandings.[77]

Is it any help to say "with Luther against Luther"? In that case we could offer the relatively conciliatory Luther of 1523 or 1515–1525 against the radically anti-Jewish Luther. That is Peter von der Osten-Sacken's argument.[78] Jewish interpretations of Luther in the nineteenth century already moved in that direction in order not to have to abandon the Reformer completely to the anti-Semites.[79] Eduard Lamparter offered a similar argument only a few years before the Nazi seizure of power.[80] But one-sided interpretations and idealizations could not and cannot rescue Luther.

Moreover, if one wants to appeal to Luther's attitude in 1523, the question of a Jewish mission clearly arises. In the Reformer's thinking the Gospel is not to be withheld from Jewish dialogue partners, but rather offered to them. In 1523 Luther wanted to "do a service to"[81] the Jews and "win some to the Christian faith."[82] Thomas Kaufmann points out that Luther, although he was not active as a missionary to the Jews, offered a "theological-didactic basis for the Jewish mission."[83] The question of a missionary responsibility toward all, and hence also toward the Jews, is by no means answered by a reference to Luther's fundamental failure. Perhaps here again we should distinguish: Christians who speak German, the language of the concentration-camp thugs, and in fact members of the Lutheran Church as a whole, in view of the connections between Luther and the Shoah that, though indirect, are still visible, should not feel themselves called to any form of mission to the Jews. This does not exclude the possibility that other churches, as their representatives, could and should accept responsibility for bearing witness, to Jews as well as others.

Luther was by no means simply filled with blind hatred for the Jews and everything Jewish; he thought that in his battle for the truth he had to protect Lutheran territories from the danger of infiltration by any anti-Christian spirit. Precisely therein lay his tragedy. Judaism, in the legalism he presumed existed there, was for him the clear and direct contradiction of the message of justification. Burning synagogues, he thought, was something to be done for the honor of God, as divine service.[84] He was fixated on his own understanding of what the truth is and thought he had to represent it conscientiously and as best he knew how; in this struggle he thought all verbal means were justified. Therefore he arrived at a "reduction of complexity"[85] both with regard to his opponents and in his own theological position. He was—as concerns his attitude toward Judaism—a theology professor led astray[86] who overestimated his own role; he is thus an admonitory example for all those who work toward a proper evangelical theology.

Thus Luther's anti-Jewish statements at the same time present us with a strong impetus to read his other writings with the greatest degree of critical attention. We must ask in very fundamental terms whether the results of his work reveal the shadow of a reductionist concentration on Christology and a certain forgetfulness of the Trinity. In any case, in his invectives against the Jews the Reformer put clearly before the eyes of the churches dependent on him the truth that they cannot revere him as an idealized saint, but that he himself was in need of the justification of the ungodly of which he elsewhere spoke and wrote so movingly.

INTOLERANCE? LUTHER AND ISLAM

In Luther's mind the only existing non-Christian religions seem to have been those of antiquity that had been overcome by the Christian faith and—as the great contemporary threat—Islam,[87] essentially as presented in the form of the Turkish religion of his time. He of course was unfamiliar with the concept of "Islam," and for that reason he spoke of the religion or faith of the Turks and occasionally of the Tartars, a Mongol people mingled with Turkish elements, as a tribe considered wild and daring. He took scarcely any note of the religious-theological implications of the discovery of America.[88] The religion of the Greeks and Romans had, so to speak, collapsed of itself; at most it might still play some part in the form of pagan Epicureanism.[89] Thus Luther's attention was directed entirely to Islam, which he studied rather closely and which he was not hesitant in judging.

CONTEMPORARY QUESTIONS

The difference between the religious situations in the sixteenth and twenty-first centuries in Europe is so great that it is almost impossible to find any questions that relate the two. Is September 11, 2001, comparable to the appearance of the Turks before Vienna in 1529 or the defeat of the Hungarian army at Mohács in 1526? Modern migrations have led to a mostly peaceful integration of people of Muslim faith, who in the first instance, on the basis of their own feelings and the estimation of others, may appear culturally oppressed and in need of assistance. However that may be, there have in the meantime been a great many and variety of personal and institutional contacts with Muslims, whereas Luther probably never saw a real, living "Turk." It is only in connection with the rapidly rising numbers of Muslim immigrants and especially the activities of terrorists that they are seen by parts of European society as a threat. But that has less to do with religion, which Europeans themselves have in part lost track of, than with a general anxiety about the infiltration of foreign cultures and economic endangerment. Of course, Islamic traditions such as Ramadan or the head scarf may revive the subject of religion in a secularized context. A good many people, especially in the so-called two-thirds world, find it to be an alternative to a galloping capitalism. The Islamic ethos appears as something to hold onto amid the moral chaos of the liberal West. Does Luther's theology have anything to say to this tension-filled situation in society?

The religious and theological situation itself is also entirely different. A prayer for peace by representatives of different religions like that at Assisi in 1996 would have been unthinkable in the sixteenth century. The Second Vatican Council made an effort to present a theological appreciation of non-Christian religions, including Islam. "The church has also a high regard for the Muslims," reads *Nostra aetate* 3. "They worship God, who is one. . . . They endeavor to submit themselves without reserve to the hidden decrees of God. . . . Although not acknowledging him as God, they venerate Jesus as a prophet. . . ."[90] There is no trace of such respect in Luther's writings. He would never have thought of speaking of "Abrahamic religions."[91]

In present understanding Islam is only one among a number of world religions with which Christianity competes. Advocates of a pluralistic theology of religions seek to do justice to this situation and respond to it. What was

Luther's theological perspective on non-Christian religions? How did he deal with them—Islam in particular? What is the sense of even opening Luther's writings on the Turks today?

PHENOMENOLOGICAL PERCEPTIONS

Apart from the religions known in antiquity and Judaism, the Islam of the Ottoman Empire was the sole non-Christian religion that was in any way familiar to Europeans in the first half of the sixteenth century. The military and religious threat from the Turks dominated ordinary awareness. Luther regarded it as a visitation from God intended to bring God's people to repentance. Under those circumstances, was it at all legitimate to defend oneself against the Turks? The bull *Exsurge Domine* accused Luther of branding the struggle against the Turks as resistance to God.[92] While Luther's original intention was to stand against the general crusading sentiment, it is noteworthy that in his writings on the Turks in 1529 he by no means rejects defense against the Turks, but he does make a clear distinction between the political and the religious sides of the Turkish problem. In his opinion this should by no means be a religious war. If the Turks did actually join battle shouting "Allah!" it would still be wrong for those attacked to respond with the cry "Ecclesia, ecclesia!"[93] There is no place for bishops and church people in the emperor's army. Christians should, in the sense of the Sermon on the Mount, not resist the evil the Turks undoubtedly represent! But Luther calls on them to improve themselves, do penance, and to pray both in public worship and at home, lamenting before God the danger from the Turks.[94] The church has enemies other than those of flesh and blood.[95] A careful distinction must be made between "Christianus" and "Emperor Charles."[96]

Nevertheless, the Reformer did not see resistance to the Turks as illegitimate. It was the emperor's duty to defend his territory and protect his subjects. Soldiers in his service should give their best in battle against the Turks, but not as Christians fighting Islam; rather, they should act as defenders called to act against a brutal aggressor. Should they be in danger of dying as a result, they should go forward to "die in a good state," which is to be preferred to a lingering death in bed.[97] Luther wants to teach how war can be conducted with a good conscience and refers to his writing on authority, in which, a few years earlier, he had anticipated what came to be called his doctrine of the two governments.

We may well doubt whether ordinary agricultural laborers were able to make such distinctions. Nevertheless, we should not dismiss Luther's theological argumentation as a cheap alibi. He knew what his approach meant, for example, for Christians who were captured by the Turks. They were to accept their fate as sent from God and serve their new masters as their knowledge and consciences directed them. If a Christian were sold to a Turk, Luther advises: "In no case should you run away. . . . You rob and steal thereby from your master your body, which he bought. . . ."[98] The only thing forbidden in this new servile relationship was fighting against Christians.

But what was Luther's perception of Islam? He depended on contemporary information, including the account of a Dominican friar from Transylvania who had spent many years as a prisoner of the Turks,[99] a refutation of the Qu'ran by Ricoldo of Monte Croce,[100] and finally the Qu'ran itself, which, however, he first encountered in 1542—in a Latin translation, of course. He was one of the first to translate parts of the Qu'ran into German (although what he translated he took from the Latin quotations of the Qu'ran in Ricoldo's work); he would have much preferred, he said, to have translated the whole Qu'ran. That he could not accomplish. However, along with other theologians he advocated publication of the Latin edition of the Qu'ran prepared four hundred years earlier by Robert Ketton in Basel.[101] It appears from the preface he wrote that he expected that for Christians the Qu'ran would be its own worst enemy.[102] Why Luther did not engage more deeply with Nicholas of Cusa's Cribratio[103] Alcorani is an open question. It goes without saying that in his Islamic studies he did not proceed with the thoroughness and competence of an Islamic scholar of today.

Luther first attempts to get a clear idea of the Turks' religion and then, on the basis of the sources, to understand what lies behind that phenomenon. As regards the person of Muhammad he seems to repeat what was said about him at the time: that he did most of his studying in a "bed of harlotry," that forty women were not enough for him, the "whore chaser."[104] But Luther did not allow himself to be blinded by such things. "Personalia" were not of interest; one must pay attention to the teaching.[105] He observes that on the surface Islam appears[106] to reject images and elaborate sacred buildings. He admires the discipline and concentration of Muslims at prayer and notes their abstinence from alcohol and the command to fast, which, however, he regards skeptically from the outset.[107] Apparently he even knew something about the Sufi practice of meditation: "Often they are also in rapture, even at table in company, so that they sit as though dead. . . ."[108]

Luther regards the Qu'ran as a Muslim "book of sermons or doctrines,"[109] on the one hand in a certain way analogous to the Bible and on the other hand something like a set of papal decretals. In connection with his—very free—translation of Ricoldo's refutation of the Qu'ran he finds that despite all its errors it contains "quite a number of true sayings":[110] "I cannot deny that the Turk esteems the four Gospels as divine and true, as well as the prophets, and that he also speaks very highly of Christ and of his mother."[111] But the Qu'ran places Muhammad above Christ, regarding the latter as having been surpassed. Christ's task is said to be done, and now it is Muhammad's turn. Luther cannot escape the analogy of the Old Testament, which for

Christians has been surpassed by Christ.[112] That the Qu'ran does not speak of four gospels and also presents a quite different view of the prophets is not important in this context. Luther wants, in any case, to be objective. At the same time Islam appears to him to be "a patchwork of Jewish, Christian, and heathen beliefs."[113] He is outraged that the Turks approve the use of violence and that there is a lot said about the sword: captured Christians are sold, and the Turks even impale children.[114] The much-praised tolerance of the Turks should not be overestimated; Christians can neither gather in public to confess Christ nor say anything critical against Muhammad.[115] The Turks can even crow about their great numbers and their military triumphs. Here, though, Luther's religious and political perceptions seem to have gotten confused (though in Islamic understanding, in any case, the two cannot be separated).

But for the Reformer theological judgment remains the guide. It is true that Islam is aware of the sinlessness of Jesus and Mary, but it denies that Christ is God's Son, "the Savior of the world who died for our sins"; it regards him as just one of the prophets.[116] To that extent it considers itself reasonable. But what has it understood about Christ? "Father, Son, Holy Ghost, baptism, the sacrament, gospel, faith, and all Christian doctrine and life are gone. . . ."[117] What do you mean, God cannot have a Son? Luther adopts Ricoldo's argument and drives it to the point of absurdity. It is as if someone would say: "God cannot live, because he does not eat and drink, shit and piss, blow his nose and cough."[118] Luther has no sympathy for the basic Islamic creed: "Who doesn't know that God is God, and that he is great!"[119] For Luther, the tautology that God is God makes no sense: ". . . as if someone would say: 'It is not a donkey, for a donkey'. . . . Everyone knows for sure that an ox or a dog is not a donkey."[120]

In Luther's opinion, however, Islam with all its false ideas destroys the basic order of human common life. This is evident from the fact that robbery and murder can be regarded as godly works. Moreover, it is especially obvious with regard to marriage and divorce. Among the Turks a man can have as many wives as he wants, and abandon them when he feels like it; here Luther's information was evidently inexact. In a word: lying destroys the spiritual and murder the worldly status, and unregulated marriage destroys the state of marriage.[121]

His perception of Islam as lived in Turkey already reveals parallels to Luther's views on non-Christian religions as a whole. They do not rest completely on untruths. In particular, Islam knows certain virtues: in any case there is "no man so bad that there is not something good in him."[122] This can also be observed in the Greeks and especially in the Romans. But it is the devil's saints who "think that [they] will become holy, and be saved by works," and help others, "without and apart from the one savior Jesus Christ," which for Luther at the same time reveals a parallel to monasticism, aimed at earning merit, which he had rejected.[123]

The Reformer was convinced that Islam would lead itself, so to speak, into absurdity. That is why he advocated the publication of the Qu'ran. One could do nothing that would endanger the Turks more than to spread information about them. There need be no fear that people could be led astray by this: as every person equipped with sound understanding must know that it is daytime when the sun is shining, so it would be clear to every Christian that assertions deviating from the prophetic and apostolic writings could not be true—and Muhammad himself admitted that he brought a new teaching.[124] Here emerges, from this (limitedly) substantive view of the foreign religion, the judgment from the point of view of the Reformer.

THEOLOGICAL JUDGMENT OF ISLAM

Since John Damascene, Islam had been regarded in the West not as a foreign religion but as a Christian heresy; often it was traced to Arius. That is how Luther saw it as well.[125] The Augsburg Confession mentions the "Mohammedans" at the end of a series of ancient church heresies.[126] Luther's Smalcald Articles attribute responsibility for all possible heresies, among which he lists Islam, to "enthusiasm."[127] Heretics spread untruth and lies; in Luther's mind lies are—as in John 8:44—frequently associated with murder; so it was with the Arians and Donatists, and so it is at present with the Turks and the followers of Thomas Münzer.[128] Nevertheless, the Reformer seems at least to suspect that Islam is a movement that cannot be fully subsumed within the common idea of heresy. With unusual acerbity he asserts that God's wrath lies behind the threat from the Turks, though certainly his first thought is of political danger. The Turk is the rod in God's hand by which God intends to lead Christians to penance.[129] He is thus also "our 'schoolmaster.' He has to discipline and teach us to fear God and to pray. Otherwise we will do what we have been doing—rot in sin and complacency."[130] Luther often parallels the Turks with the papacy, as in his hymn: "Lord, keep us steadfast in thy Word / And curb the Turks' and papists' sword / Who Jesus Christ, thine only Son / Fain would tumble from off thy throne!"[131] At the same time the Reformer asserted that the crucial difference between the two was that the danger from the Turks was only to the body, while the pope was skilled in leading the soul astray. The Turks threaten with murder, the pope with lies; Luther considers the latter to be worse. Of course, the devil is behind both: "great power and cunning skill is his dreadful armor . . ." On the other hand, there is a difference in potency between the two corrupting powers: the Antichrist announced in Sacred Scripture is not the Turk, but the pope.[132] Both threaten the Christian in the end-time. In interpreting Daniel 7, Luther projects a mighty historical panorama that assigns the Turks, and thus the Islam they represent, a place in the end-time drama.[133] What is crucial is to trust in Jesus Christ and his coming, "which cannot be far off. For the world has come to its end. . . ."[134]

It is still striking how energetically Luther repeatedly connects the Turks with the devil. The Turk is the "very devil incarnate";[135] fighting against the Turks means engaging with the devil. The devil uses the Qu'ran to murder souls. Before undertaking a military assault on them one must "smite the Turk's Allah, that is, his god the devil. . . ."[136] It may remain an open question where Luther actually means "the devil" as such and where the devil is only employed for rhetorical emphasis.[137]

In seeking properly theological criteria for Luther's assessment of Islam we discover three that are primary. The criterion of reason is somewhat ambivalent, since on the one hand Luther denounces Islam's lack of reason[138] and on the other hand he finds statements in the Qu'ran that appeal very much to the kind of reason that will not admit the authority of God's word: "it is extraordinarily pleasing to reason that Christ is not God. . . ."[139] The Qu'ran contains "vain human reason without God's Word and Spirit. For his law teaches nothing but what human wit and reason can tolerate." Anything in the faith that is intellectually difficult to accept, the Qu'ran simply drops.[140]

But for Luther the central criterion is faith in Jesus Christ. He advises those who are in danger of being captured by the Turks to learn the Decalogue, the Our Father, and the Creed by heart, but especially the second article of the Creed, which he quotes in its entirety. "For everything depends on this article; because of this article we are called Christians," it "makes us children of God and brothers of Christ. . . . And by this article our faith is separated from all other faith on earth. . . ." Those who are captured by the Turks should constantly repeat this article, in bed and everywhere else—"so press your thumb on your finger," pinch yourself, so that you do not forget![141] The captive should keep in mind that the individual's suffering corresponds to the sufferings of Christ, for "Christ desires to be weak and to suffer with his own on earth. . . ."[142] This is said to be the real difference between Islam and evangelical Christianity: what for Luther "personally was the existential center and meaning of his life and at the same time the core of his theology, namely the *theologia crucis* anchored in Jesus' death on the cross and its practical application in one's own entry into the situation of the suffering of the cross, as well as, in its content, being led into knowledge of God the Father through the crucified Christ—for all this the Qu'ran offered and still offers no point to hold on to."[143]

This is connected ultimately with a final criterion: the message of justification of sinners. The Turk is said to know only works righteousness and the sword, but nothing of forgiveness. Morally the Turk acts in a model way. But even if he is able to present himself as an angel, he is not Christ, since even the devil can easily transform himself into an angel of light.[144] There have been and are great virtues everywhere outside Christianity, once among the Romans[145] and now among the Turks. But that leads only to a bourgeois uprightness, not to righteousness before God.[146]

CRITICAL EVALUATION

That Luther's knowledge of Turkish Islam, and much more so of other non-Christian religions, was limited, and that many of his assessments were false, goes without saying. For example, he did not know that Muhammad has a different status for Muslims than Jesus Christ has in Christianity; from the outset he did not accept Muhammad's prophetic claim but saw the "Prophet" as a morally dubious heretic. From our present point of view it is not Christ and Muhammad that stand in contrast, but Christ and the Qu'ran, "incarnation" and "inlibration." While a fatalistic trend may have been visible in the Islam of the sixteenth century, that does not for the most part represent Muslims' understanding of Islam today.

Nevertheless, we must acknowledge that the Reformer made an effort to obtain authentic information, and he made his own contribution to its dissemination, though his clear aim was to put it off limits and not to encourage interreligious dialogue. It is probably accurate to say that, despite his one-sidedness, he "understood essential elements" of Islam.[147] In interpreting the danger from the Turks as God's punishment as well as in his polemics he adopted contemporary and traditional models. That the devil had led Muhammad astray and that the Qu'ran was a devilish work "was part of the common material of anti-Islamic polemics in both Byzantine and Latin forms."[148] Still, it is unedifying that, and to what a great degree, Luther repeatedly brings the devil into his writing on the Turks, especially since Satan had a considerable theological status for the Reformer.[149] Understandable at the time but scarcely comprehensible today is the apocalyptic drama of the position Islam acquired for Luther—and this as early as 1529 and not only in the sharpening mood of the last years of his life. Certainly the Reformer's view of history, so unsatisfying today, addressed a theological question that remains unresolved, a question he left to the Christianity that came after him: how do we value theologically the fact that six centuries after Christ's birth there could arise a religion that was in large part the heir of Christianity and Judaism and was able to grow into a world movement in competition with Christianity?

What is still relevant in Luther's writings on the Turks, in the face of all these reservations? As regards social and cultural conflict it is certainly his distinction between politics and religion. Political problems must be resolved politically, and religious questions in religious terms. With that, Luther in fact "gave the deathblow" to the Crusader ideology.[150] For today this means that religiously motivated "crusades" against an "axis of evil" or any such are out of the question from Luther's point of view. Social and political conflicts must be worked out on the basis of law—whether national or international. Luther thus formulates a challenge to Islam insofar as it is not prepared to acknowledge a separation between religious and social reality. On the margins there are political counsels worthy of consideration, not covered by theology and still worth taking to heart: that anyone who will not give a guilder for peace must afterward give ten or twenty guilders for war,[151] and "A man should let lie what he cannot lift."[152]

Ultimately, however, what is striking in Luther's writings on the Turks is their pastoral element. The Reformer desires to equip individual Christians to remain secure in their faith, even in the extreme situation of capture by the Turks. He recommends memorizing the most important parts of the catechism. A captive will have no books at hand and therefore must have the essentials in head and heart so as to be able to make them present to herself or himself night and day. The captive will be distracted by a thousand things and therefore should make use of a physical trick, pinching fingers in order to remain alert. The only way to encounter a foreign religion is in a state of internal assurance, and that in turn, according to Luther, cannot be maintained without making one's own the central points of the Christian message, which by no means touch only the intellect. Luther's note should be attended to in our present situation as well; then we can acquire the composure the Reformer himself repeatedly attained in looking to his Lord, Jesus Christ. "What, then, is the Turk? What does he have besides spear and steed?" But we, as believers, have Christ on our side, and we will achieve victory.[153]

It is surprising that Luther gives scarcely any thought to a mission to the Muslims. There had been some timid attempts at mission during the Middle Ages; we may recall Francis of Assisi's conversation with the Sultan of Egypt[154] and the activities of Raymond Lull;[155] early attempts to translate the Qu'ran were also undertaken with a view to mission. Erasmus of Rotterdam spoke in favor of sending missionaries to the Turks. When Luther writes that the Pope should go himself to the Turks and preach the Gospel to them instead of leading crusades[156] he was probably serious. In a late table discussion he said that he "would like to know that the Gospel had come to the Turks," and that "could well happen." If a Pasha were to accept the Gospel, it would "open a hole" in his nation.[157] But on the whole the Reformer shared the general view that it was scarcely possible "to convert a Turk."[158] Only among the Christian captives living among the Turks did he see some opportunity for mission: by their model behavior they would "adorn the Gospel and the name of Christ." Perhaps in this way they would manage to convert "many" Turks if they "would see that the Christians are so superior to the Turks in humility, patience, diligence, faithfulness, and such virtues."[159] Knowledge of the Qu'ran could help them to defend the Gospel.[160] He argues in the sense of an existentially applied *theologia crucis*. But why did he place less faith in the power of the word of God among the Turks than among the "papists"? Mission means communication, and it seems that he regarded meaningful communication with representatives of Turkish Islam in his time as impossible. This was a limitation on Luther's part, one he had constructed himself through his christologically-conditioned rejection and his own view of history and the world—a limitation that must be overcome today.[161]

Luther's theological critique of Islam is "consistently Christocentric."[162] It is off the mark for Ludwig Hagemann to assert that Luther projected "onto Islam the image of a Catholicism that in his time was distorted and fragmented in his own pointed fashion and branded it as a religion of works righteousness of papist hue."[163] In the first place, Luther's critique of Islam was not exhausted by the accusation of works righteousness, and second, the need for self-justification was, according to Luther, not peculiar only to papists, Jews, and Turks: rather, he considered it an inborn trait of sinful humanity. The center of Luther's critique of Islam is indeed represented by faith in Christ; he is the decisive and thus distinguishing Christian element. Through him "our faith is distinguished from every other faith on earth, for the Jews do not have it, nor do the Turks and Saracens, nor any papist or false Christian or unbeliever, but only the true Christians."[164] But this leads the Reformer only to a hermeneutics of distinction; he does not inquire about possible convergences: "Whatever Turks, Jews, and other ungodly persons believe we disregard."[165] Could he not have discovered common elements if he had paid more attention to the first article of faith? Could trinitarian faith not have expanded his view? Nicholas of Cusa, with his broad philosophical horizon, was able to produce a great deal more understanding for those who believed differently. Luther, in contrast, exhausted himself in defamations that often were really beneath him. Herbert Blöchle judges that the Reformer remained "without question inferior to the tolerant basic tone of Nicholas of Cusa, whose literary efforts, with their great communicative openness to the religious views of Islam, represent a milestone in Christian theology's confrontation with Islam."[166]

Jan Slomp presents an unexpected list of possible convergences between Muslim and Lutheran faith: "Muslims will recognize Luther's concern—to let God be God . . . [n. 41, Philip S. Watson, *Let God be God: An Interpretation of the Theology of Martin Luther*] . . . Equally recognizable is the awareness of Muslims and of Luther that we live our daily lives *coram Deo*. . . . Muslims and Lutherans share a great love for the word of God. . . . And could a Muslim not say about himself what Luther said about 'Ein Christen mensch ist ein freier herr über alle ding und niemandt unterthan. Ein Christen mensch ist ein diestpar knecht aller ding und jederman unterthan?'"[167] Slomp reviewed a number of Muslim publications to discover their view of Luther and Christianity. Luther would not have agreed with his method of seeking convergence, because it trends toward a game of equivocations, and Muslims would probably regard it in the same way. It was no help to Jews, Turks, and heretics, he thought, for them to speak of God with deep reverence and seriousness and even call God "Father," for they do not know "what God is. When they speak of God, Creator, and Father, they do not know what they are saying."[168]

Nevertheless the question remains whether Luther did not lay out a trinitarian perspective that was too narrow because it was restricted by his Christology. The message of justification is misunderstood if it stops at the expression of a necessarily total devaluation of non-Christian religions.[169] In addition, the Reformer's dealing with Sacred Scripture gives us pause. When he uses the book of Daniel (though in the sense of the tradition handed down to him) as the basis for his view of history we must ask what hermeneutical standards are in play here and whether they are not related to those of today's uncritical Muslim exegesis of the Qu'ran. Likewise, his eclectic emphasis on the few passages about the Antichrist in the New Testament can only be linked by great effort to the christocentrically-oriented hermeneutics he otherwise proposed. So there is a twofold deficiency: Luther does not test various opportunities for trinitarian thought because he concentrates too much on an exclusive Christology, and as regards his hermeneutical efforts he is not consistently christological enough.

Opportunism? Luther's Stance in the Peasants' War

Contemporary questions

Luther's stance with regard to the Peasants' War has entered the common perception as his great original sin. This view rests essentially on Friedrich Engels's interpretation of the Peasants' War[170] and Marxist history after him, but of course Luther himself was responsible for it also. Did he try to remain nonpartisan, or was he in fact partisan? Did he tip over and put himself on the side of the powerful?

Even from the point of view of the non-Christian religions there have been disgusted references in his direction. Jawaharlal Nehru flogged his attitude toward the peasants with the well-known and horrible quotation: "Nice words, aren't they, especially coming from the mouth of a religious leader and reformer."[171] What questions can we bring to this problem today?

The democracy of a modern constitutional state creates a set of conditions from whose perspective the medieval class society can scarcely be perceived as anything but a system of injustice. It took centuries more before liberty, equality, fraternity could be recognized as at least a slogan; the extent to which they have now been made or can be made reality remains an open question. The issue in the sixteenth century was not, in principle, that of individual freedom, but of the "freedoms" of individual classes; city air made "free."

The "common man," that is, one belonging to a class that was not part of the nobility or the clerical order and had no share in power or learning, in fact lived in a state of dependency that could descend to the point of servitude and even slavery. Of course Luther, in his programmatic writing on "the freedom of a Christian," which still stirs us today, was not concerned with social or political problems. Nevertheless we have to ask how it was that he took so little notice of concrete situations of unfreedom among his fellow human beings who were not members of his class.

The problem of justice is no different. The discussion of wherein justice consists and how it might be achieved is still active today,[172] quite apart from the obvious examples of screaming injustice. The quest to found justice and equality on the basis of natural law has failed since, depending on one's interpretation, as for example in scholasticism, it can serve to stabilize existing conditions of injustice. Still, Nicholas of Cusa had already enunciated the idea that people are by nature *aeque potentes et aeque liberi*—endowed with the same power and the same liberty.[173] As we know, this lovely philosophical assertion has not been translated into politics. Instead, as history shows: "the effort to realize justice for all threatens to produce injustice."[174] But what has always been and remains possible is to engage on behalf of those who clearly are socially disadvantaged and weak and attempt to improve their legal situation. Why did Luther, who could speak so impressively of the justice that exists in the sight of God, pay so little attention to the cause of justice among men and women?

This brings up a third question about the justification of revolt against unjust conditions. In their "Twelve Articles of the Peasantry" the peasants first took the route of medial possibilities in their time in calling attention to their situation and asking for improvement. Luther supported this—though with some reservations. However, they did not wait to see whether anything could be achieved in that fashion, but instead took up arms. In doing so, in the view of the law in force at the time, they put themselves in the wrong. We know how Luther reacted, taking his starting point from his doctrine of the two governments. Today the question here arises: where are the boundaries of the freedom to demonstrate, and under what conditions must they sometimes be crossed? What are the criteria for when violence against things is permitted, and when even violence against human beings is unavoidable? What can be said, from Luther's point of view, about the boycott and struggle against apartheid in South Africa or attempts at political resistance to the Nazi regime in Germany? What about the possible legitimacy of terrorist acts today? We can also turn the question around: what is there in the experiences of the twentieth and early twenty-first centuries that helps us to judge Luther's position?

Finally, with regard to Luther's attitude toward the Peasants' War we must inquire about the role of the churches and of individual Christians in engagement on behalf of the weak.

NARRATIVE

It is not necessary here to trace the history of the Peasants' War in detail.[175] After followers of Thomas Münzer, following his sermon on Maundy Thursday (24 March) 1524, had plundered and burned a chapel near Allstedt, Luther published a "Letter to the Princes of Saxony Concerning the Rebellious Spirit."[176] In it he called on Elector Frederick the Wise and Count John the Steadfast to intervene, saying that God had given them their offices "to preserve the peace and to punish the wrongdoer." In this they should "not sleep nor be idle."[177] In mid-March 1525 the "Twelve Articles" of the peasants of Swabia appeared in Augsburg. Since their last point referred explicitly to the "word of God," Luther saw himself called upon to write his "Admonition to Peace, a Reply to the Twelve Articles of the Peasants in Swabia," which was printed at the beginning of May 1525.[178] But the uprising had already begun in southern Germany at the end of March, and in Thuringia in mid-April. Luther, who possessed only partial information, still believed in the possibility of a negotiated settlement and appealed in his "admonition" to the consciences first of the princes and then of the peasants. The princes should amend their lives and do penance: "It is not the peasants, dear lords, who are resisting you; it is God himself, to visit your raging upon you."[179] He appeals to the peasants not to functionalize the Gospel and the name of God for their own purposes and to realize that in the absence of an orderly authority a general chaos would break out. Even natural and earthly law says "that no one may sit as judge in his own case or take his own revenge. . . ."[180] As a Christian, in any case, one sees things differently: according to the Sermon on the Mount we should desire the good of those who defame us and do good to those who do us wrong: "These, dear friends, are our Christian laws! . . . We have all we need in our Lord, who will not leave us, as he has promised. Suffering! suffering! Cross! cross! This and nothing else is the Christian law!"[181] Christians do not fight with their fists, but with the Our Father! Since it is not a matter here of a quarrel between Christians, but of worldly concerns, one should follow the law's path and install a mediating instance that could seek a compromise: the princes should lighten their oppression: "give these poor people room in which to live and air to breathe"; on the other hand, the peasants should also submit to better teaching.[182]

But these well-meaning suggestions came too late, since the hostile clashes were already in full spate. In light of the devastation wrought by the rebels in Thuringia, Luther apparently got the impression that the rebellious peasants would get the upper hand; consequently he appended to the "Admonition to Peace" an afterword "Against the Raging Peasants," printed on 10 May 1525 and then separately published under the title "Against the Robbing and Murdering Hordes of Peasants." This only became widely known after the Thuringian peasants were crushed on 15 May near Frankenhausen, with thousands of them cut to pieces. Now Luther's charge to the princes that they should spare those who had gone along with the revolt but should proceed brutally against the instigators themselves had to sound more dreadful than, in any event, it is: "Therefore, dear lords, here is a place where you can release, rescue, help. Have mercy on these poor people! Let whoever can stab, smite, slay. If you die in doing it, good for you! A more blessed death can never be yours, for you die while obeying the divine word and commandment in Romans 13, and in loving service of your neighbor, whom you are rescuing from the bonds of hell and of the devil."[183]

Since it appeared that the fronts had shifted, and he had to absorb severe criticism from friend and foe, the Reformer added "An Open Letter on the Harsh Book Against the Peasants,"[184] which he recommended, however, only as "an awkward word in his own defense" and not as "a clarification."[185] He insisted again that if authority collapsed there would be general chaos, and he defended himself against the reproach that he should have shown more mercy. Without addressing the accusation directly, he answered: "This is not a question of mercy; we are talking of God's word. . . . Here I do not want to hear or know about mercy, but to be concerned only about what God's word requires. . . ."[186] One could sin by being merciful, too! The restoration of law and order itself was "mercy," since everyone depends on order and peace. Then, after a brief explanation of his doctrine of the two governments,[187] he repeats in all seriousness the horrible words from the "Harsh Book" we have quoted above. It is true that at the end he rails against the bad behavior of the "big shots."[188] His resigned quintessence seems to be: "if the peasants became lords, the devil would become abbot; but if these tyrants became lords, the devil's mother would become abbess."[189] That, of course, did not restore peace or effect reconciliation.

Although in his writings on the Peasants' War Luther now and then reveals a certain degree of understanding of the peasants' situation, it is clear that they did not have his sympathy. At the end of his letter to the princes of Saxony he suggests that "the mob" is all too much inclined to sedition,[190] and in the "Open Letter" he even says that the peasants had it too good; if they had to give up one of their two cows they should learn to "enjoy the other cow in peace." God, he says, knew that there is need for a strong authority: "The donkey needs to feel the whip (Sir 33:25), and the people need to be ruled with force."[191]

THEOLOGICAL ARGUMENTS

Two years before the outbreak of the peasant unrest Luther had developed, in his "Temporal Authority," his doctrine of the "two governments," as it came to be called, and which we will discuss below.[192] In his writings on the Peasants' War he also called upon this doctrine in regard both to the earthly events and the understanding of spiritual things, in which Luther saw Thomas Münzer as having been mistaken. In his "Open Letter" Luther attempts to make this clear, using himself as an example. He is called a "clergyman" and a minister of the word, but if he were under Turkish rule and saw his (current) masters in danger, he would forget his office "and stab and hew as long as my heart beat."[193] The authorities are appointed by God and do not bear their swords for nothing. It is their duty to serve their subjects, and they fulfill that duty by concerning themselves for peace and orderly conditions. The medieval class order was a matter of course for the Reformer, though he supposes that the classes should serve one another mutually; thus, in his view, the whole social system functions, and that is how God wills it.[194] The Gospel must not be misused in such a way that one class, in pursuit of its own interest, should bring the whole class order into chaos. Natural law itself takes care that no one should be his or her own judge.[195] The Bible underscores this with the words: "Vengeance is mine, I will repay, says the Lord" (Deut 32:35; Rom 12:19). Self-judgment is thus out of the question, especially for Christians. But what should one do in the face of obvious injustice? "We should not approve the injustice, but we should suffer it . . . ."[196] It is necessary to make the injustice visible as such and to condemn it; but there is an established way and there are appropriate authorities for removing it.

The attempt at self-judgment has a spiritual component. For it is above all the just person who does not absolve herself or himself, but instead is his or her own chief accuser.[197] Self-judgment is—from a theological perspective—self-justification. Luther accuses the peasants of taking matters into their own hands and thus making themselves their own "god and savior"[198]—which we might relate to the words of the Communist *Internationale*: "There are no supreme saviors, / Neither God, nor Caesar nor tribune; Producers, let us save ourselves, / We decree common salvation!!"

However, this process can also assume a sublime religious form; Luther thinks he perceives it in Thomas Münzer, whom he—contrary to historical fact—saw as primarily responsible for the peasant uprising. Münzer's people appealed to direct inspiration from the Holy Spirit. "'You yourself must hear the voice of God,' they say, 'and experience the work of God in you and feel how much your talents weigh. The Bible means nothing. It is Bible—Booble—Babel,' etc."[199] In a sermon in 1526 he says that Münzer's temptation is "that it calls one to go into a corner and offer God an empty heart into which the Spirit comes." He, Luther, has in any case not acquired the Spirit in such a way, but through reading and hearing the Scriptures and their message about the suffering and resurrection of Christ.[200] Münzer, he says, holds his own "sufferings" above those of Christ. Essentially, he could do without Christ's cross. He ridicules Luther as the "soft-living flesh at Wittenberg"; he accuses the Reformer of not practicing what he preaches. But Luther acknowledges his discontent and knows how to counter: "It is not a fruit of the Spirit to criticize a doctrine by the imperfect life of the teacher. For the Holy Spirit criticizes false doctrine while bearing with those who are weak in faith and life. . . ."[201] If Münzer and his followers only spread false teaching without causing an uproar, there would be no need to stop them. After all, even the New Testament says that sects will arise. "Let the spirits collide and fight it out. If meanwhile some are led astray, all right, such is war. Where there is battle and bloodshed, some must fall and some are wounded."[202] But Münzer wanted to accomplish the Reformation with the sword, and therefore the authorities must intervene.

Thus two theological presuppositions motivated Luther in what he said about the Peasants' War: his view of authority, founded on Romans (chap. 13), and his rejection of a mysticism that could do without the Bible, and even without Christ. Paul's saying that all authority comes from God and serves God "for your welfare" and therefore does not bear the sword for no reason could be seamlessly integrated, for Luther, with the class order he regarded as unquestionable, and the rejection of Münzer's mysticism was for him a necessary conclusion from his understanding of the Gospel.

CRITICAL EVALUATION

We cannot say, then, that Luther's attitude and arguments were not consistent, but certainly his expressions were neither diplomatic nor altogether nonpartisan. Above all, though, they stood "under the tragic umbrella of 'too late'; they only became publicly known when the situation for which they were intended had fundamentally altered."[203] The significance of media and especially the swiftness with which information travels—perhaps beginning on the threshold of modernity—is fully evident: a deliberate or unintended delivery of news at the wrong time has serious consequences. We may also call it tragic that Luther was fixated on the existing social order, even though in his own time—in Switzerland, for example—there was already some degree of democratic awareness. In his polemic against the idea that Christianity must have a clear leader, in the person of the pope, he even points out that some empires are very well governed without having a "single head": "How do the Swiss govern themselves in our own time?"[204] But in his writings about soldiers ("Whether Soldiers, Too, Can Be Saved") the conditions in Switzerland are already regarded in a negative light.[205] Like his contemporaries, the humanists, Luther had an inclination toward aristocracy, which he preferred to the monarchies known in his time. It is striking that in his writings on the Peasants' War the Reformer scarcely deals with social realities at all, even though in the years preceding he had concerned himself intensively with the problems of interest and usury[206] as well as education, even for girls.[207] Luther was "blind to the social and community components of the peasants' revolts."[208] Only in a few individual cases did he intervene on behalf of disadvantaged peasants.[209] Even after 1525 he had nothing good to say about the peasants; he repeatedly admonishes them that they are not giving enough for the support of their pastors. All this seems to show that he did not feel he had adequately succeeded in impressing the reforming message on the peasant population. The strongest support for the Reformation was found not among the peasants but among the rising classes in the towns and cities. What did that mean for Luther's central concern, the doctrine of justification? To what degree was it dependent on a certain conditioning of its recipients? The Reformer did not accept Thomas Münzer's social concerns in the least. He was altogether fixated on the latter's "mysticism," without remembering that he himself had adopted some mystical traditions. In his concern with Münzer's false teaching he lost sight of the misery of a whole social class. Should we explain this by "the high degree to which the purification of the church of Jesus Christ was his sole theme" and admire "the severe restriction of the Reformer to his own purpose"?[210] Why he "did not support the just demands of the peasants remains a challenge to Luther's attitude."[211] But what constitutes the theological explosiveness of this "challenge"?

In speaking of the universal priesthood of believers[212] Luther had enormously exalted the common human being and at the same time discovered a model for common life and work that could have been exemplary for church and political communities; it anticipates the synodal and democratic elements of later church and state constitutions. Volker Leppin sees the destruction of barriers between clergy and laity as an "anticipation of the overturning of existing law and the social order then in effect."[213] Even in his writing against the "Robbing and Murdering Hordes of Peasants" there are echoes of this approach when Luther speaks of a law of necessity that everyone—not only the authorities—has the right to exercise: against a rebel "everyone is both his judge and his executioner." In much the same way as when giving reasons for the universal priesthood in "To the Christian Nobility of the German Nation Concerning the Reform of the Christian Estate,"[214] he explains, similarly to what he writes regarding the duties of the nobility in "Against the Robbing and Murdering Hordes of Peasants," that "when a fire starts, the first person who can put it out is the best one to do the job."[215] Gottfried Maron comments: one is then acting "not in one's own interest any more than the fire department is ordinarily acting on its own behalf."[216] But the effect of these approaches was not to promote even a timid democratization; quite the contrary: Luther's interest in the universal priesthood declined remarkably in his later years, probably because of his experiences in the Peasants' War. Were the theological reasons he gave at the outset not conclusive enough? Or is it not necessary today, at least within the churches, to resolve an issue that, because of Luther's inability to remain consistent in this regard, has been largely lost sight of or not adequately brought to realization?

Another key word that ought to be mentioned here is "freedom." In his reaction to the peasants' Twelve Articles, Luther polemicized against the peasants' having made "Christian freedom a completely physical matter."[217] A slave can be a Christian "and have Christian freedom."[218] In the Open Letter he then writes, as though it were absurd: ". . . then we ought to let the sword alone, and be 'free brethren,'" and then, contemptuously: "and do as we like."[219] Luther apparently cannot really imagine a responsible political freedom. This prejudice against freedom weighs down Lutheran churches and communities even today. The occasional pulpit polemic against "self-realization" is eloquent testimony to it. Here Luther has to be set against Luther!

In spite of these considerations it is not as if nothing could be brought in Luther's defense. He did, after all, risk intervening in the difficult domestic political situation. Where were the other intellectuals of his time? Erasmus was in Basel, quite secure. The humanists devoted themselves to their studies and *belles lettres*. The peasants had appealed to Luther, but he apparently would not have hesitated to take a position in any case. He was beaten up by all sides, and he must also have been wounded by what he heard about the events in Frankenhausen. But a month after the battle there (15 May 1525) he had the courage to marry (13 June 1525). He regarded his marriage as an act of confident faith in the midst of a chaotic time.

Despite all the problems it involves, we can learn something from Luther's attitude toward the Peasants' War and the disputes surrounding it. He categorically excludes the possibility that even well-considered political goals can be clothed in the Gospel (today we would be more expansive and say "religion") and thus apparently legitimated by it. What, instead, is the church's political task? It cannot decree the resolution of political problems in the sense of a theocratic order or with the aid of biblical citations. But it must insist on the clarification of social demands; it must be engaged in order to see that an unsatisfactory state of things is not simply continued. It will thus, with determination, bring its own insights into the process of developing a democratic idea and so will definitely be partisan—on behalf of the weak and in the interests of a constant improvement of living conditions and strengthening of human rights.[220]

SUPERSTITION? LUTHER'S ATTITUDE TOWARD WITCHCRAFT AND DEMONOLOGY

CONTEMPORARY QUESTIONS

On a superficial reading there is no area in which the distance between Luther and the present is greater than in his belief in the devil and witches. To be just to history we must acknowledge that the concept of superstition, which a rationally-oriented modern person applies with disgust to such beliefs, had a quite different content in the first half of the sixteenth century, and so for the Reformer himself. What was to be understood by "superstition" derived from the dominant ideas of faith, and the difference between faith and superstition was slippery at the margins, and never quite clear.[221] Not until the Enlightenment was there any thought of having a clear criterion for separating the two, namely "reason." It was reason that created the modern understanding of these terms by first being applied to particular ideas and rituals in Roman Catholicism that appeared unable to withstand rational critique. Ultimately, however, it was applied to religion as such. "Enlightenment means liberation from superstition" (Immanuel Kant).[222] The concept of superstition is always related to a particular norm; if the latter is unclear or absent it loses its function and is only the expression of a disqualification that cannot be further specified. To the extent that reason no longer serves as a clear criterion in postmodernity it is of scarcely any use today. Nevertheless, there is a general agreement about what should be considered superstition: even religion must be able to relate to reason in a considered and systematic manner. If we want to talk about Luther's superstition we will have to look for ideas and attitudes that, in contemporary understanding, contradicted the Gospel and thus Luther's own intention. What springs to mind is what he thought, in a pre-Enlightenment sense, about witches and sorcery, the devil and demons. Does his thought in those matters still have anything to do with what people experience today, and therefore have significance now?

This raises the contrary question, in view of contemporary esoteric ideas and in a post-enlightened sense, about ideas and practices that Luther branded as superstitious: are any of them anthropologically sustainable or even helpful? Esotericism often has to do with a rediscovery of supposed or real natural energies and the longing for wholeness. Is Luther's polemic against witches and his battle with demons still relevant in this context? On the other hand, esotericism is ambivalent: some of its elements bring to light traditions that have been obscured, while others lead into shadowy realms or ghettoization, as in the case of the occult and Satanism. Is what Luther said about the devil still helpful in this regard?

A third set of problems applies to the question of witches. The issue has a long and unspeakable history, beginning in the mid-fifteenth century and ending with the Enlightenment. Who are, or were, the witches? Were they "wise women" who understood healing and herbs, "specialists in midwifery and birth control"?[223] Did they practice an underground cult—for example, of the Great Goddess or the powers of Nature? Apparently the picture changed in the course of history; how much today's "witches" have to do (or think they do) with those persecuted in the Middle Ages and the early modern period is a question that remains open and unclear.[224] Application of Luther's words on the question of witches to the present is difficult for that very reason. But the major persecutions of witches only occurred after the Reformation: was Luther the cause?[225] The topic of persecution of witches does not surface in current works on Luther's theology; the monograph by Jörg Haustein[226] is almost never cited. This fact is probably the result of a "suppression mechanism."[227] Even if there is nothing to be gained from a closer investigation of Luther's views on this matter, we must still ask how they fit with the rest of his theology and what corrections to that theology they require of theologians today who give some thought to them.

Sorcery and witchcraft

Luther grew up with medieval ideas about sorcery and witchcraft, and it is not always clear whether his remarks only repeat what he had heard or whether he is conveying his own view of things. He assumes a particular contemporary image of witches that he then reflects on theologically and interprets in particular ways on the basis of certain biblical passages. In his early period it was primarily the interpretation of the Decalogue that gave him occasion to address this topic. Ultimately it even entered into his catechisms: not abusing the name of God means that "we should not use his name to curse, swear, practice magic, lie, or deceive. . . ."[228] In his explanation of the Decalogue in 1516/17[229] he assumed that susceptibility to sorcery increased with age: adolescents are interested in, among other things, blessings for swords, love potions, and marital horoscopes, while those somewhat older are more concerned with healing spells and charms; ultimately he is unsure about where to locate astrology. But the people he singles out and brands as sorceresses are the *vetulae*, the old women: they are able to cause real damage, summon thunderstorms and lightning, and inflict sickness on cattle and human beings. They can apply the "witches' curse" and even enchant children. It is striking that women are the primary targets from the outset; supposedly the devil finds it particularly easy to make use of women.[230] At a later date Luther even suggested that witches can be recognized by their ugliness.[231] In this the Reformer completely surrendered himself to the view of those around him. The practices of sorcery he reports consisted of using the names of Jesus, Mary, or the evangelists in magical spells or using particular objects for magical rites.[232] It is clear to Luther that the human being is surrounded by demons; they dwell in the wilderness and the marshes[233] and behind the provost's office in Wittenberg;[234] they flutter over our heads like clouds.[235] He is also familiar with the idea of "succubi," demons in female form who receive male semen, and "incubi," who pass it along to women to create a "changeling." He is fairly vague about what one ought to think of this,[236] since he had to defend himself against his opponents' polemic accusation that he owed his own life to that kind of demonic manipulation.[237]

From the present point of view it is especially incomprehensible and tragic that medieval people were unable to recognize mentally handicapped people as such; they regarded them as beings in whose origins the devil must have played a part. The notion of the "changeling"[238] is probably pre-Christian, of Celtic and Scandinavian origin; in some places it endured into the eighteenth century.[239] So Luther also spoke of it, though very rarely, and explicitly only in his table talk: he sees there only a *massa carnis* without soul or spirit, something one could get rid of by drowning it. He says incidentally that he would be ready "[to] venture *homicidium* on it," venture it perhaps because in doing so he would be engaging with the devil, since such beings have Satan in them in place of a soul. He suggested that in the case of a twelve-year-old child one should apply the Our Father for healing; a year later the child died anyway. People underestimate Satan's power. The same, he says, was the case with Origen, who mistakenly supposed that the devil would be saved on the Last Day.[240] On the other hand, the Bible occasionally attributes some negative things to God so that no one would be tempted to think dualistically, as the Manicheans do.[241] Luther rejects the idea that a sexual union between the devil and a human being could be fecund.[242] As a matter of principle, however, he advised baptizing a supposed "changeling," since one can never be sure and it may take some time before it will be seen whether this is really such a case. Apparently there was all kind of chatter at Luther's table, about anything and everything. One episode found in the Table Talk is attested in several variants.[243] In any case, Luther does not acquit himself as one imparting enlightenment in this instance.[244]

From his interpretation of the biblical passages that appear to confirm the existence of sorcery and witchcraft we can discover why Luther raised so few questions about them as they were understood in the Middle Ages. Those passages include especially the story of the "Magi" in Matthew (2:1-12), to whom, of course, a positive function for "magic" could be attributed,[245] but also the concept of "sorcery" in Paul (Gal 3:1; 5:20), the mysterious passage about the sons of God in Genesis 6:1-4, and other Old Testament instances such as Exodus 7:11; 8:18; 1 Samuel 28; Deuteronomy 18:10; Exodus 22:18. Jörg Haustein has carefully examined Luther's interpretation of these passages[246] and concludes that we find the Reformer to have been "well informed about the details of witchcraft and sorcery and persuaded of the scientific basis of the notion of witches: this was the outcome of a 'normal' theological education, deepened by special engagement with catechetical literature in preparation for preaching and with exegetical literature in the planning of his courses of instruction, *undisturbed* by his inner development and the external progress of the Reformation."[247]

We are thus confronted with the remarkable fact that Luther on the one hand condemned sorcery and witchcraft in the sharpest terms, and yet the presuppositions on which his condemnation was based were what we would now call superstition. For him sorcery is disobedience to God, consisting in the fact that instead of trusting God the human being acquires her or his own means toward chosen ends. In that way, in the eyes of the Reformer, it represents a parallel to other similar attempts on the part of sinful humanity: it happens sometimes that reason is the means for attempting the very same thing, and appeals to the saints conceal the identical motive. When a Christian has understood this she or he will reject all of it. It may thus be hoped that both the cult of the saints and sorcery itself will vanish.[248] Sorcery, according to Luther, is a misuse of word and sacrament. It attempts to acquire sacramental power by—in the tradition of Augustine!—bringing the word to an element, but not the words appointed by Christ to be brought to the elements of bread and wine, which he also commanded in instituting the sacraments, but self-chosen words declared holy and applied to the elements used in sorcery, which are often very peculiar.[249] It is thus possible that witches may cause real damage to other people's bodies and lives; this is not only about "white magic," which does no one harm, but the genuine *maleficium*, which—to prevent harm to individuals and society—must be punished.

With this witches and sorcerers were criminalized in the fullest sense. Luther demands that they be put to death. In 1529 he threatened the witches he suspected of being among those present at his service with torture, and did so from the pulpit.[250] If witches are convicted of sorcery then Master Hans, the executioner, ought to collect the straw and prepare the pyre.[251] In one case the straw was actually collected: at the end of July 1537 a supposed fortuneteller and "black magician" named Johannes was burned in Erfurt, even though he had repented of the (imputed) acts. From our point of view it cannot be seen as anything but the height of cynicism for Luther to have commented at table that Johannes "did honest penance and by his example brought many to fear God, and died with a joyful heart. . . ."[252]

Behind these horrible facts lies a remarkable degree of logical and theological inconsistency insofar as the sorcerer does not perform his reprehensible acts on his own responsibility, but at the urging of the devil. For it is the demons who lend potency to magic and lead the one who performs them astray into unbelief. Moreover, this says nothing about the ultimate power who allows this,[253] and even appoints it,[254] namely God's own self. Luther sees such incidents and their bitter ends as opportunities for God to warn people and bring them to the right path.[255] We thus come to the problem of Luther's idea of the hidden God, which will be discussed later.[256] In the context of the question of Luther's superstition we must first consider his Satanology.

THE DEVIL AND DEMONS

Luther's Satanology exists on two levels. On the one it has a clear function and a precisely definable theological place in the context of what he has to say about the "hidden God" and thus appears as constitutive of his Christology; on the other it presents itself altogether in the context of late medieval ideas of the devil and demons. The fact that these two levels exist, and the question of how they are related, make up one of the problems of Luther's Satanology. It appears that on both levels his attention to the devil increased over the course of his development: in the argument over the Lord's Supper his opponents count the number of times he mentions the devil;[257] ten years earlier the subject would scarcely have interested them, but ten years later they could scarcely have kept count.

In general the relevant literature has shown how belief in the devil flourished around the turn of the fifteenth and sixteenth centuries. Luther was born into and interwoven in this demon-haunted world of superstition; polemically oriented Catholic scholarship points accusingly to this, while apologetically interested Protestant scholarship uses it as an excuse. In any case it appears that the Reformer, as he grew and developed, was unable to free himself over time from the ideas of the devil he had inherited or those that surrounded him. The curve of Luther's interest in the devil runs in exactly the opposite direction.

For Luther, as for his contemporaries, the existence of the devil was a given. This is evident in what we may say is a particularly impressive fashion in the "Sermon Preached at Erfurt on the Journey to Worms"[258] and in an episode related in connection with it. In this sermon, as elsewhere, Luther spoke about the devil. In former times the devil had attacked people, but now he makes them feel secure and complacent. The church was overflowing. At some point during the service there was a creaking in the beams of the gallery under the weight of the crowd pressing in; panic broke out and people would have broken the windows and jumped out into the cemetery, according to Daniel Greser, "if Luther had not calmed them and told them to stand still because the devil was projecting his spectre."[259] We have to blend the content of the sermon with the circumstances surrounding it in order to picture Luther's spiritual situation and that of his audience: the supernatural, of which he was speaking, can at any moment intervene in the natural world; God can do this, and so can the devil.

Luther was apparently convinced that he himself had experienced demonic phenomena. He heard the devil clearly in the Augustinian monastery in Wittenberg: "for as I began to read the Psalter, and after we had sung Matins and I was sitting in the (hall), studying and writing my lecture, the devil came" and made a grinding noise three times behind the stove. "Finally, since it would not stop, I gathered up my little books and went to bed; but I regret that I did not wait him out and see what the devil would have done besides." When he realized that it was the devil he paid it no more attention and went to sleep.[260] Sometimes the devil lets himself be seen, as he, Luther, had experienced.[261] The devil has not gone away, to India or Ethiopia, but is in your room, behind the stove, everywhere you are, sleep, talk, walk, stand— "there are the devils all around you like bees."[262]

Luther used various terms for the devil, depending on the context. In his devotional writings up to about 1521 he prefers to call him the "evil spirit"; in his conflicts with Rome he gives him the names "angel of light" and "Antichrist." The enthusiasts and the uproar of the years that followed reveal the devil as "a liar and murderer"; Luther's later utterances, which characterize the devil as the author of every imaginable evil, prefer to speak of him as the "adversary," the devil who "blocks and obstructs" [the good], the "murderer from the beginning." These ideas did not replace one another but were gradually added to the existing elements; the result was a gradual expansion of Luther's portrayal of the devil. The only element that declined over time was his reference to the "evil spirit."

Certainly for Luther the devil quickly moved beyond his traditional roles and acquired theological significance. He is the slanderer of humanity who leads believers into temptation and tries to hide God's grace from them. He fights the community on all fronts and has some success, so that on occasion one must allow the hardened "to go to the devil," to whom they belong, in any case.[263] The devil can even be perceived in the small matters of daily life. But from this perspective he can easily become a chaotic power that endangers everything and everyone. From approximately the time of the Catechisms onward the Reformer increasingly perceived Satan as the "adversary" who threatens humanity and all creation.[264] The demons are especially interested in people. Although Luther supposes they are also in the wilderness, they are said to abhor desert places and broad waters because they find no people there to harm.[265] Evil spirits want to make sure that Christians "have neither money, prestige, nor honor, and can scarcely even keep alive."[266] In essence they are against everything positive in creation. They cause storms and bad weather. The devil would like to tear out all the trees; if he could, "he would not let cows have tails."[267] It irks him to see an apple grow on a tree, and it pains and vexes him "that you have a sound finger."[268] In the Large Catechism, Luther summarizes: the devil causes "so much contention, murder, sedition, and war . . . sends tempest and hail to destroy crops and cattle . . . poison[s] the air, etc.

In short, it pains him that anyone receives a morsel of bread from God and eats it in peace."[269] None of these assertions reveals any kind of christological perspective; they are, however, founded on the Bible, primarily John 8:44 (the devil is "a murderer from the beginning" and "a liar") and Ephesians 6:12 ("for our struggle is not against enemies of blood and flesh, but against . . . the spiritual forces of evil in the heavenly places").[270]

From our perspective we must ask whether Luther contributed nothing to the "demythologizing" of the devil. Unfortunately we cannot agree that the "material coloration" of a coarse and gross idea of the devil "begins to fade in Protestant hands."[271] Still, we cannot always be sure whether the Reformer is speaking of the devil in an ontological or in a metaphorical sense. Certainly the proverbial expressions Luther also used are not to be taken seriously: "under the devil's whip,"[272] "painting the devil on the wall,"[273] "in this world the devil is abbot,"[274] and similar sayings. It is a fact that the Reformer loved vivid and graphic expressions, and references to the devil were especially well suited for his purpose. He also used the name of the devil in stereotypical fashion: he describes something bad and then comments: "that is the devil."[275] The medieval properties of the devil undoubtedly diminish also as in Luther's thinking he comes to stand alongside the Law and the wrath of God. On the one hand, in this way the Law and divine wrath acquire the character of almost personal powers, but on the other hand the devil is also in some sense "depersonalized." The association of the devil with "the world" and "the flesh" has a similar effect. The human being is placed alongside the devil as self-assertive and autonomous. Conscience is one of our "two devils."[276] Who is the devil when Luther advises that one must speak to the devil "or to your own heart" . . . ?[277] Luther's theological definition of the devil thus in many respects does serve as an implicit critique of medieval belief in the devil. He also utters explicit criticism: when it comes to superstitious popular notions one should not be ready to believe just anyone; Luther, as we have already indicated, occasionally criticized the notions of incubi and succubi.[278] He contends often and at length with the supposed "spirits" of the dead. The position he here represents helps us to understand what he meant by "superstition." Since Gregory the Great's teaching on purgatory, which lacks any foundation in Scripture, people have believed in the spirits of the dead, but that is superstition brought about by the devil himself! Such appearances are by no means restless souls, but demons themselves![279] The devil is not the object here, but in some sense the subject, the *movens* of all superstition. Finally, Luther gives a further reason why the medieval, traditional presentation of the devil is of no interest to him. He knows of no typical shape of the devil, for it is of the very nature of Satan to make no satanic impression; he appears as an "angel of light" (2 Cor 11:14). Therefore the devil is not "black and rough, with claws, as the painters paint him."[280] This shows that certain demythologizing features in the significance Luther assigned to the devil tended more to strengthen that significance or in themselves represented an intensification.

CRITICAL EVALUATION

What Luther says about the devil and demons may not be as offputting as his attitude toward sorcery and witchcraft. The demonizing of Jews and Turks, enthusiasts and papists also represents an aggressivity that diminished the opponent; the attitude toward witchcraft had direct, if second-hand, effects in the bodies and lives of concrete human beings. It is certainly correct that belief in devils and witches was common everywhere at the time of the Reformation; even the majority of later opponents of the persecution of witches probably believed in witchcraft, as did those who made the laws.[281] But that is no excuse. The question is why Luther was able to shake off so many of the late medieval traditions that were contrary to the Gospel and yet remained the prisoner of the Middle Ages particularly in regard to witches and demons. At the end of his study of Luther's attitude toward sorcery and witchcraft Jörg Haustein writes that the Reformer had "a Janus face in regard to the question of witches."[282] If only we could go so far as to speak of a Janus face! Luther's lack of clarity with regard to belief in devils and witchcraft—whether they were theologically relevant or matters of superstition—may be connected with the fact that in his time, and thus for him, there was no fixed image of "the witch" and "the devil." But we must ask why the Reformer, given his theological approach, could not attain to a clearer judgment in accord with the Gospel.

At the time of the Luther jubilee of 1983, Christoph Türcke presented a polemically pointed suggestion for interpretation that he understands in terms of social criticism.[283] For Türcke it is clear that "here appears someone who declares war against magical sorcery as a whole."[284] But in doing so Luther does not proceed on the basis of reason, but on that of faith, with reason given a new and negative value. The act of faith, says Türcke, leads to an explosive synthesis: "simultaneously the most radical critique and the most skillful self-disguising of magic, both self-reflection and self-effacement."[285] The "trick of deliberate self-effacement" is, indeed, accomplished by the individual; but the priesthood of all believers, in which the new view of things "becomes common assurance, is the priestly self-betrayal of every individual."[286] Thus reason prunes itself and its abilities. In short, Christoph Türcke's thesis is that Luther replaced medieval superstition with his own and thus made the human situation worse: people no longer felt themselves responsible for their own salvation and no longer took the initiative in defending their own rights. In this way, ultimately, they were helplessly surrendered to the authority of the day.[287]

In today's Protestantism we encounter the rejection of magic in two variants: either, in the wake of the Enlightenment, people feel themselves superior to it (this is the liberal view), or (the evangelical variant) it is seen as something to be taken seriously, and for that very reason war is declared on it in the name of the Gospel. Starting from either position one can condemn certain occult or shamanistic practices being revived today, but also accuse some of the rituals and customs of Catholicism and the Orthodox churches of being "magical" and thus disqualify them from the outset. However, it can prove to be extremely difficult to make a phenomenological distinction between what is authentically religious and what is magical. Carl Heinz Ratschow contrasts the "vivid sense" of "oneness," as magic calls it, with religious knowledge of a "division in life between the human and the world, between the human being and God."[288] But the forms of magic, such as sorcery or fortunetelling, that promise oneness are not always clearly distinguishable from Christian-oriented religious practices. Apparently magical gestures and attitudes can also be an eloquent message or become an effective medium for experiencing salvation. In view of this complicated situation the criteria for distinction must be sought elsewhere.

In this connection a reference to Luther is helpful on the one hand but an impediment on the other. It is helpful to the extent that Luther pointed unmistakably and clearly to the egocentric character of magical acts: people attempt to master something beyond their control for their own benefit. Magic thus corresponds to a fundamental characteristic of sinful humans, who seek to achieve their own goals by their own actions and by any means necessary. Thus Luther can parallel sorcery with what reason also seeks. Formally, and from a purely anthropological point of view, magic can be regarded as "the expression of a unique form of logic." But that likewise means that the behavior that apparently corresponds to faith—attending worship, receiving the sacraments, prayer—can in fact be misunderstood and misused as magical.

On the other hand, the Reformer branded as superstitious especially elements of the old religion that today—for Protestants, at any rate—certainly no longer represent any danger. Holy water, which was thought in the Middle Ages to be feared by the devil, can be rediscovered as a palpable reminder of baptism. Crossing oneself is not a magical ritual for protection but an acknowledgment of the blessing conveyed by the Cross, applied to the body. The use of salt and oil, which Luther so often flayed, has found its way into Lutheran worship, as a sign of divine care, in the form of anointing. It would be a shame, and not within the meaning of the Gospel, to discredit as magical something that, as a gift of creation, is able to touch the wholeness of the human being.[289] The criterion for what is to be regarded as "the good" (cf. 1 Thess 5:21) is faith.

Someone who has become aware of Luther's false judgments of Judaism and Islam, peasants, and superstition may be tempted to avoid any further engagement with his theology. That would be wrong for a number of reasons. First, we have to be elementally clear about something St. Paul already knew: theological reflection on earth will always be a limited activity burdened by mistaken judgments, because now we see "in a mirror, dimly, but then we will see face to face" (1 Cor 13:12). In any case, we cannot simply accuse the Reformer of anti-Semitism or opportunism; even as regards his intolerance and superstition we must make distinctions. Many of his wrong judgments are explained by his surroundings and the spirit of the times. It would be anachronistic to expect of him the better and clearer view of things that has been achieved centuries later—and probably only partially.

In view of the pathbreaking theological insights of the Reformer, which brought guidance and comfort to the people of his time and shape the churches of the Reformation even today, one must of course regret that he also left us statements that Lutheran Christians have to feel ashamed of. But in a historical view one must turn the question around and ask: how could a person who was so deeply embedded in his world and the spirit of his times so thoroughly emancipate himself of all these things that a Lutheran Reformation ultimately resulted? What is the nature of a theology that, gained in struggle for a proper understanding of the Gospel and in face of the most difficult obstacles possible at the start, was ultimately able to discover the freedom of a Christian and create a model of church that pointed to the future? That is what we must explore in the chapters that follow.

NOTES

[1] Theodor Pauls, *Luther und die Juden*, 3 vols. (Bonn: G. Scheur, 1939).

[2] Quoted from von der Osten-Sacken 2002, 280–81; see the whole chapter, "Zur Rezeption Luthers in der NS-Zeit," 275–83.

[3] Von der Osten-Sacken 2002, 15–16. The author dedicates his study to the memory of Rabbi Dr. Reinhold Lewin (1888–1942/43).

[4] Bayer 2003, 4; cf. 303.

[5] Hans-Martin Kirn, "Luther und die Juden," III.14, in *Handbuch* 2005, 217–24; the quotation is from p. 222.

[6] Hellmut Zschoch, "Streitschriften," I.3, in *Handbuch* 2005, 277–94.

[7] LW 14, 257–58 (WA 19, 595, 27-29).

[8] On this see von der Osten-Sacken 2002, 47–161.

[9] LW 10, 277 (WA 55/2, 306, 145-50).

[10] Von der Osten-Sacken 2002, 69–74, at p. 69.

[11] LW 45, 195–229 (WA 11, 314-36). For the origins of this writing see the very thorough study, undergirded by a wealth of source material and an abundance of secondary literature, by Thomas Kaufmann, *Luthers "Judenschriften"* (Kaufmann 2005), 517ff.

[12] On this cf. also WA.Br 3, 101–2, no. 629.

[13] LW 45, 199; 229 (WA 11, 314, 27-28; 325, 17-20).

[14] LW 45, 198 (WA 11, 315, 3-4).

[15] LW 45, 229 (WA 11, 336, 30-34).

[16] Hans-Martin Kirn in *Handbuch* 2005, 219.

[17] See von der Osten-Sacken 2002, 242–70.

[18] LW 45, 219 (WA 11, 330, 16-20).

[19] LW 45, 201 (WA 11, 315, 6-9).

[20] WA.TR 3, 76, 21, no. 2912a. That is correct on the one hand, but on the other hand in 1540 Pope Paul III issued a Bull calling people "to meet the Jews with tolerance, to drop the untenable accusations of ritual murder, and to stop them from withdrawing to Turkish regions, since in that case every hope of their conversion would vanish." Kaufmann 2005, 565 (with a full reference at n. 290).

[21] LW 15, 265–350 (WA 54, 28,16-18).

[22] Ibid., 322: ". . . they doubt, equivocate, fidget, and search as an inept organist gropes for the keys, or organ pipes, and queries: 'Are you the right one, or are you the right one?'" (WA 54, 4, 8-10).

[23] WA.TR 5, 220, 25.

[24] WA.TR 5, 220, 25-31, no. 5535.

[25] LW 15, 269 (WA 54, 30, 21-26).

[26] LW 15, 268 (WA 54, 29, 3-6). Therefore Luther, in exegeting the "last words of David" (2 Sam 23:1-7) is able to develop the doctrine of the Trinity in what would be regarded today as a reckless fashion.

[27] LW 45, 221 (WA 11, 332, 4-6).

[28] LW 15, 352 (WA 54, 100, 20-22).

[29] LW 15, 344 (WA 54, 74, 8-10).

[30] "As a Psalter sow" (proverb), WA 53, 620, 19-20.

[31] LW 45, 222 (WA 11, 332, 21-22). Cf. the section "Luthers Äusserungen zur jüdischen Exegese," 210–27 in C. Bernd Sucher, Luthers Stellung zu den Juden (Nieuwkoop: de Graaf, 1977), though this certainly needs development. I know of no monograph on this subject; it would be very desirable to have one.

[32] LW 45, 228 (WA 11, 335, 35–336, 5).

[33] Ibid. (WA 11, 335, 33).

[34] LW 47, 121–306 (WA 53, 417–552). On this see Kaufmann 2005, 532ff. I am passing over "Against the Sabbatarians: Letter to a Good Friend" (1538), LW 47, 57-98 (WA 50, 312-37); "On the Ineffable Name and on the Lineage of Christ" (1543), WA 53, 573-648.

[35] LW 47, 217 (WA 53, 530, 31-32).

[36] LW 47, 274 (WA 53, 528, 6-10).

[37] LW 47, 200 (WA 53, 419, 17).

[38] Ibid. (WA 53, 568, 29-30).

[39] Cf. Kaufmann 2005, 544, 549.

[40] LW 54, 445 (WA.TR 5, no. 5533).

[41] LW 47, 268 (WA 53, 522, 29-36).

[42] ". . . you shall put the inhabitants of that town to the sword, utterly destroying it and everything in it—even putting its livestock to the sword."

[43] LW 547, 269–70, 272 (WA 53, 522, 27-28; 523, 1–524, 21).

[44] LW 47, 272 (WA 53, 525, 31–526, 1).

[45] LW 47, 276 (WA 53, 529, 19-21).

[46] WA 51, 195, 39-40.

[47] LW 51, 291, no. 316 (WA.Br 11, 275, 8–276, 2 [no. 4195]).

[48] Against von der Osten-Sacken 2002, 131.

[49] WA 51, 195, 39-40.

[50] Von der Osten-Sacken 2002, 294. Kaufmann 2005, 564, speaks of elements of "an anti-Semitism specific to the early modern period."

[51] Von der Osten-Sacken 2002, 297.

[52] Quoted in ibid., 300.

[53] Cf. Paul Reiter, Martin Luthers Umwelt, Charakter und Psychose sowie die Bedeutung dieser Faktoren für seine Entwicklung und Lehre. Eine historisch-psychiatrische Studie. Vol. 2: Luthers

Persönlichkeit; Seelenleben und Krankheiten (Copenhagen: Levin & Munksgaard, 1941), 210, 375–76. Cf. also Erikson, *Young Man Luther* (New York: W. W. Norton, 1993), 138, 236.

[54] Thus Kaufmann 2005, 563.

[55] Von der Osten-Sacken 2002, 149.

[56] Cf. ibid., 292–93.

[57] Gerhard Müller, "Tribut an den Geist der Zeit. Martin Luthers Stellung zu den Juden," *EvKomm* 16 (1983): 305–8.

[58] Oberman 1981, 30–39.

[59] Ibid., 48–55.

[60] Von der Osten-Sacken 2002, 259–63.

[61] Here we should especially mention Nicholas of Lyra (1270–1349) and Paul of Burgos (1351–1435).

[62] Anton Margaritha, *Der gantz Judisch glaub* (Leipzig. Melchior Loccher, 1530–31); on this see von der Osten-Sacken 2002, 162–224.

[63] Kaufmann 2005, 559; see in chapter 12, "Marriage and family," n. 69.

[64] Leppin 2006, 342.

[65] According to von der Osten-Sacken 2002, 55–56.

[66] WA 55/2, 167, 3-11. In a way Leppin 2006, 344, follows this line when he says that for Luther the Jews, unlike the Pope and the Turks, "in a sense" represented "the works of Satan since the beginnings of creation in a still more fundamental way." But this can only be true, if at all, in a transferred sense. We may not conclude with Leppin that "a grand salvation-historical panorama suddenly blazed forth here, and this shows how deeply the polemic against the Jews was anchored in Luther's theology."

[67] Johannes Brosseder, *Luthers Stellung zu den Juden im Spiegel seiner Interpreten. Interpretation und Rezeption von Luthers Schriften und Äusserungen zum Judentum in 19. und 20. Jahrhundert vor allem im deutschsprachigen Raum* (Munich: Max Hüber, 1972), esp. 386–91.

[68] See "Function of the Law" in chapter 7.

[69] Oberman 1981, 155.

[70] Ibid., 138.

[71] See "The 'synagogue'" in chapter 11.

[72] Beyer 2007, 68.

[73] LW 15, 329 (WA 54, 80, 27-29).

[74] Cf., e.g., Martin Sasse, *Martin Luther über die Juden: Weg mit ihnen!* (Freiburg: Sturmhut-Verlag, 1938).

[75] Quoted from *Handbuch* 2005, 224.

[76] Cf. the reference to Kurt Meier in von der Osten-Sacken 2002, 19.

[77] This obligation could be approached by Lutheran churches in a number of ways; cf. also the official statements, e.g., in Rolf Rendtorff and Hans Hermann Henrix, eds., *Die Kirchen und das Judentum.* Vol. 1: *Dokumente von 1945–1985* (Paderborn: Bonifatius; Gütersloh: Kaiser, 1988), esp. 527–621. Voices of American Lutheranism are collected by Daniele Garrone in Kaennel 1999, 119–30.

[78] Von der Osten-Sacken 2002, 307–8; cf. also 301–6.

[79] Cf. Kaufmann 2005, 575–76. Until the beginning of the twentieth century Luther's writings on the Jews were accorded no special importance, as is evident also from the fact that before 1933 they were very seldom printed separately.

[80] Eduard Lamparter, *Evangelische Kirche und Judentum. Ein Beitrag zum christlichen Verständnis von Judentum und Antisemitismus* (Stuttgart: Brönner Nowawes, 1928).

[81] LW 45, 213 (WA 11, 325, 17-20).

[82] LW 45, 200 (WA 11, 314, 27-28).

[83] Kaufmann 2005, 490, 509.

[84] LW 47, 268 (WA 53, 523, 3-6).

[85] Kaufmann 2005, 566.

[86]This expression is from Kaufmann 2005, 578.

[87]Cf. Blöchle 1995; Bobzin 1995; 2004; Hagemann 1983; Ehmann 2008 (which I was unable to consult).

[88]He did mention in a sermon of 1522 that "many islands have been discovered in our time" whose inhabitants needed to have the Gospel brought to them; WA 10/3, 20-21; see "Mission" in chapter 12.

[89]See Gottfried Maron, "Martin Luther und Epikur. Ein Beitrag zum Verständnis des alten Luther," *Berichte aus den Sitzungen der Joachim Jungius-Gesellschaft der Wissenschaften, e.V., Hamburg* 6 (1988), no. 1.

[90]*Nostra aetate* 3.

[91]Cf. Isma'il Raji al Faruqi, *Trialogue of the Abrahamic Faiths. Papers Presented to the Islamic Studies Group of the American Academy of Religion* (Ann Arbor: New Era, 1986); Ulrich Dehn, ed., *Wo aber ist das Opferlamm? Opfer und Opferkritik in den drei abrahamitischen Religionen* (Berlin: EZW, 2003).

[92][Errors of Martin Luther 34]: "Proeliari adversus Turcas est repugnare Deo visitanti iniquitates nostras per illos" (To go to war against the Turks is to resist God who punishes our iniquities through them), Heinrich Denzinger, et al., eds., *Sources of Catholic Dogma* (St. Louis: Herder, 1957), accessible at www.catecheticsonline.com. For the whole subject see Thomas Kaufmann, "*Türckenbüchlein.*" *Zur christlichen Wahrnehmung "türkischer Religion" in Spätmittelalter und Reformation* (Göttingen: Vandenhoeck & Ruprecht, 2008).

[93]LW 46, 183 (WA 30/2, 128, 8-17).

[94]LW 46, 170–71 (WA 30/2, 119, 2-10).

[95]LW 46, 168 (WA 30/2, 114, 25).

[96]LW 46, 170 (WA 30/2, 116, 23-25).

[97]LW 46, 185, 195 (WA 30/2, 175, 31–176, 5).

[98]WA 30/2, 192, 31–193, 5. See the translation in Adam S. Francisco, *Martin Luther and Islam: A Study in Sixteenth-Century Polemics and Apologetics* (Leiden and Boston: Brill, 2007), 170.

[99]George of Hungary, "Libellus de ritu et moribus Turcorum," published by Luther with his own preface, WA 30/2, 205–9.

[100]Translated by Luther in 1543, with a commentary based on his own original translation, WA 53, 272–396.

[101]Further details are found in Bobzin 1995; Bobzin 2004.

[102]WA 53, 569–72.

[103]Not "Cribatio," as in *Handbuch* 2005, 230; *cribum* is the sieve (English "crib") with which chaff can be separated from wheat.

[104]LW 15, 342 (WA 54, 92, 34–93, 7; 92:21).

[105]WA.TR 5, 221, 4-5, no. 5536.

[106]On this see Blöchle 1995, 155–61.

[107]WA 46, 177 (WA 30/2, 189, 27-28; 187, 28-31).

[108]WA 30/2, 187, 5-6.

[109]LW 46, 176 (WA 30/2, 121, 31).

[110]WA 53, 340, 6-7.

[111]LW 46, 196 (WA 30/2, 140, 29-31). "Christum vero dicunt Turcae raptum esse in coelum," WA.TR 5, 221, 14-17, no. 5536. This note attests to an unusually precise state of information; cf. Qu'ran Sura 4, 158.

[112]LW 46, 197 (WA 30/2, 140, 31–141, 9).

[113]LW 46, 177 (WA 30/2, 122, 29-30).

[114]LW 46, 197 (WA 30/2, 177, 18-21).

[115]LW 46, 175 (WA 30/2, 120, 29–121, 2).

[116]LW 46, 176 (WA 30/2, 122, 2-8).

[117]LW 46, 177 (WA 30/2, 122, 19-20).

[118]WA 53, 334, 27-35. Ricoldo, in contrast, had said: "si quis dicat deum (non esse substantiam, quoniam non habet accidens) vel non vivere, quia nono comedit . . ." WA 53, 335, 14-16.

[119] WA 53, 318, 15.

[120] WA 53, 318, 7-19.

[121] LW 46, 181 (WA 30/2, 127, 13-14).

[122] LW 46, 182 (WA 30/2, 217, 21-22).

[123] WA 30/2, 187, 12-14.

[124] WA 53, 570, 35–571, 3 (preface to Bibliander's edition of the Qu'ran).

[125] E.g., LW 41, 86 (WA 50, 575, 1-3). But he could see other heretics as having been responsible for the origins of Islam: cf. Blöchle 1995, 156.

[126] Or "Mahometistas," CA I, *The Book of Concord*, 27. But cf. Thomas Aquinas, *Summa contra gentiles*!

[127] SA III, viii, 9, *The Book of Concord*, 312.

[128] LW 46, 180 (WA 30/2, 124, 20–125, 9).

[129] LW 46, 158 (WA 30/2, 120, 10-24).

[130] LW 43, 224 (WA 51, 594, 9-11).

[131] Text: LW 53, 305 (WA 35, 467, no. 32). For the history of reception see Bobzin 2004, 267–28.

[132] LW 46, 181 (WA 30/2, 125, 27–126, 5).

[133] LW 46, 180 (WA 30/2, 162, 30–164, 3).

[134] LW 46, 199 (WA 30/2, 143, 31-32).

[135] LW 46, 181 (WA 30/2, 126, 2).

[136] LW 46, 184 (WA 30/2, 129, 8-9).

[137] See "Assurance of the predestination to salvation" in chapter 6.

[138] See the end of the previous section.

[139] LW 46, 177 (WA 30/2, 122, 26-27).

[140] WA 30/2, 168, 17-20. Luther says ironically that Jews, Turks, and Tartars "with their spoonful or nutshellfull of brain . . . can comprehend the incomprehensible essence of God and say that since God has no wife, He can have no Son"—fie on all "who are the disciples of blind, deaf, and wretched reason in these exalted matters, which none but God alone can fathom . . ." LW 15, 292 (WA 54, 48, 35–49, 4).

[141] WA 30/2, 186, 1-24.

[142] WA 30/2, 173, 23-24.

[143] Hagemann 1983, 26.

[144] LW 46, 182 (WA 30/2, 127, 24-25).

[145] Cf. Blöchle 1995, 116–25.

[146] See the passages in Althaus 1962, 130.

[147] Siegfried Raeder in *Handbuch* 2005, 230.

[148] Hagemann 1983, 21 n. 56. He refers, *inter alia*, to Adel-Théodore Khoury, *Polémique byzantine contre l'Islam (VIIIe–XIIIe s.)* (Leiden: Brill, 21972), the collection of sources used by Pope Benedict XVI for his lecture at Regensburg on 12 September 2006.

[149] Barth, Hans-Martin 1967; Oberman 1983; Armin Ernst Buchrucker, "Die Bedeutung des Teufels für die Theologie Luthers," TZ 29 (1973): 385–99.

[150] Slomp 2004, 294.

[151] Cf. WA 30/2, 182, 2-4.

[152] LW 46, 199 (WA 30/2, 143, 29)—something of which, especially, one who trusts in Christ is capable.

[153] WA 31/1, 348, 33-35.

[154] Cf. Raoul Manselli, *Franziskus. Der solidarische Bruder* (Freiburg: Herder, 1989), 224–30.

[155] Cf. Helmut Riedlinger, "Lullus, Raymundus Lullus (Ramon Lull) (1232/33–ca. 1316)," TRE 21: 500–5.

[156] WA 8, 708, 29-30. But cf. WA 2, 195, 5-6 (". . . nec pastores mittit ad Turcas et alias gentes") and WA 2, 225, 4-5.

[157] WA.TR 5, 221, 1-2; 19-21; no. 5536.

[158] WA 30/2, 191, 8.

[159] WA 30/2, 194, 29–195, 4.

[160]WA 53, 572, 12-16.

[161]Immediately after Luther's death there were certainly attempts made by Lutherans to bring the Gospel to the Turks as well; see Elert 1931, 1, 344.

[162]Siegfried Raeder in *Handbuch* 2005, 230.

[163]Hagemann 1983, 32.

[164]WA 30/2, 186, 15-18.

[165]LW 15, 276 (WA 54, 35, 33-34).

[166]Blöchle 1995, 191.

[167]"A Christian is a free master of all things and subject to no one; a Christian is a useful servant of all things and subject to everyone," Slomp 2004, 293–94; he lists other issues in Luther's thought that might be fruitful for dialogue.

[168]LW 15, 314 (WA 54, 68, 21-22). Cf. Karl Barth: nothing separates Christianity and Islam "so radically as the different ways in which they appear to say the same thing—that there is only one God," *Church Dogmatics*, Study Edition 9. *The Doctrine of God* II/1 (London: T & T Clark, 2010), Section 31, p. 10 [449].

[169]Against Heinrich Fries, "Das Christentum und die Religionen der Welt," 240–72 in idem, *Wir und die andern. Beiträge zum Thema: Die Kirche in Gespräch und Begegnung* (Stuttgart: Schwabenverlag, 1966), at 256.

[170]Friedrich Engels, "Der deutsche Bauernkrieg," in Karl Marx/Friedrich Engels, *Gesamtausgabe* (MEGA) 10: *Werke. Artikel. Entwürfe. Juli 1849–Juni 1851*. Vol. 1: *Text* (Berlin: Akademie Verlag, 1977), 367–443; Vol. 2: *Apparat* (Berlin: Akademie Verlag, 1977), 962–83. Cf. also Hartmut Lehmann, "Das marxistische Lutherbild von Engels bis Honecker," 500–14 in Medick/Schmidt 2004. See Engels, *The Peasant War in Germany* (Moscow: Progress, 1974); Engels, *The German Revolutions: The Peasant War in Germany, and Germany: Revolution and Counter-Revolution*, trans. Leonard Krieger (Chicago: University of Chicago Press, 1967).

[171]*In Glimpses of World History* (London: Lindsay Drummond, 1949), 285.

[172]Cf. Lienemann 1995.

[173]Quoted from TRE 8: 435, 25–26.

[174]Lienemann 1995, 197.

[175]Cf. Brecht 1986, 172–93; Leppin 2006, 221–36.

[176]LW 40, 45–59 (WA 15, 210–21).

[177]LW 40, 51 (WA 15, 213, 4 7).

[178]LW 46, 3–43 (WA 18, 291–334).

[179]LW 46, 20 (WA 18, 295, 22-24).

[180]LW 46, 25 (WA 18, 303, 3–304, 19).

[181]LW 46, 29 (WA 18, 310, 21-29).

[182]LW 46, 43 (WA 18, 333, 21-22).

[183]LW 46, 54–55 (WA 18, 361, 24-28). Cf. Brecht 1986, 178–84.

[184]LW 46, 57–85 (WA 18, 384–401).

[185]Brecht 1986, 187.

[186]LW 46, 66 (WA 18, 386, 14-18).

[187]See "God's Government with the 'Left Hand'" and "The Cooperation of God's Left and Right Hands" in chapter 14.

[188]"I have heard that at Mühlhausen one of these big shots summoned the poor wife of Thomas Münzer, now a pregnant widow, fell on one knee before her, and said: 'Dear lady, let me * * * you.' . . . What should I write for scoundrels and hogs like that? The Scriptures call such people 'beasts' . . . and I shall not make men of them [acknowledge their humanity]." LW 46, 84 (WA 18, 400, 30–401, 2).

[189]LW 46, 84 (WA 18, 401, 3-5).

[190]LW 40, 59 (WA 15, 221, 3-4).

[191] LW 46, 76 (WA 18, 394, 11-12). On this whole subject cf. Siegfried Bräuer, "Luthers Beziehungen zu den Bauern," 457–72, 875–82 in Junghans 1983; also Jay Goodale, "Luther and the Common Man—the Common Man and Luther," 66–88 in Medick/Schmidt 2004.

[192] See chapter 12.

[193] LW 46, 81 (WA 18, 398, 29-32).

[194] Cf. Bräuer in Junghans 1983, 462–63.

[195] LW 46, 25 (WA 18, 304, 1); see above, at the beginning of "Narrative" in chapter 4. Cf. Gottfried Maron, "Niemand soll sein eigener Richter sein. Eine Bemerkung zu Luthers Haltung im Bauernkrieg," 66–80 in Maron 1993.

[196] WA 18, 285, 9-10; cf. 283, 30–286, 23. Cf. LW 46, 28: "Christ says that we should not resist evil or injustice but always yield, suffer, and let things be taken from us."

[197] For Luther the definition of justice was: "Iustitia est accusatio sui in principio et iustus primum est accusator sui," WA 1, 427, 34-35; cf. WA 5, 102, 8.

[198] LW 46, 34 (WA 18, 319, 20-21).

[199] LW 40, 50 (WA 15, 211, 27-29).

[200] WA 16, 598, 12-16.

[201] LW 40, 57 (WA 15, 218, 5-7).

[202] LW 40, 57 (WA 15, 219, 1-3).

[203] Maron 1993, 71.

[204] LW 39, 64 (WA 6, 292, 12-14 [1520]).

[205] LW 46, 106–8 (WA 19, 635, 17-18, 30-31; 636, 25 [1526]).

[206] First in 1519, and last in 1524: "On Trade and Usury," LW 45, 231–73 (WA 15, 293–322).

[207] "To the Councilmen of All Cities in Germany That They Establish and Maintain Christian Schools" (1524), LW 45, 339–78 (WA 15, 27–53).

[208] Maron 1993, 78–79.

[209] Cf. Brecht 1986, 187–88; Bräuer in Junghans 1983, 465.

[210] Thus Maron 1993, 79.

[211] Armin Kohnle in Handbuch 2005, 137.

[212] See "Universal, Mutual, and Common Priesthood" in chapter 11.

[213] Leppin 2006, 156.

[214] LW 44, 137 (WA 6, 413, 33-37).

[215] LW 46, 50 (WA 18, 358, 9-10).

[216] Maron 1993, 71.

[217] LW 46, 39 (WA 18, 326, 15).

[218] Ibid. (WA 18, 327, 2).

[219] LW 46, 83 (WA 18, 400, 11-12).

[220] I am thus pleading for a dynamization of the two-governments doctrine. For the whole, see chapter 12.

[221] Translator's note: The affinity of "faith" and "superstition" is less obvious in English than it is in German, in which the respective words are "Glaube" and "Aberglaube."

[222] Cf. Walter Sparn, "Aberglaube II. Kirchengeschichtlich und dogmatisch," RGG4 1: 56–59.

[223] Wisselinck 1991, 190.

[224] See Hans Gasper, et al., eds., Lexikon der Sekten, Sondergruppen und Weltanschauungen. Fakten, Hintergründe, Klärungen (Freiburg: Herder, 41992), 455–57 (with bibliography); Reinhard Hempelmann, et al., eds., Panorama der neuen Religiosität. Sinnsuche und Heilsversprechen zu Beginn des 21. Jahrhunderts (Gütersloh: Mohn, 2001), 283, 286–89 (with bibliography).

[225] According to Jörg Haustein, "Hexen," RGG4 3: 1719–22, we can "with all appropriate caution perceive a gradient from Roman Catholic prince-bishoprics and other territories through Lutheran territories to other Reformed areas. The worst persecutions of witches in Würzburg (J[ulius] Echter von Mespelbrunn) contrast with the Palatinate, where there were no trials." Quotations from p. 1721.

[226] Haustein 1990.

[227] Wisselinck 1991, 190.

228 *The Book of Concord*, 342.

229 WA 1, 401, 1–404, 18. For what follows cf. Haustein 1990, 38–67.

230 WA 1, 403, 18-24.

231 WA 16, 551, 36-37 (1526): ". . . they have devilish forms, I have seen some of them."

232 Haustein 1990, 113; WA 16, 551, 18–552, 23: "Occidantur magae, quia fures sunt, adulteri, latrones, homicidae," ibid., 552, 14.

233 WA 17/2, 221, 10-16 (1525).

234 WA 20, 292, 36 (1526).

235 WA 32, 177, 11-16 (1530).

236 Cf. WA.Br 7, 319, 21–320, 25, no. 2286 (1535).

237 Cf. Haustein 1990, 129–30; LW 47, 254 ("On the Jews and their Lies").

238 "Wechselbalg"; a "Balg" was, in the first place, e.g., an animal skin used as a container; cf. "Blasebalg" = bellows. See Friedrich Kluge, *Etymologisches Wörterbuch der deutschen Sprache* (Berlin and New York: de Gruyter, 1975), 46.

239 Cf. "Wechselbalg," *Handwörterbuch des deutschen Aberglaubens* 9 (Berlin and New York: de Gruyter, 2005), Appendix, 835 63.

240 LW 54, 397 (WA.TR 5, no. 5207). Haustein 1990 does not mention this passage, which is in any case unique.

241 WA.TR 2, nos. 2528-29.

242 LW 2, 11: "But that anything can be born from the union of a devil and a human being is simply untrue," WA 42, 269, 35-36. On the other hand he thought, according to a table discourse, that the devil could beget children: mermaids entice men, and the devil is an artist with a thousand wiles: WA.TR 3, no. 3676.

243 WA.TR 2, no. 2528, according to the *Handwörterbuch des deutschen Aberglaubens*.

244 The *Handwörterbuch* refers to the physician Johannes Hartlieb, who in 1445 was the first to make an effort to find a natural explanation for mental illnesses; however, he had no followers for centuries thereafter. Nevertheless, Landgrave Philipp of Hesse endowed the cloister of Haina in 1533 as a hospital, for the mentally ill as well. For the whole cf. Otto Speck and Klaus-Rainer Martin, "Sonderpädagogik und Sozialarbeit," 57–65 in Heinz Bach, ed., *Handbuch der Sonderpädagogik* 4 (Berlin: Carl Marhold, 1990); Andreas Möckel, *Geschichte der Heilpädagogik* (Stuttgart: Klett-Cotta, 1988); Gottfried Hammann, *Die Geschichte der christlichen Diakonie. Praktizierte Nächstenliebe von der Antike bis zur Reformationszeit* (Göttingen: Vandenhoeck & Ruprecht, 2003), 190–214; Schneider-Ludorff 2006, 99–126.

245 For the Reformer their arts were, on the one hand, devilish, but on the other hand they were grounded in the powers of creation; there are a great many "mysterious processes" in nature that must appear to those without knowledge as marvelous: LW 52, 161 (WA 10/1/1, 559, 11–560, 11); cf. ibid., 162 (WA 562, 14) (magic: a "natural knowledge"); WA 17/2, 360, 35 (the Magi, "natural philosophers").

246 Haustein 1990, 68–97.

247 Ibid., 97 (emphasis supplied).

248 Cf. WA 6, 12, 29-35 (1519).

249 Cf. WA 37, 636, 20–637, 18.

250 WA 29, 520, 18–521, 5.

251 WA 41, 683, 34-35 (1536).

252 WA.TR 3, 460, 34-35 (1537).

253 WA 1, 408, 5-7.

254 WA 1, 408, 31-38.

255 I consider it a stretch to therefore regard Luther as having seen sorcery and witchcraft as "belonging to the order of creation" (Haustein 1990, 107).

256 See chapter 6.

257 Cf. LW 37, 269 (WA 26, 401, 23–402, 34 [1528]). Luther counters: "Why don't they also count how often I have mentioned God and Christ"—and adds his subjective experience: "and how I fight for Christ against the devil?" (ibid., [WA 402, 3-4]). Even so, I am shocked when I look at the

German index of the WA under "Teufel" (devil) in WA 72, 766–85 (!) and the Latin index under "satan(as)" in WA 68, 77–84. (See LW 55, 77–78; 282–83.) In what follows I will refer to my essay "Zur inneren Entwicklung von Luthers Teufelsglauben," KD 13 (1967): 201–11.

258 LW 51, 60–66 (WA 7, 808–13).

259 Cf. the introduction to this sermon in WA 7, 803.

260 WA.TR 6, no. 6832; 219, 30-40.

261 ". . . sicut ego vidi," WA 37, 32, 14-15 (1533).

262 WA 34/2, 364, 17-20.

263 Cf. LW 46, 84 (WA 18, 400, 29-30 [1525]).

264 WA 45, 144, 35-36 (1537); WA 16, 552, 33 (1526); LW 37, 17 (WA 23, 166, 26 [1527]).

265 WA 38, 474, 36-40 (1538).

266 The Book of Concord, 370.

267 LW 51, 206 (WA 16, 552, 8 [1526]).

268 WA 32, 36, 30-32 (1530).

269 The Book of Concord, 431.

270 Other biblical passages that are repeatedly cited include 1 Sam 16:14–23; 2 Cor 11:14; 2 Thess 2:7–12.

271 Gustav Roskoff, Geschichte des Teufels 2 (Leipzig: Brockhaus, 1869), 427.

272 LW 45, 26 (WA 10/2, 283, 23), and frequently.

273 LW 38, 171 (WA 54, 160, 26).

274 WA 50, 43, 15.

275 Cf., e.g., WA 34/1, 196, 3; the examples are many.

276 LW 26, 26 (WA 40/1, 73, 2); WA 36, 397, 5-8.

277 ". . . diabolo vel cordi tuo," WA 5, 172, 34 (1519–21).

278 And yet the existence of "incubi" and "succubi" is uncritically presupposed, e.g., in WA 1, 410, 8; 407, 5 (1518). Luther is often reserved in his attitude: "Somniarunt hoc loco incubos et succubos, quos tamen non negamus esse . . ." WA 14, 185, 29 (on Genesis 6; 1523/24). "Sed quod ex Diabolo et Homine possit aliquid generari, hoc simpliciter falsum est," WA 14, 269, 35-39 (see n. 242 above).

279 ". . . apparuit ei" (namely, to Pope Gregory) "nequissimus Diabolus, exortus ab inferno ad illudendum toti generi humano," LW 7, 297: "the specter which appeared to him was the devil in all his wickedness, who came out of hell to mock the whole human race" (WA 44, 519, 35; 520, 10).

280 WA 34/2, 360, 28-361, 19 (1531).

281 The embarrassing laws of Charles V, the so-called "Carolina" of 1531, assigned the death penalty for sorcery that caused harm.

282 Haustein 1990, 182.

283 Christoph Türcke, "Luthers Geniestreich: Die Rationalisierung der Magie," in idem and Friedrich Wilhelm Pohl, Heilige Hure Vernunft. Luthers nachhaltiger Zauber (Berlin: Wagenbach, 1983).

284 Ibid., 46.

285 Ibid., 56.

286 Ibid., 56–57.

287 We cannot further explore Türcke's eccentric interpretation of the message of justification (esp. pp. 52–55, 58–59) and the doctrine of the two kingdoms (esp. pp. 62–67) at this point.

288 Carl Heinz Ratschow, Magie und Religion (Gütersloh: Bertelsmann, 1947), 152.

289 Cf. Adolf Köberle, "Der magische Weltaspekt und seine religiöse Bedeutsamkeit," 43–55 in idem, Heilung und Hilfe: Christliche Wahrheitserkenntnis in der Begegnung mit Naturwissenschaft, Medizin und Psychotherapie (Moers: Brendow, 1985), and G. Marcel Martin, "'Schamanismus' im Dialog des Christentums mit den Weltreligionen," 336–50 in Schönemann/Maassen 2004.

PART II

Perceptions: Luther's Theology as Provocation

5

Alternatives: Between Cross and Self-Determination

"Theology of the cross" has become a kind of brand name for Luther's theology. "Cross alone" constitutes his theology.[1] It finds in the cross its criterion and its confirmation.[2] At the same time, this may be one reason why Luther's theology is not very well liked and seems not to have much about it that is attractive.

We find the symbol of the cross nowadays in every conceivable context, from the corners of rooms in hostels in upper Bavaria to decorative pendants around people's necks, even in Asia, and it has for the most part become dumb and speechless, for many people a puzzling "plus sign" on top of the church tower. In theology it seems to have become a frozen and empty formula, associated with no concrete memory of the agonizing death of Jesus of Nazareth. Consequently it has been suggested that we should no longer speak of the "cross of Christ" and instead talk of Jesus' execution.[3] On the other side it can continue to be interpreted as the symbol of an unjustified claim to power by an almighty church that is out of place in a secular, pluralistic society. The cross, or rather the crucifix, has become a run-of-the-mill object that says nothing or else an aggressive challenge, as discussion about the so-called crucifix decision showed a few years ago.[4] In this situation how can Luther's "theology of the cross" find a place for itself or bear any fruit?

Memory of the cross of Jesus Christ, in any event, stands in opposition to elementary needs at least of the well-situated people of the Western world, who have no desire to be deprived of the opportunity to make good on their ambitions. Western, well-off people see it as their task to make the best of their lives and accept responsibility for themselves. In the best case this also includes responsibility for other people or for society. In this context the memory of the crucified Jesus of Nazareth can only be a disturbing factor.

On the other side are the marginalized people who find no connection to the boom in self-realization. What use is the cross of Jesus Christ to them? It does not help them to cope with the concrete crises of their daily lives and try to catch up with those who are better off. Looking at the cross is more of a hindrance than a help in their quest to break out and become active. For example, for centuries in Latin America the cross's function was crippling. Women in particular feel damaged by references to passion and crucifixion; they have experienced too much of their own passion and crucifixion to be able to do much with the crucifix.[5]

Within Christian theology the idea of a representative sacrifice, traditionally associated with the cross of Christ, has become obsolete for many. It is said to be one of the ideas we need to part with,[6] based as it is on the idea of a sacrificial ritual that has nothing to do with Jesus' proclamation. It is considered anachronistic to speak of a "redeeming sacrifice." In fact, devotion to the passion has rapidly diminished in Lutheran congregations in recent decades; the Lenten "passiontide" has silently transformed into the "fasting time," sometimes promoted as "seven weeks without" or even "with"—though not so much "with" recollection of Jesus' suffering and death!

A theology of redemptive sacrifice, according to Klaus-Peter Jörns, arose in the interests of sacramental practice.[7] In fact we do find here—although with different presuppositions than those Luther had—an anchor for the theology of the Mass and the idea of clerical office associated with it, and in turn the claim of the Roman Catholic Church to be Christ's sole representative. Would not an insistence on the traditional implications of a theology of the cross prove to be positively anti-Protestant?

Finally, there is the head-scratching lack of understanding on the part of non-Christian religions and all our enlightened contemporaries: why should the execution of this one human being have significance for all humanity—and what is supposed to be consoling about it?

For all these reasons, would it not be appropriate to stop putting so much emphasis on Luther's *theologia crucis* and making it so central, as was at least partly the case in the twentieth century?[8]

Luther formed the concept of the *theologia crucis* in the spring of 1518. In the Heidelberg Disputation, in which he had the opportunity to present his views before the chapter of his order, he succeeded in giving a clear account of his concept. He considered the *theologia crucis* a direct counter to the *theologia gloriae* only in the years thereafter, namely in his lectures on the Psalms in 1519–1521[9] and in his interpretation of the Magnificat.[10] But the theology of the cross was not merely formative in a particular phase of Luther's development. It is in the background of his distinction between the revealed and the hidden God. It changed in the course of the dispute over the Lord's Supper and remained, in a form supported by the doctrine of two natures in Christ, as the supporting ground for the Reformation message about the justification of the ungodly. It represents a theological approach that accompanied the Reformer throughout his life and at the same time corresponded to a particular way of doing theology and a lifestyle in accord with it.[11] Luther's whole theology is, we might say, colored by and soaked in the blood of the Crucified and the suffering of the world.

THE APPROACH

BIBLICAL BACKGROUND

There are two primary New Testament passages, plus one reference from the Old Testament, on which Luther's exposition of a *theologia crucis* rests. The "message about the cross," Paul writes (1 Cor 1:18-25), is "foolishness to those who are perishing, but to us who are being saved it is the power of God." This is the way God chose "since, in the wisdom of God, the world did not know God through wisdom." The Jews demand "signs" and the Greeks ask for "wisdom," but Paul preaches to them "Christ crucified, a stumbling-block to Jews and foolishness to Gentiles." The Crucified is "the power of God and the wisdom of God. For God's foolishness is wiser than human wisdom, and God's weakness is stronger than human strength." This could be read together with the beginning of Romans, where Paul laments that God's "eternal power and divine nature," evident in the divine works, are not understood by human beings. "Claiming to be wise, they became fools" (Rom 1:18-23). In the Old Testament it is reported that Moses prayed to be able to see God's "glory." He received the answer: "you cannot see my face; for no one shall see me and live." Moses is told that he will be placed in a cleft of the rock and God will pass by; ". . . you shall see my back; but my face shall not be seen" (Exod 33:18-23). The Vulgate has two words here that Luther seized upon: God's "glory" ("Ostende mihi gloriam tuam") and the permission to Moses to see at least the back of God, to perceive the other side of God ("posteriora mea").

But it would be a mistake to see Luther's *theologia crucis* as having a biblicist foundation. His concern is rather with taking the cross of Christ, which cannot be slotted into human categories of wisdom and strength, with the utmost seriousness.

THESES

The basic statements of the *theologia crucis* can best be enunciated from Theses 19–24 and 28 of the Heidelberg Disputation.[12] "That person does not deserve to be called a theologian who looks upon the invisible things of God as though they were clearly perceptible in those things which have actually happened" (Thesis 19). According to Romans 1:22, in fact, such a person should be called a "fool." Access to the knowledge of God by way of creation, or reason that analyzes creation, is closed. Human beings have misused this way by confusing the creation with its Creator, and now the reverse path from the visible to the invisible is no longer possible. God has chosen a new way—in Christ. The one who does proper theology is instead the one "who comprehends the visible and manifest things of God seen through suffering and the cross" (Thesis 20). What is at issue is recognizing God hidden in suffering, in the lowliness and shame of the cross. Consequently, true theology and knowledge of God are found in the crucified Christ.[13] Anyone who does not understand this and does theology for his or her own glory—as a *theologus gloriae*—calls what is evil good and what is good evil (Thesis 21). It is clear to the theologian of the cross, on the other hand, that God can only be found in the cross and suffering. Therefore the "friends of the cross" know that the cross is, in truth, good, because through it works righteousness and the old Adam are crucified. The theologian of the cross knows "that he is worthless and that his works are not his but God's."[14] The attempt to know God in some other way puffs up, makes the person altogether blind and hardened (Thesis 22). Those who do not practice the theology of the cross misuse the best thing God has to offer, namely Christ. They are then not immediately "brought to zero," reduced to nothing, but for those who are reborn through suffering and awareness of the presence of death it matters not whether they themselves can act or not; it is enough for them if they are more and more destroyed and made nothing through cross and suffering.[15]

Basic statements

Luther's Heidelberg Theses argue for the cross and against human self-determination and self-glorification. They thus have both a positive and a negative, limiting character.

Positive statements

Knowledge of God (and thus an adequate theology) comes only through the cross—the cross of Christ and that of whoever believes in him. Luther's concern is that Christ and faith find one another. In order to bring our faith to Christ, God must counter our natural feelings. Only in Christ can we encounter the eternal God, who does not allow sinners to know him in any other way. Luther expresses this in his lectures on Romans as follows: "For what is good for us is hidden, and that so deeply that it is hidden under its opposite. Thus our life is hidden under death, love for ourselves under hate for ourselves, glory under ignominy, salvation under damnation . . . heaven under hell, wisdom under foolishness, righteousness under sin, power under weakness." It is universally true that whatever we say is good is hidden under the denial of it. Only in this way can faith find space and attain to God, the God who in human perspective appears to be a *negativa essentia*, the opposite of goodness and wisdom and righteousness.[16] With this the *theologia negativa* rises to a new level: human beings negate themselves in their thoughts, actions, feelings, and being. Faith, as the only adequate affirmation, implies the realization of the negation of human possibilities. This is true of believers, that is, the subjects of faith, but can also be formulated with respect to the object of faith. In *De servo arbitrio* Luther asserts that faith is about what we do not see (Heb 11:1): but in order for there to be room for faith it is necessary that everything that is believed should be hidden. And it cannot be more deeply hidden than by contrary perceptions and experiences.[17]

Thus for Luther the consequence of taking the cross seriously is in fact a revaluation of all theological values previously held. At the same time this is associated with an attack on natural human feelings. In a sermon Luther summarizes: "For God has established a fixed rule: everything that is high and praised of men is disregarded and abominable in the sight of God. . . . God turns all this upside down. Everything we call beautiful, jolly, rich, etc., he calls poor, sick, weak, impotent. . . ."[18] Because Christ "considers that evil which we consider good and vice versa, he takes away that which we delight in and gives everything that vexes us."[19]

The power of the God who awakes the dead is demonstrated in the Crucified; in human nothingness God is creatively realized. God creates what is pleasing to God and is not pleased with what the human being tries to present to him as pleasing.[20] Human beings live from sympathy, treasuring what seems to them to be worth treasuring. They seek themselves in the thing they love. God, in contrast, loves what from a human perspective is not worth treasuring, namely the sinner, the weak human being turned away from God, in order to make her or him righteous and whole. It is not our being or doing, but God's valuing of us that reveals that value of our life. Sinners are not loved by God because they are lovely; rather, they are lovely because they are loved by God.[21]

Luther is convinced that the theology of the cross formulates the way to life that is offered and commanded by God. He sees the only chance for human life in the radical reversal of our values and attitudes. Life will succeed through love for the cross. Although believers will neither boast in their activities nor be upset by their failure, the theology of the cross obviously has ethical consequences. Believers will be prepared to take on themselves the cross of others.[22]

Luther's *theologia crucis* is expressed very simply in his interpretation of the Magnificat (Luke 1:46-55): God exalts those of low degree;[23] Mary is a simple, lowly maiden and for that very reason is allowed to experience great things;[24] human beings look up, above themselves, to things that are splendid and glorious and showy, while God looks into the depths, chooses what is inconspicuous, what is nothing. It is "his manner" to look into the depths and behold things that are disregarded.[25] "For where man's strength ends, God's strength begins"—and the reverse as well.[26]

All in all, then, we can say that Luther was convinced that the theology of the cross says what "the thing actually is."[27] Knowledge of God in Christ leads to a theology appropriate to its subject by accomplishing the revaluation of all values, making evident the qualification that is valid before God, the only one that offers a chance for a successful life and makes room for an adequate ethos. No longer is there need to inquire in general about good and evil, but only about love for the cross of Jesus Christ. A theology so defined draws its conclusions from the knowledge that "nothing seems to be more nothing than God Himself."[28] This must be applied to believers and ultimately to the whole church if they want to remain true to "the thing itself."

Critical statements of rejection

Luther objected to a number of variations on the theology of "glory":

Its intellectual variant, he said, was a reliance in theology on the abilities of reason, supposing it could make ultimately valid statements about God. Scholasticism was, for Luther, an example of such a theology, though one must admit that "the concept of *theologia gloriae* for Scholasticism cannot be accepted as historical."[29] But Luther is not interested in a phenomenological description; he is making a theological judgment. Self-glorifying theology means for him something that is not conceived on the basis of the cross of Christ, a theology that of its own accord adopts traditions not covered by the Gospel and bases itself on them in order to claim validity for itself in the church, and sometimes in society as well. It avoids suffering, and it certainly does not suffer on its own behalf. It is opinionated and is not oriented to the cross and resurrection of Jesus Christ. It is arrogant, whether it presents itself in the robes of scholastic learning or in fundamentalistic "know-it-allness."

The psychological variant Luther finds made concrete in the works-righteousness of late medieval devotion. The human being does what she or he can, and feels good about it. But this is to seek to instrumentalize God, to make use of God in various aspects of life. Miracles are sought and found, even invented. So-called "saints" are the perfect representatives of a *theologia gloriae* in practice. Here, too, the point is not a general debunking of late medieval spirituality, but Luther wants to make it clear that human spiritual experience is deceiving and does not provide an adequate starting point for theology. To the extent that human beings want to rely on their own moral integrity they must face up to the radical claims of God's law. "That is surely true; if things followed the rule of feeling, I would surely be lost. . . ." There is scarcely "so much as a small spark" of life and righteousness in me, "but no matter how feeble it is, as long as the Word and a small spark of faith remain in the heart, it shall develop into a fire of life which fills heaven and earth and quenches both death and every other misfortune like a little drop of water."[30] Nor do any other experiences people may encounter furnish an appropriate starting point for theology. "The dead repose under the ground, long decomposed or devoured by maggots and all sorts of other vermin, or they are turned to dust, or they lie dispersed everywhere; but in the Word which we believe and profess they are assuredly alive and risen."[31] God may directly entrust me with experiences that I must not take as my starting point. The Canaanite woman had to find herself rejected by Jesus (Matt 15:21-28), but she resisted. She did not let herself be cowed by the first impression. So also the human being must "grasp the deep, secret 'yes' beneath and above the 'no,' holding fast in faith to God's word."[32]

In its ecclesiological variant, theology seeks the glory of an impressive church that can prove itself phenomenologically to be unified, "holy," and all-encompassing. In its desire to impress it pursues strategic considerations; it must be morally capable and proclaims its global claims. It legitimates itself as "apostolic" by means of arguments not drawn from Sacred Scripture, and it realizes itself institutionally through a hierarchical order at the apex of which stands Christ's representative on earth. Luther did not live to see the splendor of the later Baroque churches and the media-amplified impact of televised synods and worship services, but he would probably have counted both as parts of the *theologia gloriae*. The true church, in contrast, he thought less impressive; it shares the shadowy existence and shame of the Crucified.[33]

For Luther there was also a political variant of the *theologia gloriae*. It is realized on the one hand in a politically powerful church that knows how to share in shaping social life in line with its norms. But it can also appear in political movements that misuse and instrumentalize the Gospel for purposes that are entirely their own, as was evident, in Luther's opinion, in the Peasants' War. The theology of glory strives for theocracy: God's law must be sovereign! For Luther the Marxist expectation that human welfare can be fought for and organized would fall just as much under the perspective of the theology of glory as do theocratic tendencies in Islam.

MODIFICATIONS

DISCUSSIONS ABOUT THE INTERPRETATION OF THE LORD'S SUPPER

In the confrontations with Karlstadt, Oeculampadius, and Zwingli, Luther's theology of the cross found, we might say, a new field of application. Against Karlstadt, Luther wanted to show that Christ did not desire to serve believers merely as a model; otherwise it would have sufficed to hold on to the medieval theology of imitation and repentance. Against Zwingli he insisted on the foolishness of human reason, which of course was not able to comprehend Christ's real presence in the Eucharist. If we were to orient ourselves to that alone we would have to accept a great many more conclusions as well and ultimately also say that God did not become a human being and the crucified Jesus Christ was not God.[34] Instead, "grope . . . where the Word is."[35] Christ's glory is shown above all in his weakness. He has been "made sin for us" (2 Cor 5:21), he became "a curse for us" (Gal 3:13). Part of this weakness is his presence in bread and wine. Of course, God could have arranged everything differently. But if it is God's will "to give salvation to you through the humanity of Christ, through the Word, through the bread in the Supper, who are you, insolent, thankless devil, that you dare to ask why he does not do it in a different way and without these means?"[36] In fact, God loves to do precisely "what is foolish and useless in the eyes of the world,"[37] thus shaming those who think they are wise, especially the "fanatics." God, so to speak, meets people in indirect ways, because if God wanted to encounter them directly, human beings would meet the "naked" God, and that would be disastrous for them. It would be the expression of a misleading, speculative, self-glorifying theology. While it was important to Luther in his early years to be aware of the divinity in the humanity and suffering of the Crucified, he now emphasizes the fact that divinity and humanity are joined in Christ and in the Lord's Supper. The real presence of Christ in the Supper is, however, even now only one moment in God's action, hidden under its opposite, *sub contraria specie*.

Certainly Luther can also insert this method of arguing into a context in which it threatens to be counterproductive. He attempts to found the presence of Christ in bread and wine on, among other things, the divinization of the human nature of Christ and his consequent omnipresence: the presence everywhere of the divine-human nature of Christ makes possible, so to speak, the presence of the body and blood of Christ in bread and wine.[38] But that cannot be secured by a theology of the cross! The argumentative figure of the *theologia crucis* must not become an alibi for any and every kind of logically unprovable theological statement. Here the person of Christ is no longer reflected upon in light of the *theologia crucis*; rather, a particular christological position is supposed to be supported or legitimated by that theology. The *communicatio idiomatum*, according to which divine and human features in the person of Jesus Christ had complete exchange with one another, is adopted in Luther's late theses on Christ's divinity and humanity without any further regard for the cross of Christ.[39]

THE SERVANT OF GOD

Luther's interpretation of Isaiah 53 offers a beautiful witness to how he spoke of the theology of the cross toward the end of his life. The heavily edited printed version relies on the notes made by Georg Rörer; it seems redundant and apparently contains mistakes and formulations that are seldom found in Luther. But it does indicate the quiet tone in which the Reformer now spoke of the cross of Christ, as well as the clear shaping he was able to give to his late theology of the cross. The word "servant" of God gives him an opening for this. Christ's "servanthood" is said to have consisted of his service, and in particular his service of proclamation. Christ had no means of power at his disposal; he had only the word.[40] Christ reigned in the form of a slave, and people said of him, "Oh, he won't do it,"[41] not much can be expected of him; he won't make it. He is not to be grasped by rational philosophical thought, nor does he make an effort to serve through arguments addressed to reason.[42] As far as reason is concerned, it seems clear that "if he is God he cannot be a servant; if he is a servant, he cannot be God . . ."[43] His kingdom consists, then, not in wealth and power, but is a "word-kingdom," spiritual and eternal.[44] But Christian wisdom consists of "believing the unbelievable."[45] The deepening of the *theologia crucis* gained from the disputes over the Lord's Supper took hold and was repeatedly modified: it speaks of Christ, in whom the divine and human natures have mutual exchange even though reason raises objections.[46] The council (of Ephesus) is said to have been absolutely right in calling Mary *theotokos*, "God-bearer."[47] But the humility of Jesus Christ is expressed especially in this, that he was born of her and was a real human being who ate, drank, and often wept.[48] The Reformer no longer looks only to the cross, but considers all the wretched circumstances of the life of the one who had nowhere to lay his head (Matt 8:20). Luther is certain that all this was in service of redemption. Christ sensed the wrath of God, and the devil was "with him in the Garden," in Gethsemane.[49] He let himself be imprisoned under the Law and identified with sinners by calling himself a sinner.[50] He did all this in order to reconcile human beings with God and to heal their wounds. This should have its result: he wanted to be "effective in us";[51] he died in order at least "to fill the world with justice, salvation, and life. . . ."[52] The theology of the cross in all its forms of expression serves the message of the justification of sinners.

Theologia crucis as COMPREHENSIVE THEOLOGICAL PERSPECTIVE

For the theologian of the cross, the cross of Christ, the cross of the individual Christian, and the cross of the whole church belong together. The cross is not an idea that can be made present in the abstract. Only those who surrender themselves to the cross understand what the cross is all about. Hence in Christian theology the cross is not one theme among many, but *the* theme. God's glory is not made present in impressive and believable fashion, as we would wish, in the form of the projections we—to adapt Ludwig Feuerbach—attribute to it, but in the cross of Jesus Christ. Feuerbach should be asked whether human beings would really, on their own, wish to receive redemption through a crucified man. But by learning to associate the event of the crucifixion with the realization of God's glory they come to salvation in its totality. In the suffering and death of Jesus Christ, God's glory and the salvation of the human being intersect.

THE CROSS OF CHRIST

The theologian of the cross does not find God in any and every place and at every point in time.[53] He or she does not share the opinion of Ignatius of Loyola that God is to be found in all things. Instead, she or he knows that God lets God's self be found in the weakness and obscurity of Christ, and of the people who follow him. In his interpretation of the Magnificat Luther remarks how people are always looking up, orienting themselves to what is important, but God looks into the depths, at what is of no value; God regarded the lowliness of his handmaid (Luke 1:48).[54] In the same way, human beings should not orient themselves to what is intellectually, psychologically, and religiously impressive, but should begin where God began: in the manger, in the stable, on Golgotha: ". . . Take hold of God as Scripture instructs you. . . . Therefore begin where Christ began in the Virgin's womb, in the manger, and at His mother's breasts." From this there can be only one conclusion: "Therefore whenever you are concerned to think and act about your salvation, you must put away all speculations about the Majesty, all thoughts of works, traditions, and philosophy—indeed, of the Law of God itself. And you must run directly to the manger and the mother's womb, embrace this Infant and Virgin's Child in your arms, and look at Him—born, being nursed, growing up, going about in human society, teaching, dying, rising again. . . . This vision will keep you on the proper way, so that you may follow where Christ has gone."[55] Luther develops the meaning of this for believers in his interpretation of the justification of the ungodly.[56] In the first place it is about believers' affirming Jesus' path to the cross as important for themselves and thus learning to surrender to their own cross.

THE CROSS OF THE BELIEVER

The cross of Christ and the cross of believers go together. The meaning of Christ's cross becomes visible precisely to those who suffer. Therefore believers should not try to avoid suffering. They need not seek it, of course; God will send it in God's own good time! What a person must suffer is the true treasure of his or her life. Christ has sanctified it through his own suffering.[57] Thus faith does *not* mean liberation from suffering and all sorts of difficulties, but the courage to abandon oneself to the God concealed in Christ's suffering and out of it to understand and accept one's own suffering as well. It means taking up the cross! The cross of Christ is "nothing other than abandoning everything and clinging only through faith to the heart of Christ, or: to leave everything and to believe—that is, to bear Christ's cross."[58] This should not be confused with a self-satisfied mysticism of suffering. Thomas Münzer strikingly formulated it in his polemic against Luther: those who will not take the bitter Christ will eat themselves to death on honey![59] But for Luther an appeal to the cross must not in turn become another kind of attitude and theology of self-glorification. The "abandonment" he calls for requires, above all, that the believer "abandon" the self—in the twofold meaning of the concept, namely, surrendering the self and trusting entirely in Christ. For in the self a believer has nothing on which she or he can rely, no inherent spiritual quality (*sanctitas inhaerens*), but only Christ.[60] Thus the believer as such is hidden from herself or himself; the path of the righteous is not one grounded in experience or reason but is solely an advancing in faith, which in the darkness of the present remains certain of what is invisible.[61] Believers are aware of their vulnerability in temptations, through doubt, failure, and concrete guilt; the individual believer is neither morally nor otherwise an impressive figure. Our external life is like a sack that arouses disgust—but everything depends on what it contains; there is "beautiful gold in it!"[62]

THE CHURCH'S CROSS

A church that takes seriously the cross of Jesus Christ and that of the individual believer cannot appear in triumphal garb. It falls short of itself if it seeks a form that is not shaped by the cross.

Surprisingly, the same is true for Luther with regard to doctrine: the teaching of the true church is constantly attacked and disputed; it is under threat and one must make an effort to keep it pure. Therefore the Reformer wrote poetically, "Lord, keep us steadfast in thy word and curb the might of enemy swords, who Jesus Christ, thy only Son, fain would tumble from off thy throne."[63] The devil may "shell" the church heavily with the artillery of offenses and with gangs, which must produce irritation; Godself can conceal it behind all kinds of faults, "so that you necessarily become a fool and pass false judgment on it. Christendom will not be known by sight, but by faith . . ." which "has to do with things not seen."[64] There is no doctrine in the church that has not been attacked; the church shares with its Lord the resistance, misunderstandings, and attempts at manipulation he also encountered.

In light of this, the church's praxis must certainly be subject to testing. One cannot discern the true church from the fact that it can demonstrate pastoral, missionary, or social success. Statistics lie! The pope and the Turk, Luther thought, have it easy because they can boast of such great successes.[65] The true church corresponding to its crucified Lord, on the other hand, is hidden—sometimes under its opposite. Church history stands in clear opposition to what church really should be, or what the true church actually is, but the church is hidden, the saints unknown.[66] What, then? The church is really an article of faith!

Finally, suffering in the concrete, external sense also comes to the church. No church can exist without martyrdom. Suffering is its treasure, its "holy thing," but also and at the same time the instrument through which it is made "holy." In the late writing "On the Councils and the Church" (1539) Luther enumerates seven signs of the church. The seventh of these is suffering: "Seventh, the holy Christian people are externally recognized by the holy possession of the sacred cross." It must accept every kind of misfortune and persecution, attacks and other evils. It will suffer fear, sorrow, and weakness, "outward poverty, contempt, illness, and weakness, in order to become like their head, Christ." Add to this that Christians will be called "heretics, knaves, and devils, the most pernicious people on earth. . . . Wherever you see or hear this, you may know that the holy Christian church is there . . . This too is a holy possession whereby the Holy Spirit not only sanctifies his people, but also blesses them." In this way God gives the church not only "daily sanctification and vivification," but eternal blessedness as well. Hence, according to Luther, one can regard suffering even as a kind of "sacrament."[67]

Can Protestantism understand its present situation, which has become so lamentable, in this sense? Luther formulates it dialectically: the church's cross is in truth what lifts it up.[68] But that is certainly not meant as an alibi! Nevertheless: the more Satan rages, the more should Christians laugh, for Christ raises up precisely those who are thrust down; God's own motto for action is: "From nothing, everything": "ex nihilo omnia!"[69]

CRITICAL EVALUATION

Objections could be advanced from several sides against Luther's strong emphasis on the cross and suffering. Can it be explained, and therefore relativized, by psychology? What are its political consequences? Finally: what about the resurrection?

THE PSYCHOLOGICAL OBJECTION: MASOCHISM?

Lutheran piety has proved fruitful and powerful, often especially in times of suffering and political difficulties. The loveliest chorales in the Lutheran hymnal were written during the Thirty Years' War and in the years immediately after it. During the church struggles at the time of National Socialism and under the challenges of the regime in the former DDR there was something here as well. Huguenots, Waldensians, and the Salzburg Exiles confessed their faith under extreme pressures, but when the danger was past, church life and personal devotion often fell back into slumber. Does suffering make one susceptible to the Gospel, to "last questions"? Probably the religious consequences of challenges should be regarded as ambivalent. Suffering not only teaches us how to pray, but also how to curse.

Why did Luther put so much emphasis, even overemphasis, on suffering? Is it an expression of male brutality? Should we, as feminist theology suggests, suspect sado-masochistic or necrophilic tendencies here? Luther would probably answer that masochism is present when suffering is sought to increase one's own pleasure—in the sense of the *theologia gloriae*. In that sense, of course, it must be rejected; if it serves as a self-affirmation it certainly does not correspond any longer to the cross of Jesus Christ. The cross may not be regarded as an impulse, certainly not an imperative, to masochism. On the other hand, however, according to Luther one should not seek to avoid suffering. It has its own God-given function for human beings, even if they do not recognize it at first; here, as always, one must let God be God. Faith does not repress suffering but faces up to it; it is realistic.

Some of the Reformer's formulations do in fact sound masochistic, especially when taken out of context. We may criticize his view for being too undifferentiated. He speaks impressively about the suffering that results from following Jesus and can ultimately lead to martyrdom, but he does not emphasize clearly enough the extent to which human life, because it is conditioned by mortality, necessarily brings suffering with it and so evokes the theodicy question. Finally, he does not distinguish between self-incurred and undeserved suffering. He calls on people to accept suffering but he gives too little consideration to the places where suffering must be opposed and reduced by human activity, or perhaps even banished from the world altogether.

The function of suffering is not always clear either. One is called upon to will oneself into the way of Christ and conform oneself to the will of God. Suffering and assaults repeatedly renew the vivification of the human. But Luther speaks more often of the killing of the old Adam than of new life! In view of cross and suffering the good gifts of creation threaten to fade into the background and be considered of lesser worth. This is not as clear with Luther himself as in later Protestantism when this critical attitude toward enjoyment combined with a Kantian awareness of duty. The Catholic Bavarian, in contrast, as Johann Baptist Metz wittily wrote, has an earthy relationship to religion and a mystical relationship to beer! Gratitude for creation and obedience to the discipleship of suffering do not always seem well balanced in Luther's thought.

POLITICAL IMPLICATIONS: THE CROSS AND THE PEASANTS' WAR

What was the role of Luther's *theologia crucis* in the Peasants' War? As we described above,[70] the Twelve Articles of the Swabian Peasantry appeared in March 1525, demanding among other things the elimination of the tithe and serfdom, free access to the hunt and the forest, and freedom from obligatory services and contributions to the state. The peasants appealed to individual biblical passages and even offered to withdraw any demands that did not correspond to Sacred Scripture. Probably it was the appeal to Scripture that moved Luther to say anything in the first place. His "Admonition to Peace" was probably in press at the beginning of May. He supplemented it after hearing of the plundering and excesses by the peasants, adding an Afterword printed on 10 May 1525 and later appearing as a separate document, "Against the Robbing and Murdering Hordes of Peasants," a writing that still makes the Reformer the object of considerable antipathy. In the "Admonition" Luther addressed both sides. He told the princes "you must become different men and yield to God's word. . . . It is not the peasants, dear lords, who are resisting you; it is God himself. . . ."[71] The aristocracy are "not appointed to exploit their subjects for their own profit and advantage, but to be concerned about the welfare of their subjects."[72] Luther tries in turn to make it clear to the peasants that the rulers have a duty given them by God (Romans 13), and that the true Christian does not rebel against the suffering God sends her or him. "We have all we need in our Lord, who will not leave us, as he has promised. Suffering! suffering! Cross! cross! This and nothing else is the Christian law!"[73]

Thus in principle Luther certainly distinguishes between the commandment to Christians to bear their own sufferings and the necessity for an order that serves to limit suffering. But this distinction is subject to a threefold restriction: according to Luther the elimination of suffering is a duty that can only apply to the suffering of my fellow human beings, not to my own. This duty must necessarily be fulfilled by institutions that organize the struggle against poverty, assure the necessary financing, and oppose the deficit in education. The "common purse"[74] and the founding of schools are necessary. Such institutions are not self-legitimating, however; they are to be created by the authorities instituted by God for the purpose. It is remarkable and also tragic that Luther, who pleaded so impressively for the universal, mutual, and common priesthood of the faithful, could not imagine a democratic political order. He forbade Christians to act against their own suffering, but he did emphatically call for participation in removing the suffering of others. He did not consider that it is precisely through one's own suffering that one becomes able more deeply to understand the suffering of others and that, very pragmatically, the elimination of the suffering of others often includes alleviation of one's own.

THE THEOLOGICAL OBJECTION: WHAT ABOUT THE RESURRECTION?

This question is posed to Luther today particularly from circles practicing feminist theology. Is it the purpose of the theology of the cross to put people down and keep them down? Should not the positive be more strongly emphasized than the negative and destructive? Ought not more weight be given to life than to death? Similar voices are heard in ecumenical circles. Christ, after all, is the Living One! Does Luther's theology neglect the resurrection and ignore the joy of Easter? That is how it looks from the viewpoint of Orthodox theology. Roman Catholic Christians have not been prepared to judge the church only in terms of its crimes and difficulties. Christian life, after all, does not consist only of guilt and failure; with the aid of grace it is possible for people to live "saintly" lives. Fundamentalist and evangelical groups within Protestantism insist that the goal is a sanctification of life, its growth and transformation.

All these objections are based to some extent on misunderstandings of Luther's theology since, for example, his Easter sermons adequately demonstrate what he had to say about the joy of Easter and the new life. Obviously faith meant transformation and growth for him as well. But it was elementally important to him that in all this the cross should not be ignored. It has a twofold task: it remains a corrective to human religious efforts; reality must not simply be set aside by enthusiastic piety. Faith offers no opportunities to escape from or suppress its difficulties. Faith is a grasp on reality and to that extent is the precondition for a constructive engagement with it. Hence: the cross serves to open up new life! The cross is not the goal of faith, but its precondition and current form. It is precisely to the Crucified that resurrection is promised. The resurrection does not happen except in the tomb; it is not made more effective by forgetting the manger and the cross.[75]

Under the conditions of this world the Risen One is encountered as the Crucified—and the Crucified as the Risen One. Suffering is the place where liberation takes place, and conflict itself is the place of resolution; the tomb is the place out of which new life grows. Anyone who does not dare to approach the tomb cannot encounter the power of the Risen One.

In summary, then, we can say that the theology of the cross emancipates from everything that gives itself the halo of power, superiority, and "glory." In that very way it shows itself to be a "theology of resurrection." Theology of the cross and theology of resurrection must not be played off against one another. The creative power of the God who raises the dead is demonstrated in the crucified Christ and thus at the same time in the "crucified" experience of Christian existence, the "crucified" form of the church and a "crucified theology."[76]

THE ANTHROPOLOGICAL OBJECTION: WHAT ABOUT THE HUMAN BEING?

Anthropological objections to Luther's theology of the cross have been and are stated from two extremely different starting points, on the basis of an option oriented to traditional Catholic doctrine and in the name of the autonomy of the modern person.

As an example for the approach of a Catholic theologian to the *theologia crucis* that seeks the greatest possible understanding of it we may take the dissertation by Hubertus Blaumeiser on Luther's theology of the cross in his "Operationes in Psalmos."[77] Blaumeiser seeks intensively to sense what the about-to-be Reformer was saying, to understand it, and to absorb it spiritually. But he seems almost relieved when after all, if only on the margins, he finds traces of a theology that seems familiar to him and that he wants to rescue: Luther was able, after all, by reference to 2 Peter 1:4, to speak of a human "sharing in the divine nature" and in another place even of a new *concupiscentia*, now positively understood! So was he not also concerned about a "mutual glorification of God and the human"?[78] In that case even the concept of *cooperatio*, such a crux of theological controversy, can appear in a positive light![79] Blaumeiser seeks "perspectives from which the Catholic *et-et* and the Lutheran *aut-aut* are not simply alternatives."[80] He finds them, and asserts: "the cross, in all its severity, and a consequent non-being (*aut-aut*) always remains—Luther opened our eyes to this—inscribed in the mutual relationship of God and human beings (*et-et*), but it is not simply a nothingness; it is the verso of a new *being* given ever again by God."[81] In this way the author is able to value Luther's *theologia crucis* as an "enriching encouragement to thought"[82]—and the Catholic position is saved: the insistence on the God-given "relative self-status of the human person."[83]

Today's Protestant theology that is concerned with human possibilities for self-development prefers also to hold in favor of this relative self-status. One example of this we may recall is a work by Roselies Taube. She investigated Luther's interpretation of Galatians[84] and concluded that Luther left no room at all for human self-responsibility and freedom since the justified person, who lives only in God and the neighbor, no longer exists in her- or himself and as such! That person is no longer, for only God and the neighbor remain; the believer's "self-status" is absorbed by faith and love, though this is a love in which there is no genuine reciprocity. The empirical "I" comes out empty. The author senses in Luther an "ultimate estrangement between the I and God, the I and oneself, the I and the other."[85]

Some feminist theologians have supported this position with additional arguments that speak against a theology of the cross: the suspicion of sado-masochism, the accusation of an ethics of subjection, and the supposed implicit encouragement of violence. The theology of the cross, in this inter-pretation, in no way leads to liberation, but instead holds the human being fast in a constant feeling of inferiority and nothingness.[86]

Luther would probably suspect the existence, in the classic Catholic as well as in the modern Protestant reproaches, of the same "interest guiding their perceptions": the natural human being is not prepared to kneel before the message of the cross. But to those who, in the power of the Holy Spirit, have bowed before the cross Luther attributes some powerful opportunities. Precisely the person who lives out of forgiveness is able to realize himself or herself in freedom and with all her or his powers—within the Christian community and for the benefit of his or her fellow human beings. Such a one will spend all the abilities given her or him by God and yet will admit before God to being nothing but a "useless slave" (cf. Luke 17:10).

THE HOMILETICAL OBJECTION: WHO IS ENLIGHTENED BY THIS?

In essence—at least in the enlightened Protestant world—at the latest since Schleiermacher the framing conditions for understanding Luther's *theologia crucis* no longer exist. The possibility of a "last judgment" has shifted to the utmost margins of the imaginable. Any awareness of sin and guilt before God seems to exist only in a much reduced form. The idea that the wrath of God must be taken as seriously as the love of God is no longer comprehensible. The content of the preaching of the cross, which Luther assumed as a matter of course, namely the reference to Christ's atoning sacrifice before God or his battle with the devil, possesses no plausibility any longer. From a practical-theological viewpoint one can say that "the older links" of the theology of justification "to forgiveness (sacrifice, atonement, satisfaction, punishment) are no longer considered conclusive. If guilt is spoken of, then it is as guilt toward our fellow human beings, for which forgiveness from God, who has nothing to do with the offense, makes no sense."[87]

Has Luther's theology of the cross, the trademark of his theological approach, been made obsolete? How should we approach it today? The sugges-tions inherited from the nineteenth century are unpersuasive. They do rescue the basic figure of positive thinking *sub contraria specie*. For Schleiermacher all life consists of contradictions to be overcome; the "constant force" of the Redeemer's awareness of God, however, is able to overcome suffering in such a way that it can be interpreted as the expression of self-denying love: "The *theologia crucis* has been absorbed by the *theologia gloriae*."[88] Hegel, who sought to regard the opposition between life and death with radical seriousness, sees the so-called "speculative Good Friday" as a transitional stage, shown to be necessary as a negation of negation. "The unity that exists at the beginning of the dialectical movement returns, by way of alienation, to a higher unity."[89] The historically real and concrete cross on Golgotha thus not only fades into the background: for Schleiermacher it becomes a sign of triumph, while for Hegel it can be dispensed with. The symbol of the cross can, in a sense, be exchanged for the phoenix: "The goal of nature is to kill itself, to burn itself as the phoenix does, in order from this external form to appear, made youthful, as spirit."[90] However, theories of that kind cannot be communicated much more successfully than the statements of the Reformer.

It could be tempting, then, to simply pass over the message of the cross in Luther's sense and to place other parts of the Gospel's content in the foreground. This did, in fact, take place, especially in the ethical wave of the second half of the twentieth century. The Sermon on the Mount seemed more important than the cross, the ethical imperative more helpful and effective than the indicative. One should not suffer, but should actively combat suffering, lessen it and, if possible, eliminate it. The "ecumenical justice movement" raised its voice: "The time has come. . . ."[91] The suffering that comes with the struggle against suffering was neither forgotten nor avoided, but Christ's suffering was at most a model; Christ remained—to use Luther's vocabulary—only an *exemplum*, but no longer an *exemplar*.

In the meantime the limitations of this approach have become apparent. The cross of Christ appears, particularly for believers, as the great, unsolvable riddle. If we attempt to deal with it in terms of theistic presuppositions we must admit that there is no explanation for why God desired to have human beings come to salvation by way of the execution of a human being with whom God identifies, and why God did not act differently. Nevertheless, it is clear that the first believers also had a hard time understanding what the cross of Jesus Christ was supposed to mean. The pericope of the disciples on the road to Emmaus seems to be an eloquent testimony to that fact. The execution of Jesus of Nazareth must be accepted as a fact. It presents more questions than it answers. Was Luther's answer too hasty?

In any case, the question of God is thus reopened. God encounters us, if at all, differently from the way we humans imagine or hope. It is thus not impossible that God may make God's self present also in human suffering or in major catastrophes. If the doctrine of two natures, which for Luther was a constitutive component of his theology of the cross, is no longer comprehensible, still there remains the "message of the cross," that is, that God identified with the suffering Jesus of Nazareth and that as a result God shows an intention to identify with all suffering. Those who can identify with it have the chance at experiences that point to the Easter message.

THE RELIGIOUS-CRITICAL OBJECTION: WHY THE CROSS OF CHRIST AND NOT THE "WHEEL OF INSTRUCTION" OR THE "PROPHETIC CALLING"?

The message of the suffering and execution of Jesus of Nazareth must be announced today within a pluralistic society. The difficulties thus encountered, as Ingolf U. Dalferth has summarized them, are

- that the message of the cross is tied not only to history but essentially to a contingent historical event,
- that it is not merely moral preaching but is intended to be life-shaping,
- that it is not a universal symbolic key to life or death but opens a specific perspective on life and death,
- that it does not satisfy our longing for survival but corrects it by being a message of judgment on our life before God and a message of salvation about God's life, and shifts the accent from our wishes and longings to God's action and promise.[92]

That was the state of the problem at the turn of the twentieth to the twenty-first century. In the meantime the situation has become more serious: not only must the message of the cross be conveyed to secularized Christians who are weary of the Gospel or living at its margins, it must be convincingly communicated under competitive pressure from alternative religious offerings. And as we know, the truth and exclusive claims of a particular religious option cannot be proven.

This new state of things for Christian preaching and theology was only a marginal problem for Luther, and one that he certainly did not know how to resolve in a satisfactory manner with his anti-Jewish and anti-Islamic tirades.[93] His insistence on the cross, grounded in faith in the Risen One, must be called decisionism when we look at it from outside the faith. Nevertheless, his certainty about the necessity of suffering for individual Christians and for the church if they truly witness to Christ expresses a point that can lead us farther. The church of Jesus Christ is church for others, and being a Christian means being a man or woman for others. This should be verified also in regard to non-Christian religions and their adherents. With the message of the cross and of the meaning of suffering the church intends to protect individuals, and humanity itself, from destroying themselves in their intoxication with success and self-determination.

The harsh assertion that we are "obligated to the message of the cross, not the equality of all religions"[94] is inadequate. Rather, the message of the cross determines the place of the Christian church among the religions: the church of Christ understands itself, to use Franciscan terminology, as the *soror minor*, the "lesser sister." It should not try to avoid that through a dialectic of sublime identification of superficial service and factual claims to sovereignty. Thus Luther's approach in speaking of the cross could be unexpectedly fruitful in a new field.

The Buddhist monk Thich Nhat Hanh finds no positive emanation from the crucifix.[95] This might suggest that Christianity, and especially Protestantism, should instead make its central symbol that of the madonna, smiling at her child and radiating kindness. But the symbol of madonna and child is interchangeable, from Isis to Guanyin, with other symbols of the ancient human longing for security. The image of the crucifix, instead, is linked to all suffering and all those who suffer, whether from external or internal tortures. Those who are able to grasp the identification of the ultimate ground of reality with the crucified Jesus Christ are close to the resurrection.

Notes

[1] "CRUX sola est nostra theologia," AWA 2, 319, 3.

[2] "Crux probat omnia," AWA 2, 325, 1.

[3] Cf. Klaus Peter Jörns, *Notwendige Abschiede. Auf dem Weg zu einem glaubwürdigen Christentum.* Gütersloh: Gütersloher Verlagshaus, 2004.

[4] Cf. Hans-Martin Barth, "Das Kreuz als Kriterium. Luthers Kreuzestheologie und das Kruzifix-Urteil," *MdKI* 47 (1996): 23–28. The reference is to a court judgment in 1995 regarding the constitutionality of the display of crucifixes in schoolrooms in Bavaria.

[5] Cf. Elisabeth Moltmann-Wendel, "Zur Kreuzestheologie heute. Gibt es eine feministische Kreuzestheologie?" *EvT* 50 (1990): 546–57.

[6] Jörns 2004, 286–334.

[7] Ibid., 303ff.

[8] In the *Luther Handbuch* edited by Albrecht Beutel (2005) it is almost completely ignored!

[9] Cf. Blaumeiser 1995.

[10] Cf. Jos E. Vercruysse, "Maria alla luce di una teologia della croce. Martin Lutero commenta il Magnificat," 229–42 in Clara Burini, et al., *La madre del Signore*, Parola, Spirito e Vita 6 (Bologna: EDB, 1982).

[11] Cf. Walther von Loewenich, *Luthers Theologia crucis* [1929] (Munich: Kaiser, 41954); Jos E. Vercruysse, "Gesetz und Liebe. Die Struktur der 'Heidelberger Disputation' Luthers (1518)" [1974], *LuJ* 48 (1981): 7–43; idem, "Luther's Theology of the Cross at the Time of the Heidelberg Disputation," Gr 57 (1976): 523–48; Edgar Thaidigsmann, *Identitätsverlangen und Widerspruch. Kreuzestheologie bei Luther, Hegel und Barth* (Munich: Kaiser, 1983), 14–61. There is a good overview of the progress of research in Blaumeiser 1995, 31–72.

[12] LW 31, 35–70 (LDStA 1, 35–69).

[13] "Ergo in Christo crucifixo est vera Theologia et cognitio Dei": For this reason true theology and recognition of God are in the crucified Christ," LW 31, 53 (LDStA 1, 52, 27-28).

[14] ". . . donec sciat se ipsum esse nihil, et opera non sua, sed Dei esse," LW 31, 53 (LDStA 1, 54, 10).

[15] ". . . qui nondum est destructus, ad nihilum redactus per crucem et passionem . . ." LW 31, 53 (LDStA 1, 56, 19ff.).

[16] LW 25, 382–83 (WA 56, 392, 28–393, 3): "Et universaliter omnis nostra affirmatio boni cuiuscunque sub negatione eiusdem, ut fides locum habeat in Deo, Qui Est Negative Essentia et

bonitas et Sapientia et Iustitia. Nec potest possideri aut attingi nisi negatis omnibus affirmativis nostris."

[17] LW 33, 62. Cf. LDStA 1, 286, 4ff. With reference to "newer Protestant exegesis" Pope Benedict XVI objects to this interpretation of Heb 11:1 in his encyclical *Spe salvi* (30 November 2007), AAS 179, 7–8. See n. 60 below.

[18] LW 51, 37 (WA 1, 268, 9-18).

[19] LW 51, 39–40 (WA 1, 270, 22-24).

[20] "Amor Dei non invenit, sed creat suum diligibile, Amor hominis fit a suo diligibili": "The love of God does not find, but creates, that which is pleasing to it. The love of man comes into being through that which is pleasing to it" (Thesis 28), LW 31, 41 (LDStA 1, 60, 7-8).

[21] LW 31, 41 (LDStA 1, 60, 16-17).

[22] Cf. Martin N. Dreher, "Luthers Theologia Crucis und die Anliegen der Theologie der Befreiung," 38–54 in Ulrich Schoenborn, ed., *Evangelisch-Lutherische Kirche in Brasilien: Nachfolge Jesu—Wege der Befreiung* (Mettingen: Brasilienkunde-Verlag, 1989).

[23] LW 21, 299 (WA 7, 546, 32-34).

[24] LW 21, 301 (WA 7, 549, 25-27).

[25] LW 21, 313–14 (WA 7, 560, 21–561, 7).

[26] LW 21, 340 (WA 7, 586, 12-13; 586, 23).

[27] "Theologus crucis dicit, id quod res est" (Thesis 21), LW 31, 40 (LDStA 1, 52, 32-33).

[28] ". . . nihil magis nihil esse videtur, quam Deus ipse," LW 4, 355 (WA 43, 392, 17-18).

[29] Lohse 1981, 58.

[30] LW 28, 73 (WA 36, 497, 26-32).

[31] LW 28, 72–73 (WA 36, 495, 9-11).

[32] WA 17/2, 203, 31-33.

[33] See "The church as identifiable" in chapter 11.

[34] LW 36, 338 (WA 19, 486, 14-22).

[35] LW 36, 342 (WA 19, 492, 23-24).

[36] LW 37, 140 (WA 23, 268, 3-5).

[37] LW 36, 336 (WA 19, 484, 13-14).

[38] Cf. Lienhard 1980, 189, 280.

[39] LW 38, 239–42 (LDStA 2, 469–79).

[40] *Enarratio 53. capitis Esaiae* (1544; printed 1550) (WA 40/3, 683–746), at 688, 34-36; 693, 3-5.

[41] WA 40/3, 694, 22.

[42] WA 40/3, 688, 35-36.

[43] WA 40/3, 701, 30-31.

[44] WA 40/3, 693, 32: ". . . regnum eius verbale, doctrinale, spirituale, aeternum. . . ."

[45] WA 40/3, 702, 21: ". . . ut illud incredibile credant."

[46] WA 40/3, 702, 29. Here Nestorius, Arius, and other heretics were brought into the arena; ibid., 704, 31-32; 708, 7-12.

[47] WA 40/3, 708, 15-21. Did Luther himself really confuse Chalcedon with Ephesus?

[48] WA 40/3, 712, 20-22.

[49] WA 40/3, 716, 13-15.

[50] WA 40/3, 706, 15 (that is, in the Psalms; cf. Pss 40:13; 69:10).

[51] WA 40/3, 726, 26: ". . . efficax . . . in nobis. . . ."

[52] WA 40/3, 732, 17-18.

[53] ". . . ubique praesentem," LW 31, 227 (WA 1, 614, 19).

[54] LW 21, 312–24 (WA 7, 559, 31-33).

[55] LW 26, 29–30 (WA 40/1, 77, 23–80, 14).

[56] Cf. B.6.4 below.

[57] LW 31, 225 (WA 1, 613, 23-28).

[58] WA 1, 101, 19-21: "Crux Christi est nihil aliud nisi omnia relinquere et per fidem cordis Christo soli adhaerere, Vel sic: omnia relinquere et credere, hoc est crucem Christi ferre."

[59] *TRE* 19: 764.

[60]LW 26, 89–90 (WA 40/1, 197, 25–198, 15). In his interpretation of Heb 11:1 and 10:34 Pope Benedict XVI works instead, even with reference to the Vulgate, with the concept of "substance": "new 'substance' that is given to us." In martyrdom and asceticism, he says, "the new 'substance' proves itself to be genuine 'substance' . . ." However, the dispute is not so much about the "reality" conveyed in faith but about whether this reality may be understood as a quality and thus as a possession of the believer. Luther sees it as altogether grounded in the relationship to Christ. Cf. Benedict XVI, encyclical *Spe salvi*, nos. 7-8, and see n. 17 above.

[61]LW 14, 309 (WA 5, 45, 32-33): ". . . via non sensus, non rationis, sed solius fidei in caligine et invisibilia videntis."

[62]LW 17, 388 (WA 31/2, 562, 23-24).

[63]LW 53, 305 (EG 193, 1 [revised version]).

[64]LW 35, 409–10 (WA.DB 7, 418, 38ff.).

[65]LW 4, 356 (WA 43, 392, 19-21).

[66]LDStA 1, 322, 27: "abscondita est ecclesia, latent sancti, Quid?"

[67]LW 41, 164–65 (LDStA 5, 604, 28–605, 13).

[68]"Crux ecclesiae est eius exaltatio . . ." (WA 40/3, 90, 6-7).

[69]Ibid., 90, 10.

[70]See p. 51 above.

[71]LW 46, 20 (WA 18, 294, 37-38; 295, 4-5).

[72]LW 46, 22–23 (WA 18, 299, 23-24).

[73]LW 46, 29 (WA 18, 310, 28-29).

[74]Cf. Albrecht Steinwachs, "Der Gemeine Kasten. Eine oft übersehene soziale Leistung der Reformation," *Luther* 78 (2007): 32–34.

[75]According to Thomas J. Altizer, resurrection must not be understood as "jumping back into heaven"; cf. Hans-Martin Barth, "Tod-Gottes-Christologie. Der christologische Ansatz der nordamerikanischen Tod-Gottes-Theologie," *KD* 17 (1971): 258–72, esp. 265–67.

[76]"This theology is 'itself crucified theology and speaks only of the cross' (Karl Rahner)." Jürgen Moltmann, *The Crucified God: The Cross of Christ as the Foundation and Criticism of Christian Theology*, trans. R. A. Wilson and John Bowden (Minneapolis: Fortress Press, 1993), 69. Unfortunately, Moltmann does not provide a reference for the Rahner quotation.

[77]Blaumeiser 1995.

[78]Ibid., 483.

[79]Ibid., 490.

[80]Ibid., 482.

[81]Ibid., 550.

[82]Ibid., 547.

[83]Ibid., 534.

[84]Roselies Taube, *Gott und das Ich. Erörtert in einer Auseinandersetzung mit Luthers Lehre über Glaube und Liebe in seinem Galaterkommentar (1531/35)* (Frankfurt and New York: Peter Lang, 1986).

[85]Ibid., 514.

[86]Cf., e.g., Elisabeth Moltmann-Wendel, "Zur Kreuzestheologie heute. Gibt es eine feministische Kreuzestheologie?" *EvT* 50 (1990): 546–57; Dorothee Sölle, "Kreuz," 225–36 in Elisabeth Gössmann, et al., eds., *Wörterbuch der feministischen Theologie* (Gütersloh: Mohn, 1991).

[87]Rolf Schäfer, "Erfahrungsbericht: Theologie des Kreuzes in Gottesdienst und Predigt," *KD* 39 (1993): 90–99, at 96.

[88]Cf. Werner Schultz, "Die Transformierung der theologia crucis bei Hegel und Schleiermacher," *NZST* 6 (1964): 290–317, at 314.

[89]That is how Schultz interprets it: ibid., 317.

[90]Quoted from Johannes Hirschberger, *Geschichte der Philosophie*. Part 2, *Neuzeit und Gegenwart* (Freiburg: Herder, 41960), 385. English: *The History of Philosophy*, 2 vols., trans. Anthony N. Fuerst (Milwaukee: Bruce, 1959).

91Cf. Reinhard Frieling, *Der Weg des ökumenischen Gedankens* (Göttingen: Vandenhoeck & Ruprecht, 1992), 326–27.

92Ingolf U. Dalferth, "Das Wort vom Kreuz in der offenen Gesellschaft," *KD* 39 (1993): 123–48, at 142.

93See "Antisemitism? Luther and the Jews" and "Intolerance? Luther and Islam" in chapter 4.

94Dalferth, "Wort vom Kreuz," 144.

95The cross "is a very painful image for me. It does not convey joy or peace, and this does not do justice to Jesus," Thich Nhat Hanh, *Going Home: Jesus and Buddha as Brothers* (New York: Riverhead, 1999), 46.

6

Breakthrough: From the Hidden to the Revealed God

CONTEMPORARY QUESTIONS

Luther, like most of his contemporaries, assumed as given something that is not a given any longer: that God exists. Under that assumption one could discuss where God was revealed or to what extent God remains hidden. At present many people are not curious about God at all, whether hidden or revealed. It is often said that Luther was concerned about whether God is gracious, while today the question is simply whether God is. The question of a merely existent but otherwise irrelevant God, however, has been settled. From that point of view classic atheism has long since ceased to be a problem. It appears, we might say, to have dissolved along with belief in God. When aggressive advocates for atheism speak up nowadays their interest is not so much in God as in battling religion and piety. Religions have too often misused the name of God for their own inhuman purposes for us to say that this protest is unjustified. Can Luther's distinction between God in God's hiddenness and in God's revealedness be of any help in this situation?

The Reformer spoke of a "hidden" God. That could mean that God was still "present," even though hidden. But today's sense is more of an "absence" of God, which can, but need not, imply God's "death." It is perhaps still conceivable for our contemporaries that the idea of God—in whatever manner and in whatever unexpected form—might return to human consciousness, and in light of neuro-physiological processes might even be found to fit within that consciousness. That this idea could have found a historically tangible and normative interpretation two thousand years ago in the person of Jesus of Nazareth is an idea that is difficult to accept today. Does Luther's theology offer some approaches to the idea that God could make Godself present, and thus "revealed" today—perhaps in a way that transcends all previous images of the world and of God?

If God exists in hiddenness—or as "absent"—we can only know of God or at least suspect something about God if God occasionally or to a certain degree shows the divine self. The religions speak of such self-revelations of deities or the divine, though the Buddhists prefer to speak of awakening rather than of transcendent existence. For Christianity as a whole the question is why it should be only the man from Nazareth who makes Awakening possible, and not Buddha Shakyamuni; why Christians can trust that Jesus Christ is the one in whom God reveals Godself, and not Vishnu or Krishna or the message of the prophet Muhammad. Does Luther have an answer for that?

Finally, in this connection we should listen to another objection from classical atheism. If in the figure of Jesus Christ a hidden, almighty God is really made present, how can we explain all the misery that fills the world—the immeasurable misfortune of individual human beings, natural catastrophes like droughts, earthquakes, tsunamis, and the infinite suffering human beings have imposed on each other and continue to bring about? Luther speaks about sin and the wrath of God. How can his answers take us forward in the face of these questions when, in fact, they only lead to new questions? How, given the assumption of the existence of an almighty and loving God, can evil and sin exist; how could there be an "original sin"? How does God's all-powerful love jibe with the idea of a wrathful God whom we know not only from the Bible but also in the history of religions, and whom we are tempted to interpret as a projection of human passions?

The distinction between the hidden and the revealed God seems further burdened in a twofold respect: the suspicion of dualism and the idea of a determinism that cannot be theologically justified. The very terminology, "the revealed God/the hidden God" suggests that we should think here of a twofold, self-contradictory will in God, if not of two different deities in Marcion's sense. But the hidden God who, impenetrable to human perception and immune to human influence, fatally determines and shapes all events seems to leave no room for a loving will in God that would contradict that other. Is the Reformer's thought lacking all stringency here?

Hence it is not surprising that talk about a hidden God is generally absent from Christian preaching. In private piety the "loving" God dominates, and in freely formulated liturgical prayers God is addressed as "good and gracious." But this also makes God implausible in light of the misery surrounding all humanity and coming to dwell within them. Is the church condemning its message about God to irrelevance precisely when it gives the impression that faith can only be in a mild and loving God? Have modernity and postmodernity lost interest in the God of Jesus Christ because they have lost the ability to speak about the "hidden God," because the sense of God's impenetrability and resistance has vanished? If faith no longer serves a fuller appreciation of reality, religion becomes an opium. A religious mendacity about reality, even through appeal to the "loving" God, leads us into the empire of illusions. It is possible that faith must be spelled out anew and regained in terms of the hiddenness of God.[1] So should we argue again on behalf of Luther's illogic?

Or is God hidden today behind the apparently obvious things that are being said and even preached about God? The great catastrophes of recent history, including the crimes committed—Auschwitz, Vietnam, September 11, 2001—as well as the little catastrophes in individual lives give us ample reason to ask about a hidden meaning. God is experienced, if at all, as absent. This puts the question to theology: where else can God be present except in hiddenness?

Before Luther's discourse about the hidden and revealed God can be discussed we must clarify where, in his view, the question of a perception of God can take its starting point, what makes the distinction between the *Deus absconditus* and the *Deus revelatus* necessary for him, and in what kind of conceptual framework it can be phrased.

Initial Clarifications for Understanding the Distinction between the Hidden and the Revealed God

Starting point: the question of knowledge of God

There has always been reflection on the question of what human beings, in and of themselves, know about the existence and nature of God. The so-called proofs of God have a long history extending back to pre-Christian times. For Luther "proofs" of God's existence were something laughable; originally they were, in any case, intended only as "ways," and not in the sense of mathematical demonstrations. The conviction that one could conclude from the creatures to the Creator found its most concise formulation in Scholasticism. The Fourth Lateran Council formulated the doctrine of the *analogia entis*, the correspondence between beings and the ground of being, both cautiously and concisely: "between the Creator and the creature so great a likeness cannot be noted without the necessity of noting a greater dissimilarity between them."[2] This was a philosophical reflection based on Platonic-Aristotelian premises, which as such would not have interested Luther. He was convinced that the human being can know of God only what God's own self causes to be known, that is, on the basis of God's self-revelation and only within those limits. No one can speak better about God than Godself![3] The question of the capacity of reason or conscience is not to be determined on their own ground when there exists a medium through which God has opened the divine self explicitly to human beings, namely God's own word in Jesus Christ, as expressed to the full in Holy Scripture. The Bible itself contains indications that God makes Godself present to human beings through creation. This is spoken of in some of the Psalms (Pss 8, 19, 104), in Romans (Rom 1:20), and in the Acts of the

Apostles (Acts 17:27-28). For Luther the book of Jonah also belongs in this list. Hence for him it was true that human beings know that God exists, but they do not know who God is and what God intends with us. Reason is indeed able to grasp that all unearned good things come from God, but it does not know how this generous God responds to human beings and their—perverse—behavior.[4] So people either invent a mild sort of God who does not take wickedness very seriously, whose *metier* is to forgive (Heinrich Heine), and who agrees with the wishes of the "childish I," or else an implacable and strict God who strikes on earth with all sorts of suffering and in eternity with the punishments of hell and thus corresponds to the expectations of the "parental I."[5]

Thus the Reformer comes to the following set of arguments: knowledge of the existence of God, and even of the unity of God—that is, monotheism—is rationally achievable, but not the recognition of the triune God who turns to humanity in Law and Gospel. Human reason is unable to distinguish between God and the devil. That distinction is only possible in view of Jesus Christ! Finally: what would have been the use of Christ's coming if reason were wise enough in and of itself? Luther develops his arguments for the distinction between the hidden and the revealed God especially in his arguments with Erasmus of Rotterdam. But it would be wrong to adduce his writing "The Bondage of the Will" in isolation.

Necessary distinction between the hidden and the revealed God

It could have seemed logical for Luther, on the basis of God's revelation in Jesus Christ, to stop speaking of a hidden God, as was demanded centuries later—and in explicit protest against Luther—by, for example, Karl Barth.[6] Why did he nevertheless insist on this distinction? Why did he, in fact, impress it so firmly on his readers and hearers?

Resistance of the biblical witness

From a biblicistic point of view Luther could appeal to a biblical passage in which the concept of the "hidden God" was explicitly mentioned: "Truly, you are a God who hides himself, O God of Israel, the Savior" (Isa 45:15); a few verses earlier, in a monologue of Yhwh, we read: "I form light and create darkness, I make weal and create woe; I the Lord do all these things" (Isa 45:7). God "kills and brings to life; he brings down to Sheol and raises up" (1 Sam 2:6). The Reformer saw another point of reference for talk about the hidden God in the hardening of Pharaoh's heart, which the biblical account explicitly attributes to Yhwh's action (Exod 4:21, and elsewhere). In addition, in this connection Israel's attitude of resistance to faith in Christ could serve as an illustration. Paul's argumentation in Romans offered further material: "I will be gracious to whom I will be gracious, and will show mercy on whom I will show mercy" (Exod 33:19; Rom 9:15). God has mercy "on whomever he chooses, and he hardens the heart of whomever he chooses" (Rom 9:18); Jacob he "loved" and Esau he "hated" (Mal 1:2-3; Rom 9:13). The human being has no right to sit in judgment on God: "Has the potter no right over the clay, to make out of the same lump one object for special use and another for ordinary use?" (Rom 9:21). God is completely sovereign and free in making decisions. Ultimately, Luther also saw his thesis confirmed by the New Testament statements regarding the Antichrist, who "opposes and exalts himself above every so-called god or object of worship, so that he takes his seat in the temple of God, declaring himself to be God" (2 Thess 2:4). But God cannot cease to be God; hence God must also be beyond the God over whom an "opponent" can exalt himself—the hidden God! Luther here presents an argument that seems grotesque today, but one whose content is comprehensible enough.[7]

The language of experience

That one must speak of the hidden God is something the Reformer also concludes from human inflexibility and the rejection encountered by the Gospel. How else can it be explained that so many people do not find their way to faith, except by the work of the hidden God? That sin is mighty among human beings and that there could have been an original sin at all must have to do with the hidden will of God, says Luther. But also the inexplicable suffering people have to bear is for Luther an indication of God's hiddenness. Still, the theodicy problem is not as grave for him as we feel it to be today. The fact that it is possible to reject God weighs more heavily for him than the fact that people are confronted with immeasurable suffering. The fact of ongoing temptations presented to the faithful also requires explanation. Where do they come from? What do they have to do with the Gospel of Jesus Christ? Luther himself felt continually challenged by the hidden God; he did not live with Ignatius of Loyola's conviction that God can be found at all times and "in all things."[8] In his experience God continually withdraws, even from the believer!

The soteriological motif

By no means should speaking of the hidden God compromise the Gospel or shake people's confidence in it, as Karl Barth feared. How can believers find firm ground, even though they encounter so much evil within themselves and without, if, as the biblical witness says, God's hidden working is behind the evil and the rejection of grace? Those who accept God's hiddenness in faith realize at the same time that in and of themselves they have no way of opening themselves to grace and contributing to their own salvation. Everything depends on God's gracious decision, as it must be preached on the basis of the Gospel. Only Godself can be the guarantor of God's grace; the cross of Christ is the expression of God's self-definition.⁹ Behind Luther's distinction between God in hiddenness and revealedness stands the theology of the cross. In the cross of Christ we encounter no cheap "love of God," but a love that sustains itself against everything that might contradict it. Without the distinction between the hidden and the revealed God, the love of God would become a banality, a generalized "truth" that would no longer permit me to grasp the dynamics of God's love and God's actions.

Mystical background?

Luther, as we know, was not the first to speak of the hidden God. Apophatic theology has a long history beginning with Neoplatonic thought outside Christianity. Dionysius the Areopagite knew that God can ultimately be described only in terms of what God is not and how God is exalted above all the things people can say about God.¹⁰ Two generations before Luther, Nicholas of Cusa had very effectively revived this tradition. Mortal human beings can only make contradictory statements about the eternal God; to that extent God is hidden from them. Nicholas reasoned: ". . . the place wherein Thou art found unveiled is girt round with the coincidence of contradictories, and this is the wall of Paradise wherein thou dost abide. The door whereof is guarded by the most proud spirit of Reason, and, unless he be vanquished, the way in will not lie open."¹¹ In God all oppositions and contradictions come together; God *is* the *coincidentia oppositorum*. Consequently, God's being is such that it "exists or it does not exist; or that it both exists and does not exist; or that neither does it exist nor does it not exist. Nothing more can be stated . . . ."¹² Luther did, in fact, say some things that sound similar, namely that God is "no such extended, long, broad, thick, high, deep being. He is a supernatural, inscrutable being who exists at the same time in every little seed, whole and entire, and yet also in all and above all and outside all created things. . . . Nothing is so small but God is still smaller, nothing so large but God is still larger, nothing is so short but God is still shorter, nothing so long but God is still longer, nothing is so broad but God is still broader, nothing so narrow but God is still narrower, and so on. . . ."¹³ However, Luther develops these reflections not in connection with the discussion of the *Deus absconditus* but in his argument about the proper understanding of the Holy Sacrament. His problem is not the rational incomprehensibility of God, which is clear to him in any event. Trying to philosophize about it seems ridiculous to him; he calls Dionysius the Areopagite stupid. Luther's question is altogether different: is there self-contradiction in God? What about the predestination of human beings to eternal salvation or damnation? How can one believe in a gracious God in light of the challenges with which the hidden God confronts human beings?

CONCEPTUALITY

In *De servo arbitrio*, Luther contrasts the *Deus absconditus* with the *Deus revelatus*. Paul Althaus interprets this as "God in himself" and "God in his revelation." Luther uses different formulations: he can speak of the *Deus absolutus*, of God "in his majesty," the "naked" God, and contrast this with the God who is "clothed" in the divine promises, the God who has in some sense "become like" us or been "veiled" for our sake. The Reformer thus argues, depending on the context, either from the side of God or from the side of the human: God conceals Godself in absolute divine freedom and sovereignty; on the other hand God is hidden from human beings in any case insofar as they cannot comprehend God. All that can and should interest believers is the revealed God, who "binds" Godself to the word and is "preached." God, who has made the divine promise clear and sealed it in Christ, who is self-revealed in words and signs, is the one to be brought forth against the "vague" God who tempts us to "speculation."[14] It is obvious that these contrasts do not exactly match. A separate problem, to which we will have to return later, is the question: to which side of this distinction does the concept of *Deus ipse*, "God's own self," belong?

THE HIDDEN GOD

Luther experienced God's hiddenness as a challenge, as in fact is the experience of every Christian who finds it a threat to his or her own life and faith. Those who have to preach suffer especially deeply from the fact that they are unable to make God's reality and love perceptible and believable through palpable and unmistakable evidence. But Luther also knew that God's hiddenness can mean grace for human beings: "No one can see God and live" (Exod 33:20). Looking directly into the sun's furnace would destroy human eyesight. So also, in the encounter with God human beings require protection from the light: therefore God comes to us "covered," God "makes for us a mist and a shadow."[15] The human being is not in a position to encounter God directly and enter into an immediate relationship with God, not only because of the limitations of human reason but above all because of humanity's sinful constitution. Therefore God chooses the indirect, even the opposite way, acting as if God were not God, but even a demon. God works *sub contrario*—exactly contrary to what people expect of God. Here, for Luther, are the points of contact with his *theologia crucis*, the "theology of the cross."[16] God does not encounter us on earth in any other way than in the dialectic of hiddenness and revealedness: revelation is not the end of God's hiddenness, while the hiddenness of God is, in turn, an impulse to inquire anew into revelation.

GOD'S "MASKS" IN CREATION AND HISTORY

God's hiddenness and revealedness in suffering are clear for Luther especially in the realms of creation and history.[17]

Creation

For Luther, God is essentially Creator: "nothing and everything are our Lord God's materials."[18] Creation, "call[ing] into existence the things that do not exist" (Rom 4:17): that is God's domain. Luther is amazed at God's work in creation, the new trees, birds, and fish that constantly appear on earth. He finds formulae shaped by mysticism to express God's relationship to creation: God must "be present and must make and preserve his creation both in its innermost and outermost aspects. Therefore, indeed, he himself must be present in every single creature in its innermost and outermost being, on all sides, through and through, below and above, before and behind, so that nothing can be more truly present and within all creatures than God himself with his power."[19] Despite this, God is also hidden in these divine works, in which one should be able to recognize God. A stirring leaf can terrify someone who is not right with God. Certainly human beings can rightly conclude from the creation around them to the Creator, but what the Creator's plan for them is remains a puzzle to them. Believers assert that all creatures are masks and costumes God chooses to have cooperate with God, even though God "can and does do everything without their cooperation."[20] God conceals Godself, dresses, wears costumes! But only faith perceives this; nonbelievers must experience that "all creatures are God's rods and weapons when he wants to punish."[21] It is God who, so to speak, hides behind creation and all its motions; God is at the same time partially recognizable in it for believers and hidden from nonbelievers. But faith and unbelief are always at war with one another within the human being!

History

Matters are no different in the realm of history.[22] It is a trivial matter for God to make a radical change in political power relationships in the blink of an eye, to destroy one empire by means of another: "Do you not see the gun being loaded?"[23] God "shot" the Jews with the Romans, the Romans with the Goths and Wends, the Chaldeans with the Persians, the Greeks with the Turks—and God will find a bullet for us Germans, too![24] The whole world is God's "tournament and cavalry." The Turks and the pope are God's "carnival." God punishes one scoundrel with another.[25] "Whichever prince wins a battle, it is seen that God defeated the other by him."[26] God dresses in the form of Hannibal or Alexander the Great and guides history in that way. The Reformer would probably not have hesitated to see God at work even in Napoleon, Hitler, or Stalin. What was true in the past was equally true for current history and people's participation in it: it is God who is working through us; we are only God's "masks" beneath which "he hides himself and works all in all"—Luther adds, "as we Christians surely know."[27] It is a matter of seeing through God's masks, though that is possible only through faith.

GOD'S HIDDENNESS AS A CONSEQUENCE OF SIN AND THE FETTERED CONDITION OF THE HUMAN WILL

Evil

Luther was unable to resolve the problem of how to regard the relationship between God and evil by recourse to the assertion, which goes back to Neoplatonism, that evil is really "nothing," only a dulling or an absence of good. Centuries later Karl Barth took up that line again.[28] But according to Luther, Satan and the enemies of God are not "nothing"; they possess reality and an explicit will, though in a corrupt constitution. The wicked human being desires to be his or her own self, to decide for herself or himself and in no way to be obedient to God and believe that one has an obligation to one's neighbor. But as God's work and God's creature the wicked person is like the devil in being no less subject to God's almighty power than are God's other creatures and works. This leads Luther to the conclusion: God, in divine omnipotence, moves and effects everything; Satan and the ungodly are no exceptions. But God "acts in them as they are and as he finds them."[29] Their destructiveness does not feed on itself; it depends on the dynamic of divine omnipotence without which nothing can exist. God cannot be made responsible for the wickedness of the devil or of human beings. Luther is not shy of using very simple examples: a rider on a sick horse, a carpenter who has nothing but a chipped and jagged axe can only work with what is available, no matter how clever she or he may be. "The fault is thus in the tool . . . ." This explains why "the ungodly man cannot but continually err and sin, because he is caught up in the movement of divine power and not allowed to be idle, but wills, desires, and acts according to the kind of person he himself is."[30] God cannot abandon the divine omnipotence for the sake of sinful human beings, and sinful human beings are not in a position of their own accord to change their sinful constitution.[31] Wanting to see God's omnipotent power limited would mean "wanting God to cease to be God on account of the ungodly."[32] God did not create what is evil in us, but still must deal with the existing evil conditions in order to remain identical with Godself.

Of course it is also clear to Luther what the next objection to his argumentation will be: how do we explain the fact that God finds Satan and the ungodly in such aversion to a God who did not create them that way? First the Reformer relies on familiar, traditional, but utterly unsatisfying answers: the will of Satan became evil "through God's deserting [Satan's will] and Satan's sinning." But how should we imagine being deserted by God in view of God's omnipotence and universal action?[33] Here Luther passes. Next question: and why does God, in divine omnipotence, not alter the evil will God drives on by his universal action? Luther's answer: this touches "the secrets of his majesty, where his judgments are incomprehensible." It is "not our business to ask this question, but to adore these mysteries . . . . He is God, and for his will there is no cause or reason"; no one can dictate anything to God. Instead, the divine will is the measure and guideline "of all things."[34] This, at least, is certain, and even natural reason is forced to accept it: God would be a ridiculous God "if he could not and did not do everything, or if anything took place without him."[35]

Luther's argumentation is easier to understand if we try to make clear in our minds what his intention is. If God must be understood *per definitionem* as the one who is omnipotent and everywhere active, and if the sinful human being *per definitionem* is the deficient instrument who is unable to alter his or her own situation, then it is certainly true that God cannot partially or wholly abandon divine omnipotence, and the human being, aided by the power of the will, cannot effect any partial or whole alteration toward the good. Under the presuppositions he has put in place Luther's argumentation appears conclusive; his refusal, then, to suggest a believable solution is also plausible. But his interest is not in proclaiming ontological theses about the hidden God; it is, rather, to draw attention away from God's mystery and impenetrability and steer it to Jesus Christ, in whom is shown God's true face, the one that is obligatory for us. Luther's tortured statements about the hidden God are made in service of his message about the God who is revealed in Jesus Christ and who is enflamed with love for sinful human beings. If we separate what Luther writes from this intention it will lead us into a thicket of contradictions and groundless or anxiety-provoking assertions. Luther argues for the purpose of working out the constitutive significance of Jesus Christ for salvation.

No matter how strange and perhaps even repellent this line of thinking may appear, it is not simply inconclusive even today. Why did God not create human beings perfect from the beginning? Believers must admit that they do not know—otherwise they would be God! An adequate theology admits that there is much it does not understand or know. But three things are clear to Luther: God cannot cede anything of the divine omnipotence, or God would be ridiculous. Then—however we may think of God's universal action, I, the sinner, must admit my sins.[36] But ultimately I can dare to do it because in Christ, through the Holy Spirit, God is reaching out to me.

The will as unfree

In view of the human situation as thus depicted, a natural, free ability to open oneself to God and live a life pleasing to God simply does not exist— for one thing, because in any case it is only God who possesses sovereign authority and power over human beings, and also because human beings find themselves irreversibly turned away from God.[37] Luther is convinced that thus the human will, under these conditions, is anything but free; it is, instead, bound to the destructive will of the devil, who is the ruler of this world. Thus human beings by no means sin against their own intention, but freely, we might say with complete personal consent. In Luther's opinion human beings are always within the sphere of power either of God or of the devil; there is no third possibility. Of course there is a certain flexibility in everyday matters, but insofar as salvation is concerned humans are not free. Hence Luther compares the abilities of the human will with a beast of burden being ridden either by God wherever God wills, or by Satan. The human ability to will is only an object of contention; the battle itself is played out between the two riders, Satan and God.[38] According to Luther "freedom of the will" can be predicated only of God; for human beings it exists, from the outset, only insofar as God withdraws them from Satan's rule and thus conveys freedom on them.

It is thus not at all disputed that human beings, as regards their earthly needs, do indeed have a variety of opportunities to choose. But even in those decisions, however they may turn out, what comes about is ultimately what God regards as necessary. Luther does not in any way concede a universal determinism. As regards human freedom he distinguishes two perspectives: with respect to what is immediately beneath them (*respectu inferioris*)[39] human beings certainly have relative freedom, though freedom, from a psychological point of view as well, is in any case never absolute: it is realized within certain conditions such as those presented by psychosomatic and socio-cultural determinants. But as regards the things that are "above" human beings (*quae supra nos*) they have no individual opportunities to choose or decide. Here we can only speak of a passive disposing quality (*aptitudo passiva*), a certain "aptitude" to be seized by the Spirit and filled with the grace of God.[40] But it is God's sovereign freedom and decision whether or not to make use of this passive aptitude of human beings and bring them to salvation. The dispute over human free will was off track to the extent that Luther was accused of totally negating it. What is hard to accept in his position today is his distinction between a sphere within which human beings can decide and act responsibly with (relative) freedom and one in which they must simply remain passive.

God's freedom and honor

The Reformer sees in this question the sovereignty of God, indeed, God's God-ness, at risk. When he insists on God's universal active power and, correspondingly, on the restriction of the human will, he does not intend to evoke "the positively bloodcurdling notion that God is the motor in a gigantic machine that no one can bring to a stop, not even when people are seized by it and ground to pieces."[41] He supposes, rather, that a God like the one Erasmus imagines can ultimately abdicate. He expresses this in terms of his contemporaries' questions: would not a God who allowed Godself to be deprived of the freedom to predestine become an unnecessary and fatal force that abandons everything to a mechanical determinism or to pure accident? Would people not, in that case, be saved or damned without God's needing to know anything about it? Either God does everything or God need do nothing more: Luther saw this alternative acutely, and subsequent Western intellectual history has impressively confirmed it. What tasks remain for the grace of God and the Holy Spirit if human beings can freely decide for themselves? It is God's honor and glory that God's very self creates the salvation of human beings. Here appears the vanishing point of all Luther's reflections on the hidden God: God's revealed and indisputably good will in Jesus Christ.

CONFUSION OF GOD AND THE DEVIL

The human condition

Sin, death, and the devil dominate the human situation, indeed all of creation and history. Luther starts from the overarching structural conditions everyone can observe, even if one only becomes fully aware of their radical character through the law of God: human beings aim at self-preservation; they cannot live except at the expense of others. At the same time they are caught in a chain of vicious circles from which they cannot extricate themselves by their own efforts. This is not a moral judgment but a trans-moral situational analysis. Sin is not primarily moral depravity; it can even be linked to the highest moral achievements, just as the highest technical know-how can be put to work in the organization of concentration camps or the perfecting of atomic weapons. Sin means distance from God, being turned away from God and the neighbor and concentrated on the self. The characteristic attitude of human beings is not that of an open shell willing to be filled by God, but the opposite: a "turning in on oneself," *incurvatio in se*,[42] that concentrates on the self and cuts one off from genuine life. By nature humans cannot "want God to be

God." Instead, they want (if only they could!) "to be God, and [do] not want God to be God."[43] For those who turn away from the source of their lives, death is the natural consequence of sin, "the wages of sin" (Rom 6:23). The devil is fully in command of this situation: he guards his palace and remains the unchallenged ruling power (Luke 11:21-22) as long as he is not attacked by one who is stronger.

Satan

Luther's statements about the devil are multilayered.[44] He shared the beliefs of his time in devils and demons. The legend that he threw an inkpot at the devil while he was at the Wartburg can be attested as early as the seventeenth century, and it is a "clever invention," since Luther fought the devil with pen and ink. He traced his personal challenges to the devil as well. Undoubtedly he felt his belief in devils and demons was confirmed by Jesus' expulsions of demons and by other New Testament passages to the point (e.g., Eph 6:12). The suspicion that a radicalization of belief in the devil was instigated by Luther is not entirely unjustified.

Despite his captivity to medieval belief in devils there are also some beginnings of a "demythologization" of Satan in Luther's writings. The medieval requisites for the devil are dismissed as inessential; the devil is by no means recognizable by his ugliness. It is in his nature not to give a satanic impression; on the contrary, he knows how to disguise himself. He presents himself in a seductive, attractive form, as an "angel of light" (2 Cor 11:14). But referring to the devil, according to Luther, offers no alibi for human beings, because they love to follow him. Satan does not seduce primarily, as was thought in the Middle Ages, to amoral behavior, but instead to unbelief, to abandoning trust and the desire to live. He throws people back and forth between overestimating themselves and despairing. In all this he remains dependent on God; he is "God's devil."[45] Luther by no means advocates for dualism: the devil is for him not an independent power.[46] Of course, it is only faith that can recognize him for what he is.

God and the devil as indistinguishable

For human beings, God and the devil are interchangeable because the devil can disguise himself and present himself in the most beautiful colors, and because on the other hand God chooses the contrary path for making Godself present in this situation: the divine work is carried out *sub contraria specie*— under the appearance of its opposite. What looks like divine action can in reality be devilish, and what appears demonic can in fact be traceable to God. The works of God and the devil cannot be distinguished phenomenologically;

only in Christ are God and the devil separated. "In short, God cannot be God unless He first becomes a devil. We cannot go to heaven unless we first go to hell. We cannot become God's children until we first become children of the devil. All that God speaks and does"—in the eyes of the world—"the devil has to speak and do first. . . . I must grant the devil his hour of godliness and ascribe devilhood to our God." But this is a matter only of "an hour"; ultimately it is also true that "'His faithfulness and truth endure forever.'"[47] Since God can act devilishly and the devil divinely, for human beings—without Christ—God and the devil are indistinguishable. Luther denies human beings the ability to determine by means of an existing table of "characteristics" who is God and who is the devil. He knows of only a single possibility for distinguishing between God and the devil: it is only in light of Jesus Christ that, for believers, God and the devil separate. Therefore the devil stakes everything on blocking our view of Jesus Christ, and therefore Luther meets him where he meets Christ. Luther regards him as the one who is trying to take Christ's place. We can make Luther's idea clear in terms of what we may call the spatial perspective: God above, Christ and the devil in the middle, the human being below. As long as there is no belief in Christ, as long as he does not stand in the middle, between God and the human, the devil stands there in his place. God, who looks down at human beings, then sees people ruled by the devil: sin. In turn, the human being who looks up to God can see only a God covered and disguised by the devil: the wrathful God. But if Christ stands in the middle, God sees the human being in Christ and the human sees God in Christ. Human beings, who since the Fall have attributed devilish characteristics to their God and divine features to the devil, must realize in Jesus Christ that God is God and the devil is the devil.[48] Luther's whole theology is, to that extent, aimed only at sharpening the distinction between God and the devil—a distinction this theology sees as being made perceptible only in Jesus Christ.

THE REVEALED GOD

GOD IN CHRIST

Thus everything depends on my grasping God as God desires to be grasped by me, that I not define God differently from the way God has defined God's self. God has fully defined God's self in Christ, as God for us, who predestines human beings to salvation and reveals this to them through the Holy Spirit.

With this it is clear to Luther that in Christ there is an end to the hiddenness of God that threatens us. The wrath of God, beneath which God's face seemed transformed into the devil's grimace, is revealed for those who believe in Christ not as a threat (*ira severitatis*), but as a turning of God to humanity in compassion (*ira misericordiae*). God, as becomes evident in Christ, is not the severe judge and executioner who must be presumed by the conscience oppressed by the Law, but the Father who himself creates reconciliation. Christ serves as the "mirror of the fatherly heart" of God;[49] in Christ we see "into the depths of the Father's heart, indeed, into the fathomless and eternal love of God that he bears for us and has borne from eternity."[50] God is newly and utterly "defined" in Christ; only in him can the true God be known. Knowing Christ means knowing God *sub carne crucifixa*, under the flesh of the Crucified. "Now you see," Luther preached on John 3:16, in which he found God's revealedness in Christ expressed with special clarity, "that the Christ does nothing else but make the Father sweet for us and bring us to the Father through himself, and that is the end of everything Christ does, that we should acquire a fine, loving confidence in the Father. . . ."[51] I must grasp God "where he is softest," and think: "Yes, that is God, yes, so is God's will and pleasure, that Christ does that for me."[52]

Of course, God's revealedness in the unprepossessing, weak, crucified human being Jesus Christ is also a form of hiddenness. Apparently God is acting here too, and especially, *sub contraria specie*, and it is important not to be shocked or disappointed by it. In Jesus Christ we can read a "stylistic law" of divine action. Recognizing that, and grasping God's revealedness beneath the hiddenness in Jesus Christ is something that, indeed, only faith can teach, the faith Godself creates through the word.

FLEEING FROM THE HIDDEN TO THE REVEALED GOD

What is the relationship between God in the one form and in the other? In *De servo arbitrio* Luther first establishes that one must "dispute" in different ways, depending on whether one is speaking about the preached, revealed will of God or the not-preached, unrevealed God who is not worshiped. "To the extent, therefore, that God hides himself and wills to be unknown to us, it is no business of ours." It is true in this case that "quae supra nos, nihil ad nos."[53] This expression, of course, should not be applied cynically as an alibi argument,[54] but we must agree with the Reformer that people really have and should have nothing to do with God in God's eternal majesty. We must look to the word in which God reveals the divine self. Otherwise it should be enough for us, in order to know and accept the hidden will of God, that God is at work for us, in small things as in large, in a way that is impenetrable to us.

For Luther, knowing about the hidden God concentrates our attention still more on the revealed God: "If you dispute about God's goodness and power apart from Christ, that is horrible and the devil is there."[55] Anyone who wants to make God visible outside Christ sees only "hellish fire."[56]

Although the Reformer occasionally seems to separate the hiddenness and revealedness of God as if they belonged to two different Gods, for him everything depends on the one God who has revealed God's self in Jesus Christ, but who surpasses our ability to comprehend. Hence it is necessary, so to speak, for our nature to "make its way to God against God and pray to Him."[57] To that extent faith is for Luther "embattled faith."[58] The believing person experiences God differently from the one who does not believe, and the person who has entered into God's glory—so Luther adds—is also different from the believer. In the "light of nature" human beings cannot understand why God allows evil to flourish; they stand at a loss before the riddles of life. Believers, however, recognize in "the light of grace" that this apparent injustice of God will not continue in the "life after life," and—so we may add—they will then begin to see through some of God's hiddenness in nature, history, and their own fate. The mystery of predestination, however, remains closed to us on earth. Neither the light of nature nor grace offers a plausible solution to this problem. Only in the "light of glory" will God's incomprehensible righteousness be perfectly disclosed.[59] This discussion of the three lights, of course, is not about what we might call stepwise and increasing degrees of holiness. In light of the expected revelatory power of the eschatological light of glory, nature and grace come together once again on the same level; the preliminary limitations of both cannot be denied.[60] Nevertheless, the plan of Luther's argument remains visible: God, who enlightens believers through his grace in Jesus Christ, will reveal Godself to them in his perfect righteousness. *De servo arbitrio* concludes with this hope,[61] underscoring once again that Luther means to preach the God of Jesus Christ and no other. If you have Christ "then you also have the hidden God together with Him who has been revealed."[62]

ASSURANCE OF PREDESTINATION TO SALVATION

For medieval people the primary question was not how to get the most out of life, but whether one's life before God would succeed or fail. In view of a comparatively short life expectancy and multiple catastrophes and threats, people lived with the knowledge of eternity: *sub specie aeternitatis*. The expectation of resurrection and the last judgment was part of the common imagination. Eternal life or eternal damnation: that was the question toward which everything pointed. For Luther the problem was exacerbated by his concept of God, which assumed that God determines and causes absolutely everything. He was persuaded that the question of God's hiddenness culminated in this. He knew how to deal with more superficial attacks.

Superficial challenges

The problem of theodicy could be resolved to a degree, at least for believers when they considered their own situation, by reference to the positive consequences that could emerge even from the negative. Luther attempted to apply this idea especially with regard to the growth and deepening of faith: God digs around the vineyard so that it will bear more fruit, and cuts off useless shoots: "'See, I am being fertilized and cultivated as a branch on the vine. All right, dear hoe and clipper, go ahead. Chop, prune, and remove (the unnecessary leaves). I will gladly suffer it, for these are God's hoes and clippers. They are applied for my good and welfare.'"[63] The Reformer regards it as a matter of course that Christians have to suffer opposition and temptation. After all, their faith is a provocation to the devil.[64] For Satan can probably tolerate "pious people, but he cannot abide Christians."[65] Consequently, "a Christian must have evil days and suffer much."[66] There are many tasks allotted to temptation: it preserves faith because God tempts believers only so "that faith may be strong and solid and the old Adam and unbelief be throttled, which clings only to present things it sees and feels; God tempts us in order to free us from present things, so that we hold to the word alone."[67] But temptation also guards against arrogance and presumption: for believers it must be "so well salted and mixed that they do not always sense only the strengths of the Spirit, but sometimes their faith flutters and their heart hesitates, so that they see what they are. . . ."[68] The old Adam is killed by people who "antagonize us, assail us, disquiet us, and oppose our will in every way. . . . We should really pay such assailants all our goods . . . !"[69] The devil and wicked people work together, so to speak, so that faith may be strengthened and be able to develop its true strength.

Doubt of predestination

Another dimension of temptation is certainly reached when it seems that God has turned against one. This is the "high" temptation that causes people to "want to grope for God and his grace, to see whether they are there."[70] Believers come to doubt whether their sins are really forgiven. In this, according to Luther, there are two stages, two potentials for sin: sin as such and the despair that does not trust God to forgive. God becomes suspect in human eyes.[71] The "demonization" of God is most oppressive for individuals when it is about one's own salvation. All temptations reach their climax and goal in doubts regarding predestination. This may be most palpable from a present-day point of view when a person finds life not only meaningless but positively nonsensical and absurd.

It is quite certain that some of Luther's own experiences are reflected here. Are there not good reasons to reckon with a predestination not only to blessedness, but also to eternal damnation? Why did the late medieval church not repent? Why did the Jews not join the Reformation? Why do all people not find their way to faith; why do so many live their lives without feeling any interest at all in the question of eternal salvation? Finally, there are biblical passages that suggest we should not expect all people to find their way to eternal salvation: "Many are called, but few are chosen" (Matt 22:14). Of course Luther also thought in this connection of the hardening of Pharaoh's heart, though without a clear realization that this was not about eternal blessedness or damnation. Certainly he himself was more concerned with his own predestination than with the theoretical resolution of the problem of predestination in general.

What solutions are possible in view of this situation, which is so stressful for faith? For Luther the way offered by the late medieval church was out of the question—self-assurance through mystical or sacramental piety, participation in the church's life, and use of what it had to offer—and certainly not financial or existential sacrifices. Naturally Luther was just as unlikely to advocate the solution that appeared in later Calvinism, the so-called *syllogismus practicus*, that is, the idea that election could be deduced from, among other things, well-being on earth. In contrast to these, Luther knew of three ways, though he did not give them equal weight throughout his life. In his early years he speaks of a *resignatio ad infernum*, that is, the possibility of entrusting oneself to the will of God and leaving it to God whether God would decide to send one to hell.[72] From a religious point of view this might well represent an extreme form of obedience to God and human humility but it has nothing to do with Christian faith inasmuch as it does not respond to the unconditional saving will of God; it could even be seen as an arrogant refusal of the way God desires to help people to salvation in Jesus Christ. That is probably the reason why Luther did not pursue this "solution" further.

A second way, for Luther, was to uncover the doubt about predestination and so to relativize it: it should be revealed to be an unjustified seeking of signs and certainty that is not in accord with faith. Worrying about one's own predestination to salvation or damnation proves completely fruitless; it distracts us from the message of the Gospel. Consequently the temptation to doubt about predestination should be seen as an attempt by the devil to lead people astray into care for themselves.

Hence for Luther there was finally only one way to get clarity over the temptation regarding predestination: namely not to speculate on the abilities of reason but to believe the promises of the Gospel and rely on the word of God: "Anyone who believes has eternal life" (John 6:47). Knowledge of God's hiddenness concentrates the sight even more strongly on the God revealed in Christ. "Faith depends on the word alone." It closes "eyes and ears and everything" and at the same time wraps itself in the promise that Christ is the Savior.[73] We must let God be God: predestination to salvation is God's concern and God's alone; it is safer in God's hands and is better preserved to the consolation of human beings than if it depended on themselves.[74] But how does one achieve such assurance of salvation?

THE ACTION OF THE HOLY SPIRIT

How do I come to faith, to the assurance of my predestination to salvation? How do I find my way to faith in Christ, despite the resistance of the hidden God? Luther gave too little explanation of this in *De servo arbitrio*. However, by reference to John 6:44 he declared that no one could, of oneself, "come" to Christ. Rather, it is required that "the Father himself draws and teaches him inwardly." The result is that "Christ is set forth by the light of the Spirit, so that a man is rapt away to Christ with the sweetest rapture . . ."[75] The fundamental Lutheran experience of justification can find expression here in mystical terms: "that I may hear your secret whispering within: your sins are forgiven you."[76] This, unfortunately, describes no method by which one can make faith one's own. But Luther assumes that this "secret whispering within" does not take place independently of the external word, and that consequently listening to the Gospel must represent the first step. The Holy Spirit works in the preaching of the word. The Spirit's "sanctifying" is "nothing other" than that the Spirit brings us to Christ in order to convey to us the possession of redemption we could not achieve of ourselves.[77]

The Reformer formulated this impressively in his interpretation of the third article of the Apostles' Creed in the Small Catechism. He confesses: "I believe that by my own reason or strength I cannot believe in Jesus Christ, my Lord, or come to him." Everything must here be resigned to the work of the Holy Spirit, for "the Holy Spirit has called me through the Gospel, enlightened me with his gifts, and sanctified and preserved me in true faith."[78] The Holy Spirit gives faith in Jesus Christ, and does so through word and sacrament. In his Confession of 1528 Luther formulated it thus: through the Holy Spirit "as a living, eternal, divine gift and endowment, all believers are adorned with faith and other spiritual gifts, raised from the dead, freed from sin, and made joyful and confident, free and secure in their conscience. For this is our assurance if we feel this witness of the Spirit in our hearts, that God wishes to be our Father, forgive our sin, and bestow everlasting life on us. . . ." This assurance in the heart is conveyed by the Holy Spirit: "He teaches us to understand this deed of Christ which has been manifested to us, helps us receive and preserve it, use it to our advantage and impart it to others, increase and extend it. He does this both inwardly and outwardly—inwardly by means of faith and other spiritual gifts, outwardly through the gospel, baptism, and the sacrament of the altar, through which as through three means or methods he comes to us and inculcates the sufferings of Christ for the benefit of our salvation."[79]

THE TRIUNE GOD

Luther scarcely reflected on the relationship between his faith in the triune God and his remarks in *De servo arbitrio* about the hidden and revealed God. This is an area still in need of investigation.[80] But Luther's doctrine of the Trinity as such has certainly been the subject of discussion in recent decades.[81]

CONFESSING THE TRINITARIAN DOGMA

The trinitarian basis

The Reformer shared the faith of the ancient church. "To try to understand or describe the Christian faith without the Trinity would be to try to present it without the foundation on which it is based."[82] The Trinity is one of the "sublime articles of the divine majesty" about which there is no "dispute or contention, for both parties confess them."[83] It may be that Luther was mistaken about this,[84] if one considers the soteriological and ecclesiological implications of the trinitarian confession. At any rate this was not the primary interest of Luther's theology. He did not undertake any determined study of the ancient church's doctrine of the Trinity or the trinitarian disputes; neither the Small nor the Large Catechism develops the trinitarian doctrine as such. Nevertheless, it is striking that he interprets the Apostles' Creed, which previously had been divided into twelve sections matching the twelve apostles, in trinitarian terms: it concerns creation, redemption, and sanctification. This makes it clear that the Reformer's interest was not in the clarification of inner-trinitarian relations but in the significance of the persons of the Trinity for the economy of salvation.

The eschatological reservation

Luther took a critical stance toward attempts at a theological explanation of the doctrine of the Trinity; "threefoldness [Dreifaltigkeit]" seemed to him "bizarre" and "threeness [Dreiheit]" an ironic expression. The whole trinitarian vocabulary—person, essence, substance—he thought problematic.[85] Should we call the Trinity "a three-thing [gedritt; Dreiheit]?" "I cannot give it a name."[86] Luther's basically anti-speculative attitude appears particularly with regard to the doctrine of the Trinity: ". . . when it comes to the things of God, however, we must stammer and speak as we can, especially in this article, which is the highest in our holy faith and in the holy Christian church."[87] It seems wrongheaded to try to derive a trinitarian ontology that is supposed to have shaped the whole thought of the later Reformer from an early Christmas sermon in which Aristotle was used in the interpretation of John 1 and given limited acceptance.[88] As regards the fine-tuned doctrine of the Trinity as the theologians of the schools presented it, Luther warned: "But if you do not wish to fall into the net of the evil foe, forget about their clever distinctions, their obscuring explanations, and their subtleness, and cling to these divine words; press into them and stay within them as does a rabbit in a cleft in the rock."[89] His later efforts, especially regarding the axiom *opera trinitatis ad extra sunt indivisa*, attributed to Augustine, show[90] that throughout his life Luther made it his task to communicate the trinitarian confession. But what occupied him were not ontological definitions; instead it was the question of how the one God, whose work *ad extra*—according to the Augustinian formula—must be undivided, can be thought of together with the idea of a trinity of acting persons. Everything has been made by a single "maker"; it is not as if each of the trinitarian persons were active in his own task.[91] We must therefore make a distinction: seen absolutely, God's works are the result of the common action of the three persons; from a relative point of view, however, they are attributable to the individual persons, depending on the "usage" of the economy of salvation within which they stand.[92] "We assign creation to the Father, redemption to the Son, and to the Holy Spirit the power to forgive sins" and "make joyous." These are like "different garments, so that one may not confuse the persons with one another." It is always about works that, although they are so different, the triune God can effect without one's necessarily having to attribute them to individual trinitarian persons. But the trinitarian persons are "clothed" in various manners of appearance.[93] Here Luther adopts an interesting variation on modalism: Father, Son, and Spirit are not, as such, three forms of being of the one God, but instead their differentiation is explained by their functions in the economy of salvation. In this way Luther rescues the idea of God's unified action, though he only thinks it through more thoroughly in connection with the first article of the creed: creation is the result of the one trinitarian action. But what about redemption and perfection? Here again the individual trinitarian persons appear more forthrightly in their specific functions.

Luther could value a clear conceptual framework especially when combating anti-trinitarian tendencies. That he succeeded in "translating the doctrine of the mystery of the Trinity, previously formulated in Greek or Latin, into the language of the people"[94] can certainly be disputed. In general we must maintain with Gerhard Müller that as far as trinitarian dogma is concerned Luther opposed "speculation" as well as "neglect."[95]

Soteriological relevance

For Luther what was essential in the ancient church's confession of the triune God was its soteriological relevance. He did not pay much attention to the relationships within the Trinity. The Holy Spirit does not teach us "how things go on within the Godhead."[96] It is a matter of course for him that theology has to express itself in different terms from those of mathematics. It speaks a "new language." The categorical difference between the previous meaning of a word and the meaning the same word has received "in Christ" cannot be ignored.[97] But what is more important for the Reformer is what he is to preach about the triune God, namely not at all "who He is in himself beyond all the garments and works, simply in his divine nature."[98] Luther confesses the triune God "who has given himself to us all wholly and completely, with all that he is and has."[99]

THE TRIUNE GOD AND THE DISTINCTION BETWEEN THE HIDDEN AND THE REVEALED GOD

The distinction in service to the creed

How does Luther understand the relationship between the triune God and the counterpoint of the hidden and revealed God? Certainly the one cannot be played off against the other. In no way can the distinction between the hidden and the revealed God replace the trinitarian confession; in turn, the trinitarian confession by no means makes unnecessary the distinction, so important to Luther, between the *Deus absconditus* and the *Deus revelatus*. Each of these approaches has its specific function. In the explication of the creed given in the catechism the idea of the hidden God does not appear; here the subject is God's saving work on behalf of humanity. In *De servo arbitrio*, on the other hand, scarcely anything is said about the triune God; here Luther's trinitarian doctrine is "curiously undeveloped as such."[100] In that writing his whole purpose was to cause the limitations of the natural human being's ability to know to be recognized and grasped, so that in this way the God revealed in Christ should gain the upper hand. The distinction between the *Deus absconditus* and the *Deus revelatus* thus points in turn, without becoming the subject of discussion, to the status of the trinitarian confession: God reveals God's self in a threefold way. It is precisely in terms of the distinction between the hidden and the revealed God that the trinitarian confession is understood and grasped as constitutive in its significance for the economy of salvation.

The christological concentration

In Luther's view the individual persons of the Trinity can serve the hiddenness of God that aims at the revealing of his grace. God can conceal God's self as Creator just as God can become threatening in Christ when the latter is understood as lawgiver and judge. In a late disputation Luther even asserted—probably not only under a certain systematic pressure—that ". . . likewise the Holy Spirit: when he, with his finger, writes the Law on the stone tablets of Moses, then he is in his majesty and knowingly cries out against sin and terrifies hearts."[101] Hence the hidden and the revealed God can certainly not be identified with certain trinitarian persons—for example, in the sense that the hidden God is equated with God the Father and the revealed God with Christ, leaving no essential function for the Holy Spirit.

Individual statements by Luther may point in this direction: the Son is the "mirror of the fatherly heart"; through the Son we see into the Father's heart.[102] But according to Luther we discover the Father as Father through the Son, not the *Deus absconditus* as loving. The *Deus absconditus* remains, in fact, the God who is hidden from us, even in light of God's trinitarian self-revelation. Camaraderie is not in view: God remains sovereign, but God lives a sovereignty that does not threaten human beings. The believer experiences this in the encounter with the witness of Jesus the Christ.

Luther obviously finds the intersection of the distinction between the revealed and the hidden God on the one hand and trinitarian confession on the other in Christology. God wants to be known "as He reveals Himself. And God is particularly concerned about our knowledge of the revelation of His Son, as seen throughout the Old and the New Testament. All points to the Son. . . ."[103] In Christ, God discloses Godself as the Triune One, and in Christ it is made clear to human beings that, despite all their negative experiences with the *Deus absconditus*—indeed, with the devil!—God's attitude toward them is one of friendship.[104] Only now can the believer truly appreciate the working of the triune God, and not only the work of the Holy Spirit in believers themselves and in the church, also not only God's work in reconciling and justifying for the sake of Christ, but likewise the work of the Creator. So all creation begins to speak. For now "our house, farm, field, garden, and everything is full of the Bible, where God not only preaches through his marvelous works but also knocks on our eyes, touches our senses, and illumines our hearts directly, if we will allow it. . . ."[105] Now the human being is in a position to hear when the seed says to her or him: "Rejoice in God, eat, drink, use me and with me serve your neighbor!"[106]

CRITICAL EVALUATION

We could call *De servo arbitrio* Luther's tract "De Deo," his doctrine of God (Gerhard Ebeling). Luther himself regarded this writing, together with the two catechisms, as his best work. Even so, *De servo arbitrio* has not made its way into the Lutheran confessions. Does that mean that Lutheran Christians may, or even must in some sense distance themselves from it? Two primary questions must be posed here: did Luther present an ambivalent picture of God? and: did that ambivalence do damage to his pastoral intention? Or does he keep the God-question open for secularized people especially by his insistence on God's hiddenness?

AN AMBIVALENT PICTURE OF GOD?

Luther tried, in *De servo arbitrio*, to achieve the utmost acerbity of thought and theological radicality. Quite often he takes issue with Erasmus in a biting, ironic and polemical style. Should we say that in this confrontation his horse bolted? Some of his formulations invite us to suspect him of dualism. God as preached is concerned "that sin and death should be taken away and we should be saved. . . ." And yet "God hidden in his majesty neither deplores nor takes away death, but works life, death, and all in all."[107] God "does not will the death of a sinner, according to his word; but he wills it according to that inscrutable will of his."[108] How does Luther know that?

Location within the history of theology

We can attempt to locate Luther's attitude within the history of theology, in which case we may say, for example with Otto Ritschl, that Luther's "dualistic construction of the concept of God most embarrassingly" recalls "Marcionite dyotheism."[109] Reinhold Seeberg blames the heritage of Ockham for Luther's radical statements: it was Ockham, previously, who had distinguished between an absolute and an ordered power of God.[110] But that does not say anything yet in systematic theological terms.

Should we join Albrecht Ritschl in simply saying that Luther overemphasized God's wrath, or agree with Theodosius Harnack in taking the reality of God's wrath seriously? Werner Elert has argued that we should connect the wrath of God and the hidden God with that terrible "primal experience" in which "the person without Christ experiences God's fateful power."[111]

Attempts at qualification

Some psychological suggestions could be associated with Elert's reflections: the contradiction Luther expresses does not lie in God but in the human. For the one who thinks God is wrathful, God "is" wrathful; for the one who sees God as gracious, God "is" gracious. "If you believe, you shall have all things!"[112] Luther modified this saying in a number of ways: as you believe, it will happen to you;[113] you have it because you believe that you receive it;[114] insofar as one believes, one has.[115] According to Luther, faith undoubtedly has a creative function; it "makes" God, as unbelief and false belief are able to create idols. In its disjunctive function faith knows how to distinguish between God and the devil, the hidden and the revealed God.[116] But if we try to use nothing but the argument from projection here we would not only fall into the traps of Feuerbachian critique of religion, we would fail to grasp the radicality of Luther's discourse about the hidden and the revealed God.

Therefore it is also inadequate to argue in terms of a special Lutheran "form of discourse." Oswald Bayer asserts that Luther speaks "neither of the *deus absconditus* nor of the devil as an assertion in the rhetorical form of statement."[117] But he most certainly does! Of course the Reformer is aware that theological speech is always kerygmatic and subject to eschatological reservation. But we cannot use this to place limitations on a prominent part of what he has said. We gain nothing here by speaking of a special form of discourse.

The following points may be useful in formulating an opinion:

Luther, in *De servo arbitrio*, orients himself to the biblical witness. He offers no polished position statement; individual biblical passages are explained, which makes the reading of the document tiresome. The Reformer wants to bring the biblical message into force. It does indeed speak of God's wrath and rejection, but that is not the center or even close to having equal weight with what is said of God's love. In the meantime what the Reformer had to say in reference to the individual biblical passages he used in his contrasting of the hidden and revealed God has become highly problematic. For example, the hardening of Pharaoh's heart is by no means about eternal damnation! Paul Althaus has said, somewhat reticently, that Luther's concepts go beyond Sacred Scripture.[118] From a formal point of view we have to say that in his interpretation of the *Deus absconditus*, if we look at it in isolation, Luther deviated from Scripture. Did the exegete fall victim to the systematician? Certainly he is not proposing a theory about how to speak of God here or suggesting a doctrine of God, most definitely not a philosophical one. He has no allegiance either to a philosophical determinism or to a religious fatalism.[119] He only wants to point as clearly and powerfully as he possibly can to the only reliable basis he knows: Jesus Christ. Concentration on the proclamation of Christ brings him to a radicalization, or perhaps an overinterpretation or false exegesis of individual passages of Scripture.

The suspicion of dualism can only arise from isolating some individual statements of his. This shows also that Luther indeed paid too little attention to the connections between the pointed distinctions in *De servo arbitrio* and his trinitarian thought. It may have contributed quite a bit to the misunderstanding of his thought as dualism that as a rule he speaks of "the" hidden and "the" revealed God instead of about the one God in God's hiddenness and God's revealedness. We should therefore pay attention to the overall flow of *De servo arbitrio* and at the same time to the guiding perspective of Luther's theology. For him there were clear correspondences involved in the contrasting of the hidden and the revealed God. He distinguishes between God's "alien work," the *opus alienum*, and God's proper intention, the *opus proprium*, again finding the basis for this distinction in a scriptural passage: ". . . strange is his [God's] deed! . . . alien is his work!" (Isa 28:21). What seems not at all appropriate to God ultimately serves God's true purpose. The wrath God allows to govern in the divine severity, the *ira severitatis*, shows itself to be a wrath God must apply out of mercy, as *ira misericordiae*.[120] The relationship between Law and Gospel, which we will discuss later,[121] is developed in the sense of this dynamic. Luther believed he had to emphasize the hiddenness of God in his argument with Erasmus, though otherwise he wants to present God's saving self-revelation in Jesus Christ. Apparently he thought it sensible to place the accent differently according to addressee. Here it is not an analysis of the rhetorical form but attention to the addressee that serves to clarify the issue. In any case, the discourse about the hidden and the revealed God may not be used as a schematic formula. Contrary to what the construction with the perfect passive participle would indicate, this is not about a static contrast but about a dynamic relationship between the now hidden, now self-revealing God! For believers what is at stake is to allow themselves to be drawn into this dynamic. If, in view of experience of an adverse fate and knowledge of their own guilt and failure, God's hiddenness is an obstacle, they must throw themselves into the open arms of the Crucified and Risen One.[122] Faith, according to Luther, is not inner harmony and psychic balance, but struggle;[123] however, the outcome of the struggle is not open. Faith in Jesus Christ is "the victory that has overcome the world" (1 John 5:4).

Luther is thus by no means interested in the alternative between the hidden and the revealed God as such, but in the attempt to point as clearly and persuasively as possible to the genuine God who is turned toward human beings in love. The exposition in *De servo arbitrio* thus stands in the immediate context of the *particulae exclusivae* of Reformation theology. To this the Christian, distressed by the hiddenness of God, should and may repeatedly return: "Sacred Scripture alone" should be valid for believers, not speculation," "grace alone," and not works, "faith alone," and not speculative judgments and human capacities, "Christ alone," and not a "hidden God"!

DOCTRINE OF GOD AS PASTORAL CARE?

The distinction between the *Deus absconditus* and the *Deus revelatus* must also be understood in terms of Luther's pastoral intention: God alone creates the salvation of humans, and God will not let that be taken away! The fundamental intention of the Reformer's theology is also obvious here: God's glory and the salvation of human beings. God's glory is realized in the nothingness of the human. "Where can he go who hopes in God, if not into his own nothingness? But where should he go who goes into nothingness if not to the place from which he came? But he came from God and his own nothingness, which is why the one who returns to his own nothingness returns to God. For it is impossible that anyone can fall out of God's hand who falls outside himself and all creatures, which are contained on all sides by God's hand."[124] Bernhard Lohse finds that according to Luther "God and the nothingness of the human appear almost to converge . . . The nothingness of the human is equated with the being of God, or with the hand of God."[125] Sacred Scripture, according to Luther, may not be interpreted except as saying "that the human being is nothing and Christ alone is all."[126] My chance lies not in my being-something, but in my being-nothing! For God is the one who makes something out of nothing—and makes nothing out of what is something.[127] To leave the freedom entirely to God: this alone is appropriate— as a Christian I pray to the free and unsearchable God. The glory of creating salvation for human beings belongs to God alone; it is exclusive. It excludes my initiative, but it includes consequences of the highest significance: ". . . by God's grace I am what I am" (1 Cor 15:10).[128]

God's justice thus achieves its purpose in an unexpected and at first quite implausible way. God applies the divine unsearchable power and freedom not for divine self-assertion and thus against human beings, but for their benefit: God is "unjust" in that God helps human beings, enmeshed in sin and turned away from God, to eternal community with God's own self. People have lost the measure of what is "unjust." God is "unjust" in that God allows divine grace to prevail!

In this way the believer is given assurance of salvation. If everything rests on God's free election and if God promises me my election in Christ, I really need have no concerns at all; my salvation cannot be more deeply and firmly grounded. Karl Barth did not understand Luther when he criticized him for speaking here of a God outside and apart from Christ; Luther, he says, "had been foremost in adding to the christological reference the equally definite reference to a divine decision which took place apart from Christ, a decision hidden and unsearchable, but not on that account any the less real." He asks rhetorically: "Is there not something necessarily spasmodic and artificial about the reference to Jesus Christ when in fact it is accompanied by the assertion of a quite different *voluntas maiestatis*?" If Luther were understood in the sense of the absolute decree taught by Calvin, one would in fact have to cry out: "what an abyss of uncertainty is opened up!"[129] But Luther's aim, after all, was the best possible securing of certainty, namely in God's self-affirmation in Jesus Christ. In a certain sense, however, he brought the misunderstanding on himself through his formulations, which were pointed too narrowly toward his discussion with Erasmus. In particular, it was a cardinal fault to call the hidden God "God him/herself," *Deus ipse*.[130] He is quit of this linguistic *faux pas* in a number of places in which his true intention is expressed: "Christ is God himself!"[131] Luther should have made a distinction: "God him/herself" is the triune God who is self-revealed to believers as the loving Creator, Redeemer, and Perfecter and who nevertheless in all that remains the one who is and remains hidden and withdrawn from believers, dwelling in unapproachable light (1 Tim 6:16).

Nevertheless we may ask whether Karl Barth ultimately had better success in causing the grace of God in Jesus Christ to shine with a brighter light. With him, certainly, it readily acquires a triumphalistic note, the appearance of a joyful and saucy self-elevation above all difficulties. Luther was concerned not to draw people into a false security and not to let God's grace be corrupted into a truism that would lead people into inertia. For him the assurance of salvation had to be gained again and again by breaking through the alterations and disguises of the devilish-appearing hidden God and making one's way to the revealed God who is shown in Christ to be love itself. In Luther's experience faith does not live by satisfied agreement but by "nevertheless." "Amen" is a battle cry and a protest against superficial reality that contradicts faith!

God's hiddenness as challenge

What can be the meaning of Luther's doctrine of God for people who simply do not ask about God, who see themselves surrounded by a wealth of religious offerings or who are unable to bring the church talk about "God's love" into any contact with their everyday lives and therefore have had quite enough of it?

For agnostics and atheists Luther's distinction between the hidden and the revealed God expresses the fact that even for Christians faith is not something obvious and to be taken for granted. Christians also experience God as absent, incomprehensible, and they have doubts about whether God exists at all. Reason, so Luther finds, is forced, in face of the horrors in the world, to say that "either there is no God or God is unjust," and he cites Ovid, who said of himself, "Oft I am moved to think there are no gods!"[132] What Luther says about God in hiddenness, however, leaves the God-question open. It could even be that the apparent nonexistence of God only represents a facet of divine hiddenness. In that case, we might say, we ought first to seek God's hiddenness and discover it as such. Luther surmises it in all that is resistant and inexplicable as well as in shocking events in his own life and in world history.

This, of course, raises the question of where, if at all, God could "out" Godself. The religions give a multitude of mutually contradictory answers. Where among these, and within the whole of religious history, should we locate Luther's insistence on the *Deus revelatus*? Must we not, there also, speak of the hidden workings of God and, by the measure of the message of Jesus Christ, even of a revealedness of God? Luther did not have that problem, although he was certainly inclined to see God at work behind the behavior of the Turks, adherents of Islam. For him it is clear that God is self-revealed in Jesus Christ! But this assertion has to be interpreted, and that is impossible without the individual context in which it is to be done. According to Luther's conviction there can be no new revelations beyond the one unlocked for human beings in Jesus Christ. But that judgment in no way prevents us from understanding Jesus Christ in ever new contexts and interpreting him out of unaccustomed contexts. Faith in Jesus Christ as the person in whom God has given a binding promise of forgiveness and a future, fulfillment and a successful life must be newly articulated today in confrontation with agnosticism and atheism, the world religions,[133] and a roving religiosity; in the process it may also achieve a new revelatory form. The Reformer would take great care that in the process nothing of the Gospel in its original form be lost, but he would also be able to connect this task with the Holy Spirit, who "comes and gives himself to us also, wholly and completely. He teaches us to understand this deed of Christ which has been manifested to us, helps us receive and preserve it, use it to our advantage and impart it to others, increase and extend it."[134] None of this can take place without consideration for and laying claim to the respective circumstances of the time and of our lives. The "new language" spoken by Christian faith and its theology will again and again enter into relationship with the changes in language, thought, and feelings, and will have to overtake them ever and again as well.

For that reason, if for no other, monotonous talk about the "dear" God should not enter in. A one-sided and undifferentiated talk about God's love— contrary to all good intentions—kills the Gospel! Those who are able to talk about the love and mercy of God without being moved by it are blind to God in the living nature of the divine relationship to human beings and to the whole creation. Love itself has a multitude of forms, and according to Luther it can certainly express itself in God's unreasonable demands. Christian faith is not a "wellness" religion. God works on believers and nonbelievers through self-revelation and self-concealment.

NOTES

[1] Cf. Dietrich Stollberg, "'Sola fide.' Allein aus Glauben. Realität und Redlichkeit lutherischer Theologie am Beispiel des 'Deus absconditus,'" *WzM* 37 (1985): 41–47.

[2] ". . . inter creatorem et creaturam non potest tanta similitudo notari, quin inter eos maior sit dissimilitudo notanda," *DH* 806 (old numbering 432).

[3] ". . . thus I know this, that no one can speak so well of God as he himself." WA 34/2, 58, 20–59, 7.

[4] LW 26, 399–400 (WA 40/1, 607, 28-32).

[5] The mechanisms described by Transactional Analysis are apt for the description of the projections Luther complained of.

[6] Cf., e.g., *Church Dogmatics*, II/2, 66; Gerhard Ebeling, "Über die Reformation hinaus? Zur Luther-Kritik Karl Barths," 85ff. in Karl Hauschildt, et al., *Luther und Barth*, Veröffentlichungen der Luther-Akademie Ratzeburg 13 (Erlangen: Martin-Luther-Verlag, 1989).

[7] Cf., e.g., Church Dogmatics, II/2, 66; Gerhard Ebeling, "Über die Reformation hinaus? Zur Luther-Kritik Karl Barths," 85ff. in Karl Hauschildt, et al., Luther und Barth, Veröffentlichungen der Luther-Akademie Ratzeburg 13 (Erlangen: Martin-Luther-Verlag, 1989).

[8] Cf. "Finding God in all Things," 119–21 in Joseph A. Tetlow, SJ, *Making Choices in Christ: The Foundations of Ignatian Spirituality* (Chicago: Loyola Press, 2008).

[9] LW 26, 37–38 (WA 40/1, 93, 2-7).

[10] Luther at first referred to the Areopagite, but soon and increasingly felt him to be too speculative. Cf. Reinhuber 2000, 102.

[11] Nicholas of Cusa, *The Vision of God* [1453], trans. Emma Gurney Salter (New York: Cosimo, 2007), 44.

[12] ". . . Ut neque sit neque non sit neque sit et non sit neque sit vel non sit. Sed omnes istae locutiones ipsum non attingunt," *De Deo abscondito*, quoted from Reinhold Weier, *Das Thema vom verborgenen Gott von Nikolaus von Kues zu Martin Luther* (Münster: Aschendorff, 1967), 172 n. 5; cf. *Nicholas of Cusa: Selected Spiritual Writings*, trans. H. Lawrence Bond, CWS (New York and Mahwah, NJ: Paulist Press, 1997), 94.

[13] LW 37, 228 (WA 26, 339, 33–340, 1).

[14] Cf. the table in Althaus 1962, 34.

[15] WA 30/1, 245, 4: ". . . facit nobis nebulam et umbram."

[16] See chapter 5.

[17] In what follows I am adapting material from Hans-Martin Barth, *Die christliche Gotteslehre. Hauptprobleme ihrer Geschichte* (Gütersloh: Mohn, 1974).

[18] ". . . nihil et omnia sunt unser Herrgotts *materia*," WA 39/1, 470, 1.

[19] LW 37, 58 (WA 23, 135, 1-6).

[20] WA 17/2, 192, 28-30.

[21] WA 17/2, 59, 5-6.

[22] Cf. Wieland Kastning, *Morgenröte künftigen Lebens. Das reformatorische Evangelium als Neubestimmung der Geschichte. Untersuchung zu Martin Luthers Geschichts- und Wirklichkeitsverständnis* (Göttingen: Vandenhoeck & Ruprecht, 2008); and see chapter 14.

[23] LW 14, 74 (WA 31/1, 126, 13).

[24] Ibid. (WA 31/1, 127, 4-7).

[25] LW 46, 116 (WA 19, 644, 1).

[26] LW 21, 340 (WA 7, 586, 1).

[27] WA 23, 8, 36-38.

[28] *Church Dogmatics* III/3, §50.

[29] LW 33, 176 (LDStA 1, 465, 1-4 / 464, 2-4).

30 Ibid. (LDStA 1, 465, 16-23 / 464, 13-17).

31 Ibid., 177 (LDStA 1, 465, 31-33 / 464, 23-25).

32 Ibid., 180 (LDStA 1, 471, 37-39 / 470, 27).

33 Ibid., 178 (LDStA 1, 469, 4-5); the active role of God and Satan in this process is more clearly expressed in the Latin text: ". . . deserente Deo, et peccante Satana."

34 Ibid., 180–81 (LDStA 1, 471, 42–473, 13 / 470, 30–472, 9).

35 Ibid., 189 (LDStA 1, 489, 7 / 488, 6).

36 Against Beiner 2000, 135 n. 4: while Luther certainly reflected "on the origins of sin," he almost never explicitly traces it to God (cf. Barth, Hans-Martin 1967, 194–96). Beiner then writes cautiously that he comes "ultimately to *attribute evil* also to the *power* of God" (ibid., emphasis supplied). Likewise what the Reformer intends "to think through theoretically" is subject to an intention, namely that of the Confession, which ultimately is acknowledged also by Melanie Beiner when she distinguishes between "attribution" and "assumption" of responsibility (ibid., 156).

37 Cf. "The Misery of Human Limitation" in chapter 9.

38 But see "The Misery of Human Limitation" in chapter 9.

39 LW 33, 70 (LDStA 1, 297, 16-24 / 296, 18-19).

40 LW 33, 67 (LDStA 1, 293, 35-36 / 292, 25): ". . . ut Sophistae loquuntur dispositivam qualitatem et passivam aptitudinem." Lexutt's translation is not very helpful: "a dispositive quality or a passive aptitude."

41 Ebeling 1964, 306.

42 Cf. LW 25, 345 (WA 56, 356, 5-6): an expression Luther does not often use, however.

43 LW 31, 10, Thesis 17 (WA 1, 225, 1-2).

44 Cf. "The devil and demons" in chapter 4.

45 Cf. Barth, Hans-Martin 1967a, 155, 162.

46 Althaus 1962, 148.

47 LW 14, 31–32 (WA 31/1, 249, 15-29; 250, 35-37). Cf. Hans-Martin Barth, *Der Teufel und Jesus Christus in der Theologie Martin Luthers* (Göttingen: Vandenhoeck & Ruprecht, 1967), to which I refer in what follows; also Oberman 1981a, esp. chaps. VII, IX, and X.

48 Against Beiner 2000, 135 n. 4: it may well be that "talk of the hidden God" threatens to "cut the ground out from under the preaching of Jesus Christ" (Barth, Hans-Martin 1967, 185, quoted in Beiner 2000, 135); but this does not succeed because Luther's preaching of Christ is stronger! Luther assumes that God desires to be believed as the God of Jesus Christ and not regarded as a "devil." But for the Reformer faith is not a "filter" but the perception of the true situation (Beiner 134; apart from the fact that the image of a "filter" does not fit with what I have been describing above).

49 WA 30/1, 192, 5.

50 WA 20, 229, 13-15.

51 WA 10/3, 161, 4-7.

52 WA 10/3, 155, 2-4.

53 LW 33, 139 (LDStA 1, 405, 20-22 / 404, 15-17), "things above us are no business of ours."

54 Cf. LW 31, 52 (LDStA 1, 232, 10-19); and cf. Eberhard Jüngel, "Quae supra nos, nihil ad nos. Eine Kurzformel der Lehre vom verborgenen Gott im Anschluss an Luther interpretiert," *EvT* 32 (1972): 192–240.

55 WA 40/3, 303, 10.

56 WA 45, 87, 3.

57 LW 19, 72 (WA 19, 223, 15-16).

58 Reinhuber 2000.

59 LW 33, 292 (LDStA 1, 653–57).

60 Reinhuber 2000, 186–233, points this out especially, speaking of a "break in the distinction of the lights": "For Luther, the progress of the lights conceals a regress!" ibid., 206–7.

61 LW 33, 293–95 (LDStA 1, 653–57).

62 LW 5, 48 (WA 43, 461, 26-27).

[63]LW 24, 195 (WA 45, 638, 17-20, Sermon on John 15:1).

[64]Cf. WA 40/2, 435, 15: If you teach the ungodly the way of God ". . . provocas diabolum cum inferno, mundum cum inferno, mundum cum sapientibus, Sanctis, Et teipsum contra teipsum, provocas cor tuum").

[65]WA 29, 267, 16.

[66]WA.TR 2, 255, 32-33 (no. 1899).

[67]WA 24, 249, 13-17.

[68]WA 17/2, 22, 22-25.

[69]LW 42, 44 (WA 2, 101, 27-33).

[70]WA 11, 27, 27-29.

[71]Cf. Barth, Hans-Martin 1967a, 22–23, 28–29, 138–43.

[72]LW 25, 378 (WA 56, 388, 10-11).

[73]WA 20, 281, 26–282, 2.

[74]Cf. WA 24, 566–81 (sermon on Jacob at the Jabbok), as well as Eberhard Jüngel, "Quae supra nos," 192–240.

[75]LW 33, 286 (LDStA 1, 645, 31–647, 19): ". . . dulcissimo raptu . . ."; raptus is probably better translated "being raptured" or even "kidnapping"; 646, 14-15.

[76]WA 1, 190, 1.

[77]The Book of Concord, 345.

[78]Ibid.

[79]LW 37, 366 (WA 26, 505, 31–506, 12). Cf. Herms 1987, though without reference to De servo arbitrio; see also Asendorf 1988, 218–26.

[80]But cf. Schwarzwäller 1970, who addresses the problem on pp. 201–12, something Reinhuber 2000 (cf. 141ff.) unfortunately did not take note of. In the context of a twentieth-century theology relying on Luther this question was investigated by Thomas Gerlach, Verborgener Gott—Dreieiniger Gott. Ein Koordinationsproblem lutherischer Gotteslehre bei Werner Elert (Frankfurt and New York: Peter Lang, 1998).

[81]Cf. Albrecht Peters, "Die Trinitätslehre in der reformatorischen Christenheit," TLZ 94 (1969): 561–70; idem (1991): 36–55; Reiner Jansen, Studien zu Luthers Trinitätslehre (Bern: Herbert Lang, 1975); Markschies 1999; Helmer 1999; Christoph Schwöbel, "The Triune God of Grace. The Doctrine of the Trinity in the Theology of the Reformers," 49–64 in James M. Byrne, ed., The Christian Understanding of God Today (Dublin: Columba Press, 1993); Müller, Gerhard 2004.

[82]Müller, Gerhard 2004, 540.

[83]Smalcald Articles I, Book of Concord, 292. But Luther struck out the statement that both parties "believe them," as the original text formulated it.

[84]This is suggested even by the statements on Christology that follow.

[85]WA 41, 270, 2-23; 272, 1-13; 52, 338, 1-10; cf. Lohse 1995, 225.

[86]WA 46, 436, 5-17.

[87]WA 46, 436, 5-17.

[88]Against Tuomo Mannermaa, "Hat Luther eine trinitarische Ontologie?" 43–60 in Joachim Heubach, ed., Luther und die trinitarische Tradition: Ökumenische und philosophische Perspektiven (Erlangen: Martin-Luther-Verlag, 1994).

[89]LW 52, 50 (WA 10/1/1, 193, 11-13).

[90]Cf. LW 37, 360–72 (WA 26, 499–509 [1528]); LW 34, 197–229 (WA 50, 262–83 [1538]); LW 15, 267 (WA 54, 28ff. [1543]), as well as Luther's sermons on the Trinity.

[91]LW 15, 276 (WA 54, 56, 13-15).

[92]LW 15, 276–77 (WA 54, 56, 29).

[93]". . . the three persons . . . differently, each from the other, clothed in a particular work . . ." WA 41, 276, 39–277, 1.

[94]Lienhard 1980, 124.

[95]Müller, Gerhard 204, 555–56.

[96]WA 28, 60, 31-32.

97 Cf. Markschies 1999, 64–67.

98 WA 41, 270, 18-20.

99 LW 37, 366 (WA 26, 505, 38-39).

100 Schwarzwäller 1970, 201. Schwarzwäller asserts that elsewhere as well we find in Luther from time to time "a conglomerate of orthodox sayings about the Trinity, not apparently thought through and lacking an illuminating theological thread."

101 WA 39/1, 370, 18-20.

102 See "Contemporary questions" in "Superstition? Luther's Attitude toward Witchcraft and Demonology" in chapter 4.

103 LW 15, 338 (WA 54, 88, 9-12).

104 Hence it seems to me mistaken to suppose that Luther had a "doctrine of the Trinity as distinct from a general doctrine of God," as Bayer suggests (Bayer 2003, 306ff.). According to Luther any and every "general doctrine of God" must repeatedly be penetrated by faith in the triune God and so abandoned.

105 WA 49, 434, 16-19.

106 WA 46, 494, 16-17.

107 LW 33, 140 (LDStA 1, 405, 36–407, 2 / 404, 31–406, 2).

108 Ibid. (LDStA 1, 407, 7-9 / 406, 6-8).

109 Quoted from Lohse 1981, 176.

110 Ibid.

111 Ibid., 177.

112 LW 31, 348–49 (WA 7, 24, 13; WA 2, 733, 35, and frequently).

113 WA 16, 551, 30.

114 LW 31, 104 (WA 1, 543, 8-9).

115 LW 26, 440 (WA 40/1, 444, 1).

116 Cf. Barth, Hans-Martin 1972, 92–95; and cf. "By faith" in chapter 8.

117 Bayer 2003, 189–90.

118 Althaus 1962, 241.

119 See "The believer: the liberated beast of burden" and "The assurance of faith" in chapter 11.

120 See "God in Christ" in chapter 6.

121 See chapter 15.

122 ". . . ad deum contra deum confugere," WA 5, 204, 26-27; cf. LW 19, 74 (WA 19, 223, 15-16).

123 Thomas Reinhuber interprets Luther's saying that God is "a glowing furnace of love, reaching even from the earth to the heavens" (LW 51, 95 [WA 10/3, 56]) as ambivalent: he of course speaks clearly here "of the love of the revealed God; but in the background, in view of the ambiguity of the metaphor of fire and furnace, there are also hints of the mysterious and oppressively ungraspable multiple meanings of the hidden God" (Reinhuber 2000, 231). "No preaching and no theological discussion" can move "much beyond such an [ambivalent] metaphor" (ibid., 232). Reinhuber's study ends with this resigned statement, which disavows Luther's whole theology. We may hope that he has not thus succeeded in destroying Luther's image of the "glowing furnace of love"!

124 WA 5, 168, 1-6.

125 Lohse 1981, 179.

126 ". . . Quam quod homo nihil sit, et solus Christus omnia," WA 15, 527, 35-37.

127 WA 1, 183, 39–184, 10; cf. ". . . where man's strength ends, God's strength begins, provided faith is present and waits on Him. . . . where man's strength begins, God's strength ends . . ." LW 21, 340 (WA 7, 586, 12-13).

128 Cf. Barth, Hans-Martin, 2002.

129 Church Dogmatics II/2, 65– 66, at 64.

130 LW 33, 140 (LDStA 1, 406, 3 / 407, 5).

131 Cf. LW 25, 203, 253 (WA 56, 204, 27-28; 255, 26); LW 37, 75 (WA 23, 141, 23-25); LW 41, 172 (WA 50, 642, 15-16); LW 26, 401–2 (WA 40/1, 441, 33); see also the second verse of "A Mighty Fortress": "dost ask who that may be? Christ Jesus, it is he, Lord Sabaoth his name, from age to age the same . . . ."

[132] LW 33, 291 (LDStA 1, 653, 41-42 / 652, 33-34).
[133] Cf. Barth, Hans-Martin 2008.
[134] LW 37, 366 (WA 26, 506, 5-7).

7

Tension: Between Law and Gospel

For Luther this pairing "contains a summary of all Christian doctrine."[1] He "reflected deeply on the distinction and relationship between Law and Gospel with the most attentive precision and an almost cruel stringency,"[2] according to Albrecht Peters. Today there are serious difficulties in approaching this topic. At the same time we should consider that it has not been of equal importance throughout the whole history of the church. Even within the history of Lutheranism it has not always had the weight Luther claimed for it.

Contemporary Questions

The expression "Law and Gospel" is a basic formula in Lutheran theology that needs to be broken open and unlocked. The very word "Gospel" is something secular people can scarcely comprehend, and in any case it is difficult to locate. What does it mean, insofar as one is not satisfied with the "good news" as advertised and with the promise of a happy life, and to the extent that it is not simply a matter of the struggle for survival. The question of the forgiveness of sins is by no means prominent in all this. Consequently it is primarily the churches of the Reformation that have the most difficulty communicating its message.

Access to the concept of "law" seems less fraught with difficulty. It is evident that some point of reference is necessary. But must it be "law"? Nowadays "law" is more a juridical than a religious concept. But in this very context it appears ambivalent: on the one hand people would rather not come into contact with the law, and certainly not be in conflict with it, while on the other hand "law and order," as threatening as it may turn out to be, is ultimately indispensable. Then there are the psychological aspects. On the one hand it may well be that many young people have had unpleasant encounters with "the law" as found in the family home, at school, or in other places; in fact, many forms of law are misapplied and abused. On the other hand there is a longing for a clear orientation, as shown religiously by fundamentalism and socially by extremist political groups. Apparently it depends on the individual human psychic constitution whether one finds the law to be helpful or threatening. Basic forms of anxiety, as described, for example, by Fritz Riemann, are also reproduced here. Finally, from a religious point of view the law seems nowadays to be something that is no longer acceptable; Roman Catholic confessional practice appears, at least in Europe, to have declined markedly in acceptance, and the Lutheran churches in Germany were even able to concede the elimination of the annual Penitential Day as a public holiday. On the other hand, it is said that strict Catholic orders and certain sects that insist on the keeping of rules are found attractive. That Islam draws many people may have to do with the same phenomenon. At the same time Sharia, with its draconian penalties such as amputation of hands or even execution by stoning, is instilling fear and revulsion. What shall we say about the laws people lay on themselves because of their religious origins, such as head covering for women and prescriptions regarding food and fasting? Apart from such apparently superficial commandments, is there such a thing as a basic rule for all people like that articulated in the "Golden Rule"? What about human rights?

Finally, from an anthropological point of view, who or what is the ad-dressee of a law, however we may choose to understand it? For Luther it was conscience by which the ethos of the individual was directed. But it is broadly felt today that ethics are oriented solely to juridically-defined legality; what is not juridically forbidden is regarded as permissible and apparently requires no separate ethical justification. While in everyday speech we sometimes refer to conscience, the word has nearly disappeared from the terminology of psychology, sociology, pedagogy, and philosophical ethics. It is not clear "whether it is intended to mean an inner judge (enlightenment), God's voice (inspiration), a superego (psychoanalysis), a desire for the good (Catholic), the assured authority of faith (Protestant), a system-regulative mechanism (systems theory), or something else."[3]

Finally, the question must be posed to current preaching in the Reformation churches insofar as it is reduced primarily to a superficial assistance for living and the message of a loving God: has the Gospel sacrificed its power to illumine because it no longer stands before the dark background of an implacably demanding law? Is the "forgiveness of sins" no longer needed because violations of a divine law are not even recognized? According to Luther the doctrine of Law and Gospel concerns "in a sense the logic of the subject of theology."[4] How could it be reclaimed with the aid of Luther?

RELATIVE IMPORTANCE OF THE DISTINCTION AND LOCATION OF LAW AND GOSPEL WITHIN LUTHER'S THEOLOGY

The distinction between Law and Gospel was not regarded throughout Christian history as constitutive of a serious theology. It came to the fore whenever faith appeared to be threatened either by lax or libertine practices or, on the other hand, by legalism. Paul considered Christ "the end of the law" (Rom 10:4) and adjured the Galatians not to be re-enslaved to the law; on the other hand, the letter of James insists that the law must be kept. This tension was reproduced in the struggle between Augustine and Pelagius; the latter held an optimistic view of humanity and presumed the freedom of the human will to keep the commandments. Despite Augustine's protest, a semi-Pelagian line dominated medieval piety, to which Luther first objected by contrasting "commandment" and "promise" (*praecepta* vs. *promissio*). Yet it became clearer and clearer to him that what stood over against the promise of the Gospel was not a congeries of individual commandments but the radical claim of the divine will. So there arose the "real dialectic between Law and Gospel."[5] Later Lutheran theology did not maintain that dialectic; it was not even understood, especially in the nineteenth century. But in the twentieth century it acquired a new meaning in the clash between Karl Barth and Lutheran theology as represented especially by Werner Elert and Paul Althaus. This resulted in serious misunderstandings on both sides. Werner Elert interpreted law as a basic anthropological category, which Karl Barth regarded as a slide into natural theology. The then-current way of speaking about "law" and especially "popular *nomos*," in which supposedly the will of God could be discerned as it was expressed in a people, with its ominous consequences, did still more to obscure Luther's view. Why did the contrast of Law and Gospel play such a major role in his theology?

"Nearly all of Holy Scripture and all theological knowledge depends on a right understanding of the Law and the Gospel," the Reformer found.[6] In his dispute with Erasmus he worked out that the Law is more than the collection of moral precepts that are to be kept. In his confrontation with the Antinomians, who considered a preaching of the Law superfluous,[7] he insisted on the validity of the Law for believers as well. On the other hand he complained that in late medieval preaching the function of the Gospel itself was redefined, so that it lost its consoling power. Instead, the contrast of Law and Gospel was the best way, he said, "to treat and to hand on Christian teaching,"[8] the "highest art in Christianity."[9] In the distinction between Law and Gospel lies a living, existential task for a Christian and especially for a theologian. The one who masters it may rightly be called a "Doctor of Sacred Scripture," but without the Holy Spirit it is impossible to make the distinction in appropriate fashion. The Reformer acknowledges that "I experience in myself and see daily in others how difficult it is to separate the teaching of the Law and the Gospels from one another"; here the Holy Spirit must be "master and teacher."[10] Thus what is at issue here is more than one theological principle among others, a figure in the argumentation. The questions that are decisive for faith are in play, namely: what does God demand; what does God give? In what does God's sacred will consist?

In view of the significance this distinction had for Luther in his own life, he acknowledges in one of his table discourses that he thought for a long time that "Christ differed from Moses only in time and in the degree of perfection. But when I discovered the distinction that one is the Law, the other the Gospel, I made my breakthrough."[11] He believed that the distinction is so difficult because Christ himself can be understood both as gift and as example, and hence as "law": in the way he dealt with his fellow human beings he naturally serves Christians as a model or example, but "in that Christ is no more useful to you than any other saint." At that point one does not yet know whence the strength for such an attitude is to be drawn. Therefore it is essential "that before you take Christ as an example, you accept and recognize him as a gift, as a present that God has given you and that is your own."[12]

Formally, the distinction between Law and Gospel is probably so essential for Luther because he commonly thinks in terms of alternatives. He differentiates between the hidden and the revealed God, between God's external and God's own proper work, between a "wrath of severity" and a wrath in service of mercy.[13] These distinctions correspond to that between Law and Gospel, which in turn have their specific effects, depending on the one to whom they are applied: those who feel they are in the right should hear the Law, and those who are sad at their own inadequacy should hear the Gospel. So what we have here are not flat correspondences but background contexts.

At this point we touch the substance, the nerve of Luther's theology, because the distinction between Law and Gospel is about avoiding confusions that are life-threatening. Late medieval theology had, in his view, presented the Gospel as a kind of law to be followed, and the Law as a kind of gospel that people are, in fact, able to follow. But the factual result was that people were handed over to the pressure of the Law (and many additional ecclesial decrees), while the consolation of the Gospel was withheld from them. For Luther's perception, however, it is precisely through the radicality of the divine law that the depth of the Gospel is visible; it is in God's claim that God's promise is evident, as the value of health is newly appreciated against the background of a severe illness. He wrote pointedly: "Life is a help only to those who are dead, grace only to [sinners]. . . ."[14]

LAW

DEMANDS OF THE LAW'S CONTENT

Where do we encounter the will of God? What is its content? Luther again orients himself to the Bible and thus sees confirmed an opinion about which, to begin with, there is no dissent. The pagans, who do not have an explicit divine law like the Torah at their disposal, show by their behavior "that what the law requires is written on their hearts" (Rom 2:15). Thus the human being knows by nature what he should do and not do. Certainly this is made more precise for Christians. The demands of the Law are encountered on four levels: Thomas Aquinas already began with a natural knowledge of good and evil; Luther sees natural law paradigmatically summarized in the Decalogue. Of course, at the same time the general knowledge of natural law is thereby transcended, especially since for Luther the point of the Decalogue lies in the first commandment, whose meaning in turn is expressed in a special way in the twofold commandment to love. But Luther can also appeal to the Golden Rule: "What you will have done and not done to you, do and do not do to another; the light lives and shines in the reason of all human beings."[15] There is no one who would not agree with that. But what God demands appears most vividly and impressively when one places the figure of Jesus Christ before one's eyes: in him it is clear what it means to fulfill the will of God.

The voice of the Law is heard in human consciences. It speaks very concretely with regard to the relationships within which a person finds herself or himself. Luther makes this clear in terms of the classes and professions of his own time: "If you are a manual laborer, you find that the Bible has been put into your workshop, into your hand, into your heart. It teaches and preaches how you should treat your neighbor. Just look at your tools—at your needle or thimble, your beer barrel, your goods, your scales or yardstick or measure—and you will read this statement inscribed on them. . . . 'Friend, use me in your relations with your neighbor just as you would want your neighbor to use his property in his relations with you.'"[16] We can thus speak of a "double" initiative of God toward human beings: "From within he seizes our consciences with the help of the Golden Rule, and from without he incorporates us into the coordinated system of classes and professions."[17]

Thus it is not a matter of the wording of the codified Ten Commandments or the many instructions contained in Sacred Scripture, but of the basic and overall situation of the human being, a person's ultimate horizon of meaning and responsibility in the face of fellow human beings and God. Why is a human being in the world; what is she or he required to do? In this connection, for Luther, the distinction between generalized knowledge of God and revelation in Christ is again replicated. People do have a feeling that they are responsible not only to one another but to an ultimate authority. But they do not know how they should imagine that ultimate authority. Therefore they compose for themselves—to speak within the horizon of the sixteenth century—a God who from the outset is gentle and can be pleased by good works, or else a wrathful God to whom no one can bring enough sacrifices. As a rule, Luther is convinced, they do not have a clear enough idea about the demands of the Law to understand the weight of sin. Such an awareness can come only from the radicality of the first commandment of the Decalogue or from the Sermon on the Mount. It is in faith that one begins to grasp what a transgression of the Law, indeed, a life in a context of constant transgression of the Law must mean. From this comes Luther's remarkable statement that sin as such can only be understood in faith: "Sola fide credendum est nos esse peccatores. . . ."[18] It is precisely for believers that, in view of the demands of the Law, "the wide world is too narrow."[19] Therefore the precondition for grasping the Law in the whole breadth and depth of its demands is faith in God and the expectation of the last judgment. But this very precondition causes Luther to inquire not only about the content of the demand but above all about the function of the Law.

THE FUNCTION OF THE LAW

The Reformer starts from the assumption that in the course of salvation history the Law has had different functions at different times. In their original condition humanity happily obeyed God's command as a matter of course; at that time it was pleasant for them, filled them with joy and love, and these in all perfection![20] When a relationship is in good condition the one person knows what the partner desires of him or her, and it is a pleasure to comply. But after the Fall the Law received a new function, since humans could and would no longer comply with it. What originally had been a joy to humanity now fills them with annoyance and sadness–or they have not grasped how the situation has changed and think that by behaving in compliance with the Law they can retain or reconstitute their relationship with God. Luther learned above all from Paul that "the way to salvation pointed out by the Law is no longer open."[21] In this situation the Law acquires a twofold function, a twofold task that Luther calls "use," usus.

Social function

In its social function—Luther speaks of the usus politicus or civilis—the law organizes human life in society, which otherwise would hamper lives or even bring about conflict, as we may conclude from the story of Cain and Abel. Thus the law belongs to those broad spheres of life in which human existence develops and is sustained. In Luther's view these are the three "arch-hierarchies," namely *oeconomia*, *politia*, and *ecclesia*, that is, the economic, social, and institutional ecclesiastical life. Although destructiveness has been at work in all these, chaos does not break out. However, since people by their nature are neither pious nor good Christians, "God through the law puts them all under restraint so they dare not willfully implement their wickedness in actual deeds."[22] The authorities who supervise the keeping of the law therefore have a duty to maintain human society, and indeed creation as a whole. The Reformer confesses a pessimistic view of human morality: "When I refrain from killing or from committing adultery or from stealing, or when I abstain from other sins, I do not do this voluntarily or from the love of virtue but because I am afraid of the sword and of the executioner." This shows clearly what the Law is good for: "Therefore just as a rope holds a furious and untamed beast and keeps it from attacking whatever it meets, so the Law constrains an insane and furious man lest he commit further sins."[23] The application of the social function of the law thus requires, on the one hand, some clear prescriptions in its content, and on the other hand the authorities that execute the law: "For the devil reigns in the whole world and drives men to all sorts of shameful deeds. This is why God has ordained magistrates, parents, teachers, laws, shackles, and all civic ordinances, so that . . . they will at least bind the hands of the devil. . . ." This civic compulsion is said to be highly necessary and ordered by God for the preservation of public peace, and also so that the progress of the Gospel may not be hindered by chaotic conditions. In extreme cases capital punishment may be imposed, of course not as an act of vengeance or as an expiation, but only for the restraint of evil.[24] But from a theological point of view, according to Luther, the law has a very different task.

Spiritual function

The spiritual function (*usus theologicus*) lies, for Luther, in the task assigned to the law in connection with the event of justification. Justification before God is by no means to be achieved in that the law—even with God's help—can be more or less fulfilled. According to Luther this was the false way that suggested itself to the natural human being. The Jews tried to keep it by a meticulous observation of an abundance of prescriptions. The "papists" thought they had to augment God's commandments with recommendations for how one could respond to the will of God through special ascetic achievements. For Luther both are examples of the fact that the law is simply in close affinity with human reason, which "does not know anything except the Law."[25] The natural human being tries, if possible, to "do everything right" and expects to be rewarded for it. But Luther, with Paul, assumes that the law is unable to lead to salvation. Hence it is clear to him what conclusions can be drawn from a radicalization of our understanding of the law: if living according to the law yields nothing, "let us live as the Gentiles do."[26] The Gospel thus meets a twofold resistance: on the one hand human beings cannot believe that everything is to be given to them, but if they do accept that they are tempted to let themselves go. Luther comprehends the negative social consequences of this attitude and admits that they horrify him; still, he is convinced that as long as the law is regarded as the way to salvation it terrorizes people. But what function can it have if it is no longer to be regarded as the way to salvation?

Luther assumes that the voice of the law is never silent and that no one can deliberately shut it off. If it no longer leads someone on the path to salvation, it still serves to point us to our inability to keep the law. God's law convicts individual persons not only of their moral incapacity but also of the fact that even in their best moral achievements they are self-centered. We should serve God, our Lord, alone; we should bless our fellow human beings who curse us—but we cannot. And even if we should achieve it to a certain degree we are satisfied with that and proud of it and thus show how much we remain the prisoners of our own selves. The law addresses the conscience and joins with it. Those who are honest will admit that they contradict and resist the will of God—even when they are most honorable—with the innermost impulses of their hearts and the deepest drives of their existence. A "bad conscience" draws our attention to something that is not as it should be.[27] Hence the law serves not only to make us aware of individual failings and transgressions but also the "disclosure of the fundamental sin,"[28] the knowledge of humanity's basic sinful condition. It is "hereditary sin or natural sin or personal sin . . . the truly chief sin. If this sin did not exist, there would also be no actual sin. This sin is not committed, as are all other sins; rather it *is*. It lives and commits all sins and is the real essential sin which does not sin for an hour or for a while; rather no matter where or how long a person lives, this sin is there too."[29] The result, for Luther, is that "the other use of the Law is the theological or spiritual one, which serves to increase transgressions. . . ." Hence "the true function and the chief and proper use of the Law is to reveal to man his sin, blindness, misery, wickedness, ignorance, hate and contempt of God, death, hell, judgment, and the well-deserved wrath of God."[30] When the law accuses an individual and burdens her or his conscience, it is in its proper domain. It then not only enunciates morality but delivers an "ethical shock" by making the individual aware that he or she has no right to life, but must sink, before God and humanity, into the earth beneath. God, the devil, and human conscience thus combine, so to speak, to cause this shock! To that extent the devil belongs in the Gospel "as does the serpent in Paradise."[31]

The destructive function of the law, of course, is not an end in itself. Rather, God uses it for God's own purposes, takes the devil as his aide, and uses the human conscience as a medium for pointing people to the only way in which they can find rescue. "But what is the value of this effect, this humiliation, this wounding and crushing by the hammer? It has this value, that grace can have access to us. Therefore the Law is a minister and a preparation for grace." For God, a God of the humble, the miserable, and the afflicted, "is the almighty Creator, who makes everything out of nothing." The law, with its horrible effects on the human conscience, thus "does contribute to justification—not because it justifies, but because it impels one to the promise of grace and makes it sweet and desirable." The "function and use" of the law is thus "not only to disclose the sin and wrath of God but also to drive us to Christ."[32] Its working is positive in the sense that in a negative way it creates the preconditions for the seeking and acceptance of the Gospel.

Formally, Luther sees this confirmed by Paul's assertion that the Law has been "our disciplinarian until Christ came, so that we might be justified by faith" (Gal 3:24). Only when one grasps and accepts that one is sick will one take advantage of medical aid. The clearer the diagnosis, the more promising will be the therapy, if one puts oneself in the hands of a competent doctor. "The Law discovers the illness, and the Gospel gives the medicine."[33]

From an exegetical as well as a psychological and a theological perspective a number of questions must here be addressed to Luther the Reformer. But in any case we can say that he was "apparently the first in the whole history of dogma and theology" to reflect on and appreciate the law from the point of view of its fundamental function.[34] "For Luther, law is an existential category."[35]

GOSPEL

It has always been striking that in Luther's discussion of Law and Gospel, the Law is more often in the foreground than the Gospel. This may be related to the historical situation as Luther found it. But it could also be explained by the fundamental situation of humanity; we are more easily able to speak about what we find negative than about what appears "positive"; Dante's description of hell is more interesting than his account of heaven! But for Luther the reason was probably that he saw the relationship of Law and Gospel as asymmetric: the experience of the Law speaks for itself, but ultimately we can speak of the Gospel only in connection with the Law, since without the background and opposition of the Law, the Gospel itself would become Law.

THE PROMISE OF THE GOSPEL

Luther does not speak of "gospels" in the plural, but of the "Gospel" as a summary of the salvation-bringing message of Jesus Christ: "for 'gospel'

[*Euangelium*] is a Greek word and means in Greek a good message, good tidings, good news, a good report, which one sings and tells with gladness." He compares it to the news of David's victory over the giant Goliath: what an outpouring of joy there must have been among the Israelites! "Thus this gospel of God or New Testament is a good story and report, sounded forth into all the world by the apostles, telling of a true David who strove with sin, death, and the devil, and overcame them, and thereby rescued all those who were captive in sin, afflicted with death, and overpowered by the devil. Without any merit of their own he made them righteous, gave them life, and saved them, so that they were given peace and brought back to God."[36] So it is about a victory and its consequences, the end of a conflict, liberation from distress, recovery after an illness, a breakthrough to life. Luther summarizes what the Gospel brings in the words "forgiveness, life, and blessedness," for "where there is forgiveness of sins, there are also life and salvation."[37] In Christ, God has created a new situation; our response must be to accept it in faith. How this happened and what its consequences were, these Luther develops in his doctrine of justification, which will be discussed below. For the present we must note that, in contrast to the Law, the Gospel announces this new situation. It is given, but it must also be sought ever anew, so to speak; it must be "realized" in the twofold sense of the word. Human beings of themselves can neither create it nor have it at their disposition nor maintain themselves within it. They must continually rely on an ever-new encounter with the Gospel.

The function of the Gospel

In contrast to the Law, the Gospel has as its function the halting of the steadily turning carousel of human self-accusation. Only faith is equal to the challenge of the Law. The Gospel opens up the fountains from which people can truly live. The promise gives them perspective and assurance. They find themselves subject to the effective power of grace and discover in themselves the desire to fulfill the will of God. The center of their existence begins to be transformed. Faith "makes us altogether different [people], in heart and spirit and mind and powers. . . ."[38]

How is this function of the Gospel carried out in believers? The message is given, and in face of the proclamation a person has the opportunity to grasp it as true and allow it to have its effect. Preaching seeks and creates the "amen." In absolution and the use of the sacraments the Gospel reaches its goal. The community must accept an important role in all this: "where two or three are gathered in my name, I am there among them" (Matt 18:20). There is need of the sister or brother "who will comfort such a person, oppressed and bruised by the Law, with the Word of God."[39]

RELATIONSHIP OF LAW AND GOSPEL

As the Law acquired different functions within the framework of the history of salvation, it also has different tasks in the personal salvation history of individual believers. It has a different position with respect to the event of justification than in the existence of the justified human being, although, on the other hand, the two cannot be separated.

LAW AND GOSPEL IN THE EVENT OF JUSTIFICATION

It is the task of the Law to make people aware of their situation before God. The human being is a sinner and stands accused. The Law drives the person still further into entanglement in sin; in a sense it "increases" sin. According to Luther human beings have an invincible need to justify themselves, which only concentrates them still further on themselves. Or else they fall victim to despair, which ultimately represents an equally radical self-centeredness. Hence a human being must struggle with God, like Jacob at the Jabbok (Gen 32:23-31): there Jacob had to "shed his old skin" and allow himself to be broken. He no longer had firm ground under his feet. Struggling with God, that is, is nothing else than battling the wrathful God who acts toward a human being as if that person were God's worst enemy. If God "is after one's life he does not grab the skin, but reaches inside so that the marrow melts and the bones become as soft as flesh. . . ."[40] In truth, what God wants to achieve by this is only to draw the person into the divine arms; by using the Law God drives one toward the Gospel: "God has given the world two sorts of words: the Law, which rages and causes death, and the Gospel, with which he consoles and gives life. . . . But when the word by which he offers us grace is spoken, one should never again let it go, even though the Law twist it forward or backward. . . ." The believer should under no circumstances allow it to be taken away again![41] Faith sees through the stance of God, which only appears to be directed against the person. It learns that overcoming God means overcoming "what he is in our conscience and is felt to be."[42]

The result of this is that the Gospel is not reduced to cheap grace and diverted into a "sweet security."[43] The message of the Gospel is not "you're okay!" It helps believers to bear the fact that they are not okay, because God bears it. Now they learn to live with their limitations and their failures, and as a result their lives will, in fact, be changed. According to Luther's understanding and experience the Gospel can only be understood in its seriousness and depth in tension with the Law. Moses and Christ: in the fullest sense neither can be understood without the other.[44]

These considerations culminate in Luther's view that from a formal point of view Law and Gospel can encounter one another in the same word. The first commandment of the Decalogue is for the Reformer the essence of the

Law on the one hand and of the Gospel on the other. "We should fear, love, and trust in God above all things."[45] This demand can make us see that it is altogether impossible really to fulfill it, and on the other hand it can invite us to entrust ourselves utterly to God. Christ himself can become an unattainable and therefore accusing model for human beings even though he is the essence of God's grace. The petitions of the Our Father humble us insofar as we admit within them that we do not hallow God's name, live according to the ways of God's reign, and do God's will. But at the same time they show us how we should act in this situation and to whom we should turn. "Every word of God terrifies and comforts us, hurts and heals; it breaks down and builds up; it plucks up and plants again; it humbles and exalts."[46] Phenomenologically, it may be that Law and Gospel cannot be separated! Rationally, we can be clear that a word of Sacred Scripture has these two functions. But allowing oneself to be drawn not to the Law's side, but to the side of the Gospel is the work of the Holy Spirit alone.[47] Thus the event of justification is again completely separated from human initiative and altogether given and entrusted to the action of God.

LAW AND GOSPEL IN THE ENTIRETY OF CHRISTIAN EXISTENCE

But what meaning can the Law have for those who have grasped the Gospel? Is it not superfluous for them, or could they at times have need of it as an aid to orientation?

First of all, Luther emphasizes that the Gospel creates freedom: a Christian needs no one to tell him or her what to do or not do; whatever appears as a concrete task "he does whatever the occasion calls for, and all is well done."[48] A Christian lives from the source that is God's own self. The Reformer basically argues here as Augustine did in his famous exhortation: "love, and do what you will!"[49] With Augustine, of course, the imperative, namely to love, precedes. For Luther, on the other hand, love comes from hearing the liberating Gospel. It is precisely the one who is no longer under the Law who is in a position to fulfill it.[50] Hence Christians are no longer bound to the Decalogue; they are even free to establish new Decalogues: "For if we have Christ, we can easily establish laws and we shall judge all things rightly. Indeed, we would make new decalogues," as can be seen in Paul's letters and in Christ himself. These will be much clearer than what Moses had to offer. If even the Gentiles knew of the Law (Rom 2:14), "how much more is Paul or the perfect Christian, full of the Spirit, able to set in order a certain decalogue and judge most correctly about all things!"[51] Of course, this statement is relativized in the theses that follow inasmuch as Luther admits that unfortunately the presence of the Spirit of Christ cannot always be presumed, and that in all Christians, as long as they live, the flesh will arise against the spirit. But in principle he insists on what he had formulated in his arguments about the validity of monastic vows: that evangelical freedom is "of divine law."[52]

It was thus probable that voices would be raised saying that the law is completely superfluous. Johann Agricola was the most prominent representative of these "Antinomians," as Luther called them. In Agricola's opinion the law belonged from now on only in city hall and not in the pulpit, and in the early days when he was friendly with Luther he appealed to the young Reformer. Luther, in contrast, feared that people of this opinion would ultimately come to regard the Gospel in legal terms, and that without the Law they would miss the point of the Gospel. In a single writing[53] and no fewer than six series of theses for disputation[54] he sought to defy this misunderstanding. Those who would abolish the Law must ultimately cease to speak of sin.[55] The Law is "God's hammer that breaks rocks in pieces, as Jeremiah says; it confines everyone under sin."[56] It does not accomplish justification, of course, but as a precondition it is a constitutive part of the event of justification.[57] Even in the justified person, so long as he or she lives in this world, "the flesh" and sin are still active—in spite of their being fundamentally accepted by God. In Luther's view a person is faced throughout her or his life with the damning judgment of the Law that drives one again and again into the arms of the Gospel. This is true even though there are real transformations and new life in a Christian: "We need the Decalogue not only to apprise us of our lawful obligations, but we also need it to discern how far the Holy Spirit has advanced us in his work of sanctification and by how much we still fall short of the goal, lest we become secure and imagine that we have now done all that is required. Thus we must constantly grow in sanctification and always become new creatures in Christ."[58] We need the Decalogue as an examination of conscience that points out to us what in our lives does not, or does not yet, correspond to the will of God: "Insofar as Christ is risen in us, to that extent we are without law, sin, and death. But insofar as he is not yet risen in us, to that extent we are under the law, sin, and death."[59] The ongoing dialectic of Law and Gospel gives zest to Christian existence and leads it onward!

Certainly it is a disputed question whether according to Luther the Law can really have a positive significance for the orientation of the justified. In that case there would be a third function (*tertius usus*) for the Law as applied to believers. The Law should then "be kept so that the saints may know what works God demands, in which they can practice obedience to God."[60] This passage, as Werner Elert has demonstrated, was interpolated into Luther's text. At the same time, of course, there are many statements by Luther in which the Old Testament commandments or the New Testament instructions are received positively. But for believers they no longer function as a "law" that threatens them; their fulfillment is a matter of course for serious Christians.[61]

The good tree bears good fruit without needing any instructions or aids to orientation!

CRITICAL EVALUATION

Objections can be raised against Luther's teaching on Law and Gospel from the most varied points of view. We may ask whether this approach is not necessarily understood in a mechanical sense. And then: is the sequence of first Law, then Gospel correct, or must we admit that Karl Barth was right in seeing the sequence as lying in the contrary direction? This at the same time suggests some exegetical inquiries. Beyond that, the pastoral implications of this distinction must be considered. Moreover, there are critical points of view in light also of ecumenical discussions, and finally, we must test whether and how Luther's teaching on Law and Gospel can be productive within today's horizon of understanding.

MECHANISMS?

Luther's doctrine of Law and Gospel—to use an image—gives the impression that he recommends throwing someone into the water in order afterward to be able to pull him or her out again. In his dispute with the Antinomians he did in fact recommend a corresponding "method." He finds that there is no better way "to hand on and preserve pure doctrine than by following this method, namely dividing Christian doctrine into two parts, that is, Law and Gospel."[62] Is this simply about what Luther himself had found helpful and then elevated it to something universally applicable? Some of his sermons appear to have been constructed on that plan. But we should not misunderstand this. The preacher's task is not first to preach morality and then to offer opportunities for psychic balance. Preaching the Law is not preaching morality. Instead, it aims at a trans-moral self-perception of the human being before God. It leads to an ethical shock that can be understood by analogy to Paul Tillich's "ontological shock." Preaching of Law and Gospel cannot be regarded as a mechanical sequence, if only because the "use of the Law to convict" only functions if it is not related from the outset to the Gospel and thus relativized or made impossible. Instead, it wants to bring before people's eyes a twofold reality: first, that God's demands are unconditional, and second, that a human being cannot fulfill them. The second does not make the apprehension of the first unnecessary. Human beings cannot get away from the fact that they stand under the demands and thus under the judgment of God. But Luther's approach cannot be understood in a mechanical sense also because it does not proceed on the assumption of an automatic working of the Law. If someone allows the Law to point her or him to the Gospel and really comes to faith, in Luther's understanding this is the work of the Holy Spirit. Luther's intention is thus in fact anti-mechanical!

Of course, the extent to which this intention was understood and adhered to afterward is a matter for another day. Luther himself used the formulaic distinction "Law and Gospel" only beginning with his commentary on Galatians in 1531/35. It then acquired a certain fixed character in the Lutheran confessional formulae.[63]

WRONG SEQUENCE?

Karl Barth in particular, in his lecture "Gospel and Law"[64] and in the corresponding part of his *Church Dogmatics*, protested against the formula "Law and Gospel."[65] He was motivated not only by his Reformed tradition but above all by his engagement with the idea of law as he found it in the Lutheran theology of his contemporaries. Werner Elert spoke very firmly of the law of God, which he found written not only in Sacred Scripture but also in history and in personal fortunes. Against this idea Karl Barth argued that the Law can only be known from the Gospel; the covenant precedes the Law. The Law is in the Gospel "as the tablets from Sinai were in the ark of the covenant."[66] On the other hand, however, the Law could come to stand as a "form of the Gospel." The "you must!" should be seen as a "you will!" Now certainly Luther presupposed a natural human knowledge about the claims under which we stand. But on the other hand it was clear to him that the Law could only be understood in its full depth and ultimate meaning through the Gospel. It is radically threatening especially for believers! The Gospel does not relativize the Law—quite the contrary! But Luther could not regard the Law as a "form of the Gospel." It is true that Law and Gospel encountered him in the same words, for example in the first commandment of the Decalogue: "I am the Lord your God. You shall not have other gods besides me." But for Luther these words have a diametrically opposite meaning depending on whether they are heard as "Law" or as "Gospel." Luther felt himself altogether bound to Paul's understanding of the Law, while Karl Barth oriented his thinking to the Old Testament, where the Law was seen as helpful and encouraging, as the pointer that directs human beings onward and offers them a sheltering order. Psalm 119 describes this in detail; it is palpably expressed even today in Judaism, in the feast of Rejoicing in the Law (Simhat Torah). The solution probably lies in the distinction between "law" and "commandment."[67] The ethical imperative can be understood as "law" that burdens and reveals our inability to fulfill it, and as "commandment" that gives helpful orientation. Christ is "the end of the law" (Rom 10:4) and thus enables us to follow the "way of the commandments" with pleasure, which in turn is not to be identified with the fulfillment of the "Law," which was accomplished by Jesus Christ alone.

It is true that for Luther there were two preconditions that no longer exist for people today. Talk of Law and Gospel had its vanishing point in the idea of a last judgment and the possible eternal failure of some human lives. This raises the question of how God's claim can be radically articulated and understood within the conditions of our contemporary thinking. Then we must point out that, according to today's knowledge, it seems that Luther misunderstood one of the texts that served as an essential support for his argument. When Paul says that the Law "was our disciplinarian until Christ came" (Gal 3:24), the intent is to say something not about existential anthropology but about salvation history. The *paidagogos* of whom the original text speaks was, in the ancient household, the slave entrusted with the protection and raising of the next generation. But according to Paul this function of the Law came to an end with Christ. In any case, the *usus elenchticus legis* can no longer be unconditionally founded on Paul's statement.[68]

The connection between Law and Gospel thus cannot be established in the sense of a clear sequence. Insofar as human beings are in a position at all to apprehend a radical appeal addressed to them, a demand they are unable to meet, that imperative will not necessarily lead them to the Gospel. But it could raise the question of a "Gospel," a possibility of attaining to the meaning of life. On the other hand, the Gospel does in fact make God's claim radically clear—in retrospect, we might say. Through it believers become aware of their resistance to God and their fellow human beings. It appears that they cannot break this resistance by themselves, and that in fact the very attempt to do so causes the resistance to hybridize and harden. To that extent Law and Gospel are in fact mutually related, and it is the task of the believer to seek ever anew the way from Law to Gospel—and the reverse—and to walk in it. Believers thus submit themselves to a dynamic that transforms their lives. We must, of course, admit that there are other, less extreme and dramatic encounters with Christian faith whose authenticity and legitimacy may not be denied.

Pastoral aspects

For Luther everything depends on the distinction between Law and Gospel. "Distinguishing" is for him one of the principal tasks of the theologian. "The model of distinguishing Law and Gospel is not the harmless and peaceful business of a logical operation, a process of definition, as when one attempts to separate two entities or subjects that are mutually related in some way or other, such as the distinction between a novel and a romance or between murder and homicide." The model, Gerhard Ebeling finds, is instead "the process of a legal action, in which a concrete choice must be made among various claims to justice regarding a highly complicated matter . . ." or else a battle fought between fronts that are misty and wedged within one another.[69] For the Reformer this is not primarily a theological theory; it presents him with a task that must be approached pastorally. He has seen in himself and in others how hard it is to deal with the constant "you must!" Luther's concern is to identify the Law as law and allow himself to be pointed by it to the Gospel. Everything depends on the actual carrying out of the distinction. I must not pretend to myself that I can fulfill God's law and lead a meaningful life on my own; but I must also not allow myself to be crushed by the experience of my limitations and failures. I cannot give up on myself, as if God had no claim on my life or, on the other hand, was no longer interested in whether my life succeeds or not. Hence Law and Gospel describe an existential process in which God "realizes himself and the human being."[70] Luther can describe this as his most personal experience: "I did not learn my *theologiam* all at once, but had to brood deeper and deeper, my *tentationes* (temptations) brought me there...." That is missing in the enthusiasts and the mobs: they do not have the one who would be their adversary, "the devil, he can be a good teacher."[71] In laboring with Law and Gospel believers feel themselves drawn into a process of experience in which they become more and more deeply aware of God's grace.

Ecumenical implications

Catholic and Orthodox theology are clueless in face of Luther's distinction between Law and Gospel; they cannot understand it. Luther himself observed that "for many centuries" there was "a remarkable silence about this in all the schools and churches."[72] The approach in Roman Catholicism or Orthodoxy is: the law is difficult to fulfill, but with the help of God's grace it becomes more and more possible. Law and grace are not in opposition to one another but are mutually related, undialectically and unilinearly, as two positive entities. Christ becomes a source of strength on the path to an ever-increasing fulfillment of the law, but in this way he is never "the end of the law" (Rom 10:4); a genuine liberation from the tyrannical function of the law, from the "tyranny of values" (Wolfgang Schmidbauer) never occurs in this way. Here the center is not confession of the saving Gospel but the human expectation of being able to lead a saintly life with the help of God. With the aid of the law and grace a person can become a "saint." But one "learns to have faith" in the opposition of Law and Gospel.[73] Is this really nothing more than a difference in terminology?

Against this is the New Testament, if it must be understood as the witness to a saving action of God exclusively in Jesus Christ. If the law of God is fulfilled only in Jesus Christ there is no way to relativize it or to realize it (at least partially) through human initiative. For then law and freedom are fundamentally and mutually exclusive. Without this basic contradiction the cross of Christ can by no means be fully understood and adequately appreciated. Luther is convinced that Sacred Scripture may not be interpreted except as saying "that the human being is nothing and Christ alone is all."[74] The person for whom "Christ is all" finds precisely there his or her dignity and energy.[75]

THE CRITICAL FUNCTION OF THE DISTINCTION BETWEEN "LAW" AND "GOSPEL"

In Luther's view the critical function of the distinction between Law and Gospel is theologically indispensable. The Gospel must not become law. This is the purpose of the warning that the Sermon on the Mount, for example, must not be misunderstood as a private guideline and certainly not as a comprehensive social order. The Gospel does not yield the utopia of an ideal world for whose realization one must exert oneself. In fact, the Gospel should not even come to stand for something that one "must" or "should" believe— because then it has become law!

In turn, however, the Law must not be regarded as Gospel: moral activism and orthopraxis may be psychologically satisfying but they are not capable of leading to real freedom and so to a successful life.

It is necessary to understand that the Law expresses a more radical claim than any moral order. In its trans-moral power it drives human beings into a crisis that confronts them with themselves and with God and thus requires of them the acquisition of a painful consciousness of reality. In the same way, the Gospel is not to be understood in the sense of a merely psychic stabilization: despite the limitations perceived under the claims of the Law, it leads human beings to reconciliation with the ground of their existence. It enables them to affirm themselves as affirmed, even though they recognize that they can find much in themselves to reject.

LAW AND GOSPEL IN THE HORIZON OF THE PRESENT

Have we thus answered the contemporary questions directed at the Reformer? Those who are socialized as Christians, or certainly as Lutherans, could well say "yes" to this. But they too must engage with the self-concept of people today. People who feel themselves to be autonomous within the limitations of earthly existence will not bow to the dictation of a morally unpalatable law unless it is absolutely necessary. Besides, in view of the constitutional limits of human existence they do not regard themselves as guilty. They are more likely to ask about what authority they should address with their complaints that again and again there are catastrophes that cry out to heaven, in individual and social life and even in the realm of nature beyond the human. But ultimately they have lost the ability to reckon with any such authority. How can one speak of Law and Gospel under the conditions of an "etsi Deus non daretur" [as if there were no God]?

Matthias Kroeger presents an interesting attempt. He sees the "Law" as a "primal phenomenon," a "condition of life." It exists in a constant state of "formal alteration" and thus cannot be reduced to the problem of sin and transgression; rather, the unavoidability of the law is expressed in the most varied "aporetic experiences." In the "concrete form of the law at each moment," however, human beings begin "to inquire beyond themselves": "The law helps us . . . to reach repeatedly beyond ourselves—into the *extra nos* of our experience." This kind of expanded concept of the law, he says, puts theology in a position to take into account the conditions of the "new paradigm" that must be supposed to exist in the present: "the reception of the concept of religion, the realization of interreligiosity and autonomy as well as the question of the non-objectivity of the divine in non-theism."[76]

The task of orientation exists for secular people as well, and in light of the postmodern "anything goes" it is more urgent for individuals now than it was for some earlier generations. A general idea of good and evil, which Luther took as his starting point simply as a matter of course, is largely nonexistent now. But the need to choose a particular ethical option still exists. In the context of the globalization that is extending its tentacles ever more broadly, the task confronts not only individuals but whole societies, in fact, all of humanity. Unfortunately the notion of what are fundamental human rights and how they are to be obtained is not something that is eternally established. An intersubjective, interdisciplinary, and intercultural effort is required for the struggle to clarify this question, and the Reformation position should be applied also.

In view of all the existing obscurities on the one hand and the apparently unequivocal directives for behavior on the other, it is necessary to sharpen human consciences. In the individual this requires an openness to a possible plurality of options and decisions, and simultaneously an intensive engagement with the question of what should be the common task of humanity throughout the globe. One thing worth considering is the benefit of an order oriented to the Golden Rule.

But this again raises the question that stirred Luther under the conditions of his own time, namely: where shall we get the strength to translate even partially into deeds the options and *desiderata* we recognize as reasonable? Philosophies and religions will offer different answers, and these should be tested by Christians and used insofar as possible. The Gospel, as Luther understood it, could have the critical task here of constantly questioning apparent solutions, refusing to despair at those that are inadequate, and motivating to the development of more and more new ones that better meet the needs of humanity and the nature surrounding it. What should serve as the starting point is not an existing experience of the Law and a fixed concept of the Gospel but the search for new Decalogues and for the Spirit that fulfills and transcends them. In this search, as Luther was convinced, the Gospel will develop its true power.

NOTES

[1] LW 26, 117 (WA 40/1, 209, 16-17).

[2] Peter 1981, 23–24.

[3] Reinhold Mokrosch, "Gewissen. Praktisch-theologisch," RGG4 3: 906–7, at 906. For the whole subject cf. idem, *Gewissen und Adoleszenz. Christliche Gewissensbildung im Jugendalter* (Weinheim: Deutscher Studien-Verlag, 1996), 245–426.

[4] Gerhard Ebeling, *Dogmatik des christlichen Glaubens III* (Tübingen: Mohr, 1979), 289.

[5] Ibid.

[6] WA 7, 502, 34-35.

[7] See "Against the Antonomians" in chapter 9.

[8] WA 39/1, 360, 1-2.

[9] WA 36, 9, 28-29.

[10] WA 36, 29, 32-38.

[11] WA.TR 5, 210, 12-16.

[12] LW 35, 119 (WA 10/1/1, 11, 13-15).

[13] See "God in Christ" in chapter 4.

[14] LW 39, 185 (WA 7, 656, 30 [reading "sin" instead of "sinners"]).

[15] WA 17/2, 102, 8ff.

[16] LW 21, 237 (WA 32, 495, 29–496, 2).

[17] Peters 1990, 81.

[18] LW 25, 215 (WA 56, 231, 9-10): "by faith alone we must believe that we are sinners."

[19] WA 39/1, 456, 7 (in the Latin text).

[20] WA 39/1, 364, 10-13.

[21] Peters 1981, 35.

[22] LW 45, 90 (WA 11, 250, 26-29).

[23] LW 26, 308 (WA 40/1, 479, 17-26).

[24] Ibid. (WA 40/1, 479, 30–480, 25). The reference to capital punishment (p. 480, 5-6) is missing from the printed edition.

[25] LW 26, 305 (WA 40/1, 474, 22-23).

[26] Ibid. (WA 40/1, 474, 28-29).

[27] ". . . lex semper accusans nos et mortificans (the Law always accusing and mortifying us)," WA 39/1, 412, 2-3: later dogmatics spoke therefore of a *usus elenchticus*, the "convicting" use of the Law.

[28] Peters 1981, 43.

[29] LW 52, 152 (WA 10/1/1, 508, 20–509, 4).

[30] LW 26, 309 (WA 40/1, 480, 32–481, 16).

[31] WA 46, 114, 16.

[32] LW 26, 314–15 (WA 40/1, 488, 11–490, 16 [trans.]).

[33] WA 10/3, 338, 9-10.

[34] Lohse 1995, 203.

[35] Ebeling, cited in Lohse, ibid.

[36] LW 35, 358 (WA.DB 6, 2, 23–4, 8).

[37] *The Book of Concord*, 352.

[38] LW 35, 370 (WA.DB 7, 11, 6-7).

[39] LW 26, 318 (WA 40/1, 493, 18-19).

[40] WA 24, 575, 36-37; 577, 28-33.

[41] Ibid., 578, 12-14.

[42] Ibid., 578, 28-30.

[43] LW 47, 111 (WA 50, 471, 36-38).

[44] WA 39/1, 547, 20-21.

[45] Interpretation of the first commandment of the Decalogue in the Small Catechism, *The Book of Concord*, 342.

[46] LW 42, 37 (WA 2, 95, 16-18).

[47] Interpretation of the third article of the Creed in the Small Catechism, *The Book of Concord*, 345.

[48] LW 44, 26 (WA 6, 207, 4-5).

[49] "Dilige, et quod vis fac," MPL 35, 2033, on 1 John 4:14.

[50] WA 10/1/1, 359, 21-22.

[51] LW 34, 112–13 (WA 39/1, 47, 25-34 [trans.]), theses "De fide," 1535.

[52] "Ea enim libertas divini iuris est," LW 44, 296 (WA 8, 613, 9).

[53] "Against the Antinomians," LW 47, 99–119 (WA 50, 468–77); cf. "Against the Antonomians" in chapter 9.

[54] WA 39/1, 342–58; see also "Theses for the first Disputation against the Antinomians" (1537) in LDStA 2, 447–59.

[55] LW 47, 113 (WA 50, 471, 15).

[56] LDStA 2, 457, Thesis 16; cf. Jer 23:29.

[57] Cf. WA 39/1, 469, 13-19.

[58] LW 41, 166 (WA 50, 643, 19-25).

[59] ". . . quatenus Christus in nobis est suscitatus, eatenus sumus sine lege, peccato et morte. Quatenus vero nondum est in nobis suscitatus, eatenus sumus sub lege, peccato et morte," WA 39/1, 356, 15-18, Theses 40 and 41.

[60] Cf. WA 39/1, 485, 16-24 (quoted from 485, 22-24).

[61] Cf. Wilfried Joest, *Gesetz und Freiheit. Das Problem des Tertius usus legis bei Luther und die neutestamentliche Parainese* (Göttingen: Vandenhoeck & Ruprecht, 1961).

[62] WA 39/1, 361, 1-4.

[63] "Formula of Concord, Epitome V: Of Law and Gospel," *The Book of Concord*, 477–79. Cf. Gunther Wenz, *Theologie der Bekenntnisschriften der evangelisch-lutherischen Kirche. Eine historische und systematische Einführung in das Konkordienbuch*, vol. 2 (Berlin and New York: de Gruyter, 1998).

[64] Karl Barth, *Evangelium und Gesetz*, TEH n.s. 50 (Munich: Kaiser, 1956); English in *Community, State, and Church: Three Essays* (Garden City NY: Doubleday, 1960). Cf. Fulvio Ferrario, *Frammenti di teologia dogmatica. 1, Dio nella Parola* (Turin: Claudiana, 2008), 76–82.

[65] Cf. Peters 1981, 105ff.

[66] Barth, *Community, State, and Church*, 80.

[67] Cf. Paul Althaus, "Gebot und Gesetz. Zum Thema 'Gesetz und Evangelium,'" 201–38 in Ernst Kinder and Klaus Haendler, eds., *Gesetz und Evangelium. Beiträge zur gegenwärtigen theologischen Diskussion* (Darmstadt: Wissenschaftliche Buchgesellschaft, 1968).

[68] For the exegetical situation cf. Ulrich Wilckens, *Der Brief an die Römer*. Vol. 2: *Römer 6–11* (Zürich and Neukirchen: Benziger/Neukirchener Verlag, 1980), 83–101; for the history of its influence see ibid., 101–17.

[69] Ebeling 1964, 122.

[70] Dietrich Korsch, in *Handbuch* 2005, 95. However, in Luther's view "salvation" does not consist, as Korsch writes just before this (p. 94), in the "establishment of the *immediacy* of the relationship to God" (emphasis supplied), but in the establishing of peace with God. Korsch calls Luther's

theological approach a "guiding religious idea"; I consider this an understatement as regards the Reformer.

71 WA.TR 1, 146, 12-16.

72 LW 26, 313 (WA 40/1, 486, 24-25).

73 Cf. Dietrich Bonhoeffer, Letters and Papers from Prison, ed. Eberhard Bethge (London: SCM, 1956), 369.

74 Cf. Ibid.

75 This will be considered more thoroughly in the discussion of the doctrine of justification; cf. "The believer: 'both sinner and justified'" in chapter 6 and "The Decalogue" and "The Sermon on the Mount" in chapter 9.

76 Matthias Kroeger, Im religiösen Umbruch der Welt: Der fällige Ruck in den Köpfen der Kirche. Über Grundriss und Bausteine des religiösen Wandels im Herzen der Kirche (Stuttgart: Kohlhammer, 2004), 335–63.

8

Identity: "Both Sinner and Justified"

The doctrine of justification is regarded as the article by which the church stands or falls—*articulus stantis aut cadentis ecclesiae.*[1] In the Orthodox churches this place seems to belong to the Eucharist.[2] Roman Catholic theology would point to the centrality of orders for ensuring that the church stands and does not fall. The Joint Declaration on the Doctrine of Justification subscribed to by the Vatican and the Lutheran World Federation in 1999 was thus on a slippery slope from the outset, since in Roman Catholic understanding the article on justification can never be the sole foundation on which the church "stands or falls." But that was Luther's conviction: if the church ceases to communicate the message of justification it has lost its very essence, its right to exist. In the message of justification the true church finds its identity.

Certainly as regards the Lutheran churches as well one may ask whether this is a realistic view. The message of the justification of the ungodly is by no means central to their thinking and acting. In the nineteenth century the doctrine of justification for the most part led only a shadowy existence. In the twentieth century, especially in its second half, there were repeated attempts to make it comprehensible and present it as central, but thus far with limited success. The efforts of the world congress of the Lutheran World Federation in Helsinki in 1963 remained as ineffective as the theological discussions connected with the joint declaration.[3] Apparently people in church and society nowadays have different issues.

Contemporary Questions

The difficulties begin with the terminology itself. The word "justification," as a theological concept, has long since departed from everyday language. Its original meaning belonged, in fact, to the juridical context; in the Middle Ages "justification" was understood to mean the making and application of law, which could certainly include the carrying out of a verdict. Theologically, "justification" is an artificial term, both in the rare usage in *koine* Greek of the word *dikaiøsis* (which appears only twice in the New Testament itself) and in its Latin equivalent, *iustificatio*.

Translating the *Confessio Augustana* into modern Greek for the purpose of the exchange of letters between the Tübingen theologians and Patriarch Jeremias II of Constantinople required the creation of a special term. At present the term "justification" is scarcely usable outside professional vocabularies.

Moreover, the theology of justification depends on intellectual and philosophical presuppositions that apparently no longer exist, or at any rate not as a matter of course. It presumes faith in a personal God who demands a reckoning of human beings and confronts them after death with a "last judgment." The eschatological horizon that represented a given for late medieval Christians has been almost entirely lost to many people today, including those associated with the church. The "last judgment" is no longer something they think about, scarcely even "eternal life." If at all, the idea of a reincarnation in which the karma built up in the previous life is worked off, or of Allah, "the compassionate, the merciful" (Qu'ran, Sura 1), refined into the image of a fundamentally loving and forgiving God, seems more plausible. The result for human self-understanding is that they no longer need feel obligated to give account to a superior authority, but are instead to affirm and realize themselves within the limits of the given. They see themselves in the best case as responsible to themselves, their fellow human beings, possibly also coming generations and the environment. Judgment on their actions, insofar as they do not allow it to be given by other people or by society, must be formed by themselves.

In the social realm people speak of the necessity of legitimation, which in some sense adopts a concern of the old concept of justification. It is a matter of justifying oneself for particular behavior or attitudes; to that extent the pressure for legitimation is universal. Depending on particular ethical or ideological givens, the need for legitimation of one's own behavior may be greater or less. Even one's existence may require legitimation: what about the rights of unborn life or the claims of handicapped and aged human beings? There may be specific measures needed to legitimate the right to life of unproductive, suffering people. But one scarcely expects to find those in Luther's theology of justification.

On the individual level the pressure for legitimation is expressed in the context of self-justification and corresponding strategies. Internalizing norms can establish a need for self-justification; social institutions or family constellations may strengthen that need. As regards Luther the question has repeatedly arisen whether it was not precisely these sorts of problems in his biographical background that produced his theology of justification. Today, of course, the question is reversed. In certain age groups and levels of society the problem of the superego seems to have been so reduced that there appears to be scarcely any sense of a need for justification on the part of many.

If, however, guilt feelings should appear it is assumed that they are part of the *conditio humana* and thus unavoidable. If they appear destructive or disturbing they may be treated with psychological techniques. Mediation may help in concrete conflicts between persons. The application of religious points of view, such as the representative suffering and death of Jesus Christ, increasingly lacks plausibility even for Christians. If it does so at all, it seems that individual sacrifices must be offered.

This may explain why the message of justification seems scarcely to have any *Sitz im Leben* nowadays even in Lutheran congregations. Personal confession, penitential worship services, and days of penance are regarded as optional. Absolution pronounced by an agent, if still given at all, may have a counterproductive effect: it produces no changes in the lives of the faithful. There is scarcely any sense of concrete forgiveness. The places where believers may come into contact with the issue of justification are limited even within the churches. In sermons the tone is, as a rule, governed by talk of a God who is loving to all, but not about one who justifies sinners. Even so, at least the Lord's Supper is still largely understood in connection with forgiveness of sins: it strengthens believers because God makes a new beginning with them; despite their guilt they may see themselves as affirmed by God and they can turn to their daily lives with renewed confidence. But this awareness is scarcely ever developed into a theoretical reflection on the basic problems of a theology of justification, for example in concepts such as "sin," "righteousness," "judgment," or in consideration of what talk about "Christ's death" or even "Christ's blood" might mean in this context.

Thus we come to the question whether the very heart of Luther's theology can still be communicated today. Two consequences are possible: either it can be successfully translated into today's world or the focus of Reformation proclamation must be established anew and differently.

Message and Teaching of Justification

It is no simple matter to reconstruct Luther's own teaching on justification. He did not produce a monograph on this doctrine, though he had planned to do so.[4] There are series of theses on justification that Luther formulated succinctly in his later years as a basis for disputations.[5] Otherwise it is necessary to seek out what he had to say, especially in his lectures on Romans and Galatians. The writing that best expresses his approach is "The Freedom of a Christian."[6] Why did Luther not write a separate book on his understanding of justification? One reason may be that he, as an occasional writer, was always reacting to particular challenges and then, depending on which front he was fighting on, reinforced his arguments with points that seemed important to him. In his dispute with late medieval works-righteousness the message of justification was indispensable, as it was also in a sense in his confrontation with the Enthusiasts, but scarcely at all in connection with the Peasants' War.[7] Probably the Reformer put no special emphasis on the concept itself; the word "justification" does not appear in his catechisms, though the subject certainly does! What Luther wanted to say about justification is often implied in his remarks on Law and Gospel, but again there is no monographic treatment of the subject from his pen, only theses.[8] Probably he considered the subject so omnipresent that he could not conceive treating it adequately in a monograph. For him it was not a special chapter in theology; in principle it saturated every theological statement. At the same time he was not interested in a theory, a *doctrine* of justification, which would have appeared to him as abstract and thus as erroneous as a *doctrine* of forgiveness; this was the *message* of justification. The teaching on justification has its function in light of the message of justification, which it reflects. But the message is to be communicated by means of proclamation, which of course may well perform its task through a quite different conceptual system.[9] Certainly, for Luther message and teaching always belong together. His theoretical speculations were intended not only to give a basis to the message and make it transparent but at the same time to articulate it. The concept of "guiding religious idea" seriously understates his theological and pastoral interest. Luther, with his understanding of justification, was not just attempting a "systematic reworking," even one of "major proportions." He is misunderstood if he is seen as a freely acting systematic theologian, or worse, someone who juggled theological ideas. Likewise, the goal of his message of justification was not "the establishment of the immediacy of the relationship to God."[10] Rather, the Reformer was concerned with the healing of the human being's relationship to God, spoiled and broken by sin, a healing done by God's very self.

If we are to inquire into Luther's teaching about the justification of sinners we must first of all clarify what he means by sin and then consider how he conceived the event of justification. Finally, we must examine how he recognizes the result of God's justifying action.

SIN

The message of justification is addressed to sinners, but how is sin as such to be recognized in the first place? It is part of the sinful constitution of human beings that they are unaware of it and do not want to have their eyes opened to it. In that sense sin can be compared to a cancer that at first causes no pain but is still carrying on its destructive work.[11] In Luther's opinion only the preaching of Law and Gospel can bring us out of this. The threat of the Law alone would be deadly and lead to despair. But through the proclamation of Law and Gospel it becomes clear to people what sin is about: sin is a relationship phenomenon, and as such it shapes the whole human situation. Both these things can be really recognized only in faith; sin is a *credendum*.[12] Speaking of it is not the consequence of a pessimistic view of human nature. For Luther it is not part of an empirical anthropology; to that extent it has a different value for him than does radical evil in Kant's conception.[13] Nor can speaking of sin be done in isolation; it is not theologically autonomous. The focus of all talk of sin is grace: for the sake of grace we must speak of sin. When sin is forgiven, the "splendor" of life returns.[14]

SIN AS A PHENOMENON OF RELATIONSHIP

Inadequate definitions of sin

According to Luther, sin is inadequately defined if we assume that human beings are ranked by God according to what they do. In their actions, human beings can at best achieve a "civil righteousness" (*iustitia civilis*), something Luther by no means looked down on. It has an important function for human life in society. But it is shaped by human egocentricity. In any case, however, sin is more than an offense against the standards of bourgeois society.

Likewise inadequate is the idea that a human being may be judged by the attitude that underlies each of her or his actions. The division of basic human behavior into virtues and vices as presented by Thomas Aquinas and others remained unsatisfactory to Luther because it did not seem to him appropriate to speak of the moral qualities of the human being, even if they are traced to the action of God.[15] Thus also sin cannot be regarded as a negative entity that can be differentiated along a scale of "mortal" and venial sins, which can work their ill effects alongside the virtues.[16] Human sinfulness does not represent, any more than does human sanctity, an attitude traceable to a particular disposition and able to be changed in a positive or negative direction by training. Such measures, which from the point of view of today's psychology are certainly worth trying, are out of the question for Luther because they try to understand sin without, so to speak, having God in the picture. They offer concepts that basically end in individual human freedom and attribute to human persons a quality that, though created by God, makes them independent of their Creator. For Luther, in contrast, sin is a relationship phenomenon; it is about the relation between God and the human, between human beings, and within the human individual as well. The faith, love, and hope of the justified human being are contrasted with the unbelief, lovelessness, and hopelessness of the sinner.

Disruption of the relationship to God

That the human relationship to God is disordered is a truth Luther sees not only disclosed by the transgression of individual commandments but essentially consisting in the fact that a human being is not able to fear and love God above all things and to trust in God. Insofar as anyone actually attempts it, she or he does so in pursuit of personal intentions and goals. People thus instrumentalize their devotion. The Augsburg Confession speaks Luther's mind when it says that after the Fall "all . . . who are born according to the course of nature" are from birth "full of evil lust and inclinations" and "by nature" know no true fear of God or trust in God (*sine metu Dei, sine fiducia erga Deum et cum concupiscentia*).[17] Sin is thus essentially unbelief, a lack of a radically self-surrendering trust. This categorizes as sin everything that does not come from faith.[18] Sin, however, is further empowered when human beings do not trust God to forgive them! God's glory is realized in God's desire for the salvation of human beings. They rob God of it when they do not allow God to give them the gift of salvation. "There is no greater sin than not to believe this article of 'the forgiveness of sins.'"[19]

Disruption of human relationships

The disruption of the relationship to God is reproduced in the conflicted nature of human relationships. This is obvious, and it expresses itself in private and in public life, in personal quarrels and in wars between nations. But Luther does not spend much time describing this in detail because his concern is not only with concrete offenses, since externally much good may come of them; there is certainly a level of justification before human beings (*coram hominibus*) that must not be confused with justification before God (*coram Deo*).[20] "Civil" righteousness should be acknowledged as such, but it is corrupted by the ambition and thirst for glory of those who seek to attain it. Luther illustrates this especially in terms of the heroes of antiquity. Self-love, he says, poisons our relationship to God and to other human beings. It "takes from God what is his and from human beings what is theirs and gives neither God nor others anything of what it has, is, and desires."[21] Luther refers only briefly to the disrupted relationship between human beings and the nature that surrounds them. This comes into view for him only in retrospect, so to speak, in relation to the expectation of liberated and no longer sighing creation. He knows that the hog squeals with fear when it is slaughtered, and that a tree groans and creaks when it is cut down.[22] Creatures are free only in the eschaton: "All creatures will have joy, love, and gladness and will laugh with you, and you with them. . . ."[23]

Distorted relationship of human beings to themselves

Human beings seek a relationship with themselves so intensely that they lose themselves in the process. By doing what lies within their own strength, they sin—namely by seeking their own interest in everything.[24] They seek to put themselves in charge and thus become more and more entangled in a situation in which they lose their relationship to God and their fellow human beings, which ultimately leads to the rupture of all relationships, namely death. What pleases and is important to me I ultimately seek in everything I encounter, even in my devotion: "I seek in God, in all creatures, *quod mihi placet—* what pleases me."[25] Luther uses Augustine's terminology to explain this. He speaks of human love for the self (*amor sui*) and of "desires" (*concupiscentia*) that plague a person. Human beings use God and thus please themselves.[26] Of course, Luther radicalizes Augustine's categories and in part gives them new meaning. Human self-love is interpreted as a turning or incurving of the human being into itself, with the result that a person relates to the self everything she or he has to do with and seeks the self in all things. Even the religious interest, life in the monastery or prayer, can be a means of centering in oneself. Human nature "set for itself no object but itself toward which it is borne and toward which it is directed; it sees, seeks, and works only toward itself in all matters, and it passes by all other things and even God Himself in the midst, as if it did not see them, and is directed only toward itself." It "sets itself in the place of all other things, even in the place of God, and seeks only those things which are its own and not the things of God. Therefore it is its own first and greatest idol."[27] Sin is thus not primarily an individual transgression but a state of radical concentration on and fixation on oneself; individual deeds only reproduce the basic human situation. Luther at least hints that this also poisons the relationship of the human being to the surrounding creation; human beings turn "everything" toward themselves, seeking "in all creatures" what seems to them useful and profitable.[28]

By this means people lose a correct estimation of themselves. On the one hand they are subject to the temptation to overestimate themselves when they feel strong and capable. On the other hand, when something goes wrong they fall into depression. So they find themselves thrown back and forth between excessive self-esteem (*praesumptio*) and depressive despair (*desperatio*). Luther certainly made the psychological observation that "sometimes I'm up, sometimes I'm down . . ." as the spiritual says. But at the same time he finds that it lies much deeper: this is how it is with people who are oriented only to themselves! No person can perceive his or her true nature "until he sees himself in his origin which is God."[29] This is how it will be as long as the individual is reflected only in himself or herself; Luther may be thinking of Narcissus here. All those who see this differently and attribute fantastic abilities to the human being "neither understand what man is nor do they know what they are talking about."[30] The absence of the relationships for which human beings were created stands within a comprehensive context.

THE OVERALL HUMAN SITUATION UNDER THE DOMINATION OF SIN

Sin shapes the whole situation both of individuals and of all persons, and of humanity as a whole. "Original sin"[31] must be addressed in this context.

The overall situation of the individual

Luther sees the person as a whole, but this human being, understood as a whole, is "flesh" (caro), is turned away from God. No part of the person is excepted and "better" than any other, nor is any part "worse" than another: sexuality by no means has a special negative position, just as in turn the human spiritual constitution can lay claim to no special positive status. The whole human being is "flesh" (totus homo caro). Human reason is just as much subject to the power of the devil as is the will. It is an error to suppose that reason strives for the highest goals. In the same way, according to Luther, it is wrong to attribute to the human being a free ability to decide and thus to be able to choose between death and eternal life.[32]

The fundamental situation of all human beings

"Man is by nature unable to want God to be God. Indeed, he himself wants to be God, and does not want God to be God."[33] As far as Luther is concerned this is true both of individuals and of the fundamental situation of humanity as a whole. He sees it as a transsubjective reality. Human beings live under the dictatorship of "sin, death, and the devil." They move in vicious circles with their own internal connections: sin, as a turning away from life, leads inevitably to death, and here again the rule of the devil is actualized. An individual cannot rise out of this comprehensive constellation. No monastery and no court of Demeter offers that possibility. Here Luther is addressing an experience that is probably easier to comprehend today than in Luther's time. The interweaving of such vicious circles can be palpably demonstrated.[34]

This also makes it clearer what the concept of "original sin" really means.[35] It is not a matter of inheritance, certainly not a quality stamped on the human in the form of a chromosomal attribute, nor does it, as Augustine supposed, have anything to do with misdirected sexuality. The subject is more accurately described in the English term, "original sin," or "primeval sin," the fundamental determination that rules human beings on the basis of their origin (*peccatum originale* or *peccatum ordinis*). It is true that Luther accepts the story of the Fall and has no difficulty with the apparent "historicity" of what it recounts. It serves to designate sin as a transsubjective connection that governs all human beings. With Scripture he assumes "that all men have descended from one man, Adam; and from this man, through their birth, they acquire and inherit the fall, guilt and sin, which the same Adam, through the wickedness of the devil, committed in paradise; and thus all men along with him are born, live, and die altogether in sin, and would necessarily be guilty of eternal death if Jesus Christ had not come to our aid. . . ."[36] The accent does not, however, lie on the derivation of the fact that all are sinners, but on the fact itself, which individual believers must confess. Luther solidifies this with the expression from the penitential Psalm 51: "Behold, I was conceived in sin, and in sin did my mother bear me" (Ps 51:5). Luther emphasizes what is indispensably important to him in this: "I—I myself—I was conceived in sin."[37] This is not meant to offer a rational, plausible argument, but to challenge himself to acknowledge his own sinfulness. Concrete individual sin (*peccatum actuale*) is, after all, not a unique thing; it does not exist in and of itself, for in it the whole human constitution, its deviation in principle from God (*peccatum originale*) is reproduced. To that extent it is not appropriate, according to Luther, to use the word "sin" in the plural at all (although he himself occasionally does so). Consequently, this situation cannot be really changed by individual activity or qualitative improvements. "Therefore our deficiency does not lie in our works but in our nature. Our person, nature, and entire existence are corrupted through Adam's fall."[38] All the individual impulses to sin, in thoughts, words, and actions, arise out of original sin, the original human resistance to God. It is "the truly chief sin"; if not for it, there would be "no actual sin. This sin is not committed, as are all other sins; rather it *is*. It lives and commits all sins and is the real essential sin which does not sin for an hour or for a while; rather no matter where or how long a person lives, this sin is there too."[39] The serpent's head must be cut off! Only at the price of death could original sin, inevitable in every human life, be removed.

It is obvious that under these conditions the power of the will has no tools of its own at its disposal. Luther sees this attested in chapters 1–4 and 7 of Romans. But it is also clear to him simply from the fact that Christ came to earth to save humanity, which otherwise would have been altogether superfluous. Because this is a situation humans cannot alter by themselves, a solution had to be found that comes to them from without and therefore rightly appears to them "foreign."[40] On the human side there remains nothing but what Scholastic theology called a "passive ability" or "fitness" (*aptitudo passiva*), namely allowing oneself to be seized and filled by God's Spirit and grace.[41] Justification is thus not only overcoming the past. Rather, it is a matter of giving the human being a new stance, communicating the true ground of his or her identity so that the person learns to affirm and shape her or his existence.

JUSTIFICATION

Luther's ideas of sin and justification were mutually determinative. Sin, for him, is essentially a break in the relationship between God and the human being; justification must therefore be about the restoration of that relationship. Only in that way can human existence be justified. Sin affects the whole human person, and no one is excepted.[42] Hence it is impossible for a human being to achieve justification on his or her own initiative; it can only be taken charge of and effected by God. It is to be had solely through grace, *sola gratia*, "gratis." Since Luther conceives it as a relational event it must necessarily be thought of in personal categories. It is not made possible by any kind of substantial services but only through what we may call God's personal engagement in Jesus Christ—"for Christ's sake," *propter Christum*. But for that reason it can also only be received personally, that is, solely through faith, *per fidem*. These are the most important keywords that characterize the Reformation doctrine of justification in the Augsburg Confession, Article IV: "It is also taught among us that we cannot obtain forgiveness of sin and righteousness before God by our own merits, works, or satisfactions, but that we receive forgiveness of sin and become righteous before God by grace (*gratis*), for Christ's sake (*propter Christum*), through faith (*per fidem*), when we believe that Christ suffered for us and that for his sake our sin is forgiven and righteousness and eternal life are given to us."

Since this is a righteousness that is at first alien to us it must be transferred to sinful human beings. According to the article cited this takes place because "God will regard and reckon this faith as righteousness."[43] Luther interprets this in different ways, as we will see. He is not constructing a doctrine out of particular theoretical presuppositions, but instead is proceeding on the basis of the New Testament witness: Pure faith encounters him in Jesus Christ; Christ is for him "grace in person" (Werner Elert). In Jesus Christ the new, saving, successful relationship between human beings and God is made real, a relationship that is meant to be accepted and claimed in faith and consequently to have its effects in action.

BY GRACE ALONE

The message of justification receives an argumentative development and demonstration. Why we can posit a justification of humanity "by grace alone" can be demonstrated both "hamartiocentrically"[44] and "theocentrically."

Hamartiocentric foundation

If we accept what Luther says about sin his hamartiocentric demonstration is altogether plausible. Works cannot fundamentally alter a relationship as long as nothing changes in the person who seeks to produce the works. Not even relationships between human persons can be rescued by individual actions and uniquely deserving acts. The action is qualified by the person, not the person by the action. Where Erich Fromm inquired about the relationship between "having" and "being,"[45] Luther's interest was in the relationship between "action" and "being," an inquiry conducted earlier, and in impressive fashion, by Meister Eckhart. In Eckhart's case human existence was understood ontologically, in the framework of Neoplatonic thought, while Luther sees the existence of the new human that alone can be capable of new action in the justifying word of God. Luther often illustrated this by using the example of a good tree that bears fruit entirely of itself: "A good tree cannot bear bad fruit, nor can a bad tree bear good fruit" (Matt 7:18). It makes no sense to hang any kind of fruit on a barren tree; it does not change the tree. It is necessary to graft it anew—which, of course, makes this illustration also somewhat lame.[46] Works remain on a level that is inadequate for restoring community. On that level, in fact, works prove to be an additional disturbing factor: "where there is no faith, there must necessarily be many works; and where these are, peace and unity depart, and God cannot remain."[47] The "work" leads to competition— even with the best of intentions! Only a new human can act in a new way, and a human being is unable in and of himself or herself to become a person with a transformed constitution, a "new human being." A new foundation must come to the human person—"by grace alone."

Theocentric foundation

Alongside this hamartiocentric foundation Luther places a theocentric argument. God is for him simply the Creator whose glory is in creating. The justification of the ungodly is therefore "the exalted special case of divine creation *ex nihilo, sub contraria specie.*"[48] Luther illustrates the clear alternative between human and divine action with special clarity in his explication of the Magnificat: "where man's strength ends, God's strength begins, provided faith is present and waits on Him." And the contrary as well: "where man's strength begins, God's strength ends." God "withdraws His power" and lets people "puff themselves up in their own power alone."[49] Therefore "you should stop your doing so that God may do his work in you!"[50] An impressive example of this appropriate attitude, for Luther, is Mary, the mother of Jesus. She in no way builds herself up, but is glad to be "no more than a cheerful guest chamber and willing hostess" for the great Guest who has announced himself to her.[51]

FOR THE SAKE OF CHRIST

If "works" are an unusable category for reconciliation, the expression "for the sake of Christ" is not to be understood on the level of "service" or "work," any more than faith can be classified as a "work"! Christ is not a fact to be applied but the bearer and communicator of a relationship; he may not be regarded as an instrumentalizable factor. Some of Luther's formulations as well as the expressions in the Augsburg Confession and its Apology give occasion for misunderstanding in this regard. These misunderstandings are probably caused by the fact that the Reformers, when speaking of Christ, did not distinguish as later dogmatic theology did between "person" and "work." For them "person" and "work" come together in Jesus Christ, just as on the other hand—though in a negative sense—in the sinful human being person and work correspond.

Sin destroys the conditions for a successful human existence; separated from the source of life, human life lurches back and forth until it ends in death. In order to give a new quality to human life forever in community with God, and thus at the same time to accomplish divine glory, God places Godself under the conditions of an existence shaped by sin, death, the devil, and the "Law." In Christ, God takes human existence to Godself: not merely performing a service that human beings by themselves cannot do, but entering into the desolate complex of human relationships. God thus becomes the bearer of the existence of all human beings. The task God gives to Christ is to be "all humanity in person" and thus the one who has committed the "sins of all humanity."[52] Christ thus takes on the distorted relationships of humans to God, their fellow human beings, and themselves, while as a result believers can now live in a successful relationship with God, with fellow humans, and with themselves. "Jesus Christ is the person in whom I exist before God."[53] Thus I live now "not I, but Christ lives in me" (Gal 2:20).[54]

Incarnation and cross are to be understood from this fundamental perspective, though the true accent falls on the cross: the Incarnation achieves its deepest point in the cross-event. In the cross of Christ, God takes on the death of the sinner, the consequences of the situation of sin—and in doing so God creates a new counterpart on the side of the sinner: Christ, who "knew no sin" (2 Cor 5:21) "has been made sin for us" and "born under the law" (Gal 4:4).

Christ has "fulfilled" the law (in a multiple sense) and at the same time took on the consequences of unlawfulness and defiance of the law. In him the way to God is opened even for those who break the law; communication between God and the believer succeeds; the fountain of life bubbles forth and light shines on those who "sit in darkness and in the shadow of death" (Luke 1:79). Christ "redeemed us from the curse of the law by becoming a curse for us" (Gal 3:13). The *pro me* or *pro nobis* toward which Luther's argument points is thus not its subjective center of motivation but comes to be seen as a derivation: Christ died for the sins of the whole world, but since unquestionably I myself am part of the world it is necessary to say that his death also took place for the forgiveness of my sins.[55] Luther explains in a variety of argumentative processes derived from tradition where this new founding of human existence in Jesus Christ has led.[56]

The Latin model

Anselm of Canterbury had attempted to explain why God had to become human under the label of "satisfaction" to God, *satisfactio*.[57] He took as his starting point the fact that through their sin humans had dishonored God, but because of the divine holiness God could not simply overlook it. On the other hand, it was not possible for a human being to undo the damage because even if in the future one were to fully conform to the will of God one would only have done what she or he was required to do in any case. The conclusion for Anselm was that God could do nothing, so to speak, other than to act in turn, and that on the other hand the human being could not act even though this was required. Anselm's solution was that the "God human," *Deus homo*, performed satisfaction before God. Luther was able to adopt the concept of "satisfaction" easily enough in explaining the work of Christ: in his priestly office Christ had to "satisfy" God's righteousness "for us. But no other satisfaction was possible than that he offered himself and died and in his own person conquered sin together with death."[58] But this sentence itself reveals that the accent no longer lies on Anselm's rational argument but on the personal initiative of Jesus Christ. Anselm's interest was in demonstrating "the rational evidence for the mystery of the Incarnation"; Luther's focus was on the fruits of Christ's suffering for the despairing conscience.[59] Consequently Luther was also able to criticize the concept of satisfaction, saying that it was "too weak and spoke too little of the grace of Christ, and did not do enough honor to Christ's suffering."[60] In the foreground is not the sacrifice as something objectifiable; even when Luther speaks of the "blood" of Christ he thinks of it not as a thing but in relation to Jesus' surrender of his life. Christ as the high priest, as he appears in the letter to the Hebrews, did not offer something else, as a traditional priest did, or others, as some ideologues and ideologies proposed, but himself. When Luther speaks of the "merit," *meritum*, of Christ he separates it from the "merits" a pious human being hopes to acquire.[61] One is struck by how little emphasis the concept of the "sacrifice of Christ" receives from Luther.[62]

The classical model

Luther adopted the motif of the struggle against a tyrant from the ancient church: sin, death, and the devil, the Law and God's wrath are for Luther the corrupting powers that threaten and enslave human beings. Christ joins them in their condition. Luther portrays Christ as saying: "I myself will be the draft, the poison that will strangle you, death."[63] He associates this with the image, also from the ancient church, of the outwitting of the devil, who, depicted as a dragon, swallows the bait God has set for him in the figure of Christ. Too late he detects the "fishhook"—Christ's divinity! Christ is to the devil "as grass to a dog. For the Christ sticks in his throat" so that he must "vomit him out again."[64] Or again: God has "given the devil a little pill that he will devour with pleasure," but thereby God has caused "such a turmoil in his stomach and in the world" that we can only marvel at it.[65] Christ has placed himself under the tyranny of the Law, "allows the tyrant to rule over him. . . . Now I have won, the Law thinks, but did not know that it has made such a shameful mistake and has condemned and throttled God's son"—now it must "lie under the feet of the one it had condemned."[66] "That was a right wondrous strife when Death in Life's grip wallowed: Off victorious came Life, Death he has quite upswallowed."[67] The biblical reference point for Luther here is the statement of the prophet Hosea: "O death, I will be thy plagues; O grave, I will be thy destruction" (Hos 13:14).[68] The Easter jubilation of the ancient church and of Orthodoxy also echoes here.[69]

Of course, Luther is not aware that there is an alternative between the Latin and classical versions of the doctrine of redemption; he probably would not have recognized any contrast between the two, and in fact the division is probably much narrower than Scandinavian research on Luther has supposed.[70] On the whole we may say that the Latin type dominates the sermons on the passion while the Easter sermons make special use of the ancient church imagery. Both these models for describing redemption through Jesus Christ ultimately culminate in the message of the love of God.

God's redeeming love

Both the idea of satisfaction and the image of the struggle against the tyrant are intended to express what God in Christ has done out of love for humanity. "All this for us did Jesus do, That his great love he might show. . . ."[71]

The background here is the fundamental statement of the Gospel of John: "For God so loved the world that he gave his only Son, so that everyone who believes in him may not perish but may have eternal life" (John 3:16). We may leave open the degree to which a line beginning with Peter Abelard is being adopted here. God identifies with Jesus Christ: "This is my beloved Son . . ." (Matt 13:17). Mystical notes echo when Luther describes what this means for humanity: "With these words God makes the heart of the whole world to laugh and rejoice and flows through every creature with pure divine sweetness and consolation. . . . Now, how could God pour himself out more or give himself more lovingly or sweetly than by saying that it pleases him from the heart that his Son Christ should speak so kindly with me, think of me so feelingly, and suffer, die, and do everything for me with such great love. Do you not think that when a human heart truly feels how God takes such pleasure in Christ when he serves us in this way it must explode into a hundred thousand pieces for sheer joy? For then one would see into the infinite depths of the fatherly heart, indeed into the fathomless and eternal goodness and love of God that he has for us and has had for all eternity."[72]

Admirabile commercium *and* imputatio

How can this salvation effected and given by God in Jesus Christ reach human beings? It does so in that Christ identifies with the sinner and the sinner permits this identification and lays claim to it. Luther understood this identification in two different ways that are apparently contradictory and yet are constitutive of his thought.

To make clear that Christ identifies with believers Luther takes up the model drawn from tradition of the "joyful exchange" (*admirabile commercium*).[73] Faith unites "the soul with Christ as a bride is united with her bridegroom." The result of this marital union is that "Christ and the soul become one flesh. . . . It follows that everything they have they hold in common, the good as well as the evil. Accordingly the believing soul can boast of and glory in whatever Christ has as though it were its own, and whatever the soul has Christ claims as his own. Christ is full of grace, life, and salvation. The soul is full of sins, death, and damnation. Now let faith come between them and sins, death, and damnation will be Christ's, while grace, life, and salvation will be the soul's; for if Christ is a bridegroom, he must take upon himself the things which are his bride's and bestow upon her the things that are his. . . . Here we have a most pleasing vision not only of communion but of a blessed struggle. . . ."[74] So there is not only a communion of goods but an exchange as well. Christ takes on the debts of the sinner while the sinner participates in Christ's riches. "Who can understand the riches of the glory of this grace? Here this rich and divine bridegroom Christ marries this poor, wicked harlot, redeems her from all her evil, and adorns her with all his goodness."[75] Luther can use other images to describe this process: we are to become one "loaf" with Christ, in a kind of analogy to the two natures in Christ: "Now just as God and man are one indivisible person in Christ, so Christ and we also become one inseparable body and flesh. His flesh is in us, and our flesh is in Him, so that He also abides in us with His essence, etc."[76]

These euphoric expressions are, indeed, a contrast to what the sinful human being experiences. Such persons know that it is not merely a matter of the assumption of their previous guilt, but that they will continue to bring new sinfulness into the relationship with Christ. In order not to obscure or even ignore this fact, and yet not to detract from the identity won in Christ, Luther employed the idea of "imputation" (*imputatio*) of the righteousness of Christ or of faith. In doing so he was able to appeal to scholastic tradition.[77] More important for him, however, is Paul's statement: for the one who trusts "him who justifies the ungodly, such faith is reckoned as righteousness" (Rom 4:5). Believers also remain snared in sin, and yet God does not reckon it to their account.[78] Everything depends on the fact of God's "favorable regard and his 'reckoning'" righteousness to them "on the basis of grace."[79] This is about a righteousness that is foreign to human beings (*iustitia aliena*). How can it become their own? It is a remarkable righteousness we are to have, a righteousness "that is not a work, not an idea, and, in short, not at all in us, but outside us in Christ and yet is truly ours through his grace and gift and even our own as if we had achieved and earned it ourselves."[80] Thus justification and declaring righteous are identical!

Those who do not understand or share Luther's approach may object that this is only about a righteousness that is accounted, that consists only of declaration, a righteousness "as if"! But Luther wants to say that what is at issue here is not measured by the superficial criteria of positivistic thinking but by what God makes to be and addresses as the true reality. Not what the human being declares valid but what has validity in the eyes of God, that is what matters! It is not an ontology proposed by human beings that adequately expresses the case. God establishes what "is." Against all appearances, what is real is what God declares valid through his grace! But only faith grasps this.

By faith

If what is at issue in justification, and consequently also in the suffering and death of Christ on which it is founded, is not a "work" but a relationship, then naturally faith itself cannot be understood to be a "work." It by no means takes the place of "works" in the sense that one need perform no good works but must only believe! It is unfortunately the fact that Luther himself occasionally expressed himself in ways that caused him to be misunderstood when, in his early years, he called faith the "principal work": "The first, highest, and most precious of all good works is faith in Christ. . . . For in this work all good works exist, and from faith these works receive a borrowed goodness. . . . It is from faith as the chief work and from no other work that we are called believers in Christ. A heathen, a Jew, a Turk, [or] a sinner may also do all other works; but to trust firmly that he pleases God is possible only for a Christian who is enlightened and strengthened by grace."[81] Human action is deprived of its virtue by sin, while faith gives all action back its value. Therefore Luther should not have used the same word to name what has quality and what does not. The result is a misunderstanding that has had unhappy consequences to the present day. In fact, however, faith is categorically different from action; it is the basis for action before God, though the action itself is unable to give a basis for anything. In a disputation on Romans 3:28 Luther attempted to eliminate any unclarity: this is about the faith that only the Holy Spirit gives and that "shall make Christ effective in us against death, sin, and the law," and that consequently can be called "infused" faith[82]—though differently from the way in which late medieval theology had imagined an "infusion" of grace. But what function does faith have in the event of justification? Faith grasps what God offers the human being, who thereby learns to distinguish between what corresponds to the Gospel and what contradicts it; in all this it is creative.[83]

The applicative function of faith

Faith "grasps" Christ, and at the same time creates the hand, the organ for grasping, by whose aid human beings take the gift given to them.[84] Luther compares it to the prongs of a setting that holds the precious jewel.[85] The essence of faith is that it accepts, receives the living Christ, reaches for him, "apprehends" him (fides apprehensiva).[86] Such faith, naturally, cannot consist only in the communication of information (fides historica). It is insufficient for it to take notice of events in salvation history. Even the demons are in a position to believe "that" God exists—and to tremble at it (Jas 2:19). Such faith has no existential relevance. Nor can this be about a faith that is simply acquired from tradition (fides acquisita); with such a faith one would only be sharing an ideology and identifying with a particular attitude. True faith, in contrast, knows not only that Christ has suffered and that he has been raised, but that this all happened "for me, for my sins."[87] A faith superficially accepted is interested only in the possible benefits it might bring, or else it loses itself in massive speculation. True faith, in contrast, lays claim to what the passion of Jesus Christ has conveyed to human beings and leads to life and salvation. Inappropriate faith "stands like a lazy man concealing his hand under his armpit and says, 'that is nothing to me.'" "True faith with arms outstretched joyfully embraces the Son of God given for it and says: 'He is my beloved and I am his.'"[88] The "for me," "for us," if it is believed, creates true faith and distinguishes it from all other faith that only relies on external events.[89]

Luther interpreted the Apostles' Creed in this very sense in the Small Catechism. It is not a matter of ordinary truths, but that "God has created me and all that exists," that Jesus Christ "has redeemed me," and that the Holy Spirit "has called me through the Gospel, enlightened me with his gifts, and sanctified and preserved me in true faith."[90] Thus all depends not on me but on what comes to me from God. Faith is "a sure trust and firm acceptance in the heart. It takes hold of Christ in such a way that Christ is the object of faith, or rather not the object but, so to speak, the One who is present in the faith itself."[91] Faith is thus not something the human being produces but the way one opens oneself, or more properly the way in which God opens the divine self to the person. To that extent the image of open arms is still inadequate. There is no one who can in and of himself or herself open up to God. Without faith a human being does not live at all in a proper sense, since we have signed ourselves over to mortality and death. In reality the human being is only constituted by God through faith; no one "exists" before God other than in faith: faith makes one a person, grounds one's identity.[92] A believer is not constituted by her or his own ego, but through Christ who lives in him or her (Gal 2:20). The "indwelling" of Christ in me makes me "liberated from the terror of the Law and of sin, pulled out of my own skin, and transferred into Christ and into his kingdom." But "there is no spiritual way for us to grasp the idea that Christ clings and dwells in us as closely and intimately"—in his haste Luther cannot come up with the right images—" as light or whiteness clings to a wall." He wants to express, with Paul, that Christ "is fixed and cemented to me and abides in me"; Christ "lives this life that I have in me; indeed, the life that I thus live is Christ himself. Thus from this point of view Christ and I are already one."[93] The human being is united with Christ through faith even more powerfully than the partners in a marriage are united; "by it you are so cemented to Christ that He and you are as one person, which cannot be separated but remains attached to Him forever."[94] Justification is accomplished in the fact that Christ is so inseparably united with me "that He lives in me and I in Him. What a marvelous way of speaking!"[95]

Seen from the point of view of earthly existence this is indeed an "alien life, that of Christ in me."[96] It follows that faith emancipates me from myself: I no longer matter to myself![97]

The disjunctive function of faith

The faith that rests entirely in Christ and lives altogether from the Gospel is also to be understood as the ability to immediately perceive and reject what is in opposition to God. It is this faith that corresponds to the first commandment because it alone gives to God what belongs to God. To that extent faith is not about the human being but about God and God's glory. In faith God is given God's due.

But for believers this means that in faith they are torn away from their existing reality, which is shaped by sin and law, and so faith and experience conflict. "Here we need to walk in the dark and with our eyes closed, and simply cling to the Word and follow"; one must "close" one's senses, "pull them out," throw oneself on the naked Word. Summa: it sees not itself . . . it grasps not itself, it feels not itself . . . there is nothing in this or that: what one sees is pure nothing."[98] In this nothingness God and the devil can be indistinguishable. It is only by clinging to Christ, who dwells in me as something alien to my experience, that we can be led through this darkness. Faith distinguishes between God and the devil; faith is not just a rapture of spiritual, let alone bodily well-being. Faith cannot be blinded. It distinguishes between the human being and her or his experience, behavior, and actions. Faith sets me outside myself.

The creative function of faith

On the one hand faith de-realizes the old human under sin and the Law, while on the other hand it "consummates" God's divinity. In Luther's lecture on Galatians (1531) we find the statement that faith is "the creator of the Deity, not in the substance of God but in us."[99] This is not couched in mystical categories, as in the verses of Angelus Silesius: "I know God cannot live one instant without Me," or in the sense of Rainer Maria Rilke's fear: "What will you do, God, when I die / When I, your pitcher, broken, lie? / When I, your drink, go stale or dry? I am your garb, the trade you ply, / you lose your meaning, losing me."[100] God does not make God's self dependent on human beings. Faith, naturally, does not have control of God's divinity as such, so that—according to Feuerbach's model of projection—it could constitute deity itself. But Luther is convinced that faith makes God's divinity real for believers. To that extent he can say that faith "makes God."[101] In this, faith is creative: when you believe, you have—an expression Luther often repeated, and of course he did not mean it in the sense of possessions: you do not have "something," rather, God's very self is yours! Certainly that changes everything, my understanding of myself and of the world. I "have" myself anew, I perceive my fellow humans anew, I grasp all reality in a new way. In Luther's terms: sun, moon, earth, water, and air are to the nonbeliever not what they really are—namely from God. Only the believer grasps reality as what it is. This is true especially with regard to suffering, which now can no longer oppress me in any ultimate way. But Luther can also illustrate this in the Eucharist: in faith I grasp that by means of bread and wine Jesus

Christ bestows himself on me. Faith produces for itself a new ontology, one that is made valid by God! Ontology cannot be given as a framework within which the knowledge of faith would have to fit. What is valid is not what a speculative ontology says is reality but what God causes to be truly real.

But what is the relationship of this new thing to our old, familiar ontology of what exists? Luther does not consider this as a philosophical problem, but rather within the question of the relationship between faith and action.

Faith and Action

For Luther, faith and action are not on the same level and cannot mutually augment one another. Instead, faith is the ground of action that does not seek to justify itself and yet is highly effective. This effectiveness becomes the fruit of faith, though in a context that the human being, as long as she or he is on earth, cannot essentially abandon: the believer is and remains "both sinner and justified."

The power of faith

In faith the human being gains access to God's very self. Those who ask whether faith can make one holy even without works have not understood what faith is: "Faith, however, is a divine work in us which changes us and makes us to be born anew of God . . . kills the old Adam" and makes us altogether different persons "and it brings with it the Holy Spirit. O it is a living, busy, active, mighty thing, this faith. It is impossible for it not to be doing good works incessantly. . . ." Faith is "living, daring confidence in God's grace, so sure and certain that the believer would stake his life on it a thousand times. This knowledge of and confidence in God's grace makes men glad and bold and happy in dealing with God and with all creatures. And this is the work which the Holy Spirit performs in faith. . . ."[102] God's Holy Spirit develops its activity in believers, who are filled with a bold confidence in God's grace and a joyous desire to tackle doing good to both friend and foe. Luther treats this theme in a thousand variations. He is not interested merely in presenting the power of faith in general; rather, he wants to show that faith changes a person and also makes one sensitive to such changes. The believer comes to expect that God will begin and undertake something with and in him or her: "You must rather, without any wavering or doubt, realize His will toward you and firmly believe that He will do great things also to you, and is willing to do so. Such a faith has life and being; it pervades and changes the whole man."[103] Thus one should not only expect great things of

God that are conveyed by the situation or other people, but also in regard to oneself a Christian may hope for "great things"—"great," of course, in God's eyes, not career and well-being, but insights, surprising energies of love and hope—although God can by no means be pinned down here to a particular expectation. When Jesus says "follow me," he wants to express that "you yourself must take hold and await what I will do for you."[104] The believer should pay the greatest possible attention to him- or herself and to God, "as though God and he were the only persons in heaven and on earth and as though God were dealing with no one else than with him."[105] When God is at work in a person's faith it is irrelevant what particular things that person undertakes: he or she no longer sets priorities from an empirical point of view. "If he finds his heart confident that it pleases God, then the work is good, even if it were so small a thing as picking up a straw. If the confidence is not there, or if he has any doubt about it, then the work is not good, even if the work were to raise all the dead and if the man were to give his body to be burned."[106] In faith "all works become equal, and one work is like the other; all distinctions between works fall away, whether they be great, small, short, long, many, or few. For the works are acceptable not for their own sake but because of faith, which is always the same and lives and works in each and every work without distinction."[107] A believer does not give a lot of thought to what is to be done and not done and which action is most likely to lead to success, but instead "a Christian man who lives in this confidence toward God knows all things, can do all things, ventures everything that needs to be done, and does everything gladly and willingly, not that he may gather merits and good works, but because it is a pleasure for him to please God in doing these things. He simply serves God with no thought of reward, content that his service pleases God."[108] Given the often emphatic polemics the Reformer directed against late medieval works-righteousness, this pleasant and world friendly side of faith according to Luther has often fallen into the background. But his polemic was in the service of what he wanted to express in positive terms.

THE FRUIT OF FAITH

Luther liked to use the example of a tree and its fruit (cf. Matt 7:16-20) to clarify the relationship between faith and works. "Good works do not make a good man, but a good man does good works. . . . Consequently it is always necessary that the substance or person himself be good before there can be any good works, and that good works follow and proceed from the good person. . . . It is clear that the fruits do not bear the tree and that the tree does not grow on the fruits, also that, on the contrary, the trees bear the fruits and the fruits grow on the trees . . . !"[109] The tree produces good fruit of itself; it is improper to say that it "must" bear good fruit. Luther's view of the spontaneity of faith is somewhat contrary to Melanchthon's anxious observation "that such faith should produce good fruits and good works and that we must do all such good works as God has commanded."[110] But Luther can also use the example of love and marriage to illustrate how spontaneous action arises out of a good relationship. For believers the commandment is no longer a burden; in faith the first commandment of the Decalogue is fulfilled; out of faith grows the new obedience, one that does not feel itself to be such because it is not exercised under the pressure of a law felt to be heteronomous.

Faith and love constitute an inseparable unity. Luther expressed this in unsurpassable fashion at the end of *The Freedom of a Christian*: "a Christian lives not in himself, but in Christ and in his neighbor. Otherwise he is not a Christian. He lives in Christ through faith, in his neighbor through love. By faith he is caught up beyond himself into God. By love he descends beneath himself into his neighbor. Yet he always remains in God and in his love."[111] Faith and love go together like breathing in and breathing out, diastole and systole; faith "goes out into works and through works comes back to itself again."[112] That is its basic movement.

It could appear that the controversy between Reformation and late medieval theologies is founded at this point on a problem of definition: for scholasticism, faith needs to be enhanced by love (*fides caritate formata*), while in Luther's concept hope and love are always thought of as accompanying faith.[113] But Luther did not come to this idea of faith by accident. His concern is that love (and hope) must be qualified by faith if they are not to leave human beings pursuing their own goals that bind the old Adam. For the scholastics faith is "the body, the pod," while love is "the life, the kernel." It is only love that brings "living colors and the fullness itself." For Luther, in contrast, faith is by no means "an empty hull in the heart" that has to be filled with love and brought to life. To describe the miracle of faith Luther reaches for the language of the *theologia negativa*: "Thus faith is a sort of knowledge or darkness that [does not see]. Yet the Christ of whom faith takes hold is sitting in this darkness. . . ." Our righteousness is not a love that must first give form and strength to faith, but faith itself, for "in faith itself Christ is present." [114] Only a love that is supported and imbued with faith can fulfill its mission. If love is isolated from faith it can be played off against faith, in which alone God's "yes" can be grasped; then Luther regards it as extremely dangerous and mistaken. In disgust, Luther shouts in the great lecture on Galatians: "a curse on love!"[115] and yet he immediately clarifies what he means: a curse on love "that is received at the expense of the teaching of faith, to which everything must give way, love, the apostles, the angels from heaven, etc."[116]

There is a love and also a way of talking about love that has nothing to do with Christianity! But there is no faith that has nothing to do with love!

Faith defines love; out of our relationship to God all our other relationships are made right.

Certainly Luther himself knows that at the right time and in the right circumstances one must also speak of love.[117] He bitterly laments that the Reformation has not only not yielded impressive fruits but in some respects has led to a falling off of devotion. Therefore he makes it clear that faith must be preached to the unbelieving, but love to believers! He sees two basic tendencies among his contemporaries: some want to have works without faith, and others faith without works. Self-critically, he includes himself: some do not want to let go of works—and "we" do "not want to hold onto them!"[118]

How did Luther come to terms with this contradiction resulting from everyday experience?

THE BELIEVER: "BOTH SINNER AND JUSTIFIED"

Luther's assertion that a believer is "both justified and sinner" (*simul iustus et peccator*) is certainly not to be understood as a cheap escape, but it has caused a number of misunderstandings. This is by no means about a balance in which, indeed, the weight lies on the fact that one must conclude resignedly that it is impossible to overcome the situation of being a sinner. The fact that this expression is usually quoted with the word "sinner" in the second place seems to confirm this. But Luther himself could write, in the reverse order, that one who is justified is "still a sinner" and is nevertheless regarded by God as "fully and perfectly righteous."[119] The word *simul*, which Luther deliberately repeats, must not be simply replaced with *et*, as often happens; this is about two categorically different perspectives! He certainly does not mean to say that a person is partly righteous and partly sinful. No one can be partly a sinner or partly righteous any more than a woman can be only a little bit pregnant. The whole human being is sinner and righteous! But how can we merge the two in our thinking?

There are a number of alternatives: I am a sinner insofar as I perceive myself as under God's law, and I am righteous insofar as the Gospel is promised to me.[120] But the two do not stand together as things of equal weight; the Gospel calls me to surrender myself to what it promises me. Analogously, we might think: I see myself, under the laws of present reality, as a sinner, but I know that I am under the promise that righteousness is to be given to me eschatologically and therefore eternally. A third possibility would be to start from the assumption that God has begun a new creation in me and will certainly bring that work to perfection, that, although I am still a sinner, for the sake of his action already begun in me God considers me righteous.[121] All these considerations may be at play in Luther's thought, but they are concentrated in the statement: "I am a sinner in and by myself apart from

Christ. Apart from myself and in Christ I am not a sinner."[122] Whether I am a sinner or not is determined by my relationship to Christ. Sin does not represent a quality or nature in myself but a relationship that, certainly, also changes that nature.[123] A theology that can understand sin and righteousness only in the sense of qualities is certainly unable to understand how two "qualities"—black and white—can exist in tandem; the best it can imagine is a kind of muddy white or diluted black. For Luther, in contrast, what is at stake is to be in relationship with the justifying God as the sinner one is, and precisely thus, in this relationship, to change oneself. In relationship with the God who justifies me I am as holy as an angel, but in terms of nature I am full of sin.[124] But faith in Christ draws me into a process of transformation; the dim light I perceive grows brighter; it is the movement from night to morning. Therefore Luther can certainly speak of a spiritual growth: "This life, therefore, is not godliness but the process of becoming godly, not health but getting well, not being but becoming, not rest but exercise. We are not now what we shall be, but we are on the way. The process is not yet finished, but it is actively going on. This is not the goal but it is the right road. At present, everything does not gleam and sparkle, but everything is being cleansed."[125] The Christian life is a life in transition; a *transitus* that is ongoing.[126]

We come, then, to a threefold conclusion:

First, the believer may know: I am righteous insofar as I look to Christ, and I know that my identity is grounded in him.[127] There is nothing more than this acceptance in Christ—it is unsurpassable. Spiritual growth and good works attest to the presence of faith; otherwise faith would prove to be a fiction and worthless (like the foam on beer).[128] The new life serves as a seal and confirmation of the truth that something genuinely new has begun within this person. Therefore: this is not intended in the sense of a *syllogismus practicus*, understood in Calvinistic terms; the believer, too, is constantly confronted by the law of God.[129] She or he is on the way but cannot leave the path behind. Spiritual growth thus serves on the one hand as a confirmation, but at the same time it represents a process: in action I am at work taking possession of my identity. Become who you are—in faith before God! The dialectic of Law and Gospel is reproduced in the dialectic of sinfulness and righteousness of the believer—with the Gospel as the determining goal. To that extent the process does not represent natural growth but is experienced as a constantly renewed being-thrown-back onto God: for Luther, advancing means constantly beginning anew.[130] Being a Christian is therefore a matter of having an incessant "beginner's spirit," expressed in daily repentance, for "when our Lord and Master Jesus Christ said, "Repent" [Matt. 4:17], he willed the entire life of believers to be one of repentance."[131] Through "daily sorrow and repentance" the old Adam in us is to be drowned and "the new man should come forth daily and rise up"—that is Luther's understanding of what baptism means.[132] By meditating on the catechism a person is repeatedly led on this path: the commandments sharpen for her or him what one must do; the creed shows that, despite his or her guilt, it is possible to live a joyful life; the Our Father makes it clear how one is to understand and live this prayer; the sacraments confirm it to him or her in their own way. Finally: the human being is thus free to act and able to act despite all her or his limitations and inadequacy. A person thus gains the courage to accept responsibility and to make decisions even in opaque situations in which one may possibly be unable to avoid incurring guilt.

Luther himself expressed this in his famous letter to Melanchthon from the Wartburg in 1521. During his absence from Wittenberg, Karlstadt had attempted to push the reform forward rapidly; the hesitant Melanchthon felt himself under pressure and disoriented. Luther urges his friend Melanchthon, if he is a preacher of grace, to admit to his own sin. This is the context of the oft-quoted saying: "Be a sinner and sin boldly, but believe and rejoice in Christ even more boldly, for he is victorious over sin, death, and the world."[133] It is clear that Luther is not suggesting libertinism here. Instead he encourages Melanchthon to accept himself as who he is and how he is. In light of the promise of grace one can afford to do so! Here we also find the strength to make decisions, even if they may be wrong or possibly bring guilt on us. I can accept myself with my negative sides, accept my "shadows." Whatever there may be that is negative and destructive, it is "swallowed up in victory . . . but thanks be to God!" (1 Cor 15:54, 57).

CRITICAL EVALUATION

If we enter into the language and thought processes of the Reformer we will not be able to refuse him admiration for the tightness and pastoral richness of his thought. In the context of the internal distresses of his time he presents a concept of Christian existence that sheds new light on God's glory and the salvation of humanity.

Today there are five primary approaches that call Luther's theology of justification into question. Do we find here an anthropocentrism that is outmoded in light of our knowledge about social and ecological connections? Is this a completely one-sided anthropology that cannot be sustained in view of current holistic thinking? What about the exegetical foundation and the possibility of such a foundation for Luther's doctrine of justification? How does Luther's doctrine of justification appear in an ecumenical context—both with regard to the Orthodox churches of the East and to Roman Catholicism, with which there seems, since the Common Declaration on Justification, to be some prospect of agreement? But beyond that, the question remains how and whether Luther's invitation to a life consoled and empowered by justification can be communicated to people who have to exist under conditions completely different from his.

ANTHROPOCENTRISM?

Overdrawn individualism?

Luther has often been accused of irresponsible individualism and unbridled subjectivism. Is his faith really a "reflexive" one that turns everything back on itself? Over and over it is a question of the *pro me*; Luther interprets the whole of the Apostles' Creed as the confession of an individual believer and not of the church: "I believe that God has created me . . . that Jesus Christ . . . is my Lord, who has redeemed me, a lost and condemned creature . . ."[134] Is this a religious inflation of the human ego?[135] Luther would say: forgiveness is indeed applied to the individual; it is individual guilt that must be forgiven; it is, in the first place, the individual believer who is to experience joy in the Gospel! In this the Reformer is part of the history of human self-perception and the development of personality. That subjectivism has also produced some unhappy fruits is another matter. An application to the individual and her or his subjective experience is indispensable and is legitimated by the Gospel itself. But Luther was not content with this anthropological argument. Since it seems to him that everything revolves around an individual human being, God's glory is the center of his thought! The doctrine of justification is about God's divinity—God's justification. God's divinity is realized precisely in the justification of the ungodly. But a recollection of the Old Testament shows that God's glory, differently from the way Luther places the accent, can also be considered in terms of God's covenant and the "people" of believers.

Lack of ecological awareness?

What about Luther's erasure of non-human creation? Does he not empha-size the relationship between God and the human to such a degree that other creatures cannot even enter the picture? Now undoubtedly, as can be demonstrated from numerous witnesses, Luther had an extraordinarily positive attitude toward creation, so that from that point of view alone the objection cannot stand. Nevertheless, we may naturally pose the question whether the doctrine of justification is shaped so anthropocentrically that in this connection the whole reality of creation is neglected. Luther knows, of course, that sin, death, and the devil affect not only the human constitution. All creation is subjected to "futility" (cf. Rom 8:19-23). The Reformer laments that the hog squeals with fear when it is about to be slaughtered; "a tree groans and creaks when it is cut down."[136] But for human beings death is worse than for non-human creation because they anticipate their confrontation with God and know about the connection between sin and death. To that extent the doctrine of justification must in fact be primarily about human beings, for the dignity of every individual person is at stake. It is not cheaply proclaimed and it cannot be determined phenomenologically; it is theologically disclosed by the incarnation, cross, and resurrection of Jesus Christ. This is the only point from which relationships to cosmic horizons can be determined. We cannot conclude from global contexts to the dignity of the individual, but the other way around: God's turning in love to the human being yields a perspective for the universe as well; liberation and renewal are promised to suffering creation also. However, from today's perspective this still does not take creation as such seriously enough. Humanity and creation must not be understood in contrast to each other.

One-sided image of the human?

One can question Luther's anthropology from a great many and very different sides. Is this a pessimistic or—to the contrary—a much too optimistic anthropology? Are there cynical features to Luther's anthropology? Ultimately, how can it be verified empirically in light of today's anthropological insights?

Pessimistic anthropology?

It has been asked again and again whether the human situation really must be painted so "darkly" as it appears to be by Luther. Is human freedom not clearly undervalued? Does the human ability to make judgments not go unrecognized? Is not human moral capacity positively undermined by Luther's negative judgments?

Luther would certainly be misunderstood if his anthropological statements, intended theologically, were interpreted in the sense of an overall evaluation of the natural human being and humanity's possibilities. His conclusions apply to the human situation "before God" (*coram Deo*). They must be carefully distinguished from his quite extraordinarily positive expressions about the human situation as regards relationships between persons (*coram hominibus*). These two levels must be painstakingly separated. The talk of "Law and Gospel," or of the human as *simul iustus et peccator*—and in that order!—that has become so stereotypical has suggested the idea that Luther takes sin as the starting point of his theological reflection. In fact, however, the reverse is true: he speaks about sin only because he starts with grace and wants to speak about it; the "dark side" of his anthropological statements is in service of the light! With "sin" he names what the human being is unable to overcome: *God* has taken the initiative to be answerable for it and to effect redemption from evil. Human beings have no further need to repress their guilt. They can afford to accept their "shadows," something for which psychology, especially in the person of C. G. Jung, emphatically pleads. Now people can accept themselves as they know they are accepted by God. The Law challenges them to confess their sins; under the Gospel they will discover that they no longer need to soften or paper over anything. Under the Gospel there is a new, light-filled definition of the human! As a consequence, believers can be understood in terms of their justification and baptism, and it is a question whether worhip really should begin, as some liturgies prescribe, with a confession of sin or, better, with a recollection of baptism.

Over-optimistic anthropology?

If we accept Luther's argument to this point we can, of course, pose the opposite question, namely, whether he does not have a far too positive estimation of justified human beings. Does faith really produce fruit of itself? Is that Luther's own experience, and is it what believers experience in themselves? Is not the opposite, in fact, the case? Luther was self-critical enough not to make any pretenses here, and he was not sparing in his critique of spiritual carelessness in the Reformation congregations. Nevertheless, he would assert that faith is not to be confused with insight that, in Plato's sense, would lead to the actualization of the good. Nor does Luther see the Gospel as a unique impulse that would then continue to produce new good deeds of itself like a repeating detonator (as one might misunderstand the remarks in the Heidelberg Catechism about "gratitude"). Faith cannot be operationalized. It takes place in the constant movement from Law to Gospel and thus leads ever anew to spontaneous action. Certainly this leaves open the question of how one enters into this dynamic of Law and Gospel and remains held by it. Luther recommends attendance at worship, the home community, prayer. In today's terms this requires explanation: we need to recognize and apply again the values of ascesis, a spiritual order, and a spiritual way of life, without letting this lead us back into legalism.

Cynical anthropology?

Luther's anthropology could be misunderstood in two ways as cynical. On the one hand, the position of humans under Law and Gospel seems to fix a status quo: they know that during their lifetimes they will not escape the polarity of sinfulness and righteousness; they realize again and again that they are sinners and that, on the other hand, they are constantly forgiven. This changes nothing in their basic situation. The ritualized sequence of confession of sin and absolution in the liturgy seems to cement this. Luther would not see this as a fundamental questioning of his theology, but as a critique of practice. What forgiveness means can probably not be generally experienced liturgically today. Instead, it is an important value in personal pastoral care. When concrete guilt is addressed, concrete forgiveness can be experienced. In addition, concrete consequences will appear.[137]

Beyond this, however, what about the "bold sinning" Luther recommended? Does that not lead to carelessness and abuse of grace? The expression has often been taken out of its context, which clearly shows what Luther means. It is sustained and overlaid by a much bolder trust in Christ. As regards "sinning boldly," what is important to the Reformer is that one be aware of its unavoidability and justifiability. He is convinced that the self-understanding of a person who lives in faith and prayer leads to freedom, ability to act, and readiness to accept risk.[138] His position would in fact be cynical if one were to remove faith or misunderstand it as a mere question of worldview. The problem today seems rather to be "cowardly" sinning, namely, sinning with the feeling that one must unfortunately accept its inevitability instead of affirming that one is in a unique guilty situation and seeking to make the best of it, trusting in God.[139]

The empirical "I"

Finally: what about the empirical self? What can I myself contribute and do? If a Christian, as Luther writes at the end of his tractate on freedom, lives on the one hand through faith in God and on the other hand through love for neighbor, in a certain sense that person's self does not "exist"! What about the individual's ability to love and the love that is actually practiced— anthropologically, naturally, erotically?[140] It would be anachronistic to impose on Luther's theology the problem of self-realization in its present ego-related form. Luther is not interested in the individual understood psychologically. He would undoubtedly be critical of what is usually propagated today as self-realization. To love oneself in the way that is sometimes derived today from the twofold love commandment would not be something Luther would regard as conforming to either Law or Gospel. "Self-love" (amor sui) clearly has a negative flavor for him. He knows that eroticism or even social engagement need by no means involve love; the business of diakonia as such does not necessarily contain a genuine caritas! Luther is convinced, instead, that faith purifies and surpasses love, brings love to itself, one might say. Faith grounds identity; hence it is precisely in faith that a self-realization worthy of the name takes place.[141] We seldom hear about that in explanations of Luther's theology. The asymmetry that exists in principle between God's giving and that of the human, which alone gives the believer a good conscience, must not lead to a disavowal of loving surrender to God and fellow human beings.

EXEGETICAL PROBLEMS

The exegetical problematic of Luther's doctrine of justification appears especially at two points: did he not rely one-sidedly on a certain selection of passages from Scripture, and beyond that, can his interpretation of these passages stand in face of today's exegetical insights?

Eclecticism?

A classic reproach to Luther is that he was not a "full hearer" of Sacred Scripture![142] In fact, it is true that the theology of justification is essentially articulated in Paul, whereas it does not seem to appear clearly in the gospels. The Johannine writings, likewise, must first be read in a certain way if they are to be used as a foundation for a theology of justification. Besides these there are a great many statements in Sacred Scripture that appear to contradict Luther's theology of justification, beginning with Paul's notion of a "judgment according to works" (2 Cor 5:10) and ending with the relevant statements in the letter of James and in Old Testament thought in general.[143] It is true that Luther referred to individual statements in the Bible, but it was far from his intention to derive the message of the justification of the ungodly from individual biblical passages. The "full hearer" of Sacred Scripture for him was not someone who leafs through all the possibly applicable biblical passages and thus comes to a conclusion, but instead the one who grasps the center of the biblical witness. It is not on individual passages in the Bible but on the Christ event and especially the cross of Jesus Christ that the justification of the ungodly is grounded.

Example of a failed exegesis?

The passage from Romans that Luther saw as a direct confirmation that the Christian remains a sinner even when justified may serve as an example of the collision between Luther's understanding of a biblical passage and today's exegetical knowledge: ". . . I can will what is right, but I cannot do it. For I do not do the good I want, but the evil I do not want is what I do. . . . Wretched man that I am! Who will rescue me from this body of death? Thanks be to God through Jesus Christ our Lord! So then, with my mind I am a slave to the law of God, but with my flesh I am a slave to the law of sin" (Rom 7:14-25).[144] Luther sees this as having been spoken by a justified person, but Paul is referring to the still unredeemed human under the Law before the encounter with the Gospel. The New Testament undoubtedly places the accent not on the *simul* but on the "new creation" (2 Cor 5:17). Depending on the situation, however, Paul finds himself required to speak against a false claim to "new creation," as one can see in his conflict with the Gnostics in Corinth.

Paraenesis, admonitions, and guidance never seem superfluous to him, even for baptized and justified persons. The petition for forgiveness in the Our Father is never unnecessary. But the "insistent self-grounding of the believer in the alien righteousness of Christ infringes on the new obedience in love."[145] We can see that Luther emphasized the enduring sinfulness of the righteous from his adamant position against late medieval theology and piety, which refused to accept precisely this aspect of the event of justification. But that does not mean that the accent cannot be placed differently today. The longing for a deeper, more vital, more authentic faith should also be taken seriously and discussed as something that is theologically legitimate.

ECUMENICAL QUESTIONS

If we set aside the fact that even within Protestantism criticism can be expressed against Luther's doctrine of justification, for example by way of classical Calvinism or from the perspective of evangelically-oriented groups today, then we may say that especially Roman Catholic theology and, on the other hand, that of Orthodoxy have expressed reservations about Luther's understanding of justification. From both directions we hear the objection that Luther's Christocentrism might work to the detriment of a balanced doctrine of the Trinity.

Challenges from the perspective of the Eastern Orthodox churches

The fundamental tenet of Orthodox theology is from Athanasius: "God became human in order that we might become divine."[146] In the Orthodox view the goal of redemption is divinization. Now, the concept of "divinization" is subject to a high degree of misunderstanding, especially when the distinction between God's "essence" and "energies," which is critical from the Orthodox point of view, is not taken into account. Likewise, in the Orthodox understanding the "divinized" human being is not melded with the essence of God; such a one is—ultimately—filled entirely with the energies of God. The Lutheran doctrine of justification, especially when it is primarily or even exclusively interpreted forensically, appears to fall far short of this concept. Likewise the idea that the justified human must continue to confess that she or he is a sinner appears unable to approach the doctrine of *theōsis*. In fact, there are quite a few statements even in Luther that appear to point in the direction of the Orthodox notion of *theōsis*. Love makes us servants, but faith makes us "masters, yes, through faith we become gods and share in the divine nature and name."[147] The Reformer thus insists that "we are to be sharers in the divine nature and so highly elevated that we are to be loved by God not only through Christ . . . but have him, the Lord himself, dwelling entirely in us. . . ."[148] The outcome of faith is "that you become full of God."[149] Indeed, Luther formulates concisely: "Christ becomes me and I Christ."[150] Finnish study of Luther has brought a great deal of material to light.[151] However, Luther and the Orthodox authors start from completely different ontological presuppositions. It is true that one can say that "divinization belongs at the heart of Luther's Christology,"[152] but we must take care not to equivocate. Luther could probably speak of *theōsis* in the sense of a relational ontology but not a qualitative one. Another important controlling question would be whether Orthodox doctrine of divinization can be placed in a positive relationship with Luther's doctrine of justification. Orthodox theology refers to the expression in 2 Peter: "that you . . . may become participants of the divine nature" (2 Pet 1:4), which Luther also directly cites in some rare instances, but without thought for its ontological implications.

For Luther the starting point is the assertion that in faith Christ himself is present—but "Christ dwells nowhere but in sinners!"[153] It is important to the Reformer to avoid any kind of triumphalism about "sanctification" in which the "old human" would gain the upper hand again.

Challenges from the Roman Catholic perspective

The essential interest of Roman Catholic theology with regard to justification is that there is truly a perceptible transformation in the justified. It must by no means remain a fiction, an "as if" in which nothing concrete is really changed. Therefore this theology has always regarded especially the forensic doctrine of justification with a critical eye.

Luther need not be defended against this criticism by saying, for example, that he had an enormous amount to say about the effectiveness of justification—to the point of the "divinization" of the justified person. At the same time it remains important that for him the righteousness of the new human being remains an "alien" righteousness (*aliena iustitia*)[154] that never becomes a substantive quality by the aid of which one can present oneself before God. Here one of Luther's fundamental convictions comes into play: what is to be regarded as reality is not what we perceive as real with the limited means we have, but what God calls, and indeed constitutes as, "real." Things are as God sees them, not as humans see! It is not reason or the experience of apparently verifiable matters that counts before God; rather, it is God who constitutes and verifies what is and what counts.

Ecumenical discussions on the doctrine of justification have often failed to orient themselves to this fundamental difference, but instead have focused on individual questions. Thus the study *The Condemnations of the Reformation Era: Do They Still Divide?*[155] did not level out the differences. It is said to constitute a "clear difference, indeed an antithesis in the interpretation of the actual matter under discussion . . . when Protestant theology links the righteousness of the believer with the righteousness of Christ *extra se* ('outside himself'), in which the believer participates, and yet at the same time sees the justified person, as far as he himself is concerned, as still a sinner."[156] There also appears a difference in "the contrast of the formulae 'faith alone' here, and 'faith, hope, and love' there."[157] Likewise with regard to the understanding of "merit" opposing views continue to exist; the relationship among justification, baptism, and penance is seen differently.[158] But overall the conclusion is that "as regards our understanding of the justification of the sinner the mutual condemnations of the sixteenth century no longer apply to the partners today in such a way as to divide the churches."[159] The doctrine of justification becomes "a critical measure by which at all times we may test whether a concrete interpretation of our relationship to God can claim the name of 'Christian.' At the same time it is a critical measure for the church, which must be tested at all times to see whether its proclamation and practice corresponds to what has been given it by its Lord."[160] Unfortunately, this document has never received official church ratification.

The *Joint Declaration on the Doctrine of Justification*, signed at Augsburg in 1999, falls regrettably short of the statements quoted above in some respects. Here the doctrine of justification is only "an indispensable criterion which constantly serves to orient all the teaching and practice of our churches to Christ."[161] The discussions on both sides, which as a whole have been unsatisfying, and the tug-of-war over the supplementary documents—the Official Common Statement and its Annex—have probably deprived the document of much of its ecclesial and ecumenical influence.[162] The ultimate frustration has been that even the signing of the document has thus far produced no visible ecumenical effects. On the contrary: there followed, on the Catholic side, the document *Dominus Iesus*, and from German Protestantism the response, *Kirchengemeinschaft nach evangelischem Verständnis* [Lutheran View of Church Community],"[163] which also neglects to address directly the "consensus in basic truths"[164] thus achieved.

On the whole it appears that despite some formal agreements there remains an essential difference between the Roman Catholic and Lutheran convictions. The Catholic position is apparently not able to accept the fourfold *solus* of the Reformation. But that fourfold "alone" should not be misunderstood in Protestantism either:

Sola gratia—"through grace alone and without works" does not mean without the "cooperation" (Karl Barth) of the human, and that means the whole human person; justification does not take place "behind the backs" of people (Paul Althaus). Solely "for Christ's sake" and "not for our sake or that of holy merits" does not mean without the working of the Creator and the Holy Spirit! "Through faith alone" does not mean without love and without hope, even though love and hope remain subordinate and are not to be seen as augmenting faith. "Through Scripture alone" does not mean without the history and present state of its interpretation in the context of the conditions for understanding at a given time.

The *particulae exclusivae* of the Reformation are battle cries that address a very concrete opposition. They exclude what is to be excluded in light of the Gospel, but it is necessary to take care that we do not exclude what must or may remain included.

Inappropriate Christocentrism?

It is a misunderstanding to suppose that Christology should be formulated at the expense of the doctrine of the Trinity, or the doctrine of justification at the expense of the doctrines of creation and pneumatology. Luther's doctrine of justification is christocentrically oriented and thus corresponds to the New Testament witness. But this in itself means that the triune God must be seen as the author of justification. In the event of justification the action is that of both God the Creator and God the Holy Spirit, who "gives life." Both moments are contained in Luther's theology, but not always explicitly. Justification is understood as the full expression of God's divinity, the result of God's creative power *ex nihilo*; justification through Christ is not realized apart from the work of the Holy Spirit as encountered in word and sacrament. In the experience of grace that is forgiveness the graces of creation and renewal are both expressed. Justification is regarded as a holistic event in which the "whole," namely the triune God, participates and into which the "whole" human being, with body, soul, and spirit, is drawn. Luther did not consider this explicitly from a trinitarian point of view, and amending that could be a fruitful ecumenical project today.

THE PROBLEM OF COMMUNICATION

The message of justification was at one time communicable—in the context of a church and society marked by excessive but burdensome piety. Luther and other Reformation preachers had at least limited success in expressing what it is about the Gospel that brings happiness, and thus infecting people with it. The Reformer was able to move those who heard his preaching into the event of justification and awaken gratitude in them for God's endless love. The "dear Christians"[165] really did rejoice, and many even began to compose hymns. "Salvation unto us has come / By God's free grace and favor . . ." wrote Paul Speratus in 1523.[166] "A true faith sates God's wrath / a lovely fountain rises / called fraternal love / from it one knows a Christian," so Nikolaus Herman, 1562.[167] The Reformer was able to draw believers into the persuasive power of his imagery especially by his use of language rich in metaphors. The vivid and colorful way he described Christ's battle with the devil (*duellum mirabile*)[168] is perhaps the best example of how listeners were attracted with a "faithful affect into the evidence" of the event of salvation.[169] Nowadays the Dalai Lama is more successful in conveying a message with its "faithful affect" than any Lutheran pastor; the former leaves the pulpit laughing.

What does this show? The message of justification develops its function only under particular conditions; it is not the master key for every preaching situation. It is still only communicable in limited fashion to people socialized in the Lutheran Church, who understand Luther's language and that of the Luther Bible and share the Lutheran confession as their life-perspective. Certain situations in life can also present the precondition for receiving the message: involvement in personal guilt, unbearable pressure to produce, compulsion and pressure to be perfect. In this context there are also ways to translate the concept of "justification" that carry with them at least a part of its original content: relief, liberation, acceptance by God, being "acknowledged by God,"[170] being able to begin again, allowing oneself to be told by God, contrary to all experience: you are okay. The theology of justification is especially useful in a context of establishing identity[171] and self-realization, understood evangelically.[172] It must still be discovered within the discussion around human dignity and human rights. Here the liberal formula about the "infinite value of the human soul" can be meaningfully applied.

At the time of the Reformation many people could not only acknowledge intellectually but also experience and feel in their very bones what justification means. It is vital that today the message be made present as something one can experience, something by which one may orient one's life, something that is absolutely worth living; it is probably more or less hopeless to try to convey the idea of justification only verbally. In a context in which there is no corresponding ability to listen, words like sin and justification, representation and rebirth are not only incomprehensible but probably grotesque. It is cynical to speak of psychic relief if it, or at least some indications of it, cannot be experienced within a community. Talk about the dignity of the human and human rights remains mere twaddle if dignity is never addressed and is not respected in concrete ways, and when justice is not established as broadly as possible, through external sources of aid as well. It is only in such contexts that the message of justification is audible. It must be painstakingly located and answered to within a context of thought and one that is appropriate to people's lives.

But that means that the doctrine of justification is not a brand name with which one can advertise and canvass. It is a deep mystery belonging to the innermost secrets of the Christian community. It lives, in traditional language, out of confession and absolution. It is concentrated in the sacrament. Wherever people seek and are granted concrete forgiveness, there justification by God can be existentially comprehended and received.

What does that mean for the church's public proclamation? It must avoid exalting the Gospel as a useful therapeutic means, a training that promotes wellness, and it must certainly not portray it as a delicious meal that elevates the sense of living. The Gospel undoubtedly has perceptible functions; it gives an anchor for the sense of life's meaning. But if we try to ground acceptance of the message on its functions, the offer turns into oppressive legalism: you must only accept this, must only believe, but that you must do, and therefore you should go to church more often and certainly not abandon the church! But the result is not faith, only aversion. Luther did not appeal to people with his theology of justification, or on its behalf. He knew that only the Holy Spirit awakens faith and that one must be born of God if one wants to understand the Gospel message.[173] Preaching today can therefore not aim directly at justification, as might have been possible in Luther's time because of other circumstances. A Lutheran church should thus not beat the drum and shout "freedom!" as a slogan to attract people, or go around knocking on doors with the offer of justification. Rather, it should sharpen people's sense of injustice and publicly demand the overcoming of injustice and guilt. With those ideas it can make itself understood even in the secular realm.

For preaching in worship, which despite its open accessibility can no longer be regarded as something public, other conditions apply. For a long time Luther's message of justification has been communicated more in a sense of how it can be psychologically translated into existential terms. But his theology had a double emphasis: the salvation of humans *and* the glory of God. Today it seems that not only must the fact that these two belong together be rediscovered, but also the accent must be placed differently: away from a psychological functionalization of justification in the sense of an aid for living (which the Gospel undoubtedly possesses), and toward the proclamation of the glory of God, which only appears to be without function. "O Lord, open my lips, and my mouth will declare your praise!" (Ps 51:17).

What does preaching have to say, then? It must admit its poverty of plausibility and argumentative power and bravely attempt to take biblical texts seriously, to explain them and open them up for the present time. It must shed light on the figure of Jesus as presented in the gospels and reflected in the other New Testament writings. This in turn must be embedded in a lifestyle on the part of individual Christians and whole congregations that reveals acceptance and encouragement, and in an active engagement of the churches on behalf of the dignity and rights of human beings. This will create certain preconditions out of which the message of justification can at least be comprehended. Only in this way can there be a hope that, when God gives God's grace, people may gradually find their way into the secret mystery of divine justification, understand their lives anew, and from this both orient and shape what they do and do not do.

Notes

[1] ". . . isto articulo stante stat Ecclesia, ruente ruit Ecclesia," WA 40/3, 352, 3.

[2] The Eucharist "is the heart of the church, its basis, its foundation, without which the existence of the church is unthinkable," Hilarion Alfejev, *Geheimnis des Glaubens. Einführung in die orthodoxe dogmatische Theologie* (Fribourg: Universitätsverlag, 2003), 158.

[3] Cf. Eberhard Jüngel, *Das Evangelium von der Rechtfertigung des Gottlosen als Zentrum des christlichen Glaubens: eine theologische Studie in ökumenischer Absicht* (Tübingen: Mohr Siebeck, 1998).

[4] WA 30/2, 652–57.

[5] Cf. *De remissione peccatorum*, 1518 = Heidelberg Disputation, LW 31, 35–70; *Quaestio, utrum opera faciant ad iustificationem*, 1520 = Treatise on Good Works, LW 44, 15–114; Theses for five disputations on Rom 3:28, 1535–37 = The Disputation Concerning Justification, LW 34, 145–96; *De veste nuptiali*, 1537 (LDStA 2, 443–46); *De fide iustificante*, LW 34, 105–32.

[6] See "The Brilliance of Christian Freedom" in chapter 9.

[7] Peters 1984, 35, distinguishes between the "monastic front" and the "peasant front."

[8] Cf. LDStA 2, 87–91 (*Sententiae de lege et fide*, 1519); 447–60 (Theses for the first disputation against the Antinomians, 1537; cf. LW 47, 99–119).

[9] For the literature see Eberhard Jüngel, *Das Evangelium von der Rechtfertigung des Gottlosen als Zentrum des christlichen Glaubens* (Tübingen: Mohr Siebeck, 1998); cf. Gerhard Müller, *Die Rechtfertigungslehre* (Gütersloh: Gütersloher Verlagshaus, 1977); Otto Hermann Pesch, *Die Theologie der Rechtfertigung bei Martin Luther und Thomas von Aquin* (Mainz: Grünewald, 1967); Albrecht Peters, *Rechtfertigung*, HST 12 (Gütersloh: Gütersloher Verlagshaus, 1984), bibliography on pp. 326–29; Vittorio Subilia, *Die Rechtfertigung aus Glauben* (Göttingen: Vandenhoeck & Ruprecht, 1981); Schwambach 2004; for bibliography on the ecumenical problem see "Contemporary Questions" in chapter 10 and "Ministry and Orders" in chapter 11.

[10] Against Dietrich Korsch, "2. Die religiöse Leitidee," *Handbuch* 2005, esp. 92, 94, and idem, "3. Glaube und Rechtfertigung," ibid., 373–81, esp. 374.

[11] Cf. Michael Beintker, "Neuzeitliche Schuldwahrnehmung im Horizont der Rechtfertigungsbotschaft," in idem, et al., eds., *Rechtfertigung und Erfahrung* (Gütersloh: Kaiser, 1995), 137–52.

[12] Cf. Ibid.

[13] Cf. Anton Hügli, "Malum VI. Neuzeit," HWP 5: 681–706 (esp. 686–91).

[14] Cf. Christof Gestrich, *The Return of Splendor in the World: The Christian Doctrine of Sin and Forgiveness* (Grand Rapids: Eerdmans, 1997).

[15] Cf. *ST* II, 1, 55, 4.

[16] This is a remarkable "simul" pointed out by Iwand 1983, 65–66.

[17] *The Book of Concord*, 29.

[18] Rom 14:23b.

[19] LW 35, 14 (WA 2, 717, 33-34).

[20] LW 34, 151 (LDStA 2, 424/425), Thesis 1.

[21] WA 7, 212, 4ff.

[22] LW 13, 107 (WA 40/3, 537, 12-13).

[23] WA 45, 356, 18-19: ". . . et tu contra cum illis, etiam secundum corpus."

[24] LW 31, 50 (WA 1, 360, 27-28): ". . . dum facit quod est in se, peccat et sua quaerit omnino."

[25] WA 40/2, 325, 7-8.

[26] ". . . quia non quae Dei, sed quae sua sunt in ipso etiam deo et sanctis eius quaerunt suntque sibi ipsis huius operis sui ultimus (ut dicitur) finis et idolum, utentes deo, fruentes seipsis," WA 1, 425, 2-5.

[27] LW 25, 346 (WA 56, 356, 27; 357, 2ff.).

[28] WA 40/2, 325, 7.

[29] LW 34, 138 (LDStA 1, 666/667), Thesis 17.

[30] Ibid., 139, Thesis 31; accordingly, Aristotle "knows nothing of theological man," Thesis 28.

[31] The German term is "Erbsünde," literally "inherited sin."—Tr.

[32] Ibid., Theses 24, 26–30.

[33] LW 31, 10 (LDStA 1, 22/23), Thesis 17.

[34] Jürgen Moltmann, *The Crucified God. The Cross of Christ as the Foundation and Criticism of Christian Theology* (New York: Harper & Row, 1974), 300–1, 337–38.

[35] Cf. Lubomir Batka, *Peccatum radicale. Eine Studie zu Luthers Erbsündenverständnis in Psalm 51* (Frankfurt: Peter Lang, 2007).

[36] LW 37, 362 (WA 26, 502, 7-12).

[37] Ibid., 363 (WA 26, 503, 32). Bayer 2003, 174, comments: "although grammatically 'my mother' is the subject and 'I' the object, Luther in his explication reverses the order so that the subjectivity, personality, and unsubstitutable nature of my self in my sinfulness remain beyond all doubt: "'in sin did my mother bear me,' i.e., in my mother's womb I have grown from sinful seed, as the Hebrew text signifies." Of course, that is a line of argument that can in no way be persuasive today!

[38] LW 52, 151 (WA 10/1/1, 508, 6-8); cf. LW 32, 225 (WA 8, 104, 26-29).

[39] Ibid., 152 (WA 10/1/1, 508, 20–509, 4).

[40] LW 34, 153 (LDStA 2, 426/427), Thesis 27. Althaus (1961, 51) clarifies this by reference to LW 34, 178 (WA 39/1, 109, 1): "Extra nos esse est ex nostris viribus non esse. Est quidem iustitia possessio nostra, quia nobis donata est ex misericordia, tamen est aliena a nobis, quia non meruimus eam" ("To be outside of us means not to be out of our powers. Righteousness is our possession, to be sure, since it was given to us out of mercy. Nevertheless, it is foreign to us, because we have not merited it").

[41] LW 33, 67 (WA 18, 636, 6): ". . . rapi spiritu et imbui gratia Dei." What is remarkable is Luther's reference to God's patience, which bears human wickedness in order to prevent something worse, as "an ulcer, limping, or some other incurable illness in the body is tolerated out of necessity for supporting bodily life," LW 34, 152 (LDStA 2, 426/427), Theses 14, 15; cf. 19.

[42] The Law brings it to light; see "Law" in chapter 7.

[43] *The Book of Concord*, 30.

[44] From Greek *hamartia*, "failure, error, sin."

[45] Erich Fromm, *To Have or to Be?* (New York: Continuum, 2008).

[46] Ibid.

[47] LW 21, 305 (WA 7, 552, 24-25).

[48] Althaus 1962, 118.

[49] LW 21, 340 (WA 7, 586, 12-13, 23).

[50] EG 231 ("Das sind die heiligen zehn Gebote," 4 (with reference to the third commandment of the Decalogue); cf. EG 138, "Gott der Vater steh uns bei" = "God the Father, with us be," LW 53, 268–70.

[51] LW 21, 308 (WA 7, 555, 27).

[52] WA 40/1, 437, 25-26. In the same inner-trinitarian address Christ is commissioned by God: "'Tu sis Petrus ille negator,' you are the persecutor Paul, the adulterer David . . ." ibid., 437, 23-27.

[53] Lienhard 1980, 220.

[54] Cf. Barth, Hans-Martin 2002.

[55] LW 34, 110 (LDStA 2, 405), Theses 24, 19.

[56] On this cf. Barth, Hans-Martin 1967, esp. 50–82; Bornkamm, Karin 1998; Rieske-Braun 1999.

[57] In what follows I am adopting the divisions suggested and defended by Gustav Aulén.

[58] LW 52, 281 (WA 10/1/1, 720, 19–721, 1).

[59] Rieske-Braun 1999, 196.

[60] WA 21, 264, 27-35.

[61] Cf. WA 40/1, 264, 1-3.

[62] When Luther speaks of "sacrifice," "blood of Christ," or "Lamb of God" it is as a rule not in connection with the theory of sacrifice but about the depths of God's love and the measure of the salvation associated with it.

[63] WA 27, 117, 5-6.

[64] WA 20, 334, 16–335, 2.

65 WA 47, 80, 21-23.

66 WA 23, 709, 5-12. In this sermon on the Ascension (1527) Luther goes to particularly great lengths in describing how the Law was outwitted.

67 "Death Held Our Lord in Prison," v. 4, LW 53, 255–57 (WA 35, 444, 6-11 [= EG 101, 4]).

68 Thus the Authorized Version. Modern translations are different, e.g., the NRSV: "O Death, where are your plagues? O Sheol, where is your destruction?"—Tr.

69 Cf. the Orthodox liturgy of Easter, "thanaton thanato patisas. . . ."

70 Cf. the Orthodox liturgy of Easter, "thanaton thanato patisas. . . ."

71 "All Praise to thee, O Jesus Christ" (Martin Luther 1524), LW 53, 241, v. 7.

72 WA 20, 228, 28-30; 229, 7-15.

73 Cf. Raymund Schwager, *Der wunderbare Tausch. Zur Geschichte und Deutung der Erlösungslehre* (Munich: Kösel, 1986), and Walter Allgaier, *"Der fröhliche Wechsel" bei Martin Luther. Eine Untersuchung zu Christologie und Soteriologie bei Luther unter besonderer Berücksichtigung der Schriften bis 1521*, Dissertation Erlangen-Nuremberg 1966. "And through the interchange of his blessings and our misfortunes, we become one loaf, one bread, one body, one drink, and have all things in common," LW 35, 58 (WA 2, 748, 17-18); Christ has so much "crept into me, ut mea omnia habeat," WA 17/1, 188, 1-2; "Christ becomes me and I Christ," WA 17/1, 187, 9.

74 LW 31, 351 (WA 7, 25, 27-34).

75 LW 31, 351 (WA 7, 25, 27-34).

76 LW 23, 149 (WA 33, 232, 24-30); in the continuation of the quotation, certainly, Luther points out the limitations of the analogy.

77 For discussion of this see Pesch 1982, 314–15.

78 For discussion of this ibid.

79 LW 33, 271 (LDStA 1, 618, 25-26): "favente et reputante Deo." See the additional resources cited at that point in LDStA.

80 WA 46, 44, 34-38.

81 WA 46, 44, 34-38.

82 LW 34, 109–10 (LDStA 2, 403–5), Theses 1, 10, 16.

83 In what follows I am adapting ideas and passages from the text of my essay on creative faith in Hans-Martin Barth, "Fides Creatrix Divinitatis. Bemerkungen zu Luthers Rede von Gott und dem Glauben," NZST 14 (1972): 89–106.

84 In early Protestant orthodoxy faith was occasionally called "organon leptikon."

85 LW 26, 90 (WA 40/1, 165, 3).

86 LW 34, 110 (LDStA 2, 402/403), Thesis 12.

87 Ibid. (LDStA 2, 404/405), Thesis 18: "hoc totum pro me, pro peccatis meis."

88 Ibid., Theses 21, 22: "Fides vera extensis brachiis amplectitur laeta filium Dei pro sese traditum."

89 LW 34, 111, Thesis 24, " . . . illud, Pro me, seu Pro nobis, si creditur, facit istam veram fidem."

90 *The Book of Concord*, 345.

91 " . . . in ipsa fide Christus adest," LW 26, 129 (WA 40/1, 229, 15).

92 " . . . fides facit personam," WA 39/1, 283, 1.

93 LW 26, 167 (WA 40/1, 283, 26-32).

94 LW 26, 168 (WA 40/1, 285, 24-27).

95 LW 26, 167 (WA 40/1, 284, 20-22).

96 "Est igitur duplex vita: Mea naturalis vel animalis, et aliena, scilicet Christi in me," LW 26, 170 (WA 40/1, 287, 28-29).

97 Cf. Ayya Khema, *Ohne mich ist das Leben ganz einfach. Der Weg des Buddha zur vollkommenen Freiheit* (Bielefeld: Aurum, 32001).

98 LW 37, 296 (WA 26, 440, 3-4); WA 25, 238, 27; 47, 29, 23-26).

99 "Fides est creatrix divinitatis non in persona, sed in nobis," LW 26, 227 (WA 40/1, 360, 5).

100 Angelus Silesius, *Selections from The Cherubinic Wanderer*, trans. John Ernest Crawford Flitch (London: Allen & Unwin, 1932), 85 (I. 8), p. 97; Rainer Maria Rilke, "Was wirst du tun, Gott, wenn

ich sterbe?" (1899), *Poems from the Book of Hours*, Bilingual Edition, trans. Babette Deutsch (New York: New Directions, 22009), 22–23.

[101] WA 30/1, 28, 3.

[102] LW 35, 370–71 (WA.DB 7, 10, 5-10, 16-19).

[103] LW 21, 306 (WA 7, 553, 31-33).

[104] Ibid., 318 (WA 7, 565, 8).

[105] Ibid., 319 (WA 7, 565, 38–566, 2).

[106] LW 44, 25 (WA 6, 206, 10-13).

[107] Ibid., 26 (WA 6, 206, 33-37).

[108] Ibid., 27 (WA 6, 207, 26-30).

[109] LW 31, 361 (WA 7, 32, 5-12); see "Hamartiocentric foundation" above.

[110] *The Book of Concord*, 31 (Augsburg Confession VI, 1).

[111] LW 31, 371 (WA 7, 38, 6-10).

[112] LW 44, 79 (WA 6, 249, 32-33).

[113] Cf. Pesch 1982, 158–62.

[114] LW 26, 129–30 (WA 40/1, 228, 18–229, 28).

[115] Pesch 1982, 158: ". . . a monstrous saying in light of 1500 years of Christian reflection on love of God and neighbor. One quotes it with reservations, but there it is. . . ."

[116] LW 27, 38 (WA 40/2, 47, 26-27), on Gal 1:8.

[117] LW 26, 279–80 (WA 40/1, 240, 17-20).

[118] "Fides praedicatur non credentibus, charitas fidelibus. . . . Hi nolunt ab operibus auffhorn, wir nit hin an," WA 15, 435, 2-7.

[119] "Ideo et peccator est adhuc, quisquis iustificatur, Et tamen velut plene et perfecte iustus reputatur, ignoscente et miserente Deo," LW 34, 152–53 (LDStA 2, 426/427), Thesis 24. Cf. LW 25, 258 (WA 56, 272, 17-18): ". . . sed simul peccator et Iustus; peccator re vera, Sed Iustus ex reputatione et promissione Dei certa. . . ." For the reverse order see LW 27, 231 (WA 2, 497, 13): "Simul ergo iustus, simul peccator."

[120] WA 39/1, 316 (LDStA 2, 441), Theses 36, 37.

[121] ". . . propter initium creaturae suae in nobis . . ." LW 34, 152 (LDStA 2, 426), Thesis 22. For the argument between Paul Althaus and Karl Holl cf. *LuJ* (1961), 50–51.

[122] LW 38, 158 (WA 38, 205, 28-29). See other corresponding formulae in Ebeling 1989, 536–37.

[123] "The Christian, as the old creature, is to be regarded as a sinner according to his nature (*qualitas*), but in his relationship (*relatio*) to Christ he is righteous and holy," Streiff 1993, 182.

[124] ". . . in relatione tam sanctus, quam angelus. . . . Sed christianus consideratus in qualitate est plenus peccato," WA 39/2, 141, 1-5.

[125] LW 32, 24 (WA 7, 337, 30-35).

[126] ". . . qui non fuerit in transitu, hunc nec Christianum arbitreris," LW 27, 289 (WA 2, 536, 5).

[127] Here Luther's theology of baptism also enters in; see chapter 10 below.

[128] WA 10/3, 297, 18–298, 1.

[129] Cf. Peters 1984, 54.

[130] ". . . proficere, hoc est semper a novo incipere," LW 25, 478 (WA 56, 486, 7ff.). Luther recalls St. Arsenius, who prayed every day: "Adiuva me, Domine, Ut incipiam tibi vivere!—Help me, Lord, to begin to live for you!"

[131] LW 31, 25 (WA 1, 233, 10-11); first of the "Ninety-Five Theses" of 1517.

[132] *The Book of Concord*, 349.

[133] LW 48, 282 (WA.Br 2, 372, 84-85); Cf. Barth, Hans-Martin 1984.

[134] *The Book of Concord*, 343.

[135] Cf. Paul Hacker, *Das Ich im Glauben bei Martin Luther* (Graz, et al.: Styria, 1966); on this cf. also Bayer 2003, 151ff.

[136] LW 13, 107 (WA 40/3, 537, 11-13); cf. Barth, Hans-Martin 1989; and see "Sin, death, and the devil" in chapter 14.

[137] Cf. Christof Gestrich, *The Return of Splendor in the World: The Christian Doctrine of Sin and Forgiveness* (Grand Rapids: Eerdmans, 1997), 249–62.

[138]It depends on one's theological stance whether one sees the common advice on confession by Luther, Bucer, and Melanchthon (and six other theologians) to Philip of Hesse as "bold," "cowardly," or not as "sinning" at all! Cf. Leppin 2006, 315–16; Schneider-Ludorff 2006, 190–98; WA.Br 8, 638–43.

[139]Cf. Luke 16:9: "Make friends for yourselves by means of dishonest wealth. . . ."

[140]Cf. Holm 2006, as well as Roselies Taube, *Gott und das Ich—erörtert in einer Auseinandersetzung mit Luthers Lehre über Glauben und Liebe in seinem Galaterkommentar 1531/35* (Frankfurt: Peter Lang, 1986).

[141]See Hans-Martin Barth, *Fulfilment*, trans. John Bowden (London: SCM, 1980); cf. also Barth, Hans-Martin 1997.

[142]Cf. Joseph Lortz, quoted in Pesch 1982, 68.

[143]Cf. the exegetical considerations in the *Joint Declaration on the Doctrine of Justification* (Grand Rapids: Eerdmans, 2000).

[144]NRSV. Cf. LW 25, 328–36 (WA 56, 349–50). Cf. Oda Wischmeyer, ed., *Paulus: Leben, Umwelt, Werk, Briefe* (Tübingen: Francke, 2006), 240–304 (bibliography!).

[145]Peters 1984, 322.

[146]Athanasius, *De incarnatione Verbi*, PG 25, 192B.

[147]WA 17/2, 74, 2-29.

[148]WA 21, 458, 11-16.

[149]WA 17/1, 438, 14. The expression "become full of God," however, cannot be clearly parsed grammatically.

[150]WA 17/1, 187, 9.

[151]Simo Peura, *Mehr als ein Mensch? Die Vergöttlichung als Thema der Theologie Martin Luthers von 1513–1519* (Mainz: von Zabern, 1994); Tuomo Mannermaa, "Grundlagenforschung der Theologie Martin Luthers und die Ökumene," in *Thesaurus Lutheri. Auf der Suche nach neuen Paradigmen der Luther-Forschung. Referate des Luther-Symposiums in Finnland 11.–12. November 1986* (Helsinki: Finnische Theologische Literaturgesellschaft, 1987); idem, *Der im Glauben gegenwärtige Christus. Rechtfertigung und Vergottung* (Hannover: Lutherisches Verlagshaus, 1989): English (partial): *Christ Present in Faith: Luther's View of Justification* (Minneapolis: Fortress Press, 2005); Steven E. Ozment, *Homo spiritualis. A Comparative Study of the Anthropology of Johann Tauler, Jean Gerson and Martin Luther (1509–1516) in the Context of their Theological Thought* (Leiden: Brill, 1969); Reinhard Flogaus, *Theosis bei Palamas und Luther* (Göttingen: Vandenhoeck & Ruprecht, 1997); Heubach 1990, with bibliography.

[152]Ulrich Asendorf, "Die Einbettung der Theosis in die Theologie Martin Luthers," 85–102 in Heubach 1990, at 99.

[153]"Christus enim non nisi in peccatoribus habitat," LW 48, 13 (WA.Br 1, 35, 29).

[154]"Now it is certain that Christ or the righteousness of Christ, since it is outside of us and foreign to us, cannot be laid hold of by our works; But faith itself which is poured into us from hearing about Christ by the Holy Spirit, comprehends Christ. Therefore, faith alone justifies without our works, for I cannot say, 'I produce Christ or the righteousness of Christ.' . . . But I must speak thus, 'I believe in Christ and afterward I do truly good works in Christ,'" LW 34, 153 (LDStA 2, 427–29), Theses 27–29, 31.

[155]Karl Lehmann and Wolfhart Pannenberg, eds., *The Condemnations of the Reformation Era: Do They Still Divide?* (Minneapolis: Fortress Press, 1990), 47.

[156]Ibid., 53.

[157]Ibid., 56.

[158]Ibid., 72ff, 63ff.

[159]Ibid., 74.

[160]Ibid., 75.

[161]*Joint Declaration*, §18.

[162]There is an account of the origins and discussion by Beatus Brenner, *Kirchliches Jahrbuch* (1998): 55–133, with a reprinting of the documents on pp. 134–58 and bibliography on pp. 158–60.

[163] *Kirchengemeinschaft nach evangelischem Verständnis. Ein Votum zum geordneten Miteinander bekenntnisverschiedener Kirchen. Ein Beitrag des Rates der Evangelischen Kirche in Deutschland*, EKD-Texte 69 (Hannover: Kirchenamt der EKD, 2001).

[164] *Joint Declaration*, §43.

[165] Martin Luther, "Dear Christians, Let Us Now Rejoice," LW 53, 217 ("Nun freut euch, lieben Christen g'mein," EG 341, 1).

[166] Paul Speratus, "Salvation unto us has come," LH 377 ("Es ist das Heil uns kommen her," EG 342).

[167] Nikolaus Herman, "Ein wahrer Glaube Gotts Zorn stillt," EG 413; cf. Johann Agricola, "Ich ruf zu dir, Herr Jesus Christ," EG 343; Georg Grünwald, "Kommt her zu mir, spricht Gottes Sohn," EG 363; Martin Schalling, "Lord, Thee I Love with All My Heart," LH 429 ("Herzlich lieb hab ich dich, O Herr," EG 397); Benjamin Schmolck, "Weicht, ihr Berge," EKG 243; idem, "Himmelan geht unsre Bahn," EKG 248.

[168] Cf. "For the sake of Christ" above.

[169] Cf. Rieske-Braun 1999, 258.

[170] Thorsten Waap, *Gottebenbildlichkeit und Identität. Zum Verhältnis von theologischer Anthropologie und Humanwissenschaft bei Karl Barth und Wolfhart Pannenberg* (Göttingen: Vandenhoeck & Ruprecht, 2008) gives an impressive account of this (with reference to Paul Ricoeur, *Wege der Anerkennung. Erkennen, Wiedererkennen, Anerkanntsein* [Frankfurt: Suhrkamp, 2006]).

[171] Cf. Hans-Martin Barth, "Rechtfertigung und Identität," PT 86 (1997): 88–102.

[172] Cf. Hans-Martin Barth, *Wie ein Segel sich entfalten* (1979), and idem, "Rechtfertigung als Lebenselixier," 83–94 in Reiner Marquard, ed., *Reformationstag—Evangelisch und Ökumenisch. Eine Arbeitshilfe für Gemeinde und Schule* (Göttingen: Vandenhoeck & Ruprecht, 1997).

[173] "Ideo oportet nasci ex deo, non ex homine, muliere, sed ex deo, ut deus sit pater et mater, qui zeuget. Hoc scimus et de hoc loquimur, cogitamus et intelligimus . . ." WA 45, 68, 25-28.

9

Dialectics: Freedom and Limitation

Luther's remarks on freedom are concentrated in two of his writings that seem to contradict one another: *The Freedom of a Christian* (1520),[1] and *The Bondage of the Will* (1525).[2] But what is said in these two writings is not only compatible; although they have fundamentally different occasions and addressees, in their substance they belong inalienably together. The sequence of their origins is also important for understanding them.

Contemporary questions

The word "freedom" today is far from having the seductive sound it did at the time of Luther or of the French Revolution. For Lessing, the Reformer was one who freed people from the "yoke of tradition,"[3] for Goethe he brought liberation from the "fetters of spiritual bigotry."[4] As late as 1983, on the occasion of the Year of Luther, Gottfried Maron found that Luther "can, indeed must be said to have played an important, even decisive role in the history of human freedom, and can, indeed must, continue to play such a role."[5] In the interim, talk about the Reformation's emotions surrounding freedom has died down somewhat—which no doubt is connected also with the historic success of Luther's understanding of freedom. Freedom, at least in the West and the countries oriented toward it, has become a matter of course. The first article of the Universal Declaration of Human Rights (10 December 1948) declares that "recognition of the inherent dignity and of the equal and inalienable rights of all members of the human family is the foundation of freedom, justice and peace in the world."[6] The constitution of the Federal Republic of Germany (23 May 1949) seconded this: "Everyone has the right to the free development of his personality . . ." and "freedom of faith and of conscience, and freedom of creed, religious or ideological, are inviolable."[7] But despite these sweeping statements many people have the feeling that their freedom is long gone.

There have been objections from the very beginning and from the most varied directions to Luther's idea of freedom; these objections are still being articulated today. Though religiously motivated, they can seem utterly contrary: while more norm-dependent contemporaries fear that Luther's talk about freedom might lead to an indefensible liberalism or even libertinism, others find his image of the human altogether too pessimistic when he denies that humans have the ability to make a free decision before God; after all, we are undoubtedly free to do good! At present the freedom offered on all sides for self-development and personal decision is also associated with feelings of a total lack of orientation. Can these fears be defused?

From a political point of view Thomas Müntzer and the peasants of the Reformation period were the first to formulate an accusation against Luther that has not yet been silenced and was used fairly recently as a paradigm by Herbert Marcuse: Luther's idea of freedom, which applies only to the inner person, is said to be schizophrenic and serves ultimately to legitimate political and social bondage.[8] What Luther had to say about freedom also stands today in the context of worldwide theologies of liberation that have scarcely any points of contact with Luther's idea of freedom.

A third objection is that in view of global capitalism and its economic pressures the question seems no longer to be about freedom but rather, and more urgently, about justice and a sustainable ecology. What is the significance of Luther's notion of freedom in this context?

Finally, some anthropologically-based objections suggest themselves. The plea for individual self-development has shown that overinflated ideas of entitlement on the part of individuals can lead to conflicts, and even to the endangerment of whole societies. Does a guiding authority not in fact serve to give the psyche some relief? On the other hand, many kinds of esoteric methods of relaxation are now practiced, such as certain forms of meditation,[9] and these offer a certain relief from the pressures of everyday life: has Luther's talk of freedom lost its function and become outdated as a result?

But we can also ask: when brain research[10] indicates that there is in fact no such thing as a genuine free decision on the part of a human being, does that confirm what Luther says about unfreedom?

To approach an answer to these questions we must first consider that Luther makes a clear distinction between the freedom of a Christian on the one hand and the empirical opportunities for decision and action on the part of the natural human being on the other.

EMPIRICAL FREEDOM TO DECIDE

Of course Reformation anthropology also supposed that the human being is, as the Augsburg Confession has it, in "some measure" free "to live an outwardly honorable life and to make choices among the things that reason comprehends."[11] It was obvious to Luther that one can choose what to eat and drink and in other everyday matters, and he saw no need to put special emphasis on it. This kind of "freedom of the will" was something Luther "acknowledged almost naïvely."[12] In contrast to Melanchthon, who perhaps sensed a certain affinity to Erasmus of Rotterdam, Luther did find pompous talk of freedom ultimately inappropriate in this context, for how should it be possible to call people truly free when they live, after all, "under the absolute sovereignty of God (not to mention sin and death) in such a way that they cannot subsist for a moment by their own strength!"[13] But on the surface, within the limits of decisions that are relevant on earth, people of course have a choice to be morally good or evil. The Reformer caused confusion by asserting that a human being cannot decide for "the good," but of course he was speaking only of the situation in relationship to God; as far as earthly things are concerned people can, in his opinion, do a great many "good things." The best representatives of antiquity offered him impressive examples, and it could also be seen in the honesty of the Turks. But this was true only in the realm that lies under human control and so to speak beneath them. If we are talking in terms of "free choice" we must know that an opportunity to choose freely is accorded to a human being "only with respect to what is beneath him and not what is above him."[14] It has a legitimate function only with regard to choices of everyday actions and omissions. Thus Luther has to admit that "free choice" may have a certain breadth, namely "good works, let us say, or the righteousness of the civil or moral law." But that does not alter in the slightest degree the fundamental constitution of the human: the human will is not able to force itself upward into a condition of righteousness before God.[15] The high ethos of ancient philosophers ultimately does not impress Luther. He poses a rhetorical question to Erasmus: would those ancient heroes really strive for "virtue"?—people who "did not even know that virtue was?" In any case, we cannot look into their hearts; only the external appearance can be judged, and even that shows "that they did all these things for their own glory."[16] Luther refers to their accounts of themselves, but he seems to be guided also by skepticism toward himself and certainly by his theological opinion. How did that come about?

THE BRILLIANCE OF CHRISTIAN FREEDOM

With his *The Freedom of a Christian*[17] Luther did not want to put down once and for all, so to speak, what he understood "freedom" to be. Rather, it represents a reaction on the part of the Reformer as he was threatened with excommunication. It is part of his quarrel with Rome and was meant to be a last-minute communication as the papal bull of excommunication was already in the process of publication.[18] It was addressed to Leo X along with an accompanying "letter," an address that—on the certainly improbable assumption that the Pope was not adequately informed by the Curia—was meant to describe the situation once more.[19] *The Freedom of a Christian* is thus an accounting, a summary presentation of what Luther had firmly concluded under the impression given by his studies of the Bible and the preceding disputations—"the whole of Christian life in a brief form."[20] Thus this is not at all in the first place about theoretical propositions on the nature of freedom but about what it means to be a Christian, what constitutes that life. Certainly Christian life is described as being "free," or more precisely becoming "free"—and as being or becoming "subject." This designation was to tell people who felt themselves free how unfree they really were, and those who felt themselves unfree that they could be rid of what was oppressing them. Here we find three basic ideas Luther developed primarily from Paul's theology: the foundation of the freedom of a Christian, its fulfillment in love, and its realization under the conditions of earthly circumstances.

LIBERATION

Luther was fascinated by the freedom that Christ "obtained . . . and imparts . . . to and shares" with Christians.[21] All that is necessary for them is to look up and believe in Christ, in whom all grace and freedom are promised to them, for: "If you believe, you shall have all things."[22] "One thing, and only one thing, is necessary for Christian life, righteousness, and freedom. That one thing is the most holy Word of God, the gospel of Christ."[23] The Gospel tells me, who am aware of my guilt and inadequacy: if only you trust in Christ "your sins are forgiven" and you shall be righteous, free, satisfied, devout, and all the commandments fulfilled—in short, you will be free of all things,[24] "a perfectly free lord of all, subject to none."[25] All things: this includes freedom from moral pressure and pious deeds as well as from ecclesial and civil ordinances. But without faith in Christ a person is a "servant of all,"[26] living in a thousandfold dependency. Luther adapts traditional imagery to express the inner binding of the soul to Christ. As iron glows in the fire, so the soul flows in the Word of God, receives its energy, and acquires its qualities.[27] The other comparison also comes from mysticism: faith "unites the soul with Christ as a bride is united with her bridegroom." Now comes the exchange of gifts, a kind of sharing of common property between the partners, as the human gives her or his sins to Christ and Christ gives his righteousness in return. This is followed by a festal wedding banquet at which the pair serve their guests.[28]

The freedom thus described is tied to the one who creates and communicates it. In a certain sense it is not a condition; it lives out of the constant experience of being-freed. In addition, Luther is evidently not concerned in the first place about freedom of the will—for example, as a philosophical problem—but about being free from suppressed thoughts and being ensnarled in guilt and fear of failure, about freedom of conscience and relief from what burdens the conscience. It is not freedoms that are the subject of debate, but the identity of the person who in Christ must no longer define the self in terms of moral acts and omissions. This freedom "comes from divine authority"![29] It is not a natural condition, but grace. "Our freedom should be considered as grounded outside ourselves and yet in that ground coming entirely to itself."[30] Therefore it is also not subject to being "secularized,"[31] and external symptoms can tell us nothing reliable about its actual presence.

THE POWER OF FREEDOM

However, this freedom will ultimately have effects that are externally perceived. A Christian liberated into freedom acts "out of spontaneous love," simply to please God and not to make oneself God's beloved child.[32] Such a one is like Adam in Paradise, who did not think about self-justification in what he did, but acted according to the will of God, peacefully and as a matter of course. The Christian is "restored to paradise and created anew"![33] Here, too, Luther is working with images: the tree bears fruit. This comparison once again establishes that "good works do not make a good man, but a good man does good works."[34] "A good or a bad house does not make a good or a bad builder; but a good or a bad builder makes a good or a bad house."[35] Luther sees the Christian as defined not by good works, but by the deed of Christ. A Christian, "consecrated by . . . faith,"[36] is "a perfectly dutiful servant of all, subject to all"[37] through love. Christians do not do their duty while gnashing their teeth, but duty and inclination become for them a higher unity; they act of their own free will. In serving their fellow human beings they do not abandon their own freedom, but realize it. They are to their neighbors as Christ is to them.[38] They are filled with a twofold dynamic in which, so to speak, one reaches both upward and downward: a Christian lives not in herself or himself, but "in Christ through faith, in his neighbor through love. By faith he is caught up beyond himself into God. By love he descends beneath himself into his neighbor. Yet he always remains in God and in his love."[39] Love is thus not only the fruit and consequence of faith, as Luther can say in a great many other places, but an epiphany of faith and of the freedom of the Christian that is revealed in it. The Christian thus lives in harmony with the manner of God's being: God is at home in Godself in being lovingly present in human beings.[40] A Christian lives the royal freedom of the children of God.

THE DYNAMICS OF FREEDOM

And yet the freedom given to a Christian is always more than what one can live and represent at any given time. In that it "becomes our life it at the same time maintains itself as the inexhaustible ground of this actuality."[41] Luther is no illusionary and no enthusiast. He knows that the place where Christians find themselves transferred to paradise is nowhere else but earth. He is aware that he can be free from all papal regulations and commands and from the whole notion of merits, but he is not seeking the enthusiasts' illusion of absolute freedom, which can become total caprice. "We take a middle course . . . we are neither papal nor Karlstadtish, but free and Christian. . . ."[42] So in the second part of his tractate he addresses the "outer man," who might conclude "we will take our ease and do no works." Luther answers almost humorously: "I answer: not so. . . . That would indeed be proper if we were wholly inner and perfectly spiritual men. But such we shall be only at the last day." On earth it remains a matter of "begin[ning] to make some progress" toward what will be perfected "in the future life."[43] The "inner person" is the new human, the "outer" one is becoming, is in the process of acquiring the same form as the inner and corresponding to it. Between the outer and the inner person lies the eschatological tension between what "already" is and what is "not yet." On earth the new human must guide the old and attempt to make it congruent. A person is faced with the task of coping with his or her bodily existence and ordering social relationships. Here concrete behavior, even including asceticism, has its function, not as if one could thereby gain eternal blessedness, but in such a way that the outer person gradually takes on the form of, becomes "conformed" to the inner.[44] The resistance of the "flesh" makes itself felt. Now the inner person, filled with joy for Christ's sake, engages with the outer, "grabs it by the neck."[45] Wilhelm Maurer writes: "The outer is no longer the obstacle, but the tool of inwardness. . . . The body is not a dungeon for the soul, but a vessel in which the strengths needed for love's service are preserved."[46] Christians will act freely, "as servants of God," and not as "servants of men."[47] The situation with them is that their works "flow from a happy and cheerful heart, which thanks, praises, and lauds God for all the good things it has received from Him."[48] Now we know "how to live, how to defend and preserve your life against death."[49] Thus there is no question of a misuse of freedom; Luther thunders with mighty words against all who would appeal to Christian freedom as an excuse for their carelessness or caprice. But he still insists that the freedom bestowed on us in Christ must not be restricted in any sense, not even in the form of a freely chosen self-obligation toward God such as a vow. Christ "does not allow you to bind and obligate yourself to him, since he has unbound you from everything and made you free." People should not allow themselves to be fettered where Christ wants them to be free. "But in granting you this freedom God does not prevent you from putting yourself under obligation or binding yourself to your neighbor."[50] For Christians it is all the same—doing nothing and doing everything, keeping the Law and not keeping it.[51] A Christian is a "free lord" and a "dutiful servant." For Luther that is not an anachronism, but "logical" in itself: the freedom given us in Christ makes us free for a joyful service where it is needed. But the indispensable condition remains that human beings cannot obtain that freedom for themselves; they do not have control of the "inner person" because that person is constituted from outside, through Christ. This already makes it clear how Luther will answer Erasmus of Rotterdam's position on free will.

The Misery of Human Limitation

The Freedom of a Christian only begins to hint at what the Reformer would develop in his writing on the unfreedom of the will: nature by itself "cannot drive out or even recognize" the inclination to want to merit and deserve something before God.[52] But in a disputation as early as the year 1516 Luther had written that human beings, as long as they are excluded from grace, cannot of their own initiative "prepare [themselves] for grace."[53] In the Heidelberg Disputation of 1518 he then said more clearly: "Free will, after the fall, exists in name only, and as long as it does what it is able to do, it commits a mortal sin."[54] This assertion was then explicitly condemned by the papal bull of excommunication,[55] which led Erasmus of Rotterdam to compose his *De libero arbitrio*.[56] But it was already clear to the Reformer in his development that the will is only free when it desires nothing of its own but looks only to God's will without remaining attached or clinging to anything else.[57] Luther wished that the words "free will" had never been invented; after all, the notion is not in Scripture.[58] The human being after the Fall is a prisoner of the devil; in view of that, how can there be "free will"?[59] Only Christ can liberate human beings and make them free Christians.

Erasmus's writing gave Luther the opportunity to develop this in more detail. To that extent Gerhard Ebeling is right when he says that for Luther "the words about the freedom of a Christian belong inseparably with the assertion 'that the free will is nothing.'"[60] The two writings complement one another in their fundamental purpose; they represent, we might say, two sides of the same coin. It also appears to me important to observe the sequence of publication of the two: first sounds the great fanfare of the freedom of a Christian, and only later is it secured by the subsequent explanation of its implications.

LIMITATIONS ON THE ABILITY TO WILL

Luther's *The Bondage of the Will*, called in German "That the Free Will is Nothing," from the translation by his friend and colleague Justus Jonas, is couched in the style of the times in that it accuses Erasmus of unclarity, contradictoriness, and a lack of passion for discovering the truth and bombards him with many questions, some genuine and some rhetorical. Reading it in the outstanding German translation by Athina Lexutt and comparing that with the Latin formulations is over long passages an intellectual pleasure and a spiritual challenge.[61] The translation of *arbitrio* with "ability to will" is a contribution that opens up further vistas. Luther the reformer does not assert that the will as such is nothing; as already mentioned, the human being possesses the ability to decide, though "only about things that are subordinated to him." A certain ability to will thus certainly exists, but ultimately that is irrelevant. According to Luther the problem is solely what the free will can achieve before God. In the discussion with Erasmus, then, as he maintains when adopting the definition of his conversation partner, the issue is nothing other than "the power of the human will, with which the human can turn toward what leads to eternal salvation or can turn away from it." Since Luther orients his arguments to the thought process in Erasmus's writing, they are scattered and repetitive; hence we must first bring the arguments together and rearrange them. They are, with differing intensity and frequency, the following:

The mission of Jesus Christ

If the ability to will enables free action before God, Christ is superfluous.[62] We then need no physician to heal our wounds,[63] or the doctor has only a limited task, for example only to redeem part of the human affect.[64] Asserting a free ability to will means denying Christ or making of the Redeemer an implacable judge whom people then think they must mollify with the aid of Mary or the saints.[65] The work of the Holy Spirit would also be entirely superfluous.[66] And yet it is the enlightenment of the Holy Spirit by which the human is "rapt away to Christ."[67] Sacred Scripture and countless individual statements there, such as John 15 or Romans 3 and 4, to name only the most important, are misread. Justification by grace does not allow for the supposition of a free ability to will.[68] With the thesis of the free exercise of will the human being ultimately makes himself or herself "his/her own redeemer,"[69] and robs God of glory[70]; such a one ascribes divinity to her or his own free ability to will.[71]

The human need for redemption

These statements with regard to redemption correspond to those that apply to the human need for redemption. Even the temporal is not in human hands—how much less the eternal! Salvation is said to be something beyond human comprehension;[72] no one who is not "imbued with the Holy Spirit" even desires salvation![73] Of course there is a human will—but who or what guides it? If we say it is the emotions we must admit that according to Scripture the whole human is "flesh."[74] It acknowledges that humans have "persistent attraction and drive of the will toward evil."[75] Augustine had already taught that the free ability to will was good for nothing but sinning.[76]

God's universal action

Luther now sees the whole regrettable situation of the human—and here he goes beyond the arguments in *The Freedom of the Will*—as grounded in his vision of the universal action of God and the struggle between God and Satan over humanity. There is no free will because "there is no middle kingdom between the Kingdom of God and the kingdom of Satan, which are mutually and perpetually in conflict with each other."[77] "Outside of Christ there is nothing but Satan, apart from grace nothing but wrath, apart from light only darkness. . . ."[78] At the same time, human beings in this situation are not guiltless, because they assent to it, not just reluctantly, but with all their hearts. But even outside grace they remain "nonetheless under the general omnipotence of God, who does, moves, and carries along all things in a necessary and infallible course."[79] Luther knows that he is presenting an argument that is "uncomfortable"—apparently even to himself. But he sees no other possibility: one must "go all out and completely deny free choice, referring everything to God. . . ."[80]

THE BELIEVER: THE LIBERATED BEAST OF BURDEN

In this context we find the image, often cited in isolation, of the human being as a steed or beast of burden ridden either by God or by the devil: "nor can it choose to run to either of the two riders or seek him out, but the riders themselves contend for the possession and control of it."[81] It has already been observed, in different ways, that there is something wrong with this picture. Hans Joachim Iwand's criticism is that it suggests that the human will remains the same no matter who is guiding it.[82] Wilfried Härle warns that the image no longer adequately expresses "that the human ability to will is from the outset complicit in the decision for evil—not for the good!"[83] Gerhard Ebeling asserts that in confronting Erasmus Luther "portrayed the supposedly free will as a steed, with God and Satan contending with one another for the possession and guidance of it."[84] But that is imprecise because it makes it sound as if the steed, like Buridan's ass, is standing in the middle and waiting to see who will mount it. Luther himself contributed to the origin of this misunderstanding, for he contradicts himself when he says that the human will "is placed between the two like a beast of burden," while in fact he assumes no such "middle point," but rather that the center is already occupied, namely by sin, the flesh, Satan. Luther employs the image in the context of an interpretation of Jesus' discourse about the expulsion of demons by "the finger of God" (Luke 11:18–22, at 21). The point of his comparison is therefore to make it clear that when a "Stronger One" comes upon the person being held captive by Satan, "overcomes him and takes us as His spoil, then through his Spirit we are again slaves and captives—though this is royal freedom—so that we readily will and do what he wills." When God has the reins in hand, that is, the beast of burden wills to go and does go where God wills, "as the psalm says: 'I am become as a beast [before thee] *and* I am always with thee'" (Ps 73:23-24/Vulgate Ps 72:22-23). It was from this verse also that Luther took the idea of the beast of burden (*iumentum*), a comparison that in the context of the whole psalm is meant to be an image of trust. Luther uses the quotation in the sense adopted in the Vulgate, which links the two statements with an "and" and thus gives a positive view from the outset of the beast of burden that can always be with God.[85] We thus see that for Luther also the beast of burden is understood as being "with you," remaining with God. The image of a steed or beast of burden that is captive and subject to someone's ownership must be seen from the perspective of the necessary and also promised liberation! The human beast of burden liberated from Satan rejoices that it can remain with its liberator, who now guides it. This interpretation is confirmed when we add the second passage in which the image appears in Luther's document.[86] Here the Reformer assumes that the devil, as ruler of the world according to the biblical witness, "reigns in the wills and minds of men who are his captive slaves." Will Satan spontaneously release them again, so that the human person, "who is his slave and a part of his kingdom, should strive toward the good with any motion or momentum whereby he might escape his tyranny?" Never! Erasmus imagines that the free will stands "on neutral ground" and can freely decide, because God and the devil are far distant, like mere observers. But instead they are "the movers and inciters of a servile will," and so they struggle against one another. But according to Luther the starting point, if one will not make Christ a liar, is that "free choice must be nothing but a captive beast of burden"; it "can only be set free if the devil is first cast out by the finger of God." But the Gospel proclaims that liberation! Here again, then, he is not thinking of a steed in the sense in which the image traditionally appeared—as the expression of the smooth cooperation of horse and rider.[87] From the outset he is speaking of a "captive beast of burden" that is to be freed by coming under the liberating rule of Christ. To that extent one should by no means suggest a "dualistic and deterministic character" in Luther's remarks in this passage![88]

Thus one may in fact say in summarizing Luther's idea of freedom that "'the human being' is unfree—the 'Christian' is free,"[89] or more precisely: the Christian is free because of having been made free by Christ and thus—in an empirical sense as well—is free to become ever more free.

THE ASSURANCE OF FAITH

Finally, Luther also supports his view of the bondage of the human will by referring to the fact that the Jews, despite all their zeal for the Law, have not found freedom in Christ, while Paul, although he went out to battle against the Gospel, apparently did not become an apostle through his own decision.[90] At the end of the document the Reformer becomes quite personal: "For my own part, I frankly confess that even if it were possible, I should not wish to have free choice given to me, or to have anything left in my own hands by which I might strive toward salvation." That would only drive him into uncertainty, so that his conscience "would never be assured and certain how much it ought to do to satisfy God. . . . But now, since God has taken my salvation out of my hands into his, making it depend on his choice and not mine, and has promised to save me, not by my own work or exertion but by his grace and mercy, I am assured and certain both that he is faithful and will not lie to me."[91] In the Small Catechism Luther clothes this in the simple words: "I believe that by my own reason or strength I cannot believe in Jesus Christ, my Lord, or come to him. But the Holy Spirit has called me through the Gospel, enlightened me with his gifts, and sanctified and preserved me in true faith," and the same is true for all Christians on earth.[92]

There remains, of course, the question of what a human being can do at all in order to be grasped by liberation in Christ. One cannot contribute anything by action; according to Luther one only has a "disposing quality or passive aptitude."[93] This is the precondition for the human capacity to be "thoroughly imbued with the Holy Spirit"—Luther employs mystical concepts!—"and filled with grace." How does that take place? In *The Freedom of a Christian* Luther thought it appropriate that Christians form the Word and Christ in themselves in order "increasingly to strengthen faith alone."[94] Faith is deepened "by preaching why Christ came, what he brought and bestowed, what benefit it is to us to accept him."[95] The Reformer derives some advice for preachers from this: they should not merely tell stories about Christ or motivate people to identify psychologically with his terrible fate. Instead, they should preach "to the end that faith in him may be established that he may not only be Christ, but be Christ for you and me."[96] Luther has in mind people who already believe or are at least somehow within the Christian tradition;

he says nothing about what one can do if one has no relationship to faith and the church. In his writing against Erasmus he speaks bluntly: without the Spirit of God people cannot turn to God, not even if the Spirit of God should personally teach and call them.[97] The ungodly person does not come to Christ (cf. John 6:44); "even the message of the gospel itself . . . is heard in vain unless the Father himself speaks, teaches, and draws inwardly . . . which He does by pouring out the Spirit."[98] Even the work of the Holy Spirit depends for its salvific relevance on God's impenetrable choice. What, then, can a human being do? Nothing—not even surrender on his or her own initiative to the work of God. But God will do what God will do, as God has done already in Jesus Christ.

CRITICAL EVALUATION

FREEDOM BEFORE AND BEYOND PSYCHOLOGICAL INSIGHTS

Luther has high regard for the natural person as long as one is speaking about earthly matters, but absolutely none when the relationship to God is at issue. And yet he pays the highest honor to the "freedom of a Christian."

Underestimation of human autonomy?

When the Reformer is accused today of being unable to give full acknowledgment to human autonomy, the fault lies in a failure to make distinctions on the part of those who make the accusation. Luther stands between the two fronts: one side, whether they belong to traditional churches, pietist-fundamentalist, or esoteric groups, speak tirelessly of human freedom to decide; the others are convinced of human lack of freedom, whether they appeal to Kant, with his talk of radical evil, or to Schopenhauer. If we look beyond the borders of Christianity we could also think of Buddhism. But according to Luther neither the overestimation nor the underestimation of the ability to choose freely touches the true human situation. As regards responsibility for the areas entrusted to them, people should not be underestimated, but as regards their spiritual abilities they should not be overestimated. In no case can they free themselves from their own ego-bound constitution. Therefore Luther would not regard such practices as meditation, even when they are subjectively experienced as instances of grace, as leading to genuine freedom, especially since they seem more to separate people from the world than to make them free for the world.

False judgment of the human psychic constitution?

Psychology offers a quite unexpected context for Luther's understanding of the dialectics of freedom and limitation. Walther von Loewenich had already suggested that in his view of the unfreedom of the will Luther came "close to the view of the effectiveness of the collective unconscious in the human." As one with "a deep knowledge of the human psyche" he "sensed something of the limitations of control of self-awareness." The royal freedom achieved in faith could then probably be understood as "the parallel to the 'self,' the integration of the conscious ego and the unconscious."[99] Certainly one would have to say the same of the apostle Paul, who would probably consider it a gross misunderstanding of himself. For Luther the limits of the rule of the ego that is not comfortable with itself still lie on the level of what he assigns to the "subordinate" realms. But the Reformer's concern is with a level of reality that lies deeper than diastasis or the integration of the conscious and the unconscious: even the employment of one's best powers and the most successful results of psychic integration do not enable the human being to comply with the will of God and free herself or himself from guilt before God.

New perspectives from brain research?

Does contemporary brain research come to the Reformer's aid in this argument? In an interview the neurobiologist Wolf Singer concedes that a human being—in the first person—has a subjective experience of freedom, but in the scientific perspective of the third person it cannot be described as freedom. The supposition that "we are responsible for what we do because we could have done otherwise is unsustainable from a neurobiological perspective." It remains to be discovered how the descriptive system from the first-person perspective could have arisen from that of the third person. The perceptions made in the first person, although they are delimited, are—according to Singer—at the same time important for human life in community since, although the cultural environment they convey is also circumscribed, they omit their own determining factors. Singer therefore considers no profession more necessary than that of parents and educators.[100] That is, despite and on the basis of his deterministic view he would place himself entirely on Erasmus's side! But on that level Luther would not have objected either, since he is known to have done yeoman service on behalf of the education not only of growing children but of the whole society.

Probably still more firmly on Erasmus's side would be the brain researchers who either start with the hypothesis "that the brain has access to a neurological mechanism of self-transcendence"[101] or even posit a "God spot," "an isolated module of neural networks in the temporal lobe."[102] From that perspective they would always give a high estimation of the religious abilities of human beings and concede them at least a relative freedom, a position closer to Erasmus's Semipelagian thought than to Luther's view. The Reformer would probably interpret such psychological or neurobiological knowledge, if it can be sustained, in terms of God's omnipotence or in the sense of what he called the *aptitudo passiva*.

THE SOCIOLOGICAL-ECCLESIOLOGICAL DIMENSION OF FREEDOM

It is obvious that Luther applied his opinions regarding freedom and the limitations on free choice to the individual. He was concerned with the freedom of "a" Christian. This corresponded to his approach to the conscience and faith of the individual, but it was also suggested by the state of the discussion with Erasmus. At the same time, however, this meant that he was not clearly aware of the collective and social element always implied in the topic of freedom: his preaching was for individual peasants or princes, individual maidservants or noblewomen, but his goal was not the liberation of "the peasant," "the woman," or "the proletariat." This makes it difficult to connect what he said about freedom with modern theologies of liberation.

Do Reformation and liberation theological ideas of freedom contradict one another, or are they mutually enhancing? Christoph Dahling-Sander has addressed this question in a sweeping work[103] in which he contrasts Luther and Zwingli with the concepts of the American Black theologian James H. Cone and the Peruvian liberation theologian Gustavo Gutiérrez. There were already major differences between Luther's and Zwingli's ideas about freedom, despite some basic commonality; these cannot be pursued further here.[104] More difficult to bridge is the diastasis between the sixteenth and the twentieth centuries: Cone develops his idea in the context of the North American civil rights and Black Power movements while Gutiérrez begins from the social and ecclesial situation of Latin America.[105] Dahling-Sander compares the different contexts of discovery and reasoning in these four conceptions and comes to the conclusion that "freedom and liberation" are always inseparably connected and inevitably contain both "individual-personal" and "corporative" dimensions.[106] Despite the compatibility thus formulated, Luther appears as an ambivalent figure in the eyes of liberation theologians, especially because of the history of his influence on middle-class Protestantism. For Leonardo Boff, Luther's *The Freedom of a Christian* is "an apology for inner freedom," but that is his limitation: "Luther himself says that his Gospel has nothing to do with the things of this world."[107] Nevertheless, Boff honors the Reformer as "liberator of the church from Babylonian captivity," and Protestantism as "a factor in the liberation of the oppressed. . . ."[108]

Now, despite his approach by way of the conscience and faith of the individual, Luther by no means failed to recognize the overall implications for the congregation of the freedom granted in Christ. Ultimately it is precisely here that the church-critical power of the Reformation was applied and was able to make headway against the situation in which the hierarchy and existing provisions of canon law preempted the decision-making of Christians in the church. Here are also the constructive ecclesiological impulses of Luther's theology; it is no accident that in *The Freedom of a Christian* he also speaks of the universal, mutual, and common priesthood of believers: Christ shares his glory and dignity "with everyone who believes in him . . . Hence all of us who believe in Christ are priests and kings in Christ," and able to "pray for others and to teach one another divine things."[109] The word of God grounds the identity of the individual and at the same time calls individuals together. Thus a new principle of coherence is created in the church, in place of hierarchical constitution: being priests for one another, each for the other and all for all. Although this fascinating ecclesiological approach is clearly a contribution to the origins of democracy, the Lutheran churches in particular failed to buy it. Theoretically, Luther maintained it to the end of his life, but from certain pragmatic points of view he himself relativized it.[110] But above all the Reformer did not succeed in making the church a sign of freedom for society. It seems that he saw, within the framework of the two governments, that church office was responsible for showing the powerful their limits. But the churches that grew out of the Reformation, as a body, did not become pressure groups of people who engaged on behalf of the liberation of people from forced immaturity and oppression. Nor have they frequently raised their voices for the marginalized and those under threat. Rather seldom, and only belatedly, have they "heard the cry of his people."[111]

THE DIALECTICS OF FREEDOM AND LIMITATION

Despite its problematic history of influence, Luther's perception of the dialectic between freedom and limitation undoubtedly presents us with a brilliant theological concept. Certainly we already have the tradition of a statement by Seneca that obeying God is true freedom. And it is clear in our contemporary perspective as well that "in the absence of authority, liberty degenerates into licence and chaos ensues; and authority becomes tyranny unless it be tempered by freedom."[112] Besides, in mysticism there was probably always a sense of the hidden connection between freedom and obedience. Thus in the *Theologia Deutsch*, which Luther edited, we read that "whoever helps the human being to his own will helps him to the worst. For the more the human pursues and increases in his own will, the more distant is he from God and the true good."[113] Teresa of Avila, who could scarcely have heard of Luther, hears the soul calling: "O free will, what a slave you are to your own freedom!"[114] But one may rightly say that no one since Paul has suffered so thoroughly and theologically thought out so radically the dialectic of freedom and limitation as Martin Luther.

At the same time, there are questions here about Luther's anthropology as well as his doctrine of God.

Problematic anthropology?

Luther's anthropology has been attacked primarily in terms of its political implications. Herbert Marcuse zeroed in with his critique by suggesting that Luther advocates for a "conditional bondage resulting from an internalization of freedom."[115] He accused Luther of advocating for the "'inner human' while at the same time subjecting the 'outer human' to the system of secular authority."[116] Luther, he says, assumes a separation of body and spirit that led him to postulate the conditions of inner freedom as "negations of a purely external freedom."[117] What Luther said about inner freedom could therefore no longer be of any use in the struggle for external freedom, especially since the separation between the ("free") person and the office does still more to maintain the status quo of external bondage.[118]

The Reformer himself participates in this view, which is at least one-sided, by the fact that his terminology in *The Freedom of a Christian* is not really clear.[119] There he distinguishes on the one hand between body and soul, on the other between the "inner" and the "outer" human being. The distinction between body and soul suggests that in both cases he is making ontological statements on the same level, while on closer examination we see that the "inner" person of whom he speaks is in fact first constituted from outside, namely through the Gospel and the action of the Holy Spirit. At first it is unclear what Luther means when he speaks of the soul as a posited "spiritual nature" that, however, only achieves its freedom through the word and faith. Add to this that the "inner human" is identified with the "person," which, however, is the subject of its action and at the same time is to be distinguished from it. Here ancient, especially Platonic,[120] and biblical, especially New Testament, Pauline-school[121] anthropology and terminology are in contention with each other. According to Luther the inner human is the new human who can already know him- or herself to be free in Christ, and who, while still living under earthly conditions, cannot yet fully control the external human, but will shape it more and more powerfully. In any case, Luther is concerned with the whole person; in the course of his remarks his talk of the "inner" person recedes, and he speaks more and more emphatically of the "Christian"; accordingly his interest is not only in an inner world[122] but in the needs of the neighbor. The problem is not with Luther's concept of freedom but with the fact that he could only imagine it in the context of the social conditions of his time. This explains why he sees it as a matter of course that Christians, if they want to be helpful to their neighbors, "should freely serve others *and the authorities themselves* and obey their will freely and out of love."[123] Luther thinks existing secular structures can and must serve as media for such mutual responsibility—family, profession, social role. He did not see it as necessary or even permissible to call the secular structures themselves into question and remake them. Of course he was concerned not primarily with external freedom but with the inner freedom given by Christ. Nevertheless, we must certainly say that he at least contributed to creating the preconditions for greater political freedom, even though in the context of his time he was aware primarily of their concrete application in church politics and not so much in the wider social world. If the Reformer's approach, fascinating in itself and derived from the Gospel, is to be put into practice today it will be necessary to apply his ideas and make them effective not only within the context of existing systems[124] but, where necessary, even against those contexts.

Problematic doctrine of God?

The issue of Luther's doctrine of God is more difficult.[125] He sees humanity as subject to the iron law of a necessity he is convinced is a consequence of God's omnipotence. He resolves the problem that people are thus deprived of responsibility by distinguishing between compulsion and inclination: the human being is not (only) compelled to sin but does it, so to speak, with delight and love. Through Christ and in the power of the Holy Spirit, God can free a person from this situation. God *can*, but does not do so in every case. Not even if a person comes within the sound of the Gospel or is found there, not even if the Holy Spirit speaks directly to the person and calls her or him is it guaranteed that the person will arrive at the promised liberation. Logically this is consistent: it is God alone who frees or does not free from the power of Satan; *tertium non datur* (there is no third option). Has Luther thus become the victim of a compulsive system? Or should we suppose that he is aware, as von Loewenich formulates it, of the "cryptic nature of existence"?[126] Logically there is no alternative: either we must speak of predestination or of an expected apokatastasis in some form or other. The latter is out of the question for Luther on the basis of the biblical witness, and even Karl Barth, who opens this direction in his thought at least tendentially, did not dare to teach and advocate the reconciliation of all. So Luther's response to Erasmus retains a deterministic and also dualistic character. That this cannot be intended in a philosophical sense is shown by the fact that determinism, if founded on God's omnipotence, and dualism are mutually exclusive. What caused Luther, then, to insist so adamantly on the one hand on the lack of freedom in human choice and on the other hand on the sovereign freedom of the God who either chooses or rejects human beings? He sees himself forced to a twofold confession, and he chooses both: his own guilt and God's power and universal action, which cannot be limited in any way. He cannot give an answer to the question of how one could imagine God to be "righteous" under these circumstances. God's wisdom is, after all, impenetrable to humans. As with divine wisdom, so also it is "proper and indeed necessary that his righteousness also should be incomprehensible."[127] So speaks the believer who cares for nothing save that God's name be blessed, God's reign come, and God's will be done.

NOTES

[1] LW 31, 327–77 (WA 7, 20–38). The expanded Latin version Luther intended for Pope Leo X (with German translation) is easily accessible at LDStA 2, 101–85, and is fully contained in English in LW 31, 327–77. Quotations are from this version. A careful commentary on the writing based on the Latin version can be found in Rieger 2007. In what follows I will be adapting material from Hans-Martin Barth, "Freiheit, die ich meine? Luthers Verständnis der Dialektik von Freiheit und Gebundenheit," US 62 (2007): 103–15.

[2] De servo arbitrio, LW 33, 3–295 (WA 18, 600–787). Justus Jonas translated the title into German as "Dass der freie Wille nichts sei = That the free will is nothing." The version in LW 33 and WA 18 is from the Latin.

[3] Quoted according to Heinrich Bornkamm, Luther im Spiegel der deutschen Geistesgeschichte. Mit ausgewählten Texten von Lessing bis zur Gegenwart (Göttingen: Vandenhoeck & Ruprecht, 21970), 201.

[4] Ibid., 218.

[5] Gottfried Maron, "'Von der Freiheit eines Christenmenschen.' Die bleibende Bedeutung Martin Luthers," 43–57 in idem, Die ganze Christenheit auf Erden. Martin Luther und seine ökumenische Bedeutung. Zum 65. Geburtstag des Verfassers hg. von Gerhard Müller und Gottfried Seebass (Göttingen: Vandenhoeck & Ruprecht, 1993), at 55.

[6] As found on the United Nations website: http://www.un.org/en/documents/udhr.

[7] See www.constitution.org/cons/germany.txt.

[8] Herbert Marcuse, "Studie über Autorität und Familie," 55–156 in idem, Ideen zu einer kritischen Theorie der Gesellschaft (Frankfurt: Suhrkamp, 1969).

[9] There is an abundance of literature on this subject; cf., e.g., Edward Stevens, Meditieren in allen Lebenslagen. Meditationstechniken für Körper, Geist und Seele (Reinbek: Rowohlt, 1995); Almuth and Werner Huth, Praxis der Meditation (Munich: Kösel, 2000).

[10] Cf., e.g., Wolf Singer, Der Beobachter im Gehirn. Essays zur Hirnforschung (Frankfurt: Suhrkamp, 2002), and idem, Ein neues Menschenbild? Gespräche über Hirnforschung (Frankfurt: Suhrkamp, 2003). Cf. also Karl Eibl, Animal Poeta. Bausteine der biologischen Kultur- und Literaturtheorie (Paderborn: Mentis, 2004), 136: "'Free will' is a contradictio in adjecto, a logical impossibility, since every act of will that is not mere accident has its reasons. . . . It is a construction ex post. After every decision we know that there would have been other possibilities and that one or other of these possibilities might have been better: the basic experience out of which the idea of free will grows lies in the unreality of the past." This is an important idea, but it is not fully accurate insofar as the "decision" here referred to emerges from a choice between the possible "reasons."

[11] The Book of Concord, 39 ("quod humana voluntas habeat aliquam libertatem ad efficiendam civilem iustitiam et deligendas res rationi subiectas").

[12] von Loewenich 1963, 418.

[13] LW 33, 103 (LDStA 1, 347, 10ff.).

[14] LW 33, 70 (WA 18, 638, 6), "non respectu superioris, sed tantum inferioris."

[15] LW 33, 264 (LDStA 1, 607, 39ff.).

[16] LW 33, 225–26 (LDStA 1, 543, 40ff.).

[17]On this see the recent work of Rieger 2007.

[18]Cf. Brecht 1983, 385–88; Rieger 2007, 1–2. In view of the history of the writing's origins it seems groundless for Leppin to write (Leppin 2006, 160) of its pre-dating "that is probably the worst falsification that could ever be laid to Luther's account." We may also wonder what other "falsifications" Leppin is thinking of.

[19]*Epistola Lutheriana ad Leonem Decimum* (An Open Letter to Pope Leo X), LW 31, 331–43 (LDStA 2, 102–19).

[20]LW 31, 343 (WA 7, 11, 8-10).

[21]LW 31, 354 (WA 7, 20, 26-27).

[22]LW 31, 348–49 (WA 7, 24, 12-14).

[23]LW 31, 345 (WA 7, 22, 3-5).

[24]LW 31, 347 (WA 7, 22, 34–23, 3).

[25]LW 31, 344 (WA 7, 21, 1-2).

[26]LW 31, 355 (WA 7, 28, 12).

[27]LW 31, 349 (WA 7, 24, 33-35).

[28]LW 31, 351 (WA 7, 25, 26–26, 12). According to LDStA 6, 183, the word "Wirtschaft" that Luther uses here means "hospitality, dinner for guests, wedding banquet, wedding feast."

[29]LW 44, 309 (WA 8, 613, 9).

[30]Joachim Ringleben, "Freiheit im Widerspruch. Systematische Überlegungen zu Luthers Traktat 'Von der Freiheit eines Christenmenschen,'" *NZST* 40 (1998): 157–70, at 164.

[31]Iwand 1983, 87.

[32]LW 31, 359 (WA 7, 31, 6).

[33]LW 31, 360 (WA 7, 31, 17-32; the quotation is from ll. 29-30).

[34]LW 31, 361 (WA 7, 32, 5-6).

[35]Ibid. (WA 7, 32, 18-20).

[36]LW 31, 360 (WA 7, 31, 37).

[37]LW 31, 344 (WA 7, 21, 3-4).

[38]LW 31, 366 (WA 7, 35, 34-35): ". . . toward my neighbor also doth a Christian become, as Christ has become to me"; the Latin version is, "dabo itaque me quendam Christum proximo meo, quemadmodum Christus sese praebuit mihi," LDStA 2, 164, 24-25. Fidel Rädle translates: "Thus I will act toward my neighbor as a kind of Christ, as Christ has shown himself to me . . ." (ibid., 165, 32-34).

[39]LW 31, 371 (WA 7, 38, 7-10).

[40]Cf. Ringleben, "Freiheit im Widerspruch," 169.

[41]Ibid., 162.

[42]Quoted from Maron 1993, 54.

[43]LW 31, 358 (WA 7, 30, 2-6).

[44]Ibid. (WA 7, 30, 17-19).

[45]LW 31, 359 [from the author's translation] (WA 7, 30, 24-25).

[46]Wilhelm Maurer, *Autorität in Freiheit. Zu Marcuses Angriff auf Luthers Freiheitslehre* (Stuttgart: Calwer, 1970), 26.

[47]LW 30, 78 (WA 12, 333, 11-12).

[48]LW 30, 77 (WA 12, 332, 3-8).

[49]LW 23, 411 (WA 33, 666, 3).

[50]LW 44, 314 (WA 8, 615, 33-37).

[51]WA 15, 602, 3-4.

[52]LW 31, 363 (WA 7, 34, 7-9).

[53]WA 1, 147, 10-12.

[54]LW 31, 40 (LDStA 1, 47, 15-17).

[55]*Exsurge, Domine*, 15 June 1520 (www.papalencyclicals.net/Leo10/10exdom.htm), and see DES 1486 (= *Sources of Catholic Dogma* 776, 36, www.catecheticsonline.com).

[56]Desiderius Erasmus, *Controversies: De libero arbitrio DIATRIB, sive collatio, Hyperaspistes 1*, trans. Alexander Dalzell et al. (Toronto: University of Toronto Press, 1999).

57 LW 42, 48 (WA 2, 104, 37-38 [1519]).

58 LW 32, 94 (WA 7, 449, 24-25 [1521]).

59 LW 32, 92 (WA 7, 446, 12).

60 Ibid.

61 Gerhard Ebeling, Frei aus Glauben (Tübingen: Mohr [Siebeck], 1968), 14.

62 LW 33, 279 (LDStA 1, 635, 18-22).

63 LW 33, 281 (LDStA 1, 641, 8-9).

64 Ibid.

65 LW 33, 280 (LDStA 1, 635, 38ff.).

66 LW 33, 107 (LDStA 1, 355, 19-21).

67 LW 33, 286 (LDStA 1, 647, 15), "being rapt . . . with the sweetest rapture": "qua rapitur homo ad Christum dulcissimo raptu," cf. LDStA 1, 626, 14-15.

68 LW 33, 191 (LDStA 1, 617, 1-5).

69 LW 33, 228 (LDStA 1, 547, 34).

70 LW 33, 226 (LDStA 1, 545, 25).

71 LW 33, 106 (LDStA 1, 353, 4-5).

72 LW 33, 105 (LDStA 1, 351, 1-2).

73 LW 33, 105–6 (LDStA 1, 351, 24ff.).

74 LW 33, 214 (LDStA 1, 543, 26-28).

75 LW 33, 216 (LDStA 1, 528, 8-9); cf. Gen 8:21.

76 LW 33, 108 (LDStA 1, 367, 3ff.).

77 LW 33, 227 (LDStA 1, 547, 12-14).

78 LW 33, 282 (LDStA 1, 639, 25-27).

79 LW 33, 240 (LDStA 1, 567, 36-39).

80 LW 33, 245 (LDStA 1, 577, 20-22), "Ideo ad extrema eundum est . . ." LDStA 1, 576, 15.

81 LW 33, 65–66 (LDStA 1, 291, 33-39).

82 Iwand 1983, 90.

83 LDStA 1, xxxiv.

84 Ebeling, Frei aus Glauben, 32.

85 LW 33, 65. The Vulgate (reflecting the Septuagint) does not consider that the et here is intended adversatively in the original Hebrew text, as it then appears appropriately in Luther's translation (after 1545): ". . . I was a beast before you. Nevertheless I am always with you, for you hold me by my right hand, you lead me according to your counsel. . . ." (Ps 73:23-24).

86 LW 33, 236 (WA 18, 561, 27–573, 10).

87 Gerhard Ebeling, "Der kontroverse Grund der Freiheit. Zum Gegensatz von Luther-Enthusiasmus und Luther-Fremdheit in der Neuzeit," 9–33 in Bernd Moeller, ed., Luther in der Neuzeit, Wissenschaftliches Symposion des Vereins für Reformationsgeschichte (Gütersloh: Gütersloher Verlagshaus G. Mohn, 1983), 33 n. 84, refers to Gabriel Biel, Coll. II. dist. 27. q. un. a.3 dub. 2: a horse's pace depends "ab equo et sessore dirigente equum. . . ."

88 Against Härle, LDStA 1, xxxiv.

89 Maron 1993, 46.

90 Not "out of his [supposedly] wonderful power of free choice," LW 33, 276 (LDStA 1, 620, 23ff.; 11ff.).

91 LW 33, 288–89 (LDStA 1, 649, 42–651, 3; 651, 11-12, 16-21).

92 The Book of Concord, 345.

93 ". . . aptitudinem, seu ut Sophistae loquuntur dispositivam qualitatem et passivam apti-tudinem," LW 33, 67 (LDStA 1, 292, 24-25).

94 LW 31, 347 (cf. WA 7, 23, 7-9). (The text in LW differs widely from that in WA at this point.—Tr.)

95 LW 31, 357 (WA 7, 29, 15-17).

96 Ibid. (WA 7, 29, 7-15, quoting from lines 13-15).

[97]LW 33, 214 (LDStA 1, 525, 39ff.), "cum etiam spiritu Dei inter eos vocante et docente," 524, 33.

[98]LW 33, 286 (LDStA 1, 647, 12-14).

[99]von Loewenich 1963, 419.

[100]Wolf Singer, *Ein neues Menschenbild? Gespräche über Hirnforschung* (Frankfurt: Suhrkamp, 2003), 20; cf. esp. 24–34.

[101]Andrew Newberg, Eugene d'Aquili, and Vince Rause, *Der gedachte Gott. Wie Glaube im Gehirn entsteht* (Munich and Zürich: Piper, 2003), 199.

[102]Danah Zohar and Ian Marshall, *SQ: Connecting with our Spiritual Intelligence* (New York and London: Bloomsbury, 2000), 91–112, at 112.

[103]Christoph Dahling-Sander, *Zur Freiheit befreit. Das theologische Verständnis von Freiheit und Befreiung nach Martin Luther, Huldrych Zwingli, James H. Cone und Gustavo Gutiérrez* (Frankfurt: Lembeck, 2003).

[104]Cf. ibid., 172–84.

[105]Cf. ibid., 185–362.

[106]Ibid., 382.

[107]Leonardo Boff, "Die Bedeutung Martin Luthers für die Befreiung der Unterdrückten," 201–20 in idem, *Und die Kirche ist Volk geworden. Ekklesiogenesis* (Düsseldorf: Patmos, 1987, at 212, 214. [This essay is not reproduced in the English publication, *Ecclesiogenesis*, from Orbis.—Tr.]

[108]Ibid., 208, 217. For the whole cf. Barth, Hans-Martin 1990, 134–60, especially "Befreiungs-Ekklesiologie—Einlösung eines reformatorischen Ansatzes?" 154–60, and idem, "Die Theologie Leonardo Boffs—Eine ökumenische Verheissung? Protestantische Lese-Erfahrungen," *MdKI* 36 (1985): 107–12. Unfortunately, the book by the Brazilian Lutheran theologian Walter Altmann, *Luther and Liberation. A Latin American Perspective* (Minneapolis: Fortress Press, 1992), offers no points that advance the discussion in this regard. It scarcely refers to the Latin American context and withdraws completely from the discussion with the liberation theologians of Latin America. For the whole, however, cf. also Dalferth 1996.

[109]LW 31, 353 (WA 7, 27, 18-19; 28, 10). On this cf. Barth, Hans-Martin 1990, 29–53.

[110]Cf. Barth, Hans-Martin 1990, 48–53, against Goertz 1997.

[111]The theme of the Eighth General Assembly of the Lutheran World Federation, 1990, in Curitiba, Brazil, was "I Have Heard the Cry of My People."

[112]Stefan Zweig, *The Right to Heresy; Castellio against Calvin* (New York: Viking, 1936), 7.

[113]*Theologia Deutsch. Eine Grundschrift deutscher Mystik*, ed. and introduced by Gerhard Wehr (Andechs: Dingfelder, 1989), 118 (where Wehr by mistake writes "zustimmt = agrees" instead of "zunimmt = increases").

[114]Erika Lorenz, *Ein Pfad im Wegelosen. Teresa von Avila: Erfahrungsberichte und innere Biographie* (Freiburg, et al.: Herder, 1985), 95.

[115]Herbert Marcuse, "Studie über Autorität und Familie," in idem, *Ideen zu einer kritischen Theorie der Gesellschaft* (Frankfurt: Suhrkamp, 1969), 65–66.

[116]Ibid., 59.

[117]Ibid., 60.

[118]Ibid., 61–62, 63–65.

[119]Cf. Rieger 2007, 87.

[120]Cf. Eberhard Jüngel, "Zur Freiheit eines Christenmenschen. Eine Erinnerung an Luthers Schrift," 84–160 in idem, *Indikative der Gnade—Imperative der Freiheit. Theologische Erörterungen IV* (Tübingen: Mohr Siebeck, 2000), including the excursus, "Innerer Mensch," 157–60.

[121]Cf. 2 Cor 4:16-18; Eph 4:24.

[122]Even the image of the marital union of Christ and the soul is not adopted in the sense it had in the mystical tradition; it is not about *unio* but about a "blessed struggle and victory" (LW 31, 350).

[123]LW 31, 369 (WA 7, 37, 3-4), emphasis supplied.

[124]As suggested by the Augsburg Confession XVI, *The Book of Concord*, 37.

[125]See "Critical Evaluation" in chapter 6.

[126]von Loewenich 1963, 419.
[127]LW 33, 290 (LDStA 1, 653, 8-10).

10

Complementarity: Word and Sacrament

How does anyone come to believe? From a purely empirical standpoint we might point today to three factors: socialization by parents, religious instruction or belonging to a particular group, and one's own psychosomatic constitution, as described by Fritz Riemann in terms of basic forms of anxiety,[1] which brings particular needs to light; finally, experiences in the course of an individual's life may play a part. Of course, all those things could also lead to unbelief! In any case, this is no explanation for the origins of faith. In Luther's understanding faith arises out of the encounter with the word of God in its verbal and non-verbal forms. The Augsburg Confession summarizes, very much in line with the Reformer's idea, that: "To obtain such faith God instituted the office of the ministry, that is, provided the Gospel and the sacraments. Through these, as through means, he gives the Holy Spirit, who works faith, when and where he pleases, in those who hear the Gospel."[2] What are the questions associated with this approach today?

CONTEMPORARY QUESTIONS

In the Reformation period spoken language was meeting a high level of competition—technically because of the invention of printing and the rapidly rising level of education, at least in the cities, and in content because of the cultural significance of new humanistic ideas. In the interim that has changed decisively. On the one hand, at present we are suffering from an explosion of words: words provide the information society with such an abundance of data that an individual can no longer master it. On the other hand—especially as a result of the proliferation of television—optical impressions seem to be depriving words of their primacy. Add economic and political advertising strategies that, with or without images, seek to manipulate their willing or even unwilling recipients. In light of these developments the Sunday sermon is something of a wallflower. This can only be intensified by deficiencies within the church itself, namely when the preachers do not rely on their own theological competence and personal testimony of faith but copy their sermons from the Internet, for example, and then read them, with only minor alterations, to a bored congregation.

There are also, of course, some basic problems with regard to the function of words and speech in general, and in particular about what should be understood by the phrase "the word of God."

What can words provide, beyond mere information? It is true that linguistic analysis presumes that a performative moment is always connected with any information, but how is the performative power of a speech intensified, and what are the criteria for its legitimacy? Must speakers stand behind what they say, or is a distanced communication sufficient? Does the subjective conviction of the preacher, sometimes paired with emotion, heighten the penetrating power of the word? Words may serve to awaken or sketch memories; they can arouse expectations whose fulfillment either occurs or remains forever lacking. What situational conditions in our dealings with words can we observe?

Luther gave no thought to these things, even though he paid great homage to language itself. His problem was how to convey the word of God in such a way that it both confronted people with God's law and communicated the consolation of the Gospel. How did the word of God become the vehicle of the Spirit of God? Does it have this function of itself, automatically, so to speak, although presupposing that the Spirit has the freedom to work "when and where it pleases God"? What is the role of experience in this? What can we say if people have no experience of the word of God (and the sacrament)? Is the word of God bound in any way to human words? What about inner experiences that occur when hearing music, looking at a work of art, meditating according to a method, or in the ecstatic act of sexual love? How is the word of God embedded in overarching contexts of experience and action? How and in what way does it arouse which reactions? When preaching at worship one is supposed—here I am loosely quoting Wilhelm Busch—to "sit firmly on the chair," in church and also in school. Under those circumstances are concrete reactions even possible, such as would instigate or strengthen a process of dialogue out of which and in which faith lives?[3] Is it not quite easy to explain how the word "preach" has become a pejorative? What is the result of this situation for Christian proclamation outside of worship, in schools and adult education, in the media, in evangelization and mission?

The frequency of Eucharistic celebration and participation in Lutheran congregations in recent decades may well serve as a sign of a certain surfeit of words. In any case it is clear that verbal and nonverbal communication are felt to belong together, and today the cognitive may be more easily unlocked by emotions and affects than an affect can be induced by words.[4] There seems to be much in favor of the observation that the sacrament is currently gaining in attraction.

But there are many and varied questions regarding the sacrament as well. It seems to be perceived somewhat ambivalently at present. On the one hand it is an incomprehensible and empty ritual for those who are strangers to the church, a rudiment of the past from a religious history that has become irrelevant. On the other hand, the return of symbolic thought has had its effects also on a new understanding of the sacrament. Esotericism has created a greater sensibility for processes that cannot be adequately explained by sense experience. Even magic has its advocates. The need for wholeness and, as far as possible, sense experience as well evokes the expectation of new "sacraments." Anointing services that involve a personal blessing are desired and are frequently held. Do women need different "sacraments" from men?

The question of sacraments has taken on a new aspect as a result of Latin American theology of liberation: should the concept of sacrament be expanded to include hitherto unfamiliar symbols such as the "sacrament of life history," a "cup of water," a "cigarette butt"?[5] Should the church, in its struggle on behalf of the oppressed and the poor, be seen in an entirely new sense as a sacramental reality within history?[6]

The ecumenical problem represents another field of conflict. The Leuenberger Concord of 1973 reduced the tension between the Reformed and the Lutheran understanding of sacrament without being able to resolve it theologically. As regards the relationship between Roman Catholic and Lutheran ideas about sacraments many questions still remain open, despite some progress that, however, has not yet produced any effects on the official church worth mentioning.[7] Within Lutheran theology the question of the legitimacy of infant baptism erupts from time to time, a question that has been clearly answered in the negative by most Baptist congregations. Karl Barth's protest against the "highly distorted" practice of baptizing children is still audible.[8] There is as yet no communication between the Western churches' concept of sacraments and the Eastern churches' understanding of *mysterion*, and the Eastern churches would say that the question of images must be included as well.[9] The meaning of "blessing" and "consecrating" is disputed among all confessions. What was Luther's view—and does it offer us any help?

LUTHER'S NEW CONCEPT OF SACRAMENTS

Luther's concept of sacraments has polemical and therapeutic features, though the polemical exists in service of the therapeutic. To begin with, Luther was not interested in a general concept of sacrament but in the concrete sacraments of baptism, Eucharist, and confession, all of them discussed, however, in regard to their sacramental status. Christ is the true sacrament and should be understood as *sacramentum*, not *exemplum*, in the case of justification. As he was drawn into conflicts with his opponents, though, Luther had to make an effort to give precision to his concept of sacraments. The first of these efforts is found essentially in his writing entitled *The Babylonian Captivity of the Church*.[10]

What can be called a "sacrament"? That was the deciding question in determining their number. In the Middle Ages people had counted up to thirty different sacraments; the number seven prevailed only from the thirteenth century onward, more precisely after the Council of Union in 1274. It was not made binding until Trent. Therefore the Reformer's concern was not that the church invent new means of grace so as to make believers dependent on it. For him the criteria for a sacrament were its institution by Jesus Christ, the divine promise of an eschatological benefit, and the association of that promise with an external sign. In line with these criteria confirmation, priestly orders, last anointing, and marriage do not qualify as sacraments. But the sacramentality of baptism and Eucharist was to be maintained.[11] The Mass, however, had to be delivered from three "captivities": the withdrawal of the cup from the laity, the speculations about transubstantiation, and the notion of sacrifice.[12] Penance and confession do indeed convey the forgiveness of sins and to that extent an eschatic benefit, but here the perceptible external sign is missing.[13] Protestants may notice that as a rule a Catholic very seldom can participate within his lifetime in all seven sacraments: only in the case of a widower who is ordained a priest, since as a rule canon law makes marriage and priesthood mutually exclusive. But Luther did not advance that argument! Even in Catholicism a certain "hierarchy" of sacraments has become accepted; Eucharist and baptism are central, but the validity of Eucharist is considered dependent on priestly ordination. Luther had to sharply reject that condition. According to the biblical witness[14] the spiritual priesthood is intended for all Christians.[15] "Therefore all Christian men are priests, all women priestesses, be they young or old, master or servant, mistress or maid, learned or unlearned."[16] The priests of the old order have no right at all to assert that their "priesthood is different from that which is common to all Christians."[17] Calling the Mass a sacrifice and saying that those who preside at it must be "anointed and tonsured" priests is, according to Luther, a blasphemy against Christ and his priesthood.[18] Assignment of individuals to preach and celebrate the sacraments is grounded only in the politics of organization.[19]

But Luther had to defend his idea of sacraments not only against his contemporary theologians from the old order. He also had to ward off the ideas of the Pietists. Men like Thomas Müntzer or Caspar Schwenckfeld could not regard external actions as important in spiritual matters; on the other hand, the Anabaptists wanted to make them dependent on prior faith. So Luther's idea of sacraments is shaped by the particular position with which he was confronted: in arguing with the old order he had to defend baptism against the idea that it was only completed by penance, and that monastic vows could be understood as a second baptism. Against the Anabaptists he pointed out that baptism, as an act of God, could not depend on prior human decisions, and that therefore the baptism of infants and children was appropriate. Regarding the Lord's Supper he had to reject the old believers' idea of sacrifice and to extricate belief in the presence of Christ from philosophical discussions, while against Zwingli and the Spiritualists he had to emphasize the real presence of Christ. But these disputes were about the understanding of individual sacraments and no longer primarily about an overall concept of sacraments. In the same way, the Augsburg Confession only turns to the description of sacraments after it has developed its ideas of baptism, Eucharist, confession, and penance.[20]

In any case, in Luther's theology the sacrament cannot be separated from the word; there can be no discussion of it in isolation, and for two reasons: the word, for its own part, is understood in terms of its sacramental power and cannot be reduced to knowledge or intellect. The word is sacramental, and at the same time the sacrament is of the word. In his early period the Reformer underscored the sacramentality of the word, and in his later years the word-character of the sacrament. But the word is always central. More depends on the word than on the sign. "For I can enjoy the sacrament in the mass every day if only I keep before my eyes the testament, that is, the words and promise of Christ, and feed and strengthen my faith on them."[21] The word has the greater weight; it is, in a sense, the decisive sacrament, and so it is what is decisive in the sacrament as well! Celebrating a sacrament without the word that creates faith is like a "case without the jewel."[22] In its sacramental power the word of God acts not only as a means of information or a medium of communication; it awakens confidence, courage, and justifying faith. Therefore—contrary to the usual sequence—in what follows we should discuss the sacraments first.

POLEMIC AGAINST THE "WORDLESS" SACRAMENT

What makes any sacrament a sacrament? Here again Luther was fighting on two fronts. In the view of the older faith it was the orderly celebration. For baptism this consisted of the carrying out of the rite as prescribed and above all in the use of the trinitarian baptismal formula; the hands of the priest were not constitutive in this case. Regarding marriage also, the priest has only a secondary importance for the sacrament, which is conferred by the couple on one another. But in any case the key lay in the phrase *ex opere operato*: the sacrament was valid *de facto* through its celebration. But especially regarding the Mass, the priest's action was regarded as indispensable. In him the church, and Christ himself, acted. His action assured what Augustine said about the sacrament: the Word is joined to the elements, and they become the sacrament.[23]

On the other side stood the enthusiasts, who considered the sacrament essentially superfluous. For them everything depended on the possession of the Spirit; sanctification was crucial. Nothing essential could depend on external actions and material things. For Luther, in contrast, it was important that faith not dissolve into mere thoughts and feelings. Faith had to have something to cling to, something "on which it stands and is grounded."[24] Word and sacrament reach a person from outside the self. But what is their relationship to one another?

The sacrament is constituted by the word. It does not stand independently alongside it. Without the word there is no sacrament; it lives out of the word. Regarding baptism Luther asks in the Small Catechism: "How can water produce such great effects?" His answer is: "It is not the water that produces these effects, but the word of God connected with the water, and our faith which relies on the Word of God connected with the water. For without the Word of God the water is merely water and no Baptism. . . ." Analogously, as regards the Lord's Supper he writes: "The eating and drinking do not in themselves produce them, but the words 'for you' and 'for the forgiveness of sins.' These words, when accompanied by the bodily eating and drinking, are the chief thing in the sacrament, and he who believes these words has what they say and declare: the forgiveness of sins."[25]

Word and faith are not things of equal weight, but are related to one another from the outset. Luther's understanding of sacrament exists within the tension of promise and faith. The word is certainly not misunderstood as having magical power; it develops its power by opening and confirming to the believer the promise that is given in the sacrament. Of course, the word is not lacking in the celebration of the sacraments according to the old rite, but it represents only a part of the *opus operatum* rightly performed, and it is not considered especially in its relationship to faith. But in Luther's view the Eucharistic words aim ultimately not at a belief that the host is truly the body of Christ; their aim is the trust that the forgiving and renewing grace of God is incarnately present and will have its effects. It is only in conflict with the enthusiasts and the "heavenly prophet" that the Reformer finds it necessary to present ontological arguments.[26] Word and faith, in interaction, constitute the sacrament, which to that extent is in principle viewed in terms of its "use." There is no Eucharist in itself without someone's receiving it. It is not a separate action of the priest at the altar; its function lies in its being received by believing people. Faith does not constitute baptism, but receives it![27] The word of God constitutes the sacrament as sacrament, and faith receives the sacrament as sacrament.

POLEMIC AGAINST THE SACRAMENT "WITHOUT CONSEQUENCES"

Luther's polemic against the "wordless" sacrament was directed at his opponents from the old faith. With his polemic against the sacrament "without consequences" he turned to his own Reformation camp. When the sacrament is received in faith it brings consequences with it. This is true both of baptism and of Eucharist. "What does such baptizing with water signify? It signifies that the old Adam in us, together with all sins and evil lusts, should be drowned by daily sorrow and repentance and be put to death, and that the new man should come forth daily and rise up, cleansed and righteous, to live forever in God's presence."[28] Something should and does "come of" baptism! Baptism sustains and shapes a Christian's everyday existence: "A Christian life is nothing but a daily baptism, received once and lived in forever."[29] Therefore no re-baptism is necessary, only "re-believing."[30] Claim is laid to baptism ever anew in confession and penance. "If you have fallen out of the ship, climb back in again!"[31] Baptism begins the process of mortification of the old human; seen thus, it finds its goal in the death of the body. "Therefore the life of a Christian, from baptism to the grave, is nothing else than the beginning of a blessed death. For at the Last Day God will make him altogether new."[32] Hence a believer will regard every adversity along this path as meaningful and appropriate, and be able, in God, to grasp and accept it with determination.[33]

Luther is also aware of the consequences of Holy Communion. In his early period he thinks not so much of individuals as of the community of believers: "For just as the bread is made out of many grains ground and mixed together, and out of the bodies of many grains there comes the body of one bread, in which each grain loses its form and body and takes upon itself the common body of the bread; and just as the drops of wine, in losing their own form, become the body of one common wine and drink—so it is and should be with us, if we use this sacrament properly." Here Luther adopts the ancient image from the *Didache*[34] to illustrate the consequences of participation in the Lord's Supper. "Christ with all saints, by his love, takes upon himself our form, fights with us against sin, death, and all evil. This enkindles in us such love that we take on his form, rely upon his righteousness, life, and blessedness. And through the interchange of his blessings and our misfortunes, we become one loaf, one bread, one body, one drink, and have all things in common. O, this is a great sacrament. . . ." Communion and exchange of gifts with Christ lead us to communion with and love for one another: "Again through this same love, we are to be changed and to make the infirmities of all other Christians our own; we are to take upon ourselves their form and their necessity. . . . In this way we are changed into one another and are made into a community by love. Without love there can be no such change."[35] Faith and love go together; in the Eucharist this is made clear sacramentally. In the argument with Zwingli and the enthusiasts, unfortunately, this point of view in Luther's eucharistic theology retreated, but it was revived in another way as part of his baptismal theology, where he returns to the development of the universal, mutual, and common priesthood of believers.

If the sacrament is not considered to the neglect of the word, the consequences must follow. Luther would later underscore this point of view in the sense of a self-criticism of the Reformation. Even in his early period, however, he thundered against the possible dangers of his approach. If so much depends on faith, and if the sacrament can be received spiritually in faith, "what need is there then to observe mass in the church?" Luther answers: faith is enough, it in fact accomplishes everything. But how does one attain it and remain in it? Without a concrete encounter with word and sacrament "visibly . . . in certain designated places and churches," it would probably be all over with it in short order. We must mutually "enkindle in one another such faith"; no Christian can do without the word of God. Moreover, God has instituted it.[36]

But if we take God's word seriously and do not let it be swallowed up in ritual its consequences become evident. The ethical imperative grows out of the sacramental indicative. So it is—so it should be! Luther's ethics are anchored in the theology of justification and simultaneously in sacrament. This is true both of baptism and of Eucharist.

BAPTISM

We can observe several stages in the development of Luther's theology of baptism. In the years before 1520 the "actualization of the grace of baptism" is in the foreground; this is about God's covenant with the baptized and the return to baptism in penance; the accent is on the significance of baptism for the individual believer. In the phase between 1520 and 1523 Luther primarily develops the ecclesiological implications of baptism; here he obtains his great insights on the universal priesthood of believers. In the years thereafter he had to defend against a relativization of baptism through a "rebirth" such as the enthusiasts demanded. Finally, in the period of the catechisms Luther's theology achieved its "mature form."[37] Baptism grounds the spiritual identity of the individual and thus also of the congregation.

BAPTISM AS PARADIGM OF JUSTIFICATION

The pastoral-therapeutic function of baptism

The remembrance of baptism was repeatedly a consolation and encouragement to Luther himself. In phases of exhaustion and internal conflict, it is said, he wrote in chalk on his table, "baptisatus sum—I am baptized!" Baptism gives believers an unshakeable ground for their living and acting. It is altogether independent of human activities; it rests solely on God's initiative. Baptism is "water used according to God's command and connected with God's Word";[38] God commanded it; ultimately it is not a human being but God himself who baptizes.[39] The baptismal water becomes a "water of God" that Luther could describe as "divine, heavenly, holy, and blessed."[40] It is no longer a natural "watery water,"[41] but "sweetened through and through with the name of God."[42] Through baptism God opens an irrevocable saving relationship with the baptized: "It effects forgiveness of sins, delivers from death and the devil, and grants eternal salvation to all who believe, as the Word and promise of God declare."[43] It is an exorcistic action with eschatological relevance.[44] God makes an eternal covenant with the individual baptizand. That person's whole life and everything that may happen in it is now surrounded by the grace of baptism. Baptism frees from sins and thus at the same time has eschatological significance: it bestows citizenship in heaven. But it also helps us to endure earthly life: "Christ is our protection, covering, shade, our mother hen under whose wings we dwell." This is true even if we are unable to keep the covenant: "Christ does not fall from the chair of grace because of my misdeed."[45] The ship is steady; if anyone should fall out, that one should swim and see to it that he or she gets back in![46] If you have not believed, then believe now![47] Confession and penance are ways of laying claim to baptism anew. Life in baptism is for Luther a personally applied message of justification. Preaching may not reach me because of my inattention, but in the sacrament I understand that the message is for me, that the Gospel touches me in my psychosomatic wholeness.

Infant baptism and the child's faith

Of course, Luther has to submit to the question of how these noble statements are to be understood and maintained with regard to the theology and practice of infant baptism. He does not have any particular difficulty with the answer: the baptism of immature children is for him the essence of what happens in justification: human beings cannot bring any kind of prior merits or preconditions with them; God acts sovereignly in divine grace. But how can this be understood in light of Luther's assertion that it is only faith that opens itself to this event and knows how to use it?

At the outset the Reformer can certainly rely on biblical points of view. The institution of baptism, as described at the end of Matthew's gospel, is universal; why should children be excluded? Likewise, the Acts of the Apostles speaks of the baptism of whole "houses," that is, entire families and household communities (cf. Acts 16:15); certainly these also included children. Luther has no difficulty in applying the so-called "children's gospel" (Mark

10:13-16) to baptism; if children are supposed to come to Jesus they should certainly also be allowed to receive baptism! Finally, what would the people of God be without children—surely an eccentric idea! But—quite contrary to his arguments in another place—Luther can also appeal to tradition: infant baptism is affirmed "by the infusion" of the Holy Spirit;[48] if infant baptism was not true baptism in the sense in which it was instituted there would have been no church for more than a millennium, since as a rule it was children who were baptized, and not adults.[49] Finally, we must consider the witness of those who were baptized as children and have shaped the church's history by their thoughts and actions. By appealing to tradition here the Reformer appears to reveal himself as altogether inconsistent; but this is a consistent inconsistency—aimed, that is, at the center of Christian faith as he understands it: the justification of human beings by faith alone.

But what about the relationship between baptism and faith if baptism can only be received through faith? First of all, the Reformer considers it possible to baptize children in light of the faith of the godparents, who bring a child for baptism and thus pray that the baptizand will find his or her own way to faith. But this contradicted his basic assumption that there can be no substitution for a person in regard to faith; therefore he quickly abandoned that argument. Nevertheless, a point of view continues here that could be important for the later development of the understanding of baptism: children are baptized not because of the godparents' faith or that of the church, but "the faith of the godparents and [all] Christendom begs and acquires for them their own faith, in which they are baptized and believe on their own account."[50] Baptism leads to a process of socialization within the Christian community that can and should contribute to the instigation of faith in individuals.

In speaking of "childhood faith" Luther developed a thoroughly original idea.[51] How can we know that immature children really cannot believe? That they do not yet have the use of reason as adults do is no argument, since faith is a gift of God to which in any case reason can only assent after the fact. God can make an ungodly person become a believer, so why not a child? Ultimately Luther even introduces a biblical argument for childhood faith: when the pregnant Mary visited Elizabeth, who was also expecting a child, namely John, who would become the Baptizer, "the child leapt" in her womb—an act of homage to the yet-unborn child Jesus (Luke 1:41). For Luther this argued that John was "believing and sanctified" when Christ spoke to him through the mouth of his mother.[52] Luther sees the point of this incident, however, not in the excitement of the fetus but in the ability of Jesus to make himself present even to those yet unborn.[53] The Reformer was not concerned about what happens in baptism on the human side; the issue for him was God's sovereign act. God also gives faith to adults freely and without any precondition; why should this power be denied in the case of an immature child? Luther's idea of childhood faith, as naïve and absurd as it may at first sound, fully matches his understanding of the relationship between baptism and faith.

Faith and baptism

Of course Luther does not deny for a moment that faith is indispensable for the realization of what is offered to people in baptism. It is true also of adults who submit to baptism after making a clear decision in faith that they cannot avoid recurring to their baptism again and again, ever anew, in faith. In any case, baptism, after its celebration, must be continually accepted and, so to speak, ratified in faith. That, in fact, is the fundamental form of the act of faith itself: I affirm and lay claim to what God has promised me. When faith awakens, "baptism claims its own."[54] Baptism is the outward sign and seal showing that Godself vouches for my salvation and will bring it to its goal in spite of all temptations and misunderstandings. As I can contribute nothing to my own birth, so also the preconditions for the eternal success of my life cannot be created by me. It is God who grounds my identity in this life and beyond the borders of death. To that extent baptism can be seen as the essence of the event of justification, the "sacrament of identity."[55] A repetition of baptism is thus out of the question.[56]

BAPTISM AND THE COMMUNITY

Luther's theology of baptism is conceived in terms of individual believers. The connection between baptism and the idea of community, however, became clear to him in the course of his efforts at church renewal.[57] He determines that the authorities that are supposed to care for the well-being of the community, namely bishops and the pope, are more interested in other things and leave the church subject to multiple misunderstandings and misuses. What should be done in this situation? Luther turns to Christians who are not part of the hierarchy but are baptized, belong to the Christian church, and therefore should take action: the "Christian nobility of the German nation."[58] When a fire breaks out, he argues, we cannot wait for the mayor; every citizen is then obligated to take part. Every Christian, in an emergency situation, is responsible along with all others for the well-being of the community. The idea of the right of necessity had already been acknowledged for a long time, even in the medieval church, as applying to the possibility of emergency baptism by laypeople.

The proper weight of Luther's argument is borne by his idea of baptism. With great emphasis he formulates and repeatedly reiterates that we are "all consecrated priests through baptism." A spiritual difference in rank between priests and laity cannot be maintained. "All Christians are truly of the spiritual estate";[59] "all of us that have been baptized" are "equally priests."[60] The thesis is then developed theologically and reflected upon especially in *The Babylonian Captivity of the Church*.

Why does baptism have such a fundamental significance? It is through "spiritual birth" in baptism that the human being becomes a new creation.[61] Because of their baptism Christians are free and not dependent on any kind of impositions from clerical authorities. The blessing of baptism makes the church a space of freedom.[62] The Christian is anointed with the oil of the Holy Spirit and made holy in body and soul—what does a further anointing to priesthood mean? Whoever "comes out of the water of baptism can boast that he is already a consecrated priest, bishop, and pope."[63] The way in which every Christian comes into the most direct contact with Christ through baptism is simply unsurpassable by anything.

Of course, when Luther sees the universal priesthood grounded in baptism he is not thinking of an effectiveness of the sacraments through their celebration alone. He knows that baptism needs faith and that faith is awakened through the preaching of the word. Therefore he often places baptism within the broader context in which it belongs and in which it can also be understood in connection with the rationale for the universal priesthood. We are all members of the spiritual estate because we all "have one baptism, one gospel, one faith, and are all Christians alike; for baptism, gospel, and faith alone make us spiritual and a Christian people."[64] Through our new birth in baptism we are all brothers and sisters of Christ. "My dear friend, in your baptism you have entered into a brotherhood with Christ, with all the angels, with the saints, and with all Christians on earth"; within the congregation, distinctions can have only functional significance.[65] Thus a Christian may also be Christ to another;[66] there is no higher calling. All may "be priests for one another."[67] Serious consequences follow for Luther's understanding of Orders.[68] A preacher or ordained priest is assigned, "made" such, but a priest in the true and spiritual sense of the word is "born"—namely by water and Spirit in the celebration of baptism.[69] Baptism is the calling to the universal, mutual, and common priesthood of believers.

The emancipatory and church-critical side of this approach was grasped relatively soon. The constructive impulse—the calling to priestly action, especially in community, to spiritual mutuality—proved more difficult to accept. If this side of the baptismal event has been neglected in the ongoing history of Protestantism, one reason for it is that Luther himself did not give more deliberate attention to making it effective. Thus the Catechism does not pay explicit attention to it and it appears only marginally in Luther's confessional writings. Nevertheless, through the centuries Luther made his Small Catechism an instrument of the universal, mutual, and common priesthood!

The Lord's Supper

A number of stages may also be observed in Luther's understanding of the Eucharist, the Lord's Supper. The accent shifted according to the specific confrontation in which the Reformer was engaged. In his "Sermon on the Blessed Sacrament of the Holy and True Body of Christ and the Brotherhoods" (1519)[70] his concern is with communion with Christ and the heavenly world and also with the community of believers that results. In "The Misuse of the Mass" (1521),[71] as in *The Babylonian Captivity of the Church*, Luther speaks against the Mass as sacrifice. In both cases the issue is the spiritual benefit the Lord's Supper brings to the individual and the community. Beginning in 1524 the real presence of Christ is in the foreground of the conflicts, as Luther contended with Karlstadt, Oeculampadius, and Zwingli. This is the context of the writing "That These Words of Christ, 'This is My Body' Still Stand Firm Against the Fanatics" (1527) and finally "Concerning Christ's Supper," with its appended "Confession" (1528). This phase concluded, then, with the Marburg Colloquy of 1529. Here we reach the "mature form" of Luther's eucharistic doctrine; the presentation in the Catechisms was able to do altogether without any kind of polemic.[72]

In interpreting Luther's understanding of the Lord's Supper one must pay attention so as not to read it to the detriment of the left or the right. On the one hand there could be a temptation to give the word priority over the sacrament in such a way that the accent lies more strongly on the sign-character and the Lord's Supper itself ultimately seems superfluous. On the other hand, it would not be adequate to Luther's view to place the sacrament above the word, to see it as an independent entity with its own status and as constitutive for Christian faith as such. According to Luther word and sacrament may not be played off against one another. If the sacrament truly cannot be thought of without the word, nevertheless both are unique gifts of God instituted and commanded for human salvation and the glory of God. During his lifetime the Reformer engaged both the great themes that made themselves known even in his early understanding of the Eucharist: communion with Christ and the communion of believers with one another.

The ecclesiological significance of the Eucharist

The common eating and drinking seems today to be the primary revealer of the meaning of the Lord's Supper: it is about sharing with one another and practicing communion. For Luther this communicative side of the Eucharist was a matter of course, but since it arises only out of communion with Christ it is subordinate.

Functional mutuality

The sacrament of the altar, Luther wrote in his early period, means "the complete union and the undivided fellowship of the saints."[73] Christ forms a union with all the saints resulting in an exchange of goods. As in the human body, all the members care for one another: "if anyone's foot hurts him, yes, even the little toe, the eye at once looks at it, the fingers grasp it, the face puckers, the whole body bends over to it, and all are concerned with this small member."[74] Individuals may also lay claim to this: "'Though I am a sinner and have fallen, though this or that misfortune has befallen me, nevertheless I will go to the sacrament to receive a sign from God that I have on my side Christ's righteousness, life, and sufferings, with all holy angels and the blessed in heaven and all pious men on earth."[75] The Holy Eucharist "seeks" people who need it.[76] The sacrament must not be "made," but "used in faith."[77] Here the issue is, so to speak, a mystical union with the heavenly world; the christocentric pointing is not yet complete. The fact that ethical consequences follow from the reception of the Eucharist follows as a matter of course from this mystical reality. But after the great confrontations over the real presence Luther could also make use of the ancient church's image of the grains of wheat and the grapes, which lose their form and become an inseparable whole.[78] Now, however, communion among believers appears more prominently as an ethical consequence of communion with Christ; this is a reminder of it. The difference between communion with Christ and that of believers with one another comes more to the fore.

Common creed

The late Luther, perhaps inspired by his encounter with Zwingli, regarded participation in the Eucharist as also confessional. When I go to Holy Communion I witness that I, too, "am one who would praise and thank God."[79] Simply existing "in the midst of the multitude" has its ecclesiological function.[80] In this way I contribute to keeping the memory of Christ present in the world, and in doing so I help to honor God.[81] In sharp distinction from the doctrine of the Mass as sacrifice in the late medieval tradition, Luther propagates in this connection the idea of a "sacrifice of thanksgiving," though it is not always clearly evident whether he understands the eucharistic action or participation in Holy Communion as the sacrifice of thanksgiving. Here an anti-right interpretation of Luther's theology of the Eucharist can take hold and protest that the Reformer "also left some room for the ancient church's designation of the Lord's Supper as 'Eucharist.'"[82]

Why does Luther not make the celebration of the Lord's Supper the responsibility of the universal, mutual, and common priesthood?[83] He requires fathers to preach the word within the family, and if necessary even to baptize, but he radically denies them the independent celebration of the Eucharist! Is this not a remnant of late medieval sacramentalism that has not been overcome? A conservative interpretation of Luther could conclude here that Luther after all, in some sense, clung to the priest's power of consecration. But he also polemicized against private Masses, as they were requested in his time for a particular intention and payment was given, and they could be celebrated by a priest without the presence of the congregation ("Winkelmesse," "Mass in a corner"). This in no way accorded with the meaning of the sacrament! Luther decidedly viewed the Eucharist as a "public action of the community."[84] The celebration of the Lord's Supper should be public, and should be presided over by a servant of the community publicly appointed for that purpose.[85] Luther even recommends that, if none of the authorized servants is available, it would be better to do without the celebration of the Eucharist, since as such it is not necessary for salvation. While in the first years of his activity, then, he emphasized the inner side of the ecclesiological significance of the Eucharist, in the second half of his life the fact that the Christian community gathers for the sacrament of the altar and thus gives public testimony to the glory of God came to the fore.

THE CHRISTOLOGICAL CENTER OF THE EUCHARIST

For Luther, Jesus Christ is the center of the event of the Lord's Supper, and this in three respects: as the one who gives himself through the sacrifice of his life, as the one who commissions us to celebrate the Supper, and as the one who becomes present to his own in the celebration. This is already implicit in the ecclesiological statements, but it was more clearly worked out in the arguments about the concept of sacrifice, the words of institution, and the real presence of Christ.

Christ's sacrifice

In the Eucharist Christ gives himself to his own by making the sacrifice of his life efficacious for them. The words of institution articulate Christ's testament, which Luther can interpret in the sense of a guarantee attested by a notary.[86] In his "Sermon on the New Testament," which is not about the New Testament as a book but about the Eucharist, he formulates this idea so one-sidedly and intensely that one gets the impression that Jesus died solely in order to be able to leave behind this testament for the benefit of his own.[87] The doctrine of satisfaction, which is otherwise closer to his thinking, retreats here. At the same time a subtle theory of sacrifice appears: for Christians, sacrificing means offering themselves in the sense of the Lord's Prayer: "Thy will be done!"[88] Christians can bring such a sacrifice of thanksgiving and praise at any time and everywhere and let it be conveyed to God through Christ as their "priest or minister."[89] Nevertheless, it is probably misleading to speak of Luther's "theology of the sacrifice of the Mass," since Luther is not interested in a specific theology of the Mass as sacrifice; his aim is to recover an understanding of the Eucharist that corresponds to the Gospel. In addition, such ideas are found almost exclusively in the Reformer's early development, and they are unclear in many respects.[90]

The words of institution in the Eucharist point to the death of Christ, the elements to the life they promise. "Given for you and poured out for the forgiveness of sins"—"for you" and "for the forgiveness of sins" are repeated three times, highlighted, in the explanation of the sacrament of the altar in the Small Catechism. In the Eucharist God makes us participants in and certain of his self-sacrifice in Christ. The late medieval theology of the Mass, however, had turned that around: according to a saying attributed to Pope Gregory I, the priest repeats the sacrifice of Christ in an unbloody manner. In the formulation of the canon of the Mass, which still echoes in expressions currently in use, the church, or the priest, offers the sacrifice.[91] Luther scourges the "misuse of the Mass."[92] "Where is it written, that the mass is a sacrifice . . . ? Christ has sacrificed himself once; henceforth he will not be sacrificed by anyone else." The church has changed the meaning of the Eucharist on its own initiative; the New Testament knows of no sacrifice except the sacrifice of Christ on the cross and the believers' sacrifice of praise. The "nature and character" of the sacrament are thus "completely" changed. Sacrificing and trusting God's promise are mutually exclusive. "A sacrifice is a work in which we present and give to God something of our own. The promise, however, is God's word, which gives to man the grace and mercy of God." If a prince hands his goods over to someone and that person wants to give them back in order to enrich the prince and present himself or herself as the benefactor—would that not be madness? But anyone who sees the Mass as a sacrifice means to enrich God with God's own gifts! The church has taken charge of the Eucharist and invented the sacrifice—in its own interest. "'Eat and drink!' That is all that we are to do with the sacrament"—and remember Christ and proclaim his death. "He who sacrifices wishes to reconcile God." But when people try to reconcile God on their own initiative they turn the Gospel into its opposite. The promise of the Eucharist should entice and excite us to accept what God gives us. "What greater gift could he have promised than forgiveness of sins, which is nothing other than grace, peace, life, inheritance, eternal honor and blessedness in God?" Therefore the Mass may not be celebrated as a sacrifice, and the canon of the Mass must be altered accordingly![93]

Luther warns that "we who desire to be Christians" should "aid in doing away with such masses."[94] Has this injunction been fulfilled?[95] The idea of the Eucharist as sacrifice has not been made so precise in recent developments in Catholic doctrine or corrected in such a way that Luther's critique would be altogether unjustified.[96] For Luther the theology of the Mass as he found it was a reversal of the Gospel, and that is why he called it "the greatest and most horrible abomination" of the papacy, "the supreme and most precious of the papal idolatries,"[97] especially since a host of misunderstandings, misuses, and superstitions have attached themselves to it: the doctrine of purgatory, with pilgrimages, brotherhoods, indulgences, the notions of "poltergeists" growing out of it, and more. Instead, we ought to remember what the New Testament has to say about the Lord's Supper!

The text of the words of institution

Luther appealed for both the positive development of his eucharistic doctrine and the exclusion of misunderstandings of the words of institution. He proceeded in two trajectories: the wording spoke against the withdrawal of the cup as practiced by the old believers: "All of you drink of it!" It is true that at the beginning of his work Luther shared the so-called doctrine of concomitance according to which it was sufficient for the body and blood of Christ to be presented only under the form of bread. In his *The Babylonian Captivity of the Church* he turned against the withdrawal of the cup, above all because he saw it as a self-empowered intervention by the church in the words of Sacred Scripture. It is true that, beginning with the conflicts with the Hussites, the cup had taken on church-political and even secular-political implications. We can still see on the tombstones of clerics that the cup was a special mark of priests and constituted their dignity—but the Hussites had demanded that the cup be offered to every Christian. The chalice, as, for example, it stands resplendent on the gable of the Teynkirche (the Old Hussite Church) in Prague, became a symbol of protest against Rome!

The other trajectory of the words of institution had to do with spiritualization, as Luther perceived it especially in Karlstadt and then Zwingli. The bread and the cup are communion in the body and blood of Christ (1 Cor 10:16); Luther considered this statement by Paul "a thunderbolt on the head of Dr. Karlstadt and his whole party." But for Luther it is medicine and consolation,[98] for one may rely on what Christ himself has offered us! The more closely our celebration of the Eucharist resembles the way Christ himself celebrated it,[99] the more certain the ground on which we stand. Luther is not disturbed by the fact that the wording appears differently in different parts of the New Testament. On the contrary, he regards this as a confirmation of what is attested, because "the Holy Spirit studiously arranged that no evangelist should agree with another in exactly the same words. Yet these evangelists ought to have been more in agreement . . . than we. . . ."[100] Luther himself did not hesitate to harmonize the various texts into a "text for memorizing."[101] He thus purified the version used at Mass from expressions that framed and adorned it, and recalled the text in its original form, which must be seen as a unity: "This is my body" must not be isolated from the command, "Take and eat!" It is in light of the latter that the "Hoc ist corpus meum" must be interpreted![102] In this sense he insisted, at Marburg, on the wording: "My dearest sirs, since the text of my Lord Jesus Christ reads *Hoc est corpus meum*, I cannot pass over it. . . ."[103] At the beginning of the colloquy he wrote on the wooden surface of the table at which he was sitting: *Hoc est corpus meum*, and then drew the tablecloth back over it. When Zwingli sought to drive him into a corner with his arguments,

> Luther removed the velvet cloth and showed him the passage, "This is my body," which he had written for himself on the table with chalk, and said: "Here is our Scripture passage. You have not yet wrested it away from us, as you volunteered to do. We have no need of another passage." Zwingli asked whether he had no Scripture passage, argument, or testimony other than this one alone. Luther answered: "Indeed I have others, which you will hear after you have succeeded in taking this one away from me; since I have a sure word of God which no one can wrest from me, why should I let go of it and look about for another? Overthrow this argument, then you can expect to hear what additional arguments I have."[104]

What Christ has commanded is what counts, even if it appears impossible to understand. Luther prefers to accept what he cannot understand from the divine lips rather than take what appears understandable from human beings! In Marburg he insisted that if God told him to eat dung and he knew that it would be for his health he would certainly do it.[105] Zwingli recoiled in horror: God does not command such a thing!

Why does Luther show so little flexibility here? He is certainly not concerned about the wording in a biblicist sense, because it is written, but about what the wording announces, namely the promise it contains. In the bread and wine Christ promises himself to his own, and that is not to be doubted! Everything depends on the "is." The word "signifies," which Zwingli had adopted from the Dutch jurist Cornelius Hoen, opens a soteriological distance between Christ and the communicant that contradicts the promise of the words of institution. This is about the presence of the body of Christ, not its representation.[106] "Do this in memory of me" must be interpreted in terms of the "is" and not the other way around. There must be no cognitive-spiritualizing dissolution of the gift of the Lord's Supper, for this is about the effective memory of the effective promise. Nevertheless, the concept of memorial opens a narrow bridge between Luther and Zwingli. For the Zürich reformer, for whom the "night meal" is, after all, the proclamation of community and a sign of covenant, and so at the same time public thanksgiving (*eucharistia*), the memorial (*commemoratio*) is seen as a recalling that makes present what is remembered.[107] Luther might have been able to speak of a creative memory that incorporates the word of promise,[108] but that, too, would have been theologically inadequate for him.

Still it remains astonishing that the dialogue partners in Marburg were ultimately able to assent to fourteen points of agreement. Even the fifteenth, regarding the Lord's Supper, contained a series of common opinions: they together opposed the idea of the Lord's Supper as a sacrificial Mass, and together they confessed the "spiritual enjoyment" of the body and blood of Christ and the saving function of the sacrament together with the word of God, namely in moving weak consciences to faith through the Holy Spirit.

Christ's presence

With regard also to the question of the way in which Christ is present in the elements Luther had to fight on two fronts: on the one side against the doctrine of transubstantiation and on the other against a spiritualization of Christ's presence as represented by Karlstadt, Zwingli, and others.

The soteriological starting-point. In Luther's time the idea of transubstantiation was a relatively new concept; it had first been officially recognized by the Fourth Lateran Council in 1215. It said that at the priest's words of consecration the bread and wine were "essentially transformed" into the body and blood of Christ, in such a way that the substance changed while the accidents (color, taste, consistency) remained the same. This was intended, in the medieval frame of thought, to ward off two types of misunderstanding: Christ is in the elements not as, for example, a king is in his palace ("doctrine of impanation"); on the other hand, the accidents are not reduced or destroyed (annihilation of the accidents).[109] For Luther that was "the specious learning of the sophists."[110] Nevertheless, he approved the earlier condemnation of the symbolic eucharistic doctrine of Berengar, a condemnation that in principle rested already on the basis of the later doctrine of transubstantiation. Luther would rather have "only blood" with the pope than "mere wine" with the fanatics.[111] It was important to him that Christ is really and bodily present, with all his gifts, in the bread and wine of the Eucharist, and communicates himself there. The details of how we should conceive that reality may remain open. I ought not to "encircle" God;[112] "we may well allow it to be said that it is in the bread, it is the bread, it is where the bread is, or whatever you wish. Over words we do not wish to argue, just so the meaning is retained that it is not mere bread that we eat in Christ's Supper, but the body of Christ."[113]

Luther himself is not bothered by what he cannot see through intellectually. He takes his reason "captive to the obedience of Christ" and clings "simply to his words."[114] He does not consider it "necessary" that bread and wine be transubstantiated so that Christ is present beneath their accidents, but "both remain there at the same time, and it is truly said: 'This bread is my body; this wine is my blood.'"[115] If anyone wants to speak of transformation, it would be better to say that the food of the Lord's Supper "transforms us into itself and out of fleshly, sinful, mortal men makes spiritual, holy, living men."[116] According to the explanation of the sacrament of the altar in the Small Catechism, the body and blood of Christ are, "under the bread and wine, given to us Christians to eat and drink."[117] Occasionally Luther uses the particle "in" as well as "under," but never Melanchthon's "with."[118] The formula "under, with, in" has only been used in Lutheran theology since the Formula of Concord.[119]

Philosophical constructions as supplementary aids. However, in some contexts Luther himself summoned philosophical constructions to his aid. For example, he refers to the linguistic figure of synecdoche, by which one speaks of a part as standing for the whole; we point to a sack of coins and say: "This is a hundred gulden."[120] The Reformer deals with the problem of metaphors at length.[121] It is possible that he had learned "that the Scripture is most artfully arranged, if . . . one looks at it in terms of its rhetorical style."[122] The concept of ubiquity, the omnipresence of the body of Christ, which was employed against the Swiss, also represented such an auxiliary construction. The phrase "real presence," incidentally, does not come from the usage of the Reformer himself. But it was essential for him—both as regards God, who binds the divine self to bread and wine, as well as human beings who are to participate, in that bread and wine, in the reality of the risen Crucified—that nothing should detract from the real, personal presence of Christ. How this happens, "we do not know and are not meant to know. God's Word we should believe without setting bounds or measure to it."[123] Luther rejoices, somewhat naively, that "the simple faith of this sacrament is still to be found, at least among the common people. For even if the common people do not understand, "neither do they dispute whether accidents are present without substance, but believe with a simple faith that Christ's body and blood are truly contained there."[124]

Invention of theological language. So the issue is not at all one of a theory of consubstantiation over against a doctrine of transubstantiation; it is one of "establishment of identity."[125] In the course of the conflict Luther makes good on this approach in linguistic terms: in Christ the concepts we normally use acquire a new meaning: "Not that they describe a new or different thing, but they describe it in a new and different way, unless one should want to call that in itself a new thing."[126] Notger Slenczka calls this "newly defined reality."[127]

This view is grounded in Luther's notion of the creative power of the word of God. God's word is simultaneously "command-word" and "action-word"![128] In the terminology of contemporary linguistic analysis it is a performative utterance. The words of institution, if they are not meaningless, must have their own linguistic status, as is the case—in a different way—with poetry, for example. A spoken word changes perspectives and situations; the speech-gesture can create presence "and thus cannot be completely contained in the model of mere representation."[129] This is, of course, an inadequate description of Luther's notion of the power of the word of God. Add to this that, in turn, it is the words of Sacred Scripture that teach us to recognize the power of the word of God, and thus the new reality it creates, for what they are. The words, and not, for example, symbolic actions, "push us toward faith."[130] In the Eucharist Christ "also now exceeds any grasp, and you will not catch him by groping about, even though he is in your bread, unless . . . he himself gives meaning to the bread for you, by his Word, bidding you to eat him."[131] In faith, bread and wine are perceived as what they are: the body and blood of Christ.

To that extent the expression "Christ's making himself present" is not an adequate description of this process.[132] It is a fact that this self-making-present by Christ occurs neither through a representative sacrifice nor through memory, but on the basis of the promise of Christ himself, which produces faith. In Luther's understanding, Christ's making himself present is his self-promise in taking possession of the bodily reality, which therefore also has its effects even in the physical realm. To that extent Luther can say "the bread is the body of Christ,"[133] and yet he knows that this is a statement that can only be made in faith, and only in faith can it become fruitful for me. For "of course no one can drive these words through the throat into the stomach, but he must take them to heart through the ears."[134] Both the physical and the spiritual eating are necessary: the "sacramental unity" (*unio sacramentalis*).[135]

Problematic implications. Luther's approach has implications that, if taken in isolation, occasion misunderstandings. Thus he defends the *manducatio oralis*, the reception of the body and blood of Christ into the mouth. This of course raises the question of what happens if the Eucharist is taken without faith (cf. 1 Cor 11:29). On the one hand Luther can say that anyone who "does not believe has nothing";[136] on the other hand he defends the *manducatio impiorum*, for even the ungodly will be confronted with the reality of "Christ's sacrificial body and covenant blood."[137] Even those who misuse the Eucharist encounter the perspective of promise, though for them it turns into a perspective of ill. Thus in Luther's interpretation there is a tension: on the one hand precisely they should come to the Lord's Supper who are fearful and despairing and hope for forgiveness, for "he is truly worthy and well prepared who believes these words: 'for you' and 'for the forgiveness of sins.'"[138] But on the other hand there is an unworthiness that leads to judgment, as we can see in the Corinthians who made the sacrament "physical gluttony."[139]

Another difficulty in Luther's approach lies in the doctrine of ubiquity. Without using the word he applied this idea against the fanatics and Zwingli's doctrine. He may have adopted it from Ockham by way of Gabriel Biel, who described the omnipresence of God as ubiquity, namely, a non-objective presence.[140] Luther postulated ubiquity for the exalted Christ, including his human bodiliness. For Zwingli, on the other hand, a bodily presence that no one can see or touch is impossible to imagine. For him, in any case, the material could not have a constitutive spiritual significance: "The flesh is useless" (John 6:63). After all, if Christ is bodily in heaven since his ascension, he could not be present in the same way in the Lord's Supper. For the Zürich theologian only the idea of a "spiritual partaking" was sustainable. Luther, on the other hand, understood "heaven," the "right hand of God," in the sense of an ubiquity that of itself made possible the bodily presence of Christ in the Eucharist. But Luther gave little thought to the fact that a distinction between the idea of ubiquity and the notion of a special presence of Christ in the Lord's Supper would necessarily raise new questions. Of course, he did not see his thoughts on ubiquity as a confessionally binding doctrine, but as a possibility and a help for thinking about the issue.

Christological alternatives. Behind Luther's and Zwingli's different ideas of the Lord's Supper stood some definite christological options. For Zwingli, as later for Calvin, Christ sits at the right hand of God and thus outside the earthly dimension: *finitum non capax infiniti*—what is temporal is incapable of receiving into itself what is infinite. The exaltation of Christ to the right hand of the Father must be taken seriously, and God's sovereignty must be upheld! Karl Barth would say: God is in heaven; you are on earth! Reformed doctrine of the Lord's Supper rests on the christological *extra Calvinisticum*. Behind it, ultimately, stands the Antiochene christology of separation.

Luther, in contrast, asks: where is the right hand of God? It consists of the sovereignty of God's grace and love! God's freedom is demonstrated in that God binds God's very self—for the benefit of humans. God became human so that human beings may participate in God: this has been a basic axiom of Christian theology since Athanasius. God's saving will must be upheld! "[T]he glory of our God is precisely that for our sakes he comes down to the very depths, into human flesh, into the bread, into our mouth, our heart, our bosom; moreover, for our sakes he allows himself to be treated ingloriously both on the cross and on the altar."[141] The background here is the fundamental soteriology of Alexandrine christology, if you will, with a monophysite tendency. Both options represent legitimate theological intent: for the Swiss Reformation the unconditional awareness of God's sovereignty and transcendence, for Luther the radical self-promise of Christ extending even to the physical realm.

THE THERAPEUTIC FUNCTION OF THE EUCHARIST

The therapeutic aspect is present in Lutheran eucharistic piety from the very beginning. It is not only about an obedient liturgical celebration according to the directions of the one who instituted it, or the correct carrying out of a testament. The very word "testament" inspired Luther to take an interest in what the testator is handing on.[142] "What is the benefit of such eating and drinking?" he asks very pragmatically in the Small Catechism.[143] Five points should be made here.

Personal and total appropriation of salvation

Theoretically we of course know more today about psychosomatic connections than did the theologians of the sixteenth century. But expressions and proverbs indicate that the psychic dimensions of eating and drinking have been known for quite a long time: "Eating and drinking keep body and soul together," and "you get to the heart through the stomach!" Eating and drinking are the most intensive forms of "taking to oneself," "absorbing" in the fullest sense of the words: ". . . when we eat the sacrament we absorb Christ into ourselves and he does the same."[144] It is about concrete eating and drinking, so that—according to the Large Catechism—"the sacrament may be mine and be a source of blessing to me."[145] This is a wholistic inclination and appropriation: "The heart cannot eat it physically nor can the mouth eat it spiritually. So God arranges that the mouth eats physically for the heart and the heart eats spiritually for the mouth, and thus both are satisfied and saved by one and the same food."[146] Now of course Luther knows that one cannot acquire "forgiveness of sins, life, and blessedness" through the organs of chewing and swallowing. He protests against a confusion of the consecrated elements with psychopharmaceuticals by pointing out that such eating and drinking receive their meaning and function solely from the word of God. "Such a gift and eternal treasure cannot be seized with the hand."[147] But Christ's promise of himself combined with the physical elements extends into the physicality of those who receive them in faith, even into the stomach.[148] For those who receive it, then, the Lord's Supper has a therapeutic function that touches even the most elementary functions contributing to life, reaches the psychosomatic whole person, and effects the most radical and comprehensive absorption. This connection is not alien even to the critics of religion, for example when Ludwig Feuerbach sarcastically asserts that "man is what he eats."[149] As regards the Eucharist, Luther would not dispute the connection but he would interpret it soteriologically.

Integration into the Body of Christ

For Luther the motif of community among communicants was of the highest importance. In the sermon already mentioned, "The Blessed Sacrament of the Holy and True Body of Christ and the Brotherhoods" (1519), he recommends especially that people who are in crisis should receive communion and entrust themselves to the community of believers.[150] It is the same as what we experience in our own bodies: if "the smallest toe" is in pain, the whole body reacts and the whole person gives her or his whole attention to eliminating the cause of the damage and getting rid of the pain.[151] The Lord's Supper reveals its therapeutic power by integrating the individual, with all his or her adversities and also all his or her gifts, into the community of salvation, so that the individual on the one hand receives relief and on the other hand finds a field of affirmation into which one can bring oneself, both as sufferer and as active. This idea later fell into the background of Luther's thought, but it remained present: when I receive the sacrament, community happens.[152]

Identification with Christ

Certainly Luther never considered that salvation could lie in the communion of persons as such, or that their common eating and drinking would in itself be therapeutically effective. It is all about communion with Christ! He, "with all saints, by his love, takes upon himself our form, fights with us against sin, death, and all evil."[153] Food "enters into" the people who receive it, so that the eater and the eaten can—unlike things that are nailed or cemented together—no longer be separated: "Thus in the sacrament we too become united with Christ, and are made one body with all the saints"; he cares for us and acts on our behalf, "as if he were what we are."[154] According to Luther the therapeutic function of the Lord's Supper, however important for it the group is, as the basis for the experience and the field within which we are tasked, grows directly out of what cannot be explained simply by human community and common action. It lives out of the alien and alienating to which it refers—namely, that Christ initiates a "joyful exchange"[155] with sinful human beings. That is why it is so important to Luther that there be no doubt about the real and personal presence of Christ in the Eucharist.

Catharsis: reconciliation with the ground of being

"[Given] 'for you' and [shed] 'for the forgiveness of sins.'" These words are repeated three times in the Small Catechism in a way that is almost monotonous and unimaginative. They describe the use of "such eating and drinking"; they speak of the "chief thing" in the sacrament because the one who accepts these words in faith receives what they proclaim: "the forgiveness of sins." Finally, we are to understand from them who is "truly worthy and well prepared" to receive the Eucharist, namely the one who believes these words.[156] In the self-gift bound up in the bread and wine believers encounter, in a bodily fashion, the ground of their being, which releases and delivers life from everything destructive. But that ground is—as expressed in words—the sacrifice of Christ that consists in his self-gift; God personally guarantees it and thus reconciles the world with Godself. God destroys the destructive and chaotic that inseparably saturates our lives, not by a word of power but by subjecting Godself to it, suffering it, taking it on and being responsible for its consequences. In Luther's metaphoric language, which in some way can be called more realistic than logical or theological abstraction, this means: "I . . . let him—Christ—eat what is evil in me"; at the same time I let him "lap up" what I have "ladled out" for him with my destructiveness; "but from him I receive faith, joy in chastity, etc., and live from it"; I gain confidence for my life and joy in shaping it spontaneously and freely. So now "I, in turn, let myself be eaten and drunk" by my fellow Christians, as in the reign of Christ each stands at the disposal of the other with everything she or he has.[157] We should use the sacrament "as a precious antidote [lit.: *thyriak*]" against the poison that is in us; Luther is speaking here of a medicine applied in the sixteenth century against infection from animal bites or snake venom. "For here in the sacrament you receive from Christ's lips the forgiveness of sins, which contains and conveys God's grace and Spirit with all his gifts, protection, defense, and power against death and the devil and all evils."[158] The ancient image of the sacrament as a *pharmakon* is adopted here,[159] though brought up to date and by no means referring only to immortality. It is here dynamized and personalized: we are not talking about heavenly materiality misunderstood as magic. Rather, the Christ who gives himself in his grace in a way that relates to the body makes that body and the soul healthy. This is the working of the "pure, wholesome, soothing medicine which aids and quickens us in both soul and body. For where the soul is healed, the body has benefited also."[160] So in Luther's view the therapeutic function of the sacrament of the altar consists essentially in the invitation to believers to identify with the ground of their being. Thus it has an eschatological perspective and also an eschatological relevance. We may find it regrettable that in the explanation of the Eucharist in the Small Catechism there is a one-sided emphasis on the forgiveness of sins. But it is idle to argue whether in Luther's theology of the Eucharist it is the forgiveness of sins or *unio* with Christ that is central. For him both belong inseparably together and are two sides of the same thing.[161]

Emancipation from all that is destructive and chaotic

Reconciliation, refreshment, consolation, and strengthening of those under attack are always correlated in Luther's thought with equipping, enabling, and making free to act in a threatened world. The mythological language in which he expresses those ideas is alienating today: "Your devil does not rest, and the world and the flesh do not take a holiday."[162] Armed for battle by the Eucharist, we take up the fight against chaos. We do not get rid of it; we will not eliminate it, just as "our Lord Christ himself could not entirely avoid [it]."[163] But we are not handed over to it either; it will not devour us: Christ assures believers of this in a quite specific way through the sacrament of the altar. Christ draws believers into his eschatological battle against the power of chaos; he stakes "all he has and his blood for you, as if he were saying: Fall in behind me without fear or delay, and then let us see what can harm you . . . !"[164] It is a matter of eternal salvation, and to that extent the therapeutic points of view in Luther's theology of the Eucharist are always surrounded by a soteriological and eschatological horizon. Even in his early sermon on the Eucharist of 1519 he calls the sacrament "a ford, a bridge, a door, a ship, and a stretcher, by which and in which we pass from this world into eternal life."[165] But a view toward and hope for the world beyond can never mean neglecting the concrete earthly situation. On the contrary: in faith in eternal life and its indisputable meaning the gift and task of the moment are fulfilled. Those who participate in the sacrament in faith comprehend to the depths even of their bodies the confidence that their lives, despite all sins and failures, are moving toward an eternal fulfillment.

CONFESSION

The question of sin and forgiveness appears nowadays to have passed largely into the secular realm of psychology and psychotherapy, but it does not seem to have been done away with. That it is primarily secular institutions that are made use of may also have to do with the neglect of confessional practice in the Lutheran churches. Originally it was Lutheranism in particular for which confession was an extraordinarily serious matter,[166] and here and there surviving Lutheran confessionals still express that fact. Still, a good deal of traditional confessional practice has continued, in a sense, in client-centered pastoral care. For Luther, who all his life strove to explain and proclaim the message of justification, confession was at the center of his thought and spiritual practice. Hence confession must have been especially close to his heart. As a result he also found himself in an important field of conflict with late medieval theology and the church. He had to explain whether confession should be understood as a sacrament, and if not, what constituted it and what was the nature of individual confession.

IS CONFESSION A SACRAMENT?

In the late medieval church confession was a disciplinary instrument of the first order. Beginning with the Fourth Lateran Council of 1215 every believer was obligated to go to oral confession at least once a year and confess his or her sins. "Mortal sins" were to be described in detail; venial sins could be omitted. Everything depended on the priest's speaking the *ego te absolvo*, which was to be accepted as *ex opere operato*, valid by virtue of the mere celebration of the sacrament, but it was associated with certain conditions. God's forgiveness did not imply reconciliation with the church and relief from temporal punishment. Here indulgences helped; these the church could bestow by drawing on the "treasury" of merits of Christ and the saints. There were, in turn, certain opportunities for spiritual or even financial engagement associated with gaining an indulgence.[167]

It would have been attractive to Luther to treat confession as a sacrament. It was instituted by Christ and conveys eschatological graces. But it lacks a symbolic material element. The uncertainty of the location of confession within Reformation theology is still reproduced in the sequence of the articles in the Augsburg Confession: Articles XI and XII, on Confession and Repentance, follow immediately after the articles on Baptism and The Holy Supper of Our Lord (IX and X), but precede the summary statements on the use of the sacraments in Article XIII. In the Small Catechism the chapter "On the Office of the Keys and Confession" was inserted in the second edition in 1529.[168] Luther sees the institution of confession in the relevant accounts in Matthew's and John's gospels (Matt 16:19; 18:18; John 20:22-23), which speak not only of "loosing" and "forgiving" sins, but also of "binding" and "retaining." Luther wants to take both of these seriously; confession should lead to the relief of burdened consciences but must not serve to promote libertinism. Confession is about life and death. The church has two keys: the "binding key," namely the power to confront impenitent people with their attitudes, acts, and omissions or to exclude them from the congregation, and the "loosing key," namely the authority to absolve from sins and promise eternal life. One key promotes the work of the Law, the other that of the Gospel.[169] Inasmuch as believers on earth remain both justified and sinners, both "keys" are relevant to them. According to Luther confession has two aspects: those who confess declare their sins and acknowledge them clearly, and they receive the absolution spoken to them in faith. These rules are established against the opinion of the late medieval church according to which the conditions for a valid confession are "sincere contrition" (*contritio cordis*), oral confession (*confessio oris*), and satisfaction (*satisfactio operis*). Contrition, since it represents a psychological phenomenon and could be misunderstood as a psychic work, cannot be regarded as a precondition. It will happen, but it is not to be produced by human beings; it comes from God. The confession of sins need not be done orally; it can also be part of a prayer to God. Effects on the level of behavior and action will not be lacking, but they are not to be understood as conditions for forgiveness.

Admission of Sin

Being a Christian means for Luther that one acknowledges one's own sins, allows oneself to be absolved, and lives out of God's grace. Thus it is a constitutive element of Christian existence that one admit one's own failure and guilt. This is attested, in its own way, by the Our Father, with the never-superfluous petition "and forgive us our sins, as we forgive those who sin against us!" Indeed, the whole Our Father implies such a confession for Luther, because what is our prayer but "a confession that we neither have nor do what we ought and a plea for grace and a happy conscience?" Such a confession "should and must take place incessantly as long as we live," for Christian existence consists in this, "to acknowledge ourselves sinners and to pray for grace."[170]

Besides this, however, Luther also recommends making oneself aware of individual sins; we should not be content with a "cloudy generality."[171] How do I become aware of my sins? "Reflect on your condition in the light of the Ten Commandments: whether you are a father or mother, a son or daughter, a master or servant; whether you have been disobedient, unfaithful, lazy, ill-tempered, or quarrelsome; whether you have harmed anyone by word or deed; and whether you have stolen, neglected, or wasted anything, or done other evil."[172] Thus the criteria are, on the one hand, the concrete commandments as they can be found, for example, in the Decalogue, and on the other hand my current place in society. A commandment is not seen as an independent norm; it confronts me with the radical claims of God. Situational prescriptions or church rules can help me to perceive this. But it is certainly not a matter of listing individual sins; instead, I am to become aware before God of my guilty involvement. When, in this sense, I know my situation and come to seek the relief offered by the promise of forgiveness, a "joyful fear and trembling" fills me before the face of God.[173]

Absolution and the "Lesser Ban"

Luther considered absolution the second constitutive element of confession, along with the confession of sins. What is essential is that the forgiveness be explicitly pronounced: the person confessing and in need of consolation must hear spoken aloud "that through a man God looses and absolves him from his sins."[174] Hence going to confession will not be a burdensome duty for a Christian, or a good work, for in confession one receives something thoroughly useful for one's life: relief and the enabling of confident and responsible action.

In the Reformer's view a brother (and certainly a sister is implied) may pronounce absolution for another. Luther thus takes up the practice of lay confession, known before his time but forgotten in the interim. He was also able in this instance to appeal to the early Christian rule (cf. Matt 18:18; Jas 5:16). God, he says, has poured out charisms on Christians and "filled every corner of them with forgiveness of sins so that they may not find that forgiveness in the congregation alone, but also at home, in the fields, in the garden, and wherever one comes to another, there shall he find consolation and rescue."[175] For it is an enormously consoling occasion when one draws the other's attention to his or her own inner deficits and helps him or her to overcome them in God's name.[176] The *mutuum colloquium* and *consolatio fratrum* are for Luther essential duties and opportunities for the universal and mutual priesthood. Nevertheless, there is still an imbalance here: in the Large Catechism Luther speaks of the "neighbor" but in the Small Catechism of the "confessor," who is to be addressed as "Dear Pastor."[177]

Of course, it is not true that absolution must be pronounced in every case. The "office of the keys" is "a function and power given to the church by Christ to bind and loose sins, not only the gross and manifest sins but also those which are subtle and secret and which God alone perceives,"[178] but to retain the sins of the unrepentant as long as they do not do penance. The seriousness of forgiveness is clear especially from the fact that it is given only to those who truly desire it and are ready to draw consequences from it. The extended instruction on the office of the keys was only subsequently added to the Small Catechism, and the "exhortation" to the Large Catechism as a kind of "self-critique of the Reformation" (Walter von Loewenich). The Large Catechism says the Lutherans "learned it only too well; they do whatever they please and take advantage of their freedom, acting as if they will never need or desire to go to confession any more."[179] The Reformer is quite familiar with the refusal of absolution and so of a form of excommunication, the so-called "lesser ban," though in clear contrast to the "greater ban" practiced by the late medieval church, consisting of the withdrawal of all the rights appertaining to membership in the church, including the consequences in civil law.[180] The "lesser ban" had nothing to do with civil consequences and consisted essentially of refusal of the sacraments. It was intended as a therapeutic means in the sense of the argument already presented by Paul (cf. 1 Cor 5:5) and as a deliberately undertaken exclusion should serve the end of reintegration into the body of Christ. But undoubtedly the question of forgiveness was in the foreground for Luther, as it should be accomplished in every sermon through Law and Gospel, since no Lutheran preacher could "ever open his mouth . . . without speaking absolution."[181]

INDIVIDUAL CONFESSION AND "PUBLIC SIN"

Luther by no means rejected individual confession; on the contrary, he valued it highly. The "secret confession" between two Christians "when some problem or quarrel sets us at one another's throats and we cannot settle it, and yet we do not find ourselves sufficiently strong in faith" should allow us "at any time and as often as we wish [to] lay our complaint before a brother, seeking his advice, comfort, and strength."[182] In individual confession (highly subject to misinterpretation when it is called "private confession") the seriousness and the gift of confession are expressed in extraordinary measure. Luther only rejects compulsion to oral confession, which has something tyrannical about it and lacks any foundation in Sacred Scripture. If it is undertaken freely a great blessing rests on it, "for here God's word and absolution are spoken privately and individually to each believer for the forgiveness of his sins, and as often as he desires it he may have recourse to it for this forgiveness, and also for comfort, counsel, and guidance." Luther regards it as "a precious, useful thing for souls, as long as no one is driven to it with laws and commandments," and "as long as one is not forced to enumerate all sins but only those which oppress him most grievously, or those which a person will mention in any case."[183] In individual confession the word is addressed "to your person alone."[184] In the proclamation at the worship service the assurance of grace flies "into the congregation," while in individual confession it touches "no one but you alone."[185] The Reformer also regarded individual confession as extraordinarily helpful for himself and used it often. The pastoral conversation and advice connected with it were important to him: even if that were all there was, for that reason alone he did not want to do without individual confession.[186]

Nevertheless, there were the beginnings of general confession, the so-called "open accusation," even in the Reformation period, with some pre-Reformation tendencies coming into effect. These were penitential prayers, which could be combined with the liturgically prescribed listing of individual sins, followed by petitions or the proclamation of forgiveness.[187] Luther himself could regard the Our Father as a common confession and the exchange of the peace as a public absolution.[188] On the whole, however, confession had a problematic history in the Lutheran territories: in many places it was combined with an examination prior to the Lord's Supper at which the catechism must be recited. The rule that confession and examination were to be held before the local pastor could not be felt to be anything but compulsory and ultimately could only be maintained by means of regulations that were completely contrary to the Gospel.[189] This development, alongside other intellectual or personal factors, contributed to the fact that individual confession, but in the course of time common confession as well, have been almost entirely abandoned, at least among Protestants in central Europe, and that there the practice of confession can only be said to be neglected—in a church that regards itself as the church of justification!

Luther himself gave very little consideration to the relationship between the fundamental preaching of justification and the necessity of confession. Why, if justification was given once for all in baptism, must one pray again and again for forgiveness? It may have been clear to the Reformer himself that human beings on earth, even though justified, remain lawbreakers and must continually creep back into baptism, need to hear again and again the preaching of the law that points them to the liberating Gospel. Luther underscored this in his argument with his former friend and colleague Johannes Agricola.[190] But as in the course of time justification and freedom became common truths of Protestantism it no longer seemed so reasonable. In any case, it remained theologically unclear whether for people who live in faith in the message of justification there is some sin that is not forgiven. Unquestionably, the pronouncing of forgiveness strengthens the assurance of justification. But is that only an anthropologically significant action, or is it important before God? Luther would answer: in the pronouncing of forgiveness there is always a new outpouring, actualization, and application of justification. The penance that endures throughout a lifetime arises out of the faith in justification, as does the longing for the word of forgiveness, which is to be grasped in deeper and deeper ways. This was probably so obvious to him that he did not regard a systematic questioning of the necessity for explicit confession and forgiveness as something important.[191]

The Word of God

The Reformer's theology is sustained by trust in the word of God. That is why he makes such an effort to differentiate it clearly from traditions that threaten to add to, distort, or misuse it.[192] It is an indispensable medium of salvation. The sacrament lives out of the word, and the word points to and grounds the sacrament. Contrary to the superficial opinion that Reformation notions of sacraments, because oriented to the word, tend to rationalism, one must insist on Luther's view: his understanding of the word itself is sacramental. The word acts not only for the future of humanity but affects each person's whole psychosomatic existence. Here we are thinking essentially of the oral word, the word concretely proclaimed. Word and sacrament are the "means" and at the same time the "instruments" through which the Holy Spirit is given, as the Augsburg Confession (Article V) formulates it. Preaching, as the proclamation of the word of God, is thus for Luther not the object of theological lectures. He preaches about preaching, but not about problems in preparing to preach, as is sometimes the case today; he speaks about the essence of the sermon, its kerygmatic shape, and ultimately the office of preaching. But he assumes a society socialized by Christianity; consequently, the theme of "mission" appears only marginally.

THE SERMON

The sermon, for Luther, is an act that gives honor to God. This is evident from the way he often begins his sermon: "In order that we may give glory and thanks to our Lord God, let us listen to the gospel."[193] The sermon creates a space for God in which God is glorified: "When I cry to him in my sermon and with my praise, and preach about him, what a mighty and excellent God he is, then he is exalted and made known."[194] An essential element of the sermon is thus simply a grateful acknowledgment of God's mighty deeds.

The greatest deed of God is that God has given the Son. Hence Luther can summarize the program for all preaching with laconic brevity: "*Nihil nisi Christus praedicandus*—nothing is to be preached but Christ!"[195] It is of course insufficient to present Christ's life and work only superficially, "as historical facts,"[196] because then nothing would happen! Preaching must truly communicate Christ: "I preach the gospel of Christ, and with my bodily voice I bring Christ into your heart, so that you may form him within yourself."[197] In this way "we are with him there above and he with us here below; through preaching he comes down, and so we through faith rise up."[198] In fact, his coming consists of nothing else but that he preaches throughout the whole world.[199] We may regard it as disappointing that Jesus Christ should be present only in the naked word. But this is at the same time the great spiritual exaltation of the word, an enormous hope for all who preach and listen to preaching. For the Reformer the preached word is always accompanied by the "cooperative working and inculcation of God."[200] These formulations, dictated by mysticism, would later be replaced by Luther's expressions about the Spirit. The preacher and the audience must assent to the word from within themselves outward: "'Eia, vere sic est'"—"'Ah, this is true!'"[201] Of course, this remains utterly out of our reach. Because Luther knows that, he assumes that Christ not only speaks in the preacher but also listens in the hearer—"ipse in te audit."[202]

The word is the central location of the Spirit of God, the point of contact between God and the human being. Therefore it is necessary to understand and magnify the majesty and authority of the word.[203] This happens through the "crying out" of the grace of God; the "living voice" is "queen and empress."[204] Luther knew that it is not enough to press written material into the hands of people distanced from the church. What is decisive happens in direct address and listening: therefore the event of preaching also does not depend on how close to being ready for publication a sermon is; rather, what matters is that it be received by the hearer as "living," that is, addressed to her or him. The Reformer had his "Postilles" printed in order to provide material for situations in which there were scarcely any pastors familiar with the Reformation faith. But the very idea that, as today, Lutheran preachers who have many semesters of theological study behind them and are practicing Christians would copy their sermons from the Internet and read them from the pulpit would disgust him.

Luther preaches preaching. The famous statement of Angelus Silesius, that what matters is not only Jesus' birth in Bethlehem but also his birth "in you," was anticipated by his critique a century and a half earlier: "If Christ had died a hundred thousand times" it would have been no use if it were not preached![205] In preaching, God's self-surrender is realized. Through the sermon, as miserable or annoying as it may sometimes be, "he shakes out his very person, as widely as the world extends."[206] Luther also uses the image of a love affair with God begun through the sermon: in it God offers the divine self to us as our "paramour," and through the preacher "he seeks to see who wants to be his bride."[207] The preacher—lovers' go-between, marriage broker between God and the human being!

THE PREACHING OFFICE

In his early days Luther spoke emphatically about preaching by the laity. Referring to 1 Peter 2:9, he said: "Since all Christians are called out of darkness, each one is bound to declare the might of Him who has called him."[208] This was explicitly true for women also—despite the apostolic admonition that they should be silent in the congregation (1 Cor 14:34-35). Of course, no one would seek as preachers any who are dumb or inarticulate, for one who preaches should have "good voice, good eloquence, a good memory and other natural gifts." In that view it is men who are more likely to have those skills. But the principle is that "if no man were to preach, then it would be necessary for the women to preach."[209] Faith itself is the "proper priestly office," and for that very reason "all Christian men are priests, all women priestesses, be they young or old, master or servant, mistress or maid, learned or unlearned."[210] Luther sees the universal, mutual, and common priesthood not as competition to the priestly office; on the contrary: the calling of all requires that one from among them should take on the office of preaching and administration of the sacraments. "If everyone were to preach, who would listen; if they all preached at once there would be a bawling such as the frogs make: Kar ker ker. . . ."[211] That is not an absolutely conclusive argument, because the members of the congregation could take turns. But democratic ideas had not advanced that far in Luther's mind, and his experiences with peasants, fanatics, and enthusiasts were not so ideal as to invite him to develop them further.

So as a rule the preachers have the task of proclaiming the Gospel. For laity their chief duty in regard to preaching heard in worship was to do their homework afterward. If the Gospel was not vigorously considered and discussed in homes, "it will not hold its place in the pulpit."[212] Without a congregation that works at what it has heard there will be no place left for preaching. Certainly Luther counts prayer as part of the homework to be done: "good prayer belongs after a good sermon, to give strength to the word."[213]

Apparently because he was shaken by the utterly individualistic religious activities of the fanatics, Luther was ambivalent about the laity's engagement with the Bible: on the one hand he found it good that two or three people should speak together about questions of faith; on the other hand he sharply rejects the idea that the Gospel should be talked about in taverns as if it were a fable about Dietrich of Bern.[214] Luther regarded that as a problematic method of mission, and one that was inadequate to the message.

This explains what Luther had to say about the authority of the preacher. He presents his congregation with the picture of the kind of "masters" preachers are: They have their own sphere of mastery, namely the duty to proclaim the truth.[215] But that is not often perceived in them; so it happens that some will gladly go a hundred miles to a church "because our Lord God himself speaks there."[216] But in reality everyone who speaks the word by commission from Christ's community may assume that his or her mouth is "Christ's mouth."[217] Luther himself seems astounded at the possibility that through a preacher thousands can come to faith, and he advises that if anyone knows a good preacher he or she should thank God "that one has experienced it."[218] It is said to be a truly remarkable event if God "let us hear a comforting and strengthening word" through a preacher or in any other way.[219] From there he comes to the bold conclusion about words that, used as a false claim to authority, have caused a great deal of evil: preachers, like parents—one may well add "equally"—are "gods" to those entrusted to them because they carry out duties that properly belong to God, namely helping, advising in all crises, and doing good.[220] Luther assigns a crucial position to preachers—one, it is true, that makes harsh demands on them.

It is well known that the Reformer was no Donatist; he considered it possible for a preacher to bring many to God and yet not be personally pious and ultimately to go to the devil.[221] He, Luther, wished that if Judas were still living people would not reject his preaching, because when God's word is preached it is still God's word whether spoken by a Peter or a Judas.[222] Suspecting that a colleague has impure motives is no reason for not taking his theology seriously. That "the pastor himself doesn't believe" cannot, according to Luther, serve as a cheap pretext for staying away from worship. At the same time, naturally, he expects that the lives and teachings of those in office will correspond as much as possible.

However, he sees the greatest danger for preachers in an altogether different place. The resignation that characterizes so many pastors nowadays did not seem to him the great challenge, although in truth he, too, knew something about the failures of his own spiritual office. He heard the peasants saying: "What Gospel? Money!" That struck so deep in him that years later he still repeated it in the original dialect.[223] But he saw the greatest danger for preachers and sermons in superficial success! He, Luther, never wanted to be a preacher if everyone thought him a good one—God protect us from preachers who please everybody![224] He observed the element of modishness that affects the choice of preachers even today, and he presents some cutting pictures of star preachers.[225] He pounds it into his students: the Gospel was not given to us so the people will acclaim us![226]

For Luther preaching is a dangerous business because it involves engaging with powers that are opposed to God.[227] Paul Althaus—altogether according to the mind of Luther—calls the problematic preacher a "public hazard."[228] Those who preach the Gospel clearly and so as not to be misunderstood must reckon with resistance, not applause. Like the child in the manger whom they are to proclaim, they will be turned away from their places and sent to the barn. Their hidden work, their lack of success correspond to the style of the God of Jesus Christ, who can conceal himself under his opposite and is powerful in the weak. Word and sacrament share in this inconspicuousness, in the God— the child in swaddling clothes, the man on the cross—who wants to encounter human beings.

MISSION

The concept of "mission" in the modern sense was, of course, something Luther knew nothing of. He did not found any missionary societies and he did not send out missionaries. Nevertheless, he was not altogether ignorant of the idea of mission.[229] In his work "That Jesus Christ Was Born a Jew" he did think about how to motivate Jews to convert to (Reformation) Christianity.[230] He at least hinted at spreading the evangelical witness among the Turks.[231] In both cases, of course, he was skeptical about the result. But God could be trusted to complete "the miraculous work" and perhaps even to convince a Turkish Pasha to adopt the Christian faith.[232] Arguing with a Jew, in any case, was like "beating an anvil with a straw."[233]

Luther gave three reasons for mission to the heathen, insofar as he engaged it at all. In the first place he assumed that the blessing of God's promise would extend to both Jews and pagans. The Gospel is like a stone, he said, that one throws into the water so that waves spread out from it in circles.[234] The reign of Christ would accomplish itself; God's reign comes in any case "of itself without our prayer," but we ask in the second petition of the Our Father "that it may come to us."[235] Accordingly, Christians are called upon to bring the Gospel to the heathen; it should spread like fire in straw and dry wood and make a place for the reign of Christ.[236] Werner Elert interprets this: "The Gospel is steadily attacking those who do not want to hear it."[237]

The addressee of the Gospel—the second reason for mission—is the whole world; God wants to be God for all people. It is true that the message has gone out throughout the world, but it has not yet reached every place. Therefore preaching must continue until the Last Day.[238]

But ultimately, according to Luther, it is the word of God itself that breaks the road and effects its own reception. To that extent even the regular community worship assembly is a missionary event. It is also true that authentic faith cannot hold back: it "breaks out and confesses and teaches" the Gospel—even if it costs the believers their own lives.[239] In a word: where there is faith, there also is mission. It is striking that Luther scarcely ever argues— as the later pietist mission did—that pagans must be preserved from hell. It is true that Luther by no means shared Zwingli's belief that even pagans like Socrates and other great persons from antiquity would be redeemed.[240] But he could speak of people who, in his opinion, are seeking the truth and, without knowing it, are waiting for the saving message to be brought to them.[241] Regarding Cicero, whom he especially admired, he said in his Table Talk that he hoped God would "be gracious to him and those like him," but of course it is not our business to assert such a thing.[242] Despite his firm rejection of universal redemption in principle, his idea of mission is not soteriologically but theocentrically oriented and motivated. He proceeds entirely on the basis of his experience with the effectiveness of the word of God in and of itself. Hans-Werner Gensichen interprets this to mean that according to Luther it is clear to believers "that God, Christ, the word himself is the subject of mission to the world." For that very reason he is also aware "of God's mission as a matter for all Christians."[243]

Carrying out mission in no way implies compulsion in any form; Crusades and a crusading mentality are utterly out of the question.[244] But it is a matter of course for the Reformer that every Christian has the duty to witness to the Gospel; it is part of Christians' dignity, since the universal, mutual, and common priesthood of the baptized is accorded and committed to them.[245] He also considered model behavior by Christians to be effective for mission. In addition, he actually considered sending preachers among the pagans.[246] If one wanted to be active in witnessing to the Gospel one might have to learn a foreign language; Luther regretted that he did not know Arabic. His advocacy of the translation and publication of the Qu'ran is certainly to be understood in terms of his apologetic-missionary engagement.

It remains remarkable that Luther took no concrete steps toward missionary activity, even though as early as 1519 he accused the pope of not doing justice to his missionary duties to the Turks.[247] Herbert Blöchle suggests three reasons, though they are only partly convincing:[248] first there was the political and military tension between the Turks and the Empire, which was not a good environment for missionary activity. But could not a peaceful mission—on the model of Francis of Assisi and his dialogue with the Sultan of Egypt—have contributed to alleviating that tension? Second, the expected approach of the Last Day made an extensive mission unnecessary or even impossible. But could it not instead have been a motivation to missionary haste? Finally, Luther's attitude to the Turks was more apologetic-defensive than missionary-offensive. This of course raises the question of Luther's reasons for that attitude. One major one could have been the simple fact that in the sixteenth century responsibility for the Christian message was regarded more or less territorially. Hence Portugal or Spain, not Saxony, seemed obligated to undertake the mission.

We may ask ourselves why the Reformer had so little trust in the effective power of the word of God among the Jews and Turks. Of course, he did not count on the word's being automatically effective. He knew that it is a grace when the word comes over a land "like a passing shower of rain," which indeed can rapidly move on.[249] Nevertheless, it remains to be explained how, with regard to the conversion of the Turks, Luther seems to have relied more on modeling than on proclamation.

CRITICAL EVALUATION

Critical questions directed at Luther's theology of word and sacraments come from many directions: does the Reformer's thought represent an isolating overvaluation of the word? Is his doctrine of sacraments marked by a "sacramental positivism" inherited from the Middle Ages? What philosophical assumptions and prejudgments no longer shared today have shaped what he says about word and sacrament? Finally: in his interpretation of word and sacrament is the church as a necessary precondition neglected? To these problems, immanent to the system of Luther's theology, we may add some contemporary questions that are at least in part associated with those problems.

WORD-FETISHISM?

Luther assigns an exalted position to the word. He himself had certainly experienced the creative and innovative power of the word, and he made good use of it. He regarded the word sacramentally, and at the same time he saw the sacrament in terms of the word, resulting once again in a preponderance of the word.

The effective results of this were highly problematic. In the age of orthodoxy, but especially in the period of the Enlightenment and afterward, this led to an intellectualizing of Protestant Christianity. Pietism and parts of the Awakenings in the nineteenth century were able to legitimate spiritualizing tendencies by reference to the word. The inflation of the word in the twentieth century resulted in a banalization that led, especially within Protestantism, to an exhaustion with preaching.

On the other hand, linguistic analysis has opened new opportunities of access to the word; a line of poetry can express more and different things than purely factual information. Symbols are being rediscovered as something not less valuable than positivistic statements and actually going beyond them. They point to a reality not grasped by normal communicative language. That this also offers opportunities for charlatanism and manipulation is another matter. Nevertheless, symbolic speech as such must first be accorded its value. Propositional language also contains implications that point to the religious field. Whoever says "I" is required, as such, to question and determine the position of this "I" in the midst of its surroundings and experiences.[250] Finally, the perception of performative language, as profiled by John L. Austin and now seen as a fundamental element of human speech, appears to affirm Luther's understanding of the word.[251]

Luther himself had derived his ideas about the word from the Bible, especially Old Testament interpretation, in which word and thing fused. When God "speaks, it happens; when he commands, it comes to be" (Ps 33:9). This is reproduced in the New Testament: "only speak the word," says the centurion at Capernaum to Jesus, "and my servant will be healed" (Matt 8:8). As regards the Old Testament one can, of course, ask whether the theological conviction about God's power in the word precedes the Hebrew usage, or whether theological consequences are being drawn from a particular idea of language. In the context of today's perception of the differences in language behavior and conceptualization throughout the world we must, in any case, incorporate linguistic possibilities that contradict Hebrew and Indo-Germanic grammar and include, among other things, the possibilities of expression within Asiatic language families.

That the word of God can encounter people through hearing and speaking was for Luther not a language-immanent possibility, of course; it was something he attributed to God's omnipotence. He was not bothered by the fact that the same sermon heard by a number of people at the same time was meant to address individuals and so its effect, from a human point of view, was dependent on rather accidental factors on the part of the hearers as well as the preacher. In the word, Luther found, God used a specific opportunity to encounter a person—in preaching and pastoral care. As regards the word of God, its effects in the human person would not fail. Rudolf Bultmann took up this hint of Luther's understanding of the word in his idea of the "kerygma" that existentially touches and changes people. In Gerhard Ebeling's language about the "word event" linguistic analysis, theological scholarship, and exegesis come together. Luther's understanding of the word of God is altogether supported by these.

Luther neither isolated the word with regard to the sacrament nor with regard to the life it releases from itself. He is by no means talking of "hypostatization"; the word does not become an independent entity with its own relevance. It is important today, rather, to rediscover with Luther that preaching is not directed only to the conscious mind. The word, as that of the triune God, points beyond itself to what cannot be adequately expressed by means of language, not only grasping the conscious mind but leading to an awareness of the nearness of God that encompasses the whole human person.[252] Luther thus would probably have understood that the word is conveyed by other media. Music and the chorale were close to his heart in any case. As someone who made intensive use of the means of communication of his own time—printed books and open letters—he would certainly recommend to the church today that it get more deeply involved in the world of media. He was sensitive to the needs of the society around him and he knew how to apply the Gospel to experience. For him the word of God did not exist in the abstract but always in relation to a particular situation. He could speak it in such a way that it evoked either resistance or assent. He reported naïvely and gratefully on the successes of the word of God. He did not let himself be discouraged by failures because he entrusted the effects of his preaching to the will and governance of God.

Sacramental positivism?

The accusation that Luther's idea of sacraments could represent an inappropriate materializing of the spiritual was expressed during the Reformation itself, both by the Reformed group and by the enthusiasts. The Enlightenment suspected magic and superstition here. Does Luther's sacramental theology not contain a massive and insupportable amount of medievalism? The idea that a sacrament, while it does not work *ex opere operato* (by its very celebration), does have its effect simply through the speaking of a word that is received in faith was hard to distinguish from the traditional Roman Catholic idea of sacraments. Is it not true that this medieval overburden is evident in Luther's reasons for infant baptism, in which tradition represented an important part of the argument? Did Luther "pursue a wrong path to its end"?[253]

Obviously we must admit that Luther was in fact a child of his time and could not simply divest himself of inherited ideas. But his sacramental theology is clearly anchored in the whole of his theological thought; it corresponds precisely to his theology of the word of God. The word transcends itself and so requires the sacrament. A human being does not live only from word to word; people are not appealed to only through words and they also react to the things that appeal to them by other means than words. A wholistic self-perception on the part of the human being in awareness of both hemispheres of the brain corresponds altogether to the mutuality of word and sacrament as Luther describes it. But more important for him was the theological argument, namely that it is God's intention to grasp the human being as a whole and thus make Godself present to and communicate with each person totally—which includes the bodily dimension, to the depths of the material, psychosomatic self.

Nevertheless, the question remains whether the Reformer did not accept or propose inconsistencies that detract from rather than adding to his thought. We may refer to his notion of "childish faith," his talk of the *manducatio oralis* of the unworthy and of the "ubiquity" of Christ, exalted in his human nature as well. The strong equation of the interpretation of the water of baptism as "Godly water" with the presence of Christ in the eucharistic elements is not persuasive either exegetically or in terms of systematic theology. Certainly, if we look more closely we can see that the points I have listed are by no means intended to ground theological statements; rather, they represent conclusions, consequences that no longer fit well within the picture and have no sustaining function in the architectonics of Luther's theology. The Reformer may himself have regarded them as indispensable, but as derived notions they are not dogmas; they are only possibilities he thought of, suggested, and tested. Today, however, no one is obligated to accept them. Certainly he saw more clearly than some later theologians that theology cannot exist only as a sum of intellectually satisfying "consistencies"!

A third objection arises, certainly, from current exegesis: what is the historical status of the institution of the sacraments by Jesus himself? For Luther it was obvious. Both the command to baptize and the account of the Last Supper have, however, become matters of controversy. The last word has not been spoken just yet; New Testament scholarship appears no longer to be as skeptical here as it seemed to be after Rudolf Bultmann. At the same time it is clear that the New Testament itself traced baptism not to the historical but to the risen Jesus, and that the words of institution at the Supper were liturgically shaped by the first communities. Of course this does not make baptism and Eucharist rituals that have nothing at all to do with the historical

Jesus. They are deeply anchored in what the gospels say about Jesus, in Jesus' own baptism and his meal practice. To that extent it is appropriate to speak not of an "institution" of the sacraments, but of a clear "context of institution" within which they stand.[254] The memory of the context of institution could perhaps be an aid today especially to those who are unable to "see" and "taste" "how gracious the Lord is" in physical eating of bread and drinking of wine. Such persons may see themselves—in fulfilling the "meal" that traces to Jesus' table fellowship with the suffering and oppressed and in this sense has been repeated over the centuries—concretely connected to those gathered at table with Jesus and with Jesus himself. In any case, the direct biblicistic argument for an "institution by Christ" cannot be maintained in the way Luther used it. This opens up the concept of sacrament as well.

That is to say, can we determine such a "context of institution" for other language acts and liturgical gestures as well? In connection with psychosomatic knowledge and esoteric wish-fantasies a new sensibility has arisen for the possibilities of expression in word and gesture. Women seem especially open to these things. Thus, for example, "anointing," which is certainly attested in the New Testament (Jas 5:14), has found a place in Lutheran worship. The transparency of external processes and actions is being discovered. Luther would assign this area to his idea of proclamation but not to sacrament. He might also fear that the clarity of God's self-gift in baptism and Eucharist would be endangered by it. Under the condition that today these will no longer be subject to magical misunderstandings he might feel more sympathy for crossing oneself or for holy water, which recalls baptism, than for freely invented new symbolic actions. As regards baptism and Eucharist he was certain that here God encounters us with a divine self-gift, applied on the basis of God's word, with its physical application to my physical side as well. But questions remain here also.

It is in line with the insights of recent exegesis and liturgical scholarship when in current Lutheran theology and also in the documents reflecting theological differences the Eucharist is no longer interpreted in the first instance on the basis of the *verba testamenti*, but as a whole event. The elements are to be seen in their functional context, and that in terms not only of individual communicants but also of the whole congregation. At the same time it is important that the Holy Eucharist be retrieved from the christological narrowing imposed on it by Luther, for obvious reasons, and be seen as a trinitarian event.

LACK OF A TRINITARIAN ANCHOR FOR THE DOCTRINE OF BAPTISM?

Luther's baptismal doctrine was drawn altogether from the forgiveness of sins and thus was christological in its orientation. The baptismal formula itself, however, is trinitarian: ". . . baptizing them in the name of the Father and of the Son and of the Holy Spirit!" (Matt 28:19). Lorenz Grönvik, in a study that still repays reading, sought to interpret Luther's baptismal doctrine on the basis of a salvation-historical context understood in trinitarian terms.[255] God the Father gives himself in creation—a gift that has been obscured by the Fall. The Son gives himself and reconciles the Father—a gift that is only realized when the Holy Spirit distributes it "inwardly" through faith and "outwardly" through the Gospel and the sacraments. Here baptism finds its salvation-historical-systematic place.[256] Thus it has a trinitarian anchor in Luther's thought, corresponding to the baptismal formula in Matthew. In baptism all three of the trinitarian persons are active: the Father with his light and majesty, the Son with his blood, the Holy Spirit with his fire.[257] Hence without question the "God of baptism" is also the "God of creation,"[258] especially since in the element of water created things are made part of the process.

But the role of the Creator remains clearly underemphasized in Luther's texts on baptism. Moreover, the question arises: what function can creation really have? Because of the Fall it is, after all, negatively programmed.[259] The unbaptized person, although created by God, can only be regarded as subject to sin and death. But this not only contradicts the instinctive sense even of a Christian; it is contrary to a doctrine of the Trinity that—to quote Augustine freely—says it is impossible to separate the "outward" (ad extra) works of the Trinity. But if God the Creator must be seen simultaneously as the Redeemer and Perfecter, baptism cannot stand solely in a negative relationship to the created reality of a human being. In baptism, rather, the true intention of creation is put into action. This may be connected to the question of how that should be defined and to what it extent it can be connected to what the spiritualists and Anabaptists attempted to address as an inner world. Today we would think in this connection of the human capability for transcendence as expressed in the question of meaning and the longing for fulfillment. If we also incorporate the Reformer's harsh judgments on the Anabaptists—to the point of recommending capital punishment for them![260]—we would refuse to follow Luther's baptismal doctrine, elsewhere so grand, on this point at least. Nor will one be able to share his emphatic plea for infant baptism except when there are appropriate conditions for socialization provided for the baptizand by the parents and the congregation, so that the baptized child has real opportunities to understand, as an adult person, what it means to be baptized.

PHILOSOPHICAL AWKWARDNESS IN THE DOCTRINE OF THE EUCHARIST?

Luther has repeatedly been accused of having made too little effort to free himself from the ideas of the nominalistic philosophy that helped to shape his theological education. William of Ockham had taught a certain revelatory positivism of the word. The distinction between God's omnipotent action and God's "arbitrary" ties to particular orderings made it possible to see the sacraments as contingently established. Everything depended on what God willed and how God decided. Duns Scotus grounded Mary's immaculate conception in the fact that God "could do it," that it "was appropriate," and that therefore God "did it."[261] Did Luther think similarly, in principle, as regards the Eucharist—rejecting the doctrine of transubstantiation but then resolving the problem in Aristotelian fashion as biblically supported because he could not imagine the real presence except as substantial? It would be a step in the right direction if the real presence could be conceived at least apart from qualitative, quantitative, and localizing conditions; still, in Marburg he refused to cede the phrase *substantive et essentialiter*, which he understood as "wahrhaftiglich," "truthful."[262] The conflict with the Reformed group over the Lord's Supper proved to be a problem not only of philosophical terminology; Luther had to hold on to the real presence, precisely as a spiritual event, through a naïvely applied Aristotelian concept of substance. A *significat* could not be preserved except as an *est*! Today, however, the situation is reversed: how can the *est* be communicated except by means of its *significat*? The "is" can only be effective through what it "means," though in a sense that transcends cognitive apprehension. Luther's interest was not in a philosophical definition but in the fundamental soteriological intention. Under the philosophical conditions of 1529 the *est* contained a surplus of soteriological meaning over *significat*. Today the opposite is true: the popular-positivistic assumptions in terms of which the "is" is perceived must be disrupted. Something can be more than it *is* (positivistically considered), and this is clear precisely in the fact that the positivistically understood "is" is clarified by what it "means."

ECCLESIOLOGICAL DEFICIENCY?

In relating word and sacrament to individual believers Luther took his starting point from the message and experience of justification. To what extent did he thus neglect the church? If we start with what Luther wrote about the sacraments in the Small Catechism we could certainly get the impression that there is a deficient ecclesiology here. This can be explained from a situation in which, at all events, the church—as an institution that rendered people dependent—was at least implicitly present in every theological statement. Luther's historical service here consisted precisely in liberating word and sacrament from the institutional clutches of a church that regarded itself as indispensable. In fact, the word of the Gospel is aimed at individual believers, at their "conscience." To that extent Luther inculcated the category of the individual, together with his or her freedom and responsibility.

Nevertheless, it is too bad that at least in his doctrine of baptism and Eucharist he often did not fully develop the ecclesiological points of view that in other places he was able to expand upon. Thus in his explanation of the universal, mutual, and common priesthood he certainly spoke of baptism, but in his explanation of baptism he does not even mention his insights on the universal priesthood, much less make use of them. Something similar is true of his explanation of the Lord's Supper. In a sense the ecclesiological implications of the understanding of the Eucharist as the early Luther was able to develop them, in broad and impressive terms, were largely lost in the battle over the real presence. But they can be retrieved, precisely by reference to Luther! He should not be accused of having given too little attention to the outlines of his own reformational ecclesiology. The presentation of his doctrine of the church will make this clear.[263]

For Luther preaching, baptism, and Eucharist are basic functions through which individual believers and thus the whole church lives. They are what a person needs for life and death, with earthly life at first altogether in the foreground. Word, water, bread, and wine are among the elementary data of human living; they represent human basic needs to be cleansed or to cleanse oneself, to take nourishment, to be spoken to and to speak.[264] Luther also maintained the eschatological relevance of baptism and Eucharist for individual believers when he said of the Eucharist that in it we are given "forgiveness of sins, life, and salvation," and when he saw as the purpose of baptism that people should "rise up, cleansed and righteous, to live forever in God's presence."[265] These statements are intended as both present and future. But—at least in the Small Catechism—they are not developed in terms of the community of believers or the renewal and transformation of the world. The narrowing we can see here is another result of concentration on Christ and the justification given through him. But Luther scarcely developed this approach at all in ecclesiological or trinitarian terms in his most influential writings, which certainly would have been possible.

POTENTIAL ECUMENICAL CONFLICTS AND RESOLUTIONS

There is no area in which ecumenical conflict is more acute than with regard to the sacraments. This dispute has strained the relationship between Reformed and Lutheran churches for centuries. In 1973 the Leuenberg Agreement sought to reconcile the two approaches. Article 15 of that document says: "In the Lord's Supper Jesus Christ, the Risen One, imparts himself in his body and blood, given in death for all, through his word of promise with the bread and wine. He assures us thereby of the forgiveness of sins and sets us free for a new life of faith. He allows us to experience anew the fact that we are members of his body. He strengthens us for service to humankind."[266] Modern exegesis has liberated both parties from substantial-ontological thinking and brought the soteriological function of the Eucharist into the foreground. It is true that Luther would probably not have agreed with the formulation "with the bread and wine," but the accent is no longer on the controversy between "is" and "signifies." Instead, the focus is on the fact that Jesus Christ "imparts himself." This is likewise no longer attached exclusively to the words of institution but incorporates the whole liturgical celebration of the Lord's Supper.

The Roman Catholic Church, despite a long phase of intensive dialogue, has repeatedly distanced itself from the Lutheran understanding of sacraments. The Agreed Statement on Baptism in 2007[267] represents no progress, since in Catholic understanding baptism must be augmented by a second "sacrament," namely confirmation, if one is to become a full member of the church; Lutheran baptism as such is thus not ecclesiologically sufficient. The differences in the understanding of the sacrament of the altar appear insurmountable, since the magisterium of the Catholic Church makes the validity of the Eucharist dependent on the "sacrament" of priestly orders, a subject that cannot be further developed here.[268] The Catholic Church interprets Christ's presence in the Eucharist on the basis of its own self-understanding, though it has to struggle with problems here and there. The more the church as an institution moves sociologically and factually into crisis, the greater are the chances that it may realize that it is not the church that supports the sacrament; rather, the sacrament, together with the word, supports and sustains the church.

The challenge for a theology oriented to the Reformation is to bring Luther's approach and knowledge into the ecumenical context and to protest against developments that, from this point of view, run contrary to the Gospel. This includes an objection to the opinion that a worship service without sacramental celebration is but a spiritual torso. A service of the word, even when ecumenically organized, and however deficient it may be from the standpoint of other churches, is, so the churches of the Reformation are convinced, a worship service in the fullest sense. The longing for a common celebration of the Eucharist may arise out of psychologically or pastorally justified feelings, but it does not correspond to a Lutheran understanding of worship.

The Orthodox theology of the Eastern churches is not in accord either with the Reformation churches' exaltation of the word of God or with the Roman insistence on a priestly power of orders; it lives, we may say, in its own more pneumatologically shaped world.

Lutheran theology can certainly learn from ecumenical experience. Catholic eucharistic piety is deeply engaged with the idea of "transformation." The notion of a transformation of the communicant through the reception of the Lord's Supper is not only not foreign to Luther but follows from his understanding of God's self-gift in word and sacrament. The old Lutheran formula for distribution, "may it strengthen and sustain you in true faith . . ." should thus be expanded by expressions such as "and sanctify you entirely" (cf. 1 Thess 5:23-24). The Eucharist transforms; it gives strength, courage, and zest.

An appreciation of Orthodox spirituality, with its devotion to icons, would help Lutheran believers to discover the image, not as a means of illustration as Luther himself used it, but as a medium through which, in meditation, God's word reveals itself.[269] In addition it could prevent a certain breathlessness in Lutheran worship insofar as it aids the cultivation of calm and silence. The Lutheran theologian and religious philosopher Rudolf Otto suggested nearly a century ago that silence should be introduced into Lutheran piety as a third sacrament, so to speak.[270]

Finally, there is a further point of ecumenical controversy that has scarcely played any part in dialogue thus far: how to understand blessing. Reformed theologians are tempted to reject blessing as word magic; blessing can only be asked for, not "bestowed." Catholic theology, on the contrary, contains a broad selection of acts of blessing and consecration that can be applied to people in every situation in their lives, and even to animals and objects. Lutheranism sees blessing as a performative speech-act that, received in faith, communicates the saving presence of God.[271] Common to all confessions is the conviction that it is the triune God who cares for creation by blessing it.[272] Given that, should it not be possible and ecumenically productive, despite all our differences of interpretation, for one church to proclaim and pray for— whether in liturgical form or not—the blessing of the triune God on the other churches?

NOTES

[1] Fritz Riemann, *Anxiety: Using Depth Psychology to Find a Balance in Your Life*, trans. Greta Dunn (Munich: Reinhardt, 2009).

[2] *The Book of Concord*, 31. The Latin formula is clearer in some ways: "Ut hanc fidem consequamur, institutum est ministerium docendi evangelii et porrigendi sacramenta. Nam per verbum et sacramenta tamquam per instrumenta donatur spiritus sanctus, qui fidem efficit, ubi et quando visum est Deo, in his, qui audiunt evangelium."

[3] Hans-Martin Barth, *Theorie des Redens von Gott. Voraussetzungen und Bedingungen theologischer Artikulation* (Göttingen: Vandenhoeck & Ruprecht, 1972), 99–108, 174–75.

[4] Cf., e.g., Gerhard Marcel Martin, *Sachbuch Bibliodrama* (Stuttgart: Kohlhammer, 1995), or Wolfgang Riewe, "Stufen des Lebens. Religionsunterricht für Erwachsene," in *Brennpunkt Gemeinde* 1 (1995), ed. Arbeitsgemeinschaft Missionarische Dienste, Box 101142, 70010 Stuttgart.

[5] Cf. Leonardo Boff, *Kleine Sakramentenlehre* (Düsseldorf: Patmos, 1976; 7th ed. 1984).

[6] Gustavo Gutiérrez, *A Theology of Liberation: History, Politics, and Salvation*. With a Foreword by Johann Baptist Metz (Maryknoll, NY: Orbis, 1973; rev. 15th ed. 2000), ch. 12, "The Church: Sacrament of History," 143–61.

[7] Cf. Joint Lutheran/Roman Catholic Study Commission on the Gospel and the Church, *The Eucharist* (Geneva: Lutheran World Federation, 1980); Karl Lehmann and Wolfhart Pannenberg, eds., *The Condemnations of the Reformation Era: Do they Still Divide?* (Minneapolis: Fortress Press,

1990); World Council of Churches, *Baptism, Eucharist, & Ministry* (St. Louis: Association of Evangelical Lutheran Churches, 1982).

[8] *Church Dogmatics* (London: T & T Clark, 2010), IV/4, 1–206.

[9] Cf. Hans-Martin Barth, "'. . . sehen, wie freundlich der Herr ist.' Das Verhältnis von Wort, Bild und Sakrament im Protestantismus," *KD* 39 (1993): 247–62.

[10] LW 36, 3–126 (StA 2, 173–376). For Luther's understanding of sacraments cf. Ulrich Kühn, *Sakramente* (Gütersloh: Gütersloher Verlagshaus Mohn, 1985); Althaus 1962, 297–338; Lohse 1995, 91–93, 143–53, 316–33.

[11] LW 36, 18, 92, 106–7, 117–18, 123–25 (WA 6, 550, 7-16, 22-32; 560, 20-24; 568, 8-14).

[12] Cf. "The christological center of the Eucharist" below.

[13] See "Confession" below.

[14] Luther refers to 1 Pet 2:1-5, 9; Rev 5:10; 20:6 (LW 36, 139–40 [WA 8, 487, 15–488, 2]), and also to Hebrews. See "Universal, mutual, and common priesthood" in chapter 11.

[15] LW 36, 138 (WA 8, 486, 27-29).

[16] LW 35, 101 (WA 6, 370, 25-27), "all Christen man pfaffen, alle weyber pffeffyn. . . ."

[17] LW 36, 140 (WA 8, 488, 7-8).

[18] LW 36, 141 (WA 8, 489, 37-40).

[19] WA 8, 405, 24-34; cf. the engagement with 1 Cor 14:34-35 (women should "keep silent in the churches"), culminating in the statement: "but if no man were to preach, then it would be necessary for the women to preach," LW 36, 152 (WA 8, 497, 19–498, 14).

[20] Augsburg Confession XIII, *The Book of Concord*, 35–36.

[21] LW 35, 91 (WA 6, 363, 9-11). Christ himself "is more concerned about the word than about the sign"; without the particular words he spoke he would not have instituted the Eucharist (LW 35, 106; WA 6, 373, 32-33).

[22] LW 35, 91 (WA 6, 363, 19-20).

[23] "Accedat verbum ad elementum et fit sacramentum = When the Word is joined to the external element, it becomes a sacrament," to which Luther appeals, for example, in the Large Catechism, *The Book of Concord*, 448.

[24] WA 30/1, 215, 25-26.

[25] *The Book of Concord*, 349, 352.

[26] See "The christological center of the Eucharist" below.

[27] WA 30/1, 218, 30-31.

[28] *The Book of Concord*, 349.

[29] WA 30/1, 220, 22-23. Luther formulates a wordplay here: "Semel es baptisatus sacramentaliter, semper baptisandus fide, semper moriendum comperquo vivendum," LW 36, 70 (WA 6, 535, 10-11).

[30] LW 40, 261 (WA 26, 172, 35).

[31] WA 34/1, 97, 25-26.

[32] LW 35, 31 (WA 2, 728, 27-29).

[33] Cf. LW 35, 33–34 (WA 2, 730, 30–731, 2).

[34] Cf. *Didache* 9.

[35] LW 35, 58 (WA 2, 748, 8-26).

[36] LW 35, 104 (WA 6, 372, 23-25, 28-30).

[37] Thus Kühn 1985, 28–32. For Luther's baptismal theology cf. Grünvik 1968; Martin Ferel, *Gepredigte Taufe. Eine homiletische Untersuchung zur Taufpredigt bei Luther* (Tübingen: Mohr, 1969); Horst Kasten, *Taufe und Rechtfertigung bei Luther und Thomas von Aquin* (Munich: Kaiser, 1970); Karl-Heinz zur Mühlen, "Luthers Tauflehre und seine Stellung zu den Täufern," in Junghans 1983, 1: 119–38; 2: 765–70; Peters 1993.

[38] *The Book of Concord*, 348.

[39] Cf. WA 30/1, 213, 12-16.

[40] WA 30/1, 213, 31; 214, 11.

[41] "Ideo non aqualis aqua, sed divina, celestis, in qua deitas ipsa est," WA 37, 264, 25-28.

[42] WA 37, 642, 33.

[43] *The Book of Concord*, 348–49.

[44] Cf. *LBW*, "The Rite of Holy Baptism," especially parts 2, 10, 13-16.

[45] Cf. WA 46, 199, 36-37.

[46] WA 30/1, 222, 1-6.

[47] WA 30/1, 219, 12-13.

[48] WA 30/1, 218, 15-16.

[49] Cf. LW 40, 256–57 (WA 26, 168, 27-29).

[50] WA 17/2, 83, 9-12.

[51] Karl Brinkel, *Die Lehre Luthers von der fides infantium bei der Kindertaufe* (Berlin: Evangelische Verlagsanstalt, 1958; cf. Grönvik 1968, 164–72.

[52] LW 40, 242 (WA 26, 159, 14-18). For the arguments regarding the baptism of children cf. esp. Erich Geldbach, *Taufe* (Göttingen: Vandenhoeck & Ruprecht, 1996).

[53] LW 40, 239 (WA 26, 156, 34–157, 1).

[54] LW 40, 243 (WA 26, 160, 5).

[55] Cf. Barth, Hans-Martin 2008a, 607ff.

[56] Cf. "Concerning Baptism. A Letter of Martin Luther to Two Pastors," LW 40, 229–62 (WA 26, 144–74).

[57] Cf. "Theological basis" in chapter 11.

[58] In what follows I am adapting material from Barth, Hans-Martin 1990, 31–40.

[59] LW 44, 127 (WA 6, 407, 13-14, 22-23).

[60] LW 36, 112 (WA 6, 564, 6-7).

[61] LW 36, 68 (WA 6, 534, 24-26).

[62] Cf. LW 36, 70 (WA 6, 536, 7-18; 537, 19-31).

[63] LW 44, 129 (WA 6, 408, 11-13).

[64] LW 44, 127 (WA 6, 407, 17-19).

[65] Cf. LW 44, 193 (WA 6, 452, 32-34).

[66] LW 31, 366 (WA 7, 66, 3-4): "Dabo itaque me quendam Christum proximo meo, quemadmodum Christus sese praebuit mihi . . . ." The German version in WA 7, 35, 34-35, "werden ein Christen, wie Christus mir worden ist," is variously interpreted. Manfred Jacobs translates ". . . be a Christian as Christ has become for me . . ." (Insel ed. 1:260). Bertram Lee Woolf translates: "I will therefore give myself as a Christ to my neighbor, just as Christ offered himself to me" (Bertram Lee Woolf, trans., "The Freedom of a Christian," 42–85 in John Dillenberger, ed., *Martin Luther. Selections from His Writings* [New York: Anchor Books, 1962], at 75). Cf. Rieger 2007, 297, 303–4, and B.7.3.2 above.

[67] Cf. Barth, Hans-Martin 1990.

[68] See "Ministry and Orders" in chapter 11.

[69] LW 40, 37 (WA 12, 178, 7-14; 26ff.).

[70] LW 35, 49–73 (WA 2, 742–58).

[71] LW 36, 127–230 (WA 8, 482–563).

[72] Kühn 1985, 49–52, or Althaus 1962, 318–23, who place the accent somewhat differently. For Luther's eucharistic theology as a whole cf. Hans-Martin Barth, "Die therapeutische Funktion des Heiligen Abendmahls," *PT* 73 (1984): 512–25; Hans Grass, *Die Abendmahlslehre bei Luther und Calvin* (Gütersloh: Bertelsmann, 21954); Eberhard Grötzinger, *Luther und Zwingli: Die Kritik an der mittelalterlichen Lehre von der Messe—als Wurzel des Abendmahlsstreites* (Zürich: Benziger; Gütersloh: G. Mohn, 1980); Kühn 1985, 45–67; idem, "Luthers Zeugnis vom Abendmahl in Unterweisung, Vermahnung und Beratung," 1: 139–52; 2: 771–75 in Junghans 1983; Eckhart Lessing, *Abendmahl* (Göttingen: Vandenhoeck & Ruprecht, 1993); Gerhard May, ed., *Das Marburger Religionsgespräch 1529* (Gütersloh: Gütersloher Verlagshaus Mohn, 1970); Erwin Metzke, "Sakrament und Metaphysik. Eine Lutherstudie über das Verhältnis des christlichen Denkens zum Leiblich-Materiellen," 158–204 in idem, *Coincidentia oppositorum. Gesammelte Studien zur Philosophiegeschichte* (Witten: Luther-Verlag, 1961); Peters 1993, 129–89; Simon 2003.

[73] LW 35, 50 (WA 2, 743, 21-22), "gemeynschafft und ein leybung."

74LW 35, 52 (WA 2, 744, 2-4).

75LW 35, 54 (WA 2, 745, 10-14).

76LW 35, 55 (WA 2, 746, 33-34).

77LW 35, 63 (WA 2, 751, 37-38); here Luther inserts his polemic against the concepts of *opus operatum* and *opus operantis*.

78Cf. WA 30/1, 26, 25-31.

79LW 38, 109 (WA 30/2, 604, 30-31).

80Ibid. (WA 30/2, 604, 34-35; 605, 1).

81Ibid. (WA 30/2, 604, 20-23).

82Kühn 1985, 64, with reference to WA 30/2, 614, 27. Cf. LW 38, 122.

83Cf. "Ministry and Orders" in chapter 13.

84Kühn 1985, 65.

85WA.Br 7, 339, 21; cf. 366, 44.

86LW 35, 86; cf. 88 (WA 6, 359, 1-3; cf. 361, 5-7).

87LW 35, 85 (WA 6, 358, 21-24).

88LW 35, 98 (WA 6, 368, 5-7).

89LW 35, 99 (WA 6, 369, 8-9).

90I find obscure, for example, WA 6, 371, 24-25 (LW 35, 101). But cf. the highly analytical and instructive presentation by Wolfgang Simon, *Die Messopfertheologie Martin Luthers. Voraussetzungen, Genese, Gestalt und Rezeption* (Tübingen: Mohr Siebeck, 2005).

91Eucharistic Prayer I (the Roman canon): ". . . we pray you, gracious Father . . . accept and bless this holy and perfect sacrifice . . ."; Eucharistic Prayer IV: "we offer you his body and blood, the acceptable sacrifice which brings salvation to the whole world." Cf. Joint Lutheran/Roman Catholic Study Commission on the Gospel and the Church, *The Eucharist* (Geneva: Lutheran World Federation, 1980); full text available online at http://www.pro.urbe.it/dia-int/l-rc/doc/e_l-rc_Eucharist.html. Dietrich Korsch contrasts the model of "sacrifice as memorial" with the "Zürich way," which is "memorial instead of sacrifice." The Wittenberg alternative, on the other hand, would be: "Ever-renewed self-re-presentation." But here he shifts the level from the action of the priest or the congregation to Christ's action: ultimately all three models interpret the action in the sense of "self-immediacy"; the question, however, is in what manner the church is active in it—by an action that makes present, or by memory, or by altogether renouncing any operationalizing action and simply claiming what is given: "Take, eat . . ." Korsch 2005, 1–18.

92"The Misuse of the Mass" (1521), LW 36, 127–230 (WA 8, 482-563).

93LW 36, 146–47, 168–70, 173, 175–76 (WA 8, 493, 20; 494, 4-11; 506, 10-12; 511, 22-26; 512, 12-18; 512, 31–513, 4; 515, 21-22).

94LW 36, 198 (WA 8, 536, 22-27).

95Dietrich Korsch formulates generously: "What matters is to understand the basic conception in each confessional form—as a way in which the presence of Christ is realized as that which is absolutely valid." Remaining to be decided, then, is "the question, to which of these forms of presence does each individual Christian know himself or herself to belong and be able to recognize it as binding—out of one's origins, but also with conviction" (Korsch 2005, 18).

96Cf. Gerhard Ludwig Müller, *Katholische Dogmatik. Für Studium und Praxis der Theologie* (Freiburg: Herder, 31998), 706–7, 709, 711; encyclical *Ecclesia de Eucharistia* of Pope John Paul II (17 April 2003), §§ 11–13. Incidentally, Luther observes that Eucharist, as thanksgiving, excludes the idea of sacrifice: the one who sacrifices petitions God, but whoever "thanks does not pray that it will be acceptable, but rejoices that something is given to him" (LW 36, 171 [WA 8, 513, 22-24]).

97Smalcald Articles II, 1, *The Book of Concord*, 293.

98LW 40, 177 (WA 18, 166, 33).

99LW 36, 52 (WA 6, 523, 25-27): "Iam Missa quanto vicinior et similior primae omnium Missae, quam Christus in caena fecit, tanto Christianior."

100LW 36, 165 (WA 8, 508, 23-26).

[101] Cf. Peters 1993, 151ff.; but cf. LW 37, 151–372 (WA 26, 448, 26–481, 28; 481, 29–487, 8; 487, 9–498, 12, 27), "Confession Concerning Christ's Supper" (1528), where Luther explains all four of the relevant texts.

[102] Schwarz 2005, 20–25.

[103] LW 38, 48 (WA 30/3, 137, 9).

[104] "The Report of Osiander," in The Marburg Colloquy, LW 38, 67. For the whole cf. Gerhard Müller, "Martin Luther in Marburg 1529. Anlass, Vorgeschichte, Entscheidungen," 115–32 in Norbert Stieniczka, ed., "Mit dem Glauben Staat machen." Beiträge zum Evangelischen Philipps-Jahr 2004 (Darmstadt and Kassel: Verlag der Hessischen Kirchengeschichtlichen Vereinigung, 2005).

[105] Cf. LW 38, 54 (WA 30/3, 116, 27-28).

[106] Cf. von Soosten 2005.

[107] Cf. Gottfried W. Locher, Zwingli's Thought: New Perspectives, trans. Duncan Shaw (Leiden: Brill, 1981), 303–39; Ulrich Gäbler, Huldrych Zwingli: His Life and Work, trans. Ruth C. L. Gritsch (Philadelphia: Fortress Press, 1986), esp. 131–35.

[108] In analogy to the "subversive" memory of which Johann Baptist Metz sometimes speaks.

[109] Cf. Müller, Katholische Dogmatik, 696ff.

[110] Smalcald Articles III, 6, The Book of Concord, 311.

[111] LW 37, 317 (WA 26, 462, 4-5).

[112] LW 37, 128 (WA 23, 249, 26).

[113] LW 37, 65 (WA 23, 145, 29-32); cf. LW 37, 230 (WA 26, 341, 16-19), where Luther delivers a roundhouse blow incorporating all the prepositions that occur to him: With "in," reason may think of straw in a sack or bread in a basket, "but faith understands that in these matters 'in' is equivalent to 'above,' 'beyond,' 'beneath,' 'through and through,' and 'everywhere.'" Apparently the Reformer is not at all concerned with precise location but only with the "that" of Christ's presence.

[114] LW 36, 34 (WA 6, 511, 18-20).

[115] LW 36, 35 (WA 6, 511, 39–512, 1-2).

[116] LW 37, 101 (WA 23, 205, 21-23).

[117] The Book of Concord, 351.

[118] LW 37, 65 (WA 23, 145, 21-32).

[119] The Formula of Concord, VII, 35, The Book of Concord, 575.

[120] Cf. LW 37, 302 (WA 26, 437, 30–445, 17).

[121] For the whole cf. Wolff 2006.

[122] von Soosten 2005, 105.

[123] LW 37, 29 (WA 23, 87, 32-35).

[124] LW 36, 32 (StA 2, 190, 6-9).

[125] Wolf-Dieter Hauschild, Lehrbuch der Kirchen- und Dogmengeschichte 2. Reformation und Neuzeit (Gütersloh: Gütersloher Verlagshaus, 1999), 310.

[126] "Disputation on the Divinity and Humanity of Christ (WA 39/2, 92–121), LDStA 2, 472/473, Thesis 24; cf. Theses 20–24.

[127] Notger Slenczka, "Neubestimmte Wirklichkeit. Zum systematischen Zentrum der Lehre Luthers von der Gegenwart Christi unter Brot und Wein," 79–98 in Korsch 2005.

[128] Cf. LW 37, 180 (WA 26, 282, 16-25).

[129] von Soosten 2005, 106–11, at 110.

[130] WA 30/1, 56, 9.

[131] LW 37, 69 (WA 23, 151, 28-32).

[132] Against Schwarz 2005, 19–20, and Dietrich Korsch (see n. 91 above).

[133] Cf. LW 37, 65 (WA 23, 145, 29-32).

[134] LW 37, 86 (WA 23, 179, 27-28).

[135] Schwarz 2005, 48.

[136] WA 30/1, 226, 27-29.

[137] Peters 1993, 159; the expression "sacrificial body offered" / "blood of the covenant outpoured" appears frequently in Albrecht Peters's explication and gives his presentation a coloration I do not find in Luther.

[138] *The Book of Concord*, 352.

[139] LW 38, 132 (WA 30/2, 622, 6-9).

[140] Cf. Lohse 1995, 192–93, as well as Jörg Baur, "Ubiquität," *TRE* 34: 225–41.

[141] LW 37, 72 (WA 23, 156, 30-33).

[142] Thus, e.g., in his "Sermon on the New Testament" (1520); cf. Erwin Mülhaupt, ed., *D. Martin Luthers Evangelien-Auslegung*, Part 5 (Göttingen: Vandenhoeck & Ruprecht, 1961), 173–76. In what follows I am adapting material from my essay, "Die therapeutische Funktion des Heiligen Abendmahls" (see n. 72 above).

[143] *The Book of Concord*, 352.

[144] WA 30/1, 27, 6-7.

[145] *The Book of Concord*, 449.

[146] LW 37, 93; 37, 87: "But since the mouth is the heart's member, it also must ultimately live in eternity on account of the heart, which lives eternally through the Word, because here it also eats physically the same eternal food which its heart eats spiritually at the same time" (WA 23, 191, 18-22; 23, 181, 11-15).

[147] *The Book of Concord*, 450.

[148] Cf. LW 37, 83 (WA 23, 156, 30ff.).

[149] Cf. Ludwig Feuerbach, *Gesammelte Werke*, ed. Werner Schuffenhauer (Berlin: Akademie-Verlag, 1967–), 10: 230.

[150] LW 35, 53 (WA 2, 745, 1-5).

[151] Cf. "Functional mutuality" above.

[152] WA 30/1, 27, 18.

[153] LW 35, 58 (WA 2, 748, 14-15).

[154] LW 35, 59 (WA 2, 748, 32-36).

[155] See "For the sake of Christ" in chapter 8 and "Liberation" and "The power of freedom" in chapter 9.

[156] *The Book of Concord*, 352.

[157] WA 30/1, 27, 7-9.

[158] *The Book of Concord*, 454.

[159] Cf. Ignatius Eph. 20.2. A study of the history of the concept of *pharmakon* in Christian theology and devotion would be highly revealing!

[160] *The Book of Concord*, 454.

[161] Cf. the argument between Albrecht Peters and Wolfgang Schwab in Lohse 1995, 331.

[162] WA 29, 218, 7-8.

[163] *The Book of Concord*, 456.

[164] LW 51, 93 (WA 10/3, 51, 7-9); cf. Barth, Hans-Martin 1967, 171ff.

[165] LW 35, 66 (WA 2, 753, 17-19).

[166] Cf. the Augsburg Confession XXV, *The Book of Concord*, 61–63.

[167] Peters 1994, 36–40.

[168] *The Book of Concord*, "[Confession and Absolution]," 349–51.

[169] LW 40, 372–73 (WA 30/2, 503, 17-33).

[170] *The Book of Concord*, 458 (WA 30/1, 235, 2-5).

[171] Kurt Frör, quoted in Peters 1994, 63.

[172] *The Book of Concord*, 350.

[173] LW 40, 377 (WA 30/2, 507, 10-11).

[174] *The Book of Concord*, 458 (WA 30/1, 235, 25-28).

[175] WA 47, 297, 40-298, 4.

[176] WA 15, 487, 29-32.

[177] *The Book of Concord*, 350 (in the original, "worthy dear Sir"); cf. 458 (formerly "brother"), and see also WA 30/3, 570, 20–571, 15.

[178] *The Book of Concord*, 311; cf. 314.

[179] Ibid., 457 (WA 30/1, 234, 11-18). [*The Book of Concord* says this of "men."] Insofar as this applied, Luther calls these people "such pigs," and says they would do better to continue to obey the pope's rules of fasting, etc.

[180] Cf. Christian Link, "Bann V," *TRE* 5: 182–90.

[181] WA 15, 485, 31-32.

[182] *The Book of Concord*, 458 (WA 30/1, 235, 15-22).

[183] LW 37, 368 (WA 26, 507, 20-27).

[184] WA 15, 586, 31.

[185] WA 15, 586, 34.

[186] Cf. WA 15, 487, 23-27.

[187] Cf. *TRE* 12: 79.

[188] LW 53, 28 (WA 12, 213, 7-11); for the whole cf. Peters 1994, 79ff.

[189] Cf. Peters 1994, 87–91.

[190] For the battle with the Antinomians, which cannot be explored in detail here, cf. Lohse 1995, 195–203; for Agricola cf. Joachim Rogge, "Agricola, Johann," *TRE* 2: 110–18, and cf. chapter 13 below.

[191] For references to further literature on Luther's understanding of confession and penance see Peters 1994, 92–93.

[192] Cf. "Tradition as a danger to the church" in chapter 16.

[193] WA 37, 134, 6. In what follows I am using material from my essay, "Luthers Predigt von der Predigt," *PT* 56 (1967), 481–89.

[194] WA 16, 196, 12-15; cf. WA 40/1, 121, 2.

[195] WA 16, 113, 7-8.

[196] LW 31, 357 (WA 7, 29, 7-9; cf. WA 5, 543, 17).

[197] LW 36, 340 (WA 19, 489, 9-10).

[198] WA 12, 565, 19.

[199] "Suum venire est nihil aliud quam quod praedicat per totum mundum," WA 20, 364, 37-38. This is the equation of the Easter preaching and the Easter event that appears occasionally in Luther's writing; cf. Hans-Martin Barth, "Historie und Identifikation. Über Luthers Passions- und Osterpredigt," *PT* 55 (1966): 70–80. Also "resurrectio est annunciatio et sage de resurrectione . . ." WA 27, 119, 4.

[200] WA 1, 175, 36; 190, 1.

[201] LW 11, 37 (WA 3, 549, 33-35).

[202] WA 20, 350, 6-7.

[203] ". . . amplificare maiestatem verbi," LW 27, 46 (WA 40/2, 57, 4).

[204] LW 26, 432 (WA 40/1, 651, 13).

[205] LW 16, 332, 5-6. But perhaps ultimately Luther and Johann Scheffler (Angelus Silesius) meant to say something similar!

[206] WA 27, 118, 32-33.

[207] WA 27, 122, 11-13.

[208] LW 36, 149 (WA 8, 495, 21-23).

[209] LW 36, 151–52 (WA 9, 497, 29-34; 498, 13-14).

[210] LW 35, 101 (WA 6, 370, 25-27).

[211] WA 10/3, 97, 5-6.

[212] WA 36, 135, 3.

[213] WA 28, 73, 5.

[214] Cf. WA 11, 85, 17 with WA 11, 82, 27-29.

[215] WA 28, 317, 2-3.

[216] WA 37, 136, 18-19.

[217] WA 8, 683, 3-15.

[218]WA 16, 617, 14-15.

[219]LW 42, 52 (WA 2, 108, 3-4).

[220]". . . sunt dii erga suos . . ." WA 28, 613, 1.

[221]LW 21, 270–71 (WA 32, 528, 31-32).

[222]WA 34/1, 198, 6-7.

[223]WA 36, 541, 12-19 (1532!); cf. LW 28, 106.

[224]WA 28, 530, 13–531, 3.

[225]Cf. LW 26, 56–58 (WA 40/1, 105, 4-5); WA 34/1, 311, 16-19; LW 21, 7–8 (WA 32, 304, 12-20).

[226]LW 27, 100 (WA 40/2, 128, 9-10).

[227]Cf. Eberhard Winkler, "Luther als Seelsorger und Prediger," 1: 225–39 in Junghans 1983; Eilert Herms, "Das Evangelium für das Volk. Praxis und Theorie der Predigt bei Luther," 20–55 in idem, *Offenbarung und Glaube. Zur Bildung des christlichen Lebens* (Tübingen: Mohr, 1992).

[228]Oral communication.

[229]For this whole subject cf. Karl Holl, "Luther und die Mission," 234–43 in idem, *Gesammelte Aufsätze zur Kirchengeschichte 3 (Der Westen)* (Tübingen: Mohr [Siebeck], 1928); Werner Elert, *Morphologie des Luthertums* I (Munich: Beck, 1931), 336–43; Blöchle 1995, esp. 58–72; 187–92.

[230]See "Stages" in chapter 4.

[231]Cf. "Critical evaluation" in the section "Intolerance? Luther and Islam" in chapter 4.

[232]WA.TR 5, 221, 17-21 (no. 5536).

[233]WA.TR 1, 161, 5 (no. 369).

[234]WA 10/3, 140, 1-10.

[235]*The Book of Concord*, 426.

[236]Cf. LW 20, 326 (WA 23, 645, 30-35).

[237]Elert, *Morphologie* I (1931), 338. Cf. the whole chapter on mission, 336–51.

[238]WA 10/3, 139, 14–140, 15.

[239]LW 35, 361 (WA.DB 6, 8, 29-31).

[240]Cf. LW 38, 290 (WA 54, 143, 15–144, 6); cf. Blöchle 1995, 52–53.

[241]LW 17, 317 (WA 31/2, 504, 35-36): "veri sunt exspectatores inter gentes, qui sciscitantur, scrutantur veritatem et salutem, donec consequantur."

[242]WA.TR 4, 14, 3-9 (no. 3925). See further references in Blöchle 1990, 306, n. 206. We may see in this instance a hiatus between Luther's dogmatic convictions and his personal hopes!

[243]Hans-Werner Gensichen, "Mission im Luthertum," *RGG3* 4: 546–48, at 546. Gensichen thus establishes the connection between Luther and the missionary theology of the second half of the twentieth century.

[244]Cf. Blöchle 1995, 69–70, and "Critical evaluation" in the section "Intolerance? Luther and Islam" in chapter 4.

[245]A moving example of this attitude is the Hessian mercenary Hans Staden, who, while serving as a Spanish rifleman, fell into the hands of cannibals in what is now Brazil. He did not conduct an active mission, but he said his prayers before a cross set up in front of his hut. He told the "wild people" that their gods could not help them, and he prayed for them when they asked him to, for the end of a storm or a threatening downpour. He sought to prepare his fellow prisoners for death. Again and again he found consolation in prayer and in singing hymns. The savages threatened him several times, saying they were about to kill and eat him. "Then I began to sing, with tearful eyes and from the bottom of my heart, the Psalm [130]: Out of the depths I cry to you, O LORD. Then the savages said: Look how he cries; now he is moaning." Or they said that "my God was a piece of dirt, in their language this is called Teuire [teøuira]." Hans Staden, *Hans Staden's True History: An Account of Cannibal Captivity in Brazil*, ed. and trans. Neil L. Whitehead and Michael Harbsmeier (Durham, NC: Duke University Press, 2008), 51, 64.

[246]LW 14, 9 (WA 31/1, 228, 33–229, 9). Of course, here Luther is speaking of the Old Testament context.

[247]WA 2, 195, 5-6.

[248]Blöchle 1995, 189–90.

[249]LW 45, 352 (WA 15, 32, 6-8).

[250]Cf. Ernst Tugendhat, *Egozentrizität und Mystik. Eine anthropologische Studie* (Munich: Beck, 2003); Hans-Martin Barth, "Egozentrizität, Mystik und christlicher Glaube. Eine Auseinandersetzung mit Ernst Tugendhat," NZST 46 (2004): 467–82.

[251]Cf. John L. Austin, *How to Do Things with Words* (Cambridge, MA: Harvard University Press, 1962); see also Oswald Bayer, *Was ist das: Theologie? Eine Skizze* (Stuttgart: Calwer, 1973), 25–27.

[252]Cf. Hans-Martin Barth, "Alpha- und Omega-Glaube. Ein Beitrag zum christlich-buddhistischen Dialog," 7–19 in Peter Neuner and Peter Lüning, eds., *Theologie im Dialog. FS für Harald Wagner* (Münster: Aschendorff, 2004).

[253]Cf. Dorothea Wendebourg, "Den falschen Weg Roms zu Ende gegangen? Zur gegenwärtigen Diskussion über Martin Luthers Gottesdienstreform und ihr Verhältnis zu den Traditionen der Alten Kirche," 164–84 in idem, *Die eine Christenheit auf Erden. Aufsätze zur Kirchen- und Ökumenegeschichte* (Tübingen: Mohr Siebeck, 2000).

[254]Cf. Ulrich Kühn 1985, 335ff., 266ff.

[255]Grönvik 1968.

[256]Ibid., 14, with reference to WA 26, 505, 38–506, 9 (LW 37, 366).

[257]Cf. WA 37, 272, 17-21; Grönvik 199.

[258]Ibid., 23.

[259]Grönvik writes that "direct communion with God on the basis of creation" is impossible, according to Luther (p. 22). But what does "on the basis" mean? According to Luther creation is "a kind of background for baptism" (Grönvik, 30). God's omnipresence in creation is distinguished from his special presence in word and sacrament (p. 31); there is a "difference between the presence of God in the creature and the presence of God for our salvation" (pp. 31, 32). But—according to Luther—is a presence of God without soteriological function even conceivable? Even if it were conceivable according to Luther, is it theologically supportable?

[260]On the one hand Luther rejected violence against the Anabaptists so long as they did not act as political agitators: "We should allow everyone to believe what he wills. If his faith be false, he will be sufficiently punished in eternal hell-fire," LW 40, 230 (WA 26, 145, 23–146, 2). On the other hand, in 1531 Luther could advocate the death penalty in horrible words: "Placet mihi Martino Luthero. Though it may be regarded as *crudele* to punish with the sword, yet it is *crudelius* that they damn the ministry of the word and do not produce a sure teaching and oppress right teaching," and so seek to destroy the world order (WA.Br 6, 223, no. 1882). Cf. also the certificate from Luther, Melanchthon, Cruciger, and Bugenhagen for Philip of Hesse (1536): "That it is the duty of worldly authority to defend against the Anabaptists with physical punishment, several thoughts from Wittenberg," WA 50, 8–15. The Anabaptist Fritz Erbe, after being held for seven years in Eisenach, was imprisoned from 1540 to 1548 in the dungeon of the south tower of the Wartburg—not far from the room where today people reverently recall Luther's translation of the New Testament. Bernhard Brons has pointed out to me, of course, that Luther's attitude was in line with imperial law.

[261]Cf. Axel Schmidt, "'POTUIT, DECUIT, ERGO FECIT.' Die Unbefleckte Empfängnis nach Johannes Duns Scotus," 149–65 in Albrecht Graf von Brandenstein-Zeppelin, et al., eds., *Im Dienste der inkarnierten Wahrheit. Festschrift zum 25-jährigen Pontifikat Seiner Heiligkeit Papst Johannes Paul II* (Weilheim-Bierbronnen: Gustav-Siewerth-Akademie, 2003).

[262]Cf. J. Staedtke, "Abendmahl III/3," TRE 1: 107–22.

[263]See chapter 11.

[264]"After the traumatic action of birth, every person is greeted by the adults by means of cleansing, feeding, and address. . . . These most elementary experiences are restored when we look from the pew to the center of the liturgical space—to the altar, font, and pulpit." Manfred Josuttis, *Der Weg in das Leben. Eine Einführung in den Gottesdienst auf verhaltenswissenschaftlicher Grundlage* (Munich: Kaiser, 1991), 147–48.

[265]*The Book of Concord*, 352, 349.

[266]LA 15, in *Sakramente, Amt, Ordination (Sacraments, Ministry, Ordination)*, Leuenberger Texte 2 (Frankfurt: Otto Lembeck, 1995), 17.

[267]*MdKI* 58 (2007), 58–59.

268Cf. the encyclical *Ecclesia de Eucharistia* by Pope John Paul II "to the bishops, priests, and deacons, men and women in the consecrated life, and all the lay faithful," on the Eucharist in its relationship to the church, 17 April 2003 (AAS 159), at www.vatican.va.

269Cf. Hans-Martin Barth, "Wort und Bild. Ein Beitrag zum Gespräch zwischen Orthodoxie und Luthertum," *KD* 35 (1989): 34–53; idem, "'. . . sehen, wie freundlich der Herr ist'" (1993) (see n. 9 above).

270Cf. Katharina Wiefel-Jenner, *Rudolf Ottos Liturgik* (Göttingen: Vandenhoeck & Ruprecht, 1997).

271Cf. Dorothea Greiner, *Segen und Segnen. Eine systematisch-theologische Grundlegung* (Stuttgart: 21999); on Luther see pp. 211–49.

272Cf. Hans-Martin Barth, "Kriterien christlichen Redens von Gott," *NZST* 17 (1975): 9–21, esp. 18–21.

11

Struggle: Between the "True" and the "False" Church

What we find today in the form of established churches, free churches, or denominations is far removed from what Luther could or wanted to imagine as a reformed and renewed church. Even the Roman Catholic Church of today no longer corresponds to the church against which Luther raised his protest in the sixteenth century. Nevertheless, the Protestant churches throughout the world are still nourished by impulses traceable to Luther's ecclesiological insights, and his critique of the Roman Church, despite its new presentation in the Tridentine form and especially in Vatican II, has by no means been made obsolete. The Orthodox churches, which are more clearly recognized by both Protestant and Catholic churches today, were already in Luther's scope; the "Muscovites," "White Russians," and "Greeks," as well as the "Bohemians" (Hussites) drew his attention to the fact that there were Christians even outside the papal church.[1]

Luther's ecclesiology developed as a critique of the Roman church. Joseph Lortz, in his description of the Reformation in Germany,[2] recognized and lamented the moral decline of the Roman church of the time. But it would be wrong to limit Luther's critique of the church to the corruption of monastic life or the behavior of the popes. Of course these things have their place in his polemic, but Luther was probably not acquainted with the details of what the popes were doing in Rome. Differently from the critique of a John Wycliff or Jan Hus, his began not with the moral situation but with the self-concept of the church of his time: in his view it tyrannized over people with invented rules and denied them access to the Gospel itself. In addition, while the church was omnipresent, ecclesiology itself had scarcely been developed.

As with most of the themes in his theology, we can observe a clear development in Luther's doctrine of the church. It does begin, insofar as it does not follow the settled lines of tradition, with the observation, which shocked Luther himself, that the pope truly could be the Antichrist announced in Scripture.[3] The first phase developed as a polemic critique of the papal church, grounded in Scripture but combined with an emphasis on the idea of *communio*. This phase includes the writings "On the Papacy in Rome" (1520)[4] and "That a Christian Assembly or Congregation Has the Right and Power to Judge All Teaching and to Call, Appoint, and Dismiss Teachers, Established and Proven by Scripture" (1523).[5] The second phase expresses the consolidation, but also a self-critique of the Reformation; here the emphasis is on order. The order of worship is regulated;[6] visitations are necessary and visitors must be instructed.[7] Also belonging to this group is the late writing "On the Councils and the Church" (1539).[8] In any case the older Luther clearly shows more interest in a developed ecclesiology than the younger had; the latter was more focused on the fact that in faith each individual human is addressed and challenged: "It is about your neck, it is about your life."[9] A final phase is represented by the apocalyptic writings in which the Reformer attacks the Roman church and the pope in a sometimes uncontrolled polemic in expectation of the imminent arrival of the Last Day.[10] The horrible writings against the Jews[11] belong here, as does the "Appeal for Prayer Against the Turks" (1541).[12]

CONTEMPORARY QUESTIONS

At present the church is regarded ambivalently both by its members and by those outside. A good deal of the evil that has been done by the church itself or in its name is strongly rooted in general awareness: trials of heretics and witches, crusades, religious wars, bloody confessional battles even in the very recent past, colonialism, restrictions on free research. While the Reformation and Protestantism were long regarded as an alternative to the model of a power-obsessed medieval church, today scarcely any distinction is drawn between the sins committed by individual churches. What seems negative in one church is accounted against the other; even the evil committed in the context of a non-Christian religion is brought to bear against religion in general and so also against Christianity as a whole. The fact that the Christian church has left not only a trail of blood, but also a much stronger trail of blessing in the world remains underemphasized; the churches' self-awareness and even their self-critical members suffer from all this. The ambivalence of the church's history is clearly reproduced in the present: are the churches really the defenders of peace and freedom or are they bulwarks of narrow-mindedness, self-assertion, and backwardness? Can looking at Luther's theology of the church communicate a positive image to both its members and those distant from it, or is he a particular representative of a backward-looking model of the church?

The church is in especially bad odor as an institution. Since the first actions of Constantine the Great on its behalf (and even more of Theodosius the Great) it has enjoyed privileges, at least in central Europe, that, as expanded by papal power politics and exploited in part by the Reformation churches as well, do not appear appropriate in our time. Will Article 144 of the constitution of the Federal Republic of Germany, which adopts Articles 136–139 and 141 of the Weimar Constitution, be sustained over the long run? What about concordats and church laws in which the special role of the church in society, schools, and universities are still established? Can such establishments be given a theological foundation—with or without Luther? State church structures with a corresponding system of payments and taxes, with bureaucratic management and dubious advertising strategies, are unattractive in a time in which individuals prefer not only to choose their pastor and congregation but to pursue their own spiritual paths and sometimes to seek out or even invent the religion that suits them. Where can we sense something of the "soul" of the institutional church? Can individuals still imagine themselves as members of a local parish at all? Is church plausible for them at most as a worldwide network of engaged individuals who are virtually connected with each other? But if we ought to consider the concrete parish, what about the structures we find there, the relationship between the producers and the consumers, the paid and volunteer workers, and the supervising officers with long-term contracts and pensions? Does Luther's theology have anything to say in this situation?

And then there is the poor ecumenical world! Can Luther be seen as anything but a disruptive factor there? What about his talk of the "Antichrist" or his distinction between the "true" and "false" church? Is one of the existing churches to be identified as "false," and if so, by what criteria? Did Luther contribute anything positive to the search for a "visible unity" of the church? Is not the quarrel between the confessions already reflected in the interpretation of his work, so that there is sometimes a clearly observable distinction between right- and left-wing trends in interpretation that could be relevant precisely for his ecclesiology? Since the Reformation the church has continued to divide into a multitude of confessions, denominations, and movements; in the last hundred years the rediscovery of charisms has played a significant role in this. Was not Luther completely blind at this very point?

Finally, there is the question of the eternal destiny of those people who cannot join the church or have always belonged to a non-Christian religion: Is Luther not a clear advocate of the opinion that there can be "no salvation" outside the church? How can this viewpoint be maintained today in the context of the world religions and of increasing irreligiosity, in Europe at any rate? Can it be brought into the interreligious dialogue?

CHURCH AS "CREATURE OF THE WORD"

Probably because of the omnipresence of the church as institution, which in Luther's view had very little to do with the Gospel, he did not especially treasure the idea of "church." He called it an "obscure" word, that is, one that has nothing to say, as well as "not German," that is, a foreign word.[13] He preferred to speak of the Christian community or assembly, of the holy Christian church, of the holy Christian people of God, "the whole Christian church on earth," as in his explication of the third article of faith in the Small Catechism.[14] For him, the church was a "crowd, assembly of people who are Christians and holy."[15]

Theologically, Luther did not proceed on the basis of the self-definition of the late medieval church with which he was familiar; instead he asked what was the origin of the community of Jesus Christ from which it reforms itself ever anew. How was it founded; what constitutes it? That must also determine how it is to be identified.

WHENCE THE CHURCH?

Luther was convinced that "thank God, a seven-year-old child knows what the church is, namely, holy believers and sheep who hear the voice of their Shepherd."[16] This he regards as self-evident. It is due to the effective power of the word that the voice of the Good Shepherd is heard and thus community is created and the people of God is constituted. The word of God is the "high sanctuary" because of which "the Christian people is called holy." God's word does not return empty (cf. Isa 55:11). It "cannot be without God's people, and conversely, God's people cannot be without God's word."[17] The church is thus no clublike gathering of the like-minded. The church is begotten, formed, nourished, brought up, pastured, strengthened, equipped, and adorned solely through the Gospel—"the church's whole life and being consists in the word of God."[18] Wherever the Gospel is spoken, there is the church, and thus it is by no means tied to particular places (such as Rome). "Where the word is, there is the church."[19] It depends on the word, not the word on it; this is true also of the church as institution: the Gospel is above the church, not the church above the Gospel. If it were otherwise it could change that word and thus everything else, and add its own ordinances.[20] But it is "incomparably" less than the Gospel, and thus categorically different from it.[21] All this is summarized in the concept of the church as "creature of the word," *creatura verbi*.[22] Thus Luther views the church primarily not in its active role but as the result of God's activity: it is a "creature," the result of God's working. It is God's Spirit who "makes," "gives," "gathers," "rules," and "preserves" the church,[23] so that the individual believer can confess that the Holy Spirit "has called me through the Gospel, enlightened me with his gifts, and sanctified and preserved me in true faith, just as he calls, gathers, enlightens, and sanctifies the whole Christian church on earth and preserves it in union with Jesus Christ in the one true faith."[24]

Nevertheless, Luther can also emphasize that and why he regards the activity of the church as indispensable. The Holy Spirit leads believers into the holy catholic church, has "placed you in the bosom of the church."[25] It is the "mother who begets and bears every Christian through the word of God."[26] Therefore "who wants to find Christ, must first find the church."[27] Hence the church is, so to speak, both mother and daughter. But speculations about whether it is "co-creatrix" or even "co-redemptrix," or at least "cooperator" in salvation are groundless.[28] The roles are clearly separated: the church is the "mother" of believers, but only because and insofar as it is the "daughter" of the word of God. Because it lives from the word of God it is founded in Paradise,[29] and for that reason "one holy Christian church will be and remain forever."[30]

When Luther concludes on the same ground that "outside the Christian church there is no truth, no Christ, no sanctification," this is clearly not intended in the sense of a necessity of the institutional church for salvation. Rather, it refers to what constitutes the inner dynamic of the church, namely proclamation. *Extra ecclesiam nulla salus* means for Luther *extra praedicationem Evangelii nulla salus*.[31] The church is, of course, "the assembly of people who believe in Christ. With this church one should be connected and see how the people believe, live, and teach. They certainly have Christ in their midst."[32] Anyone who wants to come to faith must encounter people who can testify to the Gospel and who live from it!

THE CHURCH AS IDENTIFIABLE

If the church is to be understood as the "creation" of the word of God, it clearly follows that and how it can be identified, even though, as the true church, it must at the same time be believed to be hidden. The true church is in no way identical with the institution and organization of church and its members. The distinction between the "church in the proper sense"[33] and the church as a social entity preserves the concrete, visible church against overestimation of itself and enables self-distancing and self-critique.

Visible, invisible, and hidden church

The true church filled with the Holy Spirit is, as such, not visible to the naked eye.[34] The all-too-obvious visibility of the papal church conceals precisely what the church is really about and what is invisible about it. The unity and holiness of the church cannot be discerned from external phenomena. The confession of Nicaea-Constantinople speaks of "the one, holy, catholic, and apostolic church";[35] this seemed to make it clear how one might recognize the church. But here, according to Luther, the text is not speaking of "the external Roman unity," which evidently does not correspond to holiness in the sense of sinlessness, nor does the text say "I believe in the Holy Spirit, one holy Roman church, the communion of Romans."[36] "All of us see the external Roman church. That is why it cannot be the true church, which is believed and which is a community or assembly of the saints in faith. But no one can see who is holy or who believes."[37] The issue is the unity, holiness, catholicity, and apostolicity of the church in a deeper sense, namely in eschatological perspective. Luther took action on behalf of a genuine catholicity of the church, geographically as well, extending beyond the scope of the papal jurisdiction; this is served by replacing the expression "catholic church" in the creed with "Christian church," although formally he could already refer back to late medieval usage.[38] Certainly for him apostolicity had priority, though understood in the sense not of a historically conceived apostolic succession but as a clear reference to the statements of Sacred Scripture. The ancient church's confessional statements about the "one, holy, catholic, and apostolic" church speak of its eschatological characteristics and are not phenomenological descriptions of its current earthly state. But they do release corresponding spiritual impulses and bring them into effect: the empirical church is challenged to seek its unity, to allow itself to be drawn into holiness, to become aware of its worldwide duty, and to trust itself more and more deeply to the word of God, corresponding to the apostolic preaching. What one can see about the church is sometimes not at all the church of Jesus Christ. Church, in the proper sense of the word, is an "article of faith."[39] In the Apostles' Creed we say: "I believe . . . the holy Christian church." "If this article is true, it follows that no one can either see or feel the holy Christian church, nor can anyone say, 'See, here or there it is!' For what one believes one can neither see nor feel. . . ."[40] Ultimately it is for God alone to identify God's church as such: "He does not want the world to know when he is sleeping with his bride."[41] So Luther distinguishes between "two churches"; the one he calls "spiritual, internal Christendom," the other "physical, external Christendom."[42] Certainly the two belong together, like body and soul, and one cannot clearly separate them. Without the true and genuine church there would be only a soulless body; the church would remain "alone." But then it would no longer be the church!

In the short run it appears that Luther was tempted to consider the model of an "ecclesiola in ecclesia," a special grouping of those who seriously wanted to be Christians.[43] In a sermon in 1523 he said that the sacrament should be given only to such as one knows "how he believes and that he is the kind of vessel that can contain it."[44] Here he even says that true believers should be assembled separately.[45] At least those who do not intend to draw any consequences from receiving the sacrament (!) could be excluded.[46] Similar notes can be heard in the *Formula Missae et communionis*[47] from the same year. They are repeated in the preface to the German Mass of 1526, where he rather resignedly says that he could and would "not yet" realize such a community, for "I have not yet the people or persons for it, nor do I see many who want it."[48] It was probably responsibility for the sacrament, the reception of which presupposed a knowledge of its meaning and a determination to consequential action, that caused Luther to make these remarks; likewise, the longing for a "distinct Christianity," one that every believer knows, would have played a role. But the Reformer never returned to these ideas from his early period. They would have undermined his image of the church and his whole ecclesiology and destroyed his theological approach by way of the justification of the ungodly at its core.

Nevertheless, for Luther the church was not simply "invisible," an ideal community, a "civitas Platonica."[49] The church is "hidden"[50] as Christ's divinity is concealed beneath his humanity, as God's action is hidden beneath its opposite. Nevertheless, it can be seen by its "characteristics" or "signs," the *notae ecclesiae*. The fruits of faith and sanctification cannot play a decisive role in this; they can be counterfeited.[51] The church is, however, perceptible and identifiable on the basis of its confession.[52]

Characteristics of the church

For the Reformer the most important characteristic of the church is the word of God: "Where God speaks, he also dwells."[53] The sole enduring and infallible sign of the church has always been God's word.[54] Insofar as the word also constitutes the sacrament, the sacraments themselves are part of this infallible characteristic. But if we follow his statements individually we see that he contemplated a gradation: word and baptism constitute the Christian, while the Eucharist can be subordinated to these.[55] Beginning with the word of God, there follows an incomplete and variable list of signs of the church. Thus in "On the Councils and the Church" (1539) we find: word, baptism, Eucharist, power of the keys, ordination, prayer, praise and thanksgiving, and finally suffering and assaults for the sake of the "holy possession of the sacred cross."[56] In "Against Hanswurst" he adds to word, sacrament, and office also creed, Our Father, respect for authority, praise of the state of marriage, and refusal of vengeance.[57] Apparently different consequences may follow, according to the situation, from the basic constitution of the church through word and sacrament, and these may be added as signs by which the church can be recognized. But the core is what the Augsburg Confession asserts in its seventh article: the church is the "assembly of all believers among whom the Gospel is preached in its purity and the holy sacraments are administered according to the Gospel. For it is sufficient for the true unity of the Christian church that the Gospel be preached in conformity with a pure understanding of it and that the sacraments be administered in accordance with the divine Word."[58] Thus the church is not known by the sameness of external forms or by the behavior or condition of its members, but by the powerful influence of word and sacrament that gathers, motivates, and activates the community. Where God's word is preached and the sacraments are celebrated, there— hidden, but with the most public consequences—is the church in its fullness.

The self-concept of the Reformation

This shows us what reformation can be. The church needs reformation, but it is not the task of a single human being; it is God's doing.[59] No one likes to admit that the church errs, and yet this is necessary when it teaches something apart from or even contrary to the word of God.[60] There are clear criteria: in light of the word of God "we judge both apostles and churches and angels as well."[61] It would be disastrous to acknowledge false authorities. "Cursed be all obedience to the depths of hell, be it to the authorities, father and mother, yes, even the church, if it be disobedience to God. . . . Here I recognize neither father, mother, friendship, authority, nor Christian church."[62] The appeal to the ultimate authority of the word of God serves an emancipatory function with regard to all penultimate authorities. This firm appeal to God's word must not be confused with fundamentalist biblicism. What the word of God says emerges from the fourfold "alone" of the reformational approach: faith alone, resting on grace alone, as it is given solely in Jesus Christ and attested only in Sacred Scripture. Here Luther finds also the basis for his own church-critical proceedings. Of course, he asks himself the question: "Do you really imagine that you are the only one who is wise?"[63] But we must expect errors in the church, as announced in the New Testament itself. "For we cannot trust or build on the lives and works of the fathers, but on God's word alone."[64] So Luther can say that "we" are the true ancient church.[65] He urges the clerics of the old belief assembled in Augsburg to either convert or do away with the inconvenient Reformer; he declaims: "If I live, I shall be your plague. If I die, I shall be your death. For God has set me on you. . . ."[66] But in no case would he admit that the church should be called by the "unholy name" of this "poor, stinking bag of worms." As we know, the "Lutheran" churches have not followed his demand. Despite his sense of mission, the Reformer was self-critical enough to know that even the evangelical or "Lutheran" churches could not simply identify themselves with the reign of Christ; if they had accepted such an identification they would by that very fact have become the "false church."[67]

COMMUNION OF SAINTS

COMMUNION

The "assembly of the people on earth who believe in Christ" includes those "who live in true faith, hope, and love," with the consequence that "the essence, life, and nature of Christendom is not a physical assembly, but an assembly of hearts in one faith."[68] Luther's primary accusation against the papal church in the early phase of his work, besides a lack of orientation to God's word, was the absence of genuine community. The pre-Reformation church was deeply divided—institutionally through the hierarchical division between clergy and laity, but also by moral differentiation, the consequence of a gradation between monastics and ordinary Christians. As faith results in an exchange between Christ and the individual believer, so there should be an exchange between believers. They can and should become "one loaf."[69] Luther took from the monastic tradition the phrases *mutuum colloquium* and *consolatio fratrum*—conversational exchange and mutual brotherly consolation. This exchange can have a material, moral, or spiritual side. What we have must "be in service," otherwise it exists "in theft."[70] Every person is "created and born for the sake of the other"; there has to be some sign of that in the Christian community, at least![71] But the "moral" exchange also matters. Christians back each other up; the innocent wife backs up the prostitute, the pious councilor the thief. Still more important for Luther, of course, is spiritual exchange, through which individual members of the community are assured that they belong to the church of God. It contains the witness of believers in centuries past. Luther says of the Psalter: "there you look into the hearts of all the saints. . . . This also serves well another purpose. When these words please a man and fit his case, he becomes sure that he is in the communion of saints, and that it has gone with all the saints as it goes with him, since they all sing with him one little song."[72]

Luther gives this idea a special tone by recognizing the condition of all the spheres within which community exists. Every believer belongs to three "states": each has a place in the community, in the family, and in society. Through her or his position in family and society, in economic life, and in the Christian communion, every Christian is included in each of these three states, *politia, oeconomia, ecclesia*. From these arise the duties one has to fulfill for the sake of fellow human beings and the whole of society. Each thus exists within a functional context that is important for the maintenance and growth of state, economy, and church.[73]

SAINTS

In agreement with Luther, the Augsburg Confession defines the church as an "assembly of all believers and saints" (*congregatio sanctorum et vere credentium*).[74] Corresponding to New Testament usage (cf., e.g., Rom 1:7; Phil 1:1), the "saints" for him are not primarily the perfected. In his writing in response to the canonization of Benno of Meissen, "Against the New Idol," he wrote that we must "turn away from the dead saints in heaven and turn toward the saints on earth, lift them up and honor them. That pleases God, and that has he commanded."[75] In Karl Holl's words, the Reformer "brought [the saints] down from heaven to earth." The saints who should really interest Christians live here on earth! They should be the object of our concern, and in particular active love of neighbor should take the place of honoring the saints. Luther expands on that in his "Confession" of 1528: "Again, all fathers and mothers who regulate their household wisely and bring up their children to the service of God are engaged in pure holiness, in a holy work and a holy order. Similarly, when children and servants show obedience to their elders and masters, here too is pure holiness, and whoever is thus engaged is a living saint on earth. Moreover, princes and lords, judges, civil officers, state officials, notaries, male and female servants . . ." for "whatever is contained in God's Word must be holy, for God's Word is holy and sanctifies everything connected with it and involved in it."[76]

Luther suggests a terminological distinction, one that has, however, not been accepted in Lutheran theology, namely that there is a categorical difference between the concepts of "holy" and "saved." One becomes holy through one's own work, but one can be saved only through Christ. "Even the godless may have much about them that is holy without being saved thereby."[77] That is to say that the "holiness" of Christians, as it may and should show itself in their way of life, is something derived; it grows out of the salvation promised them in Christ. Of course, this terminological suggestion is in conflict with New Testament usage, according to which the concept of "holiness" is used in a general eschatological sense. But as regards the matter itself, the Reformer agrees with the New Testament: the saint or holy person is not one who can show outstanding moral achievements, has a powerful religious aura, or is an impressive religious personality. On the contrary: it is precisely the saints who know their own deficiencies, who are aware of how far they fall short of the possibilities offered them in faith. The life of the saints is "hidden with Christ in God" (Col 3:3). Externally no one can determine who is a saint. Their sanctity is hidden from believers; they appear in their own eyes utterly imperfect. But they can know themselves in faith to be saints: more surely than that your name is Hans or Kunz, you should be certain that you are a saint![78]

The theology of the cross helps Luther to find a definition of the saints that is not rendered oppressive by the perfection of the ideal but recognizes saints as flesh-and-blood people. It is precisely the human being ensnared in guilt and failure who is called, in the midst of the chaos of her or his life—to be a saint! "This is the will of 'God, who is wonderful in his saints,' that they are simultaneously righteous . . . and unrighteous . . . sinners and saints at the same time, aware of being sinners, unaware of being saints, or sinners in reality, saints in hope."[79] The true saints rely solely on the justifying and sanctifying action of God for Christ's sake. Human beings cannot sanctify themselves or make themselves saints; they can only pray that God's name "may be sanctified among us as well." But this happens when "the Word of God is taught clearly and purely and we, as children of God, lead holy lives in accordance with it."[80]

Luther thus formulated a new profile of the saints, on the one hand with a strong anchor in the biblical witness but on the other hand unmistakably bearing the specific features of Reformation piety. Christian existence lives from and out of the word that makes holy; it stands firm against the challenges of crisis and sin; it finds its obvious field of activity within the Christian community and in the natural laws of humanity.

UNIVERSAL, MUTUAL, AND COMMON PRIESTHOOD

Luther's ideas about the common priesthood of believers rested directly on his new concept of the idea of "saints." This has unfortunately received an inadequate labeling, for it is not only about the dignity of individual Christians.[81] The point, rather, is the moments of mutuality and commonality in which this dignity is actualized. Luther finds various elements in support of his concept and so makes clear both the church-critical and the constructive ecclesiological impetus of this approach.

THEOLOGICAL BASIS

Luther's arguments for the common priesthood of the faithful did not all have equal weight, but they exist within an overall context in which they support one another. As we would expect, Luther tried to anchor his doctrine of the common priesthood in Sacred Scripture, but individual biblical passages play only a subordinate role.[82] Of course the Reformer appeals to the two fundamental New Testament statements on this topic: ". . . let yourselves be built into a spiritual house, to be a holy priesthood. . . . But you are a chosen race, a royal priesthood, a holy nation . . ."[83] and the song in Revelation: ". . . you have made them to be a kingdom and priests serving our God. . . ."[84] But Luther sees what he says about the "common priesthood" affirmed by the whole biblical witness. He regarded baptism as a calling to common priesthood; the baptized, freed for a new life in Christ, at the same time know themselves obligated to and responsible for the community. The assertion that all believers are "priests" to one another follows directly, for him, on the one hand from his Christology, and on the other hand from his belief in justification—from the closeness of believers to Christ and the resulting closeness of believers to one another. The priesthood of believers to one another, grounded in Christ and filled with life and spiritual dynamism, is thus acknowledged as the life-principle of the church of Christ.

Consequences

Important consequences follow, both for the church's doctrine and also for its praxis. These are in part critical of the church, and in part constructive in nature.

Church-critical elements

If we must begin from the direct empowerment of Christians through baptism and faith there is no more room for an official priesthood as distinct in principle from that of the laity. Priestly ordination, reserved to a particular group of people and spiritually qualified in a specific way, then has no further function; rather, it contradicts the promise of the Gospel given to all believers. This does not mean that there should not be offices and duties within the community that are indeed different, but it does mean that the fundamental distinction between clergy and laity resting on priestly ordination is eliminated. The concept of "apostolic succession" must then also be understood differently, namely in the sense not of a historical sequence of acts of ordination but as a substantive relationship to the Gospel; that constitutes the "apostolicity" of the church! Monasticism cannot then represent a higher level of Christian life; monastic vows, understood as a stage beyond baptism ("second baptism"), devalue the gift of baptism bestowed on every Christian. Hence the common priesthood means emancipation from an infantilizing hierarchy and at the same time a "democratization" of the church. This approach, though imperfectly developed and not ultimately sustained in reality, released some impulses to social criticism and is part of the early history of democracy.

Constructive ecclesiological elements

Only if one takes seriously the fact that through baptism all Christians are priests to one another can one grasp what the church is really all about: church is "brotherhood" whose unity must not be undermined and endangered by the construction of special brotherhoods. "My dear friend, in your baptism you have entered into a brotherhood with Christ, with all the angels, with the saints, and with all Christians on earth. Hold fast to this and live up to its demands, and you have all the brotherhoods you want. . . ."[85] The brotherhood resulting from baptism is realized not in special conventicles but in the relationships within which a Christian in fact stands: thus husband and wife are siblings in faith. If a husband communicates the Gospel and faith in Christ to his wife he becomes in some sense her "father in Christ."[86] By making the Gospel known to them, father and mother become apostles, bishops, and pastors to their children, for "whoever teaches the Gospel to another is truly his apostle and bishop."[87] This spiritual siblinghood consisting in being there for others is actualized, according to Luther, in a whole series of points:

Personal confession is the outstanding locus for the development of the priesthood of the baptized for one another. The believer who confesses his or her sins to a brother or sister can hear the voice of God in the words of the sibling. No institutionalized priestly office is required! In this brotherhood/sisterhood the difference between woman and man is also removed in principle; obviously the woman has the same right to hear the confession of a brother and affirm forgiveness for him as does a man with a woman.[88] This is true since "all baptized women are in a spiritual sense the sisters of all baptized men. They have in common the sacrament, the Spirit, faith, and spiritual gifts and blessings, by reason of which they are more closely related in Spirit" than by external kinship.[89] That Luther, bound up in his times, drew inadequate conclusions from his insight and, of course, did not yet consider women's ordination, is another issue.

Another important function of the common priesthood of believers is prayer. Luther develops this in a different context, with his new evaluation of the "last anointing" which, according to the New Testament, is not so much about anointing as about prayer for the sick.[90] The priestly competence given to believers through baptism is thus also expressed in the ability to identify Christian doctrine as such and to distinguish it from inappropriate teaching. How should it be, Luther asks, that Christians "do not also have the power to taste and judge what is right and wrong in faith?" Rather, they must lay claim to their competence without fear and judge what can be perceived of the empirical church "according to our faithful understanding of Scripture." Every Christian has the responsibility to understand the faith more deeply and protect it against errors. Luther develops these ideas in a document whose title states its program: "That a Christian Assembly or Congregation Has the Right and Power to Judge All Teaching and to Call, Appoint, and Dismiss Teachers, Established and Proven by Scripture."[91] There is necessarily, in consequence, a new understanding of ordination. It is not as if, in Luther's mind, the office of preaching should be simply the result of a division of labor and delegation, as in a modern democracy. God directly instituted the office of pastors "to "minister word and sacrament to a congregation" among whom they reside.[92] But in doing so God created an office to which a person should be called, as in the case of any other office, and that the official only occupies as long as he or she is not dismissed. Nothing distinguishes the officeholder's activity, as far as its value is concerned, from what a farmer does in the field or a housewife in her home; it is faith that gives their quality to all these activities.[93] Thus "the sacrament of ordination" cannot be anything but an orderly way to choose a preacher for the congregation.[94] In precisely the same sense, according to the Augsburg Confession, no one should preach publicly or administer the sacraments "without a regular call," *nisi rite vocatus*.[95]

Luther's doctrine of the common priesthood culminates in the now-familiar expression that one should become Christ to one's fellow human beings. God pours out divine gifts on me; completely free of charge God forgives me my sins and gives me the fullness of a new and blessed life—"so, thus will I . . . likewise freely, joyfully, and for nothing do what pleases him and become to my neighbor a Christ as Christ has become to me. . . ."[96] The background here is certainly Luther's idea of the Eucharist, previously discussed, in consequence of which the meal-event results in an internal joining on the one hand of Christ to the believer, but on the other hand between believers themselves.[97]

There are more or less direct consequences of Luther's approach for life in society. Luther's polemic against late medieval mendicancy, which seemed dogmatically legitimate, should be understood entirely in the context of his teaching about the common priesthood. Within a community in which one is there for the other, no one should have to beg; everyone should contribute something to the community. Luther's pedagogical engagement also belongs in this context; a better education for all is required! Luther's friend and colleague Bugenhagen founded girls' schools because "the same heaven awaits them."[98] The beginnings of the emancipation of women come into the picture as a result: if there are "exceptional pupils, who give promise of becoming skilled teachers, preachers, or holders of other ecclesiastical positions," they should be allowed to study; Luther can appeal to the fact that there have also been female saints, such as Agnes, Agatha, or Lucy.[99] So it can be said that "two clearly discernible offices were created for women: teachers of catechism and 'church servants,'" which probably also included baptism administered by midwives.[100] This had its consequences for the role of fathers also: if they wash diapers people ridicule them, but "God, with all his angels and creatures is smiling"—not, of course, because they wash diapers, but because they do so in faith.[101]

However, on the basis of the common priesthood Luther also reflected on the possibility that women could assume the office of preaching.[102] All Christians are "priests," all women "priestesses" ("pffeffyn"), "be they young or old, master or servant, mistress or maid, learned or unlearned. Here there is no difference, unless faith be unequal."[103] It is striking that Luther occasionally includes even children![104] If no man preaches, "it would be necessary for the women to preach."[105] Luther is also convinced that "among all Christians one finds many, both men and women, who can preach as well as the one who preaches at a particular place."[106] But it seems to him that women are less well fitted for the office of preaching, and besides, *est contra consuetudinem*, "it is contrary to custom."[107]

MINISTRY AND ORDERS

The question of spiritual office continues without interruption to be explosive, especially in the realm of ecumenical discussions, where it is a principal theme.[108] This issue of ministry has a different position in the Roman Catholic Church and its theology than it has in Protestantism; in the former, ordination[109] is regarded as a sacrament and the church is conceived hierarchically.[110] Add to this the problem of the papal office and the issue of women's ordination. But it would damage both theology and the church if the theme of office and ministry were left exclusively to controversial theological debates.

The interpretations of Luther's idea of ministry have often been associated with particular interests that guide perceptions. One somewhat right-leaning interpretation attempts to bring the Reformation office of preaching closer to Catholic official priesthood and to understand ordination by analogy to the consecration of the priest.[111] A more left-leaning presentation places emphasis on the common priesthood and sees the ministry of preaching as representative of it; here some congregational tendencies are visible.[112] There was also some development in Luther's idea of ministry, and this has been variously evaluated. Without question the common priesthood was in the foreground during his early period, but with the consolidation of the Reformation congregations the ordered ministry tied to ordination came more to the fore.

THEOLOGICAL FOUNDATIONS OF MINISTRY

Ministry and the common priesthood

Luther was aware that the phenomenon and concept of the "priest" was more at home in the world religions than in Christianity.[113] The foundation for the office cannot be here, then, nor is it found in the Old Testament priesthood, which reached its goal and its end in the high priesthood of Christ. "Priest" is a somewhat enigmatic concept in Luther; on the one hand, as applied to Christ he treats it in an extraordinarily positive manner, but as regards the Old Testament priesthood and especially the late medieval church he regards it very critically. His terminology is inconsistent. Add to this (and Harald Goertz in particular has pointed this out) that he speaks metaphorically about the common priesthood.[114] Since the image Luther uses for the priest is ambiguous, it cannot have a single meaning when applied to the church's reality. But it is clear that Luther had to find a new word for the holder of office: the *sacerdotium* belongs to the whole community while the officeholders have to carry out the *ministerium*. Pastors are thus—and this is the concept Luther now prefers—primarily "servants" of the word and thus of the community.[115]

Office must accordingly be grounded in the service it offers: its function is the proclamation of the word and the administration of the sacraments for the whole community. God wants to see that function exercised, and publicly, for the salvation of human beings and for God's own glory. To that extent the office of the ministry is "commanded, instituted, and ordained" by God.[116] This is the office that is described in the Augsburg Confession as "instituted" by God (Article V), though the form it is to have is by no means defined.

Certainly we can also observe the tendency to restrict this office, which in principle belongs to the whole community, to the pastorate. It is true that in principle all believers can be entrusted with the function of ministry, but not all in the same way. The spiritual office is instituted by God, but how it is exercised is a matter for the community to decide. To that extent the foundations of office "from above" and "from below" by no means lie "impartially alongside one another."[117] Rather, they are clearly related each to the other. The community has the obligation to seek and call a minister. In his remarks on the common priesthood Luther created a clear basis for the conception and perception of the ministry associated with ordination: "Because we are all priests of equal standing, no one must (may) push himself forward and take it upon himself, without our consent and election, to do that for which we all have equal authority. For no one dare take upon himself what is common to all without the authority and consent of the community."[118] Precisely because all have the same right, there must be choice and delegation.[119] Here, of course, the argumentation is no longer spiritual, but rational, or we might say that a spiritual basis grounds a rationally derived argument. But even this is only persuasive if it is applied to public worship and excludes the possibility of a rotation in which all members of the community might successively take turns. It is true that one could in some way argue on the basis of Harald Goertz's interpretation of Luther: "The ordered regulation of the exercise of service through the ordained ministry is thus not only not at all in *contradiction* to the 'priestly' authority of all believers, but on the contrary serves to *realize* the common priesthood."[120] But one would have to insist, at least with the early Luther, that the "realization of the common priesthood" is by no means entirely covered by this and that it must not be applied only to spheres in which there is no competition for "office."

Ministry through ordination

Ministry associated with ordination differs from the common priesthood of believers primarily through the fact that it belongs to a particular sphere of responsibility. We are speaking here not of a special power (e.g., the power of orders), or an unchangeable qualification (*character indelibils*), but of the public acceptance of service to word and sacrament. It is a matter of "legal *responsibility*,"[121] which must be regulated, though in principle it could be regulated differently. We can compare it to Sunday: what is to be done on Sunday could, in principle, be done on any other day, but—in this case—the day already assigned to it presents itself as appropriate.[122] The officeholder, the "one in service," differs from the laity in no way other than in his or her calling and corresponding service.[123] But God wants that service and identifies with it because God wants thereby to come to the aid of humans: this gives the office and the person who occupies it his or her authority. Like parents toward their children, so are the preachers "gods" to their hearers because they are doing God's business.[124] Of course, Luther is capable of immediately dissolving this focus on the ministry, for God "condescends to enter the mouth of each Christian or preacher."[125] The service of preaching and the celebration of the sacraments must be publicly visible; in them the church can be recognized and fulfills its mission. Therefore the Augsburg Confession requires that no one should teach publicly or administer the sacraments without a regular calling (Article XIV). Although in the sixteenth-century situation the ecclesiastical and secular publics were still closely associated, Luther would probably have been thinking here primarily of the congregational public.[126] The apostles were sent into the whole world, and Christ himself preached freely and openly; Pentecost did not happen in a corner. "The office of the ministry and the Word of God are supposed to shine forth like the sun. We should not go around sneaking and plotting in the dark," but "deal openly in broad daylight. . . ."[127] "The Holy Spirit does not come with stealth. He descends in full view from heaven."[128]

THE FORM OF MINISTRY AND OFFICES

Ordination

God desires to have God's word preached and the sacraments celebrated; this, presupposing the common priesthood, makes necessary an office tied to ordination, and so a regular calling, an "ordination" is required. It is not an act of consecration, but the appointment of a person to perform the desired task. Ordination is "nothing but a certain rite whereby one is called to the ministry of the church."[129] Luther did not consider the liturgical act necessary, but he did ordain Georg Rörer a deacon in 1525. Melanchthon was legitimated by his duties at the university, Osiander because he was called by the council of Nuremberg.[130] After 1535, however, for practical and juridical reasons supra-regional ordinations were celebrated within worship services. They were theologically grounded in baptism, regular calling, and the prayer of the congregation. They were legitimated by Christ himself: if we have him, the highest pontifex, with us, then "good night, Pope."[131] The laying on of hands as part of the ritual bestowed no special authority or gifts; it was to be understood as an "appropriate liturgical gesture"[132] associated with the Our Father and the singing of the congregation, "Now Let Us Pray to the Holy Ghost," prayers that were certain to be heard.[133]

Certainly there remained a lack of clarity in the fact that Luther still spoke of "blessing" and had blithely ignored the relevant passages in the New Testament (cf. 1 Tim 4:14; 2 Tim 1:6). This was a notarial action[134] that sealed competence in a particular field of responsibility but did not ground a hierarchical superiority. This view was in no way intended to devalue ordination but instead to represent an exaltation of every calling. The conveyance of office naturally presumed a certain aptitude and at the same time demanded a degree of education; Luther thought in particular of knowledge of the biblical languages. His pedagogical involvement is evident, though certainly not exhausted, in this context.

Divided ministry

For Luther, ministry is not simply identical with the office "of the pastor," but includes all those who work in it: "all who are engaged in the clerical office or ministry of the Word . . . such as those who preach, administer sacraments, supervise the common chest, sextons and messengers or servants who serve such persons."[135] The preaching office is multifold and within its framework the diaconal ministry should be restored to its early Christian form. The Reformer also regarded the office of the schoolmaster as important. He himself referred again and again to his calling to the ministry of "doctor of Sacred Scripture." Essentially, of course, the ministry is the office of preaching; the preacher is a servant of the word, for ultimately faith comes from preaching (cf. Rom 10:17). In preaching, Christ's coming into the world is fulfilled.[136]

The office of bishop also represents a form of the preaching ministry; it can be carried out by the "superintendents" who act within the framework of a consistory as much as by specially appointed bishops. Luther himself ultimately installed Nicholas of Amsdorf as bishop of Naumburg in 1542. He could imagine a conciliar leadership of bishops, with none holding a higher position than any other.[137] In contrast, he rejected a superordination of the pope, whether based on divine or human law, for the preservation of the church's unity or whatever: he saw Christ alone as responsible for that.[138] Indeed, at the time of the Augsburg Reichstag, when a new order was not yet in view, he even thought it possible to leave the old-believer bishops in their offices and entrust them with the jurisdiction, oversight, and installation of evangelical (Lutheran) preachers, so long as the freedom to preach the Gospel was secured; beyond that, the Reformation congregations would finance themselves.[139] Beyond that, Luther counted on it that gradually the secular authorities could be addressed regarding their responsibility, as he had already done in the appeal "To the Christian Nobility" (1520). So he came to the idea of princes as "bishops of necessity,"[140] toward whom the Reformer himself remained skeptical[141] and from whom the Lutheran churches were only able to free themselves, by necessity, after the end of World War I.[142]

THE COMMON TASK OF MINISTRY AND THE COMMON PRIESTHOOD

The church's most important task is to preach the word of God. "The first and foremost of all on which everything else depends, is the teaching of the Word of God. For we teach with the Word, we consecrate with the Word, we bind and absolve sins by the Word, we baptize with the Word, we sacrifice with the Word, we judge all things by the Word." The one to whom the word is entrusted is truly a "priest." God's word is common to all Christians.[143] Nevertheless, there are different areas of responsibility, which is why there can really be no competition. The public representation of the proclamation is assigned to the officeholder; anyone who is not in office has the duty to witness to the Gospel in his or her familial and professional field. "Where right belief is, the Spirit will not let you rest; you will break forth, become a priest and teach other people, too . . . for when your heart is full, the mouth must overflow. . . ."[144]

Ministers and laity stand facing one another on the ground of their common priesthood. The ministry serves the laity through preaching in worship and the celebration of the sacraments; the laity sustain the ministry through their prayers and support it by their participation in spiritual tasks within their own sphere. Thus arises an ideal image of Lutheran worship, which Luther describes as follows: "There our pastor, bishop, or minister in the pastoral office, rightly and honorably and publicly called, having been previously consecrated, anointed, and born in baptism as a priest of Christ . . . goes before the altar. Publicly and plainly he sings what Christ has ordained and instituted in the Lord's Supper. He takes the bread and wine, gives thanks, distributes and gives them to the rest of us who are there and want to receive them. . . . Particularly we who want to receive the sacrament kneel beside, behind, and around him, man, woman, young, old, master, servant, wife, maid, parents, and children, even as God brings us together there, all of us true, holy priests, sanctified by Christ's blood, anointed by the Holy Spirit, and consecrated in baptism. On the basis of this our inborn, hereditary priestly honor and attire we are present . . . and we let our pastor say what Christ has ordained, not for himself as though it were for his person, but he is the mouth for all of us and we all speak the words with him from the heart and in faith, directed to the Lamb of God. . . ."[145]

As far as worship is concerned, this is certainly a convincing image! It does not, of course, include the life of the congregation outside the worship service. Not in view is the fact that charisms may be alive in the congregation and awaiting their development for the good of the whole. Here is payback for the fact that Luther did not really grasp a theology of charisms. In light of his experiences with the fanatics and Paul's advice in Romans (Rom 12:6-8) and 1 Corinthians (1 Corinthians 14), the Reformer seems to have regarded them instead as a threat to the community.[146]

THE CHURCH'S APOCALYPTIC STRUGGLE

Luther formally adopted Augustine's idea that from the very beginning there had been "two churches," a "true" and a "false."[147] Abel and Cain are their first representatives; with Cain began what culminates in the Antichrist.[148] The false church has its signs, just as the true one does. In his exhortation to the clergy assembled at the Augsburg Reichstag, Luther listed thirty-seven numbered "things" that "have been practice and custom in the pretended church." These include indulgences, sacrificial Masses, abuse of the ban, purgatory, poltergeists, innumerable pilgrimages, and "the same kind of prayers without number." By association Luther adds things he regards as superfluous and inappropriate.[149] If one wants to behold the Christian church without cross and struggle, without heresies and divisions, one must wait a very long time! Where God's church is, the devil builds a chapel alongside it. Satan has his own church through which he threatens the true church from within and from without, through heresy and massive oppression: ". . . his craft and power are great."[150]

ROMAN AND FANATIC HERESIES

Heresy has been the greatest danger to the church in all times. It appears in two basic forms:

The essence of Roman heresy is the *glossa*: the word of God is not accorded the authority that belongs to it. Either people set up their own authorities and attribute exclusive interpretive power to them, as in the case of the papal magisterium, for example, or else they invent outlandish principles of interpretation such as allegoresis. One can also deprive the biblical text of its claims by alienating it with inadequate theological or philosophical concepts (e.g., *transsubstantiatio*). The result is that people do not allow the word to "stand" in its original meaning, but interpret it according to their own interests.[151] Thus arise misunderstandings, falsifications, invented burdens for the people, and harmful orders for church and society. As the example of the Mass shows, this process can even lead to a reversal of the Gospel.

Appeal to the "spirit" is the essence of the fanatical heresy, which also deprives Sacred Scripture of its power. This occurs by appeal to inner experience, which is said to be superior to the word, by one-sided selection of biblical passages, or by a superficial or supposedly "dialectical" interpretation that twists the original meaning of a biblical statement. The consequence can also be unclear thinking, against which Luther protested vehemently: it is about a clear yes or no![152] In this way the ecclesiastical and public order can be reduced or even dissolved; arbitrary lawlessness will then replace them.

But God sustains the church against all internal and external dangers! In the Arian period there were scarcely five orthodox bishops in the world, and those had been driven from their episcopal sees. Even under the heretics' rule, Christ sustained his church.[153] Luther confesses that "there is much that is Christian and good under the papacy; indeed everything that is Christian and good is to be found there and has come to us from this source. . . . in the papal church there are the true holy Scriptures, true baptism, the true sacrament of the altar, the true keys to the forgiveness of sins, the true office of the ministry, the true catechism in the form of the Lord's Prayer, the Ten Commandments, and the articles of the creed."[154] The Reformer even mentions certain usages he considers useful, for example showing the crucifix to the dying and reminding them of Christ's suffering, as well as "many good hymns and canticles, both Latin and German."[155] To that extent there are signs of the true church even in the Roman church; the struggle between the true and the false church is going on within the church itself.

Luther is less generous in his judgment of the enthusiasts: if the public ministry of preaching is cut down, as Luther fears, the light of the Gospel will remain at most only in a few individuals, "and in that fog Christ will come"— but still he will come![156]

POLITICAL PERILS

Luther sees external perils for Christianity on the one hand from the revolutionary peasants and on the other from the Turkish threat. For him, both had apocalyptic significance. "See what a mighty prince the devil is, how he has the world in his hands and can throw everything into confusion, when he can so quickly catch so many thousands of peasants, deceive them, blind them, harden them, and throw them into revolt, and do with them whatever his raging fury undertakes."[157] Ultimately the Turks seemed to him more dangerous. In 1521–1522 they had conquered Belgrade and Rhodes, won a battle at Mohács in 1526, and in 1529 they lay before Vienna; in 1539–1540 the situation again reached a crisis. It is true that Luther regarded the pope as worse than the Turks; consequently it made no sense to turn against the Turks as long as the papal heresy had not been overcome. Hence there was no question of a crusade against the Turks as far as Luther was concerned. He contended against the Turks' religious claims; he was active in promoting the publication of the Qu'ran for apologetic reasons, and in 1543 he brought it to print with his own preface.[158] Although he fought determinedly for resistance to the Turks, he first called for penance. In any case, the church should not defend itself by force. Here, to use the formula of the Augsburg Confession, what counts is not the power of force, but the word.[159] When Luther addresses the political authorities he does so in the context of his doctrine of the two governments.[160] But since the church's existence is tied up with the physical existence of believers, political perils, whether from Turks or from restless peasants, are experienced as a danger to the church.

THE "SYNAGOGUE"

Judaism,[161] as the late medieval church presented it, was regarded by Luther as in tension with the church; we may think only of the numerous defamatory depictions of Jews ("Jewish sows") in the Gothic churches. Such a sculpture was found (and is still found) in the town church of Wittenberg. But, as described above, Luther considered Judaism differently in the course of his development. On the one hand, for someone to whom Hebrew was important and who could speak fondly of the "fathers" of the Old Testament there existed an obvious affinity for Judaism. On the other hand, Luther was ultimately disappointed by the Jews.[162]

In his early period Luther expected that many Jews would recognize his sympathy for them and join the Reformation.[163] But that was not the case. On the contrary: he received reports of Jewish conversions in Moravia, whereupon he wrote his horrible anti-Jewish screeds. He no longer argued with theology alone, but allowed himself to be drawn into anti-Jewish emotions; he scolded the supposed arrogance and avarice of the Jews. Reading the book "On the Jews and Their Lies" from 1543[164] must always have been a challenge to every Christian, but since the Holocaust it is altogether unbearable. Heiko A. Oberman makes an effort to show that one should no more speak of solidarity with the Jews on the part of the young Luther than of racial hatred in the old man.[165] Unquestionably Luther stands within the tradition of his time, but that in no way excuses him. Theologically we should question whether in these cases the shadows of a christological concentration and a certain oblivion toward the Trinity make themselves felt. That would be a question to be addressed to all of Luther's theology! Are the anti-Jewish writings "slip-ups" explainable in terms of the rage of an old man, or do they point to a structural fault in Luther's theology? Certainly it is evident that his anti-Jewish, anti-

Turkish, and anti-papal polemics, especially in his last years, were affected by an apocalyptic perspective.

THE "ANTICHRIST"

For Luther the figure of the "Antichrist" summarized the devil's resistance to the true church, especially at the end of the ages: the Antichrist is the "End-Christ," as the late Middle Ages saw it. Luther himself saw the historical movements of his time and his own mission as apocalyptic, end-time events. He could attribute Antichrist features to the enthusiasts and the peasants, the Jews and the Turks, but the real Antichrist sat in Rome. The notion of the Antichrist had already played a role in anti-papal polemics in the late Middle Ages; for example, in the struggle over the ideal of poverty people pointed to the un-Christian lifestyle of the "vicar of Christ." Luther, however, was not so much concerned with the papal lifestyle as he was with the teaching. As early as his dialogue with Cardinal Cajetan the suspicion awakened in him that the Antichrist might be at work in the church. In a letter to Georg Spalatin (18 March 1519) he confesses that his studies in the papal decretals had intensified that suspicion.[166] In 1520 there followed "On the Papacy in Rome."[167] At that time he still wanted to accept the papal office, if the issue was only human arrangements. But what the pope said and decided had to be tested against Sacred Scripture: "For my part he must remain under Christ and let himself be judged by Holy Scripture."[168] It would be necessary to interpret correctly the relevant biblical passages that were (and are) adduced as a theological basis for the papacy: the rock on which the church is built, so that the gates of hell shall not prevail against it, is in no way represented by the institution of the papacy but "it means to be built, in strong and true faith, upon Christ the rock!"[169] Polemic against the papacy continued throughout Luther's whole life and only increased at the end. The pope was accused of elevating himself above God and Christ and having founded "a new, false church."[170] Christ himself is with his church and needs no representative, no vicar.[171] The papacy was instituted neither by secular power nor by Christendom; therefore it cannot come from God: it is "an institution of the devil."[172] Luther sees his opinion confirmed by corresponding passages in Scripture, which itself predicts the Antichrist (1 John 2:18). He "opposes and exalts himself above every so-called god or object of worship, so that he takes his seat in the temple of God, declaring himself to be God" (2 Thess 2:4). He sees the papacy itself as the Antichrist, making little distinction between the office and its occupant. But despite all his biting polemic the Reformer is aware that the Antichrist threatens every church and therefore can appear at any time as an "intra-church phenomenon."[173]

CRITICAL EVALUATION

LUTHER'S VISION OF THE CHURCH: AN EXCESSIVE DEMAND?

Luther had no primary interest in the church as institution. At the center of his theology stood the question of the glory of God and the salvation of humanity. Only from that perspective could the church acquire its value. It was a derived entity, but precisely as such it had its specific significance. His love for the true church corresponded to his battle against the Roman church. Aroused by the vision of the seer in the Apocalypse (Revelation 12), which in later Catholic tradition was interpreted as Mary, Luther composed a hymn to the church in the style of a love song:

> To me she's dear, the worthy maid,
> And I cannot forget her;
> Praise, honor, virtue of her are said;
> Than all I love her better. . . .
> Sore travail is upon her;
> She bringeth forth a noble Son
> Whom all the world must honor,
> Their king, the only one.
> That makes the dragon rage and roar,
> He will the child upswallow;
> His raging comes to nothing more;
> No jot of gain will follow.
> . . .[174]

Mother and Son, Christ and the church are in danger, but they will not fall. Luther belonged to that company of Christians who, in the course of the church's history, have again and again expressed their longing for a true, pure, and convincing church. It has been said that Luther chose the path from the monastery to the world in order to make the world a monastery. But the world failed, and there was no way back into the monastery either! Luther was disappointed in his expectations of Christians; how much he had hoped for from them in 1520! In 1526, in the preface to the German Mass, he again gave free rein to his imagination: "those who want to be Christians in earnest and who profess the gospel with hand and mouth should sign their names and meet alone in a house somewhere to pray, to read, to baptize, to receive the sacrament, and to do other Christian works." Here people could practice church discipline, agree on a common donation for the poor, and "center everything on the Word, prayer, and love."[175] This is the longing for what a religious order attempts to realize, a resolute way of faith and life. But, Luther then asserts with resignation, a real Christian is a "rare bird!"[176]

The Reformation model of church is demanding; it is not for people who take refuge in Mother Church and allow themselves to be led by her apron strings, but for those who, as adult Christians, take up their position in church and society. But there were not all that many of those even in the century of the Reformation. The self-criticism required by the Reformation, especially after 1527/28, caused the aspect of a communion of believers and, parallel to it, the idea of the universal, mutual, and common priesthood to retreat— an irrecoverable loss. The corresponding insights departed from the Lutheran churches and found a degree of realization in congregationally-organized communities and pietist groups.

TRAGEDY OF THE COMMON PRIESTHOOD?

Why has the idea of the common priesthood of believers had so little clear success, either in Reformation theory or in practice—in fact, not even in Luther's own theological development? There are probably not only pragmatic but also theological reasons.

The emancipatory side of this approach was easier to convey than the constructive side; the link to emancipatory tendencies in politics was fairly close. This was reproduced in the terminology that has become commonly accepted, but it expresses Luther's own idea in only limited fashion. We speak of the "common" priesthood of the faithful, losing sight of the aspect of mutuality that, for Luther, was constitutive of it. Nor does the formulation of the idea reveal that the community of believers acts together. Hence the common priesthood is regarded more as a status than as a ministry or a duty, and so acquires a tendency to draw people away from the church as institution rather than to bring them into it.

Moreover, the word "priest" is deceptive. In some sense the result was a "double bind": it is impossible to polemicize on the one hand against the concept of priesthood and on the other hand to make it one's motto. Ultimately there was a deficiency in the argument because a grounding of the common priesthood in baptism proved inadequate. Many of the baptized did not, *de facto*, pay any attention to the priesthood bestowed on them. Hence it remained unclear, even for Luther, whether there was a common priesthood of all the baptized, or only of those baptized who took their baptism seriously and claimed it. Since Luther did not take the step to the "ecclesiola," the community of those "who earnestly desire to be Christians," there remained a gap in the argumentation at this point.

Other possible foundations for the common priesthood that the New Testament might have offered were shamefully neglected by Luther. In the wake of late medieval tradition and in his battle against the enthusiasts it did not occur to Luther to think carefully and make theological use of what the New Testament has to say about charisms.

The deficiencies mentioned are regrettable, but they do not make Luther's approach obsolete. It should not be too late for the Lutheran churches to render it a reality and then to introduce it into the overall ecumenical horizon.[177]

Lack of clarity about the common priesthood was also damaging to the understanding of ministry tied to ordination. Some statements in the New Testament[178] were simply avoided rather than being applied to the concept of the common priesthood. Luther could turn his argument entirely around: while he once wrote a whole document demonstrating "That a Christian Assembly or Congregation Has the Right and Power to Judge All Teaching,"[179] scarcely a decade later he angrily demanded: "Since when are you a judge of your pastor, or for that matter, your own judge?"[180] It is true that he had not revised his fundamental notion of the common priesthood, but he did not develop it and translate it into the context of a measured theology of ministry grounded in the New Testament.

LACK OF INSTITUTIONAL INTEREST?

Luther first saw himself as taking part in the battle against the institutional church and the existing order of things. Hence the construction of a new institution, which he at first had no intention of doing, could not be his primary interest. But when that proved unavoidable he began with some clear starting points: the promise of the Gospel led to faith, and faith to love. The relationship between *promissio* and *fides* on the one hand and the obvious tie of *fides* to *caritas* on the other laid a clear ecclesiological foundation. If everything depended on the faith that grew from the promise, and if love arose of itself out of that faith, then there was the broadest possible field of possibilities for organization. This found its confessional expression in the *satis*/"sufficient" of the Augsburg Confession (Art. VII).

In fact, however, this meant that the orders then in existence or in the process of development were adopted. There is no fundamental objection to that; Catholic priests today still wear liturgical garments derived from antiquity. For Luther orders were useful if they left room for the basic relationships as stated. This opened the door both to traditional patterns of organization as manifested in the parish or Sunday worship and also to new trends like those beginning to appear in view of the rise of absolutism in the organization of state church regimes. The difficulty, of course, was that things once established could scarcely be broken off in the future. It took World War I and the collapse of the German empire to finally set the Lutheran churches in Germany on their own institutional feet.

One heritage of this unwillingness to institutionalize was probably that until today Protestantism has developed no clear relationship to power. As a rule Protestants do not trust themselves to speak an authoritative word grounded in reason, knowledge, and experience and to take public leadership. Power is despised. As a Protestant one hesitates to claim power, whether within the congregation or in society. This appears democratic and is certainly appealing in comparison to other churches. On the other hand, neither the individual nor a social group can exist without claiming its own space and exercising influence on the world around it. The Lutheran Church must stand for something, and so must the individual Christian. Luther himself resolved that personally in charismatic fashion, so to speak. The Protestantism that follows him must seek institutional solutions if it is not to lose itself in the jungle of vague relationships.

Inappropriate polemic?

It is especially in connection with what he says about the church that Luther repeatedly becomes unusually polemical. In his case polemic is not to be explained only psychologically or historically. For him faith was a struggle, preaching was a battle; the work of the church itself could not be understood except as a history of struggle by which people were to be rescued from the devil's rule. The theological and content side of Luther's polemic should therefore be carefully examined and taken seriously; it cannot simply be passed over for the sake of an irenicism appropriate to today. This is true, first of all, of his distancing himself from the late medieval church and also from the enthusiasts and the Swiss reformers. Identifying the pope with the Antichrist was not a malicious act on Luther's part; it was the expression of a deep concern for the message of the Gospel and therefore for the church as well. Luther also declared war against everything to do with the Antichrist in his own confession; the self-criticism of the Reformation is eloquent testimony to this. Luther perceived the synagogue as a false church that rejected the witness to Christ, but he saw Christian communities threatened also by political challenges and structural deficiencies, as attested especially by his writings against the Turks. Faith demands a clear stance, a "yes" in which the implicit "no" is also perceptible. That between the clear "yes" and the definite "no" there can in many respects be some latitude was something that Luther often failed to acknowledge in the heat of battle.

But what is unforgivable is the lovelessness we sometimes find in his polemic, especially in the late anti-Jewish and anti-papal writings. The fact that he saw his opponents in the perspective of an apocalyptic struggle does not excuse him. Particularly in an apocalyptic situation, love must not pale. Luther's anti-Jewish writings are an embarrassment to every interpreter of good will. Some take no position at all: Paul Althaus,[181] but also Otto Hermann Pesch[182] and Oswald Bayer[183] do not even address them. Bernhard Lohse treats them, as I have said above, only in an excursus.[184]

Heiko A. Oberman writes: "The insistence on tolerance of the Jews, though only in the sense of coexistence for the sake of conversion, he maintained to the end of his life. But the nearness of the last days drew tight the boundaries of tolerance, as to time also."[185] This is a remarkable sort of argument: for one thing, it is a strange kind of tolerance whose only purpose is conversion. For another, despite some formal utterances that could also be understood as lip-service, Luther's "insistence" is to be observed more in the direction of intolerance. "With the approach of the Antichrist, however, there was no other option," Oberman comments, "than to effect the final separation—not only from the Jews! As the days of the world grew short for the aging Luther, he was not concerned about campaigns against the Turks, or hatred of Rome or of the Jews, but about upholding the Gospel in the confusions of the end-time."[186] This may in fact have been the case for Luther, but here he most certainly chose false means for "upholding the Gospel."

How did Luther arrive at his negative judgment on the Jews? Their focus on the Law made them for him the essence of works-righteousness, which he thought he had to combat on every front. In Luther's view the rabbis "knowingly and willingly" twisted the truth about the Messiah;[187] for 1,500 years they had rejected the Gospel; Luther could regard that as hardening of the heart. In Gerhard Müller's interpretation, "the ways part over faith."[188] If only it had merely been a parting of the ways! Müller finds Luther's suggestions for a state policy toward the Jews "grounded in the fact that Luther did not acknowledge Jewish faith as a conviction."[189] This may well be a correct observation, but from today's perspective the question naturally arises: how was it that Luther was so unable to perceive or take seriously the convictions of another human being?

It is certainly not wrong to see and interpret Luther's anti-Jewish polemic in the context of his times. The massive pogroms against the Jews that took place in plague times were more than a century and a half in the past; in the interim we can count nearly ninety expulsions within the territory of the German empire. To that extent Bernhard Lohse is correct when he says that Luther only took up "suggestions that had long since been made by others"; here, he says, Luther was neither "original" nor "keener"; the laws regarding heretics were in any event much worse.[190] Religious plurality was felt to be a threat to public order and peace. Oberman points out that in any case Lutheran theologians like Justus Jonas and Andreas Osiander took a friendlier attitude to the Jews. In the approach adopted by Lutheran piety of justification it was not primarily the Jews who came to represent the murder of the Son of God; individual sinners had to discover that they themselves were guilty and confess:

"Our great sin and heavy offense
has nailed Jesus, the true Son of God, to the cross.
Therefore, poor Judas, and all the crowd of Jews,
we may not curse you as enemies,
for truly the guilt is ours."[191]

Bernhard Lohse recommends renouncing prejudices, conducting substantive dialogue with Judaism, and practicing tolerance: three things we would have expected of Luther himself! In his theses on justification the Reformer was able to speak of the "incomprehensible forbearance . . . of God."[192] But forbearance is here understood as an attitude that undertakes compromise in order to prevent something worse. As regards faith, his "forbearance" had its limits: "for love bears all, endures all. Faith bears nothing, and the Word endures nothing; the Word must be perfectly pure."[193] Faith and love must certainly be distinguished, but to separate them in this way is deadly for both: love without faith dissolves into pure emotion that knows no reason or criteria, while faith without love becomes a death-dealing weapon of the opinionated.

But this raises the theological question whether Luther's polemic against the Jews was merely a deviation that can be explained by the apocalyptic mood of the age or by sheer boorishness, or whether it was a consequence of his theological approach. The strict division he drew between Law and Gospel would not have made him more receptive to the Jews. His high estimation of the Gospel of John in particular may have caused him to accept its often hostile attitude toward the Jews without thinking: "You are from your father the devil, and you choose to do your father's desires," the Johannine Jesus says to his Jewish interlocutors (John 8:44). Jesus, "the condemned, crucified Jew,"[194] marks the extremes of closeness and at the same time of radical distance between Jews and Christians. Here we see once again that an isolating concentration on Christology such as we find in Luther has to have its boundaries broadened by Trinitarianism. Otherwise it would prove to be a flaw in the fabric of Luther's theology. But such a Trinitarian expansion is possible on the basis of Luther's approach, as can be shown from what he wrote about the Old Testament, and even in his judgments on Judaism.

DUALISTIC BIAS?

There seems to be at least a latent dualistic bias running through Luther's theology that strengthened throughout his life. As a rule the Reformer was able to preach so convincingly, joyfully, and vividly about salvation through Christ, forgiveness, and the justification of the ungodly that the implicit negative pole of his words retreated into the background. He did not threaten hell; as a believer he knew that he had escaped it. But its flames were not forgotten. He could jeer at the devil, but he saw him at work in many places: among the old believers, the Jews, the Turks, enthusiasts, peasants, and even in the congregations that joined the Reformation. Ultimately he knew of Satanic attacks from his own experience.

Luther did not repeat Cyprian's assertion that there is no salvation outside the church. Whatever may have been happening outside the church, he took only marginal interest in it, if any: danger from the Turks, the Copernican revolution, the discovery of new islands. That corresponded to the geographical location and the place in church history where he saw himself placed by God. But it was clear to him that there is no salvation apart from Christ. Therefore care must be taken, at least within the church, that salvation in Christ should be preached with full clarity and that its saving effects should not be diminished by misunderstandings and demonic false interpretations. Hence everything was concentrated on the struggle between Christ and the devil, and so between the true and false churches.

In the context of Luther's historical situation and mission that is quite understandable. There are constellations within which one-sided positions must be dared and defended. But they must be recognized as such, so that their relative character remains clear. The historical Luther, however, would scarcely have been pleased with any such relativizing. At least in his later years he saw even more clearly "the fathomless either-or that God in Christ has placed over all human beings."[195] He was no longer able, as in his earlier years, to say that the papal dominance that was so contrary to the Gospel had "not arrived . . . without God's providence," although even then he believed that this development was the result not of a gracious, but rather of a wrathful divine choice.[196] Here negative tendencies and processes were still held together under God's direction. But in Luther's late writings we read almost solely about struggle and conflict, though of course he did not question the victory. In a period of globalization, however, when human groups are growing closer and closer together, this kind of thinking does not bring us forward. It is true that an emphatic protest against everything that damages and diminishes human beings must be sustained. But the overall perspective must be Trinitarian—with a strong emphasis on God's creative governance and the inspiring power of God's Spirit. If Luther's theology cannot function without asserting a "fathomless" dualism, we must ask seriously whether it can have any future—and whether in this it really corresponds to the Gospel.

NOTES

[1] LW 39, 58 (WA 6, 286, 35–287, 23).

[2] Joseph Lortz, *The Reformation in Germany* (London: Darton, Longman & Todd; New York: Herder & Herder, 1968).

[3] Cf. Gottfried Seebass, "Antichrist IV. Reformations- und Neuzeit," *TRE* 3: 28–43.

[4] LW 39, 49–104 (WA 6, 285–324).

[5] LW 39, 301–14 (WA 11, 408–16).

[6] Cf. the Preface to "The German Mass and Order of Service" (1526), LW 53, 61–67 (WA 19, 72–78).

[7] Cf. the Preface to "Instruction to the Visitors of Parish Pastors in Electoral Saxony" (1528), LW 40, 269–73 (WA 26, 195–201).

[8] LW 41, 3–178 (WA 50, 509–653).

[9] WA 10/1/2, 335, 18-19.

[10] "Against Hanswurst" (1541), LW 41, 179–256 (WA 51, 469–72); "Against the Roman Papacy, an Institution of the Devil" (1545), LW 41, 257–376 (WA 54, 206–99).

[11] "On the Jews and Their Lies," LW 47, 121–306 (WA 53, 417–552); "A Warning Against the Jews" (1546), WA 54, 206–99.

[12] LW 43, 213–41 (WA 51, 585–625). For the whole cf. Althaus 1962, 248–96; Lohse 1995, 294–316; Kühn 1980, 21–38; Michael Beyer, "Luthers Ekklesiologie," in Junghans 1983, 1: 93–117; 2: 755–65.

[13] LW 41, 144, 143 (WA 50, 625, 5; 624, 19).

[14] *The Book of Concord*, 345.

[15] LW 41, 143 (WA 50, 624, 17). Neebe 1997, 180–81 puts together a list of terms that, however, are clearly not to be understood as equivalents, but mutually interpretive. Regrettably, it lacks conceptual acuity; ibid., 269–70.

[16] *The Book of Concord*, 315, with allusion to John 10:3.

[17] LW 41, 150 (WA 50, 629, 34-35).

[18] ". . . breviter, tota vita et substantia Ecclesiae est in verbo Dei," WA 7, 721, 12-13.

[19] "Ubi est verbum, ibi est Ecclesia," WA 39/2, 176, 8-9.

[20] WA 30/2, 682, 10-19.

[21] "incomparabiliter minor ipso . . ." WA 2, 430, 6-7.

[22] Ecclesia enim creatura est Euangelii," WA 2, 430, 6-7.

[23] Cf. *The Book of Concord*, 345; WA 30/1, 45, 9; WA 7, 219, 4.

[24] *The Book of Concord*, 345.

[25] LW 51, 166 (WA 30/1, 91, 9-10).

[26] WA 30/1, 188, 24-25.

[27] LW 52, 39 (WA 10/1/1, 148, 8-9).

[28] Against Peters 1991, 238.

[29] Cf. LW 1, 104 (WA 42, 141, 1–147, 41).

[30] CA VII, *The Book of Concord*, 32.

[31] "Outside the church there is no salvation"; "outside the preaching of the Gospel there is no salvation." Peters 1991, 236.

[32] LW 52, 39–40 (WA 10/1/1, 140, 14-17, reorderd).

[33] Apology of the Augsburg Confession VII, *The Book of Concord*, 173. To the contrary cf. Congregation for the Doctrine of the Faith, "Answers to Some Questions Regarding Certain Aspects of the Doctrine on the Church," 29 June 2007, Question 5: "Why do the texts of the Council and those of the Magisterium since the Council not use the title of 'Church' with regard to those Christian Communities born out of the Reformation of the sixteenth century?"

[34] Hence the formulation "visibility of the hidden church" (Korsch 2007, 112, 117) is problematic.

[35] *The Book of Concord*, 19 [substituting "Christian" for "catholic"].

[36] LW 39, 67, 75 (WA 6, 300, 34-35).

37 Ibid. (WA 6, 300, 38–301, 2).

38 Peters 1991, 213, 222.

39 LW 41, 148 (WA 50, 628, 18).

40 LW 39, 220 (WA 7, 684, 28–31), with reference to Heb 11:1.

41 WA 17/2, 501, 35; 510, 37-38.

42 LW 39, 70 (WA 6, 296, 37–237, 9).

43 LW 53, 64 (WA 19, 75, 3-18).

44 WA 12, 481, 7-8 (Text II).

45 WA 12, 485, 4-5 (Text II).

46 WA 12, 491, 2-6 (Text II).

47 LW 53, 15–40 (WA 12, 205–20).

48 LW 53, 64 (WA 19, 75, 18-21).

49 Luther held the concept of "invisibilis" to be not only "less" than "absconditus" (against Wendebourg 405), but used it, if at all, with great precision. The church is "visible" "per fidem" (LW 11, 136 [WA 4, 188, 17]), "ex professione" (cf. n. 52); the very obvious "visibility" of the papal church speaks against it (WA 7, 710, 2). Believers are "invisibiliter" born from the word, "thus the church grows, not indeed in outward appearance but invisibly," "ita crescit Ecclesia non in specie, sed invisibiliter" (LW 17, 407 [WA 31/2, 578, 4]).

50 "The Church is hidden, the saints are unknown," "abscondita est ecclesia, latent sancti," LW 33, 89 (WA 18, 652, 23).

51 LW 41, 167 (WA 50, 643, 6-26).

52 WA 39/2, 161, XII, ll. 8-9.

53 WA 14, 386, 28-29.

54 WA 25, 97, 32-33.

55 Cf. Michael Beyer in Junghans I (1983), 97.

56 LW 41, 164 (WA 50, 641, 35–642, 3).

57 LW 41, 194–98 (WA 51, 478, 34–485, 24), 1541. Neebe 1997, 222–34 traces the increasing list of signs and presents a chart of their hierarchizing, 228. Unfortunately, the author is more interested in secondary literature than in Luther's own texts.

58 The Book of Concord, 32.

59 LW 31, 250 (WA 1, 627, 27-30): "The church needs a reformation which is not the work of one man, namely, the pope, or of many men, namely the cardinals . . . but it is the work of the whole world, indeed it is the work of God alone."

60 LW 26, 66–67 (WA 40/1, 132, 27), ". . . if the church teaches anything in addition or contrary to the word of God, one must say that it is in error."

61 LW 38, 161 (WA 38, 208, 22-23), with reference to Gal 1:8-9.

62 WA 28, 24, 15-26.

63 LW 24, 323 (WA 46, 22, 33-34).

64 LW 38, 159 (WA 38, 206, 18-19).

65 Cf. LW 41, 194 (WA 51, 487, 18).

66 LW 34, 49 (WA 30/2, 339, 15-16).

67 Cf. Michael Beyer in Junghans I (1983), 115, and nn. 348 and 349 there.

68 LW 39, 65 (WA 6, 292, 38–293, 4).

69 Cf. LW 35, 58 (WA 2, 748, 18). It is highly one-sided to understand Luther's idea of communion only in terms of participation in the sacraments and thus to approach a Catholic communio-ecclesiology, as is attempted, for example, by Simo Peura, "Die Kirche als geistliche communio bei Luther," 131–56 in Heubach 1996.

70 WA 12, 470, 40-41.

71 WA 21, 346, 21.

72 LW 35, 256 (WA.DB 10/1, 102, 9-30).

73 This is well developed by Michael Beyer in Junghans I (1983), 104–8. Whether and to what extent Luther took account of the three states outside the Christian community is a separate

question. Wilhelm Maurer (Maurer 1970) does not deny that there were also tensions among the three hierarchies and some inconsistencies as well. The unclear reference to Dionysus the Areopagite's concept of hierarchy should probably be called a terminological mistake on Luther's part.

74 *The Book of Concord*, 33.

75 WA 15, 192, 12. In what follows I am adapting material from Hans-Martin Barth, *Sehnsucht nach den Heiligen? Verborgene Quellen ökumenischer Spiritualität* (Stuttgart: Quell, 1992), 76ff.

76 LW 37, 364–65 (WA 26, 505, 1-10). Cf. also the lovely anecdote about Antony in *The Book of Concord*, 275–76.

77 LW 37, 365 (WA 26, 505, 20-21). Luther himself did not hold to his terminological suggestion.

78 WA 32, 92, 22.

79 ". . . Simul peccatores et simul sancti, peccatores scienter, sancti ignoranter, sive peccatores in re, sancti in spe." Quoted from Lennart Pinomaa, *Die Heiligen bei Luther* (Helsinki: Luther-Agricola-Gesellschaft, 1977), 169, referring to Erich Vogelsang, ed., *Unbekannte Fragmente aus Luthers zweiter Psalmenvorlesung 1518* (Berlin: de Gruyter, 1940), 85.

80 *The Book of Concord*, 346.

81 Goertz 1997, 40, n. 21, asserts that the concept of "common priesthood" does not yet appear in Luther, since the word "allgemein/common" only came into use later. But cf. LW 36, 138 (WA 8, 488, 7): "das gemeyn aller Christen priesterthum," "a . . . priesthood, held in common by all Christians"). In Luther's view the Christian does not "become" a priest in the sense of the common priesthood; she or he is such through baptism. "It would please me very much if this word 'priest' were used as commonly as the term 'Christians' is applied to us. For priests, the baptized, and Christians are all one and the same," LW 30, 63 (WA 12, 317, 9-11).

82 In what follows I am adapting material from Barth, Hans-Martin 1990, 29–53. For the whole cf. also Volker Leppin, "Evangelium der Freiheit und allgemeines Priestertum. Überlegungen zum Zusammenhang von Theologie und Geschichte in der Reformation," *MdKI* 58 (2007): 103–7.

83 1 Pet 2:5, 9.

84 Rev 5:10.

85 LW 44, 193 (StA 2, 149, 2ff.).

86 LW 36, 100 (StA 2, 240, 27ff.), "An non baptisatus baptisatae spiritualis frater?" (240, 28).

87 LW 45, 46 (WA 10/2, 301, 23-28). Cf. Gerta Scharffenorth and Klaus Thraede, *"Freunde in Christus werden"* (Gelnhausen: Burckhardthaus, 1977), 183–286.

88 LW 36, 88 (StA 2, 232, 24).

89 LW 45, 8 (WA 10/2, 266, 15-18).

90 James 5:13-15. Cf. Hans-Martin Barth, "Heilende Seelsorge. Wort und Sakrament als Heilsmittel im therapeutischen Zusammenhang," US 42 (1987): 213–22, esp. 218.

91 LW 39, 301–14 (WA 11, 408–16); see also "Concerning the Ministry," LW 40, 3–44 (WA 12, 169–96).

92 LW 44, 176 (StA 2, 136, 19ff.). The Reformation's grounding of office is not only about the "structural irreducibility of the human word," as Korsch says (Korsch 2008, 110; cf. 106–10). In speaking of the "wordliness of faith" (p. 103), he presumably means "word-character of faith."

93 LW 36, 78 (Cf. StA 2, 225, 1ff.).

94 It is a *ritus quidam eligendi Concionatoris in Ecclesia*, LW 36, 113 (StA 2, 249, 35-36).

95 *The Book of Concord*, 36. For the whole cf. Goertz 1997.

96 StA 2, 299, 9-12; the Latin is *Dabo itaq(ue) me quendam Christu(m) p(ro)ximo meo, que(m)admodu(m) Christus sese p(rae)buit mihi,* ibid., 298, 12-14. Cf. LW 44, 301.

97 Cf. "God's creative word" in chapter 16; "For the sake of Christ" in chapter 8; "Polemic against the sacrament 'without consequences'" and "The ecclesiological significance of the Eucharist" in chapter 10.

98 Quoted from Scharffenorth 1977, 267.

99 LW 45, 371 (WA 15, 47, 13-17).

100 Scharffenorth 1977, 268.

101 LW 45, 40 (WA 10/2, 296, 27–297, 1).

[102]Cf. Goertz 1997, 252ff.

[103]LW 35, 101 (WA 6, 370, 25-28).

[104]Cf. LW 36, 138–39 (WA 8, 489, 2-6).

[105]LW 36, 152 (WA 8, 498, 13-14). The Risen Lord makes Mary Magdalene "a preacher," so that she "might be a master and teacher to the dear apostles. . . ."

[106]LW 30, 135 (WA 12, 389, 10-11).

[107]WA.TR 5, 10, 6-7.

[108]Cf. Roman Catholic-Lutheran Joint Commission, The Ministry in the Church (Geneva: Lutheran World Federation, 1982); Karl Lehmann and Wolfhart Pannenberg, eds., The Condemnations of the Reformation Era: Do They Still Divide? (Minneapolis: Fortress Press, 1990), 154–57; Bilaterale Arbeitsgruppe der Deutschen Bischofskonferenz und der Kirchenleitung der Vereinigten Evangelisch-Lutherischen Kirche Deutschlands, Communio Sanctorum. Die Kirche als Gemeinschaft der Heiligen (Paderborn: Schöningh, 2000), 64–99; World Council of Churches, Baptism, Eucharist, and Ministry (Geneva: World Council of Churches, 1982), §§15 18. For the whole see Reinhard Frieling, Amt. Laie, Pfarrer, Priester, Bischof, Papst (Göttingen: Vandenhoeck & Ruprecht, 2002).

[109]This sacrament "by the anointing of the holy Spirit, puts a special stamp on them [priests] and so conforms them to Christ the priest in such a way that they are able to act in the person of Christ the head," Presbyterorum Ordinis 2, in Austin Flannery, OP, ed., Vatican Council II. The Basic Sixteen Documents (rev. trans. Northport, NY: Costello, 1996), 319.

[110]Lumen Gentium, chap. 3, in ibid., 25–43.

[111]Cf. Helmut Lieberg, Amt und Ordination bei Luther und Melanchthon (Göttingen: Vandenhoeck & Ruprecht, 1962); on this cf. Goertz 1997, 17–18.

[112]Cf., e.g., Klaus Peter Voss, Der Gedanke des allgemeinen Priester- und Prophetentums. Seine gemeindetheologische Aktualisierung in der Reformationszeit (Wuppertal: Brockhaus, 1990). My own version is also oriented primarily to the development of the common priesthood and is less interested in the question of orders; cf. Barth, Hans-Martin 1990, 29–53.

[113]LW 40, 35 (WA 12, 190, 12-14).

[114]Cf. Goertz 1997, 33–79. Goertz, however, distinguishes too little between the metaphorical statements and those that are apparently not metaphorical, both of which Luther uses to describe the common priesthood.

[115]Cf. LW 36, 116 (WA 6, 564); LW 39, 154 (WA 7, 636, 6-18); LW 14, 32 (WA 31/1, 251, 2-13); WA 37, 13, 9-11; WA.Br 1, 239, 26-27.

[116]LW 41, 171 (WA 50, 647, 8).

[117]Against Althaus 1962, 280.

[118]LW 44, 129 (WA 6, 408, 13-17).

[119]"Thus who, e.g., in the worship assembly seizes the word without being asked by the congregation thereby forces all others to be silent and so robs them of their own right. Thus precisely because in the common priesthood every Christian has the same individual authority to serve word and sacrament, it can only be preserved if all those who are equally authorized 'call' a particular person from among them, i.e., in mutual agreement give the assignment to exercise this service representatively and publicly for all. Thus Luther grounds not the service itself but the necessity of delegating its regulated public exercise to particular persons, that is, the constitution of the institutional ministry, in the common priesthood," Goertz 1997, 195.

[120]Ibid., 212.

[121]Ibid., 185.

[122]Cf. ibid., 227.

[123]LW 36, 116 (WA 6, 567, 19): ". . . a laico nihil differat nisi minsterio"; LW 36, 113 (WA 6, 464, 13): ". . . sacerdotium aliud nihil est quam ministerium." Such statements are sometimes terminologically misleading since, e.g., in the passage cited it is not the common sacerdotium of believers but the sacerdotium as ministerium that is referred to.

[124]WA 28, 613, 15-17. Cf. Luther's interpretation of Ps 82:6 (e.g., LW 13, 71 [WA 31/1, 215–17]).

[125]LW 24, 66 (WA 45, 521, 27-28).

[126]For an explanation of *publice* in Augsburg Confession XIV cf. Maurer 1 (1976), 217ff.

[127]LW 21, 8 (WA 32, 303, 17-19).

[128]"Against Infiltrating and Clandestine Preachers" (1530), LW 40, 379–94, at 384 (WA 30/3, 518–27).

[129]LW 36, 116 (WA 6, 566, 31-32). Melanchthon thought he could accommodate to the old believers here by also designating and understanding ordination as a sacrament (Apology of the Augsburg Confession XIII, *The Book of Concord*, 212).

[130]He had received priestly ordination in 1520. Bernhard Brons pointed this out to me; see Gottfried Seebass, "Osiander, Andreas (1496–1552)," *TRE* 25: 507–15, esp. 508.

[131]WA 41, 241, 36.

[132]Goertz 1997, 316ff.

[133]Cf. the formula of ordination in LW 53, 122–26 (WA 38, 423–31).

[134]WA 53, 257, 6-9.

[135]LW 37, 364 (WA 26, 504, 31-35).

[136]WA 20, 364, 38.

[137]WA 50, 217, 5-17.

[138]WA 50, 217, 23–218, 18; WA 50, 215, 14–217, 9.

[139]LW 34, 52 (WA 30/2, 341, 25–342, 34).

[140]Cf. WA.Br 8, 396, 14-15.

[141]Cf. WA.Br 10, 436 (no. 3930).

[142]Cf. Hans-Walter Krumwiede, "Kirchenregiment, Landesherrliches," *TRE* 19: 59–68.

[143]LW 40, 21 (WA 12, 180, 5-9), "verbum est idem omnibus." The office of preaching is one: "prorsus unicum et omnibus commune," LW 40, 23 (WA 12, 181, 17-18; cf. 182, 22; 190, 18-19; the same is true of the office of the keys, WA 12, 183, 30-31). But Luther can also characterize the common spiritual ministry as "that common and spiritual priesthood by which we all sacrifice ourselves mystically," *sacerdotium, quo nos mystice omnes nos ipsos sacrificamus*, with reference to Romans 12: LW 9, 124 (WA 14, 645, 19).

[144]WA 10/3, 311, 27–312, 2.

[145]LW 38, 208–9 (WA 38, 247, 12-29).

[146]Cf. Goertz 1997, 241–52; Kärkkäinen 2006.

[147]LW 41, 194 (WA 51, 477, 30-33).

[148]Barth, Hans-Martin 1967, 85; Höhne 1963, 87.

[149]LW 34, 54–57 (WA 30/2, 347, 25–349, 29).

[150]"A Mighty Fortress" (EG 362, 1).

[151]Ibid., 4.

[152]Cf. LW 40, 168 (WA 18, 158, 23-29).

[153]Cf. Asendorf 1967, 152, n. 125.

[154]LW 40, 231–32 (WA 26, 147, 13-18)—though in the midst of it all the "Antichrist" is pursuing his ends (ibid.; WA 26, 147, 26-33).

[155]LW 38, 177–78 (WA 38, 221, 18-35).

[156]LW 17, 254 (WA 31/2, 457, 30-31).

[157]LW 46, 51 (WA 18, 358, 28-32).

[158]See above, chapter 4.

[159]". . . not by human power, but by God's Word alone," . . . *sine vi, sed verbo* (CA XXVIII), *The Book of Concord*, 84.

[160]See chapter 12.

[161]See "Antisemitism? Luther and the Jews" in chapter 4.

[162]For the whole cf. Oberman 1981b; idem, "Luthers Stellung zu den Juden: Ahnen und Geahndete," in Junghans I (1983): 519–30; also WA 53, 579–648, "On Shem Hamphoras and the Ancestry of Christ" (1543).

[163]"That Jesus Christ was Born a Jew" (1523), LW 45, 195–229 (WA 53, 417–552).

[164]LW 47, 121–306 (WA 53, 417–552).

[165]Oberman 1981b, 156.

[166]LW 48, 114 (WA.Br 1, 359, 29-31), no. 161.

[167]LW 39, 49–104 (WA 6, 285–324). For the whole see Hubert Kirchner, "Luther und das Papsttum," 441–56 in Junghans I (1983).

[168]LW 39, 101 (WA 6, 322, 8-9).

[169]LW 39, 93 (WA 6, 315, 5-21).

[170]LW 41, 206 (WA 51, 494, 27–495, 23).

[171]WA 7, 742, 13-16.

[172]This comes from the title of Luther's writing, "Against the Roman Papacy, an Institution of the Devil," LW 41, 257–376 (WA 54, 206–99).

[173]Dorothea Wendebourg in *Handbuch* 2005, 413.

[174]LW 53, 294 (WA 35, 462–63). That the church must bear the "noble Son" is to be understood, in Luther's thought, as meaning that whoever would find Christ must first find the church that proclaims him (LW 52, 39 [WA 10/1, 140, 8]).

[175]LW 53, 64 (WA 19, 75, 5-15).

[176]WA 20, 579, 21; "seltzam" can mean both "remarkable" and "rare." Cf. LW 17, 186 (WA 31/2, 407, 5): Christians are "sparsely sown."

[177]There is an attempt in this direction, oriented to Luther, in Barth, Hans-Martin 1990, 191–250.

[178]1 Cor 12:28; cf. also the corresponding statements in the Pastorals and Paul's own understanding of his mission.

[179]LW 39, 301–14 (WA 11, 408–16).

[180]LW 40, 386 (WA 30/3, 520, 27-28). Cf. Barth, Hans-Martin 1990, 48–53.

[181]Althaus 1962.

[182]Pesch 1982.

[183]Bayer 2003.

[184]See chapter 2 above; Lohse 1995, 356–67. Cf. also Johannes Brosseder, *Luthers Stellung zu den Juden im Spiegel seiner Interpreten. Interpretation und Rezeption von Luthers Schriften und Äusserungen zum Judentum im 19. und 20. Jahrhundert vor allem im deutschsprachigen Raum* (Munich: Hueber, 1972); and see also "Antisemitism? Luther and the Jews" in chapter 4.

[185]In Junghans I (1983), 528.

[186]Ibid., 529.

[187]Lohse 1995, 365.

[188]Gerhard Müller, "Antisemitismus VI," *TRE* 3: 143–55, at 148.

[189]Ibid.

[190]Lohse 1995, 366.

[191]The language has been smoothed; the German text is quoted from Heiko A. Oberman in Junghans 1 (1983): 530. This motif was then taken up by Paul Gerhardt: "My burden in Thy Passion, Lord, Thou hast borne for me, for it was my transgression which brought this woe on thee . . ." *The Lutheran Hymnal*, 172, 4 (*EG* 85, 4; cf. also *EG* 81, 3).

[192]WA 34, 152 (StA 5, 149), Thesis 14: "Sed ad incomprehensibilem tolerantiam et sapientiam Dei minus malum ferentis, ne maiore malo omnia subvertantur."

[193]LW 9, 166 (WA 14, 669, 14-16): "Charitas omnia suffert, omnia tolerat, fides nihil suffert et verbum nihil tolerat, sed perfecte purum esse debet verbum."

[194]Cf. WA.Br 8, 90, 24 (No. 3157).

[195]Peters 1991, 236.

[196]LW 39, 100 (WA 6, 321, 31-36).

12

Division of Labor: God's Left and Right Hands

The so-called two-kingdom or two-government doctrine is among Luther's most controversial ideas. Especially in the twentieth century it led to some sharp clashes. In part it was theologically falsified and politically misused. It evoked a flood of secondary literature[1] and quite a few misunderstandings. In particular, it makes clear what a great historical distance exists between the present and the time of the Reformer. Add to this the difficulties involved in the concepts he used, which today sometimes appear opaque or confusing. Finally, Luther stood within a history of tradition that he partly adopted, partly modified, but that no longer belongs to us at all. In what follows I do not propose to offer new theses on this vast subject or try to describe the complicated discussion. It is more important, as concerns Luther's idea of the two "kingdoms" or "governments" to ask what about them is "evangelical" in the proper sense, what in all this serves the glory of God and the salvation of humanity. The concrete ethical implications of the concept represent a theme that must be handled separately.

CONTEMPORARY QUESTIONS

CHANGING TIMES

Luther made his core statements on the two-kingdoms or two-governments doctrine in his 1523 writing, "Temporal Authority: To What Extent It Should be Obeyed,"[2] but "authority" in the sixteenth-century sense no longer exists. It has been replaced by the state built on equal rights and by democracy, to the origins of which Luther did, after all, contribute. When Luther engaged with the relationships between what we would call state and church, church and world, Christian and civil responsibility, he could assume as a matter of course that his addressees were essentially citizens of the Holy Roman Empire

313

and Christians of the German nation; in the meantime we now have a Europe in which Christianity plays at best a marginal role and that must seek its place somewhere between non-Christian religions and religious indifference. The "Constantinian age of the church" is declining to its end; in Germany this is signaled by court proceedings against crucifixes in schoolrooms and against the pealing of church bells loudly enough to be heard; Sunday retains only limited protection, and church taxes are under scrutiny. In a counter-movement, Islam is raising theocratic demands. Head scarves, the building of mosques, and the cries of muezzins carried over loudspeakers are the point of the spear. Despite the continued state support of the churches, and despite the immense diaconal engagement of the churches on behalf of society, the mutual relationship of the functions church and society have for one another needs a new theological clarification. Freedom of religion is up for discussion. Will the development of a "world ethos" reconcile the religions and cultures with each other, or do we need something like Luther's two-kingdoms/two-governments doctrine to protect a constructive mutuality and peaceful regulation of conflicts?

Infinitely much has also changed in detail. Luther, in developing his teaching, was constantly concerned with "classes" or "orders." Today not even the concept can be used; it survives only in such combinations as "professional order" or "class politics." Work and calling, in the face of unemployment on the one hand and the preservation of free time on the other, have acquired a new caliber; marriage and family are largely in the process of dissolving, while the economy seems to be flourishing "independently of any laws," and threatens so to destroy the possibilities for individual survival and the horizon of meaning for many. Capital markets and scholarship go their own, sometimes common ways. In this situation is it the duty of a church that appeals to Luther to make an effort to maintain or create structures and institutions that can be of assistance to individuals or groups?

The society in which Luther lived was marked by the overwhelming power of the Roman church, which affected all aspects of life. In this context Luther's interest had to lie in setting limits to the influence exercised by a controlling ecclesiastical system. Church should again be church in the true sense and at the same time give the world back its own dignity and value. Today, at least in Europe, the situation is reversed: economic and social policies also shape the lives of churches and congregations. The warning or encouraging voice of the Gospel rings out over sparsely inhabited pews; in the media it is drowned out by the chatter of mutually neutralizing talk shows. The relationship between society and church needs to be rebalanced. In particular, Protestantism has to seek out its place in the midst of a globalization process rushing forward within an irrational religiosity and an ultimately disoriented secularism.

The most urgent ethical challenges are clearly at hand: the problems of stem-cell research and the exploration of the universe, understanding of the limits of life, its beginning and its end, responsibility for the world in view of AIDS, hunger, and climate change. How can all this be understood in terms of Luther's idea of God's action, and what are the necessary consequences? As a helpless individual I will ask myself how anyone can live his or her faith as a Christian in the face of overpowering economic and political developments. What solutions does Luther offer us?

A RETROSPECTIVE VIEW OF THE PROBLEMS

One thing that burdens the discussion of the doctrine of two kingdoms or two governments is the way it is misused. Particularly in the first half of the twentieth century people thought they could give a theological foundation to the "independent legal system" of the world by appeal to this teaching. In fact, Luther said that the world's government has its "own nature,"[3] though he did not believe this "nature" was independent of God's commandment and ordinance, or that it should emancipate itself from them. Representative voices of Lutheranism have wrongly interpreted Luther in this matter, as Ulrich Duchrow in particular has pointed out in several publications.[4]

In the realm of political and social questions Luther hardly ever theorized in the abstract. That makes him highly vulnerable. His publications all attempted to intervene in current affairs. His ideas about authority were probably influenced in a positive direction by the authorities he himself encountered in the person of his own sovereign, the Elector Frederick the Wise. In turn, Thomas Münzer may have served for him as the epitome of an insubordinate attitude toward authority, contrary to Sacred Scripture. Proponents and opponents of the two-kingdoms or two-governments doctrine are called upon to consider to what extent Luther saw his own theological ideas confirmed by the chaos of the Peasant War. Historians must agree that even the introduction of the Reformation was in many cases "anything but a parade example for the application of the two-kingdoms doctrine."[5] Was the two-kingdoms/two-governments doctrine condemned to failure from the outset?

DIFFICULTIES OF ACCESS

CONCEPTUALITY

Luther himself does not speak about a doctrine of two kingdoms or two governments, but he does talk about two "kingdoms" and two "governments"—what is their relationship?[6] Understanding this today is made all the more difficult by the fact that in the language of the sixteenth century "kingdom" or "empire" (Reich) could refer both to a territory and to its government. "The kingdom of God" can mean both at the same time: the realm within which God rules. Luther uses the two concepts synonymously, but also as distinct from one another. The word "Reich/kingdom" can probably in certain cases also include the concept of "government," or "rule," but "government" can never entirely be replaced by "kingdom/rule."[7] We find statements in Luther in which the "kingdom of God" is contrasted with the "kingdom of Satan," and others in which he speaks of God's government or rule, with its "right" and its "left." Consequently, some authors even speak of a "three-kingdoms doctrine."[8]

Apparently the background for Luther's idea of two "kingdoms" is Augustine's notion of two *civitates*, which Ulrich Duchrow translates as "governmental units," and behind the talk of two governments is the medieval notion of two *potestates*, two "powers."[9] In fact, Luther clarified his idea and gave it more precision over time. For the Reformer of the early 1520s God's kingdom and that of Satan stand over against one another in the sense of an eschatological dualism. The kingdom of God contains believers, that of Satan all other people. God's secular government thus applies only to non-Christians, since Christians do not need it! In the course of his later deliberations, however, it became clear to Luther that the "secular" consists not only of politics and authority; marriage, family, and economy are also parts of it—essentially, it encompasses the whole realm of creation. Moreover, he had defined the Christian as *simul iustus et peccator*, "justified and sinner alike," and the necessary consequence was that secular government was also responsible for Christians insofar as they had to be seen as sinners. The rule suggested by Heinrich Bornkamm makes sense: "kingdom" should be understood to mean "sphere of government" and "government" God's "way of ruling."[10] In that case the point of Luther's approach was that he saw God's twofold "way of ruling," or today perhaps better "way of governing"—with the aid of the "right" and the "left hands"—as engaged in battle with the "realm" or "kingdom" of Satan. Accordingly it would be better to speak of a "two-governments doctrine" than of a "two-kingdoms doctrine." In any case, the term "two-kingdoms doctrine" was created in 1922 by Karl Barth and was immediately used as a polemical weapon.[11]

Another, and not only terminological problem consists in the fact that Luther speaks not only of two governments but also of three orders or "hierarchies," namely economy, politics, and church.[12] How can the two concepts of government and order or condition be related to each other?

HISTORICAL BACKGROUND AND BIOGRAPHICALLY-CONDITIONED CLARIFICATIONS

The historical background for Luther's two-governments doctrine has often been recited. For the Reformer it probably existed primarily in the context of the late medieval idea of a division of power between the emperor and the pope. The investiture controversy had resulted in a bitter conflict over the relationship between the two. The "doctrine of the two swords," which developed its own significance in the struggle between Philip the Fair and Boniface VIII and was given theological precision by papal critics like William of Ockham in the sense of a separation of powers, could have reached Luther by way of his Ockham-oriented education, or simply as the mood of the times.[13] A poem from the era of Emperor Frederick II had sung:

Two swords in one sheath
quickly spoil each other;
if the pope seeks empire,
both swords come to ruin.[14]

A unique source for Luther's ideas, of course, was Augustine's teaching about the two *civitates*, which emphasized that the *civitas Dei* was realized in the earthly church (though it was not identical with it), and thus the *civitas terrena*, which was shaped by the Evil One, stood against it.[15] Any number of unclear passages or ambiguities in Augustine's writings could have transferred themselves to Luther. The contrast between the "city of God" and the world seems, in any event, to have offered a handy instrument for condemning the history and present state of the church and the world by application of the two-swords theory. Ulrich Duchrow sees (somewhat schematically, but nevertheless accurately) the links between Augustine's doctrine of the *civitates*, the notion of the two swords, and Luther's approach as follows: "It is true that up to about 1516 Luther primarily treated Augustine's doctrine of the two *civitates*, which he exploited for his own purposes. But while not abandoning it, he then combined it—e.g., in the broader framework of the class ethos—with elements of the medieval *potestates*-theory, and in the process especially the latter, but also the former, saw their original forms altered; the result was a new whole made up of the two."[16]

This begins to address the fact that Luther's view of the two governments changed and was clarified in the course of his life, something that certainly was also related to his perception of various situations. In the beginning of his conflict with authority it seemed to him obvious that Christians gladly suffer injustice when it is done to them,[17] but by the time of the Augsburg conference he thought it permissible to "go to court" and object to injustice and violence, so long as one's heart remains free of self-interest.[18] In the disputation over the "three hierarchies" he acknowledges that Christians have the right to defend themselves and to join the military for self-defense as well.[19] To evaluate this we must consider that it was only in 1486 (and not without a time limit until the King's Peace of 1495) that feuds, and in a sense the general indulgence of fighting, were forbidden; this may at least partially explain the positive attitude toward authority the Reformer reveals in many of his writings.[20] It would certainly be a mistake to interpret the two-governments doctrine in isolation and solely as a result of his experience in the Peasants' War. His initial view of the two methods by which God rules was maintained throughout his life. That he occasionally argued differently, when he required help from authority or was threatened by it, and that a purely formal definition of authority was "the result of this hectic sequence of defenses,"[21] is an assertion that does not bespeak a very good knowledge of the sources.

Essential for Luther, however, were not only the strands of tradition we have mentioned, and the historical circumstances, but also the materials to be drawn from Sacred Scripture. On the one hand there are things in the Sermon on the Mount that can create an impression that secular rights and laws have no validity at all any more for those who believe: "But I say to you, Do not resist an evildoer . . ." (Matt 5:39). Christ's kingdom is "not from this world" (John 18:36). On the other hand, Paul urges: "Let every person be subject to the governing authorities; for there is no authority except from God, and those authorities that exist have been instituted by God" and "the authority does not bear the sword in vain" (Rom 13:1, 4). First Peter also says, among other things, that Christians should "for the Lord's sake accept the authority of every human institution" (1 Pet 2:13). The soldiers to whose consciences John the Baptizer appeals are in no way encouraged to lay aside their calling, but simply to do no injustice and be content with their pay (Luke 3:14). All this quite apart from what the Old Testament has to say about making war and "authority"! Luther undoubtedly had to attempt to relate these different instructions to one another, and to that extent one can rightly say that he "as elsewhere, as an exegete made a distinction between the two kingdoms."[22] The distinction between two "kingdoms" resulted, for him, not from observing the social situation around him but from his perception of the kingdom of Christ and the divine grace within which such different laws are in effect from those found in the "kingdom of the world." Thus he came to the conclusion that one must "divide the children of Adam and all mankind into two orders, the first belonging to the kingdom of God, the second to the kingdom of the world."[23] Here Luther's terminology is still unclear. The "kingdom of God" for him includes "all the true believers who are in Christ and under Christ." But a few lines later he indicates that of course the kingdom of the world is also subject to God's governance. God desires, on the one hand, to preserve the world, encourage peace, and turn aside evil, and on the other hand to convey salvation to human beings through the Gospel; Luther formulates succinctly: "For this reason God has ordained two governments: the spiritual, by which the Holy Spirit produces Christians and righteous people under Christ; and the temporal, which restrains the un-Christian and wicked so that—no thanks to them—they are obliged to keep still and to maintain an outward peace."[24] Elsewhere he speaks, simply and in a way designed to impress pedagogically, of God's working with "right" and "left hands."[25]

God's Government with the "Left Hand"

First we should note that Luther does not speak of "God's kingdom on the left," as if this were a separated sphere that God would allow to lie aside, to the left, or might finish off "with his left."[26] It is true that for Luther the Christian and theologian God's government with the "right hand" is more important, but that by no means signifies for him that God's government with the "left" is a matter of indifference to God. On the contrary, this is about creation and its preservation, so that God can achieve God's spiritual goal for humanity. At the same time, with the "left hand" God protects creation from destroying itself.

In order to develop this idea Luther speaks of three "classes" or "orders" or—and this is easily misunderstood today—"hierarchies."[27] The background of his doctrine of orders or classes may also have been the ancient idea of the orders of "instruction, defense, and nourishment," as well as the divisions of moral philosophy that prevailed in the late Middle Ages, namely monastic, economic, and political ethics.[28] But these were not intended in the sense of a fixed class order; rather, it was about designating the different spheres of life, the "basic states of life" within which a person exists.[29] The orders designate functions, and the transition to the different callings within which these develop is fluid. Luther can speak schematically of *politia*, the sphere of society and politics; *oeconomia*, the field of marriage, family, and economy; and *ecclesia*, the earthly, institutional side of the church, though the spiritual side must also be included. To a certain degree these "orders" correspond positively to the classic monastic vows of obedience, chastity, and poverty: human life is always about the relationship to the secondary and primary authority, whether in sexuality, marriage, and family or in dealing with possessions and property. In monasticism these problems are concentrated in a particular "order" or "condition" and legal restrictions are placed on them. Monasticism and papacy cannot be included within Luther's positive scheme. They feature as special "orders" grounded not in creation but in human arbitrariness, serving neither the salvation of the human nor the glory of God.[30]

In his confession of 1528 the Reformer summarizes:

> But the holy orders and true religious institutions established by
> God are these three: the office of priest, the estate of marriage,

the civil government. All who are engaged in the clerical office or ministry of the Word are in a holy, proper, good, and God-pleasing order and estate, such as those who preach, administer sacraments, supervise the common chest, sextons and messengers or servants who serve such persons. These are engaged in works which are altogether holy in God's sight. Again, all fathers and mothers who regulate their household wisely and bring up their children to the service of God are engaged in pure holiness, in a holy work and a holy order. Similarly, when children and servants show obedience to their elders and masters, here too is pure holiness, and whoever is thus engaged is a living saint on earth. Moreover, princes and lords, judges, civil officers, state officials, notaries, male and female servants and all who serve such persons, and further, all their obedient subjects—all are engaged in pure holiness and leading a holy life before God. For these three religious institutions or orders are found in God's Word and commandment; and whatever is contained in God's Word must be holy, for God's Word is holy and sanctifies everything connected with it and involved in it.[31]

Christian love is realized in these three "institutions and orders"; as "the common order" it penetrates all orders and thus also excludes their becoming fixed and unchanging.

THE "AUTHORITIES" (politia)

Contradictory arguments

What Luther says about authority can appear contradictory. In view of the failures of the official representatives of the church he appealed to the Christian nobility in Germany in 1520 to intervene and lay claim to their own spiritual competency. In 1523 Count George of Saxony, among others, forbade the selling or purchasing of Luther's translation of the New Testament. At this point Luther inquired "how long" the "arm" of authority should be, if it is not to go too far "and encroach upon God's kingdom and government."[32] Thus in the first part of his writing on authority he clarifies its legitimate competency, while in the second part he describes its limits. For Luther that is not a contradiction, because he is concerned to show those in authority that they should see to it that "Christ will remain Lord," and yet not make Christ's commandments into civil laws.[33] He has no problem in referring to his "Open Letter to the Christian Nobility" (1520), which obviously took a different tack: it addresses, at least tendentially, the authorities who were inclined to support the Reformation, the "Christian" nobility, while "Temporal Authority: To What Extent it Should Be Obeyed" (1523) is influenced by the resistance of princes who held to the old belief; it insists that political authority, whether Christian or not, must recognize and accept its limitations, for "the soul is not under the authority of Caesar."[34] Is this a legitimate distinction?[35] It is true that the address to the nobility was not about compelling people to believe but about establishing structures that were helpful for faith, but Count George and his old-believing colleagues could have adopted the same arguments. With his idea that a prince could function as an emergency bishop[36] Luther then returned in a sense to his position of 1520, although he was aware that not only Christians in general but Christian princes in particular are rare birds.

Duties and tasks of those in authority

The problem of the duties of those in authority is not only about their relationship to faith and the church. In his "Whether Soldiers Too Can Be Saved" (1526)[37] the Reformer boasts that the secular sword and authority had not since the time of the apostles been so "clearly described or so highly praised" as in his writings.[38] What was his basis for the exaltation of earthly authority? He was convinced that "governing authority is by its very nature such that through it one may serve God."[39] Natural law traditions may be in the background here. God guides history and sustains the creation through the ordinances God has given. These extend beyond the boundaries of the Christian world; this Luther observes, for example, in the fact that even among the Turks there is an orderly state polity. Within an exegesis of Psalm 82:1 that sounds somewhat bizarre today—"God has taken his place in the divine council; in the midst of the gods he holds judgment"—he develops the idea that offices within a community are "a divine ordinance."[40] Thus God wills to let those holding earthly power "be gods over men"; their task is "a divine thing," and therefore they should be called "divine, godlike, or gods."[41] Rule is seen as a servant exercise of power for the good of humanity. For this purpose, however, there needs to be real earthly power, effectively applied. If someone wanted to try to rule an entire country with the Gospel, according to Luther this would be as if a shepherd were to pen up wolves, lions, eagles, and sheep together without further concern. "The sheep would doubtless keep the peace and allow themselves to be fed and governed peacefully, but they would not live long . . . ."[42] When Elector Frederick the Wise and Count Johann the Constant hesitated to punish plunderers and arsonists who had been roused by Thomas Münzer in the name of the Gospel, Luther advised them that they could proceed in good conscience since "your power and earthly authority are given you by God in that you have been bidden to preserve the peace and to punish the wrongdoer." Therefore the Elector should "not sleep nor be idle"; he will have to answer before God if he uses the sword carelessly.[43] Three essential duties are assigned to the wielders of authority: to punish the wicked, to protect the good, and to preserve the peace. As a doctor, faced with a severe illness, must now and then undertake an amputation, so the one with earthly rule must not hesitate to use the means entrusted to him. For Luther it is thus clear "that war and killing along with all the things that accompany wartime and martial law have been instituted by God." In cases of necessity, when there is no other way out, a limited war must be accepted to restore peace. "This is why God honors the sword so highly that he says that he himself has instituted it. . . . For the hand that wields this sword and kills with it is not man's hand, but God's; and it is not man, but God, who hangs, tortures, beheads, kills, and fights. All these are God's works and judgments."[44] This explains the horrible lines in Luther's "Against the Robbing and Murdering Hordes of Peasants" (1525):[45] "Therefore, dear lords, here is a place where you can release, rescue, help. Have mercy on these poor people! Let whoever can stab, smite, slay. . . ."[46] There was no question for Luther that those who engage in war could be "in the state of grace." On the other hand, if a soldier is sure that he is going to be forced into an evidently unjust war he should withdraw and obey God rather than human beings (Acts 5:29).[47] Otherwise he should throw himself into battle with a good conscience. At the end of this writing Luther formulates a prayer for soldiers before going to battle: "'Heavenly Father, here I am, according to your divine will, in the external work and service of my lord. . . . I thank your grace and mercy that you have put me into a work which I am sure is not sin, but right and pleasing obedience to your will." Then the soldier can say the creed and the Our Father, and "commit body and soul into God's hands, draw your sword, and fight in God's name!"[48] These bloodthirsty tones should not deceive us into denying that Luther argued in pacifist fashion overall and, simply on the basis of reason, repeatedly discouraged making war. Only in exceptional situations of defense could war occasionally be legitimate. The primary duty of authority, according to Luther, was of course to care for the citizens, both with material goods and through giving them access to education. In the Large Catechism he says that a prince should prefer a loaf of bread to a lion on his escutcheon, and the "councilmen of all cities in Germany" are urged to establish and maintain "Christian schools."[49] And yet in Luther's eyes society was clearly hierarchical: every person is at the same time a "subject" and a "superior," on the one hand dependent on others above her or him and on the other hand superior to those who are beneath her or him and for whom she or he is responsible.[50] People stand over against their superiors as individuals, but toward those dependent on them their role is as "persons in general" who should act responsibly not only for themselves but also for those dependent on them.[51] But this hierarchical order, because of the mutual relationships of all within it, also contains a democratic moment.

Governing as paradigm of rational action

In secular government—for Luther the paradigm for acting in secular matters in general—reason or, as we would probably say today, the "sound mind" has the final say. In public affairs "you do not have to ask Christ about your duty. Ask the imperial or the territorial law!"[52] This is "subject to reason,"[53] and therefore it makes sense to consult even pre-Christian "heathen" authors about political problems.[54] This basic idea of Luther's is evident also in the fact that he frequently argues in terms of contemporary proverbs and even prepared his own collection of such sayings. In this context Luther can also adopt and make use of traditions of natural law.

MARRIAGE AND FAMILY, BUSINESS, WORK, AND OCCUPATION
(oeconomia)

At first glance it may appear remarkable that Luther could treat questions of marriage and family within the same category as problems of business, work, and occupation, though his terminology is not consistent in every case. Often he lumps together occupational problems and difficulties in marriage as things Christians must deal with. One should pray to God for help "before entering into managerial duties or marriage."[55] This combination, which seems peculiar to us today, may be grounded in the fact that in the first half of the sixteenth century the management of a household or estate was closely related to general problems of business and economy, as we can illustrate in the role of Katharina von Bora. But it also relates to the fact that Luther saw both marriage and occupation as "orders" or "estates" in which one can and should serve God.

Marriage and family

The Reformer had no regard for premarital and extra-marital relationships or for partnerships resembling marriage. But it is interesting to examine the reasons for this. Certainly the ground did not lie in hostility to the body or a sourpuss morality! For him, being married is an "order," not to say a "calling" and "occupation." He wrote "The Estate of Marriage" three years before he himself entered into the order of marriage. We should not object that he understood nothing of such things! "I base my remarks on Scripture, which to me is surer than all experience."[56] He learns from the account of creation that marriage was willed by God, indeed, that it had its origin in Paradise.

The main aspect of his view of marriage that has been widely accepted is that marriage is a "worldly matter."[57] Weddings and the state of marriage are "worldly business,"[58] and Luther gives a basis for this by pointing out that marriage also exists outside Christendom and among nonbelievers.[59]

The espousal, as a legal action, well into the late Middle Ages took place at the church door, that is, outside the church itself. Thus the church as institution had nothing to do with it in the first place. Nevertheless, a multitude of canonical regulations had grown up that, Luther was convinced, had narrowed, overgrown, and undermined a Christian understanding of marriage. Marriage is not a sacrament! It conveys no eternal graces and blessings. Luther had already expanded on this in his "On the Babylonian Captivity of the Church."[60] The fact that Luther did not regard marriage as a sacrament has led some to conclude that in Protestantism it is less highly esteemed, namely as something "only" worldly. But that is by no means the case. Luther himself places worldly matters on a very high plane—as God's creation, though fallen. Marriage has "God's word in its favor and was not invented or instituted by men. . . ."[61] The tie between a man and a woman is "of divine law";[62] there is "a divine sanction on married life";[63] marriage is a "blessed estate pleasing to God."[64] Luther places it above any spiritual or other secular order.[65] Apart from any kind of sacramental character, Paul Althaus's accurate formulation applies: "'worldly' and 'holy' or 'godly' do not represent opposites for Luther."[66] It is true that he makes a distinction between merely being married and recognizing what it means![67] There can be no question of divorce for Christians. For them, after all, marriage is not something compulsory but a means by which fornication and unchastity may be checked and eliminated. But for unbelievers, in Luther's opinion, divorce should be allowed.[68] The Creator desires to act through married couples, their common life and their sexuality. Consequently, adultery is a cardinal sin, for which the Old Testament therefore prescribes stoning! Luther carries this observation to the point of making it a thesis that adulterers should be executed, and if the authorities are not ready to do so—as he evidently presumes they are not—anyone who has committed adultery should leave the district and be regarded by the betrayed partner as dead, unless the two can reconcile.[69] The deceived partner should be free to remarry.

This is not the place to evaluate or discuss Luther's view of marriage as a whole.[70] But it is important in our context to see how he argues in the context of his doctrine of orders. He proceeds in terms of natural law and theology: "We were all created to do as our parents have done, to beget and rear children. This is a duty which God has laid upon us, commanded, and implanted in us, as is proved by our bodily members, our daily emotions, and the example of all mankind."[71] Luther was evidently convinced of the powerful nature of the sex drive. If you put fire to straw, shouldn't you expect it to burn?[72] With very few exceptions, in his opinion, no one could escape the power of his or her drives. Therefore he advises wives that, if their husbands are impotent, under certain conditions and with the partner's consent they should seek other means.[73] This suggestion recalls his later confessional advice to Landgrave Philip the Magnanimous, which had such important consequences. In doing so Luther was applying a custom that was at the time even juridically sanctioned in German states.[74] However, Luther sees his counsel as legitimated by creation and the Creator himself. Christians know "that God himself instituted [marriage], brought husband and wife together, and ordained that they should beget children and care for them."[75] God also gave special dignity to marriage by protecting it with a separate commandment: "You shall not commit adultery!" (Exod 20:14; Deut 5:18). "For the estate of marriage does not set well with the devil, because it is God's good will and work."[76] There may be many difficulties in marriage and family life, but faith opens the eyes and makes the partners aware that the activities involved "are all adorned with divine approval as with the costliest gold and jewels." Some may wrinkle their noses and say: oh, washing diapers, making beds, smelling the stink! But if I know that I as a man am created by God and that this child was begotten by me I will confess to God "that I am not worthy to rock the little babe or wash its diapers, or to be entrusted with the care of the child and its mother." If a man washes diapers and people ridicule him, still he should say: "God, with all his angels and creatures, is smiling—not because that father is washing diapers, but because he is doing so in Christian faith."[77] If a woman has trouble in her pregnancy she should be consoled by the fact that God is acting in her, and with the radicality that is typical of him and is nearly unbearable for us today Luther continues: "should it mean your death, then depart happily, for you will die in a noble deed and in subservience to God."[78] The New Testament also has something to say about marriage: after all, Christ accepted an invitation to a wedding! In a sermon on the marriage at Cana, Luther says that Christ also shows here how one should overcome difficulties in marriage. "This is the word of God, that you should turn water into wine, and a sour marriage into pleasure." The heathens and unbelievers do not know this; "therefore their water remains water and will never be wine."[79]

Marriage and family are outstanding fields in which to serve God, "for the father of a household who rules his house in the fear of God, brings up his little children and servants in the fear and knowledge of God, in discipline and honesty, is in a blessed, holy estate. Likewise a woman who sees to the provision of food and drink, cleaning and bathing her children need seek no holier estate and none more blessed by God."[80] Through motherhood and fatherhood God cares for us "like a kind and loving mother."[81] If I encounter a woman who is more beautiful than my own wife, as a Christian I can say to myself: "though I may look over all the women in the world, I cannot find any about whom I can boast with a joyful conscience as I can about mine: 'This is the one whom God has granted to me and put into my arms.'"[82] For Luther, being married and having children is the obvious fulfillment of the human condition and of being a Christian. One should not desire to be wiser or more pious in this regard than God is. "God says, 'It is my will that you have a helper and not be alone; this seems good to me.' Man replies, 'Not so; you are mistaken; I vow to you to do without a helper . . . !'" God gave the woman to the man as his helper, but the pope disputes that and asserts that a wife is instead "a hindrance in serving God."[83] Without having modern singles in mind, Luther does not consider the state of "virginity" illegitimate, so long as it is not chosen for egoistic reasons. "Let each one act as he is able, and as he feels it has been given to him by God."[84] Marriage and parenthood have an important function in God's government with the "left hand," for from their authority "everything else flows and spreads."[85] Thus the estate of marriage serves the entire society, "whole cities and countries."[86]

And yet this role also extends into the sphere of God's government with the "right hand," since parents have "spiritual and worldly power" over their children: "Whoever teaches the gospel to another is truly his apostle and bishop," for "teaching the gospel produces apostles and bishops."[87] Here there is some overlap, something Luther probably did not adequately reflect on and that he would probably seek to clarify by calling upon his distinction between Law and Gospel. The two ways of governing touch at this point, but their mutual relationship is not made clear.

Work, occupation, and business

The sphere in which God operates with the "left hand" includes work, occupations, and the business economy. God works in our working; "through us he preaches, shows mercy to the poor, consoles the afflicted."[88] This does not mean that he has no other hands but ours, but that he takes our whole existence into his service. "What else is all our work to God—whether in the fields, in the garden, in the city, in the house, in war, or in government— but just such a child's performance, by which He wants to give His gifts in the fields, at home, and everywhere else? These are the masks of God, behind which He wants to remain concealed and do all things."[89] Work conveys God's blessing to us, and so becomes itself a blessing.[90] Its dignity lies in this, independently of how burdensome or unacknowledged it may be. Work is worship; it is all "pure holiness and leading a holy life before God."[91] The traditional value of activities is reversed: at the apex are no longer contemplation and asceticism but farm work and crafts. Such worship of God can take place in every calling. God says to workers: ". . . so hear what your work is: it is the holiest thing, by which God is made glad and through which he will give and grant you his blessing." This exaltation of work should be applied to all tools, even "written on the brow and nose when they perspire from working. . . ." So see that "a devout Christian farmer write on his wagon and plow, a shoemaker on his leather and awl, a smith and a carpenter on their wood and iron this verse: 'Rejoice, for it is well with you!'"[92] People should see themselves as coworkers of creation.[93] The same is true of trade, which Luther regarded critically; however, it is necessary and can probably "be practiced in a Christian manner."[94] Therefore secular government has the duty to see to it that contracts are complied with and, for example, that money on loan is repaid.[95] But because people know that in their work they are serving God they do not overestimate their own abilities and clearly understand that "we serve God also by resting, indeed by doing nothing more than resting."[96] It is said that at table Melanchthon was busy with his "Apology of the Augsburg Confession" and wrote even while he was eating; Luther stood up and took the pen from his hand.[97] But work also deserves to be paid (cf. Luke 10:7; 1 Tim 5:18). Luther soberly writes that someone who has nothing can give nothing. But not to give "violates the nature of possessions,"[98] an argument from natural law, which has its own weight in God's government with the "left hand." Paul Althaus says accurately that, while Luther did not subscribe to the idea that "property is theft," still he finds that "property *becomes* theft if the excess beyond one's personal needs is not used to benefit one's neighbor."[99] If a Christian sees someone who has nothing to put on, "he says to his money: 'Out you come, Squire Guilder! There is a poor, naked man who has no coat; you must serve him. There is a sick person with no refreshment: out you go, Squire Annaberg; out you go, Squire Joachimsthal, you have to go and help him!'"[100] Without exerting pressure in a legal or moral sense Luther makes it clear that it is God who desires to work and give aid through my money.

In his 1519 sermon on usury Luther distinguishes three degrees or ways of dealing with money and goods: the first and highest is to let it be taken from one, the second is to give generously, and the third and, so to speak, the weakest is to lend without demanding interest.[101] This last would today be something like working with an eco-bank. One can in fact say, with Hans-Jürgen Prien, that Luther "insisted on the social obligations of property."[102] The Reformer put no greater effort into any topic in business ethics than usury: in two sermons on usury (1519 and 1520),[103] in his "Trade and Usury" (1524),[104] and in his instruction "To Pastors, That They Should Preach Against Usury" (1540),[105] as well as in his weekday preaching on the Sermon on the Mount.[106] Luther suggested that interest should be kept low, around 5 to 6 percent, and the lower the better; he opposed speculation and dealing in interest as well as monopoly. This is not the place to go exhaustively into the subject of Luther's business ethics.[107] He did not understand why a debtor who could not pay his or her debts should be imprisoned, because to do that was to value money more highly than a human being.[108] Lending money should be done only out of love, not for the sake of gain; otherwise it would directly undermine all community.[109] Luther's polemic against usurious use of capital stood counter to early capitalism, but he did not comprehend its laws. However, Luther at the same time declared war on beggary, which had held a legitimate place in the framework of late medieval works-righteousness.

Everyone is obligated to contribute to the good of society, and those who withdraw from that duty forfeit their place in society.[110] But those who are truly needy should be helped out of a "common chest," that is, a fund administered by the commune or the parish. Luther intensively supported the establishment of these "common chests." He was convinced that secular laws alone were insufficient, so that "Christian love" must take action in this instance.[111] He often appeals simultaneously to Christian love and to natural law or the Golden Rule.[112] It is clear in many of these references and suggestions that Luther is not thinking solely of worldly governance but counts on a cooperation of both the spiritual and the secular.

THE CHURCH AS INSTITUTION

It may seem surprising that the church appears as a third element in Luther's doctrine of the three orders, alongside authority, marriage, and family. His use of language is, in fact, confusing, so that we need to distinguish a number of things.

Luther sees the church as founded on God's commandment to Adam to eat of all the trees in Paradise except the tree of the knowledge of good and evil (Gen 2:16-17). "Here we have the establishment of the church before there was any government of the home and of the state . . . After the church has been established, the household government is also set up . . . there was no government of the state before sin, for there was no need of it. Civil government is a remedy required by our corrupted nature."[113] But what does he mean by "church"? Luther is on the one hand aware that he cannot speak in the same breath of "government of the state" and "household government" and of the church; this is evident, for example, in the fact that he can contrast faith in Christ with the economic and political sphere.[114] When he asserts that "these divine stations continue and remain throughout all kingdoms, as wide as the world and to the end of the world,"[115] he cannot mean "church" in the proper sense, but only a social form of religion belonging to it as a reality in society. Luther apparently can regard this structure of church as founded in natural law. He sees the truth that human beings have the need to worship a God as founded equally in creation and in the fact that marriage and family or state governments exist.[116]

But the relativizing of social structures by creation applies also to the church in the proper sense. As a social reality with its subdivisions, orders, and functions it is part of the sphere God rules with the "left hand" and that is to be shaped by human beings with the aid of their reason. Otto Hermann Pesch writes accurately: "All action, whether civil or ecclesial, that is not an immediate application of the Gospel (together with the accusing law!) is part of God's worldly government, the kingdom of the world." Consistently, then,

"Lutheran theology counts this action of the church in the form of laws and administration as part of God's worldly government."[117] Questions of order within the church can therefore no longer be founded on divine law; they are open to being shaped freely according to what is proper and necessary.

Is the church not part of God's government "with the right hand"? We considered in previous chapters what Luther had to say about its duties and offices.[118] But the church is clearly more than an arbitrary union of people or a party, since God's word is preached and the sacraments celebrated in it! In that regard it does not belong to the kingdom of the world. Here Luther thinks not so much of the universal, mutual, and common priesthood of believers as of the preachers, "the angels and watchmen of our Lord Christ."[119]

This raises the question not only of how God's two governments are related within the church but also of the relationship among the three estates or orders themselves. Insofar as Luther expects that it will be Christians who find their respective roles within all three orders, he speaks of their cooperation. Thus, for example, marriage is for him the "source" of family and state and the "nursery of the church."[120] But insofar as the subject is not Christians, or rather insofar as it is Christians as human beings who are simultaneously sinners and justified, the church must also separate itself from economy and authority and, when needed, wield the word against them.

Luther intensified his approach after 1539 by speaking also of three "hierarchies" and so linking to Dionysius the Areopagite's doctrine of angels.[121] Apparently he wants to say that human society does not organize itself, in the sense of Plato's orders of nourishment, defense, and instruction, but that in these three basic functions Godself is at work, together with his heavenly powers.

Luther's doctrine of three orders is certainly not intended to show individual Christians their place. But they are confronted with the question of where they belong. On the one hand they are in a sense obligated to all three orders, as appears particularly from the grounding of the schema in natural law. On the other hand, as regards their function in society or in the church they must enter primarily into one or at most two orders. Again the question arises: how do these different "roles" relate to each other?

The principal problem behind these difficult definitions is the way in which Luther's doctrine of the three orders relates to that of the two governments. It is further complicated by the fact that the Reformer could also use the word "government" for "estate" and "order."[122]

What is the solution for relating the doctrines of two governments and three orders? It is unsatisfying to say that neither of the two concepts should be interpreted to the detriment of the other, and to speak of Luther's "agility," as Oswald Bayer does.[123] He also finds that in Luther's own understanding the doctrine of the three orders has "much greater weight" than that of the two governments.[124] His solution thus consists in the degrading of the two-governments doctrine in contrast to that of the three orders. It is likewise unsatisfying to give priority to the two-governments doctrine in the early Luther and the three-orders doctrine in his later years, although there are certain indications of that. Or should we simply let the two concepts stand alongside one another as two schemata of interpretation?[125] That does not satisfy either, inasmuch as the two-governments doctrine apparently interferes with the three-orders doctrine. Probably most enlightening is the suggestion of Max-Josef Suda that we should see the two-governments doctrine as political— I would prefer to say theological—theory and the teaching on orders as preaching for Christians.[126]

In any event there remains especially in this context the exquisitely difficult question of the relationship between God's working with the left and the right hands. We are surely not to assume that the left hand does not know what the right hand is doing!

The Cooperation of God's Left and Right Hands

Remarkably enough, Luther sees no problems here. On the contrary: in his opinion problems only arise when the distinction between God's two governments is not maintained. Bishops should act within the realm of God's government with the right hand and concern themselves with the proclamation of the Gospel. Instead, if they are prince-bishops and endowed with political authority they interfere in civil matters. Thomas Münzer, on the other hand, should be a preacher of the Gospel, and instead he thinks he can use violence to establish the reign of God. In the Peasants' War, which was turning everything topsy-turvy, both of God's governments seemed to be in danger. It was necessary, therefore, to understand that every Christian is located in a different set of life-circumstances and has to act accordingly. She or he receives orientation for that purpose from the Sermon on the Mount and from natural law, although it is not intended that the world should be directly ruled in terms of the Gospel.

God's government with the left and right hands

As so pregnantly formulated in Luther's document on authority, God has "ordained two governments: the spiritual, by which the Holy Spirit produces Christians and righteous people under Christ; and the temporal, which restrains the un-Christian and wicked so that—no thanks to them—they are obliged to keep still and to maintain an outward peace."[127] God uses these two governments to withstand the realm of Satan. Luther speaks of power[128] where today we would more likely think of authority, and that can make reading these texts disturbing. "For the sword and authority [Gewalt], as a particular service of God, belong more appropriately to Christians than to any other men on earth."[129] But if the exercise of power is service to God, "then everything that is essential for the authority's [Gewalt] bearing of the sword must also be divine service."[130] In the secular realm the sword rules, but in the spiritual sphere it is the word. That also makes it clear where the boundaries of secular power lie: "No one shall or can command the soul unless he is able to show it the way to heaven; but this no man can do, only God alone." The reason for this is clear: "for God cannot and will not permit anyone but himself to rule over the soul."[131] The preacher in turn should not attempt to accomplish anything in the sphere of world order by use of violence. He or she works only "with the powerless word with which the preacher must always at the same time put his or her own existence in play—political impotence is part of her or his spiritual power."[132] God works in different ways within the two governments with the same goal, namely to resist the realm of Satan and redeem human beings from it. How does that look from the human side?

The Christian in various aspects of life

Luther contrasts the doctrine of the two governments with his idea of the three orders or estates. Christians live both in the field in which God rules with the left hand and in the sphere in which God works with the right. These two spheres and methods of God's government must not be confused or mixed together, for then they cannot fulfill their common task. But Christians also live in different orders, and these, too, must not be mixed together, though in them all are Christians and can carry out their service. While what is at stake in God's two governments is a set of clear distinctions, the doctrine of the three orders is about integration and cooperation.

The Christian under the two governments

A Christian lives in two basic relations, namely before God and in community with his or her fellow human beings. "According to your own person you are a Christian," but in relation, for example, to your servant you are "a different person, and you are obliged to protect him."[133]

This means that "the two persons or the two types of office are combined in one [person.]"[134] A Christian has to carry within himself or herself two persons "simultaneously,"[135] for she or he "should not resist any evil; but within the limits of his office, a secular person should oppose every evil."[136] If we want to think in terms of the concept of person as we use it today we would probably have to say that one person has two different and even mutually contradictory roles to fulfill. But the idea of a "role" is inapplicable to the extent that one can play a role in part, or from time to time, or in rotation. Luther, however, is talking about the two duties given by God and allotted to a Christian together with his or her existence in this world.

Lohse points out that the idea of a *duplex persona* existed already in the Middle Ages, especially as regards the twofold function of a ruler.[137] As a Christian I can and should accept injustice, but that my fellow human being should be the victim of injustice is something I cannot allow under any circumstances! Privately, so to speak, I am in a position to swallow a lot of things, but as a person who also has a certain responsibility in the public sphere I must engage on behalf of the elimination of injustice. As far as one's own life is concerned, it is indeed true for the Christian that "Suffering! suffering! Cross! cross! This and nothing else is the Christian law!"[138] But as a "worldly person" one has a different obligation than as a "Christian person."[139] In the Middle Ages being an executioner was a dishonorable profession. The executioner, before carrying out his deed, had to apologize for his action as if he himself had committed murder. But according to Luther he is doing nothing wrong; rather, he is fulfilling his office, which is assigned to him within God's worldly government and by doing which he does his legitimate part. The office of the sword, "out of great mercy," must be "unmerciful."[140] It is no different for a judge: it is painful for him to condemn the guilty and he is sorrowful that he has to impose the death sentence. It appears that only anger and disfavor are at work here. But in the heart of the judge, if he is a Christian, it looks quite different: his "meekness" does not die, despite his gruesome deed; instead it "torments" his heart severely when he—Luther writes "she"!—"has to be angry and severe." The Reformer summarizes: "I must not regard my own possessions, my own honor, my own injury, nor get angry on their account; but we must defend God's honor and commandment" while preventing "injury or injustice to our neighbor. The temporal authorities [have the responsibility of doing this] with the sword; the rest of us, by reproof and rebuke."[141] We may find it impossible today to understand how little sense Luther apparently had of the tension thus addressed when he writes: "In this way the two propositions are brought into harmony with one another: at one and the same time you satisfy God's kingdom inwardly and the kingdom of the world outwardly. You suffer evil and injustice, and yet at the same time you punish evil and injustice; you do not resist evil, and yet at the same time, you do resist it. In the one case, you consider yourself and what is yours; in the other, you consider your neighbor and what is his." As regards yourself and what is yours, "you govern yourself by the gospel and suffer injustice toward yourself as a true Christian"; in what concerns others, however, "you govern yourself according to love and tolerate no injustice toward your neighbor. The gospel does not forbid this; in fact, in other places it actually commands it."[142] Luther even names an "order of neighborliness" that obligates a Christian to care for his or her fellows and protect them from injustice.[143] This "neighborly office" or "estate of neighborliness" can be understood as a direct analogy to the universal, mutual, and common priesthood of believers. In the worldly sphere a Christian is to exercise the "order of neighborliness" and in the spiritual realm answer her or his calling to the universal priesthood.

Christian existence in terms of the three orders

In principle every person belongs to all three orders or estates. Although Luther can also give reasons from natural law for his doctrine of orders and therefore can see it confirmed even by societies outside Christendom, he develops it primarily in view of Christian existence. A Christian has a particular place within the family, in public life, and finally also within the institutional church. It does not matter whether one finds oneself in a position of service or one of leadership. This furnishes the point of view for his testing of consciences: "Reflect on your condition in the light of the Ten Commandments: whether you are a father or mother, a son or daughter, a master or servant. . . ."[144] The school is a classic example of a field of activity that extends to all three orders: here everything is about education, enabling for a meaningful life within society, and establishing a relationship to the Christian community.[145] The orders or estates, as the "orders created by God are his workshops, the people living within them his workers and handymen."[146] Although fundamentally the Christian is thus obligated to each of the three orders, because of his or her calling to one or the other order he or she may be responsible in a particular way for one of them. Accordingly, Luther added a "table of duties" to his Small Catechism, collecting in it biblical sayings intended to make clear to the individual orders what their orientation should be. These instructions end with a reference to the significance of love for work in all orders, and with the mnemonic:

> Let each his lesson learn with care
> And all the household well will fare.[147]

If the activities of the various orders do not get in each other's way, but interact appropriately, the whole society benefits. Since this is about God's ordering of things, Luther sees the angels cooperating and fighting in the background, as he elucidates especially in a sermon for the feast of St. Michael in 1530.[148] "So every prince, citizen, householder, in sum every Christian has his angel who watches over him."[149] Here again Dionysios the Areopagite's teaching on angels is clearly in the background of Luther's doctrine of the three orders; however, it was only after 1539 that Luther adopted the concept of "hierarchy" as the designation of an "order" without thinking in the Neoplatonic sense of an ontological distinction among the various "hierarchies."

THE POLITICAL DUTY OF THE INDIVIDUAL CHRISTIAN AND OF THE CHURCH

Occasionally Luther points out that the two governments depend on each other:[150] worldly government creates the precondition for the church's development of its own activity.[151] The preaching office, on the other hand, serves the authorities by keeping the public peace. But for Luther this includes as an essential component a protest against inappropriate behavior by the political powers. It is true that the world cannot be ruled "according to the Gospel and Christian love,"[152] but preachers certainly have the duty of appealing to the consciences of the authorities: it is necessary to speak the word of God to the "clodhoppers!"[153] So Luther certainly approves of political preaching. He raises his voice against speculators who "devour" the world[154]—an almost prophetic projection in view of today's rampant capitalism. He suggests that a maximum price should be established[155] and measures should be taken against unjust distribution of wealth.[156] The Reformer engages in battle against usury and denounces greed.[157] He recommends that one refuse to serve in an unjust war.[158] If the princes do not do their duty, then "let us be bishops, that is, be attentive and watch!"[159] The concept of an "office of guardian of the church," which could easily be misunderstood in the sense of a self-appointed office of oversight, is not at all to the point: this is about the duty to protest, to be a Protestant! Christians as individuals and as church must testify to the truth.[160] They should "apply their ethical standards in society."[161] Direction should come, on the one hand, from the Sermon on the Mount,[162] on the other from natural law. In this realm Luther apparently read the Sermon on the Mount, the second table of the Decalogue, and ideas from natural law together, with the Golden Rule evidently serving as something like a common denominator.[163] If it is a question of unfair business dealings, agreements and contracts should sometimes be broken because "what is against God, law, and nature is null," it is invalid; in this case a prince should intervene "directly, tear up seals and letters," and not care what others say about him.[164] The Reformer certainly did not intend to advocate for legalistic preaching or a know-it-all morality but to raise a prophetic protest on behalf of what is good for people and what their rights are.[165] Luther from the beginning took it as given that human beings are endowed with certain basic rights[166] that may not be violated. To that extent his approach also belongs within the history of the origins of modern human rights.

CRITICAL EVALUATION

The difficulty of providing a critical evaluation of Luther's view of God's two governments is evident simply in the fact that the central concepts, such as "authority," "order," "kingdom," "government," "office," "hierarchy" are all things of the past and are very hard to relate to present social realities. A critical evaluation will primarily address four problems: what are the historical strains burdening this teaching of Luther and how should we deal with them? Did Luther take his position in relation to the social conditions of his time, and thus to an order of things that is today, and perhaps in principle even then, passé? Then: what should we do with the accusation that Luther here advocates a double morality? Finally: what theological deficits or desiderata can be addressed in terms of Luther's doctrine of the two governments?

HISTORICAL BURDENS

The historical strains burdening Luther's doctrine of the two governments appear first in the difficulties in the theological material he has inherited and then in the illustrative material the Peasants' War seems to represent for Luther's two-government teaching.

A difficult inheritance

Three theological traditions that do not fit together smoothly shaped Luther's doctrine of the two governments: Augustine's teaching about the two *civitates* and the associated idea of a struggle between the city of God and the kingdom of Satan; then the so-called theory of the two swords, with its plea for the superiority of the spiritual sword over worldly government; and finally the Areopagite's vision of various "hierarchies" serving the glory of God. The theory of the two swords may have derived from generalized recollections of the investiture controversy, whereas the doctrine of the three orders, in its developed catechetical form—for example in the work of Johannes Gerson[167]—was still very present. The three elements could be related to each other, as Luther in fact attempted, but they by no means dissolve into one another. This explains the difficulty Luther had with the terminology, a problem he thus left to his interpreters: it took a long time before the concepts of "kingdom/realm" and "government" could be distinguished from each other.[168] However, in the interim it has been clarified that in Luther's view God, with God's "governments," opposes the "kingdom" of Satan and in this way builds up his own "kingdom." The relationship between the two-governments teaching and the three-orders doctrine is more difficult to define:

there is still discussion of the question whether the governments doctrine can be incorporated into the three-orders teaching,[169] or whether the teaching on the three orders belongs within God's worldly government. Luther did not make consistent use of the concepts he employed.

Biographical implications

Although Luther's doctrine of governments was differently accentuated in the course of his theological development, we cannot speak of a clear expansion or change. Certainly there were some clarifications in the wake of his writing on authority; in his struggle with Rome and the Roman system Luther was at first concerned to distinguish the two governments. As the Reformation communities consolidated, the doctrine of the three orders became the focus of Luther's attention. And yet there is no clear caesura here. Not even the Peasants' War[170] led to any major changes. Luther attempted to tell both the princes and the peasants what had to be said to each within the framework of his understanding of the two-governments doctrine. We cannot call it anything less than tragic that the arguments in the 1525 "Admonition to Peace, A Reply to the Twelve Articles of the Peasants in Swabia"[171] had no effect because that document was printed together with "Against the Robbing and Murdering Hordes of Peasants," written only a few weeks later.[172] The latter was then circulated separately and acquired its own significance. The "Open Letter"[173] urging the authorities to mercy and leniency was unable to change anything at that point. Unfortunately one must say of Luther that "he did not make an effort to bring about a general peace."[174] Still, we may recall that Luther's final mission, days before his death, though on behalf of a comparatively unimportant cause, was for the purpose of reconciling two opponents and thus securing peace.[175]

The Reformer understood the order established by God in such a way that one had to obey it. For him that meant that no one was to obtain his or her own goals by force. Christians should employ only the word. As early as 1522, three and a half years before the outbreak of the Peasants' War, he had published his "Faithful Admonition to Avoid Revolt and Rebellion."[176]

Certainly it appears that Luther was psychologically constructed in such a way that revolt and rebellion aroused an elementary loathing in him. This may seem strange, since within the church he brought about one of the most profound "revolts" in its history. It may be that there was a mutual psychological influence at work here: one who dares to engage in radical protest in one area needs a certain stability in another. But from our perspective today this in no way raises our opinion of Luther for writing, in his work on soldiers, "We dare not encourage the mob very much. It goes mad too quickly," and recommending instead: "it is better to take ten ells from it than to allow it a handsbreadth, or even a fingersbreadth in such a case." "The mob neither has any moderation nor even knows what moderation is. And every person in it has more than five tyrants hiding in him."[177] Such an attitude was, of course, not calculated to appreciate and reflect on the nuances of social crises.

FALSE ORIENTATION TO AN OUT-OF-DATE ORDER OF THINGS?

In any case it is clear that from our perspective Luther's social ideas are outmoded. But a more penetrating question would be whether his vision of society was not also part and parcel of his past era. His contrast of divine governance with the right and with the left hand makes it clear, after all, which hand was more important for him. For him, too, the spiritual government is more essential than what goes on within the world's government. Above the household law in effect in the family stands the city law, while the law of the church has a separate status of its own.[178] Certainly we would not accuse Luther of having theocratic tendencies. A governance of the church over society is out of the question for him. Nevertheless, we cannot avoid the impression that he has in view an orderly *Corpus christianum* and wants to prevent its breakdown. If he can acknowledge that the world, under the government of God's left hand, has a relative independence it is probably because in terms of common natural-law philosophy it seemed generally clear what should be done in the realm of civil justice. At present this has long since ceased to be true. The more that common morals and Christian ethics diverge, the stronger is prophetic protest demanded of the church and its members.

It would be anachronistic to expect that Luther would have engaged on behalf of a profound transformation of society in favor of a democratic order in our sense. Nevertheless, we must maintain that scarcely any other sixteenth-century theologian "emphasized more sharply the limits of secular power and fought more in principle against Machiavellianism and the idea of power politics overall, and advocated more strongly for the linking of secular power to the preservation of divine and human rights" than Luther.[179] But on the other hand it is altogether unsatisfying to hear the Reformer saying: "A slave can be a Christian, and have Christian freedom, in the same way that a prisoner or a sick man is a Christian, and yet not free." After all, a worldly kingdom "cannot exist without an inequality of persons, some being free, some imprisoned, some lords, some subjects, etc." Paul's socially explosive statement—"neither slave nor free, but all one in Christ Jesus" (Gal 3:28)—Luther sees as confirming the status quo, namely that "in Christ the lord and the servant are equal."[180]

The criticism required of Luther's overall view of society applies also in some ways to a number of details. Undoubtedly Luther enhanced the value of secular activity by regarding it as worship and disputing the priority of asceticism, monasticism, and the ordained priesthood. Each person may know that she or he is called by God to her or his profession or work. For Max Josef Suda, Luther's ideas about work and calling in a sense summarize his whole ethics: "In the faith that makes us righteous we recognize our whole life as a calling, or a call, in which we work together with the creating God."[181] This is certainly a supportable thesis, although Luther would not have expressed it in terms of "calling." He thought more of the concrete profession or work in which one lives. Therefore it was also necessary to remain true to one's own calling,[182] though Luther also observed sympathetically that many a one rises to the highest degree of social recognition.[183] Godself, that is, has in that case altered the situation of the people in question. Nevertheless, we can no longer say, as was possible even half a century ago, that "it was Luther who first gave the word *calling* [or profession: Beruf] the deep and full tone it has today."[184] Luther's ethos of calling is confronted today with an exploitative salary-dumping on the one hand and a job mentality on the other, to say nothing of unemployment and the shifting of work overseas. But even in his own time Luther did not adequately understand the socio-economic problems of his era. The overarching social and economic-political factors that led in his time to poverty and misery were outside his awareness. He was probably not, as Marx thought, the "oldest German national economist,"[185] and certainly not the best. In particular, he had an inadequate understanding of what we today would call an "institution." It is true that attempts have been made to confront Luther's view with the modern concept of institutions and to make it useful in that regard.[186] It is also true that his critique touched what we would today call early capitalism, but without truly comprehending its internal laws. His eye fell rather on the damage that had to result from the mutual self-suppression of any sense of community. This is a point of view that needs to be brought into effect within our current social reality as well.

Double standard of morality?

Does Luther's idea that a person lives as a Christian according to different laws than she or he does as a person of the world tend toward a "double standard of morality"? That apparently was Ernst Troeltsch's impression: "That is in every form a double morality according to utterly contrary principles."[187] This view could harden into the idea of an "autonomy" that prevails in God's worldly government. But there had to be some very determined interests guiding the perceptions that could have led to this false interpretation of Luther. More serious is the objection brought against Luther's two-governments doctrine under the label "royal reign of Jesus Christ." Karl Barth suspected that in Luther's thought the Law had made itself independent of the Gospel, and that it was in this way that he had arrived at his decisive separation of the two governments. The second thesis of the Barmen Declaration opposes "the false doctrine that there could be areas of our life in which we would not belong to Jesus Christ but to other lords." Karl Barth presents his counter-model to the two-governments doctrine in his "The Christian Community and the Civil Community."[188] In the meantime it has become clear, of course, that according to Luther a Christian also lives and works under the rule of Christ in her or his secular activities. The conscience of a Christian shaped by the Sermon on the Mount finds its expression in accepting responsibility in the public sphere. According to Luther, believers know of no private Christian morality that could not be translated into concrete action. To that extent there is certainly, for Luther, a tie between faith and social or political institutions. Believers are also aware of their responsibility in political and economic life. They know themselves to be made "answerable for the world," although that concept would not have pleased Luther since he was convinced that it is God who "answers for" the world. Still, the question of how and by what concrete steps Christians can do justice to their responsibility does not dissolve the two-governments doctrine. This difficulty echoes now and then in Luther's interpretation of the Sermon on the Mount. As a "secular person" I may assemble treasures, and these may also serve the needs of others, "yet not too much," so that I would become a "greedy belly."[189] I must care for my children, but I should take care that I do not become a miser, excusing myself by saying I want to "provide for them generously."[190] I can deceive myself by judging my fellow human beings under the pretense that it is not about the person but the thing.[191] But these examples show that the two-governments doctrine is only a name for the coordinates within which I must make my decision. In other words, it points to the conscience of the individual Christian.

THEOLOGICAL DEFICITS AND DESIDERATA

Although a good deal of unnecessary and probably also ideologically moti-vated strife has been created in the struggle over Luther's doctrine of the two governments, there still remain a number of unresolved theological questions, both as regards his own presuppositions and concerning our own contemporary perceptions.

Inadequate biblical foundation?

The first problem has to do with the New Testament basis for Luther's doctrine of the two governments. Is it not true that here the history of theology and devotion had a stronger influence than the New Testament itself? We need to inquire seriously whether the Reformer could have developed his two-governments doctrine solely on the basis of biblical material, without the mediation of Augustine's *civitas* teaching and the medieval theory of the two swords. Luther's exegetical reflections on the Sermon on the Mount and Romans 13 and related biblical passages need to be reviewed. Luther, elsewhere highly sensitive to traditions that were foreign to the Bible, in this instance apparently did not consider it necessary to apply his critical standards with the same acerbity.[192] Where, in particular, is New Testament eschatology? Was it not, despite Luther's eschatological and even apocalyptic consciousness, consumed by the bourgeois ideas of the sixteenth-century world?

Absence of a systematic-theological basis?

Where is Luther's doctrine of the two governments located within the whole of his theological thought? Was the *theologia crucis* that was so important to the young Luther inserted in an unsustainably one-sided way into the framework of the two-governments doctrine,[193] so that Luther could commend "suffering, suffering, cross, cross" to the peasants? Or was it entirely overlooked and omitted in this context? What was the relationship between Luther's doctrine of two governments and the distinction he made and sharpened between Law and Gospel? Here it is certain that until recently too little attention has been paid to the internal distinctions in Luther's concept of law in its political function, which has its significance in the secular government, and its spiritual function in light of the reign of Christ.

Finally: how does the two-governments doctrine relate to the center of Luther's hermeneutics, "what promotes Christ"? What in it "promotes Christ," is promoted by Christ? It highlights the witness to Christ before the world, but is not the world thereby put at a disadvantage? How can it bear fruit in regard to the justification of the ungodly? It would certainly have been Luther's intention to develop it in a way that makes it clear how it unfolds and enables life—the life of a Christian in faith and in responsibility for what he or she is assigned to do. But that connection is not always clear. Is the doctrine of two governments a "theological" theory at all, in the full sense?[194]

Inconsistent doctrine of God?

A final problem lies in the very idea of contrasting divine action with the right and with the left hand. How much room does that contrast leave for the working of the Holy Spirit? It belongs on the side of the reign of Christ, but can Christ and the Holy Spirit be set dialectically or even antithetically over against the action of the Creator? Luther is convinced that Christ has a spiritual kingdom: for example, he pays no attention to the filling of offices in civil contexts; he does not worry about the thunder, for God does that![195] He does not care for political or economic matters; his task is to destroy the kingdom of the devil and save human beings.[196] But here Luther had not read his Bible carefully enough: what about the stilling of the storm or Jesus' healing miracles? The idea that God is supposed to work with the left and the right hand certainly does not rest on a well-thought-out doctrine of the Trinity. The ancient axiom attributed to Augustine, that God's outward works are indivisible, *opera divinitatis ad extra sunt indivisa*, is not applied at all. That is remarkable, since Luther affirms it in many places[197] and even in a sense radicalizes it.[198] Regarding the two-governments doctrine, Wilfried Härle speaks of something "dual," but not to be understood as "dualistic";[199] but how, then, is it to be understood? Here further reflection is certainly needed. Eilert Herms has noticed this difficulty and summarizes God's action in the two governments under the concept of "striving toward the goal of salvation," speaking even of "striving toward the goal of salvation by the created world-event."[200] This puts him closer to Karl Barth than to Martin Luther.[201]

As a theological theory of the relationship of church and world, or of state and church—if it was ever meant that way—the two-governments doctrine has failed. But neither is it the "theological theory of a specifically Christian politics," certainly not its "guiding theory."[202] Luther most assuredly wanted not to create a Christian politics but to preserve the right and dignity of the world. On the other hand, the two-governments doctrine is underestimated when it is called only a "situational address to the consciences of certain people."[203] It is also probably more than an elixir for clarifying processes that are hard to see through.[204] Its strengths are best revealed if we read it as an ethical pointer to the place for the lives of believers in a world in which not everyone is a Christian. "Christians and non-Christians are co-subjects of God for the preservation of creation."[205] Of course, it can function appropriately only as an indication of place, not of how to act,[206] although Luther's formulations often give the impression that clear directives could be derived from them. The Reformer seems to have observed this limitation only rarely, and even then leapt over it intuitively. In this sense he lived and used his concept of the two governments. It is astonishing what he had to say, despite these weaknesses, not only to Christians but to the society of his time. His engagement against usury and on behalf of care for the poor as well as his urgent appeals to value education and keep the peace present an impressive commentary on his doctrine.

The perception of two different divine governments gave Luther the basis for liberating himself from the theocratic system of the papal church. At the same time, it was foreign to him to install a Reformation-oriented theocracy in place of it; the two-governments doctrine preserved him also from that. It was ultimately confirmed, long after his death, in the terms of the Peace of Westphalia. Strife between confessions or religions cannot be banished from the world by the victory of one or the other side. Only a clear legal basis creates the precondition for the different religious options to live together. This approach, which has succeeded in modern times so that it now seems obvious, may well continue into the future. Luther's two-governments doctrine—sometimes with inadequate theological means—opened the way for it.[207]

NOTES

[1] For bibliography see *TRE* 36: 782–84, 788–89, 792–93, and also Johannes Haun, et al., eds., *Zur Zwei-Reiche-Lehre Luthers* (Munich: Kaiser, 1973); Uwe Rieske-Braun, *Zwei-Reiche-Lehre und christlicher Staat* (Gütersloh: Gütersloher Verlagshaus, 1993); Dalferth 1996; Suda 2006, 117–97.

[2] LW 45, 75–129 (WA 11, 245–281).

[3] LW 13, 163 (WA 51, 238, 29 [1534/35]).

[4] Ulrich Duchrow, ed., *Zwei Reiche und Regimente. Ideologie oder evangelische Orientierung? Internationale Fall- und Hintergrundstudien zu Theologie und Praxis lutherischer Kirchen im 20. Jahrhundert* (Gütersloh: Mohn, 1977); idem, ed., *Umdeutungen der Zweireichelehre Luthers im 19. Jahrhundert* (Gütersloh: Mohn, 1975); idem, *Christenheit und Weltverantwortung. Traditionsgeschichte und systematische Struktur der Zweireichelehre* (Stuttgart: Klett, 21983). On Duchrow's interpretation of Luther's doctrine of two kingdoms cf. Dalferth 1996, 96–106.

[5] Gerhard Müller, "Luthers Zwei-Reiche-Lehre in der deutschen Reformation," 417–37 in idem, *Causa Reformationis. Beiträge zur Reformationsgeschichte und zur Theologie Luthers* (Gütersloh: Mohn, 1989), at 425. Müller also asks how the Augsburg Confession, subscribed to by princes and the councils of free states within the empire, matches up with the concept of the two kingdoms; ibid., 426.

[6] Cf. Härle 2004, 784–85.

[7] Gänssler 1983, 68.

[8] Duchrow 1983, 526. Gänssler 1983, 135–38 even asks: "Luther's four kingdoms?"

[9] Cf. Duchrow 1983, 526. Duchrow, it is true, makes a suggestion here that has not been adopted in the continuing discussion, that in future we should speak of a "three-kingdoms doctrine."

[10] Cf. Lohse 1995, 338.

[11] Reference in Lohse 1995, 172, n. 499.

[12] E.g., WA.TR 5, 218, 15-16. See below, "God's government with the 'left hand'" and "The Christian in various aspects of life" and "Historical burdens."

[13] Cf. Mantey 2005, 14–161.

[14] Bornkamm, Heinrich 1960, 255.

[15] Cf. Duchrow 1983, 183–319.

[16] Duchrow 1983, 440.

[17] LW 45, 96 (WA 11, 255, 9-12 [1523]).

[18] LW 21, 111 (WA 32, 392, 18-21 [1532]).

[19] WA 39/2, 46, 20–47, 3; 50, 21–51, 13 (in relation to a war initiated by or in the interest of the pope [1539]).

[20] Cf. Müller, Gerhard 1989, 417–18.

[21] Gänssler 1983, 152–53, at 153.

[22] Pesch 1982, 237.

[23] LW 45, 88 (WA 11, 249, 24-25 [1523]).

[24] LW 45, 91 (WA 11, 251, 15-18).

[25] E.g., WA 1, 692, 8-11 (interpreting Psalm 109/110, v. 1; here both kingdoms are "subject to Christ"); cf. WA 9, 134, 24-27 (1518, with reference to Augustine); WA 36, 385, 7-11 (1532); WA 52, 26, 23-27 (1544).

[26] Cf. Althaus 1965, 62, n. 69.

[27] This last is derived from Dionysius the Areopagite's concept of "hierarchy," without attention to its implications.

[28] Cf. Prien 1992, 164; Pawlas 2000, 67–68; and Suda 2006, 59.

[29] Bayer 2003, 112; also "basic conditions," ibid., 113.

[30] As regards the papacy cf. WA 39/2, 48, 15-20 (1539).

[31] LW 37, 364–65 (WA 26, 504, 30–505, 10 [1528]).

[32] LW 45, 104 (WA 11, 271, 28-29; 261, 31 [1523]).

[33] LW 45, 83 (WA 11, 246, 7).

[34] LW 45, 111 (WA 11, 266, 18).

[35] Gänssler 1983, 81–90 disputes this; Müller, Gerhard 1989, 422–23 points to the changed "angle of vision."

[36] Cf. H.-W. Krumwiede in TRE 19:59–62.

[37] LW 46, 87–137 (WA 19, 623–62).

[38] LW 46, 95 (WA 19, 625, 15-17).

[39] LW 45, 100 (WA 11, 257, 32 [1523]).

[40] LW 13, 39–72, at 44 (WA 31/1, 189–218, quoting from 191, 33 [1530]).

[41] Ibid. (WA 31/1, 191, 26; 192, 3-4).

[42] LW 45, 92 (WA 11, 252, 8-10 [1523]).

[43] LW 40, 51 (WA 15, 213, 4-9 [1524]).

[44] LW 46, 96 (WA 19, 626, 22-27 [1526]).

[45] LW 46, 45–55 (WA 18, 357–61 [1525]).

[46] LW 46, 54 (WA 18, 361, 24-25 [1525]). Cf. "Opportunism? Luther's Stance in the Peasants' War" in chapter 4.

[47] LW 46, 130 (WA 19, 656, 22-29 [1526]).

[48] LW 46, 135–36 (WA 19, 661, 9-26).

[49] LW 45, 339–78 (WA 15, 27–53).

[50] LW 46, 103 (WA 19, 643, 15-17).

[51] LW 46, 122 (WA 19, 652, 25–653, 14).

[52] LW 21, 110 (WA 32, 391, 5 [1532]).

[53] LW 13, 198 (WA 51, 242, 1-2 [1534/35]).

[54] Ibid. (WA 51, 242, 36-42).

[55] WA 40/3, 213, 28-29 (1532/33).

[56] LW 45, 43 (WA 10/2, 299, 10-11 [1522]). For his "confessional advice" to Philip of Hesse, see below.

[57] Cf. LW 53, 110–15, "The Order of Marriage for Common Pastors," at 111–12 (WA 30/3, 74, 3; 75, 16); "an external, worldly matter," LW 46, 259–320, "On Marriage Matters," at 265 (WA 30/3, 205, 12); "a rather secular and outward thing," LW 21, 93 (WA 32, 376, 38 [1532]).

[58] The Book of Concord, 371.

[59] Cf. LW 36, 92 (WA 6, 550, 33-37 [1520]).

[60] Cf. LW 36, 92–106 (WA 6, 550–60).

[61] LW 53, 112 (WA 30/3, 75, 16-17 [1529]).

[62] LW 36, 98 (WA 6, 555, 4-5 [1520]).

[63] Cf. The Book of Concord, 393.

[64] Cf. WA 30/1, 161, 28 (1529); The Book of Concord, 394.

[65] The Book of Concord, 393.

[66] Althaus 1965, 94.

[67] LW 45, 38 (WA 10/2, 294, 21-22 [1522]).

[68] LW 45, 31 (WA 10/2, 288, 19-22).

[69] LW 45, 32 (WA 10/2, 298, 8-17). Cf. the argumentation against the Jews in chapter 4, "Attempts at explanation," n. 62.

[70] See the bibliography in Suda 2006, 158; and see Jane E. Strohl, "Luther's New View on Marriage, Sexuality and the Family," Lutherjahrbuch 76 (2009): 159–92.

[71] LW 45, 155 (WA 12, 242, 8-11).

[72] LW 45, 26 (WA 10/2, 284, 8-9).

73 Cf. LW 36, 103–4 (WA 6, 558, 20-32 [1520]).

74 Cf. *Luthers Werke. Volksausgabe in acht Bänden. Erste Folge: Reformatorische Schriften*, 2 (Berlin: C.A. Schwetschke, 21898), 482, n. 1, with reference to Jakob Grimm, *Weisthümer* (Göttingen: Dieterich, 1840–78) 3, 42, 48, 70, 311, and the comment: "This self-aid according to German custom appears in Luther in *legalized form* as a secret marriage, but one acknowledged by the nominal husband."

75 LW 45, 38, 41 (Cf. WA 10/2, 294, 33; 298, 26 [1522]).

76 LW 45, 37 (WA 10/2, 294, 10-11).

77 LW 45, 39, 40 (WA 10/2, 295, 18–296, 6; 296, 27–297, 1).

78 LW 45, 40 (thus the text in CL 2, 253, 1-4; Cf. WA 10/2, 301, 13-14).

79 WA 17/2, 62, 29-30 (1525).

80 WA 52, 112, 8-10, 19-24 (1544).

81 LW 45, 43 (WA 10/2, 299, 30).

82 LW 21, 87 (WA 32, 372, 21-24 [1532]).

83 LW 45, 145, 144 (WA 12, 234, 22-25; 234, 6-7 [1523]).

84 LW 45, 46 (WA 10/2, 302, 6-7).

85 WA 30/1, 152, 20-21 (1529).

86 LW 45, 44 (WA 10/2, 300, 3-4).

87 LW 45, 46 (WA 10/2, 301, 29).

88 LW 33, 243 (WA 18, 754, 15-16 [1525]). For what follows cf. esp. Dalferth, Silfredo B. 1996, 157–74.

89 LW 14, 114 (WA 31/1, 436, 7-11 [1532]).

90 WA 40/3, 280, 18-29 (1532/33).

91 LW 37, 365 (WA 26, 505, 7 [1528]).

92 WA 40/3, 280, 20-29.

93 Suda 2006 sees Luther's understanding of profession and call as at the heart of the Reformer's ethics: "But in the faith that makes us righteous we recognize our whole life as our profession, rather our calling, out of which we work together with the creating God," 199.

94 LW 45, 246 (WA 15, 293, 29-31 [1524]).

95 LW 45, 258 (WA 15, 302, 14-18).

96 WA.Br 5, 317, 40 (1530).

97 According to Althaus 1965, 108 n. 20.

98 LW 14, 219 (WA 19, 562, 3 [1526]).

99 Althaus 1965, 71–72.

100 WA 10/1/2, 376, 14-18 (1526). Annaberg and Joachimsthal were figures stamped on coins.

101 LW 45, 273 (WA 6, 3, 8-19 [1519]).

102 Prien 1992, 200.

103 LW 45, 273–310 (WA 6, 3–8, 36-60).

104 LW 45, 231–73 (WA 15, 293–322).

105 WA 51, 331–424.

106 LW 21, 1–294 (WA 32, 299–544). On this cf. Gerta Scharffenorth, "Die Bergpredigt in Luthers Beiträgen zur Wirtschaftsethik. Erwägungen zur Theorie ethischer Urteilsbildung," 314–38 in Scharffenorth 1982.

107 On this cf. Prien 1992; Pawlas 2000.

108 Cf. LW 9, 241–42 (WA 14, 714, 31-32 [1525]); WA 16, 542, 14-16 (1524–1527).

109 Cf. Prien 1992, 216, 222, 224.

110 This, and not a concrete challenge to act, is probably what is meant when Luther bluntly suggests that lazy people who refuse to work should be hanged. Cf. WA 51, 383, 17-22 (1540).

111 LW 45, 189 (WA 12, 14, 7-8 [1523]).

112 E.g., LW 45, 247, 250 (WA 6, 5, 25-26; 6, 8, 16-17 [1519]).

113 LW 1, 103–4 (WA 42, 79, 3-9 [1535–1545]).

114 Cf. LW 13, 369 (WA 32, 50, 38–53, 20).

115 AW 13, 361 (WA 31/1, 410, 16-17 [1530]).

[116]Nevertheless, I consider it erroneous to treat Luther's ideas about rational knowledge of God and universal revelation, as he presents them, for example, in his exegesis of Jonah, under the title "ecclesia" (against Bayer 2003, 115–28, who in this connection thinks he can even see possibilities for interreligious dialogue). In any event they were at most formal in nature.

[117]Pesch 1982, 233, 234. Pesch adds, self-critically, in n. 14: "Luther himself never says it this way, as far as I can see." But this view resulted from his idea of the priesthood of all believers, his rejection of an ontological distinction between priests and laity, and his making secular institutions responsible for the interests of the church and, for example, regarding councils as human institutions. Pesch could have pointed out that Luther was able to apply his idea of the "duplex persona" to the church as well: "For the church is a twofold person in one and the same man," LW 49, 385 (WA.Br 5, 493, 46-47 [1530]).

[118]See "The ecclesiological significance of the Eucharist" in chapter 10 and "Lack of institutional interest?" in chapter 11.

[119]LW 38, 99 (WA 30/2, 597, 19-24 [1530]).

[120]". . . fons Oeconomiae et Politiae est et seminarium Ecclesiae," LW 2, 131 (WA 42, 354, 23-24 [1535–1545]).

[121]On this see esp. Maurer 1970. Or was he impressed by the idea ("Angelica Hierarchia")?

[122]Cf. Maurer 1970, 31, with reference to WA 47, 853, 20-24, and 854, 2-6 (1539). Maurer even says in n. 117: "Strictly speaking, then, we cannot treat a doctrine of the two governments in Luther, but we must speak of *three* governments"; he refers to WA 43, 523, 16-19 (on Gen 27:27-29; LW 5, 138).

[123]Bayer 2003, 115.

[124]Ibid., 114.

[125]Reinhard Schwarz, "Ecclesia, oeconomia, politia. Sozialgeschichtliche und fundamentalethische Aspekte der protestantischen Drei-Stände-Theorie," 78–88 in Horst Renz and Friedrich Wilhelm Graf, eds., *Troeltsch-Studien 3: Protestantismus und Neuzeit* (Gütersloh: Mohn, 1984).

[126]Suda 2006, 180.

[127]LW 11, 91 (WA 11, 251, 15-18 [1523]).

[128]Translator's note: the German word Luther uses is "Gewalt," which LW translates "authority," but that represents a softening; "Gewalt" primarily means power and even violence.

[129]LW 45, 100 (WA 11, 258, 1-3).

[130]LW 45, 103 (WA 11, 260, 32-34).

[131]LW 45, 106, 105 (WA 11, 263, 3-5; 262, 9-10).

[132]Bornkamm, Heinrich 1960.

[133]LW 21, 109 (WA 32, 390, 30-32 [1532]).

[134]Ibid. (WA 32, 390, 10).

[135]LW 21, 110 (WA 32, 391, 24).

[136]LW 21, 113 (WA 11, 393, 38-39). The situation is further complicated or made murky by the fact that Luther suggests an additional distinction. He writes: "Here we have [= there come to be] two different persons in one man. The one is that in which we are created and born, according to which we are all alike—man or woman or child, young or old. But once we are born, God adorns and dresses you up as another person. He makes you a child and me a father, one a master and another a servant . . ." LW 21, 23 (WA 32, 316, 18-23).

[137]Lohse 1995, 341 n. 556.

[138]LW 46, 29 (WA 18, 310, 10-11 [1525]).

[139]WA 19, 648, 19-22 (1526); see the further passages cited by Pesch 1982, 235 n. 19.

[140]LW 46, 73 (WA 18, 391, 30-32 [1525]).

[141]LW 44, 102–3 (WA 6, 267, 21-26, 32-35 [1520]).

[142]LW 45, 96 (WA 11, 255, 12-21), with reference to preaching and Jesus' demand: give to Caesar what belongs to Caesar, and to God what belongs to God.

[143]Cf. Prien 1992, 218.

[144]*The Book of Concord*, 350.

[145]Cf. Maurer 1970, 32.

146 Ibid., 22.

147 *The Book of Concord*, 566.

148 WA 32, 111, 15-19 (1530).

149 WA 32, 116, 6-7 (1530).

150 God himself is the "founder, lord, master, protector, and rewarder of both kinds of righteousness," LW 46, 100 (WA 19, 629, 30–630, 2). Nevertheless, one cannot simply say with Suda 2006, 122, that "neither of the two governments can succeed without law, but also not without the Gospel" (better formulated: "or without . . ."). Similarly inaccurate (at least as regards the late Luther) is his assertion that "the reign of Christ, in which God rules openly for all, is his union with the world empire."

151 LW 13, 44 (WA 31/1, 192, 21-25 [1530]).

152 LW 45, 263 (WA 15, 306, 28-33 [1524]).

153 WA 51, 406, 4 (1540).

154 Luther calculates how, with interest at 40%, a peasant or city-dweller, knight or noble, even a prince or a king would be "devoured" within a year. The one lending the money has neither risk nor effort, "sits by the stove and roasts apples," WA 51, 365, 1-12 (1540). Karl Marx quotes this passage, as well as others, explicitly in *Capital: A Critique of Political Economy* (New York: Random House, 1932), 1: 649–50 n. 1.

155 LW 45, 249 (WA 15, 296, 11-16 [1524]); cf. Werner Elert, *Morphologie des Luthertums*. Vol. 2, *Soziallehren und Sozialwirkungen des Luthertums* (Munich: Beck, 1953; 1st ed. 1931), 483.

156 WA 51, 366, 9–376, 9. The usurer and miser is not even really a human being—much worse than a tyrant, a robber, or a murderer, he is a "bear-wolf," a monster possessed by Satan. A miser should be hunted down, cursed, beheaded, especially those who "deliberately make things dearer," that is, drive prices up by manipulating their wares, WA 51, 421, 5-14.

157 See Ricardo Rieth, "Habsucht" bei Martin Luther. *Ökonomisches und theologisches Denken. Tradition und soziale Wirklichkeit im Zeitalter der Reformation* (Weimar: Hermann Böhlaus Nachfolger, 1996), and idem, "Luthers Antworten auf wirtschaftliche und soziale Herausforderungen seiner Zeit," 46–57 in *Main Address. Luther Congress 2007*.

158 LW 44, 100 (WA 6, 265, 21-24 [1520]).

159 WA 51, 367, 10-13 (1540).

160 LW 21, 112 (WA 32, 393, 9-13 [1532]), with reference to John 18.

161 Prien 1992, 204. That Luther at the same time expects "actions directed to structural change" from the authorities, as Prien suggests (p. 134), is doubtful; he thinks more of law within the framework of existing structures. Revealing of his thinking are statements such as that judging and punishing are "all part of the secular realm, which is not our concern here and which we will therefore permit to act the way it should and must act," LW 21, 211 (WA 32, 473, 31-32).

162 For Luther's interpretation of the Sermon on the Mount cf. Duchrow 1983, 536ff., 548ff., 575ff., 585ff., 590ff.; Scharffenorth 1982, 314ff.; Prien 1992, 200ff.

163 Cf. Prien 1992, 209.

164 WA 51, 366, 9–367, 1 (1540).

165 Cf. Prien 1992, 156.

166 Cf. WA 7, 578–85; also Martin Heckel, "Menschenrechte im Spiegel der reformatorischen Theologie," in idem, *Gesammelte Schriften*, vol. 2, ed. Klaus Schlaich (Tübingen: Mohr [Siebeck], 1989); Scharffenorth 1982, 232ff.

167 Cf. Johannes Gerson, "Tractatus de modo vivendi omnium fidelium," in Peters 1994, 102–3.

168 Cf. Johannes Heckel, *Im Irrgarten der Zwei-Reiche-Lehre* (Munich: Kaiser, 1957), and Pesch 1982, 230ff.: "in a snare of confusing distinctions."

169 Cf. Bayer 2003, 295–96.

170 See chapter 3 above, and cf. Gottfried Maron, "Bauernkrieg," *TRE* 5: 319–38, with bibliography; Horst Buszello, Peter Lickle, and Rudolf Endres, eds., *Der Deutsche Bauernkrieg* (Paderborn: Schöningh, 1984; 31995).

171 LW 46, 3–43 (WA 18, 291–334).

172 LW 46, 44–55 (WA 18, 357–61).

173 LW 46, 57–85 (WA 18, 384–401).

174 Wolf-Dieter Hauschild, *Lehrbuch der Kirchen- und Dogmengeschichte*, Vol. 2, *Reformation und Neuzeit* (Gütersloh: Gütersloher Verlagshaus, 1999), 97.

175 See Brecht 1987, 362–68.

176 WA 8, 676–87.

177 LW 46, 105 (WA 19, 635, 7-15 [1526]).

178 Cf. Maurer 1970, 30. God must maintain this "ring or circle" and "do everything in all of life's vocations, indeed, in all creatures," LW 41, 176–77 (WA 50, 652, 7-9 [1539]). This is not about superiority, but about mutual influence.

179 Heckel, "Menschenrechte," 1125. His reference is to the document on authority.

180 Luther is here interpreting Gal 3:28 (LW 46, 39, [WA 18, 327, 24-25 (1525)]).

181 Suda 2006, 199; cf. 125, 138ff.

182 Cf. WA 29, 566, 36-39 (1529); LW 5, 130 (WA 43, 512, 16-17); LW 8, 75, 83 (WA 44, 657, 9-23 [1535–1545]).

183 Cf. WA 37, 170, 34-35 (1533); LW 46, 250 (WA 30/2, 575, 9–576, 7 [1530]): "It is not God's will that only those who are born kings, princes, lords, and nobles should exercise rule and lordship. He wills to have his beggars among them also."

184 Bornkamm, Heinrich 1960, 277.

185 Karl Marx, *Grundrisse der Kritik der politischen Ökonomie* (Berlin: Dietz, 1953), 891. For Marx's interpretation of Luther's economic ethics cf. Günter Fabiunke, *Martin Luther als Nationalökonom* (Berlin: Akademie-Verlag, 1963).

186 Ernst Wolf tried to understand the "orders" or "estates" in the sense of "institutions." Cf. Trutz Rendtorff, "Zum sozialethischen Problem der Institutionen," in Lutheran World Federation, *Glaube und Gesellschaft. Beiträge zur Sozialethik heute* (Stuttgart and Berlin: Kreuz-Verlag, 1966), 42ff., and Hans Schulze, "Begriff und Kriterien einer theologischen Handlungslehre—im Gegenüber zu paränetischer und ordnungstheologischer Ethik," *EvT* 29 (1969): 183–202.

187 Ernst Troeltsch, *Gesammelte Schriften 1: Die Soziallehren der Christlichen Kirchen und Gruppen* (Tübingen: Mohr, 1912), 488 n. 223.

188 Karl Barth, "The Christian Community and the Civil Community," in idem, *Community, State and Church: Three Essays* (Garden City, NY: Doubleday Anchor, 1960). Cf. Ernst Wolf, "Königsherrschaft Christi und lutherische Zwei-Reiche-Lehre," 207–29 in idem, *Peregrinatio 2* (Munich: Kaiser, 1965).

189 LW 21, 171 (WA 32, 441, 9 [1532]).

190 LW 21, 185 (WA 32, 452, 21-24).

191 LW 21, 223 (WA 32, 483, 32-34).

192 Bockmühl 1987, 106, suggests that Jesus Sirach might have been the godparent here. Es frommt dir nicht, dass du nach dem gaffst, was dir nicht befohlen ist, und was deines Amtes nicht ist, da lass deinen Vorwitz. ["Do not meddle in matters that are beyond you, for more than you can understand has been shown you"] (Sir 3:23 NRSV); Gott hat von Anfang seine Werke wohl geordnet, und einem jeglichen sein eigen Werk gegeben, und erhält sie für und für in solcher Ordnung, dass sie ihr Amt immerdar ausrichten (…) und keines das andere hindert ["When the Lord created his works from the beginning, and, in making them, determined their boundaries, he arranged his works in an eternal order, and their dominion for all generations . . . they do not crowd one another"] (Sir 16:26-28 NRSV). But Luther does not refer directly to such biblical passages. Hence it could also be that these and similar translations can be traced instead to Luther's previous theological decisions. In fact, the translation of the Apocrypha did not take place until 1523–1534. Bockmühl warns "that the Reformation was eager to find New Testament content for its dogmatics, but in ethics it remained stuck on the level of canonical and apocryphal Old Testament materials," 107.

193 Cf. the thesis of Lee Brummel, "Luther and the Biblical Language of Poverty," *Ecumenical Review* 32 (1980): 40–58.

[194]Luther can at the margin even refer to the juridical phrase "friendly to the person but hostile to the sin," LW 21, 76 (WA 32, 365, 4). Cf. Prien 1992, 152.

[195]"Christus non curat tonitrum, sed Deus," WA 11, 202, 32 (1523). But in one of his last letters to Käthe he speaks of his expectation that Christ will care for him, "he lies in the cradle and rests on a virgin's bosom, and yet, nevertheless, he sits at the right hand of God, the almighty Father," LW 50, 302 (WA.Br 11, 286–88).

[196]"Christus non curat politiam aut oeconomiam, sed rex est ad destruendum diaboli regnum et ad salvandos homines," WA.TR 1, no. 932.

[197]". . . confiteri, quod unus Deus et unissimus," WA 49, 466, 11 (1544).

[198]"As the works of the Trinity to the outside are indivisible, so the worship of the Trinity from the outside is indivisible," LW 15, 311 (WA 54, 65, 23-24 [1543]).

[199]TRE 36: 785.

[200]Handbuch 427, 423.

[201]This is correctly put to him by Michael Roth, "Die fundamentalethische Bedeutung der Unterscheidung von Schöpfung und Erlösung. Bemerkungen zur Zwei-Reiche-Lehre," NZSTR 46 (2004): 184–206.

[202]Herms 1991, 102, 117.

[203]Gänssler 1983, 151, with reference to Ebeling.

[204]Cf. Matthias Kroeger in TRE 36: 792.

[205]Dalferth, Silfredo B. 1996, 187. The comparison of Luther's two-governments doctrine with Latin American theology of liberation is enlightening, for example as undertaken by Dalferth. Despite all the differences, Dalferth works out some existing commonalities.

[206]The doctrine of orders expresses this more clearly than does the two-governments scheme; cf. Müller, Gerhard 1989, 435–36.

[207]The two-governments doctrine as such, however, by no means unites the obligatory nature of faith with "acknowledgment in principle of ideological pluralism." Against Herms 1991, 122. In thinking of God's government with the left hand Luther did not have in mind a pluralism of religious options and claims.

13

Christian Existence: Secular and Spiritual

If we consider all its different aspects Luther's theology appears not to be simple; rather, it is intellectually demanding. How can it be translated into Christian everyday life? According to the Reformer's conviction what is important is "in the first place, that doctrine be completely correct and perfect, and then, that life move and be regulated according to it."[1] But the cross instead of self-determination, the breakthrough from the hidden to the revealed God, the tension between Law and Gospel, being both sinner and justified, simultaneously bound and free—what does all that mean for concrete living? We are tempted to suspect that this could only be about purely internal, invisible processes, even if they need not be understood in the sense of "innerliness" (Max Scheler) or even "quietism" (Herbert Marcuse).[2] How does Christian life look from this perspective? Can we "see" it at all, or is it instead "hidden with Christ in God" (Col 3:3)? Can its contours be described and made clear in comparison to the Christian lifestyle of other confessions, or to the life demanded by a purely humanistic ethos?

CONTEMPORARY QUESTIONS

Can we learn anything from Luther today about shaping and living a Christian life? He is supposed to have said: "Whoever loves not wine, women, and song remains a fool his whole life long." It is clear from the outset that these words do not correspond seamlessly to his theology. But is there a kernel of truth in them? A joyous affirmation of the world and the pleasures it offers—that concept is more often practiced today by non-Christians. Religious people seek a different spirituality. There are calls for civility. The strictest orders attract the most entrants; the implacability of Islam is attractive. Even evangelical Protestants profit from this mood. On the other hand, mysticism of all stripes, from esotericism to classical Buddhism, has an increasing number of adherents. Even within Christianity charismatic movements are advancing.

Illuminating examples of self-surrender such as Francis of Assisi or caritative engagement on the model of Mother Teresa are as impressive as ever. Can devotion shaped by the Reformation relate to these types of spirituality? Or does it fade into a kind of vague churchiness with nothing to offer besides church attendance and bourgeois virtues?

Added to all this today are spiritual goals and tendencies that have never before existed, at least not to this degree. "Seekers" do not want to buy any packaged religious systems. They choose from among the various religions what seems useful to them: patchwork spirituality. Luther's threefold "alone" is in radical contradiction to such a practice. Spirituality is supposed to refine, deepen, and enrich life; the psychic budget demands inner growth, harmony, and well-being: wellness spirituality. Is this desire damnable in the Reformer's eyes, or is there some justification for it, even for Christians?

Protestantism still adorns itself with the word "freedom." Lutheran ("Evangelical") Church = "Church of Freedom."[3] But is it still an actively "liberating" church with a "liberating" theology? Freedom has long since become a common expectation—sometimes in a way the Reformer would abhor and that he began to flay even in his own time. Could it have anything to do with Luther's theology that today it is above all those parts of Europe where the Reformation succeeded that are among the most secularized regions of the world?

From today's perspective the question arises whether Luther's ethics were not extraordinarily backward-looking. Are they nothing but a counter-model to late medieval piety and thus imitative of it, and consequently passé? Can we find any kind of impulses here that could lead us onward?

Luther argues fairly often in terms of natural law, as is still the case in Roman Catholic moral theology. Is Luther aware of any *proprium* of Christian, or even Lutheran/Evangelical ethics?

THE NECESSITY FOR ETHICAL ORIENTATION

Luther's advice for daily life is simple. He distinguished only phenomenologically between secular and spiritual activities, in the sense of his two-governments doctrine, but not in principle. This "shattered the idea of the scholastic social order, with its division of labor, according to which some pray for salvation while others work for those who pray."[4] For Luther all behavior and action is qualified by faith, be it "so small a thing as picking up a straw."[5] Work is proper to humanity. The human being is "born to work as are the birds to flying."[6] They should rejoice that God trusts them to make something.[7] They can be God's coworkers, the instruments of divine action.[8] In his early years the Reformer thought that a Christian did not need any real instruction in how to act; the good tree would bear good fruit of itself. Believers know what they should do, just as lovers do. Even someone who is obsessed with money does not need to be told that and how she or he should protect it against theft.[9] Johannes Agricola appealed to such statements when he denied the necessity of law for believers.[10] But Luther objected.

AGAINST THE ANTINOMIANS

In the very first of his Ninety-Five Theses, Luther postulated that repentance represents a lifelong requirement for Christians. "When our Lord and Master Jesus Christ said, 'Repent' etc. [Matt. 4:17], he willed the entire life of believers to be one of repentance."[11] What became of that beginning in the course of development of the Reformer's theology? It was clear from the beginning that a merely ritual act of repentance, through contrition, oral confession, and priestly absolution with the performance of an assigned penance, would no longer suffice. It is true that for Luther also contrition is associated with the awakening of remorse at one's own sins,[12] but forgiveness depends not on remorse, but on faith. "Beware then, of putting your trust in your own contrition and of ascribing the forgiveness of sins to your own remorse."[13] Sorrow for sins, awakened by the encounter with God's implacable Law, instead points people to the Gospel, sends them straight back to their baptism, and does so every day.[14] Repentance is not a plank to cling to alongside baptism in the sea of ruin, as the church father Jerome saw it.[15] Repentance, in principle, includes "both Law and Gospel."[16] The working of the Law is thus factually a precondition for forgiveness. Of course, contrition and sorrow could also be awakened by beholding the innocent suffering of Christ.[17] But in principle it is true that anyone who abolishes the Law will abolish sin along with it, and if there is no more sin, "then Christ is nothing."[18] Hence Luther never tires of "stimulating" people to repentance. Because Christians are both sinners and justified throughout life they remain obligated to repentance and forgiveness as long as they live. They thus understand that, despite all obstacles, they may always begin anew. The concept of repentance thus loses its gloomy medieval sound. The young Luther confessed that no word had become sweeter or more pleasant to him than this one, after Staupitz had made it clear to him that true repentance begins "with love for righteousness and for God."[19]

But what about the possibility of growth in faith? This happens under the ever-new blessing-rich working of Law and Gospel. Does the Law in this remain restricted to its most important function, namely making us aware of sins, or can it also acquire an orienting function for Christians?

The Reformer did not speak explicitly of a *tertius usus legis*, a third function of the Law for those who believe and are reborn.[20] But his writings are full of statements about what a Christian should do and not do. In his great lecture on Galatians he emphasizes that, just as right faith must be taught, so also love and "true" good works must be insisted upon.[21] In "On the Councils and the Church" (1539) he explains that we need the Decalogue not only so that it can tell us "of our lawful obligations, but we also need it to discern how far the Holy Spirit has advanced us in his work of sanctification and by how much we still fall short of the goal, lest we become secure and imagine that we have now done all that is required. Thus we must constantly grow in sanctification. . . ."[22] Luther sees a function for the Law that corresponds to the Gospel. Wilfried Joest has called it *usus practicus evangelii*; he thinks it more appropriate in this context to speak of "commandment" rather than "law."[23] In his conflict with the Antinomians the Reformer emphasizes both: that the Law is for all people, as the hammer of God that shatters the rock, but that it is to be received by believers as the light yoke of Christ.[24] The Law remains, but it no longer oppresses, because the burden Christ lays on us is easy and sweet. It is true that the content of this sweet law is nothing other than what leads to knowledge of sin: that is, first and foremost the Decalogue, the Sermon on the Mount, or the twofold commandment of love.

THE DECALOGUE

Within the framework of his conflicts with the Antinomians Luther points out that he himself, "as old and learned as I am," recites the commandments daily like a child, "word for word."[25] Besides this, he says he has presented any number of expositions of the Decalogue, and that was in fact the case: in 1518 the "short explanation," in 1520 the "short form," and especially the sermon "On Good Works," sermons on the catechism, and the catechisms themselves. Klaus Bockmühl speaks of an "omnipresence of the catechism and especially of the Decalogue in the churches of the Reformation."[26] But Luther was also aware of the limitations of the Mosaic ten commandments insofar as they were cultically obsolete and in a certain sense no longer in force because of Christ.[27] To what extent can the Decalogue still be relevant for believers?

The Reformer, like the tradition before him, is convinced that the Decalogue corresponds to natural law.[28] You would have to preach the Law for a hundred thousand years to an ox, ass, or steer before they could receive it, even though they have ears, eyes, and a heart, but human beings agree spontaneously; the Law is written in their hearts.[29] In their heart of hearts they know that one should fear God and love one's neighbor.[30] The Golden Rule is a significant example. According to Albrecht Peters, Luther locates "the middle position of the Decalogue between God's primal command, written in all human hearts," and the "twofold commandment of selfless love of God and neighbor."[31] This is incorrect to the extent that the Reformer scarcely connects the Decalogue to the Sermon on the Mount. On the other hand it was clear to him that natural knowledge of good and evil "[does not by itself] make us Christians."[32] He expresses this especially in his "Treatise on Good Works."

The new and special accent the Reformer gives the Decalogue is clear already from the fact that here the explanation of the first three commandments is nearly twice as long as that of the remaining seven. Luther makes his point in one of the first sentences: "The first, highest, and most precious of all good works is faith in Christ." Of course, "work" is used here in a categorically different sense from what it usually means: faith alone gives value to the act. In the view of faith all works are the same and there is no longer any distinction between important and unimportant activities; faith knows that every act and omission in accordance with faith is pleasing to God. Nor does faith require any instruction regarding action: "a Christian . . . who lives in this confidence toward God knows all things, can do all things, ventures everything that needs to be done, and does everything gladly and willingly."[33] Luther apparently sees no contradiction in the fact that in his sermon he also gives a considerable number of detailed instructions about what works are in accord with the various commandments. He even creates a hierarchy: "After faith we can do no greater work than to praise, preach, sing, and in every way laud and magnify God's glory, honor, and name."[34] The third commandment is important inasmuch as it puts an obstacle to high-handed action and insists "that we let God alone work in us and that in all our powers . . . we do nothing of our own."[35] Likewise the fourth commandment is given a special position: it emphasizes obedience and service to all "who are set in authority over us"— which in Luther's view means especially parents and superiors, for in some way every person must be "ruled and subject to other men."[36] The Reformer can also assert immediately, without losing his train of thought, that on the last day Christ will not ask "how much you have prayed, fasted, pilgrimaged, done this or that for yourself, but how much good you have done to others, even to the very least."[37] For this doing of good is also not given its value of itself, but only by faith.

So what is the function of the Decalogue for believers? Elsewhere the Reformer can speak of it as an examination of conscience. The Ten Commandments are "a mirror of our life in which we can see wherein we are lacking."[38] But the Decalogue is also a space for living in which Christians are at home, can move about freely, guided only by faith in Jesus Christ. Klaus Bockmühl criticizes Luther, saying that the content of his teaching is only a "behavioral ethics" with "very little consciousness of the goal."[39] What about a *proprium* in the content of Christian ethics? Does Luther's understanding of the Sermon on the Mount help us here?

THE SERMON ON THE MOUNT

Chapters 5–7 of Matthew's gospel are among the Synoptic passages Luther cites most frequently. While supplying for Johannes Bugenhagen, the pastor of the church of Wittenberg, in 1531 and 1532 he gave weekday sermons on the Sermon on the Mount that were published in 1532. In his interpretation he was fighting on two fronts. The old believers were convinced that Jesus' radical commands could not be for everyone, but must be seen as "counsels" for the small group of those especially dedicated, thus primarily those in religious orders. The Reformer considered that an excuse. On the other hand, the enthusiasts appealed to the Sermon on the Mount by attempting to meet its imperatives as literally as possible. This Luther thought impossible; the "sectarian spirits" did not fully grasp the radicality of Christ's claims. Luther saw two possibilities: one was to interpret the Sermon on the Mount in the sense of an implacable law that led to a shattering of moral endeavor and so pointed to the Gospel. In that case it would convey the knowledge that "by our own ability we cannot properly fulfill an iota," a dot, "of it," even though "once we have become Christians through Baptism and faith, we do as much as we can."[40] Or he could seek a counter-position by supposing that in the Sermon on the Mount Jesus was speaking solely of the fruits of faith, and one must speak of justification and grace elsewhere.[41] But even in that case the question would remain: how are the ethical imperatives to be understood in face of the fact that Christians, though now "transferred to another and higher existence,"[42] are supposed to live in the midst of the world according to the Sermon on the Mount? The hermeneutical key is given him by the two-governments doctrine: since they live in the grace of Christ, believers are in a position to do without and to suffer in their own regard, but since as long as they are in the world they also are subject to God's rule with the left hand they must—precisely as Christians—act on behalf of their fellow human beings. The "solution" is "for oneself" and "for others."[43] In the Sermon on the Mount, Christ teaches his own how they should "live and behave before God and in the world."[44] In this way Luther is able to avoid both the temptation to theocracy and reduction to a quietistic individual ethics. The imperatives are not blunted, and yet they cannot be applied in every situation. Gerta Scharffenorth is even able to encapsulate this procedure in a clear, four-part schema for making ethical decisions that she derives from the Reformer's arguments: "Determining the problem (situational analysis), exegesis and interpretation of basic related texts, confrontation of available ways of behaving with what the Bible says, invitation to self-testing before decision."[45] This probably applies especially in concrete questions such as selling at interest and usury.

But if we run through the weekday sermons on Matthew 5–7 we get the impression that the accent tends to fall more and more on the aspects of relief in the solutions presented. Luther arrives at the conclusion that "real citizenship (!), when carried on in a Christian manner is ten times as hard as a Carthusian routine."[46] What is the whole foolish work of monks and hermits in contrast to "one pious child, servant, or maid who is obedient and faithful in the performance of his duty"?[47] And if someone were to do miracles like the apostles, Luther continues, "I would rather be a shoemaker's apprentice or a dishwasher on the basis of the Word of God. I would elevate this occupation above all your suppositions, even if you were able to raise the dead."[48] To have pious citizens, women, children, masters, menservants and maidservants like this—that would be heaven on earth![49] The Reformer interprets Paul as saying "If you have Christ through faith, then let everyone be obedient and subject to the government and practice mutual love in your station. You see, there you have the true mirror of a Christian life."[50] Certainly if one were asked to forsake the Gospel it would be necessary to be radical and refuse,[51] but normally everything seems to come down to the principle with which the table of duties in the Small Catechism concludes:

> Let each his lesson learn with care
> And all the household well will fare.[52]

No doubt the Reformer thus succeeds in assigning a precise place to love of neighbor and giving it a clear profile. But what about love of God?

THE TWOFOLD LOVE COMMANDMENT

Luther often preached on Matthew 22:34-46 because it was the old church's chosen pericope for the Eighteenth Sunday after Trinity. At first the text gave him an opportunity to repeat his fundamental themes: Law and Gospel. Who could be in a position to love God and neighbor with the whole heart, soul, and strength? Consider how often you have loved your neighbor just as yourself—you will find "a thin list!"[53] Only Jesus Christ fulfilled the twofold commandment. Those who wanted to serve God had already thought out for themselves how they would attempt it—Luther lists the whole arsenal of late medieval piety—enter a monastery, make pilgrimage to Rome or Santiago, fast, celebrate, honor the saints.[54] But it is precisely your "own" self-created "observance" that is to be avoided.[55] God does not desire to be courted with monstrances and the erecting of altars.[56] "Do you wish to love me," God asks, "do me a favor that will please me? Help the poor . . . I will be quite close enough to you in every poor person in need of your help and teaching: I am in their midst. . . ."[57] God does not need my activities, or any particular behavior of mine, not even my preaching. "Don't gape at heaven and say: oh, if I might once see our Lord God, how I would offer him all possible service! . . . You have him in your house, in your household servants and children."

So the world is "full, full of God; in every street, before your door you find Christ."[58] "Come down, come down, Christ says; you will find me in the poor; I am too high for you in heaven, you will be stranded."[59] Such words, which give a new value to everyday life, even in its "most contemptible" works,[60] are impressive on the one hand, but on the other hand they create the impression that there is no place left for a "unique" love of God: love for the neighbor is the "unique" or "proper" love of God. According to Luther, God "melts" the two commandments "into one another,"[61] but in such a way that essentially only the commandment of love of neighbor remains. But the Reformer also addresses the question of the commandment to love God, apart from God's identification with love of neighbor. Loving God could consist, for example, in loving to hear God spoken of, desiring to be with God.[62] If we were to produce true love for God we would have no more need of commandments; everything would follow of itself.[63] But he considered it hypocrisy for someone to withdraw, thinking: "Oh, I will love God! Oh, how I love God, who is my father!" People only say such things when all is well with them. But true love of God says: "Lord God, I am your creature; do with me what you will."[64] For Luther, the love of God consists in trust in and obedience to God; that, for example, is how he interpreted Abraham's obedience.[65] His interest, however, was not in individual acts; on the contrary, he was focused on the self-surrender of the whole person: "your whole life as you live it in your body, in the five senses, and what you do with your body, all that should be directed to giving God praise. . . ." With his command to love God, Christ means to say that everything must be done for the love of God, "whether you sleep or wake, work or stand idle, eat or drink. . . ."[66] Only Christ could really fulfill such a command.

And yet the twofold commandment is precisely for believers. "For that very reason we teach the faith, so that the law may be fulfilled."[67] It tells people: "That is how you were" (namely, in Paradise), "and so shall you yet be and become."[68] It is by no means true that you will be blessed if you "only believe" (!), and that no harm is done if you do not keep the commandments: "No, dear sir, that is no way out." That is why preaching should be about the "raising up of our body and our soul, so that we will again be in the state of one who exists to love God and the neighbor from the heart." This is to be perfected in the next life, "but begin here in this life."[69] For Christ's sake is given to us that our heart be made "sweet" and "through the Holy Spirit enkindled and driven so that it begins to love him again and again, from day to day, more and more."[70] A "new flame and fire" is to be kindled in us. We should remain under Christ's "wings," under which the sin that is yet in me shall be no sin. Christ desires to feed us, as the hen feeds her chicks, namely "give us the Holy Spirit and strength so that we begin to love God and keep his commandments," and continue thus until the Last Day.[71]

In spite of such words there is still a remarkable restraint. It is impossible for human beings to love God in majesty; such love does not belong to this earth. "Love God in creatures; he does not desire that you should love him in his majesty."[72] There seems to be an element of sorrow in these sayings, a knowledge of the incapacity of the human heart and at the same time hope for an eternal fulfillment. "In that life there will no longer be faith, but perfect love. . . ."[73] This is the sense in which Luther interprets Paul's saying that faith, hope, and love will abide, and that the greatest of them is love (1 Cor 13:13): faith endures only through time; it has "only to do with God in our hearts in this life, but love has to do with God and the whole world forever."[74] What does all that mean for faith in everyday life, for the lifestyle of believers?

FAITH AND MANNER OF LIFE

According to Luther, Christians are not characterized by a particular lifestyle but by the way they live their lives. "I am not a Christian because I do this or that, but because Christ is born and given for me."[75] This way of living is characterized by faith and an ethos corresponding to it, as well as by the joy that comes from a life lived in faith. A good deal of what the Reformer had to say about the Gospel and justification, and about life under God's two governments, could be repeated at this point. What is striking is that the church, or even the concrete congregation, seems to have only a subordinate place and value in this scenario.

FAITH AND DAILY LIFE

Believers do their duty as indicated by their order or estate. They work without worrying about the yield. They rejoice that they are able to be God's coworkers, for God desires that we work, even though he could let "things well baked and boiled, grain and wine grow on the table." He wants us to apply our reason: "He gives us wool, which he causes to grow on the sheep, but there will be no cloth made of it unless we work and make cloth of it"—and then the cloth is still not clothing![76]

Christians, justified before God, live in peace with God and rejoice. They need fear no one, and they know how to deal with death and the devil: in all their doing they are certain of God's presence.[77] "A Christian is something precious. There is nothing so insignificant in him that it does not please God."[78] This is "such a man as our Lord God made."[79] Christians do not commit any monstrous deeds, but otherwise they live like everybody else. At the same time they are aware of their sins and feel themselves to be stronger than unbelievers.[80] Our ethical successes are not ours, but those of Christ, who lives and works in us. What is "our own" is nothing but sin, but in Christ it is "concealed and blotted out through the forgiveness of sins; and daily it is put to death through the same grace of the Spirit, until we have died to this life altogether."[81] Faith and love make up the life of a Christian, though externally a Christian is scarcely different from other honest people.[82] Nevertheless, a difference from bourgeois honesty remains, in the fact that Christian couples may not divorce; at least, one should counsel them to remain together. If they do divorce, they should not remarry.[83] Christians also treat the Golden Rule differently from other people; they are not confined to the measure of mutual requests, but act spontaneously out of love.[84] Luther sometimes emphasizes the positive sides of being a Christian and sometimes gives more weight to the difficulties. A Christian life is "a blessed [original: 'wunnselig'] and joyful life, and the yoke of Christ is soft and sweet," even though in our unbelief it sometimes seems hard and bitter to us, according to a homily of 1525.[85] The one who is filled with the Spirit runs around as if drunk.[86] On the other hand, Christian existence is stressful, because it is constantly attacked and challenged; it creates resistance and must resist in turn; it is necessary "to wage war and risk one's life."[87] The devil has nothing against religious people, but he cannot stand Christians.[88] So a Christian easily becomes Satan's footscraper.[89] On the whole one may get the impression that in his early years the Reformer placed the positive and exhilarating elements more in the foreground, and in later years the burdensome ones. In his exposition of the Our Father in 1518 Luther could say euphorically that a truly righteous person is made so much like God that he or she can be indifferent to time and place as well as to other people, for every day is a festival for such a one.[90] About a decade later, in his treatise on the Sermon on the Mount, he says that a Christian leads a hard life, "as if he were walking on a narrow path, in fact, on nothing but razors."[91] The common thread, of course, is love, "after all, that is why we live together on earth, so that we might serve and help one another."[92] But "Christian existence does not consist in outward behavior," for everything depends on faith; a Christian knows that. "For this reason he walks, stands, eats, drinks, dresses, works, and lives as any ordinary person in his calling, so that one does not become aware of his Christianity. . . ."[93] Luther sounds resigned when he laconically observes in the lectures on Galatians: "We live as we can."[94] But this is the expression not so much of resignation as of a sober, realistic view of Christian existence, which equally knows itself sustained by God's presence and is assured of it in prayer.

For Luther the great inner counterpoint to the rather unprepossessing outward face of Christianity was prayer. From it comes also the Reformation style of life in the proper sense, which in turn derives its strength from listening to God's word. Obviously Luther was familiar with all forms of personal and liturgical prayer.[95]

Prayer as an internal event

For the Reformer, faith is "pure prayer."[96] Faith and prayer can be identified; in fact, they are virtually interchangeable. Luther does not regard prayer as a spontaneous natural human impulse; the sinner as such has neither the right nor any real opportunity to pray. Rather, prayer is grounded in God's commandment and promise. "Call on me in the day of trouble; I will deliver you, and you shall glorify me!" (Ps 50:15), says the Old Testament. "Ask, and it will be given you . . . !" says Christ in the Sermon on the Mount. From such sayings Luther concludes that prayer does not arise out of free human initiative. Rather, it is an act of obedience. The Reformer's intention is not to institute a legal demand for prayer but instead to encourage to prayer, because God has commanded it and therefore it must make sense. That is why no one should in any way despise her or his own prayer.[97] Luther himself prays in this way: "My God, you have commanded me to pray and to believe that my prayer will be heard. For this reason I come to you in prayer and am assured that you will not forsake me but will grant me a genuine faith."[98] Genuine faith will "catch" God with God's own words.[99] Prayer should teach us "to recognize who we are and who God is,"[100] that is, how needy we ourselves are and how more than richly God wants to shower us with gifts. Prayer is thus not only sustained by God's commandment but gains its special power from the fact that it takes place in faith in Jesus Christ, who has opened for us sinners access to God. "If you do not pray in and through Christ, and he himself in you (!), it is in vain."[101] Christ himself takes on the voice of my prayer! God guarantees it. But Luther can also trace it to the work of the Holy Spirit: "You must feel the Holy Spirit's call in your heart, for it is also your heart that calls. . . . He calls and cries with all his strength, that is, with his whole, his full heart, so that everything lives and moves with such confidence."[102] What can seem dry dogmatics in the doctrine of "justification" or of the Trinity here finds its living, existential application.

Genuine faith makes us "bold and thirsty" for true prayer.[103] In faith the human heart is "permeated" by God, and the Spirit sees to it that we are able to pray.[104] A Christian prays without anyone's being able to observe it, but "one's heart nonetheless does beat incessantly . . . with sighs such as these: 'Oh, dear Father, please let Thy name be hallowed. . . .'"[105] Christian prayer is full of expectation and yet it does not constrain God.[106] Ultimately it asks for nothing but the Holy Spirit and the consolation of the divine word.[107] Luther can use mystical expressions[108] and yet he rejects the idea that prayer leads to union with God; this thought, he says, could break your neck.[109] Those who think they are disposed to prayer should be especially careful; sinking deep in meditation to the point of tears could also be brought about by the devil.[110] True prayer is struggle, confrontation with the powers that are opposed to God, even with God's own self, as Luther illustrates in the story of Jacob's struggle at the Jabbok.[111] Christian prayer will not be lacking the "awful cry." "But Christ's spirit shall and must outshout that cry!"[112]

It may help Christians to keep in mind the words of the Our Father. But Luther himself admits that when he meditates on a petition in the Our Father he "gets lost among so many ideas" that he forgoes the other six. "If such an abundance of good thoughts comes to us we ought to disregard the other petitions, make room for such thoughts, listen in silence. . . . The Holy Spirit himself preaches here, and one word of his sermon is far better than a thousand of our prayers." Luther says he has often "learned more from one prayer than I might have learned from much reading and speculation."[113]

The Our Father as a model

For Luther the starting point for Christian prayer should normally be the Our Father.[114] He interpreted it often and in a variety of contexts: "An Exposition of the Lord's Prayer for Simple Laymen,"[115] in catechetical preaching and in the catechisms, in the framework of his preaching on the Sermon on the Mount,[116] and in his instructions on prayer for "Master Peter."[117] Add the Our Father hymn he wrote, still found in the Lutheran hymnals.[118] For Luther the sequence of the petitions is significant: first is the Name, the kingdom, and the will of God, and only then follow the matters of importance to the one praying. This brings Luther, in a brief interpretation in 1519, to the original idea that most believers only get inwardly involved, so to speak, in the second half of the Our Father, where it is about themselves. But it is important to begin the Our Father at the beginning and not at the end.[119] Almost the most important thing to him is the beginning, the address, "Father." "This is indeed a very short word, but it includes everything. Not the lips, but the feelings are speaking here. . . ."[120] It is the name of God, out of which "the whole Godhead swells and overflows. . . ."[121] With this name God seeks to "encourage us to believe that he is truly our Father and we are truly his children."[122] Therefore everything depends on our being able to call God "Father" from our hearts— then we will be blessed. Luther says of himself that he cannot do it, but he wants to try to, "and begin as a little child seeks its mother's breast." Luther uses an expression here that can scarcely be translated into modern German:

"als ein kindlin an seinem zitzlin zu nueseln"—the way an infant pushes its nose against its mother's breast, seeking the nipple.[123] The trusting address, "Father," matches the assurance of the "Amen" at the end. In the "amen" spoken in full confidence, the prayer returns to its beginning: "Our Father— Amen!"

Prayer as external action

Although for the Reformer prayer belongs to the innermost sphere of faith, he also gives indications of how it is to be carried out externally. He is aware of the obstacles that appear spontaneously when one tries to pray. "'Ah,' we say, 'you are not yet ready to pray! . . . Your daily sinning makes you unworthy. . . . Do you suppose that God heeds and hears your prayer?" Then I should make it clear to myself that I will not be more skillful in half an hour or eight days later.[124] One should not use many words in prayer; if we pray and sing for hours and hours without being altogether present in heart it will become too strenuous; "any day laborer would prefer to work at threshing for an entire day to just moving his mouth for two or three hours in a row or staring straight at a book."[125] On the other hand, pre-existing words can be an impetus for the soul; in that case they function like a trumpet, a drum, or an organ, "or any other sound which will move the heart and lift it upward to God."[126] But it seems better to Luther to follow the model of the church fathers, who recommended "short, fervent prayers, where one sighs toward heaven with a word or two"; those can also be combined with any secular activity.[127] "In other words, prayers ought to be brief, frequent, and intense," a prayer that "proceeds from the heart."[128] Prayer requires intense concentration. Luther explains this to Master Peter, the barber, in terms of his trade: "So, a good and attentive barber keeps his thoughts, attention, and eyes on the razor and hair and does not forget how far he has gotten with his shaving or cutting. If he wants to engage in too much conversation or let his mind wander or look somewhere else he is likely to cut his customer's mouth, nose, or even his throat."[129] Luther gives most of his attention to individual prayer. He does not consider it necessary, though it is useful, to withdraw into one's "closet," where one may pray "in a free and uninhibited manner, using words and gestures that he could not use if he were in human company."[130] But even if one prays alone, "Never think that you are kneeling or standing alone, rather think that the whole of Christendom, all devout Christians, are standing there beside you and you are standing among them. . . ."[131]

Meditation

In the course of the encounter with esotericism and East Asian spirituality, attention has been directed to the question of meditation styles in the Christian tradition, and also in Luther's case.[132] Luther knew the word *meditari* from the Latin Bible: "Happy are those who . . . delight in the law of the Lord, and on his law . . . meditate day and night" (Ps 1:1-2). He also belonged to a broad medieval tradition of meditation, though he distanced himself from it in characteristic fashion. Like many before him, he recommended *ruminare*, the re-chewing of a text when going to sleep and when awaking the next morning.[133] In meditation the soul becomes pregnant with the seed of the word of God until it bears fruit.[134] Medieval meditations on repentance and the passion left their traces in Luther's feelings and thoughts. But the more important the external word became to him, the closer meditation approached scriptural interpretation. It opens up the biblical text. If one reads it aloud one is better protected against subjective conceits like those of the enthusiasts. Meditation does not lead to visions or other mystical experiences, but to combat with temptations and assaults.[135] *Contemplatio*, silent contemplation, is replaced by *tentatio*, active conflict with existential resistance. Here what has been gained in meditation proves itself, and so comes the experience of God. Therefore it is advisable to have biblical passages at hand to which one can refer and also cling.[136] Luther thinks that in the case of the letter to the Romans it is worthwhile that a Christian "not only . . . should know it word for word, by heart, but also that he should occupy himself with it every day, as the daily bread of the soul." The more one deals with it, "the more precious it becomes and the better it tastes."[137] In believers' dealings with Sacred Scripture the Holy Spirit develops his activity. It is possible that he may interrupt one's cognitive engagement with the text; Luther interprets the word "Sela," which is difficult to explain and tends to appear suddenly in certain psalms, in this sense.[138] It is worth remembering and sometimes writing down what the Spirit says to me.[139] In his instruction for the Master Barber Peter, Luther recommends a four-step process for meditating on the Decalogue: "I think of each commandment as, first, instruction, which is really what it is intended to be, and consider what the Lord God demands of me so earnestly. Second, I turn it into a thanksgiving; third, a confession; and fourth, a prayer." He calls this "four parts . . . a garland of four strands."[140] In principle this procedure can be applied to every word of the Bible—and of course to individual passages in the catechism.

A LIFE SHAPED BY THE CATECHISM

Luther was never tired of insisting on how important to him personally the catechism was. Although he was a doctor of theology and a preacher, he acted like a child being taught its catechism: he would speak, in the morning or whenever he had time, "word for word" the Our Father, the Ten Commandments, the Credo, or the Psalms. He had to "remain a child and pupil of the Catechism," and he loved to do so.[141] Max Josef Suda rightly points out that the Reformer in saying this did not mean his own explanations of the catechism but the central parts of the catechetical material: the Decalogue, Credo, and Our Father.[142]

The place of the catechism in daily life

Luther was annoyed that pastors who joined the Reformation and so were released from the burden of the Daily Office did not "morning, noon, and night read a page or two of the catechism, a prayer book, the New Testament, or something else from the Bible, and pray an Our Father for themselves and the people of their parish. . . ."[143] He explains in the Small Catechism how the father of a household should "hold up" the Decalogue, Credo, and Our Father to his family and explain the sacraments to them. It is true that a Christian always lives in the spirit of prayer, and yet external, oral prayer should not fall silent. Luther suggests to his congregations that everyone "in the morning and in the evening, at table and whenever he has time" should pray a benediction or the Our Father, the creed or a psalm. Common prayer is also very powerful.[144] Thus a Christian's life moves between the morning and the evening blessing. "In the morning, when you rise, make the sign of the cross and say, 'In the name of God, the Father, the Son, and the Holy Spirit. Amen.'" Following this prayer, and perhaps the creed and the Our Father, "after singing a hymn . . . you should go to your work joyfully." On the same model, then, at night one should make the sign of the cross, say the creed and the Our Father, "then quickly lie down and sleep in peace."[145] A Christian should "cultivate the habit of falling asleep with the Lord's Prayer on your lips every evening when you go to bed and again every morning when you get up."[146] This is about the shaping of the day, with every day seen as a spiritual unit—perhaps on the model of farmers' daily round. It is striking how and in what contexts Luther uses the word "daily": God provides for believers "daily and abundantly," "daily" forgives them "abundantly" all their sins, and expects that the old Adam will daily be drowned and a new human being "come forth daily and rise up. . . ."[147] The Our Father and the creed should be prayed daily;[148] we also need daily repentance.[149] The Bible should be used every day.[150] Sunday recedes in importance, even though, in accordance with the traditional order, it remains a significant day;[151] it serves for bodily refreshment, listening to God's word, and prayer. But it is appropriate also to pray and allow oneself to be moved by the word of God on weekdays; as far as the Reformer is concerned what is important is not a particular day, but every day, for "at whatever time God's Word is taught, preached, heard, read, or pondered, there the person, the day, and the work are sanctified by it."[152]

The spiritual dynamic of the catechism

The first three major sections of the catechism were not arbitrarily or accidentally arranged by Luther; they constitute a dynamic context: in the Decalogue every person learns what is to be "done and omitted," in the creed where, in view of everyone's inability to match up to the Decalogue, one should "take and seek and find," and finally, in the Our Father, how one is to "seek, take, and bring" grace to oneself.[153] This order, already appearing in the Middle Ages, with the Decalogue before the creed, had a fundamental significance for Luther inasmuch as it is capable of illustrating the basic problem of Law and Gospel. While the first section formulates the demanding will of God, the second recalls God's gracious action. The interpretation of the Our Father introduces an existence face to face with the God who constitutes the source and goal of one's life. If believers add the remaining major sections, on baptism and the Lord's Supper, they will, by considering their baptism in conflict with their former lives and through the Lord's Supper, find themselves placed in a new frame of existence. The whole is not thought of as a single process, a system of steps, or a method, but as a centripetal power field that shapes Christian existence—through the repeated penetration of individual impulses ever anew into consciousness. The structure of the catechism makes it clear that this is not meant to be a summary of Lutheran dogmatics but an aggregate of strengths that is again and again able to open to people new orientations, sources of energy, and spaces for living. In Luther's conception the catechism attempts to drag people into God as into a whirlpool. It is not a short theory of Christianity, nor is it a kind of handbook of operations; it is simultaneously fuel, an injection of energy that can put our existence into motion.

CRITICAL EVALUATION

Luther refused to separate Christian existence into secular and spiritual sides. By faith the whole person is newly valued in all his or her doings and omissions. In this way the Reformer gave believers an internal basis for action in the world and a good conscience about it. In his or her particular calling, a Christian should be active on behalf of fellow human beings and thereby also serve the whole society. With this approach Luther certainly contributed indirectly to the rise of the modern social state. Of course, we do not know to what extent maidservants sweeping stalls and menservants carrying off the dung in the sixteenth century really saw their activity as service of God. In the

Lutheran village in Franken where I grew up there were, in any case, farmers who stopped to call on God in silent prayer when the bell rang in the morning and evening, when they sowed their seed and when they brought in their crops. That may have been a long-term effect of a piety initiated in the Reformation, but undoubtedly it also had its problematic consequences.

DANGER OF SELF-SECULARIZATION?

Luther battled for a theological revaluation of the secular. Work is divine service. He quotes the church father Jerome: "everything a believer does is prayer." He repeats the proverb: "who works faithfully prays twice." Does this proverb indicate a tendency to secularization that was already showing itself in Luther? In any case, Luther affirms that "such thoughts and such faith" undoubtedly make work "a prayer and a sacrifice of praise." And yet there is the immediate "but": "Yet we must be careful not to break the habit of true prayer," and finally become lax and lazy. Ultimately, God has commanded us to pray, promised to hear us, and through Christ has taught us the Our Father.[154] For Luther this argument is conclusive, but for his hearers it may come to seem nothing but advice. After all, the Reformer himself relativized a good many pious actions. A "real citizenship" lived as a Christian seemed to him more valuable than the asceticism of a Carthusian monk.[155] If there were a great many pious citizens in a city, "we would have the kingdom of heaven on earth. We would not need any monasteries. People would not have to fast or pray and sing all day long in church but simply do no more than what their various stations and occupations required."[156] Could we not simply add here, in modern style, "and have no need to go to church"? Luther is aware of the danger of his approach and tries to avoid it, but his argument is apparently insufficient. Therefore he begins to rail against the meanness that has the evangelical preachers starving. He ultimately demands that nonbelievers in his congregations should "be driven to sermons for the sake of the Ten Commandments, so that they at least learn external works of obedience."[157] They should be forced to go to sermons so that they may acquire knowledge about their social obligations.[158] Melanchthon was godfather to this stance, church ordinances were prepared, and yet in the period afterward attendance at worship had to be secured by social control, sometimes even by political means.[159]

LOSS OF CHRISTIAN FORMS OF LIFE

Luther polemicized unstintingly against monasticism, "hoods" (the monastic habit), and "flatheads" (clerical tonsures), against pilgrimages, fasting, and the use of money to found institutions. At the time of his treatise "On Good Works" he said people thought the first commandment could be fulfilled by "singing, reading, playing the organ, reading the mass . . . founding and decorating churches, altars, and monasteries, collecting bells, jewels, garments, trinkets, and treasures, and running to Rome and the saints." If this were done in faith, it was praiseworthy, but only because of the faith shown, not because the works as such were virtuous.[160] However, basically Luther was very soon unable even to imagine that such things could really be done out of faith. Although he knew that faith could move the intimate emotions, he thought that weeping during prayer was more probably caused by the devil;[161] the "gift of tears" of which the spirituality of the Eastern Church speaks was foreign to him. He regarded it as a phenomenon revealing the unrepentant person focused on the self. Specific forms of spiritual expression he saw as hypocrisy. Only fasting yielded a certain meaning for him, if it was not associated with arrogance or the idea of gaining favor through works, in which case it was a "nice external discipline."[162] He could even imagine a worldly fasting, perhaps one required by authority; as an external order of discipline it would do some good.[163] He also recommends periods of fasting or individual fast days, not as a special service to God but as "memorial days" or "distinctive days"; he considered Friday evening especially suitable.[164] However, he does not wish to introduce such a thing himself, especially since he has to continually battle against false ideas.[165] Thus ultimately there remain only the bourgeois ways of life that are identified with the Christian lifestyle. Feminist groups have noted that as a result women did not even have the option of going into a monastery to escape pressure from their immediate family and their relations.[166] The foundations and women's convents that remained, at least in Lower Saxony and Westphalia, were only partially able to assume the functions of the monasteries, especially since they were largely reserved for the nobility. Now, it is true that the women's monasteries and convents of the late Middle Ages may not have been such hives of emancipation as feminists seem to imagine. Nevertheless, they are right to point to an actual reduction in the opportunities for various forms of Christian life in the Reformation churches, a decline whose reversal began only with the preaching Pietist women of the eighteenth century and the deaconesses of the nineteenth. Klaus Bockmühl finds that it was no accident that Lutheran Protestantism, having expelled monasticism from itself, took two hundred years before it rediscovered mission and three hundred before it re-adopted church diaconal service.[167] He could have mentioned the Lutheran communities that formed a century later.[168] The Reformer was evidently so deeply engaged in struggle with the forms of late medieval piety that on the one hand were misdirected and on the other hand had become soulless that he was largely unable to accord any genuine meaning to external actions and lifestyles. Add to this that he rejected the scholastic teaching of a *habitus*, an inborn grace,[169] because the idea could have formed the basis for human autonomy before God. However, Luther did not distinguish between the fact that a human being can neither develop a stable "condition" before God nor adopt an "attitude" grounded in the self and yet that one must certainly acquire an attitude in the context of this earthly life that is formed by insights and habits. He therefore gave too little effort to the building up of such an attitude in his congregations.

CHRISTIAN ETHOS WITHOUT A MATERIAL PROPRIUM?

The *proprium* of Christian ethics is for Luther the faith out of which love grows. In his view, however, love can scarcely develop in any way other than in the secular world. It is true that there was a categorical difference, for him, between something that happens in faith and love and cases in which this is not true. But materially, Christian behavior can scarcely be distinguished from the bourgeois morality of his time. Klaus Bockmühl, who otherwise is unjust to the Reformer in many ways, is right in deploring that in Luther's catechisms there is no specific material Christian ethos: where is there any spirituality, such as that expressed in the biblical stories of the anointing of Jesus in Bethany or the widow's "mite"?[170] Catechetical instruction should "make Christians" of people, though Luther apparently was not thinking only of young people.[171] But the idea of mission, which should actually be addressed in this context, plays no role at all. Likewise, the specific ethos of the common, mutual, and universal priesthood is not a theme in the catechisms or in Luther's interpretation of the Sermon on the Mount.[172] Where, in his later period, are the young Reformer's references to the fact that Christians should advocate for one another in prayer and accuse each other of their sins and pronounce forgiveness?

For Luther, Christian existence is not characterized by specific duties and opportunities within the congregation but, insofar as he describes it at all, by confession and suffering. "Before I forsake Christ and the Gospel, let my wife and children, my body and goods, sun and moon and all the creatures be gone."[173] Luther scarcely ever has in view that one's lifestyle within the congregation and the specific ethos of community could be a witness. The presupposition for his broad identification of Christian and bourgeois ethos was, of course, the congruence of Christian and public morality, something that was still a given in the dying Middle Ages even though atheistic tendencies were already emerging.[174] The more that Christian and common ethical consciousness diverge, the less can Protestantism orient itself to Luther in this regard.

ONE-SIDED IMAGE OF GOD?

Luther found two things to be important for everyday Christian existence: knowledge of sin and forgiveness, and trusting God as the one who rules the world in small things and in great. The childlike way, seemingly naïve today, in which Luther, as a grown man, a preacher, and a doctor of theology (as he often emphasized) spoke to his God or trusted himself to the words of the Our Father has something touching about it, though it may force a smile from some modern readers. We should not fault the Reformer for not challenging the theistic concept of God, especially since he knew that the God to whom he prayed could also be thought of quite differently and must then be seen as "our Father in heaven," "... a supernatural, inscrutable being who exists at the same time in every little seed, whole and entire, and yet also in all and above all and outside all created things."[175] He by no means had a sexist attitude; this is shown, for example, by his frequent comparison of God or Christ to a hen who protects and feeds her chicks. Trinitarian features are not absent, though as a rule they are applied to individual persons of the Trinity and though Luther rather seldom envisions the triune God when he is at prayer. If he reserves the fulfillment of true love of God for the eschaton, that expresses the longing he seems to have had for it. But we may well reproach him that love of God had for him—in contrast to the tradition—"no place of its own and apparently no specific content."[176] Better said: it had only a single place, namely in love for the neighbor. Is this the reason why modern Protestants are characterized by intensive diaconal efforts but not really by love, that those efforts seldom have anything to do with love for the congregation, the expressions of its life, or even the church building? Is it a sinful presumption for a person to wish to practice and recommend love for God apart from love of neighbor? That seems likely for Luther, and it also explains his ambiguous relationship to mysticism. On the one hand he repeatedly makes use of its language and imagery; on the other he distances himself emphatically from the idea of a *unio* with God. In the context of Luther's thought that may be more or less consistent, but it should certainly not serve as an argument that Lutheran Christians should follow him in this. The challenge today is to discover how the profound trust that characterized Luther's prayer and faith can be retained or newly won in the face of a situation in which the theistic concept of God is beginning to dissolve out of general awareness. Add to this the difficulty that contemporary Christians, educated in exegesis and aware of hermeneutical problems, cannot approach the Decalogue, the creed, and the Our Father in the same naïve and simple fashion as Luther could. Here we need new efforts in catechesis, and these should include the experiences of other confessions and religions.

LIMITED ESCHATOLOGY?

New Testament eschatology has come more clearly into perspective for Christians only since the end of the nineteenth century. To that extent we should not reproach Luther for the fact that it played a limited role for him.[177] The *Supputatio annorum mundi*, written in his last decade, shows how much he was concerned with the question of the approach of the Last Day, though he did not presume to calculate a concrete date.[178] In any case, the end seemed to him to be near. Nevertheless, it is striking that impatient expectation of the reign of God did not play a central motivating role for him. What was important in his eyes was that people cannot bring about the reign of God by their own activities; it comes, that is, "of itself without our prayers." We pray "that it may also come to us," that with the help of the Holy Spirit "by his grace we may believe his holy Word and live a godly life, both here in time and hereafter forever."[179] But it does not seem that concrete future changes in the life of the individual or the congregation are required, to say nothing of social goals, and certainly not utopias. If faith awakens and is joined to a corresponding bourgeois way of life, the reign of God is present. It will be accompanied by resistance and suffering. Anyone who does not have "haters, slanderers, and persecutors" is not yet a Christian or at any rate has not demonstrated his or her Christian confession in deeds.[180] But it is suffering that is in the foreground, not the deed. Luther does indeed take note of the activities of the old believers; they are not lacking in deeds, though they only choose to do what they themselves have thought of and not what Christ desires of them. The Reformer makes a comparison: "If we [Protestant] Christians were as diligent in our works as they are in theirs, we would be nothing but saints. Still neither side really gets anywhere: we are lazy and indolent; they are entirely too active." He comes to the conclusion: "And so, thank God, we still have the advantage, in that we have started believing and loving a little and are on the right track, however weak our progress may be."[181] Is that honest modesty, or is it also resignation? My feeling is that the eschatological impetus is lacking here as regards both individuals and the congregation; there is nothing of the avid expectation of God's action about which the young Luther in particular certainly spoke. A church unable to blaze with visible successes should be more inclined to long for the palpable inbreaking of the reign of God than a church institution that, like the Roman Catholic Church, presents itself as the reign of God already present on earth. The strong emphasis on justification and salvation in the "now" of faith, however, has over time not only failed to open a perspective on the coming reign of God on the Reformation side as well; it has instead caused it to fade.

MAXIMAL PROGRAM FOR A MINORITY?

It has been said that Luther left the cloister in order to make the world a monastery. In fact, there are some amazing parallels between the monastic lifestyle and the way Luther characterized Christian life as a whole. In his discourse on the states of life he even spoke of "orders," probably as a deliberate antithesis to late medieval monasticism, which he himself was happy to have escaped. The classic monastic vows (poverty, chastity, obedience) are reproduced in the ethics of the orders or estates: obedience to the local authority, happy and orderly marriage and family life in place of chastity, and a responsible dealing with money and property in place of poverty. The Christian already has behind him or her the ordination that the monk-in-becoming had at first pursued, in the form of baptism. Comparable to the status of the rules of an order was the "Table of Duties, Consisting of Certain Passages of the Scriptures, Selected for Various Estates and Conditions of Men, by Which They May be Admonished to Do Their Respective Duties."[182] The liturgy of the hours was replaced by the catechism and prayer in the morning, at table, and in the evening. Did the whole thing come to anything different from the well-known *ora et labora*, now applied no longer to a monastic community and instead directed to the whole church? But was that in itself too much to expect of the general population? Luther occasionally remarked on how few believers there were. A Christian is a "rare bird."[183] In terms of numbers, he estimated the ratio of Christians to non-Christians at about one to a thousand.[184] In the preface to "The German Mass and Order of Service" (1526) he could still imagine that those "who want to be Christians in earnest" would come together, pray together, hold divine service, and live a life committed to love.[185] But he does not yet have "the people or persons for it," and does not "see many who want it."[186] There are many who come to worship but "do not believe and are not yet Christians. Most of them stand around and gape, hoping to see something new." Did Luther fail to take seriously the extremely unfavorable ratio he observed between believers and unbelievers? What was the consequence of his observation, as far as he was concerned? He prepared a new order of worship intended to serve as a public means "to move [such people] to believe and become Christians."[187] He makes pedagogical suggestions about how to use the catechism; he supports the visitation of the Saxon pastors and congregations. He never returns to his suggestion that serious believers should be gathered. Ultimately, in his view, they also remain sinful human beings and thus belong at the same worship service as those who have yet to come to faith. But the problem of profiling Christian existence has not only remained an ongoing theme of Lutheran piety; in face of a society that is increasingly bidding farewell to Christianity it is more acute than ever. Following Luther's thought, one could say that the challenges of the non-Christian world exist to make believers into genuine

Christians. Luther knows people who "mock not only our worldly actions but also our good spiritual works, such as our prayers, our fasting, our acts of kindness, who, in brief, are never at peace with us." That is a priceless blessing: "We should really pay such assailants all our goods!"[188] They exist today in adequate numbers and variety. If only they would bring us individual Christians and our congregations to draw the right conclusions! The profile of Lutheran Christianity needs to become sharper again.

Notes

[1] LW 21, 129 (WA 32, 406, 21-23).

[2] Cf. Heckel, Martin 1989, 1127–28.

[3] Cf. Kirchenamt der EKD, ed., *Kirche der Freiheit. Perspektiven für die evangelische Kirche im 21. Jahrhundert. Ein Impulspapier des Rates der EKD* (Frankfurt: Gemeinschaftswerk der Evangelischen Publizistik, 2006).

[4] Pawlas 2000, 51.

[5] LW 44, 25 (WA 6, 206, 9-11).

[6] WA 17/1, 23, 39-40, with reference to Luther's (wrong) translation of Job 5:7.

[7] WA 30/1, 149, 17-22.

[8] WA 40/3, 211, 24-30.

[9] WA 20, 513, 23-28.

[10] Cf. "Relationship of Law and Gospel" in chapter 7.

[11] LW 31, 25 (WA 1, 233, 10-11).

[12] LW 6, 325 (WA 44, 275, 19-22).

[13] LW 36, 85 (WA 6, 545, 25-27).

[14] Cf. *The Book of Concord*, 433, 441–42; WA 30/1, 704, 34.

[15] Peters 1993, 94–95.

[16] WA 39/1, 414, 11-12.

[17] WA 50, 471, 1-5.

[18] WA 50, 471, 17-18.

[19] Cf. Lohse 1995, 197.

[20] See "Law and Gospel in the entirety of Christian existence" in chapter 7.

[21] "Therefore it is as necessary that faithful preachers urge good works as that they urge the doctrine of faith," LW 27, 53 (WA 40/2, 68, 17-19 [printed 1535]).

[22] LW 41, 166 (WA 50, 643, 19-24), with reference to 2 Thess 3:18 and 1 Thess 4:1, 10.

[23] Joest 1961, 77–78.

[24] WA 39/1, 346, 15-16, Thesis 16; 381, 3-7. For more detail see Schulken 2005.

[25] LW 47, 109 (WA 50, 470, 27 [1539]).

[26] Bockmühl 1987, 41.

[27] WA 39/1, 374, 5-11.

[28] Cf. Peters 1990, 71–72.

[29] WA 16, 447, 26-34.

[30] WA 39/1, 374, 3-6.

[31] Peters 1990, 71.

[32] *The Book of Concord*, 419.

[33] LW 44, 27 (WA 6, 204, 25-26; 207, 26-28).

[34] LW 44, 39 (WA 6, 217, 8-11).

[35] LW 44, 72 (WA 6, 244, 5-6).

[36] LW 44, 80, 82 (WA 6, 252, 1-2).

[37] LW 44, 71 (WA 6, 244, 22-25).

[38] LW 33, 173 (WA 16, 380, 23-25); cf. WA 24, 14, 28-29; WA 39/1, 374, 2-5.

[39] Bockmühl 1987, 90.

[40] LW 21, 72 (WA 32, 359, 15-27).

[41] "Ideo ista tria capita tantum sunt referenda ad opera & contra falsam doctrinam hypocritarum. Et alio loco, de fide seu operum radice dicendum," WA 38, 459, 12-13.

[42] LW 21, 108 (WA 32, 389, 17-18).

[43] Duchrow 1983, 540.

[44] LW 21, 108 (WA 32, 389, 30-31).

[45] Scharffenorth 1982, 333.

[46] LW 21, 256 (WA 32, 511, 38-39).

[47] Ibid. (WA 32, 512, 10-15).

[48] LW 21, 261 (WA 32, 515, 33-37).

[49] LW 21, 257 (WA 32, 512, 30-32).

[50] LW 21, 262 (WA 32, 516, 23-26).

[51] LW 21, 258 (WA 32, 513, 30-37).

[52] The Book of Concord, 356.

[53] WA 32, 129, 9-10.

[54] E.g., WA 52, 490, 30-33.

[55] WA 52, 490, 11-12.

[56] WA 20, 515, 22-23.

[57] WA 20, 515, 25-29.

[58] WA 20, 514, 27-30 (rearranged).

[59] WA 20, 517, 31–518, 12.

[60] LW 51, 105 (WA 10/3, 343, 6-8).

[61] WA 20, 514, 21.

[62] WA 20, 512, 19-20.

[63] WA 20, 513, 21-23.

[64] WA 10/1/2, 406, 24-25.

[65] LW 51, 105 (WA 10/3, 342, 30-37).

[66] WA 10/1/2, 406, 31-33, 37-38.

[67] WA 45, 147, 32-33.

[68] WA 45, 146, 28-29.

[69] WA 45, 147, 11; 148, 25-30.

[70] WA 45, 149, 30-32.

[71] WA 45, 154, 15-19.

[72] WA 11, 189, 5 (trans.).

[73] WA 45, 148, 31-32. In the catechisms love of God appears as subordinate to obedience: "to love, praise, and thank him without ceasing, and, in short, to devote all these things to his service, as he has required and enjoined in the Ten Commandments" (Large Catechism, The Book of Concord, 412); "We should therefore love him, trust in him, and cheerfully do what he has commanded" (Small Catechism, The Book of Concord, 344).

[74] WA 17/2, 171, 14-15.

[75] WA 16, 127, 1.

[76] WA 10/1/2, 379, 12-15.

[77] Cf. WA 5, 120, 1-3.

[78] LW 5, 277 (WA 43, 619, 41).

[79] LW 7, 83 (WA 44, 361, 23-24).

[80] WA 34/1, 275, 19–276, 7.

[81] LW 21, 205 (WA 32, 469, 19-22).

[82] "Christianus sol peccator bleiben; foris non multum differt ab honestis civiliter," LW 26, 376 (WA 40/1, 573, 5).

[83] Cf. LW 21, 94 (WA 32, 378, 4-15; 379, 25-34).

[84]Cf. Peters 1990, 83–84.

[85]WA 17/2, 433, 20-24.

[86]WA 24, 52, 4.

[87]WA 34/2, 372, 19-21.

[88]WA 29, 267, 16-17.

[89]"Christianus ist ein fustuch Satanae . . ." WA 28, 192, 11.

[90]WA 1, 437, 1-2.

[91]LW 21, 245 (WA 32, 502, 38-39).

[92]LW 21, 137 (WA 32, 413, 21-22 [in parentheses in WA]).

[93]LW 52, 38 (WA 10/1/1, 137, 18–138, 3).

[94]"Sic vivimus, ut possumus," LW 26, 376 (WA 40/1, 573, 3-4).

[95]Cf. Schulz Frieder 1976; Wertelius 1970; Mikoteit 2005.

[96]WA 8, 360, 29.

[97]WA 30/1, 194, 9-11.

[98]LW 42, 114 (WA 2, 697, 3-5).

[99]WA 17/2, 203, 34-35.

[100]LW 21, 145 (WA 32, 419, 33-34).

[101]WA 34/1, 384, 1-2.

[102]WA 10/1/1, 372, 10-16.

[103]WA 8, 356, 1.

[104]LW 24, 87 (WA 45, 540, 15).

[105]LW 24, 89 (WA 45, 541, 18-31).

[106]WA 1, 181, 25-34; WA 10/1/2, 265, 37–266, 4.

[107]Cf. Schulz 1978, no. 56.

[108]Cf. Heiko A. Oberman, "Simul gemitus et raptus: Luther und die Mystik," 20–59 in Ivar Asheim, ed., Kirche, Mystik, Heiligung und das Natürliche bei Luther (Göttingen: Vandenhoeck & Ruprecht, 1967); zur Mühlen 1972; Gerhard Wehr, ed., Martin Luther: der Mystiker. Ausgewählte Texte (Munich: Kösel, 1999); Volker Leppin, "Mystik," in Handbuch (2005), 57–61.

[109]WA 34/1, 384, 11-14.

[110]WA 34/1, 382, 5-6.

[111]E.g., WA 24, 571–81.

[112]WA 10/1/1, 373, 5-8.

[113]LW 43, 198 (WA 38, 363, 11-16), "A Simple Way to Pray."

[114]Cf. Georg Nicolaus, Die pragmatische Theologie des Vaterunsers und ihre Rekonstruktion durch Martin Luther (Leipzig: Evangelische Verlagsanstalt, 2005). Especially instructive are chap. 3, on the Our Father "in concrete confrontations," chap. 4, "Our Father and God," and chap. 5, "Our Father and Eschatology."

[115]LW 42, 15–81 (WA 2, 80–130 [1519]).

[116]LW 21, 142–48 (WA 32, 420, 9–427, 40 [printed 1532]).

[117]LW 43, 187–211 (WA 38, 358–75 [1535]).

[118]Lutheran Hymnal 458 (EG 344).

[119]A brief, good interpretation of the Our Father before and behind is in WA 6, 21–22 (1519).

[120]LW 26, 385 (WA 40/1, 586, 20-21).

[121]WA 17/1, 430, 26-27.

[122]The Book of Concord, 346.

[123]WA 46, 345, 25. For Luther's interpretation of the Our Father in general cf. Martin Luther, Amen. Das Weitere findet sich. Gelebtes Vaterunser, selected and introduced by Hans-Martin Barth (Freiburg: Herder, 1989).

[124]LW 24, 385–87 (WA 46, 78, 15, 28-28; 79, 12-13, 26-27).

[125]LW 21, 142 (WA 32, 417, 25-28).

[126]LW 42, 25 (WA 2, 85, 21-24).

[127]LW 21, 143 (WA 32, 418, 4-8).

[128]Ibid. (WA 32, 418, 19).

129LW 43, 199 (WA 38, 364, 5-11).

130LW 21, 139 (WA 32, 415, 1-4).

131LW 43, 198 (WA 38, 362, 32-34).

132Cf. esp. Nicol 1984.

133WA.Br 1, 396, 15–397, 2, no. 175.

134LW 11, 513: "that I might conceive Your seed in the womb of my soul and nourish and cherish it there until it becomes a fetus of a good work, and this cherishing is meditating on it (ut conciperem semen tuum in utero anime mee et ibidem illud alerem ac foverem usque in foetum boni operis, quod fovere est ipsum meditari), WA 4, 376, 27-29.

135See "Oratio, meditation, tentatio: theological method" in chapter 15.

136Cf. Nicol 1984, 99.

137LW 35, 365; Nicol 1984, 175–82, interprets Luther's experience in the tower as occurring in meditation.

138AWA 2, 130, 26–131, 8.

139LW 43, 201 (WA 38, 366, 14-15).

140LW 43, 200-9, at 200 (WA 38, 364, 28–372, 28, at 365, 1-4).

141The Book of Concord, 359.

142Suda 2006, 28.

143Ibid.

144LW 21, 139 (WA 32, 415, 12-20).

145The Book of Concord, 352–53.

146LW 24, 387 (WA 46, 79, 29-30).

147The Book of Concord, 349.

148LW 35, 56, 65 (WA 2, 750, 23), referring to the Mass.

149LW 46, 171 (WA 30/2, 118, 17-19).

150WA 52, 24 (WA 10/1/2, 73, 28).

151Cf. Luther's interpretations of the third commandment of the Decalogue: Peters 1990, 162–79. It really cannot be said that Luther emphasizes "the special character and excellence of Sunday and its worship service," against Lexutt 2008, 120. Even the Sunday worship service is seen altogether in the context of the weekday worship services and everyday devotion.

152The Book of Concord, 377.

153WA 7, 204, 14-18.

154LW 43, 191–92 (WA 38, 359, 12-13; 359, 13).

155LW 21, 256 (WA 32, 511, 27-34).

156LW 21, 257 (WA 32, 512, 29-35).

157WA.Br 5, 136, 13–137, 15 (no. 1466).

158LW 49, 234, cogendi ad conciones, "compelled to attend" (WA.Br 5, 137, 15), no. 1467.

159Revealing in this respect is Peter Cornehl, "VIII. Evangelischer Gottesdienst von der Reformation bis zur Gegenwart," TRE 14, esp. 55–61.

160LW 44, 32 (WA 6, 211, 14-18, 23-25).

161WA 34/1, 382, 5.

162WA 30/1, 391, 5.

163LW 21, 159 (WA 32, 431, 6-19, 32).

164Ibid. (WA 32, 431, 32).

165Because of the misuse of fasting, Luther would rather see "a gorged pig" than "a saint like this, even if he fasts most strictly on bread and water," LW 21, 158 (WA 32, 430, 31-34).

166"Women in Protestantism had it worse. Luther took the nun as his wife and thus closed off the space for a celibate life," Catharina Halkes, Gott hat nicht nur starke Söhne. Grundzüge einer feministischen Theologie (Gütersloh: Gerd Mohn, 1980), 109. Mary Daly interprets it thus: "instead of having 'the nun' as a religious ideal, Protestant women have been offered the picture of 'the minister's wife.' Clearly, this has hardly been a liberating image," Beyond God the Father: Toward a Philosophy of Women's Liberation (Boston: Beacon, 1973; 1985), 85.

[167] Bockmühl 1987, 111.

[168] On this cf. Johannes Halkenhäuser, *Kirche und Kommunität. Geschichte und Auftrag der kommunitären Bewegung in den Kirchen der Reformation* (Paderborn: Schöningh, 1985).

[169] Cf. LW 44, 25 (WA 6, 206, 24-28); cf. Joest 1967, 248, 268, 323, 366–67.

[170] Bockmühl 1987, 515.

[171] LW 51, 64 (WA 19, 76, 11-15) (catechism). Cf. LW 51, 62 (WA 19, 73, 10-14; 74, 23-26), with reference to the German Mass.

[172] Cf. Barth, Hans-Martin 1990, 48–49.

[173] LW 21, 258 (WA 32, 513, 31-32).

[174] Cf. the Latin index of WA under *atheus*; Gottfried Maron, *Martin Luther und Epikur. Ein Beitrag zum Verständnis des alten Luther* (Göttingen: Vandenhoeck & Ruprecht, 1988); Barth, Hans-Martin 1971, 20 and *passim*.

[175] LW 37, 228 (WA 26, 339, 34-35).

[176] Bockmühl 1987, 84.

[177] See Andreas Lindemann, "Eschatologie III. Neues Testament," *RGG4* 2: 1553–60; also Berthold Lannert, *Die Wiederentdeckung der neutestamentlichen Eschatologie durch Johannes Weiss* (Tübingen: Francke, 1989).

[178] WA 53, 22–184; cf. Ole Modalsli, "Luther über die Letzten Dinge," in Junghans 1983, 1: 331–45; 2: 834–39, esp. 1: 333–34 and 2: 835–36.

[179] *The Book of Concord*, 346.

[180] LW 21, 248 (WA 32, 505, 5-10).

[181] LW 21, 282 (WA 32, 533, 24-30).

[182] In the Small Catechism, *The Book of Concord*, 354.

[183] WA 20, 597, 20-21.

[184] ". . . seeing that the whole world is evil and that among thousands there is scarcely a single true Christian," LW 45, 91 (WA 11, 251, 12-13). Cf. LW 44, 32 (WA 6, 211, 32): "there is not one in a thousand who does not put his confidence in the works"; WA 51, 411, 22-25: "a majority of our Christians are now non-Christians"; WA 38, 560, 39–561, 7: "If we were not to tolerate some weeds there would be no church." See also LW 12, 151 (WA 51, 270, 15-20); WA 16, 242, 19-27.

[185] LW 53, 64 (WA 19, 75, 5-8).

[186] LW 53, 64 (WA 19, 75, 20-21).

[187] LW 53, 63 (WA 19, 74, 25-27).

[188] LW 42, 44 (WA 2, 101, 31-32).

14

Intercalation: Time and Eternal Life

CONTEMPORARY QUESTIONS

There are few themes in Luther's theology in which the foreignness of his thought to today's current ideas seems clearer than in the case of eschatology. Here the crucial question is whether his message can have any future at all outside its eschatological frame. On the whole it will be impossible to return to his image of the world, despite massive efforts undertaken in that direction by proponents of creationism and North American dispensationalism. Our perception of the world today is shaped by the idea of a development that seems to have begun with something like a "Big Bang" and will end somewhere in nowhere. Of course, theology no longer has to contend with the concept of eternity of matter, as was the case in the time of Thomas Aquinas, for example. But the history of time as Stephen Hawking describes it,[1] or the end of humanity as Michel Foucault anticipates it,[2] are scarcely theological concepts that are easier to deal with. Can Luther's theology live with them?

Add to this the question of history. Luther saw God in it, but according to the common idea today it runs by itself. Marxism, with its idea of a comprehensible and goal-directed development, could still have produced a certain understanding of Luther's view. But in the meantime it has come to seem that history drives itself onward according to the laws of market economics—in view of the advancing exploitation of the world connected with globalization—possibly in the direction of catastrophe. Fears that can be compared to those of Luther's time are spreading: comprehensive crises in finance and economy, world-political power shifts, terrorism, the self-infantilization of human beings.

Individuals, insofar as they are aware of such processes, see themselves helplessly confronted with the demand to affirm their lives even without a future prospect and despite the blows one must necessarily expect, or else to end life at one's own hand. It is not the thought of death that evokes terror, but dying itself; that, however, can be ameliorated. Passing life on to others, begetting and bearing children and raising them at personal cost can appear, in view of such an absence of meaning, as an unnecessary requirement

377

imposed from outside. Those who cannot bear the absurd situation of their existence can find a broad spectrum of religious options open to them, competing with Christian hope if not trumping it with a certain kind of rationality or psychological plausibility. How can we even understand Luther's view of the "last things" in view of this situation, to say nothing of accepting it and letting it bear fruit?

Preconditions for Understanding

It is difficult to find an appropriate title for Luther's eschatology, because for him eschatology is not a separate topic. In the history of theology, research in eschatology began only at the end of the nineteenth century and then gained greatly in interest in the second half of the twentieth. But this could not be the source of Luther's primary controversy with his opponents. It is true that he took a critical stance toward the doctrine of the immortality of the soul, made a dogma in 1513[3] in opposition to the abandonment of belief in an afterlife in Italian humanism and the Renaissance. It was not that Luther simply denied the immortality of the soul, but the philosophical foundation for the assertion, namely that the soul is the human "form," was something he felt to be contrary to Scripture. In his view the primary objection was its lack of orientation to Christ's significance for humans' eternal salvation. In addition, his eschatology was altogether "present" in its character: his concern was with the present Christ, who through the justification of the ungodly helps to overcome death. On the other hand, Luther's theology was partly shaped by elements of late medieval apocalypticism, especially the then-current extreme fear of the last judgment. To that extent eschatology shaped the whole of the Reformer's theological thinking, even though he did not find it necessary to take a fixed position on individual questions about the "last things."[4] If we are to give an appropriate evaluation of what Luther had to say about the "last things," two prior observations are necessary:

Luther Shared the Apocalypticism of His Time

On the whole a general mood of catastrophe was rampant at the beginning of the sixteenth century, a "UFO atmosphere"; illustrated flyers that aroused great anxiety were in circulation, and there was much talk of prophecies and remarkable events. Comets appeared, as well as new and inexplicable diseases; syphilis played an ominous role.[5] Luther observed a "cracking" in the fabric of the world. He applied his observations of human aging to the history of the world: before someone dies "he first falls ill, takes a fever, plague: these are signs that he is passing away. So the world is also falling ill; the heavens, the earth, people, the sea, the stars, etc., all appear to be sick."[6] The world is growing old; creation says "I am tired."[7] But the sign that must really be taken seriously, showing that the world will soon end, is that word and sacraments are despised, that the Gospel of Jesus Christ is being obscured and darkened.[8]

It is true that Luther did not know what to do with the Revelation of John, since it had given rise to too much speculation: numerous interpreters have "brewed it into many stupid things out of their own heads."[9] But he then does succumb to individual suggestions for interpretation, though he does not maintain them consistently but rather shifts them in close connection with his own perceptions and experiences.[10] So he interpreted the Turkish advance against Vienna in 1529 in apocalyptic categories, with Daniel 7 and various passages from Revelation playing an important role.[11] The "thousand-year reign" is supposed to have begun at the time Revelation was written down, and thus is already at an end (Revelation 20). The devil is no longer bound; now, with the appearance of the Turks, the last day is at hand. Individual images in Revelation are interpreted in terms of the history of Christianity and thus show what hard times the church has always endured. This estimation is shown, for Luther, by the appearance of the Antichrist; as early as 1518 he sees the circumstances of the last day approaching.[12] According to one opinion found in Judaism[13] and reflected in the *Letter of Barnabas*, the world will last for six thousand years. Luther calculated in 1540 that in that year the number of the world's years had reached exactly 5,500. Hence the end of the world was now to be expected; the sixth millennium would not be fully completed.[14] Michael Stiefel, a friend of Luther's, expected the world to end on 19 October 1533 at eight in the morning. Luther did not care to participate in such calculations: "but about that day and hour no one knows . . ." (Matt 24:36). And yet the question of the end of the world occupied him a great deal, especially in his last years. This is more than obvious in his *supputatio annorum mundi*, "Reckoning of the Years of the World," in 1541. Here he developed a salvation-historical schema beginning with Adam and leading in a first period to Abraham, in a second to Pentecost, and in a third to the last day; each of these units lasted two thousand years. For Luther, history was now nearing its end.[15]

HERMENEUTICAL PROBLEMS

Although in principle Luther had no difficulty in understanding biblical statements literally, he was aware of the special hermeneutical task involved in interpreting eschatological passages.[16] He knew he had to distinguish between direct statements that must be taken literally, symbolic elements that are nevertheless easy to interpret, and finally those symbolic elements that really must be interpreted as allegorical and must not be read literally.[17] We need to distinguish among his own expressions in the same sense! Luther is capable of allegorizing unhesitatingly, for example when the Gospel of Luke says that signs will be seen in the sun (Luke 21:25-26); he is certain that this means that Christ ceases to shine and the Gospel will no longer be preached. Stars fall: faith declines to nothing. Reading Paul's apocalyptic sayings in 1 Thessalonians (4:15-17), the Reformer finds that these are paraphrases, allegorical words.[18] The trumpet of the judgment will not be one such as we know in this world, but God's trumpet.[19] It is clear to Luther that things in the eschaton are different from what we now see; consequently there is no need here for a special "demythologization." In order to perceive the world that will be infinitely more beautiful we will require organs of perception that are also infinitely clearer.[20] This also gives Luther the freedom to treat things in the realm of what our earthly eyes can see in very drastic and malleable fashion. He understands that all this is meant "figuratively": the comparisons are packing material, "paper bags,"[21] little cloths into which one can put what is said about the resurrection. Just as a child before its birth does not know what is to come, so also with us: "we know as little about eternal life as children in their mother's womb know about their arrival."[22] Luther can relativize the form of what can be said about eschatology because he is certain about the content of Christian expectation beyond death.

God's Working in Time and History

Luther did not really give any fundamental consideration to the nature of time like that of Augustine. His concern was with the "now,"[23] the present, specific, especially important moment in history. More important than his concrete historical speculations and judgments is the fact that he was certain of a beginning and end of history: time is limited both as regards individual human lives and for the history of humanity. Luther knows of a "life in which there is no time."[24] But for him time and beyond-time are not truly opposites, for when God, through grace, gives us the Holy Spirit we will "believe and live a godly life, both here in time and hereafter forever."[25]

God, who is above all things, acts in time and history, though in hidden ways.[26] In the course of history, especially in the church, God wears a mask.[27] The same is true of military conflicts: "whichever prince wins a battle, it is seen that God defeated the other by him."[28] God acts through us and we are "only his masks beneath which he hides himself and effects all in all."[29] History is God's card game.[30] We cannot see God's cards. He determines when this or that event is to take place. Only then can one do anything, "when the hour comes that God gives."[31] The decisive hour for Germany has dawned with the Reformation: "The time is at hand, do penance, Germany, at the hour of grace!"[32] God meets us graciously, and we should show gratitude.[33] It is in this context that the Reformer understands his own mission. He is to warn his country. God uses one great political power to destroy another; God will "also find a bullet for us Germans, to hit us and not miss."[34] What would the Reformer have to say to Germans today? Would he threaten them with Sharia law?

For Luther, on the one hand, the meaning of historical events can only be discovered after the fact.[35] On the other hand, he thinks he can discern God's judgment and grace in them.[36] He is quick to interpret negative events as God's punishment, but he also clearly sees God's kind intervention in historical happenings. Thomas Müntzer's dreadful end is for him a "public judgment of God," though he remains aware that God might not yet have spoken the last word about him.[37] But it is not only historical events that he traces to God's intervention; he does so also with regard to everyday doings: at Tambach he is delivered from the unbearable pains of his kidney stones, and he writes to his wife in relief that many prayers had brought it about "that God opened my bladder this night."[38] There is a time for everything, and one cannot dictate to God. When the "hour" comes, however, it cannot be prevented by anything. On the other hand, if "the hour has not come, one cannot accomplish anything, do what one will. If it is not meant to be, nothing will come of it."[39] God appoints the time, and this is especially true of our last hour.

Being Able to Die

In the late Middle Ages a whole genre of literature developed for pastoral care of the dying, an "art of dying," *ars moriendi*. The "block-letter books" in which they circulated were often provided with woodcuts in which the dying were vividly presented with the temptations they must contend with: demons held up their sins before them, but there was no dearth of angels to comfort the dying. Luther, in fact, was less interested in dying than in death itself, recognizing it as what constantly threatens Christians, together with sin and the devil, but also as the ultimate liberation from entrapment in sin and as what has been overcome in Jesus Christ.

Sin, death, and the devil

Death, for Luther, is of course not primarily a medical or biological problem. According to Paul, death is "the wages of sin" (Rom 6:23). Thus it represents a challenge not primarily to our somatic existence but to our awareness. Death confronts us with the law and makes it clear to us that life is over. No animal, no creature fears death as much as the human being does. Our fear of death shows that we are created for living.[40] Luther devises expressions that remind one of twentieth-century existentialism. His famous sermon on Invocavit Sunday in 1522, after his return from the Wartburg, begins with the words: "The summons of death comes to us all, and no one can die for another. Every one must fight his own battle with death by himself, alone. We can shout into another's ears, but every one must himself be prepared for the time of death, for I will not be with you then, nor you with me. Therefore every one must himself know and be armed with the chief things which concern a Christian."[41] Life, he says elsewhere, "is not a span of time but, as it were, a violent toss which catapults us into death."[42] There is never a time when death is not very close to us. Luther wrote an expansion of the hymn, going back to the eleventh century, "In the midst of earthly life snares of death surround us." He added: "In the midst of death's dark vale, powers of hell o'ertake us . . . In the midst of utter woe, all our sins oppress us. . . ."[43] Life, essentially, does not reveal itself going forward, but always and only in retrospect.[44] "Our years come to an end like a sigh" (Ps 90:9). Luther does not interpret "sigh" negatively, but uses it to shed light on the fleeting nature of life and the frailty of human speech: what human speech is substantially, no one knows—where does it come from, where is it going, what constitutes it? Is it anything more than a mere sound, an echo, a fleeting movement, and yet sent out irretrievably? The nightingale fills heaven and earth with her voice, yet "we do not know where the sound of its voice begins and where it ends. Our life is just like this."[45] But for human beings death is worse than for non-human creation. The grass grows and dies because of God's ordering of things, while "God nods his approval and laughs."[46] It is true that innocent creation does not suffer without pain; the hog squeals in fear when it is to be slaughtered; "a tree that is cut down does not tumble to the ground without a creaking noise."[47] But it is human beings who experience death most dreadfully: they are "not created for death."[48]

DEATH AS THE END OF RESISTANCE TO GOD

Knowing about the connection between sin, death, and the devil had an altogether positive side for Luther. With death, sin also reaches its limit and comes to its end. In death, finally, it comes to pass that "all sin ceases and the will of God is satisfied in all things to the fullest."[49] Now death becomes medicine for sin: "So it is a blessed thing" if we die willingly.[50] Death is taken into God's service and so must serve believers as well: for them it is nothing but "pure grace, indeed, a beginning of life," "a healing thing for all who believe in Christ, for it does nothing but corrupt and make nothing of everything born of Adam, so that Christ alone may remain in us."[51] In death, Christians attain to perfect divine worship.

Death, the little death

Fear of death should be disclosed as something the devil uses to terrify us—in God's service! Ultimately we must relate everything we encounter, both death and life, to God; God lives and rules "manifestly" beyond what we experience and what oppresses us.[52] Then we can judge our situation rightly. The Holy Spirit teaches us to "number" our days, and so we learn to pray Psalm 90: "Lord, you have been our dwelling place in all generations . . ."—the very beginning of this psalm "breathes life."[53]

Those who believe in the God of Jesus Christ know that they need no longer take death too seriously: it is only a "little death."[54] Death has no longer any claim on them and no power over them; it is a "painted death," a dummy. I am frightened when I see a snake, even a dead one, and even when I discover that it is no longer alive and cannot be dangerous to me. If we orient ourselves to our five senses "it hurts," and so we should listen to what Sacred Scripture tells us about our future.[55] If I let myself be guided by faith there will be for me only a "sweet" death.[56]

How did Luther imagine the time of transition between the moment of death and the last judgment? This was the traditional problem of an "intermediate state," which late medieval theology had sought to resolve in various ways: there was a special place where the Old Testament ancestors waited (the *limbus patrum*), and one for dead but unbaptized children (the *limbus infantium*). The Reformer did not engage in that kind of topology of the beyond. But he knew how to offer consolation to women "for whom childbirth has gone badly": the heartfelt cry and deep longing of the mother is heard by God; everything is possible for those who believe; God has not bound Godself so as to be unable to make us blessed without the sacrament, as God then hears our "unspoken yearning"; Luther recalls the widow of Nain (Luke 7:11-12), the daughter of the Canaanite woman (Matt 15:22-28), and the healing of the son of the royal official (John 4:47).[57] Perhaps this may be seen as an indirect contribution to the question of universal reconciliation.

Luther, like generations before him, was concerned with what happened to a person in the hour of death, where body and soul went. The idea that it went to purgatory Luther first understood in the sense of an experience of dread,[58] but then radically rejected.[59] On the one hand there is no basis for the doctrine of purgatory in Sacred Scripture; on the other hand it has produced so much superstition that it must be radically extirpated. The image of sleep seemed to Luther the most appropriate one: this comparison "satisfied" him.[60] No one knows how long he or she has slept; we do not hear the clock strike the hours.

This is the anthropological argument. On the other hand, Luther points to the categorical difference between our world and God's. The psalmist had already known that with God a thousand years are like a day (Ps 90:4): there is no time there; "before God everything happens at once. There is neither before nor after."[61] With God "everything is an eternal moment."[62] Eternity is not an extension of time but is athwart every moment of time.

In death, believers come definitively under Christ's protection: "as a mother lays her child in its cradle in the chamber, not so that it will die, but so that it will sleep and rest softly, so . . . all the souls of believers are placed in Christ's care."[63] Luther also "names" the place where dead believers rest: he does not work with the idea of an intermediate kingdom, an anteroom of hell; the proverbial "bosom of Abraham" is, he says, a symbol for God's word.[64] Here, that is, believers find their rest and their place: "The word is the place of infinite breadth. So the chambers of rest for souls are the word of God or the promises in which we sleep. . . . If we grasp this in faith and fall asleep in the word, the soul enters into an infinite space. . . ."[65] God's word is "the space of infinite fullness." When someone dies, the soul enters this infinite space; the promises are its resting place, and there it can sleep. God becomes our refuge, our resting place, our house—"our dwelling place in all generations" (Ps 90:1). God consoles believers: "My word is eternal and in this Word you are eternal."[66] For Luther, God's self and God's promise become one. Neither heaven nor earth will be our eternal dwelling, and not Paradise either, but "God himself."[67]

Preparation for Death?

Luther at first adopts the medieval tradition and speaks in the same vein of "preparing to die."[68] The basic idea is: deal with dying while you are still alive! When you find yourself in the last throes of death with all its assaults and fearful fantasies, it is too late. We should practice seeing things as they really should be seen—that is, in God's eyes—and as they really will be. As early as his lectures on Romans, Luther says that Paul "calls our attention away from a consideration of the present and from the essence and accidents of things" and teaches us to look to their future state.[69] A truly valid ontology comes not from human observation or empirical investigation, but is grasped in faith. What is real is what is true before God. Therefore you must "look at death while you are alive and see sin in the light of grace and hell in the light of heaven."[70] Word and sacrament will help you; Christ, the angels, and all the saints surround you!

But the later Luther did not address preparation for death directly. Those who live as justified are reconciled with God, the world, and themselves; they have no need to concern themselves constantly with death. They can soberly decide to what extent they should expose themselves to the danger of death in concrete situations. This question was very current during the plague of 1527; Luther here calmly discusses to what degree one should avoid the danger of death or expose oneself to it for the sake of suffering fellow human beings.[71] The point is to oppose death, because that is the will of God. Pastoral care is part of that resistance. The "communion of saints" described in a sermon of 1519 does not lose its meaning for Luther in later years, but it is transformed into a communion of prayer and advocacy, of those who stand in solidarity and mutual support, and finally the communion of believers in which each consoles the others, in sisterly and brotherly fashion, with the word of God. The sacrament, which is accorded special attention in 1519, is questioned even then as to what promise it offers to the dying. In Luther's later writings the word of God becomes so much more weighty that the sacrament fades into the background as mere assistance. In contrast to our own perceptions today, then, for Luther the question of "dying" is not central; the problem of death is not reduced to the phenomenon of dying. The challenge of death is indeed reproduced in our fear of dying, but that is not even remotely an adequate account of the whole. That is: the phenomenon "death" cannot be appropriately discussed if one neglects the problem of human identity and the responsibility connected with it and avoids the question of an ultimate horizon of meaning and fulfillment. The human situation must be delivered from death's dominance if steps toward freedom are to be made possible in this regard.

RESURRECTION

Luther is more interested in the resurrection and the salvation of individual believers than in the fate of humanity or the future of the universe. Even the question of judgment was at first for him of lesser interest because it was, so to speak, put to rest by justification. The relationship among the individual elements of Christian eschatology—the point of death, resurrection, the last day, judgment—represented no problem for Luther. He had no trouble dealing with different and even contradictory ideas and images. Faith in God's promise relativizes everything.

RAISING OF THE DEAD

People of the late Middle Ages seem to have made no clear distinction between the idea of a resurrection and that of the immortality of the soul. It is true that in the sixteenth century the hope for eternal life had also lost its sustaining value for many; jokes were made about it by freethinking cardinals in Renaissance Italy. This explains why on the eve of the Reformation, as we have already noted, the doctrine of the immortality of the soul had to be pointedly made into a dogma, at the beginning of the Fifth Lateran Council in 1513.[72] That the soul could survive alone, however, seemed to Luther a foolish idea: this "distinction is rubbish. I will attack it." One must say: "'The whole Abraham, the whole man, shall live!'"[73] Thus people retain the gender identities that belong to them through creation;[74] it is the earthly body that has received baptism and enjoyed the Lord's Supper, that will become a new, transformed spiritual body united with the soul.[75] The pre-Reformation Easter hymn also fully expresses Luther's conviction: "Christ is arisen from the grave's dark prison. We now rejoice with gladness; Christ will end all sadness."[76] Christ has become a bridge for us, bearing us across the abyss of death.[77] Through baptism and eucharist we belong to him; we are incorporated into him. He has already broken the boundary of death; the head is already through and will draw the members with it. In relation to the one who fills heaven and earth the human being is only a *punctulus*, a little drop; it is merely the husk that needs to rise, for the kernel is already in eternal life. With Jesus' resurrection, mine has already begun.[78] The beginning of the new life thus occurs this side of the bounds of death. Both beyond and on this side of death, all that matters is that God acts on the human being and the human lets God act: "it is our function passively to receive God and His working within us."[79] As an embryo in the womb lets itself be "made" by God, so we hold still for God.[80] Gerhard Ebeling interprets: "The being of the human" is "God's acting on him."[81] The same is true on both sides of death! God remains the Creator out of nothing, and this is no less true of the overcoming of death than of the justification of the ungodly. The earthly human being is for the Creator nothing but "the simple material of God for the form of his future life."[82] This may be for human beings as it is with a piece of wood being worked by an artist. It wants to protest loudly: "Stop, stop, you are ruining me!" But that is just how the new thing comes to be.[83] Luther has many images for this process. In death the *mortificatio*, the killing of the old human, reaches its goal; in the resurrection the new and everlasting life is accomplished. The Reformer does not hesitate to describe it, and yet in doing so he transcends the level of human description: we will "have so much in God that no food, no drink, no malmsey can be so precious. . . . In short, in place of whatever we must now derive from all creatures here and there singly and piecemeal—although this, too, comes from Him and is given by Him—we shall have Him directly. . . ."[84]

Thus resurrection means renewal and transformation; it applies to the individual and to the whole creation. Luther paints it broadly: the sun will be seven times brighter and our eyes a hundred thousand times sharper; the whole world will be transfigured and a hundred thousand times more glorious than it is now.[85] Aging will cease, and the nursing of infants as well; Luther provides a wealth of vivid detail.

The outlook toward the new and the look back to the old creation seem to touch in this instance; the third and the first articles of faith come together. What we see in creatures witnesses—in its preliminary way—to future glory. Luther's doctrine of creation, as Ulrich Asendorf accurately formulates it, is "eschatologically wrapped, so to speak." Luther does not see creation as it is; such a view would most certainly lead to different conclusions! Instead, he sees through it "to the future form of all things."[86] For him, the resurrection of the dead is painted in every creature, in the grain, in the trees. In creation one can also read how life is only made possible by the passage through death. Look at a seed grain, which appears to rot in the earth, "is a little wet thing, gets a little tail"—who could guess that barley could come of that, and even beer?![87]

So Luther can confidently surrender himself to death as well. In Eisleben, on his last journey, a few days before his death, he said in a mood of black humor: "when I get home to Wittenberg again, I will lie down in my coffin and give the worms a fat doctor to feast on."[88] Then he will sleep until Christ comes "and knocks on my little tomb and says: Get up, Dr. Martinus, get up! Then in an instant I will rise and will be happy with him forever."[89] There is really no place left for a last judgment in this kind of direct expectation and unshakable awareness of salvation. But Luther can also express his hope by speaking about the last day.

THE LAST JUDGMENT

The idea of judgment has clearly receded. In the Small Catechism the last judgment is passed over with only an indirect reference: Christ will, on the last day, "raise me and all the dead" and "will grant eternal life to me and to all who believe in Christ."[90] From many points of view Luther is, in modern terms, an advocate of "present eschatology." In Christ, believers already have the judgment behind them. "Those who believe in him are not condemned." (John 3:18).[91]

On the other hand, Luther had no difficulty with the idea that those who do not believe and remain unwilling to repent are destined for eternal punishment. In his confession of 1528 he formulates, with the tradition, that "the godly will live eternally with Christ and the wicked will perish eternally with the devil and his angels."[92] Luther did not teach universal salvation. He paints hell in late medieval colors as fire in which there is not "a little drop of water,"[93] and yet as something that can no longer threaten those who believe. The last day will bring the final victory over the devil and all the ungodly.[94] The return of Christ will bring about the final division. However, the Reformer did address the question of universal salvation.[95] He mentions Origen's *apokatastasis* doctrine and is able to name biblical passages that may be adduced in its support. But if Christ is the ladder to the heavenly Father, how can we ignore him and bypass him and presume to ascend to heaven by our own reason?[96] The statement of Scripture, he says, is clear. When it says in 1 Timothy that God desires all to be saved (1 Tim 2:4), that only says that we should pray for all and preach to all. However, Luther does admit that God may give faith to someone who is dying, or even after death, and so save that person. "No one, however, can prove that he does do this."[97] Luther is not fully consistent on this question either, as is hinted in his consolation to mothers whose children could not be baptized before death;[98] he could hope that even Cicero might be saved.[99] Moreover, how can we understand a rejection of universal salvation if hell is the place to which Christ descended, to the "last and utmost depth," deeper than anyone else?[100]

Ultimately Luther had to face the fact that there are quite a few passages in Scripture that speak of "reward." How does that relate to the doctrine of justification? It is striking that in the second half of his life Luther again begins to speak more frequently of judgment, though it is not a judgment "according" to works, but "on" works. Precisely because for him faith is not to be regarded as requiring works, the latter have their own value independent of faith. Luther can thus speak unconcernedly of a reward for the faithful. Thinking of reward is said to be characteristic of human beings, since they consider the future and are not fulfilled, as animals are, in the present. Works are pleasing to God, who affirms them. In them we have confidence and reputation "before God," though not in relation to God![101] In a sermon on the parable of the judgment (Matt 25:31-46), Luther explains: this gospel speaks of mere works, because "one must also preach about good works. That is simply a good thing."[102] In his interpretation of the Sermon on the Mount he adds some pages of his own devoted to the distinction between "grace and merit."[103] There can be no merit before God, but grace is promised to believers as their reward. As regards faith all are equal, and none is less holy than Peter or Paul. But their faith bears fruit in different ways. It could be given to a believer that her or his prayer benefits an entire country, keeping it free of war and pestilence. Others are gifted in different ways. Moreover, a Christian routinely has much to suffer and endure. But we should not think that our "works, troubles, and sorrows have been lost and forgotten."[104] All the stars are in the heavens, but they have different luminosity and clarity (cf. 1 Cor 15:41); therefore, for example, Paul will be "more brilliant, more bright and clear than others."[105] Life, in the whole sum of its everyday minutiae, will be valued and purified at the last judgment.

THE DEAR LAST DAY

The Reformer interprets the last day on the one hand in terms of salvation history, on the other hand existentially, without attempting to relate the two or create a seamless joining.

Luther obviously takes the salvation-historical interpretation from the biblical witness. Christ came bodily in his birth, he daily "comes into our heart through the gospel," but that cannot be perceived with earthly eyes. At the end of days Christ will show himself publicly and irrefutably.[106] This later became the doctrine of Christ's threefold advent. For Luther, the salvation-historical and existential interpretations of the last day could shift immediately into one another: "you should be prepared for the Last Day, for it will come soon enough for everyone after his death. Then he will say: 'Behold, I died only a short time ago!'"[107] But for Luther the existential interpretation of the last day is foremost. It is not primarily the day of wrath, *dies irae*, but the day of redemption, which one may await with uplifted head (Luke 21:28). Then we will at last be free from sin. Luther concludes from this that no one is better prepared for the last day than the one who desires to be freed from his or her sins. At that point both preaching and faith will come to an end. Then we will "be blessed forever with the dear angels who behold God's face, something we have here only in hearing and faith. Therefore this, a kingdom of the word and faith, will become another kingdom where we will no longer hear and believe, but see God the Father and Christ before our eyes. . . ."[108] Therefore Luther speaks of the "dear last day," which he awaits with longing and knows to be near. The question about the time of the end he answers "with a 'soon' whose eager anticipation can scarcely be surpassed."[109] He expresses his longing especially in his letters: "Come, dear last day, Amen."[110] One should live in expectation! We should understand what awaits us; if only our hearts could grasp that "the Day of Judgment will be a time of rejoicing for you . . . since condemnation and the terrible judgment are gone."[111] Without denying human responsibility in earthly things, Luther advises that we should apply ourselves to the demands of the passing world only, so to speak, with the left hand and half-heartedly, while believing and confidently expecting "that" day.[112] For then God will be all in all.[113] The copyist taking down Luther's sermon inserted an "etc." here, even though then there will be no more "etcetera."

CRITICAL EVALUATION

Luther's strangeness to us is more than clear in his eschatological writings in particular. Those who work with him today are often tempted to see and regard him as a direct conversation partner, but they should consider what a completely different worldview the Reformer lived with. It was simply a matter of course that a narrow span of time had been planned for the world: it had been created six thousand years before and its time seemed now to be running out. The earth was the center of the universe and humans, insofar as anyone was aware, were the center of the world. Salvation history was regarded as the center of world history; cultural spheres and even non-Christian religions were for the people of the time—and so for Luther—"marginal phenomena" in a twofold sense of the word. Given all that, it continues to astonish us how directly the Reformer is still able to address today's readers. Despite that, of course, a good many questions remain open.

Entanglement in contemporary apocalyptic ideas?

The significance of apocalyptic for Luther is variously interpreted, but it is undisputed that he sometimes allowed himself to be infected by panics over comets and other fears of his time. He recognized much in late medieval piety as superstition, but he only reduced superstition to the measure already present in the Bible. He did not question the ideas about demons that had made their way into the New Testament. He undoubtedly saw his opponents and his own mission in eschatological perspective. In light of this, to what extent can his eschatological ideas and statements still claim validity today?

Undoubtedly, Luther's theology contains individual moments of "demythologization." Heaven, for him, is not the place where the clouds float by or the realm of the spheres; where a person believes, there is God's realm. Hell is not a place of tortures that one can vividly imagine with the aid of sick fantasy; what "hell" means can be intimated from the tortures of a bad conscience.[114] Christ experienced the "descent into hell" in his fears on the cross. Here we can observe theological criteria that must also be applied hermeneutically in reading Luther.

Luther reveals a certain scent for the distinction between apocalyptic and eschatology. He distinguishes at least in preliminary fashion between the image and the thing. What is important is not the apocalyptic scenario but the eschatological expectation that may be expressed there. I therefore do not consider it appropriate to speak of an "evangelical apocalyptic" or "Lutheran apocalyptic."[115] Above all, the future is seen entirely in the perspective of the present, and the present, in turn, from the perspective of the future. The accent lies on justification here and not on blessedness beyond death, on the slaying and renewal of the human being today and not on his or her physical death, on new life in the present and not on any kind of speculations about the future.

Nevertheless, Luther's theology is a reminder that Christian faith requires, and offers, a future perspective extending beyond the bounds of death.

Otherwise it would not exhaust its potential. Would it not likewise be robbed of its ultimate basis?

MEDIEVAL ALIENATION FROM THE PRESENT WORLD?

Luther speaks a great deal about the new life, but—as regards the earthly realm—this consists essentially of the need for me to see through it, see it differently, and not that I should change it. Luther's ethics are not organized in terms of eschatology, but on the basis of creation and redemption. The arrangements seem to be established in advance; within their limits I, as a Christian, bring into action the love that grows out of my faith.[116] The renewal that comes from assurance of eternal salvation is the property of the individual; it is not about the renewal of structures, certainly not about transforming the world. Here Calvin is by far the more modern reformer! Luther's piety seems to correspond more closely to that of eastern Orthodoxy than to Calvin or even a secularized Calvinism. Concrete social action is not outside Luther's horizon, but it is always something produced by the individual transformed in faith: a Christian, "as a new man," should see through superficial reality, have "far different, even completely opposite thoughts," and thereby be able to "boast and glory." When things go ill with them, Christians should be aware that even in prison they have a "mighty prince and lord," and on their sickbeds they are "superlatively strong." One should keep clearly in mind "that he only becomes a new, living man when he dies here and now," and that here is "a prelude of the life to come," which can only be grasped in its whole and novel quality in faith.[117] Undoubtedly Luther himself actively intervened in his world and changed it; it would seem that his eschatology did not inspire him to that activity, but at least it did not put on the brakes! The question remains whether that is sufficient in face of the New Testament view of hope.

OPEN THEOLOGICAL QUESTIONS

Luther's eschatology concentrated powerfully on the problem of resurrection and the eternal destiny of the individual.[118] Let me emphasize just three of the problem areas that remain insufficiently clarified:

What about the eschatological future of the church? That was not a topic of interest to Luther. The multitude of the perfect was not the center of interest for him. When God becomes all in all, the question of the "church" takes care of itself. But if we understand the church, as Luther himself was inclined to do, not as an earthly institution but as the Body of Christ, we open up additional angles of vision that he himself did not consider. Then the institution of the church on earth, with its whole history up to the last day, must be evaluated in terms of eschatology. Its task and its nature can then not be extinguished at the end of the world.

What about the future of the universe? Luther did not see it as the result of an organic development but as the consequence of a rupture. The question of how the identity of individual believers or of "the world" could be thought of beyond that rupture did not concern him. He took Paul's advice not to think too much about "how this will happen," but simply to be content to "leave that to God."[119] Insofar as he did seek an answer he found it in his faith in God as the Creator. Identity can only be grounded in God and God's word. The relationship God–human or God's glory–human salvation is so much in the foreground that the question of the "destiny" of creation recedes. As his interpretation of the relevant passage in Romans (Rom 8:19-22) shows, he certainly knows how to say something about the promise bestowed on creation as well.[120] He describes in vivid imagery how this promise will be fulfilled, but then retracts that through his idea of a new creation *ex nihilo*. Some clarification is needed here.

Next: what about *apokatastasis*, the "bringing back of all things"? Luther on the one hand seems to have desired it deeply, but on the other hand he wanted to see the destruction of his opponents. In any case, though he could not teach it on the basis of the biblical witness, he did not altogether exclude it. On the whole it sufficed for him to feel sure of the promise for believers and invite to faith in those promises. His christocentrically designed theology could only work consistently if all those who did not come to this center in Christ must be regarded as thereby excluded. He consoled himself that in the light of God's eternal glory all questions and problems regarding the predestination of humans to salvation or damnation would be resolved. Today the issue would be to demonstrate in light of the Gospel that Luther's exclusive concept of Christ is inclusive, and to give reasons for that: Christ alone, and at the same time Christ for all, given for the life of the world.[121] Exclusive inclusivity could be the direction a resolution might take. The anchoring of Christology in a comprehensive and integrative Trinitarian thought ought to open some angles of vision that could shed more light.

Finally, in light of the whole of the Reformer's theological thought the question arises: does the message of justification ultimately rest solely on the expectation of the last judgment? Does it collapse without the biblical view of the future? What can it say to people who do not live within an eschatological horizon shaped by traditional Christianity? This could correspond to the historical situation that caused the young Luther to begin to look for a gracious God in the face of the threat of God's judgment he felt weighing on him, and so to come upon Paul's statements about the justification of sinners. But it seems to me that at the end of his theological and spiritual development things were quite the opposite: it was not eschatology that conditioned the theology of justification, but the assurance of justification that shaped Luther's eschatology[122] and enabled him even to allow contradictions in its presentation without finding them problematic. It is precisely in the founding of his eschatological hope in the assurance of justification that his way of dealing with the "last things" can link to today. Many questions seem to remain open, but not the answer that relativizes all of them.

The Lutheran response

We cannot say that Luther was "uninterested in a development of material statements about future perfection."[123] Such a lack of interest would not be sustainable today either. Christians should know why they do not share Islam's ideas of Paradise, why they do not expect reincarnation, and how their faith goes beyond Buddhist ideas of Nirvana. A reference to the sustaining power of faith during our life on earth is also inadequate consolation at the grave. The Reformer knew a way that neither involved itself in wild fantasies nor led into a night that offered no orientation.

He pled for a faith that sees through the superficial reality of the here and now. Experience will follow faith, but first we have to believe against experience—and "feel what we do not feel."[124] We should see the world differently from how it presents itself to our earthly eyes: "See, that is the way and the nature of faith!"[125] What is a farmer thinking while sowing seed? He or she does not "dwell on the kernels which fall into the ground to rot," but "looks forward to and awaits the coming summer. . . ."[126] So we should "have a cloak placed around [our heads]" and allow ourselves to be led to the one in whom we believe.[127] Luther turns Feuerbach's suspicion of projection back on him: we see earthly reality as if through a painted glass, but eternal life "with clear, open eyes."[128] This, of course, does not change his estimation of life on earth. "We are now in the dawn of the future life, for we begin again to acquire the knowledge of creatures we have lost through Adam's fall. Now we see the creatures rightly . . ." We begin to "recognize" God's glorious works and miracles "in the little flowers, when we think how omnipotent and kind God is. . . ."[129] Knowledge of eschatology does not consist of information about the post-mortal world, but unlocks the present and thus develops an anticipatory power.[130] "It must all be left behind, and we must freely, boldly, and with sure confidence take the leap into God. That's what he wants of us."[131] On "that day" we will then mock ourselves: "Phooey on you, that you were not bold" in believing in Christ.[132]

So Luther knows, when it comes to dying, how to place his soul in Christ's hand rather than his own; otherwise the devil would long ago have torn it away as a vulture seizes chicks.[133] In his early sermon on preparing to die he had insisted: "Seek yourself only in Christ and not in yourself and you will find yourself in him eternally."[134] Faith in God who is gracious in Christ brings everything with it[135]—and at the same time it lets go of "all visible things in the world, including the self"; it surrenders itself entirely and remains only "in the word of God."[136] It gives its whole self away, and in just that way it is sustained.

NOTES

[1] Stephen W. Hawking, *A Brief History of Time: From the Big Bang to Black Holes* (Toronto, et al.: Bantam Books, 1988).

[2] Michel Foucault, *Von der Subversion des Wissens* (Munich: Hansser, 1974), 106, would "certainly wager that the human being will vanish like a face in the sand of the seashore."

[3] Cf. Lateran Council V, bull "Apostolici regiminis," DS 1440–41 (old numbering 738).

[4] Cf. Asendorf 1967; Ole Modalsli, "Luther über die letzten Dinge," in Junghans 1983, 1: 331–45; Hans-Martin Barth, "Leben und Sterben können. Brechungen der spätmittelalterlichen 'ars moriendi' in der Theologie Martin Luthers," 45–66 in Harald Wagner, ed., *Ars moriendi* (Freiburg: Herder, 1989); Notger Slenczka, "II.9. Christliche Hoffnung," 435–43 in *Handbuch* 2005.

[5] WA 10/1/2, 104, 2–105, 12 (1522).

[6] WA 37, 204, 9-13 (Latin parts translated by author).

[7] WA 32, 230, 9.

[8] Kastning 2008 attempts to interpret Luther's theology in terms of an opposition he thinks he sees in the Reformer's thought between a "time of wrath" and a "time of grace." God, he says, is putting "the river of history . . . in tension between self-withdrawal and self-appearing" of his word (p. 385). Already, in view of his perception of the rule of the Antichrist, Luther is said to have feared the beginning of the "time of wrath" (pp. 272ff.); at the end of time, according to Luther, there will be a silencing of the word of God (p. 390). The Reformer is said to see "no teleological connection between wrath and grace" (p. 365). This interpretation shifts the Christ event to the margins of Luther's theology and forces it into the coordinates of wrath and grace; as a result, the connection between the two is lost. Even though Luther knows that God can withdraw and conceal himself (cf. p. 304, and "The Hidden God" in chapter 8 above), he does not expect the end of all things to be "the day of the irreversible presence of the time of wrath" (p. 390).

[9] LW 35, 400 (WA.DB 7, 408, 14-15).

[10] Cf. esp. the careful study by Hans-Ulrich Hofmann, *Luther und die Johannes-Apokalypse* (Tübingen: Mohr, 1982).

[11] Ibid., 371–82.

[12] WA.Br 2, 211, 34-35.

[13] Cf. b. *Sanh.* 97a; *Abod. Zar.* 9a; *Barn.* 15:4-9

[14] WA 53, 171.

[15] WA 53, 28–182. Cf. Kastning 2008, 18. To that extent suggestions about Luther's "self-stylization" and his "creation of his own *memoria*" (Leppin 2006, e.g., 80, 339) lack any basis.

[16] On this see esp. Hofmann 1982, 45–72; 239–335.

[17] LW 35, 400 (WA.DB 7, 408, 4-30).

[18] "Das ist periphrasis," LW 51, 252 (WA 36, 266, 4–267, 4); "Das sind verba Allegorica," LW 51, 253 (WA 36, 268, 1).

[19] LW 51, 253 (WA 36, 268, 21).

[20] Cf. WA 45, 231, 22-23; WA 34/2, 126, 6-10.

[21] Luther says "scharnitzel," LW 28, 175 (WA 36, 640, 10).

[22] WA.TR 3, 276, 26-27 (no. 3339).

[23] "We have, of all time, only the *now* . . . [de omni tempore nihil habemus, quam quod NUNC est]," LW 13, 300–1 (WA 40/3, 525, 15). For Luther's understanding of history cf. esp. Kastning 2008.

[24]". . . ex tempore in talem vitam, in qua nullum est tempus," LW 13, 99 (WA 40/3, 522, 28), on Ps 90:4.

[25] *The Book of Concord*, 346.

[26]Cf. Zahrnt 1952; Kastning 2008, 199–205, and *passim*.

[27]LW 45, 331 (WA 15, 373, 7-17).

[28]LW 21, 340 (WA 7, 586, 1-2).

[29]WA 23, 8, 36-37.

[30]WA.TR 6, 32, 25-29 (No. 6545).

[31]LW 21, 207–8 (WA 32, 471, 9-10).

[32]"Poenitentiam age, Germania, tempore gratiae! It is time!" WA.TR 4, 134, 40-41 (No. 4096).

[33]LW 50, 58 (WA.Br 6, 326, 19-21, No. 1943).

[34]LW 14, 74 (WA 31/1, 127, 4-7). Cf. "God's 'masks' in creation and history" in chapter 8. Cf. "God's 'masks' in creation and history" in chapter 8.

[35]". . . when I have done it you will see, and not before," WA.TR 5, 221, 29-33 (No. 5536).

[36]WA 50, 385, 15-17.

[37]Cf. WA 18, 373, 20-37; 367, 1-21.

[38]LW 50, 167 (WA.Br 8, 51, 11-15, No. 3140).

[39]WA.DB 10/2, 115 (on Qoh 3:9).

[40]Cf. WA 39/2, 367, 1-24.

[41]LW 51, 70 (WA 10/3, 1, 7–2, 2).

[42]"Significat enim non cursum, sed ceu impetuosum iactum esse, quo ad mortem rapimur," LW 13, 100 (WA 40/3, 523, 23-25).

[43]LH 518, 1–3 (EG 518, 1–3).

[44]LW 13, 118 (WA 40/3, 555, 23-25). In what follows I am adapting material from my essay, "Leben und Sterben können. Brechungen der spätmittelalterlichen 'ars moriendi' in der Theologie Martin Luthers," 45–66 in Harald Wagner, ed., *Ars moriendi. Erwägungen zur Kunst des Sterbens* (Freiburg: Herder, 1989).

[45]LW 13, 120 (WA 40/3, 557, 11-26; 558, 21-23).

[46]"Deo favente et ridente," LW 13, 106 (WA 40/3, 536, 15).

[47]LW 13, 107 (WA 40/3, 537, 11-13).

[48]". . . homo . . . talis creatura, quae . . . non est creata ad moriendum," LW 13, 94 (WA 40/3, 513, 24).

[49]WA 17/2, 13, 25-26.

[50]WA 10/3, 76, 1-3.

[51]WA 24, 112, 31-32; WA 1, 188, 20-22.

[52]Cf. LW 13, 117, 136 (WA 40/3, 547, 14-17; 570, 20-23).

[53]LW 13, 83 (WA 40/3, 496, 24-27).

[54]WA 22, 100, 13-14.

[55]Cf. WA 22, 100, 2; LW 51, 240 (WA 36, 250, 16-17).

[56]Cf. WA 22, 100, 7-8; 102, 14.

[57]LW 43, 247–50 (WA 53, 205–8).

[58]Cf. LW 31, 126 (WA 1, 555, 26–559, 5).

[59]LW 34, 54 (WA 30/2, 267–90), in the list of "things which have been practice and custom in the pretended church."

[60]WA 43, 360, 37.

[61]WA 12, 596, 30-31.

[62]WA 10/3, 194, 11-12.

[63]WA 43, 360, 42–361, 3.

[64]Cf. Asendorf 1967, 292.

[65]WA 43, 361, 12-16.

[66]LW 14, 134–35 (WA 31/1, 456, 8).

[67]LW 13, 85 (WA 40/3, 498, 24-26).

[68] "A Sermon on Preparing to Die" (1519), LW 42, 95–115 (WA 2, 685–97).

[69] LW 25, 360 (WA 56, 371, 3-6).

[70] LW 42, 103 (WA 2, 688, 35-36).

[71] "Whether One May Flee From a Deadly Plague" (1527), LW 43, 113–18 (WA 23, 339–79).

[72] Cf. n. 3 above.

[73] LW 54, 447 (WA.TR 5, 219, 11-14). For Luther, of course, this cannot be about an immortality inherent in humanity. Rather, the resurrection of believers rests on the beginning made in the raising of Jesus and revealing its effects in the lives of believers. Christ's resurrection was for our benefit: Christ has crept out of the hole in which he had been buried; he has torn open the belly of death and sits at the right hand of God: that is our consolation (LW 28, 108 [WA 36, 543, 15–551, 3]).

[74] "Persons, such as man and woman, will remain, and also the entire human race as it was created," though without the needs of natural human beings. "Everybody will be a perfect human being and have all he needs in God," needing neither father nor mother nor an earthly lord or servant, not even a preacher (LW 28, 143 [WA 36, 595, 24-30]).

[75] LW 28, 190 (WA 36, 666, 35–667, 17).

[76] LH 187; EG 99.

[77] Cf. LW 24, 41–45, esp. 42 (WA 45, 489, 3–507, 36, esp. 498, 28–499, 8).

[78] WA 36, 161, 32–162, 8-9.

[79] LW 27, 294, ". . . nostrum agere est pati Deum in nobis operantem" (WA 2, 539, 5).

[80] WA 8, 217, 1-13 (on Ps 37:7).

[81] Ebeling 1989, 487.

[82] LW 34, 139, "The Disputation Concerning Man" (1536): "Quare homo huius vitae est pura materia Dei ad futurae formae suae formam."

[83] WA 4, 638, 1-10.

[84] LW 28, 142 (WA 36, 593, 32–594, 18).

[85] WA 34/2, 126, 33-34.

[86] Asendorf 1988, 146.

[87] Cf. LW 28, 186 [where this passage is omitted]; (WA 36, 655, 1-4).

[88] Quoted from Oberman 1981a, 11–16, at 13; English, 3–8, at 5.

[89] WA 37, 151, 9-10.

[90] The Book of Concord, 345.

[91] LW 22, 356 (WA 47, 102, 20-33).

[92] LW 37, 372 (WA 26, 509, 13-14).

[93] LW 28, 144; cf. 148 (WA 36, 596, 36–597, 13); cf. WA 36, 616, 20-23.

[94] Cf. WA 49, 741, 5-7.

[95] LW 43, 47–55 (WA 10/2, 322–26), a 1522 letter to Hans von Rechenberg on the question whether someone who died without faith might be saved.

[96] Cf. LW 43, 55 (WA 10/2, 326, 2-5).

[97] LW 43, 54 (WA 10/2, 325, 5-6).

[98] See B.12.4.3 above.

[99] Cf. Reinhuber 2000, 287–88, and "Mission" in chapter 12.

[100] Cf. WA 23, 702, 15–703, 1. Bernhard Brons suggests that perhaps here "only" the "forecourts of hell," so to speak, could be meant.

[101] WA 36, 454, 9–455, 3.

[102] WA 45, 324, 23-24.

[103] LW 21, 285–94 (WA 32, 535, 29–544, 7).

[104] LW 21, 291 (WA 32, 541, 10-11).

[105] LW 21, 293 (WA 32, 543, 7-8); cf. LW 28, 226–27 (WA 36, 635, 26–636, 20), and the argumentation in the Apology, The Book of Concord, 133 (appealing to 1 Cor 3:8).

[106] LW 51, 114 (WA 10/3, 349, 22-23); WA 10/1/1, 44, 2-20.

[107] LW 30, 196–97 (WA 14, 71, 4-5, 21).

[108] WA 49, 573, 30-34.

[109]Schwambach 2004, 108.

[110]LW 50, 219 (WA.Br 9, 175, 17): "Come, day. Amen." We customarily insert the missing "dear last" here. Strictly speaking it can mean the day of our hour of death or the bright day of eternity. But there are related formulations: "Veni, veni, Domine Iesu, veni. Tempus est faciendi, Amen" (Come, come, Lord Jesus. The time is fulfilled. Amen.), WA.Br 10, 525, 22-23.

[111]LW 22, 384 (WA 47, 102, 28-30).

[112]Cf. WA 36, 379, 27-28.

[113]LW 28, 124 (WA 36, 595, 9).

[114]Cf. WA 10/3, 192, 15-18; LW 8, 25 (WA 44, 617, 27-32); LW 19, 72 (WA 19, 225, 12–226, 5). Certainly this did not mean that in Luther's opinion there was no such thing as eternal damnation.

[115]Against Korsch 2007, 133, 143, who surprisingly avoids the concept of "eschatology" here and says nothing about Luther's ideas of resurrection, judgment, and eternal life.

[116]Cf. The Book of Concord, 38 (CA XVI, 5): ". . . manifest Christian love and genuine good works in his station of life" (in talibus ordinationibus exercere caritatem).

[117]LW 51, 244 (WA 36, 256, 18-29).

[118]On this cf. esp. the series of sermons on 1 Corinthians 15, LW 28, 57–213 (WA 36, 478–696), as well as Wiemer 2003, who, however, would like to demonstrate that Luther's whole theology is related to the idea of eternal perfection.

[119]LW 28, 175 (WA 36, 647, 17-19).

[120]Cf. LW 25, 360–62 (WA 56, 371, 1–372, 25).

[121]Cf. John 6:51; Rom 11:32; Barth, Hans-Martin 2008, 783–85; 797–98.

[122]Cf. LW 28, 176, 190, 150–51 (WA 36, 640, 23-25; 662, 31–663, 24; 529, 38–530, 6).

[123]". . . quite oddly . . ."? Against Norbert Slenczka in Handbuch 2005, 436.

[124]LW 28, 71 (WA 36, 495, 30-31).

[125]WA 12, 610, 2-3.

[126]LW 28, 177 (WA 36, 641, 27-38).

[127]LW 22, 305 (WA 47, 34, 9-13).

[128]WA 34/2, 110, 26-28. This quotation may again make it clear how far Dietrich Korsch 2007 (e.g., 46, 134, 153, and elsewhere) falls short when he constantly interprets (Luther's) faith as a self-interpretation (derived from the Bible). Theologically, the issue is the interpretation of the interpretation.

[129]WA.TR 1, 574, 8-10 (no. 1160).

[130]Cf. Norbert Slenczka in Handbuch 2005, 440.

[131]LW 51, 47–48 (WA 1, 267, 2-3).

[132]WA.TR 1, 89, 16-17 (no. 203).

[133]Quoted by Justus Jonas in his memorial sermon at Eisleben; cf. Bornkamm, Heinrich 1960, 319.

[134]LW 42, 106 (WA 2, 690, 24-25).

[135]WA 10/3, 95, 5-6.

[136]WA 12, 458, 18-22. Faith "seeks not for anyone [etwarm], that it may be sure, and so it is retained." The WA translates "etwarm" with "irgendjemandem," "anyone"; ibid., line 21 and n. 1.

15

Conflict: Between Theology and Philosophy

No one knows how Luther might have begun a summary presentation of his theology. The dogmatics of Lutheran orthodoxy begin with an exposition on theology in general, its object and its principle, on Sacred Scripture, and on the significance of the Creeds.[1] Luther, like Calvin, begins with Sacred Scripture without first choosing a central theme. Characteristically, the Augsburg Confession also has a Foreword but not a Prolegomena that would have explained its understanding of theology and its approach to the Sacred Scriptures in advance. But in looking back and reconstructing Luther's theology we can indeed extract its principles, much as the Reformer himself programmatically formulated them in his preface to the first volume of the Wittenberg edition of his German writings in 1539.[2] We find there an overall perspective he derived from Psalm 119 and within which the whole of his theological thinking and work could be described. In addition, from the beginning the Reformer was in tension with what he called "philosophy." As early as 1509 he wrote in a letter: "From the beginning I would have preferred to exchange theology for philosophy."[3] The conflict between theology and philosophy thus became an inheritance he left to the ensuing history of Protestantism.

Contemporary Questions

It was Luther's intention to liberate theology from the embrace of the philosophy he found in place, an embrace he regarded as a stranglehold. This explains the constant polemics against Aristotle and, deriving from that, against the "scholastics," especially in his early years. At present the problem seems to be entirely different: the dispute over what is reality and how it is to be interpreted is not really being carried out between theology and philosophy. The lines of interpretation have separated. The remaining points of contact between philosophy and theology seem to exist only within the realm of general theory of science. How is a proper theology conducted? What is the value of university studies? What about the philosophical competency required for a proper study of theology? Philosophical education today retains a much greater value within Roman Catholic theology than among Protestants. Has Lutheran theology lost the philosophical ground under its feet, or does it deliberately refuse to walk on it? Then what business does it have in the realm of science and scholarship at all? What answers to these questions might we expect to find in Luther's theology?

Rationality appears in a multitude of historical guises; consequently a knowledge of the history of philosophy is also valuable for those who reflect on matters of theology. The formal possibilities of rationality are irreplaceable; therefore logic is necessary. But what is the relationship of philosophically responsible logic and theological plausibility? Luther testified at Worms: "Unless I am convinced by the testimony of the Scriptures or by clear reason (ratione evidente) . . . my conscience is captive to the Word of God."[4] What is ratio evidens, and what is its scope? Liberal Protestantism has, as a whole, accorded considerable value to reason, regarding itself as the promoter of science and progress. In the shadow of that approach, theology struggles today to be recognized as a scientific discipline without always taking into account the fact that the idea of reason has suffered repeated and severe crises. Within the last fifty years alone the concept of reason has changed materially at least twice, first in the wake of Critical Rationalism and the Frankfurt School after 1968, and then in light of the New Age movement, beginning in the 1990s. How can theology assert itself in such contexts, shifting as they are in themselves?

In a certain sense a relationship must first be reestablished between theology and philosophy. This is made difficult by the fact that philosophy is no longer seen as a primary dialogue partner for theology (and vice versa), since the humane and social sciences, especially psychology and sociology, but also medical anthropology, put their questions to theology much more directly than does philosophy. What is demanded is not dogmatic indoctrination but ethical orientation. Add to this the challenge posed by the theologies of non-Christian religions, the scientific study of religions, and an atheism that is reasserting itself. Can Luther have anything to say to all that? For him, what was on trial was the contemporary philosophy that surrounded him, while he regarded the theology that opened up to him through the Gospel as liberating.

Philosophy Put to the Test

Luther staged a brutal attack above all against the philosophy of Aristotle, while on the other hand he repeatedly appealed to reason and showed himself, in his discussion with Erasmus, to be an astute dialectician of the highest order.[5] How do we explain the tension between the two?

THAT ROGUE ARISTOTLE AND SCHOLASTIC PHILOSOPHY

At the beginning of the sixteenth century the authority of Aristotle was no longer undisputed, and long before the Reformation era Absalom of St. Victor had asserted that "the Spirit of Christ does not reign where the spirit of Aristotle rules."[6] But for centuries the Stagirite had counted simply as *the* highest authority in philosophical questions, the "Philosopher" pure and simple. To orient oneself to a certain subject one did not inquire of experience, but of Aristotle. Luther himself held a lecture series on the Nicomachean Ethics in 1509. He definitely recommended an engagement with Aristotle as beneficial in the education and intellectual training of young people.[7] But when someone said that Christ is like the sun, whose light illuminates much more brightly when reflected in the mirror of Aristotle, Luther found that "with this pretty similitude pagan teaching was introduced into Christianity as well."[8] Aristotle would apparently have left the Reformer cold if it had not been that Aristotelian thought had muscled its way into theology in the form of scholasticism. Luther's polemic is therefore directed in the same breath against Aristotle and against the scholastic theologians, whom he addresses in his lectures on Romans—in the midst of the Latin text—as "pig-theologians."[9] He calls Aristotle a "gas-bag" (*fabulator*),[10] a "rancid philosopher."[11] For him Aristotle is "the blind heathen teacher . . . this damned, conceited, rascally heathen . . . this wretched fellow."[12] Aristotle is said to propound an unsustainable notion of God; he speaks of a deity who, as being itself, considers only itself instead of beholding the world's misery, and thus he denies the God in whom Christians believe.[13] Aristotle's god "sleeps" and "snores."[14] He is like a nursemaid who is supposed to watch a child and does not notice when the cradle tips over.[15] Luther thinks one ought to "bark a warning" against such a philosophy.[16] We can give three examples of his conviction.

Theses against scholastic theology

In 1517, even before publishing the Ninety-Five Theses, Luther had presented a hundred theses "against scholastic theology." They often conclude by naming a concrete opponent: "contra Gabrielem" (Gabriel Biel), "contra Scotum" (Duns Scotus), or a generalized group ("contra Scholasticos," "contra philosophos"). This corresponds to the style of disputation then in use; saying precisely against whom one was speaking no doubt frequently refined the profile of what one said. For example, he says of Aristotle that his ethics were "the worst enemy of grace" (Th. 41). According to Luther they aimed at human self-creation. He considers it an error to think that Aristotle's idea of happiness did not contradict Catholic doctrine (Th. 42). An orientation to happiness leads to concupiscence! (cf. Th. 21). It is said to be erroneous to say that one could not be a theologian without Aristotle (Th. 43). Luther goes even further: "no one can become a theologian unless he becomes one without Aristotle" (Th. 44)! In summary, he says: "Briefly, the whole Aristotle is to theology as darkness is to light" (Th. 49).[17]

Against Latomus

The theological faculty at Leuven had found itself called upon to condemn Luther's opinions, especially regarding sin and grace. Jacobus Latomus, a theologian in that faculty who makes his sole appearance in this case, tried to give reasons for his faculty's position and to make it more profound. Luther responded to him from the Wartburg, where he had no resources at hand except the Scriptures. He expressed doubt about whether Thomas Aquinas had been among the blessed, since he "wrote a great deal of heresy, and is responsible for the reign of Aristotle, the destroyer of godly doctrine."[18] It was Luther's opinion that scholastic theology was nothing but a misjudgment of reality and an obstacle that led people astray from the statements of Sacred Scripture. His advice was that "a young man avoid scholastic philosophy and theology like the very death of his soul. The Gospels aren't so difficult that children are not ready to hear them."[19] After all, how were Christians instructed in the days of the martyrs, when this philosophy and theology did not yet exist? How did Christ himself teach? Ultimately, Luther offers an argument that would scarcely occur to today's theologians: "In all these hundreds of years up to the present, the courses at the universities have not produced, out of so many students, a single martyr or saint. . . ." Scholastic philosophy and theology are known by their fruits—or the lack thereof.[20] Luther thus offers three criteria: a theological assertion should be tested by what is in Scripture and what Christ himself taught. It should also be a statement that is clear, accessible even to children. Finally, genuine theology will have existential consequences.

De servo arbitrio

In his discussion with Erasmus of Rotterdam, Luther was also quite naturally concerned, among other things, with the relationship between theology and philosophy. He elucidates it with the figure of Nicodemus in the Gospel of John (John 3:1-10), who cannot imagine what "being born again" could mean: "for whoever heard that man must be born again to salvation 'of water and

Spirit?' Whoever thought that the Son of God must be exalted, 'that whoever believes in him should not perish, but have everlasting life?' Did the greatest and most acute philosophers ever make mention of this? Did the princes of this world ever possess this knowledge? Did the 'free will' of any man ever attain unto this, by endeavors?" Reason and free will and the whole world are forced to admit that they did not know Christ and had not heard of him before the Gospel came into the world.[21] Here it is clear that the Reformer was not concerned only with the limited abilities of human reason, but at the same time with the complete inability of the human will to decide for the Gospel on its own initiative.

What did Luther have against scholastic theology influenced by Aristotle? Formally he considered it a foreign infiltration: Sacred Scripture is clear enough! Theology's fundamental orientation cannot be to a philosophical concept. Luther considered the content of scholasticism, to the extent it was not oriented to Sacred Scripture, to be a falsification of Christian faith: its interest was in the self-constitution of the human being rather than the grace of God, in human happiness instead of the glory of God, in its own ideas instead of rebirth and contrition. It has a wrong estimate of the abilities of reason and the will, for Luther was convinced that reason is limited and the will unfree. Moreover, it lacks the existential consequences that take shape in discipleship and martyrdom.

Theses on John 1:14

Late in life the Reformer apparently felt the need to give greater precision to his view of the relationship between philosophy and theology. In the theses he presented in 1539 on John 1:14[22] he engages especially (without naming them) with Pierre d'Ailli and Gabriel Biel;[23] his explicit adversary is the "Sorbonne, the mother of errors" (Th. 4). In regard to the statement "the Word became flesh" he makes clear what false conclusions can be drawn from it if it is approached using the rules of philosophy. Namely, when syllogisms are applied the premise may be quite correct, and yet the philosophical proof may lead to a false conclusion. This is not because of "the defect of the syllogistic form, but because of the lofty character and majesty of the matter," which is "not indeed something contrary to, but . . . outside, within, above, below, before, and beyond all logical truth" (Th. 20-21). It simply transcends human ability to understand. Here today's reader naturally looks for a more precise definition of the relationship between philosophical dialectics and theological statement. But for Luther it suffices to point out that even in earthly things the appropriate categories of thought must be applied: it is as impossible to measure a pint with the measure of a foot as it is to weigh a line on the scale (Th. 31-32). To that extent "the truth" is never "the same" in every context (Th. 38). This is all the more true of the difference between philosophy and theology. Luther therefore thinks "we would act more correctly if we left dialectic and philosophy in their own area and learned to speak in a new language in the realm of faith apart from every sphere" (Th. 40). Thus it is a question of different spheres; to confuse or mix them damages both: if theology is forced into a theological statement it becomes an abstract truth and thus destroys itself; if theological and philosophical statements are mixed together they become unclear and self-contradictory. The point of Thesis 40, however, is that Luther wants to locate theology outside of "every" sphere, which in fact demands a new language.[24] At the same time it is clear that Luther is not against philosophy as such, but objects to an inappropriate philosophical theology.

When Luther polemicizes against Aristotle and the scholastic theology shaped by his philosophy he intends something more than merely to set himself apart from a particular philosophical school. Rather, what he proposed for debate was the significance that should be accorded to reason in matters of faith and thus in theology.

REASON: THE DEVIL'S WHORE AND GOD'S GIFT

Luther uttered some extremely derisive remarks against reason, and also some opinions that placed the utmost value on it. What explains that?

The problem of unenlightened reason

At the beginning Luther probably approached the problem of reason more intuitively: with Christ something came into the world that reason cannot unlock by itself, but that instead calls it into question and, in fact, reveals its limitations and stubbornness. If Christ is to be taken seriously, Sacred Scripture must be taken seriously. If Christ and Sacred Scripture are not taken seriously, then the true nature of grace remains unclear, if not altogether unknown. The honor of the God who turns to sinners with abundant mercy is besmirched. Human beings do not find the way to life, but remain prisoners of the world of death. The main concern of Luther's theology—"the glory of God and the salvation of the human being!"—furnishes the guideline here. However, the Reformer is able to develop this fundamental insight in detail with a high degree of philosophical acuity. Four arguments come to the fore:

First: Reason's extent is limited. God, precisely because God is God, transcends human rational capacity. Occasionally reason, or philosophy reflecting on reason, admits this; the true philosopher knows that she or he knows nothing.[25] Moreover, this can be found in Sacred Scripture: think of Paul's statements at the beginning of 1 Corinthians (1 Cor 1:18-25; cf. also John 3:1-15).

Next: reason in turn is biased and by no means "objective." It cannot be otherwise, since we are talking about the reason of human beings, which—

understood in light of Scripture—in every respect, in its thinking, willing, and acting, is prejudiced and unfree. If we look through colored glass, everything appears to be that color.[26] The things that govern human beings are not apparently objective criteria independent of human judgment, but their guiding interests. Human beings always have themselves in mind before all else, in their thinking, willing, and acting. The whole person is "flesh," and Luther, with Paul, regards "flesh" as the sinner's existence as turned away from God.[27] Reason works as a seducer, and philosophy flatters it. Human beings seek to build themselves up in their own minds, and the fundamentally deviant direction of their lives is expressed in their wills: no one can, by nature, want God to be God.[28] Reason entices people away from listening to God's word and thus betrays them: "for they interpret God's Scriptures with conclusions and syllogisms and drive them where they will."[29]

Third: reason thus falls short not only of God, but of the human being, whom it defines falsely, or rather, human beings define themselves falsely with the aid of reason—namely as self-sufficient and free in their thoughts, wills, and actions. But how should it be otherwise as long as reason knows only itself? It sets up a whole series of interesting anthropological assertions and in doing so by no means understands itself as merely a formal aid; it makes itself the criterion of its own action. It describes the human being as *animal rationale*, a rational being, and at the same time defines what *ratio*/reason is. It defines reason by means of reason—a circular argument! If we compare reason or philosophy with theology, Luther is convinced, we must admit that the human being knows "almost nothing" about human beings.[30] Nor is there any hope that this might change as long as the human does not perceive himself or herself "in his origin which is God."[31]

Fourth and finally, reason cannot convey certainty. It may be possible for it to assert that a God exists, but it does not know who this God is and what God's attitude toward human beings may be. Reason plays "blindman's buff" with humans.[32] It adjusts God to its own ideas—as the God who rewards good with good and evil with evil and therefore is to be feared. Human anxiety about the self then shapes what reason says about God. But reason can also inflate itself to the point of saying that there is no God;[33] then the presumptuousness of fallen humankind takes full control. Whatever the outcome, reason must be content with *speculari*[34] and hence deserves no trust; one cannot rely on it. Faith, however, lives in a joyous and proud certainty! For it is not the way of a Christian heart to take no joy in clear statements—on the contrary, a Christian must "rejoice in testimony to the truth, or be no Christian!"[35] What an assent to truth (*assertio*) derived from faith evokes is "constant adherence, strengthening, confessing, attending, and unshakeable endurance."[36]

From these points of view Luther can describe reason as "the foremost whore the devil has."[37] She seduces, feeds people with untruths, nourishes passing illusions, does not take people's real needs seriously, and remains noncommittal.

Reason as the gift of God

After the Reformer has said all these critical things about reason, we are astonished to find it singled out in Luther's interpretation of the first article of the Apostles' Creed: "I believe that God has created me and all that exists; that he has given me and still sustains my body and soul, all my limbs and senses, my reason and all the faculties of my mind. . . ."[38] This is evidently to be maintained, even though the interpretation of the third article requires the assertion "that by my own reason or strength I cannot believe in Jesus Christ, my Lord, or come to him."[39] Luther accords reason the highest imaginable praise in his theses for the "Disputation Concerning Man" in 1536: "And it is certainly true that reason is the most important and the highest in rank among all things and, in comparison with other things of this life, the best and something divine." Reason is "the inventor and mentor of all the arts, medicines, laws, and of whatever wisdom, power, virtue, and glory men possess in this life." "The arts," in the medieval divisions of the university, include the subjects related to mastery of language (grammar, rhetoric, and dialectic), as well as the subjects related to mathematics (arithmetic, geometry, music, and astronomy); knowledge of these was the precondition and basis for studies in theology, among other things. Reason constitutes the essential difference, the *differentia specifica*, between human and animal and the rest of creation. Sacred Scripture also makes reason "lord over the earth, birds, fish, and cattle," for without it the *dominium terrae*, the divine command to have dominion, could not be realized (Thesis 7). Luther thus understood reason as the human instrument for ruling over the rest of creation. Reason is "a sun and a kind of god appointed to administer these things in this life" (Thesis 8). Even after the Fall, God did not "take away this majesty of reason, but rather confirmed it" (Thesis 9).[40] Thus the human is defined as a rational being. However—and this is the parenthesis within which these magnificent statements about reason are to be evaluated—this definition, as noted, applies only to the human as "mortal and in relation to this life" (Thesis 3).[41]

THE AMBIVALENCE OF REASON

Reason is thus to be esteemed highly, but in the proper context! As great as is its scope in the realm of natural life, in spiritual matters it can do very little. It is irreplaceable in the ordering of our earthly life, but it has dreadful effects when it mixes in spiritual things with a presumptuous claim to competence. Luther distinguishes between two levels, the theological and the political "forums."[42] Whoever is interested in being adept in worldly things should study secular literature.[43] The ancient authors treat questions of social life "in the best and noblest ways."[44] For understanding the meaning of the words of Sacred Scripture, too, reason is indispensable; it draws appropriate conclusions from the statements of Scripture. Luther's appeal at Worms to the *ratio evidens* is to be understood in this sense.[45] He praises the abilities of reason, including individual achievements of his own time such as printing. Its field is that of social order and professional know-how; that is why, for example, good schools are necessary. But reason's scope is limited. It belongs to the world of fallen creation, not to the order of salvation. This can also be understood as a "soteriological unburdening of reason":[46] it need not be responsible for everything.

Reason would be completely overstepping itself if it dared to put itself in the place that belongs to the Holy Spirit! A philosophy that would seek to do so would be a "perverse love of knowledge."[47] Theologians who develop their speculations on the basis of reason have sought in the wrong direction: "if they bore their heads up through the heavens and look around they will not find anyone, for Christ lies in the manger and in the woman's lap. So they fall back down and break their necks."[48] Those who seek to gather theological knowledge apart from Christ are unfaithful and make themselves guilty of the equivalent of adultery.[49] "'Pure' reason is for Luther a reason that is unenlightened and blind. . . ."[50] People have often attempted to explain this rigid opinion as something the Reformer inherited from nominalism. William of Ockham was also, in his own way, concerned with the freedom of God, which cannot be limited by human reason. That heritage is more than merely a burden. And yet Luther interpreted God's freedom not in terms of philosophy but on the basis of his theology of the cross. Still, in his sometimes positive and sometimes critical evaluation of reason he had to wrestle with the question of "double truth." In fact, he asserts the impossibility that "the same thing [can] be true in philosophy and theology,"[51] which does not entail the assertion of a double truth. Rather, Luther's concern is that faith and theology should find their own language, one adequate to their uses. He criticizes reason not in terms of theory of knowledge but on the basis of soteriology. His problem is not the relationship between reason and revelation but the simple inadequacy of unenlightened reason in spiritual things. "But reason cannot *think* correctly about God; only faith can do so."[52]

THEOLOGY, EMANCIPATED AND EMANCIPATING

According to Luther, accurate statements about reason and philosophy cannot be derived from self-reflection. This applies to both their ability and their limitations. What theology has to say determines what is important in philosophy—spiritually speaking—and by no means the reverse! Luther does not woo philosophy to recognize theology; he takes it as his starting point that philosophy cannot ever acknowledge theology because philosophy as such is in no way in a position to grasp the truth of theological statements. To that extent all theology is directed to a conflict with philosophy; it is a "conflictual science."[53] It cannot do without reason, but it must take care that philosophy does not tread the Holy Scriptures with unwashed feet.[54] Philosophical concepts must first be given a bath.[55] The Holy Spirit has its own grammar.[56] What is important is "to speak in a new language" and with the greatest freedom "in the realm of faith apart from every sphere."[57] Again near the end of his life Luther spoke of this as something desirable. He himself always strove to speak firmly and in confrontation with outdated views of the object, the method, and the function of theology.

THE JUSTIFYING GOD AND THE SINFUL HUMAN: THE OBJECT OF THEOLOGY

What is the object of theology? If we look at the meaning of the concept itself, it is "about God"—a truism that is, of course, in need of explanation. Thomas Aquinas formulated it thus: "in sacred science, all things are treated of under the aspect of God: either because they are God Himself or because they refer to God as their beginning and end. Hence it follows that God is in very truth the object of this science."[58] Luther can in principle also reply in this way. God, Christ, or faith is the object of theology. But that does not yet touch the point of his understanding of theology.

Luther's most thorough discussion of the object of theology is found, remarkably enough, in his interpretation of Psalm 51. This is a penitential psalm: "Have mercy on me, O God, according to your steadfast love . . ." (Ps 51:1). This psalm, he says, contains the main points of our religion, namely the truth about sin and repentance, grace and justification, the true and appropriate worship of God. For many these concepts are empty words, the vague remnants of a dream that flees at the day's dawning. But the knowledge of the matter here present does not arise of itself, "at home, in our hearts, but is revealed and given from heaven."[59] This psalm is by no means only about David and his sinful relationship to Bathsheba; rather, it is about the "root of godlessness,"[60] the understanding of sin and grace. The scholastic theologians—in Luther's opinion—neither understood what sin is nor what grace is; they taught a rational theology lacking the word of God. That is why they believed God could be impressed by human behavior and the only issue is finding a morally better way of life. But the psalm speaks of true repentance, and according to Luther that means two things, namely acknowledgment of sin and acknowledgment of grace, fear of God and trust in God's mercy. This must be learned ever and ever anew, for persons enlightened by the Holy Spirit still remain dependent on the word of God; they know that they are scarcely in a position even "to drink a tiny drop from the immeasurable ocean of the Holy Spirit."[61] What is open to debate is not individual sins; what must be considered is the whole nature of sin, its source, and its origin. It is deep wisdom to know and recognize that we are "nothing but sin," for sin by no means consists merely in thoughts, words, and works. Rather, sin is the whole of life—Luther writes "this whole"—that we have received from our father and mother, and individual sins arise only out of that basis.[62] The natural constitution of the human is not intact, not in the civil and most certainly not in the spiritual realm. As a result of sin, rather, people are turned away from God and seek their own honor, even with the aid of their piety. The psalm conveys a teaching that must not only be reflected on theoretically, but must be comprehended existentially.

As a foundation for this Luther argues christologically and in terms of a theology of experience. If it were otherwise, "what need would we have of Christ?"[63] The believer will feel the unbearable burden of God's wrath and experience just as palpably as the grace of God when she or he finally discovers, full of joy: I cannot stand by myself, but in Christ I am justified and righteous, made righteous through Christ, who is righteous and makes righteous.[64]

Under these conditions it becomes clear how Luther has to define the object of theology and what his intention is in doing so. Philosophy reflects the human being as a phenomenon within its environment; the physician is concerned with the sick, the jurist desires just and lawful relationships, but the theologian discusses "the human being as sinner."[65] Human beings should perceive their state before God. That will drive them to despair and so bring them to a knowledge of grace and justification.

Thus theology is not a matter of general statements about God's majesty and omnipotence, but instead "the proper subject of theology is the sinful and lost human being and the justifying God, the savior of the sinful human being." Luther judges sharply and radically: "whatever is questioned or disputed about in theology outside this subject is error and poison."[66] For that is the point of the whole of Sacred Scripture: how graciously God deals with us through Christ. Consequently theology is not about the superficial concerns of this earthly life, for which reason is, after all, responsible, but about eternal salvation, about the human being in danger of eternal death and the justifying, saving, and lifegiving God.[67]

Hence in retrospect it is easy to understand how and why the Reformation was bound to catch fire as a conflict over indulgences. Theology's concern is not with abstract statements about God and the world, but with the concrete reality of a relationship, namely that between God and the sinful human being. Theology is regarded as a "humane science" or one of the "humanities," but it is a theological humane science:[68] its object is the human being before God. This relationship is conceived wholistically, as concerning the whole human being in face of the eternal God. It is conveyed by means of the word, and that communication is itself a wholistic event that encompasses the human being in all facets and phases of his or her existence.[69]

Was Luther being arbitrary and decisionistic in defining the object of theology in that way? Is his decision psychically and biographically determined? In fact, he does point to his own experience in connection with himself and Sacred Scripture. Luther sees a twofold reason for his decision: in his perception the sinful human and the justifying God encounter one another in Jesus Christ. Any other definition of the object of theology would eliminate the true relevance of Jesus Christ. A theology oriented to the cross of Jesus Christ points out the path. "Christ is the subject of theology."[70] The whole of Sacred Scripture points to Jesus Christ by confronting human beings with the Law and the Gospel.

This confirms the fact that for Luther the subject of theology is the God who testifies about Godself to the sinful human being in the divine word. Therefore the ability to distinguish is an essential element of theology: to distinguish between Law and Gospel, between philosophy and theology, between tradition and Sacred Scripture, between letter and spirit. Hence Sacred Scripture serves as the formal principle of Luther's theology; the material principle is given in Jesus Christ, and the final principle appears as the consolation of the conscience burdened by sin. Considered in light of this definition in terms of its goal, the Reformation was, in Luther's sense of it, a movement of pastoral care.

ORATIO, MEDITATIO, TENTATIO: THEOLOGICAL METHOD

The object, method, and function of theology correspond. If the relationship between the justifying God and the sinful human being constitutes the object of theology, its method cannot consist of rational deduction or free speculation. It can by no means be restricted to the intellectual realm. Its object is the life the justifying God gives to the sinful human being; hence theology's method must also be related wholistically to life. Reduction to a single level of human existence or solely to what humans can produce by their own reason is then utterly inadequate.

In the preface to the first volume of the Wittenberg edition of his German writings Luther summarized this in a concise form.[71] "Moreover, I want to point out to you a correct way of studying theology, for I have had practice in that. If you keep to it, you will become so learned that you yourself could (if it were necessary) write books just as good as those of the fathers and councils . . . . This is the way taught by holy King David (and doubtlessly used also by all the patriarchs and prophets) in the one hundred nineteenth Psalm. There you will find three rules, amply presented throughout the whole Psalm. They are *Oratio, Meditatio, Tentatio*."[72] As Luther explicated the object of theology on the basis of a psalm (Psalm 51), so he does with its method. Psalm 119, the longest in the Old Testament, presents a virtually endless sequence of expressions of gratitude and praise for God's word and commandment, as well as advice about how one can and should approach the word of God. Here one may learn the appropriate way to study theology or, better, to study "in" theology: one can never come to the end of it, but one can plunge into it and move within it like a fish in the water. It is not enough to know the classic representatives of theology, and it is not a matter of respecting church authorities: "You yourself" should be put in a position to decide theologically and to express yourself in a theologically productive way. This is fundamentally true for all Christians![73] The Middle Ages were already familiar with individual steps in the study of the Bible, with *lectio* serving primarily as a source for *quaestio* and *disputatio*.[74] For a spiritual opening up of Sacred Scripture, Bernard of Clairvaux distinguished four steps leading to a climax: the reading of Scripture seeks the sweetness of the soul's life, meditation finds it, prayer asks for it, and contemplation enjoys it. Today these stages are still recommended as spiritual aids in the context of Roman Catholic spirituality.[75]

It is characteristic of Luther's approach, in contrast, not to begin with reading Sacred Scripture, but with prayer: "Firstly, you should know that the Holy Scriptures constitute a book which turns the wisdom of all other books into foolishness, because not one teaches about eternal life except this one alone. Therefore you should straightway despair of your reason and understanding. . . . But kneel down in your little room and pray to God with real humility and earnestness, that he through his dear Son may give you his Holy Spirit, who will enlighten you, lead you, and give you understanding."[76] This does not at all mean that the study of Sacred Scripture should not involve the highest efforts of the intellect, but Luther is concerned that "sense and understanding" should not make themselves independent, but put themselves at the service of the Holy Spirit. All theology begins with prayer, which after all is the medium in which Sacred Scripture opens itself to us. In prayer experience is articulated, in prayer it is reflected on, and in prayer the conclusions to be drawn from experience of Sacred Scripture become evident.

"Secondly, you should meditate, that is, not only in your heart, but also externally, by actually repeating and comparing oral speech and literal words of the book, reading and rereading them with diligent attention and reflection, so that you may see what the Holy Spirit means by them. And take care that you do not grow weary or think that you have done enough when you have read, heard, and spoken them once or twice, and that you then have complete understanding. You will never be a particularly good theologian if you do that, for you will be like untimely fruit which falls to the ground before it is half ripe."[77] The study of theology is thus regarded as a process of ripening that proceeds by means of an ongoing engagement with Sacred Scripture and may not be interrupted prematurely—in essence, never. Meditation here does not mean descent into one's own interior space or objectless contemplation, but the contrary: sinking into the word of God, beginning with reading, hearing, and if possible learning by heart. "For God will not give you his Spirit without the external Word; so take your cue from that. His command to write, preach, read, hear, sing, speak, etc., outwardly was not given in vain."[78] It is true that all this is about the attempt to discover "what the Holy Spirit means." In his work for Peter the master barber, "A Simple Way to Pray," Luther describes how he imagines this and how he himself practices it: He starts with central biblical texts such as the Our Father or the Decalogue, and concentrates, listening for the message the text contains; he considers what in it causes him to reflect, what leads to lament and confession, and what he should ask for. It can at any time happen that he arrives at "so many ideas" that he forgoes the rest of the content, for "if such an abundance of good thoughts comes to us we ought to disregard the other petitions, make room for such thoughts, listen in silence, and under no circumstances obstruct them. The Holy Spirit himself preaches here, and one word of his sermon is far better than a thousand of our prayers."[79]

"Thirdly, there is *Tentatio, Anfechtung*. This is the touchstone which teaches you not only to know and understand, but also to experience how right, how true, how sweet, how lovely, how mighty, how comforting God's Word is, wisdom beyond all wisdom."[80] It is necessary, then, to put faith and theological insights to the test and take resistance seriously. Luther is less concerned here about intellectual questioning than about existential engagement with the word of God that does not enlighten or is contradicted by the experience of suffering or an inability to believe. What Luther has in mind here is not mystical experience (although he uses the word "sweet," often applied to such), but the kind of experiences one hates to have but must endure. In this sense theology is a science of experience, a science of painful experiences that, however, bring one ever closer to what sustains faith: it is especially under the heaviest burdens that the power of the divine word proves itself sustaining and consoling. While today the Gospel is often praised and recommended as an aid to living, Luther thinks that ". . . as soon as God's Word takes root and grows in you, the devil will harry you, and will make a real doctor of you, and by his assaults will teach you to seek and love God's Word."[81] The resistance one draws upon oneself from within church and theology can also be part of this; Luther is convinced that he is "deeply indebted" to his papists, "that through the devil's raging they have beaten, oppressed, and distressed me so much. That is to say, they have made a fairly good theologian of me, which I would not have become otherwise."[82] Finally, the experiences thus to be gained include that "the longer you write and teach the less you will be pleased with yourself. When you have reached this point, then do not be afraid to hope that you have begun to become a real theologian. . . ."[83] It is not only the wrestling with other opinions that calls oneself into question, but also a growing degree of self-criticism that makes a real theologian.

Luther's theology thus moves between attentive listening to Sacred Scripture and a clear perception of one's own experience, between *sola scriptura* and *sola experientia*; in a table discourse he formulates it as "sola autem experientia facit theologum."[84] This, however, is precisely what makes it trustworthy; "it tears us away from ourselves," from all the experiences that seem to speak against the word of God, and places us "outside ourselves," where we can stand and remain. Give me a place where I can stand, and I will move the world: that was Archimedes's desire, and here is that place! We do not rely on our feelings, but solely on the divine promise, which now also shapes the world of our feelings.[85]

METAPHORS, TROPES, NEW WORDS: THE LANGUAGE OF THEOLOGY

Luther's whole theology is one single great effort to put the divine promise into words. But which words? His problem is not the varying capacity for speaking and hearing in his different audiences; he is able to express his theological convictions—with great flexibility in handling the particular level of reflection—as easily in a sermon as in a lecture or a programmatic writing. Ultimately, for him the various forms of discourse belong together in any case; preaching is always also teaching, and he can equate a lecture with the morning office of Lauds.[86] He thus makes no distinction in principle between the language of theology and that of faith. But what is the relation of the language of faith or theology to everyday speech, to its instrumental use, or to the "stylized" terminology of philosophy? Sacred Scripture, for example the letter to the Galatians, seems like a foreign language to ordinary people; if they do not learn the language, they cannot understand.[87] Christians and non-Christians hear the same words, but only believers are really interested in the content of the proclamation;[88] there are particular preconditions for understanding it. In our confession of the divinity of Jesus Christ "we enter a different land" from the one in which Christ walked on earth as a human being.[89] The distance from philosophical reflection is absolutely clear: philosophically, the word is only "noise," but theologically "word" means the Son of God.[90] What is needed, then, is to find words for what cannot be, or cannot adequately be, expressed in everyday language or in the professional language of philosophy.

In his preaching Luther attempted to bridge the hiatus through the plasticity and rich imagery of his discourse. He plumbed all possibilities—sought comparisons, created new words,[91] adopted models of thought from philosophy when they suggested themselves.[92] But above all he made use of an infinite number of metaphors. He sees Sacred Scripture itself as inviting him to do this, but it was by no means an open door for arbitrary interpretation and allegorizing. A multitude of metaphors should always and repeatedly give expression to the one fundamental meaning of the divine promise. Thus the metaphor—quite apart from any and all modern theories of metaphor— comes to stand not *for*, but *as* the thing itself. Indirect reference expresses not something irrelevant, but the relevant thing itself. When Luther speaks about the Crucified and his meaning for humanity, therefore, he is "to be taken metaphorically at his word."[93] The image of the risen Christ, who with the banner of victory in his hand breaks and destroys the gates of hell, is valid; one may leave the "high and incomprehensible ideas" alone.[94] Does this mean that for Luther all theology is imagery, allusive speech?

Yes and no. Yes, insofar as human beings lack a language adequate to the divine promise. Precisely as regards confession of the triune God we have to admit that ". . . we must, regarding divine things, stammer and speak as we can. . . ."[95] For this we need a new language, the language of Pentecost. Not only the disciples, but the women as well (!) then spoke in new and different tongues.[96] One must be born of God and taught by the Holy Spirit if one is to speak and understand this language.[97] The point is that the content of God's promise must be grasped at least in some way (*aliquomodo*),[98] even though in the process one must move, so to speak, in the fog.[99] Stefan Streiff has attempted to describe this new language as "medial," drawing on the linguistic analyses of Johannes Anderegg.[100] Medial language, like poetry, is able to communicate in ways that are not available to instrumental language. It is a kind of tongue that must abandon argumentation but that by its "appeal" creates space and effect. It refers to the realm of the instrumental and the functional but calls them into question and thus leads beyond them. This does not result in arbitrariness and willfulness—according to Luther—because it is secured by the constitutive reference to Scripture and dogma. However great the kinship between Luther's shaping of language and the "medial" language Streiff describes, the Reformer would have counted the latter also as "old" language. The new language given by the Holy Spirit, in contrast, uses the "old" ways of speaking, whether instrumental or medial, and transforms them. Under the onslaught of the new language human beings no longer see themselves as they thought they would, and the world no longer in the way it had appeared to natural sight. But precisely through this the Holy Spirit— with the aid of language—intervenes also in the realm of the instrumental and begins to transform it. "Indirect" speech acquires the most direct effects. But taken alone and as such it remains weak, vulnerable, and easily overlooked. It has only one way of legitimating itself, namely recourse to God's word, and only one opportunity to make itself effective, namely confession and proclamation.

THEOLOGY'S FUNCTION: SERVICE TO PROCLAMATION, TEACHING, AND CREED

Thus for Luther theology is not dry and abstract, but a practical and living matter. Its primary goal cannot consist in theoretical knowledge of such things as how to speak of the relationship between the two natures of Christ or what is to be said about inner-trinitarian relations. The teaching that is at stake for theology is not a system that serves intellectual satisfaction or institutional self-assertion. It should not be adopted as a heteronomous concept. Its task is to work out what one needs to know for life and death. The teaching reflected upon and articulated by theology serves as an orientation to how life is to be measured and how one might achieve success in life, in a comprehensive sense that is sometimes contrary to appearances. For Luther this is concentrated in the essential points of the catechism; to that extent theology for him is "systematic catechetics."[101] The sequence of Decalogue, Creed, and Our Father shows Luther what is important for a Christian person: the Ten Commandments tell him "what he should do and not do." The Creed tells him "how he should take and seek and find it"; the Our Father, finally, shows him "how he should seek and find."[102] This sounds simple and pragmatic, but of course Luther knows that theology also demands clarity, because a small shift in accent can distort God's whole offer of salvation and so endanger the honor of God. As the human being needs clear water, so the Christian needs pure teaching.

Certainly the pure teaching that is helpful to human beings is not conveyed primarily in lectures on dogma, but rather in proclamation. Luther, like other theologians of the Reformation, can use the concepts of "teaching" and "preaching" interchangeably, but teaching is understood in light of preaching, and not preaching in terms of an abstract concept of theoretical teaching. Preaching is a dynamic event, for in the sermon Christ scatters "his person throughout the wide world."[103] Proclamation is thus not primarily about information, conjecture, or appeal, but about encouragement: this you can expect of God, this you can believe! In personal pastoral care, especially in confession and absolution, proclamation as encouragement attains its utmost concentration from a psychological point of view. Here consciences are comforted; here they find relief and solace.

The content of the teaching learned from listening to Sacred Scripture and communicated by preaching ultimately leads to profession of faith—in thanksgiving and praise. This profession again represents an act of proclamation. Luther himself—from a formal point of view—presented two explicit formulations of his evangelical confession. In 1528, in the shadow of illness and frustration, he wrote his own personal profession of faith, attached to his "Confession Concerning Christ's Supper," which was directed primarily against Zwingli.[104] Almost a decade later, in preparation for the council called to meet at Mantua in 1537, which did not happen, he wrote the "Smalcald Articles," which became part of the confessional writings of the Lutheran Church.[105] The reading of the *Confessio Augustana* at the imperial diet in Augsburg was celebrated, altogether in Luther's sense, as a success. The confession of the God who justifies solely through Jesus Christ was presented in a fully public manner. With this, a goal of Reformation theology appeared to have been attained.

For Luther the function and method of theology were not yet separated from faith itself as technical processes in the sense of the later division of labor. Luther's notion of theology was formed a good two hundred years prior to the Enlightenment and differed from its new scientific-theoretical concepts. But it remains clear that the Reformer would not abandon his basic position, even though there might be a differentiation of disciplines and a technical perfecting of theological work: Theology is a function of faith and is at the same time in the service of faith, in regard both to individual believers and the community of Christians. Theology cannot grasp its object apart from the existential consummation of faith, which takes place within the community of the church, and otherwise it cannot fulfill its task.

Critical Evaluation

The relationship between philosophy and theology, reason and faith, as Luther sees it, is readily apparent in his statement before the Diet of Worms, mentioned at the beginning of this chapter: "Unless I am convinced by the testimony of the Scriptures or by clear reason . . . I am bound by the Scriptures I have quoted and my conscience is captive to the Word of God. I cannot and I will not retract anything, since it is neither safe nor right to go against conscience."[106] Contrary to later misunderstandings, this is not a plea for independent, rational evidence, and certainly not for the autonomy of conscience. Rather, what this expresses in terms of theology is that a statement is theologically responsible if I can show the extent to which I obtain it

- being brought to insight by Sacred Scripture, possibly against (Luther says "overcoming"!) prejudices and experiences,
- with the support of reason applied to the Scriptures, and
- in a conscience overcome by God's word, so that I cannot say otherwise than what I now attempt.

Finally, it is part of this that I entrust my speaking and profession to the help of God; Luther added to his Latin statement the German words "Gott helfe mir, Amen" (God help me. Amen).

What critical evaluation shall we now give of Luther's understanding of the relationship between philosophy and theology, faith and reason? What are the objections to it and how should we deal with them? Was Luther correct in his accusations against scholastic theology? What is there in his idea of "theology" that is still usable or even promising for the future, in light of our current ideas about science and scholarship?

Historical misjudgment?

From the beginning of his theological development Luther had a tense relationship with philosophy, something caused or at any rate intensified by the critical attitude toward Thomas that prevailed in the Augustinian monastery at Erfurt. Nevertheless, one must say that he made distinctions: he repeatedly defends Bernard of Clairvaux. His concentration on an interpretation of Scripture oriented to Christ seems to have been influenced, at least in part, by the contemporary "pietistic theology," especially as represented by Staupitz.[107] In his polemics he often did not adequately distinguish between Aristotle and "the Scholastics," or between Thomas and the Thomists. When he thundered against Aristotle the object of his wrath was often not the philosopher himself but his baleful influence on theology. He probably knew Thomas better than was long supposed.[108] Nevertheless, he allowed himself to be led into making generalized condemnations: "In the whole of Thomas there is not a word that would give one confidence in Christ."[109] This, of course, is unfounded. Thomas Aquinas was portrayed by his contemporaries as a deeply devout man to whom, for example, the verse-prayer "Adoro te devote" is attributed.[110] But Luther's interest was not in screening theological teachers; he was intent on describing what he considered essential: in the case of this quotation, "confidence in Christ."

However, in criticizing philosophy the Reformer did not make it sufficiently clear that, from a methodological point of view, one cannot simply contrast philosophical thought with a naïve approach to Sacred Scripture as if they were the sole alternatives. Approaching Sacred Scripture also implies philosophical thinking and basic attitudes, as was all too clear in the clash over the interpretation of "est" in the Last Supper pericope. Gerhard Ebeling rightly points to the "programmatic differences" we encounter in Luther's theology "between philosophical uses of language and the *modus loquendi* of the Bible, with some tentative appeals to the Hebrew." He concludes: "his sensing of this semantic difference in individual words and expressions, and leveraging the intent of biblical language against traditional theological language, was the crucial moment that set the course for the genesis of Luther's theology."[111] But the question remains whether the course thus set always led to clear results. The relationship between philosophy and theology is inadequately considered when Luther, on the one hand, rejects the thesis of "double truth" and on the other hand protests that what is considered true in philosophy need not be regarded as true in theology. The reason of the natural human being is rejected as prejudiced and leading to error and yet within prescribed limits is claimed as useful in interpreting Scripture.

RATIONALITY'S REVENGE?

Did Luther undervalue the abilities and relevance of rationality? Lutheran orthodoxy after the Reformation made use of rationality and many philosophical traditions as a matter of course. This was unavoidable in the face of the conflicts with Tridentine Catholicism, the Swiss Reformation, and later with Cartesianism. In the epoch of the Enlightenment historical-critical exegesis was born, adopting in its own way Luther's approach to understanding the literal sense of a text and yet to a degree setting it against him. As regards the Reformer himself it is clear that he was interested—though he expressed it differently—not in "enlightenment," but in "illumination."

Existential versus sapiential theology

Otto Hermann Pesch sees the difference between Luther and Thomas in their different theological styles: the Reformer practiced existential theology, while Aquinas's was sapiential. These are two quite legitimate types of theology, but the question remains: how far apart could they move? What prevents sapiential theology from descending into a Platonizing rationalism, and what protects existential theology from becoming nothing but a kind of decisionism? For Luther, in fact, theology is essentially *sapientia*, wisdom, even "wisdom about wisdom,"[112] and he includes *scientia* within *sapientia*. In Luther in particular the contrast between *scientia* and *sapientia* does not work, and on closer examination it probably does not apply to Thomas's thought either. A distinction between wisdom and knowledge is certainly helpful, and even indispensable in certain contexts, but especially in today's systematic theology there is an attempt not only to distinguish but also to overcome these false theological alternatives.

Add to this that philosophy is no longer the primary dialogue partner for theology; the humanities have joined it. Theology today is a science of conflicts with regard to a great many possible centers of such conflict whose fires are kindled more probably by ethical than by dogmatic questions.

Of course Luther did not recognize "methods" for theological study in today's sense.[113] The theological disciplines were not yet distinguished; Luther was neither a systematician nor a biblical theologian nor a church historian. To that extent his three "rules" can also not be understood as a theoretical scholarly guide for theology. He was a theologian in an overarching sense, which in view of today's splintering of theological specializations could certainly be regarded as a model worth striving for. If prayer, meditation, and resistance to attack cannot be functionalized as instruments of theological knowledge, they do represent a comprehensive horizon of reflection on faith within which intellectual insights can ripen and be made more profound.

Double bind

It is well known that Luther considered reason very important, a gift of the Creator, and especially for the purpose of understanding Sacred Scripture. But the reason of believers did not, for him, simply become a *ratio renata*; it remained the reason of the human being, simultaneously righteous and sinful. The result is an unclear double bind: reason, seen as positive in terms of creation but as corrupted by the Fall, serves in itself as a precondition for the reception of biblical statements. Luther himself advocated a careful attention to the original biblical languages, sought the literal meaning of a scriptural passage, and conducted theological disputes with considerable philosophical acuity. The ambivalence of reason is examined, but its valency is not clearly explained.

The heritage of Luther, a tendency to polemicize against reason and philosophy, has in many respects led to a neglect, in Protestantism, of the relationship between faith and the realm of rationality. Rational self-assurance was no longer possible without further condition; there was no instrument at hand for an effective critique of ideology. Instead, faith had to allow itself to be accused of ideological self-immunization and decisionism.

The Reformer by no means pronounced a summary discrediting of reason. What is problematic in his dealings with reason is the way he thought he could distinguish between reason's abilities with regard to form and content. He advised caution in the use of philosophical terms but did not regard it as impossible. Certainly, as we have seen, one had to bathe them first,[114] put them under the shower or bring them to the dry cleaner. But can the results of the cleaning be convincing? They just get dirty all over again, and at the same time the cause of the soiling is the capacity to receive, within which the very idea of faith itself first becomes possible. This calls for an ongoing philosophical-theological reflection that Luther—probably also because of his apocalyptic worldview—did not really foresee. Such an ongoing reflection is indispensable in theology today.

Responsibility for creation

Luther acknowledged a significant value for reason as regards the outward things of life and human responsibility for creation, but denied its competence in spiritual questions. However, can the earthly and the spiritual realms be so blithely separated? Is not reason just as self-seeking and driven by egoism in the realm of creation as in that of the spirit? The modern crises of reason seem to confirm that. Luther could still assume the universal validity of ideas of natural law (which, on the other hand, created some complications for him). Modern discussions of human rights are the heirs of this idea, but they have not been able to establish its universal validity. A society depends on the basic ethical convictions of its members unless it is governed in authoritarian fashion. Hence the apparently complete dismissal of reason by the Reformation is unsustainable today. Luther himself had hinted that it is faith that motivates reason to social engagement.[115] Faith and reason must be in touch with one another. This should not be impossible if we consider that they are made possible by the same anthropological precondition, namely the ability to transcend. The question today is not how the argument between them is to be resolved, but how the two together can use their different capacities in the service of life.

INDIVIDUALIZATION?

Luther's concentration on the individual conscience certainly contributed to an individualization of faith, which also fully corresponds to the Gospel. It is the individual human being whose sin is forgiven and who thereby gains a new courage for living. Nevertheless, we must ask whether this individualization of faith and the theology that reflects on it came at the expense of the community of the church, and whether it did not introduce a fissive bacterium into the Reformation's cause from the beginning.

The significance of theology for church and society

If one appeals to conscience and the rational insight of the individual, the necessary outcome is plurality. What function then remains to the church as a community? Ultimately we must even ask whether society itself is not enthralled to this fissive bacterium, so that it necessarily disintegrates into a multiplicity of "I, inc."s. It is true that such questions are often posed from positions that in any case are only able to see individualization and plurality in a negative light.

For Luther the individual conscience is in fact indispensable. That in turn was for him the very precondition for a church and society organized in meaningful and constructive ways. Cohesion is created precisely by the mutual responsibility of the members. Luther attempted to express this in what he said about the universal, mutual, and common priesthood. It is a matter of mutual witness by all for all, whereby all can challenge each other but can also inspire. This applies first of all to the church, but it has effects for society as well. The hierarchically organized Corpus Christianum is replaced by the responsible society in which beggary is abolished as far as possible and common funds for charity are established, in which each individual lays claim to his or her opportunities for education and contributes by her or his calling to the success of the whole.[116] Society, however, could learn a lot from Luther's thoughts on ecclesiology; his ideas about the priesthood of the baptized are undoubtedly part of the early history of democracy.

The significance of church and society for theology

For Luther the church is the community of believers in which theology is practiced. In the course of a resolute return to the witness of Sacred Scripture and its center, Jesus Christ, there arises a circularity of reception of the scriptural witness and human experience (including reason) that evokes insights from all the participants and thus points anew to Sacred Scripture on a new and altered plane. Nevertheless, the ecclesiological as well as the social context of theological work, and a corresponding engagement with philosophy, as proposed by Luther, are too narrowly developed from today's point of view. Nor can one assert that the relevance he saw for the church in the professional exercise of theology exists to such an extent that one can point to a structural identity between the characteristics of theology and those of the church, as Oswald Bayer attempts to show.[117] It may be that word, prayer, and cross, as hallmarks of the church, correspond to *oratio*, *meditatio*, and *tentatio* in the realm of theology. But where in theology are the elements corresponding to sacrament and sacramental community? They could only be recovered today in the context of a holistic approach. While Protestant theology has often engaged intensively on behalf of an awareness of social conditions and contexts, the significance of the church for the development of appropriate and progressive statements about and on behalf of society has largely remained a mystery to it.

THEMATIC REDUCTION?

Does Luther's concentration on the contrast between the sinful human being and the justifying God represent an unnecessary self-limitation of theology? Should theology not be concerned "with God and the world"? If we follow the Reformer's approach will the result not necessarily be a ghettoization of theology? From the ecumenical side we encounter the question whether concentration on Christ does not lead to a reductionism, namely an obscuring of trinitarian thought. Anthropologically speaking as well, it could be reductive to see the human being solely as sinner. Cannot theology say a great deal more about the human?

Luther would probably respond that it is a matter not of beginning with the fullness of possible perceptions and ideas but of obtaining that fullness from Christ. Christology itself, after all, demands the doctrine of the Trinity, just as it should be used on behalf of a wholistic anthropology. At the time of the Reformation the concentration on Christ—sometimes even at the price of reductionism—made sense and was even necessary. Today, however, we require a new explanation and extrapolation of Luther's approach. This means that what is said about the word of God must be developed wholistically, namely in terms of trinitarian theology. God's word is not fulfilled in the reception of words; they themselves can be understood more comprehensively by including sociological and psychological factors and nonverbal elements. God's word is threefold: it has creation-centered, soteriological, and pneumatological components.[118] Therefore it is necessary to cultivate symbolic thought and to rediscover traditional forms, not only of scriptural meditation. Lutheran scholarship for a long time displayed a broad skepticism toward mysticism and meditation. It was asserted that on the path of meditation recommended by Luther "the human being does not concentrate on his navel; he does not hide within himself"[119]—as if, for example, East Asian meditation were "navel-gazing"! The human being can by no means hear what comes to her or him from without and allow it to bear fruit unless she or he knows how to unite it with what is within and thus to that extent hear "within the self." The relationship between reception of the word of God and reception of a reason that is not understood as rationally confined could thus be reordered. In addition, in this way the whole social and cultural environment of the "sinful" and "justified" human being would appear anew as a gift and a task received.

COMMAND OF THEOLOGICAL LANGUAGE

What Luther had to say about the language of theology and of faith is undoubtedly impressive. Speaking in new languages, with new tongues, as fits the gifts of the Holy Spirit: this reveals the distance between everyday language and the language of faith and also shows the latter's relevance for the mundane. At present the field is dominated by positivistic thought and discourse, so that nonspecialists can scarcely understand even a poem as calling his or her superficial reality into question or as opening up new meaning. Therefore it is important to point to these different levels of language. Theology and preaching would be well advised to bring them again and again to the awareness of believers and nonbelievers. If we work with the concept of a mediating use of language we can say that "human beings cannot exist without an instrumental use of language. But they are equally unable to endure the world—in modernity the reverse is more and more true: the world is unable to endure human beings—without a mediating use of language."[120] This is a fact that can be verified even by anthropology; theology, through the word of God, encounters even mediating language as further transcended. But for Luther his understanding of the special conditions of theological discourse provides no charter for any and all kinds of speculation; on the contrary, he sees the language of faith and theology as grounded in and limited by a prior gift:[121] God's self-revelation in Jesus Christ, as attested in Sacred Scripture and in the dogma of the ancient church.[122]

Why the foundation of valid theological discourse should lie precisely here is something that cannot be established by argument. Luther cannot give any logical arguments for his decision against someone who would appeal to other foundations. Nor did he have any understanding for the different choices of others—heretics, for example. From today's perspective this is revelation-positivism or simple decisionism. For Luther it was a matter of experience, or rather of *his* experience. He could not see himself as someone who had decided on his own and arbitrarily for a particular understanding, one he would never surrender; rather, it was something that had grown on him in his encounter with Sacred Scripture, something he had wrested from it. To that extent the accusation of "decisionism" is not accurate. On the Reformer's part it was subjectively honest, and it is, in fact, the experience of innumerable Christians—but how can it be intersubjectively communicated? The new language of faith, categorically distinct from everyday language, must at a minimum be related to rational argumentation.[123] This is a task Luther has left to all theology rooted in his thought.

NOTES

[1] Cf. Heinrich Schmid, *Die Dogmatik der Evangelisch-Lutherischen Kirche dargestellt und aus den Quellen belegt. Neu herausgegeben und durchgesehen von Horst Georg Pöhlmann* (Gütersloh: Mohn, 1979; orig. ed. Erlangen: C. Heyder, 1847), 17ff. English: *The Doctrinal Theology of the Evangelical Lutheran Church: Verified from the Original Sources* (Philadelphia: Lutheran Publication Society, 1889).

[2] LW 34, 283–88 (WA 50, 658, 29–659, 4).

[3] WA.Br 1, 17, 42-43 (no. 5).

[4] LW 32, 112 (WA 7, 838, 4-5).

[5] Cf. Theodor Dieter, *Der junge Luther und Aristoteles. Eine historisch-systematische Untersuchung zum Verhältnis von Theologie und Philosophie* (Berlin and New York: de Gruyter, 2001).

[6] Reference in Denis R. Janz, *Luther on Thomas Aquinas. The Angelic Doctor in the Thought of the Reformer* (Stuttgart: Steiner, 1989), 17.

[7] LW 44, 201 (WA 6, 458, 26–31).

[8] WA 12, 414, 19–30 (at 27–28).

[9]LW 25, 261 (WA 56, 274, 14).

[10]WA 9, 23, 7.

[11]WA 9, 43, 5 (in a broader sense *rancidus* means "disgusting, revolting").

[12]LW 44, 200–1 (WA 6, 457, 34; 458, 4-5, 7).

[13]WA.TR 1, 57, 44-45.

[14]LW 33, 171 (LDStA 1, 456/457, 13.17; cf. LDStA 1, 654/655, 10ff.).

[15]WA.TR 1, 73, 29-31; LW 25, 361 (WA 39/1, 179, 30-34).

[16]LW 25, 361 (WA 56, 371, 17-19).

[17]LW 31, 10–12 (LDStA 1, 19-33).

[18]LW 32, 258 (LDStA 2, 397).

[19]Ibid. (LDStA 2, 395).

[20]Ibid.

[21]LW 33, 281 (LDStA 1, 637, 23-37).

[22]LW 38, 239–42 (LDStA 2, 461–67).

[23]On this see esp. Streiff 1993, 43–114, as well as Beutel 1991a.

[24]See "Metaphors, tropes, new words: the language of theology" below.

[25]LW 34, 137–44 (LDStA 1, 654/655, 27ff.). Cf. Ulrich Moustakas, "Differenz und Relation. Zum Verhältnis von Theologie und Philosophie bei Luther," *KD* 46 (2000): 92–125; Oswald Bayer, "Philosophische Denkformen der Theologie Luthers als Gegenstand der Forschung. Eine Skizze," 135–49 in Rainer Vinke, ed., *Lutherforschung im 20. Jahrhundert. Rückblicke, Bilanz, Ausblicke* (Mainz: von Zabern, 2004).

[26]WA 16, 143, 17-19.

[27]Cf. "Erläuterungen XIII. Die biblische Anthropologie," 304–97 in Martin Luther, *Ausgewählte Werke*, ed. Hans Heinrich Borcherdt and Georg Merz. Ergänzungsreihe vol. 1 (Munich: Kaiser, 31986).

[28]LW 31, 10 (WA 1, 225, 1-2).

[29]LDStA 1, 372/373, 24-27; cf. LW 31, 12, 87, 265.

[30]LW 34, 137 ". . . paene nihil scire" (LDStA 1, 664/665, Th. 11).

[31]LW 34, 138 ". . . donec in fonte ipso, qui Deus est, sese viderit" (LDStA 1, 666/667, Th. 17).

[32]LW 19, 55 (WA 19, 207, 4).

[33]LW 33, 291 (LDStA 1, 652/653, 40ff.); cf. Barth, Hans-Martin 1971.

[34]Luther also has economic and political "speculation" marginally in view; cf. WA.TR 2, 56, 26–57, 2.

[35]"Non est enim hoc Christiani pectoris non delectari assertionibus, imo delectari assertionibus debet, aut Christianus non erit," LDStA 1, 226, 16-29/227, 22-23.

[36]Ibid.

[37]LW 51, 374 (WA 51, 126, 9-10 [1546]).

[38]The Book of Concord, 345.

[39]Ibid.

[40]LW 34, 137 (LDStA 1, 664/665).

[41]Ibid., Thesis 3: ". . . haec definitio tantum mortalem et huius vitae hominem definit." For the whole cf. Gerhard Ebeling, *Luther-Studien* II/3, as well as Hans-Martin Barth, "Martin Luther disputiert über den Menschen," KD 28 (1982): 154–66.

[42]WA 39/1, 230, 2-3.

[43]LW 13, 199 (WA 51, 242, 36-37).

[44]WA 40/3, 202, 24.

[45]Cf. zur Mühlen 1995, 157–58.

[46]Ibid., 147; cf. 153.

[47]"Quia sicut libido est perversa cupiditas voluptatis, ita philosophia est perversus amor sciendi, nisi assit gratia Dei . . ." WA 59, 410, 1-2; see Dieter, *Der junge Luther und Aristoteles*, chapter 6.

[48]WA 9, 406, 17-20 (smoothed). The reference is to those commenting on the *Sentences* of Peter Lombard.

[49]WA 59, 409, 20-21.

[50]Bayer 1994, 77.

[51]LW 38, 242 (LDStA 2, 466/467), Thesis 39.

[52]LW 26, 238 (WA 40/1, 376, 24-25), emphasis supplied.

[53]Bayer 1994, 115ff.; 510–11.

[54]Cf. WA 40/1, 20, 32ff.

[55]WA 39/1, 229, 16-19.

[56]"Spiritus sanctus habet suam grammaticam," WA 39/2, 104, 24.

[57]". . . loqui novis linguis in regno fidei . . ." LW 38, 242 (LDStA 2, 466/467), Thesis 40. Cf. Dennis D. Bielfeldt, "Luther and the Strange Language of Theology. How 'new' is the 'nova lingua'?" 221–44 in David M. Whitford, ed., *Caritas et Reformatio. Essays on Church and Society in Honor of C. Lindberg* (St. Louis: Concordia, 2002). See "Metaphors, tropes, new words: the language of theology" below.

[58]*ST* I. q. 1 a 7.

[59]WA 40/2, 316, 21-22. The psalm quotations are from the NRSV.

[60]Ibid., 316, 32.

[61]Ibid., 318, 22-25.

[62]Ibid., 322, 18-23, "hoc totum."

[63]Ibid., 322, 31.

[64]Ibid., 327, 32-35.

[65]Ibid., 328, 17.

[66]". . . Theologiae proprium subiectum est homo peccati reus ac perditus et Deus iustificans ac salvator hominis peccatoris. Quicquid extra hoc subiectum in Theologia quaeritur aut disputatur, est error et venenum," WA 40/2, 328, 17-20.

[67]Cf. ibid., 328, 26-28.

[68]". . . de cognitione hominis theologica, et de cognitione Dei etiam theologica . . ." WA 40/2, 327, 36-37.

[69]Therefore the human relationship with God is inadequately described as an "exchange of words" or a "conversation": against Bayer 1994, 38; Bayer 2003, 36.

[70]WA.TR 2, 242, 4-5, no. 1868: "Christus est subiectum theologiae, de quo dicitur: Subiectum adaequatum."

[71]LW 34, 283–88 (WA 50, 658, 29–661, 8). Cf. Hans-Martin Barth, "Erfahrung, die der Glaube bringt," *WPKG* 69 (1980): 567–79, as well as Bayer 1994, 55–106.

[72]LW 34, 285 (WA 658, 29–659, 4).

[73]". . . Omnes dicimur Theologi, ut omnes Christiani, ist keiner von den anderen höher geweiht," WA 41, 11, 7-14 (with modernization of the German text).

[74]Cf. Theo Bell, *Divus Bernhardus. Bernhard von Clairvaux in Martin Luthers Schriften* (Mainz: von Zabern, 1993), 324; Bayer 1994, 29. Cf. also Ulrich Köpf, *Religiöse Erfahrung in der Theologie Bernhards von Clairvaux* (Tübingen: Mohr, 1980).

[75]"Beatae vitae dulcedinem lectio inquirit, meditatio invenit, oratio postulat, contemplatio degustat," Guigo II the Carthusian (1140–1193), *Scala claustralium*, c. 1, PL 184, 475–76 (sometimes also attributed to Bernard of Clairvaux). Cf., e.g., "Vier Freunde, die uns zu Jesus bringen": www.jenskaldewey.ch.

[76]LW 34, 285–86 (WA 50, 659, 5-12).

[77]Ibid., 286 (WA 50, 659, 22-29).

[78]Ibid. (WA 50, 659, 32-33).

[79]LW 43, 198 (WA 38, 363, 9-16).

[80]LW 34, 287 (WA 50, 660, 1-4).

[81]Ibid. (WA 50, 660, 7-10).

[82]Ibid. (WA 50, 660, 12-14).

[83]Ibid. (WA 50, 660, 25-27).

[84]WA.TR 1, 16, 13.

[85]". . . Ideo nostra theologia est certa, quia ponit nos extra nos: non debeo niti in conscientia mea, sensuali persona, opere, sed in promissione divina . . .": "And this is the reason why our theology is certain: it snatches us away from ourselves and places us outside ourselves, so that we do not depend on our own strength, conscience, experience, person, or works but depend on that which is outside ourselves, that is, on the promise and truth of God, which cannot deceive," LW 26, 386 (WA 40/1, 589, 8-9); the printed Latin text inserts after "quia" "rapit nos a nobis et"; ibid., 589, 25.

[86]Cf. LW 12, 4–5 (WA 40/2, 193, 2-3): "Omnis praedicatio vel lectio sacrae theologiae est ipsum verissimum sacrificium laudis vel Eucharistia vel gratiarum actio" (beginning of his third lecture on the Psalms, 1532). Cf. Mikoteit 2004.

[87]WA 41, 658, 27-30.

[88]WA 37, 513, 30-35.

[89]LW 37, 229 (WA 26, 340, 35–341, 5).

[90]"Philosophice heis(s)t verbum sonus aut vox, sed theologice loquendo verbum significat filium Dei," WA 39/2, 103, 9-10.

[91]This he did especially in connection with his discussion of the sacraments: "Leibsbrot [body-bread]," "Kern im Wasser [kernel in water]"; cf. Wolff 2005, 564–65.

[92]Thus "synecdoche" in the context of the arguments about the Eucharist: see the "Confession Concerning Christ's Supper," LW 37, 151–372, esp. 211, 214, 302, 330 (WA 26, 444, 1-20; 427, 13-20).

[93]Wolff 2005, 86; cf. LW 25, 135–36 (WA 56, 139, 21-23).

[94]WA 37, 63, 25-29.

[95]WA 41, 270, 8.

[96]WA 49, 753, 17-18.

[97]"Ideo oportet nasci ex deo, non ex homine, muliere, sed ex deo, ut deus sit pater et mater, qui zeuget. Hoc scimus et de hoc liquimur, cogitamus et intelligimus: per suggestionem spiritus sancti praedicatur et intelligitur," WA 45, 68, 25-28.

[98]"Ideo ut capere aliquomodo possimus, dedit Deus nobis formulas loquendi . . ." WA 39/2, 98, 15-16 (with reference to Christology).

[99]"Praescribuntur enim ibi nobis a Spiritu sancto formulae; in illa nube ambulemus," ibid., 104, 18-19.

[100]Streiff 1993.

[101]Bayer 1994, 106ff.

[102]WA 7, 204, 13–205, 3.

[103]WA 27, 118, 32.

[104]LW 37, 360–72 (WA 26, 499–509).

[105]The Book of Concord, 287–318.

[106]"Nisi convictus fuero testimoniis scripturarum aut ratione evidente . . . victus sum scripturis a me adductis et capta conscientia in verbis Dei . . ." LW 32, 112 (WA 7, 838, 4-8).

[107]Cf. Hamm 1982; Hamm 2004; also Ulrich Köpf, Gabriel Biel und die Brüder vom Gemeinsamen Leben (Stuttgart: Steiner, 1998).

[108]Mostert in Junghans 1983, 340; cf. Pesch 1994.

[109]WA.TR 2, 193, 5-6.

[110]Adoro te devote, latens Deitas, Quae sub his figuris vere latitas: Tibi se cor meum totum subiicit. Quia te contemplans totum deficit. Visus, tactus, gustus in te fallitur, Sed auditu solo tuto creditur: Credo quidquid dixit Dei Filius: Nil hoc verbo veritatis verius. (Godhead here in hiding, whom I do adore, masked by these bare shadows, shape and nothing more, / See, Lord, at thy service low lies here a heart, Lost, all lost in wonder at the God thou art. / Seeing, touching, tasting are in thee deceived: How says trusty hearing? that shall be believed; / What God's son has told me, take for truth I do; Truth himself speaks truly or there's nothing true.) English text may be found at http://feastofsaints.com/adorote.htm.

[111]Lutherstudien II/3, 6. And yet in those terms one must for the most part agree with Luther's content.

[112]See "*Oratio, meditatio, tentatio*: the theological method" above.

[113]For Luther's understanding of theology in the context of current theory of science cf. Oswald Bayer, "Glauben und Wissenschaft," 127–41 in idem, *Autorität und Kritik. Zu Hermeneutik und Wissenschaftstheorie* (Tübingen: Mohr, 1991).

[114]WA 39/1, 229, 18-19.

[115]Cf. LW 36, 104 (WA 6, 559, 2): "libera ratio, immo charitas. . . ."

[116]The social consequences of the Reformation were not primarily the origination of absolutist structures under local nobility; those go back to developments that began long before the Reformation and were very distant from the ideas of the Reformers. Consider Machiavelli's *Il principe*, written in 1513.

[117]Against Bayer 1994, 105–6.

[118]Cf. Barth, Hans-Martin 2008a, 216ff.

[119]Bayer 2003, 32. This prejudice will probably dissipate in light of the newer results of Luther scholarship. Cf. Hamm 1982, 1998, 2004; Leppin in *Handbuch* 2005, 57–62.

[120]Streiff 1993, 220.

[121]". . . secundum praescriptum est loquendum . . ." (Christians are to speak . . . according to what has been prescribed), LW 38, 240 (LDStA 2, 462), Thesis 11.

[122]This is especially true with regard to Christology (cf. WA 39/2, 98, 12-22) and trinitarian dogma (cf. WA 41, 270, 6-12). It is interesting how tradition—though of course drawn from Scripture—here appears alongside Scripture itself!

[123]Benedict XVI addressed this problem from a Roman Catholic perspective in his Regensburg lecture in 2006; cf. idem, *The Regensburg Lecture*, ed. James V. Schall (South Bend, IN: St. Augustine's Press, 2007); cf. also Knut Wenzel, ed., *Die Religionen und die Vernunft. Die Debatte um die Regensburger Vorlesung des Papstes* (Freiburg: Herder, 2007).

16

Rivalry: Between Sacred Scripture and Human Tradition

One of the key phrases of the Reformation was *Sola Scriptura*: "Sacred Scripture alone!" "Let the Word stand," and let none of one's own thoughts be added to it! This principle was to be respected in the interpretation of Sacred Scripture, and also as regards the relevance of Sacred Scripture, which is not to be obscured by added traditions or diminished in any other way. This is a difficult proposition today, for a twofold reason: a great many of our contemporaries do not warm up to Scripture, or to religious traditions either.

Contemporary Questions

Critical questions are asked today both about what the Christian churches regard as tradition and about the Bible itself, which is also perceived as traditional material. Tradition as such has acquired a bad reputation; new knowledge advances humankind! Traditions from the past are considered more of a hindrance than a help; they can only prove helpful if they lead to new knowledge and yield to it. Innovation trumps tradition. With Descartes and the Enlightenment as a whole came the reversal whereby not traditions, but new and ongoing insights and experiences came to be regarded as contributing to progress. This view still dominates the attitudes of many people, even though here and there a certain rehabilitation of older customs may be in progress.

But if we want to rely on traditions at all we are immediately confronted with the problem of what traditions are useful. In the present age a challenge is posed by the traditions of non-Christian religions. Can Luther's theology be of any help in this situation? In this regard not even the various Christian confessional traditions see eye to eye. Luther may have found it easy to polemicize against the tradition as he found it; in the meantime, however,

429

even the Lutheran churches have assembled an impressive total of traditions of their own.

It also appears difficult to separate Sacred Scripture from broader traditions, since it owes its own existence to a traditional process. Besides, there are standards of confessional interpretation from which Sacred Scripture is scarcely able to disentangle itself and that have what amounts to credal status: in Roman Catholicism, for example, the interpretation of the words to Peter in Matthew 16:18; in Protestantism the emphasis on the Pauline message of justification in contrast to what is said in the letter of James.

This problem leads to the further question of the textual basis to which the Confessions actually appeal: does the Christian canon of the Old Testament contain only those Hebrew books that are regarded as canonical, as Protestant theology generally holds, or should we also include the late writings included in the Greek Septuagint, as in the Orthodox and Roman Catholic tradition? What is the role of translations? To what extent may a translation be responsive to theology and thus also confessionally colored, as the Luther Bible undoubtedly is? Would not, instead, a truly ecumenical unified translation be desirable, like the unified texts of the Our Father and the Apostles' Creed? What role should belong to biblical translations with different theological accents, such as the *Bibel in gerechter Sprache* ("Bible in Inclusive Language")?

Most difficult, finally, is the question of a clear and appropriate interpretation of the Bible. There is no such thing as Sacred Scripture "alone"; it always stands within the context of a particular socio-cultural constellation. Its interpretation takes place in a dialogue between the text and the particular recipients. To what extent should the biblical text be able to liberate us from the prejudices we bring with us, and to what extent do particular prior understandings help us to grasp the meaning of the text? Will the Bible still be emancipatory after it has been amalgamated with a culture like that of the West? How can it be liberated from traditional forms of inculturation and made available for other and different inculturations? How and from what points of view can we attribute a normative significance to Sacred Scripture in the face of all these questions? What should be the guidelines for interpretation? Can a biblicist fundamentalism be justified—or how do we establish that there is no justification for it? What about the legitimation of historical-critical exegesis?

For Luther the clarity and relevance of Sacred Scripture were obvious on the face of it, in contrast to the traditions that surrounded it and had overgrown it. Tradition seemed to him ambiguous, while the statements of Sacred Scripture were clear and of obvious relevance as regards the glory of God and the salvation of humans. How can we hold to this approach that was so central for the churches of the Reformation?

THE AMBIVALENCE OF TRADITION

Traditions are often accepted unquestioningly and only later made the subject of critical reflection. This process is in some ways analogous to the path from childhood to adolescence: only after reaching a certain age does one question the validity of views one adopted uncritically as a child. The dogmatic traditions accepted by the Roman Catholic church are available, collected and in official form, in Denzinger's *Enchiridion symbolorum*,[1] which up to the Bull "Exsurge Domine," which threatened Martin Luther's excommunication, contains nearly 1,500 documents by modern numbering. From Trent to the end of the twentieth century another 3,500 were added. For Luther, in view of this abundance of traditions, three questions came to the fore: First, where do the priorities lie? With conciliar decisions, papal declarations, the voices of the Fathers? What has the greatest weight? Then, how should we deal with contradictions? The battle between the Thomistic-oriented *via antiqua* and the Nominalist-oriented *via moderna* had not yet been resolved; within the *via moderna* itself there was a good deal of elasticity in the notion of grace. The orthodoxy of the Eastern churches was, in any case, very slow to attract any attention. Finally, what sorts of unnecessary burdening of conscience and hostility to life did the received traditions contain?

Medieval theology did not see this problem. For it, too, Sacred Scripture was the authority, but it did not choose to see any contradiction between that and the traditions that were piling up. The tradition of the old believers therefore had no response to the Reformation's attack, with its insistence on Sacred Scripture as the sole valid criterion. Even today the problem is scarcely acknowledged in the theology of the Orthodox churches of the East, and instead is either repressed or dogmatically decided: Sacred Scripture and the teachings of the first seven ecumenical councils are valid. This rejects any further unbridled development of tradition, but it does not solve the problem of the relationship between Scripture and Tradition as it had developed up to that point. In any case, Scripture was to be read in light of tradition.[2] Protestant fundamentalist groups, in contrast, do not seem to appreciate that an isolated reference to the Bible is impossible. They reject the idea that Sacred Scripture can never be understood apart from particular traditions and contexts, and that the fundamentalist way of reading corresponds to a particular pre-understanding.

It is hard to say how we got to such a confused situation. Sacred Scripture only appears as a criterion if blind trust in a common tradition disappears and the necessity of taking a position and being responsible is accepted. But how to get there? For the Reformer the catalyst was a radical encounter with Sacred Scripture in the context of the question of God's glory and the salvation of the human being. This radical encounter was and is, according to Luther's conviction, out of our control, for the Holy Spirit works when and where it will.

TRADITION AS A DANGER TO THE CHURCH

Luther by no means rejected the church as he found it *in toto*—on the contrary, it is always astonishing to observe how conservative his attitudes were. This is especially evident in the care he exercised in making changes to the worship service. The 1523 "Formula missae et communionis" for the most part maintains the old order; only the canon and the elements referring to sacrifice are eliminated. The "German Mass" of 1526 is likewise conservative. Even under the papacy, said Luther, there was "much that is Christian and good"; indeed, all the essentials—Sacred Scripture, baptism, the Lord's Supper, the Decalogue, the Credo, the Our Father—were taken from the papal church, though there they were in part misunderstood and distorted.[3] There are "human ordinances" and "human inventions" by which people have tried to secure themselves or put themselves onstage. But in doing so one violates the glory of God and thereby also burdens human beings. Luther's repeated example is the Pharisees, who in this connection are described not as Jews but as characteristic types of human behavior. After all, Sacred Scripture itself testifies that we will have to reckon with false teachers and even with the appearance of people who claim to be Christ. This, then, is about dangers that arise within the church itself; their symbol is the Antichrist (cf. 1 John 2:18-27).

To understand Luther rightly at this point we must recall the historical situation. Many innovations had been adopted only since the millennium and thus were relatively new. Transubstantiation and the withholding of the communion cup from the laity were in place only since the twelfth century, officially since the Fourth Lateran Council of 1215; likewise compulsory oral confession once a year was introduced in 1215. Indulgences were created in connection with the Crusades and the jubilees of the so-called Holy Years. Priestly celibacy was officially ordered in 1074. The *Decretum Gratiani*, the summary of canon law, also comes from the middle of the twelfth century, and there were a great many even newer requirements for fasting and such matters.

Thus the authority of church councils was of even greater importance. Luther acknowledged their authority in principle but held it to be a fundamental truth that councils could err. He had to make that assertion in his disputation at Leipzig in 1519 with regard to the Council of Constance, a century earlier, in the course of which, notoriously, John Hus had been condemned and burned. This was about the authority of Christ and the Gospel in contrast to that of an assumed authority that appealed to hierarchical or partially democratic representation. Nevertheless, Luther only changed when change could not be avoided. Thus before 1526 the question of the real presence of Christ in the Eucharist was not really a problem for him even though he had distanced himself from the idea of transubstantiation in his "The Babylonian Captivity of the Church" in 1520. It was only the appearance of Zwingli and the "fanatics" that made it seem necessary to Luther to express himself on the matter and to assert his theological position.[4]

In Luther's time the authority of the pope was not settled to the degree that was to be established by the First Vatican Council in 1870.[5] The constitution *Dei Verbum* of the Second Vatican Council would then read: "But the task of giving an authentic interpretation of the word of God, whether in its written form or in the form of tradition, has been entrusted to the living teaching office of the church alone." This is interpreted as service to the word, but it regards tradition as included: "This magisterium is not superior to the word of God, but is rather its servant. It teaches only what has been handed on to it."[6] The authoritative collection of official texts makes it clear which decisions are regarded as infallible.[7] It had not gone that far at the time of the Reformation. In any case, Luther was clear: there are false developments and wrong decisions in theology, even though he took it as a principle that the church as a whole can never err.

Luther also observed tendencies toward wrong structural developments that resulted in deviations from the original witness of the Gospel and the incapacitation of the community. He traced both to the fact that there can be interest in such wrong developments that is traceable to the sinful makeup of human beings.

At the same time Luther did not reject tradition in principle, but asserted that it is not of itself sufficient for theological argument. In Worms he said: "I do not trust either in the pope or in councils alone, since it is well known that they have often erred and contradicted themselves."[8] Tradition, he says, must be critically examined to see whether the church is teaching something that does not correspond to the word of God or even contradicts it. In that case correction and amendment are in order.[9]

THE UNAVOIDABILITY OF TRADITION AND ITS NEED FOR CRITIQUE

The Book of Concord, which brings together the formulaic elements that make up the Lutheran confessions, is well known to contain—very much as the Reformer would have it—the three creeds of the ancient church: the Apostles' Creed, the core of which was created in the second century, the Nicene-Constantinopolitan Creed of 325 and 381, and the so-called Athanasian Creed, which had nothing to do with Athanasius and stems from the beginning of the seventh century.[10] Luther sometimes explicitly cited the conventional creed as a formal authority: ". . . so all true Christians believe and so the Holy Scriptures teach us."[11] Against objections to the virgin birth Luther says: "Here I have a little book that is called the Credo, in which is this article. That is my Bible; it has stood so long and it has not been knocked over. By this I stand, on this I was baptized, from this I live and die. . . ."[12]

Certainly more important than this formal acknowledgment is the fact that the Reformer adopted the central content of the confessional formulae of the ancient church. As regards trinitarian faith, the "sublime" articles about the "divine majesty," Luther thinks that "Concerning these articles there is no contention or dispute, since we on both sides (believe and) confess them."[13] We can see, however, that there were controversies in the offing from the fact that in the final redaction of the Smalcald Articles he struck out the words "believe and." But as regards Christology he also accepted as valid the statements in the Apostles' Creed and the Athanasian symbol, though of course he interpreted these in the sense given them in his Small Catechism. This listing, indeed, raises a number of the questions relating to Luther's Christology and doctrine of the Trinity that we have addressed in previous chapters. At any rate it is clear to Luther that on the one hand the tradition is unavoidable, since it is God who gives the church knowledge, but on the other hand it remains in need of criticism because here people get involved in terms of their own interests. The word of God must therefore serve as a critical measure; with its help "we judge both apostles and churches and angels as well."[14] The Reformer recalls the contention between Paul and Peter as described in Galatians (chap. 2). Another Gospel cannot simply be invented (cf. Gal 1:9). Thus a formal reference to "apostolicity" is no criterion: "Whatever does not teach Christ is not yet apostolic, even though St. Peter or St. Paul does the teaching. Again, whatever preaches Christ would be apostolic, even if Judas, Annas, Pilate, and Herod were doing it."[15]

THE AMBIVALENCE OF EXPERIENCE AS THE BASIS FOR A PROBLEMATIC CONSTRUCTION OF TRADITION

From the present-day point of view one may well wonder why Luther's rejection of traditions became so intense. His battle for the word of God and against human and church traditions should not be understood simply as an emancipatory initiative or a juvenile attitude, a kind of "away with Rome!" Nor is it adequately explained by saying that at that time his view corresponded to the program of humanistic education, the return "*ad fontes*: to the sources!" Rather, the Reformer sees a serious threat to the word of God not only from presumptuous earthly authorities that claimed to interpret it authoritatively but also from the basic human need to employ speculative reason to make for oneself an image corresponding solely to one's own fantasy[16] and to trust more in one's own supposed experience than in the word given us by God.

Thus in Luther's view experience has a place that must be doubly defined. On the one hand the experience of misery and crisis is the place where God's word is at work and produces a sense of its power. From this comes existential certitude. "No one can worthily speak or hear any Scripture, unless he is touched in conformity with it, so that he feels inwardly what he hears and says outwardly and says, 'Ah, this is true!'"[17] God's word must be understood with the heart,[18] and for Luther the heart is the place within the human being where soul, intellect, will, and affect come together.[19] Here thought and feeling are intertwined. Both participate in the process of understanding. That is why the translation of Sacred Scripture is such a difficult task: "It requires a right, devout, honest, sincere, God-fearing, Christian, trained, informed, and experienced heart."[20]

On the other hand, however, the word of God, Luther is convinced, takes us beyond our immediate experience. No matter how much he insists on an existential, "experienced" theology, he warns just as much against accepting one's own experience as the final arbiter. The experience of sinful human beings is corrupted, so that God's actions and words must appear nonsensical to them. Sin and the devil are, so to speak, closer to the human being than God's word; therefore reason is more enlightened by what they have to say. Therefore Luther repeatedly calls people to struggle against reason. Faith transcends and corrects experience. Luther illustrates this with the example of the Syro-Phoenician woman, who, before she can be helped, must overcome the experience of being rejected and sent away by Jesus (cf. Matt 15:21-28): "Every thought, what you feel, see, and hear—all this you should cast out of your heart," and not let yourself be guided by what you sense about death and life, sin and grace, but "cling only to the word, let it not be taken from you, orient yourself to it, then there is no want." For through apparently negative experiences God brings people to "cling to the word alone with all your heart. He wants you to stand on no other footing than the word alone that you have heard." It is God's will: "he wants you to be stripped naked. Whether you come to heaven or hell, you must hold to this word. Where it is, you also must be and say: Here I have the word, I will place myself within it, I feel what I will, I will not let myself be torn away from this word."[21] The human heart must turn away from its experience, its "feelings," and "seize the deep, secret Yes under and over the No, believing firmly in God's word."[22]

To begin with, then, God's word is regarded altogether in terms of its effect on the emotions. But this very experience of the emotions leads beyond itself to a faith that is no longer dependent on emotion, an experience that lives without and contrary to experience, an experience of a higher order. It can sustain the protest of the emotions because it trusts hearing more than all other senses; it relies on God's word. One must take the word "into the ears and then press it into the heart and hold to it."[23] Luther concludes: "the ears alone are the organs of a Christian"; one must, so to speak, put one's eyes into one's ears, for the word takes us farther than what we have before our eyes or what we sense![24]

While the Reformer, in his polemic, opposes the tradition attacked in the Roman church as fixed "experience," in his battle against new "experiences" supposedly to be gained he primarily has the fanatics in mind. They, after all, do not point to the Gospel, but to the Big Rock Candy Mountain! They do not teach how the Spirit of God comes to the human person, but how the human should attain to the Spirit of God.[25] But what is crucial is not that we make God's word our own, but that we become God's own through God's word. As early as 1515, in his lectures on Romans, Luther writes that God "thus changes us into His Word, but not His Word into us."[26] Experience takes place in this way also, but "experience in a new dimension."[27] This does contradict the way we otherwise gain experiences and deal with them. "In nature experience is the reason why we hear, and it precedes assent; in theology, however, experience follows assent."[28] This does not contradict Luther's expressions of high regard for experience, found elsewhere. He knows that faith experience contains distinctions: the assent of faith to God's word is continued in a depth experience that proves its validity against all external circumstances and maintains its assent to God's word. The word of God may not be limited by the capacities of our experience. Neither reason nor tradition nor individual experience may set boundaries to God and his Gospel. "Only where there is no standard against which to measure God's word does it encounter me."[29] But how does Luther come to regard the word of God as such an exclusive criterion, and how does he apply it?

GOD'S WORD AND SACRED SCRIPTURE

The Reformer need not be defended against the accusation of biblicism. When his hymn demands: "The word they shall allow to stand, Nor any thanks have for it" we should recall that he immediately continues: "He is with us, at our right hand, With the gifts of his spirit."[30] The word of God is by no means to be identified simply and solely with Sacred Scripture. The word of God, which works through Sacred Scripture, is not some sort of thing one can study in an objective fashion; it is an active subject that makes the hearers and readers its objects. Consequently it cannot be arbitrarily turned and twisted; it resists such manipulation. No one can speak so well about God as God's own self![31] If reason could grasp and understand spiritual things of itself, "our Lord God could well have kept his mouth shut, but it is *supra et contra rationem*"—it goes beyond reason and at the same time goes against it.[32] God is indeed everywhere in all creatures, but he does not will to be sought everywhere. He has clearly marked how and where one can find him—namely in the word. "Whoever hears his word sees into his heart."[33] But if God's word and Sacred Scripture cannot be simply identified, what is their relationship to one another?

GOD'S CREATIVE WORD

For Luther, God is the Creator pure and simple. To that extent the first article of faith already contains everything that is constitutive for Christian faith: confession of God, who must be understood as Creator in every respect, on the surface, in the natural world, and also in the spiritual, for "God made us and not we ourselves; we are his people and the sheep of his pasture" (Ps 100:3). Allowing God to create—that is the mystery of faith. The instrument the Creator uses is the word. So it was when the world was created, and so it is in the justification of the ungodly, the new creation: God calls into being what is not (Rom 4:17): "For he spoke and it came to be; he commanded and it stood firm" (Ps 33:9). This is an important difference between God and the human: when God speaks, God makes something; when the human makes something, she or he speaks![34] God's word is the primal reality that underlies all reality. Therefore we may not orient ourselves to superficial reality or allow ourselves to be blinded by it. God's word, like Godself, is almighty, and it has a great many functions. Luther illustrates this with the different concepts and comparisons that are used in the Bible itself for the word of God: "The Scriptures assign many different names to the Word of God because of its many virtues and effects. It is indeed all things and all-powerful [Heb 1:3; 4:12]. It is called 'the sword of the Spirit' [Eph 6:17], with which we combat the devil and all spiritual foes. It is termed 'a light' [Ps 119:105], 'the early and the late rain' [Jas 5:7], 'a heavenly dew' [Hos 6:4], 'gold, silver' [Ps 119:72], medicine, garment, ornament, and the like. Similarly, it is also called bread, since it nourishes and strengthens the soul, which grows strong and fat on it."[35] It is God's uterus, God's womb, "in it [God] conceives us, carries us, gives birth to us."[36] It has generative power, begets the new human, so that each one's birth takes place in the effective power of the word of God. It creates the faith of the individual and thus at the same time that of the church. In the word the eschatological new world is present.

What is the basis for this all-encompassing manner in which the word of God is at work? God communicates God's own self through it. The word points to Jesus Christ. Without the word I could not grasp Jesus Christ: "Christ on the cross and all his suffering and his death do not avail, even if, as you teach, they are 'acknowledged and meditated upon' with the utmost 'passion, ardor, heartfeltness' . . ." Luther instructs his opponent, Karlstadt. "Something else must always be there. What is it? The Word, the Word, the Word. Listen, lying spirit, the Word avails. Even if Christ were given for us and crucified a thousand times, it would all be in vain if the Word of God were absent and were not distributed and given to me with the bidding, this is for you, take what is yours!"[37] More than a century later Angelus Silesius wrote: "Were Christ born in Bethlehem a thousand times and not in you, so would you remain lost forever,"[38] incorporating the mystical tradition that speaks of God being born in the human soul; for Luther such a divine birth can only be accomplished through the word. Christ must "become word"; only thus does he nourish. Christ is of no benefit to us "unless God translates him into words whereby you can hear and know him. What does it profit you if Christ sits in heaven or is hidden in the form of bread? He must be brought to you, prepared for you, and translated into words for you by means of the inner and external word. See, that is truly the Word of God. Christ is the bread, God's Word is the bread, and yet there is but one object, one bread. He is in the Word, and the Word is in him. To believe in this same Word is the same as eating the bread. He to whom God imparts this will live eternally."[39] The word makes Christ present inwardly to the believer: just as a sunbeam is reflected on the surface of water or in a mirror, "so Christ is reflected and casts a beam of his light into our hearts." In this way we ourselves are "illumined from one clarity to another" (2 Cor 3:17), see the Lord ever more clearly, and are "transformed and illumined in the same image, so that all become one loaf with Christ."[40] Luther illustrates the relationship between the word and the believer in mystical imagery: being baked together with Christ, the union of the human heart with the divine word.[41] Luther does not understand the word here primarily as a means of communication or as a means of mutual understanding between God and the human person, but in its performative nature. It is through the word of God that God creates reality![42]

This makes clear what significance the Reformer accords to preaching: the sermon is not primarily a communication of information; it is a saving event, an effective deed in which God takes hold of human hearts and drives out the powers that are in opposition to God. It is not a moral appeal or metaphysical information; it is an exorcistic event that serves the glory of God and the salvation of human beings.[43] Hence Luther can make preaching itself the subject of preaching.[44] It acquires its power not through the psychic efforts of the preacher; this Luther makes clear in the controversy over the meaning of the word in the eucharistic celebration. Whispering and mysterious gestures are of no avail: ". . . where have we ever taught that our whispering and breathing have improved the bread?" Everything depends on the word itself.[45]

The preaching that culminates in the promise of forgiveness corresponds to reception in hearing and meditation. Mary, the mother of Jesus, is, so to speak, the perfect listener to preaching (Luke 2:19, 51). But what is the relationship between these powerful expectations of the word of God and the dry words of Sacred Scripture?

SACRED SCRIPTURE

Precisely because of his high esteem for the word of God it has always been startling to see how freely Luther could criticize the Bible. He did not believe in a verbal inspiration of individual passages in Scripture. For him the very existence of the Bible was a stopgap measure; the "putting into writing" of the Gospel could be injurious to the living character of the message. Writing books was not really in keeping with the New Testament; "rather in all places there should be fine, goodly, learned, spiritual, diligent preachers without books, who extract the living word from the old Scripture and unceasingly inculcate it into the people, just as the apostles did." For "they first of all preached to the people by word of mouth and converted them, and this was their real apostolic and New Testament work." But when false teachers appeared and spread every kind of heresy people began to bring Scripture to their aid; they wanted "to ensure that the sheep could feed themselves and hence protect themselves against the wolves, if their shepherds failed to feed them or were in danger of becoming wolves too."[46] This statement is partially correct historically; it is also Luther's retrojection of his own situation into the period of early Christianity. But what is really important to the reformer is the living nature of the message. For "the word 'Gospel' signifies nothing else than a sermon or report concerning the grace and mercy of God"; the Gospel "is not what one finds in books and what is written in letters of the alphabet; it is rather an oral sermon and a living Word, a voice that resounds throughout the world and is proclaimed publicly, so that one hears it everywhere. . . ."[47] This is about the *viva vox evangelii*. Luther would probably have rejected a Bible and tract mission that consists essentially of distributing written materials.

Luther's Bible was at first the Vulgate, though not yet in an edition based on scholarship and universally recognized; its text, too, had first to be purified. But in making his own translation Luther certainly had the words of the Vulgate in his ears.[48] His first attempts at translation into German were made in connection with his own preaching work; the text to be presented had to be comprehensible. In accordance with the humanistic ideals of his time and on the basis of his own principled convictions the Sacred Scriptures must of course be translated from the original text. The translation of the New Testament, done at the Wartburg in only seventy-three days, published in 1522 and referred to in church histories as the September Testament, has always been acknowledged as an outstanding achievement of the Reformer. The translation of the Old Testament was done only in fits and starts, so that the whole Bible first came to publication in 1534. But Luther was not satisfied.

Weekly meetings of a special commission worked to improve the text; the minutes of the meetings are partially preserved.[49] Sometimes they worked for three or four weeks to find a single appropriate word or expression and still could not.[50] The problem with every translation, even today, is to decide whether it should be oriented toward the original or the target language. Luther was concerned with the target language in the interest of the original, as indicated by the famous demand to "inquire of the mother in the home, the children on the street, the common man in the marketplace" and "be guided by their language, the way they speak. . . ."[51] Beyond that, Luther also asked artisans about the names of their tools, had Georg Spalatin explain the different kinds of birds, and got the butcher to describe the slaughtering of a ram. Nevertheless, he did not totally orient his work to the target language, but instead carefully weighed when, for substantive reasons, he had to stick closer to the Hebrew and when he could freely make use of German. His guide in all of it was his theological responsibility. The whole Bible was to him a testimony to Jesus Christ. It is repeatedly pointed out that "what inculcates Christ" was also the decisive criterion for his Bible translation, but one must also say that this is an insufficient definition of Luther's point of view. For him the forgiveness of sins bestowed in Christ is the real center of the biblical witness. This is strikingly clear in the fact that in editions of the Bible from 1533 to his death he had the expression "FORGIVES SINS" (Rom 3:25) in capitals— the only such passage in the whole Bible![52] If a passage in the text is unclear he asks whether it is speaking of Law or Gospel, the forgiveness of sins. This theological approach yielded for Luther, as Klaus Dietrich Fricke formulates it, "key reformational words"[53] that appear frequently in Luther's translation of the Bible: "console," "consolation," "preach," "grace." His creative use of language may also be partly rooted in this when the simple Hebrew "tov/good" is translated "that is a precious thing" (Ps 92:2) or "I love . . ." (Ps 18:2) with "dear to my heart is . . ." In Hebrew, Psalm 36:6 reads: "Your steadfast love, O Lord, is in the heavens, your faithfulness as far as the clouds." Luther translates: "Your steadfast love, O Lord, reaches throughout the heavens, and your truth as far as the clouds extend."[54] Of course, the Reformer also introduced his theology into the text. He was accused of this especially in regard to Micah 6:8: "It is told to you, O mortal, what is good and what the Lord requires of you, to keep the word of God and to love and to be humble before your God." Literally, "be humble before your God" should be translated "walk (walk with, live) attentively/carefully/willingly with your God." Luther was probably aware of the change, because he wrote in the margin: "to keep God's word, that is faith, love, suffering."[55] His translation of the Hebrew Bible is in fact a "deliberate Christianization of the Old Testament."[56] How can that be justified today? In his tradition-critical prefaces on the individual biblical books and in scattered marginal notes the Reformer gives his readers a clear handle on what they should be looking for as they read.[57] Should this be regarded as making up the readers' minds for them ahead of time, or as an aid to unlocking the Bible? The elimination of Luther's prefaces by the pietists was, we might say, a first step in the disempowerment of Luther's Bible.

How did the Reformer see the canon of the Bible and how did he evaluate the individual biblical writings? The idea that the Apocrypha are books that "cannot be seen as equal to the Holy Scriptures but are useful and good to read" goes back to Jerome, who in turn appealed to the *hebraica veritas*.[58] Luther sometimes permitted himself some very personal judgments on individual parts of Scripture, as in his introduction to the explanation of Psalm 118 ("Give thanks to the Lord . . ."), the "lovely Confitemini," as he called this psalm: he referred to it as "his" psalm, saying that he "was particularly directed to this psalm, that it must be and be called my own," and that it had helped him in a variety of crises. "Would to God that the whole world would claim this psalm as their own, as I do!" Luther would be happy to contend with anyone about who had the best right to call this "his" or "her" psalm. He deplores the fact that very few people "can say from their hearts to Sacred Scripture or to a single psalm throughout their lives: you are my beloved book, or: you shall be my own little psalm."[59] Thus Luther exercised something like literary criticism long before the creation of historical-critical exegesis: in the book of Jeremiah, for example, he found that everything is so confused that one gets the impression that Jeremiah himself could not have composed the book; however, one should not worry about the order or allow oneself to be hindered by the lack thereof.[60]

However, Luther goes furthest in his criticism based on theology: the "true and noblest books" of the New Testament (so he says in the preface to the 1522 edition)[61] are the Gospel of John, 1 John, the letters of Paul (especially those to the Romans and the Galatians, but also the one to the Ephesians), and 1 Peter. These are "the true kernel and marrow of all the books"; the Reformer called the Gospel of John the "one, fine, true, and chief gospel."[62] He is, so to speak, married to the letter to the Galatians; that is the epistle he has relied upon: "my Kate of Bora."[63] It seems to him that in the letter to the Hebrews "wood, straw, or hay are perhaps mixed" into it.[64] Best known and most frequently attacked is Luther's critique of the letter of James, which he thought "an epistle of straw" in comparison with the letters of Paul:[65] "I almost feel like throwing Jimmy into the stove, as the priest in Kalenberg did"—the pastor of Kalenberg, during a visit from his duchess, had used wooden statues of the apostles for heating.[66] Luther doesn't want to count "Jimmy" among the most important books in his Bible because he diametrically contradicts Paul and his message of justification. On the basis of such arguments Luther boldly altered the sequence of the biblical books, placing Hebrews and James, which had previously followed immediately after Philemon, at the end of the canon, just before the letter of Jude and Revelation. His second preface to Revelation (1530)[67] shows, however, that Luther did not regard his judgment of the biblical books as irreversible; foci in the understanding of biblical passages could alter to some degree in the course of a lifetime.

The Old Testament posed a special problem for the Reformer. On the one hand he was deeply committed to it; after all, he (and his "team") translated it from the Hebrew. On the other hand he could not fail to see that it contains a great deal that does not conform to the New Testament. So, for example, he says of Esther and 2 Maccabees, which rely to an unusual degree on the secular history of Judaism, that he wished they did not exist at all; they "Judaize" too much and contain a great deal of gross pagan stuff.[68] Some distinctions are therefore needed. As regards Luther and the Old Testament we must distinguish on three levels: first of all, it is clear that it is addressed to a particular people, namely Israel; it is, so to speak, the criminal and civil code of the people Israel, or, as Luther said at the time, the Jews' "Saxon law"; from that point of view it has nothing to do with Christians any more than the law of the German empire was valid in France. The second level is that of religion, on which, according to Luther, the Jews themselves misunderstood it to some degree, namely insofar as they were interested only in an external fulfillment of the Law. From this religious point of view, however, the Old Testament was obsolete for Christians, and it would be totally mistaken for a Christian to keep the prescriptions of the Old Testament or seek to legitimate any kind of theological opinions by reference to the Old Testament, as some of the "enthusiasts" tried to do. If one were to deal with the Hebrew Bible in that way one might as well "drive out Christ and eliminate the whole New Testament." For Moses "is given to the Jewish people alone, and does not concern us Gentiles and Christians."[69] Hence Luther does not hesitate to interpret the Sabbath commandment in terms of the Christian Sunday and in his Catechism to pass over the prohibition of images, just as the medieval church had done.

The third level, of course, is the one that can claim relevance for Christians also. Here again we must distinguish between what is as true for Christians as for all people, that is, natural law, and the preaching of Law and Gospel as accepted especially in Christian faith. Natural law is said to be nowhere so clearly summarized as it was by Moses. His important function was to present natural law to Christians, too, as divine law, for human reason is so blind that it cannot really recognize sin. On the other hand, however, Moses' preaching of the law must be seen through the lens of the Gospel, for Christ is the end of the Law (Rom 10:4). While it is true that this does not cause the commandments of the Decalogue to lose their meaning so "that one should not keep or fulfill them," but Moses' proper "office" in them, namely to accuse the people and give them bad consciences, is dissolved, since for Christians, "through Christ sin is forgiven, God is reconciled, and man's heart has begun to feel kindly toward God."[70] The Old Testament is really revealed only by the New Testament, which "is as if somebody had a sealed letter and later on broke it open."[71] The Old Testament is legitimated by the New; this is how Luther understands the challenge of John 5:39 to search the Scriptures, that is, the Old Testament, for this, he says, is what Christ is testifying to: "Here you will find the swaddling cloths and the manger in which Christ lies . . . Simple and lowly are these swaddling cloths, but dear is the treasure, Christ, who lies in them."[72]

Thus Luther does not simply refer formally to the Bible; he seeks to understand where, in fact, God's word speaks and can be found. He draws his criteria from that perspective. The distinction between Law and Gospel, discussed above,[73] is important to him. It could look as if the Reformer was completely arbitrary in his dealings with Scripture. Hence we must clarify the ways in which his personal, literary, and theological criticisms are related.

THE CENTER OF SCRIPTURE: CHRIST

In interpreting a book, even today, we first look within the work itself for major and incidental motifs, and in the process we sometimes discover contradictions. For Luther there was a central content and, derived from that, a clear criterion for interpreting Sacred Scripture and evaluating individual passages. He organized his whole hermeneutical activity around those principles.

The central content and decisive criterion of Scripture is Christ: take Christ out of Scripture, and what is left that is in any way essential?[74] "[T]he entire Scripture deals only with Christ everywhere."[75] Formally, of course, this assertion cannot be maintained, as was also clear to Luther. So, starting from his central criterion, he asserts that there are statements in Sacred Scripture that must be considered as in themselves irrelevant or even pagan. Then he traces statements that point to Christ by portraying him as model and lawgiver. This is important, he says, but it does not yet touch the center, which is found in those passages that express the Gospel offered in Jesus Christ. For Luther the dialectic between Law and Gospel unlocks the whole of Scripture. He finds this most clearly expressed in Romans, which he therefore regards as "a bright light, almost sufficient to illuminate the entire holy Scriptures."[76] On the other hand, as we have indicated, the Reformer seriously doubted that the letter of James could have been written by an apostle, since in James's opinion Abraham—altogether against Paul's thinking—is supposed to have been justified by works. Luther of course understands that James is polemicizing against those who wanted to rely on faith without works. But James thought that he could achieve something by appealing to the Law; he was "unequal to the task."[77] His assertion that he is an apostle achieves nothing at all. Not formal criteria, but those of content, are what can advance us here: "that is the true test by which to judge all books, when we see whether or not they inculcate Christ."[78] To "inculcate Christ [Christus treiben]" first of all means only formally that they teach or "treat of" Christ. But the content of the expression is something more, namely what brings Christ and all his blessings close to the person, "when the voice comes that says, 'Christ is your own, with his life, teaching, works, death, resurrection, and all that he is, has, does, and can do.'"[79] For Luther this by no means entailed a reduction of everything to Christology. If the Bible were a great and mighty tree "and all its words the branches," he could say he had tapped all the "branches."[80] The preacher, that is, must—here he uses yet another image—"sit in the middle of the Scriptures,"[81] must in fact "stick his head into the Bible day and night."[82] Luther does not appoint a "*Sitz im Leben* for the Bible" but "a *Sitz* in the Bible for its interpreters."[83] The biblical message is understood by the one who is at home in the Bible and knows how to apply all its individual passages to Jesus Christ and to understand them in his light.

Luther's guiding hermeneutical ideas arise from that approach. The individual passages of Scripture serve Christ, the king, as his servants. If they prove themselves recalcitrant they must be opposed: "if the adversaries press the Scriptures against Christ, we urge Christ against the Scriptures."[84] A critique of the fourfold sense of Scripture based on Christology is a necessary consequence. In the Middle Ages it was customary to distinguish between the literal sense (which gave information), the allegorical sense (which showed what was to be believed), the moral sense (which gave the necessary directions for action), and finally an "anagogical" sense that pointed to the church and eternal life.[85] Luther found the allegorical sense a particular abomination because it drew one away from the literal sense. An allegorical interpretation threw the door wide open to getting away from what the text really means. Allegory, as the word itself betrays, says something different from what the text offers. What is astonishing, then, is the freedom with which Luther himself uses allegoresis. In the pericope of the Good Samaritan the one who falls prey to the robbers is of course the sinful human being, while the robbers are the devil. The oil the Samaritan pours into the wounds of the one who fell among the robbers is the Gospel of God's grace; the wine stands for the Cross, which unavoidably follows faith. Then the Samaritan places the wounded person on his donkey: "That is he himself, the Lord Christ, who carries us; we lie on his shoulders, neck, and body. There is scarcely any lovelier story in the whole Gospel than the one in which the Lord Christ compares himself to a shepherd who carries the lost sheep on his own shoulders back to the flock. He is still bearing it, even today." The inn to which the victim is brought is Christianity, and the host represents preachers.[86] We can see from this example that Luther also makes distinctions in the use of allegoresis: it is appropriate as long as it expresses the Gospel in appropriate fashion. In interpreting the Old Testament Luther found many "figures" representing Christ.[87] Where Christology was concentrated in the text itself, of course, there was nothing to allegorize; in that case allegory would only lead astray.

Consequently, in explaining the words of institution in the Eucharist Luther allowed for no allegorizing whatsoever.

As far as the Reformer was concerned, Sacred Scripture is clear in both an external and an internal sense. The external clarity he sees as also founded in Christ, for he is the "center of the circle from which the whole circle is drawn . . . and whoever is oriented to him belongs within it." One must find one's own relationship to that center, and then one will clearly understand what Scripture says. For Christ is "the very center of the circle, and all the stories in Holy Scripture, when regarded rightly, are about Christ," have their goal in him.[88] The approach immanent in the work and existential interpretation are mutually joined. The result is a hermeneutics that does not teach how to understand in a distanced and cognitive sense but is intended to create an inner joining of Christ and the reader or hearer. When one looks at Christ, what is unclear becomes clear. Obscure passages in Scripture that at first seem incomprehensible acquire light and clarity from the clear and direct passages. In this way Scripture explains itself, so to speak: it becomes easy to understand in and of itself, completely open and altogether trustworthy, *sui ipsius interpres*—its own interpreter.[89] Paul Althaus has expanded this statement by saying that therefore Scripture also critiques itself, is "*sui ipsius critica*."[90] It interprets itself by articulating the witness to Christ so that it can be understood. Christ is, "so to speak, the matter of Scripture in person."[91] There is certainly an internal logic to this, because if the interpretation of Scripture could only be legitimated by a particular authority, the authority in turn would have to be legitimated—and so on.[92]

The first precondition for the possibility that the witness to Christ can be articulated in a comprehensible manner and clearly received is language. Therefore one must "hold to the simple, pure, and natural meaning of the words, in the grammar and usage God has created among humans." Otherwise Scripture would be "shaken like a reed by every wind."[93] That is why Luther insisted so strongly on the original biblical languages and reproached the Waldensians for supposedly not having done so.[94] We cannot deny that the Gospel, although it "has come and still comes every day through the medium of the Holy Spirit," still reaches us through the medium of language. This is not a general observation, but is applied to the Gospel when Luther continues: "languages are the sheath in which this sword of the Spirit is contained; they are the casket in which this jewel is enshrined." The Reformer never tires of seeking imagery for languages: they are "the vessel in which this wine is held; they are the larder in which this food is stored." The parable of the feeding of the five thousand is brought into play: languages are the baskets in which "are kept these loaves and fishes and fragments. If through our neglect we let the languages go (which God forbid!), we shall not only lose the gospel"; there will also be consequences for our command of any language: "the time will come when we shall be unable either to speak or write a correct Latin or German."[95]

God's word has but one meaning. The fountain in the marketplace is publicly visible and accessible even if those who live in the side streets cannot see it. The sun's light shines even if someone were to keep his or her eyes closed: consequently, people should "stop imputing with blasphemous perversity the darkness and obscurity of their own hearts to the wholly clear Scriptures of God."[96] Externally, the content of the biblical message is altogether discernible. But how does the external clarity produce assent to faith, and thus inner clarity?

Luther sees inner clarity as grounded in pneumatology. With regard to Christ the Scriptures are their own witness, but they gain their persuasive power not from outward authorities but from within: one "senses that this is God's word."[97] Luther summarizes in *De servo arbitrio*: "there are two kinds of clarity in Scripture . . . one external and pertaining to the ministry of the Word, the other located in the understanding of the heart." Regarding the inner clarity one must say that "no man perceives one iota of what is in the Scriptures unless he has the Spirit of God." All have darkened hearts! Therefore "the Spirit is required for the understanding of Scripture, both as a whole and in any part of it." But as regards external clarity "nothing at all is left obscure or ambiguous, but everything there is in the Scriptures has been brought out by the Word into the most definite light. . . ."[98] Certainly, inner clarity is not achieved without the external word that God has caused humans to know. God "will not come to you in your chamber and speak with you. It is appointed that the external word must be preached and must precede, and afterward, when one has taken the word into one's ears and heart, then comes the Holy Spirit, the true schoolmaster, and gives power to the word so that it sticks."[99] In his controversy with Karlstadt, Luther also includes the sacrament in the external process of communication that is followed by the action of the Holy Spirit.[100] Given his christocentric and pneumatological approach to Scripture, it is easy enough for Luther to find two passages that appear to contradict each other: God (or God's word) and Sacred Scripture are as widely different as the Creator and the creature[101]—and, on the other hand, he can write of "the Holy Scriptures, that is . . . God himself."[102] The tension is resolved in the idea that Sacred Scripture "contains" God's word.[103] The clarity of Scripture is not simply given; it yields itself ever anew to those who engage with it. This is true both of the external clarity that can be achieved by diligent philological work and reference to the center of Scripture and for the inner clarity that, of course, is not at our disposal and must be left to the working of the Holy Spirit. "Claritas" then means not only intellectual clarity but the illuminative power of the Gospel that fills the faithful.

CRITICAL EVALUATION

Some general anthropological and some specifically ecumenical objections can be raised against Luther's understanding of Scripture. There are also questions to be posed about his translation and his hermeneutics. How should we approach these?

QUESTIONING LUTHER'S TRANSLATION OF THE BIBLE

Luther's Bible translation is "partisan"—we might say it corresponds perfectly to his theology. Did he create his own basis of argument for his theological approach? If his prefaces to the Old and New Testaments and to the individual biblical books as well as his marginal notes were printed in our contemporary editions of the Bible it would only strengthen that suspicion. Martin Brecht suggested that, apart from the translation itself, the prefaces and marginal glosses in Luther's *Deutsche Bibel* made it "the most effective of all his works."[104] What are the arguments today for retaining Luther's Bible? We can, of course, mention Luther's creative power with words and his significance for the history of the German language as a whole. But that is not an adequate theological argument. Peter Steinacker points out that, in contrast to the *Bibel in gerechter Sprache* (Inclusive Language Bible), Luther's Bible preserves the "cultural memory" of German-speaking Protestantism. That is an underestimation: it preserves the spiritual memory at least of the Lutheran churches. Many generations have, to use an expression from the old Bavarian liturgy, received from it "grace and aid, teaching and consolation." The book of sayings appended to the Catechism was a further aid to keeping core expressions in Luther's language alive. The marking of key passages (which has shifted in the course of time) in boldface or italic type[105] attempts the same thing in a different way. Would German-speaking Protestantism lose its basis if it abandoned the Luther Bible?

Not only has historical-critical exegesis since the Enlightenment shown that biblical texts must constantly be translated anew; Luther himself, into his late years, worked steadily to improve his translation. Thus new translations are quite according to his own mind. The Bible is not the Qu'ran, to which Muslims accord religious validity ultimately only in its Arabic version. The message of the Bible presses from within itself to be translated, understood, heard, received, and used. Of course, that does not do away with Luther's Bible. New attempts at translation are important, but they can either match the spirit of the Luther Bible—as does, for example, the translation by Jörg Zink—or contradict it, as does the *Bibel in gerechter Sprache* in quite a few places. Lutheran theology and churches will have need, in the present time, for biblical translations of all sorts designed for different groups of readers, but they will repeatedly turn to Luther's Bible as a standard that makes it clear whether a translation really does justice to the Gospel as the Reformation understood and preached it. The Lutheran churches would do a disservice to ecumenism as well if they were to abandon the Luther Bible in favor of a new, common "ecumenical" biblical translation; they would, in fact, be guilty of depriving it of one of their most distinctive contributions.

But further work must be done on the text of the Luther Bible itself if it is to be used in liturgy and so maintain its function of bestowing identity on Lutheran congregations. Revisions will have to strive to retain the flow of language that is characteristic of Luther and preserve his style, so thoroughly impregnated with experience, while carefully adopting the changes that have taken place in the German language.[106] Exegetical insights can be brought to bear in the form of notes or text boxes, but overall it is important that the Luther Bible remain the book to which Lutheran Christians can appeal in good conscience, as modeled by Luther: "Unless I am convinced by the testimony of the Scriptures or by clear reason. . . ."[107]

ANTHROPOLOGICAL OBJECTIONS

Relevance of the word

Did Luther overestimate the relevance of the word and so introduce a trend to rationalism? Did his insistence on hearing, in contrast to seeing, tasting, and feeling, represent an anthropological reductionism? Where is human wholeness? Luther would probably answer: it is precisely the word that reaches human conscience, the human center. Forgiveness can only be conveyed to human beings through the word. The word opens future and perspective. Ultimately, a promise can scarcely be given except through the word. But what is fundamentally at issue is hearing not only with the ears but with body and soul, skin and hair. According to recent anthropological investigations, in fact, the ear seems to be a preferentially equipped sense organ. As one is dying, none of the sense organs continues its receptive ability as long as does the ear. Even physiologically, the ability to hear constitutes an essential element of the specific difference between human beings and the world of animals and plants.[108] Luther assumed the primary difference lay in the ability to speak.[109]

Relevance of the biblical word

If we insist on this specific role of the word, certainly, the question arises whether Luther, while not overestimating the capacity of human words, did perhaps overvalue the significance of the biblical word. He did not live in a religiously plural world as we do today; he could not ask himself why the Bible, and not the Bhagavad Gita or the Buddhist canon. But he did have Islam to consider; he himself wrote the preface to Theodor Bibliander's edition of the Qu'ran in 1543.[110]

But reading the Qu'ran was no temptation for him; it was clear to Luther that no other writing testifies to Christ with such validity as the New Testament, as well as the Old Testament seen through the lens of the New. Luther did not examine the testimony to Christ in the Qu'ran. Here today's Christians must proceed differently. It is possible that certain parts of the Qu'ran can be read through Christ in much the same way as the Old Testament—and many relevant discoveries made in the process![111]

Spirit and letter

In Luther's time a further anthropological objection was offered by the Pietists: everything could not depend on the letter; after all, Sacred Scripture itself says: "The letter kills, but the spirit gives life" (2 Cor 3:6). The inner witness of the Holy Spirit is essentially important for Luther. It is because of the work of the Holy Spirit that the word is able to "satisfy the heart," so to embrace and capture the human person that she or he "feels how true and right it is."[112] But the Spirit does not come "without a medium," directly, without being communicated through the word of Jesus Christ. So if God has sent the Son into the world and Sacred Scripture attests to it, that makes it clear where God wills to be found and where God is not. Thus there is no immediate encounter with God but only one that is mediated by the word of Jesus Christ. Of course, the Spirit is as inseparable from the word as the breath is from the voice. If we are speaking of faith in Christ, it certainly cannot take place apart from or without Jesus Christ, and the Holy Spirit has a constitutive function, helping the word to have and maintain the power to break through. The Spirit can make present to me a word that I may have heard ten years ago and not noted at the time. But the Spirit cannot be recognized as the Spirit of Christ without the word of Christ.

Word and deed

Finally, there is another objection that is presented especially by religious people against Luther's concept of the word of God: in the beginning was the deed! Orthopraxis is more important than orthodoxy! "You will know them by their fruits!" (Matt 7:20). Here again Luther's intention is not hard to understand. He regards the scope of human action as limited. The permanent challenge, "do well," does not bring people to ultimate fulfillment, despite their desire to act. Behavior can and must discredit the word in many cases, but words can transcend behavior. A preacher who does not know that the word of God infinitely surpasses her or his own acts and omissions and leaves them in the dust should not even bother to ascend the pulpit. It is only through the word of God that a Christian's actions have their rightness, their approval, their dignity, their freedom, and their joy. After all, Luther himself "acted"! But what he probably paid too little attention to was the fact that even action—in the sense of the word—can be a manner of hearing because it encompasses and deepens what is heard.

HERMENEUTICAL PROBLEMS

Hidden biblicism?

Was Luther's understanding of the relationship between Scripture and Tradition naïve? The Bible, after all, is a historical book. In the wake of the Reformation's initiative, historical-critical exegesis since the Enlightenment has developed this insight as an unmistakable fact. Does that make Luther's idea of Scripture obsolete? Certainly many of the ways the Reformer dealt with Sacred Scripture seem naive, or to put it more gently, simple—in the good sense. We may also regret that there seems to be a fundamentalist tendency in Luther in certain contexts. Thus it is striking that while Luther reveals a surprising freedom in his evaluation of the biblical books, within the biblical writings themselves he does not always adequately apply his christological criterion. One example of this is the way he reads some of the demonological statements in the New Testament with utter seriousness or takes the eschatological imagery seriously in an altogether biblicist fashion.[113] "What inculcates Christ" did not furnish him with an adequate criterion with which to confront superstition and the ideas of witches and sorcery in radically critical fashion.[114]

Certainly this does not detract from the fact that in other—and more essential!—contexts Luther exercised a thoroughly skilled critique of statements that seemed to him "heathenish," even though they were found in the Bible. He asked whether and to what extent the self-revelation of the glory of God in Jesus Christ for the salvation of human beings was expressed in what he read. On that basis he could, in the sense of a "second naïveté," leave some passages of Scripture without understanding them and "take off his hat."[115]

Trinitarian word!

Luther's concern is understandable: he wanted to prevent self-preoccupied people from fooling themselves. Therefore he permitted no swerves into esotericism and does not recommend religious self-development apart from Jesus Christ. That is altogether reasonable. But what about the Creator's word that makes itself evident in creation itself and about which the Reformer had so much to say? He explains the working of the word about Jesus Christ and that of the Spirit through the word, but not the word of the Creator and the language of creation. The message of the Creator and creation is developed in another place and in other contexts; as a result it threatens to become an independent "Gospel" without Christ, while the preaching of Christ loses the plausibility it gains from creation.[116] Something similar can be said about the work of the Spirit. The close connection of the Spirit to the word isolates it from creation. It is no longer in a comprehensive sense "the Giver of Life," as the Nicene-Constantinopolitan Creed says. Luther did not adequately succeed in showing that God's word is trinitarian—"three-voiced." The word of Christ cannot be understood without the cooperative aid of Spirit and Creator. The origin of faith depends not only on christological and pneumatological, but also on creation-related preconditions. My own constitution, with its created condition, cannot be omitted, and it implies also my history, my family, and my friends, ultimately even my breath—all that goes into the shaping of my experience and should be understood, from the perspective of the Christ-witness, as God's word to me.[117]

Long-term effects

Distant effects of Luther's approach are also perceptible: the historical-critical exegesis that began with the Enlightenment adopted Luther's plea for the literal sense of Scripture but at the same time failed to hold to and apply his criterion for content: the Christ message. It has only been the theology of the twentieth century that has put things back in the right order with its intensive hermeneutical discussions. Karl Barth demanded a theological interpretation—to the glory of God! Rudolf Bultmann made himself the defender of an anthropological interpretation—for the salvation of human beings! His existential interpretation was sustained by a primal Lutheran impulse: the Gospel is kerygma, a living, life-conveying message!

ECUMENICAL CHALLENGES

The Bible as the church's book

The Bible is held in high regard in Roman Catholicism also, especially since Vatican II. In the assembly hall where the council sat it lay open on a kind of throne before the eyes of the council fathers; during worship it can be honored with incense and kissed by the priest, whose right and privilege it is to read or sing the gospel. But these very gestures express the fact that the Roman church has a firm hold on the Bible. It is a book that belongs to the church! This is developed, in opposition to Luther and the church that follows him, in a number of ways.

The canon of Scripture is considered a gift and a rule of the church, which, after all, preceded it. The process of constructing the canon proved problematic and was fully completed at a relatively late period. With Luther one could object that the Christ attested in the canon is not the church's gift! It was, after all, only through his mission that the church came to be. Nor was there any church authority that established what the canon should be. Rather, it succeeded in its own right and was then subsequently accepted by church authorities, though its extent remains a matter of dispute among the various confessions. But when, at the end of the second century, a relatively clear delimitation of the core content of the canonical writings was achieved, that should be regarded as a self-limitation on the part of the church, which desired to bend to the normativity of the book. At about the same time, in fact, the basic elements of the creed and the definitions of orders were established. Apparently these represented three structural elements of the church that had proved themselves necessary as such but whose concrete shape was not yet fully determined.

Valid interpretation of Scripture

In its own view the Roman church is the authentic interpreter of the Bible. The biblical texts are occasionally unclear in themselves, and it is only in the context of the church that they are rightly understood. There is an ever-deepening process of self-disclosure of revelation; there is a *sensus plenior*— a fuller sense that only reveals itself in the course of the ages. Ultimately the church has Jesus' promise that the Spirit will lead it into all truth (John 16:13). Luther would probably object that this is a typical case of how people try to use a scriptural argument in order to escape Holy Scripture itself! Who is the church? Not primarily the hierarchy, which reserves certain rights to itself, but the "sheep who hear the voice of the shepherd" (John 10:27-28). Here Luther's idea of the universal, mutual, and common priesthood is key: the Holy Spirit works through personal and particular access to the words of Sacred Scripture, through mutual witness and mutual criticism. He enables the testing of spirits; to that extent every Christian is in principle also a critic—Luther says a "judge"—of other doctrines.[118] The history of the outcomes of the Reformation and the present condition of Protestantism unfortunately show that this is an ideal notion: on the one hand Luther's proposal has been misunderstood individualistically and has contributed to a fragmentation of the church; on the other hand the constructive strengths of the Reformer's approach have scarcely been appropriated by the established Lutheran churches. Certainly the socio-cultural conditions have changed in the meantime. The isolated relationship of an individual Christian to the Bible could have an emancipatory effect in the Reformation period, but it was protected from a complete deviation into subjectivism by the presence of the church as a matter of course and of a society shaped by the church as well. Today the Bible is often only found to be helpful when it is communicated by individuals or a group who have clearly been affected by its message.

The blessings of tradition

A third ecumenical objection points out that, after all, in essence there is no getting around tradition. Scripture itself is a piece of tradition, as Vatican II indicates when it sets "sacred scripture" alongside "sacred tradition" and so in a sense subordinates the former to the latter.[119] The Holy Spirit has not left the church alone; moreover, Protestantism has developed a great many traditions of its own. Luther would not dispute either of these last statements: for him tradition was not an evil as such, and he found that there were insights in the history of the church that lead us farther and whose content is found in the Gospel even if it is not formally part of the Bible. This explains Luther's unquestioning acceptance of the creeds of the ancient church, the classic proof of which is his attitude toward infant baptism: it "has been thus from the beginning of Christianity."[120] It comes from the apostles and has been continued since the apostolic time; this is clearly to be traced to the work of God, without which the practice of infant baptism would certainly not have continued. If there is nothing in Sacred Scripture contrary to a particular tradition, then according to Luther no objection can be made to its retention. Tradition is not negative as such; the principle of *sola scriptura* only rejects those traditions that obscure the content of the Gospel and thus do damage to life. In this way it is precisely the recourse to Scripture that assures the continuing life of the church.[121] Luther thus produces a consistent inconsistency. Formally he is inconsistent because he wants to be consistent as to content: baptism, and especially infant baptism, were for him at the heart of the justification of sinners as reflected and preached by Paul. The practice of infant baptism, though it could not be attested in Scripture, had thus led to a deeper comprehension of the Gospel.

The new traditions produced by the Reformation in its credal formulae are also to be understood and evaluated in this sense. Luther himself did not regard his theology as an innovation but as a return to the origins, as *reformatio*. His experience was that the lamp of the Gospel, long hidden under a bench, was now being brought out again. Probably he did not himself understand the extent to which his talk of sin, justification, and freedom had in fact led to a deeper understanding of the Gospel and thus to a new stage in Christian awareness. The problem that arose for himself and then for the time after his death was the rapidity with which this new stage became solidified and proved resistant to further renewal. The aim of constantly reforming the church—*ecclesia semper reformanda*[122]—did not correspond to Luther's original intention! It was a long time before it became clear that from Sacred Scripture as the *norma normans* was to be derived not only a once-for-all *norma normata* in the form of the confessional statements but also the task of constantly rediscovering and giving effect to the *norma normata* and, ultimately, the *norma normans* as well.[123]

Word, sacrament, and image

Another ecumenical objection to Luther's concept is that his approach causes the word of God, or Sacred Scripture, to become isolated from the sacrament (thus the Roman Catholic and Orthodox objection) and from the image (as in the Orthodox theology oriented to a devotion to icons). In view of Protestantism as it actually exists, one cannot disagree. The consequence was undoubtedly at least a spiritualization, but in fact also an intellectualization of Christianity and worship. Luther himself would be able to defend against this: both the sacrament and the image take their life from the word; both are unlocked by the word and so it is through the word that they can be understood. Luther certainly affirmed both sacrament and image. For him a sacrament is *verbum visibile*, though the image is only an instrument for the illustration and concretization of the word. Hearing the word takes place also through sacrament and image,[124] and in Protestantism music in particular was a further important medium of expression.

Thus in the face of current Protestantism one must certainly speak of a variety of processes leading to imbalance and impoverishment, but these can be done away with precisely by recalling Luther's approach. At any rate, for the Reformer himself it was clear that God in Jesus Christ, through the Holy Spirit, makes Sacred Scripture relevant and at the same time creates in it a clear criterion for the evaluation of traditions, which then in some cases reveal themselves as illegitimate but in others may be discovered to be helpful and even to advance our understanding.

NOTES

[1] Heinrich Denzinger, *Enchiridion symbolorum, definitionum et declarationum de rebus fidei et morum*, ed. Karl Rahner (Freiburg: Herder, 1963). English: *The Sources of Catholic Dogma* (St. Louis: Herder, 1957), accessible at www.catecheticsonline.com.

[2] Cf. Hubert Kirchner, *Wort Gottes, Schrift und Tradition* (Göttingen: Vandenhoeck & Ruprecht, 1998), 14–22.

[3] LW 40, 231 (WA 26, 147, 13-18).

[4] Cf. LW 36, 329–61 (WA 19, 482, 25–483, 19).

[5] Cf. DH 3011, DH 3074; LG 25; DV 10; KKK 85–87.

[6]*DV* 10: "Munus autem authenticae interpretandi verbum Dei scriptum vel traditum . . ." Translation in Austin Flannery, OP, General Editor, *Vatican Council II. The Basic Sixteen Documents* (Northport NY: Costello Publications, 1996).

[7]This is accomplished by printing the respective numbers in boldface. See Josef Neuner and Heinrich Roos, rev. Karl Rahner and Karl-Heinz Weger, *The Teaching of the Catholic Church as Contained in Her Documents* (Staten Island: Alba House, 1967).

[8]LW 32, 112 (WA 7, 838, 5-6).

[9]LW 26, 87–88 (WA 40/1, 132, 27-28): ". . . extra vel contra verbum Dei aliquid docet."

[10]*The Book of Concord*, 17–21.

[11]LW 37, 372 (WA 26, 509, 19-20).

[12]WA 37, 55, 12-15.

[13]*The Book of Concord*, 291.

[14]LW 38, 161 (WA 38, 208, 22-23).

[15]LW 35, 396 (WA.DB 7, 384, 29-32). This approach is lightly passed over in current ecumenical discussions: the concept of "apostolicity" becomes the Joker. Cf. Hans-Martin Barth, "'Apostolizität' und 'Sukzession' in den Konvergenz-Erklärungen von Lima," *ÖR* 33 (1984): 339–56.

[16]See "Reason: the devil's whore and God's gift" in chapter 5.

[17]". . . 'Eia, vere sic est,'" LW 11, 37 (WA 3, 549, 30-35).

[18]Cf. Isa 6:10 in Luther's translation from 1545.

[19]Cf. LW 11, 282 (WA 4, 7, 22); WA 40/2, 425, 17-20; cf. also Joest 1967, 210–28!

[20]LW 35, 194 (WA 30/2, 640, 26-27).

[21]WA 21, 113, 16-29.

[22]WA 17/2, 203, 31.

[23]WA 10/1/2, 222, 34-35.

[24]LW 29, 224 (WA 57 III, 222, 7); cf. WA 10/1/2, 222, 33-35; WA 32, 99, 6; LW 24, 31 (WA 45, 490, 30), and Barth, Hans-Martin 1989b.

[25]LW 40, 147 (WA 18, 137, 6-9).

[26]LW 25, 211 (WA 56, 227, 4-5).

[27]Althaus 1962, 61.

[28]WA.TR 1, 183, 25-27 (no. 423).

[29]Iwand 1983, 223.

[30]LW 53, 285, "Our God He Is a Castle Strong," v. 4 (EG 362, 4).

[31]WA 34/2, 59, 21.

[32]WA 37, 296, 37-38; Albrecht Beutel comments: "it is *supra rationem* because reason cannot grasp the word. But it is *contra rationem* because reason cannot grasp that either," Beutel 1991a, 93.

[33]WA 11, 225, 27-28.

[34]WA 9, 330, 18-19.

[35]LW 42, 56 (WA 2, 111, 9-15 [1519]).

[36]LW 52, 79 (WA 10/1/1, 232, 10-15).

[37]LW 40, 212–13 (WA 18, 202, 34–203, 2).

[38]Angelus Silesius, Mensch, *werde wesentlich*. Selected and introduced by Rudolf Irmler (Stuttgart: Steinkopf, 1976), 40.

[39]LW 42, 59 (WA 2, 113, 35–114, 4).

[40]WA 10/3, 425, 17-22.

[41]One must meditate so deeply on the word of God and allow it to penetrate one's inmost being, "quasi ex verbo Dei et corde tuo una res fiat, so that you become much more certain of the thing than of your own life," WA 32, 151, 18-20.

[42]See chapter 10 below.

[43]Cf. Gustaf Wingren, *Die Predigt* (Göttingen: Vandenhoeck & Ruprecht, 1959).

[44]Cf. Barth, Hans-Martin 1967b.

[45]Cf. LW 40, 212–13 (WA 18, 202, 2-13).

[46]LW 52, 206 (WA 10/1/1, 626, 15–627, 10).

47LW 30, 3 (WA 12, 259, 8-9).

48Cf. Heinz Blanke in *Handbuch* 2005, 258–59.

49For Luther's Bible translation cf. Meurer 1996; Stolt 2000, 84–126; Brecht 1987, 101–18, *Handbuch* 2005, 258–65.

50LW 35, 188 (WA 30/2, 636, 15-18).

51LW 35, 189 (WA 30/2, 637, 19-21).

52Martin Schloemann, "Die zwei Wörter. Luthers Notabene zur 'Mitte der Schrift,'" 89–99 in Meurer 1996.

53Klaus Dietrich Fricke, "'Dem Volk aufs Maul sehen.' Bemerkungen zu Luthers Verdeutschungsgrundsätzen," 24–37 in Meurer 1996, at 29.

54Other impressive examples are in Pss 90:17; 33:4; 27:14; Isa 60:3; Jer 31:3.

55Cf. the commentary on the passage in the *Stuttgarter Erklärungsbibel* (Stuttgart: Deutsche Bibelgesellschaft, 1992).

56Fricke, "'Dem Volk aufs Maul sehen,'" 27.

57Brecht 1987, 104, even thinks that "the interesting progress of Luther's theology can be traced" in the "further development of the glosses."

58For references see *TRE* 3: 293–94.

59Quoted in Hermann Barth and Tim Schramm, *Selbsterfahrung mit der Bibel* (Göttingen: Vandenhoeck & Ruprecht, 1977), 58–59.

60Preface to the prophet Jeremiah, LW 35, 280–81 (WA.DB 11/1, 192, 10-16).

61LW 35, 361 (WA.DB 6, 10, 7-35), not printed in the editions of the Bible after 1534.

62LW 35, 362.

63WA.TR 1, 69, 18-20 (no. 146).

64LW 35, 395 (WA.DB 7, 344, 27-28).

65LW 35, 362 (WA.DB 6, 10, 33-34).

66LW 34, 317 (WA 39/2, 199, 24-25).

67LW 35, 399–411 (WA.DB 7, 406–21).

68WA.TR 3, nos. 3391a, b.

69LW 40, 92 (WA 18, 76, 2-5).

70LW 35, 244 (WA.DB 8, 25, 22-26).

71LW 52, 41 (WA 10/1/1, 181, 24–182, 1).

72LW 35, 236 (WA.DB 8, 13, 6-8).

73See chapter 7.

74WA 18, 606, 29.

75LW 25, 405 (WA 56, 414, 15).

76LW 35, 366 (WA.DB 7, 2, 15).

77LW 35, 397 (WA.DB 7, 386, 13-15).

78LW 35, 396 (WA.DB 7, 385, 25-27).

79LW 35, 361 (WA.DB 6, 8, 18-19).

80WA.TR 2, 244, 20-23.

81WA 9, 664, 17.

82WA 7, 250, 23-24.

83Albrecht Beutel, in *Handbuch* 2005, 447.

84LW 34, 112 (WA 39/1, 47, 1, 19).

85See "Multiple senses of Scripture" in chapter 19.

86WA 10/1/2, 363, 38–366, 17 [the quotation is from 366, 10-14]; cf. Luke 10:30-35.

87Cf. LW 35, 247–48 (WA.DB 8, 29, 32–31, 18).

88WA 47, 66, 23-24 (referring to the Old Testament; on John 3:14).

89WA 7, 97, 23.

90Althaus 1962, 79ff.

91Beutel 1991a, 250; cf. 250–52.

92Cf. WA 7, 96, 25ff.

[93]LW 33, 162–63 (WA 18, 700, 34–701, 3). Alan of Lille found that "an authority has a waxen nose, which means it can be twisted so as to be able to accept different meanings." Reference in Denis Janz, *Luther on Thomas Aquinas: The Angelic Doctor in the Thought of the Reformer* (Stuttgart: Steiner, 1989), 22 n. 66.

[94]Rothen 1990, 50.

[95]LW 45, 360 (WA 15, 37, 3-6; 38, 7-15).

[96]LW 33, 27 (LDStA 1, 236/237, 35-38).

[97]WA 30/2, 687, 32.

[98]LW 33, 28 (LDStA 1, 238, 19-30; 235, 24-39).

[99]WA 17/2, 460, 2-6.

[100]LW 40, 146 (WA 18, 136, 9-15).

[101]LW 33, 25 (WA 18, 606, 11-12).

[102]LW 34, 284 (WA 50, 657, 26-27).

[103]LW 52, 146 (WA 10/1/2, 75, 6-7); cf. Lohse 1995, 163.

[104]Brecht 1987, 104. Or is that appellation better applied to the Small Catechism?

[105]Hartmut Hövelmann, *Kernstellen der Lutherbibel. Eine Anleitung zum Schriftverständnis* (Bielefeld: Luther-Verlag, 1989).

[106]Stolt 2000, 104–10.

[107]LW 32, 112 (WA 7, 838, 4ff.).

[108]Cf. Joachim-Ernst Berendt, *Das dritte Ohr. Vom Hören der Welt* (Reinbek: Rowohlt, 1985).

[109]LW 35, 254 (WA.DB 10/1, 100, 12-17).

[110]WA 53, 569–72.

[111]Cf. Barth, Hans-Martin 2008a, 220; but see "Phenomenological perceptions" in chapter 4.

[112]LW 52, 33 (WA 10/1/1, 130, 14-16).

[113]Cf. Barth, Hans-Martin 1967c.

[114]Cf. Haustein 1990, and "Superstition?" in chapter 4.

[115]Cf. WA 37, 45, 1-4.

[116]This is especially striking in Luther's "Presentation of the Faith, preached in Smalcald, 1537," WA 45, 11–24.

[117]Cf. Hans-Martin Barth, "Gottes Wort ist dreifaltig. Ein Beitrag zur Auseinandersetzung mit der 'archetypischen Hermeneutik' Eugen Drewermanns," *TLZ* 113 (1988): 251–54.

[118]LW 39, 306 (WA 11, 410, 29–30).

[119]*Dei verbum* II, 7-10.

[120]LW 40, 241 (WA 26, 155, 29-30).

[121]Cf. Althaus 1962, 307ff.

[122]See "Missionary ecclesiology" in chapter 19.

[123]On this, and to the contrary, cf. Härle 1995, 152.

[124]Barth, Hans-Martin 1989b.

PART III

Consequences: With Luther beyond Luther

17

What Endures

If we ask about what remains, we must be clear about one thing first of all: for whom should we demonstrate that it is enduring, and for whom must it be secured? Germanists and students of culture may regard Luther's translation of the Bible as something "enduring"; students of the history of religion might ask whether the Reformation, which was so essentially shaped by him, signifies a new step in the development of religion. Roman Catholics may find the provocation his theology represents for them as something "enduring." What in Luther's theology is of enduring value for Lutheran Christians and their churches?

"Existence" Theology

Those who consider Luther without prejudice may at first not be so much moved by what he says theologically as by the way he says it. When Luther's German was closer to everyday life, that may have been felt more strongly than it is today. In the year 1914 the President of the Bavarian High Consistory, Hermann Bezzel, asked: "Why does our soul rejoice when it savors his words, which move along so simply and yet seem like pure music, which so often touch the deepest nerve of our minds and speak to our hearts?"[1] We do not write that way any more. Nevertheless, the loving immediacy of the way in which Luther brings his theological thought into the present context is still perceptible today and may even be communicable, at least in part. Even those like Goethe who stand rather at a distance from the Reformation faith can sense something of what is special about Luther: "Between us, there is nothing in the whole business [of the Reformation] of any interest except Luther's character, and that is also the only thing that really makes an impression on a crowd. All the rest is a confused rubbish."[2]

Luther represents an authentic theology; he does not teach "like the scribes" (cf. Matt 7:29). Since Luther's time theology has been professionalized and divided into sub-disciplines, but at the same time it has been emancipated from faith. It is regarded as a function of faith and in the service of faith. Faith and theology, especially scholarly university theology, remain related and yet have diverged. There is justification for that, but it should not lead to the impression that it is possible to study and teach theology without reference to one's own faith. Luther emphasizes that vehemently: "*experientia facit theologum*"—experience makes the theologian.[3] Theology is shaped not only by the experience of faith but also by the perception of resistance to faith, experiences with the experience of faith, something that, namely, at least for a time may not even be possible to experience, so that faith may be sustained against all experience and non-experience. Luther's theology grows out of a faith under siege that does not flee to false security but allows itself to be challenged ever anew by concrete life and the questions it poses. It is aware of God's hiddenness, it is familiar with "consoled" and even "salutary despair."[4] It is a theology of the cross, the cross of Christ, the cross of human beings, of humanity, not a theology one could suspect of being wishful thinking, even if Ludwig Feuerbach tried to interpret it in that sense. It has something to say to suffering, confused, distressed people who are not simply living vegetative lives on a superficial level. Therein lie both its opportunity and its limits. Here is a person dealing with his own resistance. He has not gently resolved all recalcitrance within the self, perhaps like Francis of Assisi, nor is he in the process of fighting down all his resistance as Ignatius of Loyola attempted to do. Here is a person doing theology, thrown into a muddle of fears and doubts and yet in all of it knowing himself entrusted to the saving hand of his God. The early Sören Kierkegaard would very probably have understood him.[5] It is about life and death, about existence and therefore a theology of existence that does not seek an aesthetically satisfying system. From the outset it takes into account that theological ideas on earth can never be smoothly resolved. Perhaps it is the fault of this Lutheran heritage that the Lutheran tradition has not produced a sweeping and comprehensive dogmatic system, a "Summa" like that of Thomas Aquinas, an "Institutes" like that of Calvin, a "Christian Faith" like that of Schleiermacher, and a "Church Dogmatics" like that of Karl Barth.[6] Luther's theology of existence unfolds in tensions and polarities. It is existential theology that lays claim to the individuals who encounter it with skin and bones. Pietists have taken up this thread when they say that preaching that is not "per du" is "perdu."[7] It is also "existential" theology that is aware of the elementary conditions of human existence, of sin and death, so that Martin Heidegger was able to make use of it. But it is more. The one who engages with it stands and falls with it, lives with it or dies with it. "I am a fool," and thank God for it.[8] Here some gentle critique may be registered: is such a theology not all too subjective? Does it have anything to say not just to individuals under stress but also to those who are happy, or to a whole congregation made up of unhappy and happy people? Authentic theology withstands precisely when one finds oneself thrown off the customary track.

Luther infected his friends and colleagues, and sometimes even his opponents, with his theological ideas. In any case: if such faith fades in Protestantism and such theology is no longer practiced, it will flatten out into a copy of other churches or a mere worldview.

Theology Drawn from the Bible

Luther's Reformation theology was neither created by intellectual manipulation nor did it grow out of subjective hallucinations. In his "great testimony to himself" in the preface to the first volume of the collected edition of his Latin writings the Reformer gives information about how, according to his recollection, his theology came about: he had been working with the letter to the Romans, and particularly with the statement "for in it [the Gospel] the righteousness of God is revealed through faith for faith; as it is written, 'The one who is righteous will live by faith'" (Rom 1:17). Day and night he meditated, trying to grasp the meaning and application of these words. "There I began to understand that the righteousness of God is that by which the righteous lives by a gift of God, namely by faith." He felt himself altogether born again and that he had entered Paradise through open gates.[9] What is striking in this formulation is the matter-of-fact combination of careful exegetical study—exegetes today still attempt to clarify the context of particular constellations of words—and meditative openness, which can also include the life of feelings (Luther "felt" it, "*sensi*"). He approached the explication of biblical books in this way, "with both hands," studying Romans, Galatians, and Hebrews, the Psalms a second and third time, and Galatians once again. He stayed with individual books for years at a time, three years for the Psalms, ultimately ten for Genesis.[10] Luther himself used the most modern aids available to him, including Reuchlin's *Lehrbuch* and *Lexikon der hebräischen Sprache*. Of course exegesis has been infinitely refined since then. But the task remains the same: to begin with the literal meaning of the text and—something that today's exegesis does not accomplish, as a rule—to make it spiritually fruitful as well. The combination of the two remains a valid approach in Lutheran theology. For it we need a new, spiritual professionalism in order to be able to get beyond exegetical work and open up the content of the text through hermeneutics.[11]

The Reformer developed what he had to say with reference to biblical passages, not least in his sermons. In his occasional writings he quotes very loosely and without checking, because he swam in the Bible like a fish in water. But he did not arbitrarily or carelessly extract his arguments from the wealth of material; he followed a clear conception that was later described as the "canon within the canon": the center of Scripture is Christ. This permitted him to deal freely with individual biblical statements and even authorized him to undertake an interpretative and evaluative rearrangement of the books of both the New and Old Testaments. Theology should not develop within the jungle of tangled traditions or the undergrowth of imaginative speculations, but should be measured by the original documents of what is attested in the history of Jesus Christ and the people Israel. That a center of the biblical witness must be sought, and that individual passages are to be understood from that center, is another element of Luther's approach that can be called enduring. But critique also applies here: did Luther not, in the process, multiply distort the historical sense of the Old Testament in particular, and on the other hand did he really adhere consistently to his own approach?

Finally, we should recall his translation work, honoring not merely the result—although I still find it astonishing.[12] But Luther himself by no means regarded his translation as sacrosanct; instead, during his lifetime he worked constantly with a small committee to improve the translation. That, too, is something enduring in the Reformer's theology: the duty to toil constantly for the best possible translation of Sacred Scripture and yet to preserve Luther's translation as a heritage of the Reformation in worship and catechesis.

LIBERATING THEOLOGY

There is no need to give a special demonstration or proof of the fact that the Reformer experienced the message of the justification of the ungodly as liberating for himself and many others. The question is rather to what extent this sustaining insight of Reformation theology can be seen as something enduring and still valid today. The surrounding circumstances of human self-understanding seem to have changed so much that even many Protestants would not count justification among "enduring" elements of Luther's theology. That is owing not only to Luther but also to the demands of the applicable New Testament texts.[13] People in the Western hemisphere, at least, do not as a rule see themselves as sinners who have to receive their "justification" from a transcendent authority. But the message of justification has also been corrupted by the Lutheran churches' constant attempts to beat it into people, liturgically as well, and on the other hand extolling it in hucksterish fashion as a marketing tool for Protestantism instead of treating it as a sacred mystery: it is the secret of Christian life, developing its power and peace in very particular situations. It can undertake the greatest variety of functions in different psychic and socio-cultural situations. In the sixteenth century it obtained its significance against the horizon of the last judgment, which was thought to be imminent; liberation from that fear consequently brought forth in Luther's contemporaries a positive sense of their lives. Today it seems rather to be the reverse: justification is understandable as the encouragement to personal self-affirmation when one sees oneself confronted with one's own concrete guilt, failure, or rejection by others; it serves as the basis for gaining identity, self-realization, and the ability to act.[14] Liberation from the burden of constantly having to legitimate oneself includes confidence about what may come after death. It is still comprehensible that for Luther himself the message of justification formed an elementary basis for his life and work. That cannot be directly applied, and yet it can be sensed even today. An example for me is the famous saying attributed to the Reformer: "and if the world were to end tomorrow, we would still plant our apple trees today." That statement does not fit Luther, because the day before the end of the world he would certainly have had something else to do besides planting apple trees. And yet it is the spirit of Luther that speaks here, a confidence in a hopeless situation that has been associated with Luther's faith—in the years immediately after the end of World War II, when this saying actually originated.[15] Gottfried Benn honored it in his own way:

What did Luther Mean About the Apple Tree?
I don't care—destruction itself is a dream—
I stand here in my apple orchard
and I await the collapse with confidence—
I am in God, who beyond the world
still holds a few trumps in his hand—
if the world falls apart tomorrow morning,
I endure forever, and solid as a star—
is that what he meant, the honest old man,
and glances once more at his Käthe?
and drinks one more tankard of beer
and sleeps until it starts—tomorrow morning at four?
Then he was truly a very great man,
one we can only admire even today.[16]

In this connection Luther's humor should also be given its due![17]

NOTES

[1] Hermann Bezzel, *Warum haben wir Luther lieb?* (Munich: Müller & Fröhlich, 1914), 5.
[2] Quoted from von Loewenich 1963, 41.
[3] WA.TR 1, 16, 13.
[4] ". . . per fiducialem desperationem," "through confident despair," WA.Br 1, 35, 34 (1516); "quam salutaris illa esset desperatio," "how salutary that despair was," LW 33, 190 (WA 18, 719, 11-12).
[5] Cf. Bornkamm, Heinrich 1970, 96.

[6]This is, of course, also due to the "local method," which is not primarily interested in the internal system of dogmatics; cf., e.g., Johann Gerhard's *Loci theologici*.

[7]Translator's note: to be "per du" is to be on a first-name basis of friendship; the French word "perdu" means "lost" or "futile."

[8]LW 51, 35 (WA 1, 267, 6-7).

[9]LW 34, 337 (WA 54, 186, 3-9): "Donec miserente Deo meditabundus dies et noctes connexionem verborum attenderem, nempe: Iustitia Dei revelatur in illo, sicut scriptum est: Iustus ex fide vivit, ibi iustitiam Dei coepi intelligere eam, qua iustus dono Dei vivit, nempe ex fide. . . . Hic me prorsus renatum esse sensi, et apertis portis in ipsum paradisum intrasse."

[10]Cf. Jans Wolff, "C.I.8 Vorlesungen," in *Handbuch* 2005, 322–28. Wolff writes: "Luther's major service as professor and doctor and the abundance of his insights, as revealed not least in his later academic lectures, have to this day not been adequately evaluated or analyzed with appropriate sophistication by Luther scholars," 327.

[11]Cf. Hans Martin Barth, "'Wie verstehst du, was du liest?' Professionalität und Spiritualität im Umgang mit der Bibel," *DtPfBl* 107 (2007): 195–200.

[12]See the examples in "Sacred Scripture" in chapter 16.

[13]Klaus-Peter Jörns, *Notwendige Abschiede. Auf dem Weg zu einem glaubwürdigen Christentum* (Gütersloh: Gütersloher Verlagshaus, 2004).

[14]Cf. Hans-Martin Barth, *Fulfilment*, trans. John Bowden (London: SCM, 1980); idem, "'Ich lebe, aber nicht mehr ich . . .' Christlicher Glaube und personale Identität," *NZST* 44 (2002): 174–88.

[15]Cf. Martin Schloemann, *Luthers Apfelbäumchen? Ein Kapitel deutscher Mentalitätsgeschichte seit dem Zweiten Weltkrieg* (Göttingen: Vandenhoeck & Ruprecht, 1994).

[16]Gottfried Benn, *Sämtliche Werke*, vol. 2 (Stuttgart: Klett-Cotta, 1986), 142.

[17]Cf. Fritz Blanke, *Luthers Humor* (Hamburg: Furche, 1957), as well as Stolt 2000, 147–72, and Gritsch 2006.

18

What We Should Let Go

There is probably no Lutheran theologian today who would say that there is absolutely nothing in Luther's theology we need to let go of. On the contrary, it is within Protestantism itself that voices have repeatedly been raised to criticize, for example, the elements of "medieval origin" in his theology; Albrecht Ritschl did so even in the nineteenth century.[1] Ernst Troeltsch was able to praise the genius of the Reformer while at the same time assigning him in large part to the Middle Ages; his image of Luther resembles a "Janus face deserving admiration and accusation simultaneously."[2] The "Middle Ages" have come to symbolize the negative features that muddy the image of Luther, while that era is today more subtly understood, at least by experts, and in many ways is now viewed positively. So we cannot simply dismiss what is "medieval" in Luther's theology; perhaps some elements of that need instead to be recovered! For a long time it was a favorite practice to play off the "young Luther" against the aging Reformer—young Luther yes, and let's abandon the old one. But newer research has shown that this distinction is impossible to sustain.[3] The question remains whether, in Adolf von Harnack's sense and that of Neo-Protestantism, we can profile the "real Luther" against what is not really proper to him.[4] But what is "real"—is it simply what I like? These different opinions show that even in reading Luther we need something like a "canon within the canon" that can orient itself to what the Reformer himself understood to be the center of his faith and his theology, and that is undoubtedly Jesus Christ, as Sacred Scripture testifies to him and as he in turn constitutes its center. We then need to reflect again on this "canon" to test its coherence.

INVOLVEMENT IN WHAT IS CONDITIONED BY OUR MAKEUP AND SOCIALIZATION

Psychic constitution and socialization may have cooperated for Luther in a number of ways. This is not the place to shed light on the Reformer's psyche.[5]

But we may at least say that he was basically a conservative type. Statues of Luther from the nineteenth century that show him standing with his fist on the Bible give a false picture. Films about Luther that depict his trembling before the emperor and the empire are closer to reality. Apparently nothing was more objectionable to the Reformer than revolution and political unrest. He preferred accepting the orderly power of authority to enduring the uprising of the "mob." The class arrangement of the Middle Ages was for him a matter of course. He saw the beginnings of a move to absolutism as ethically mistaken but not as a latent and altogether dangerous political development. The fact that he showed no interest in the Swiss model of a developing democracy may be connected to the scope of his education, which was limited in political matters and scarcely extended beyond the provincial level. The bourgeois ethos that was addressed especially by the aging Reformer, supported by appropriate passages in the Pastoral letters and the Old Testament apocrypha, fits seamlessly within his view. That ethos certainly had its own justification, but Luther left it too little open to impulses that could lead beyond it. Kierkegaard was among those who reproached him for that in particular, in light of the Danish national church in the nineteenth century, which no longer had anything to do with the eschatologically-minded community of the first believers. To what extent is Luther himself responsible for this development? How is it that his pathbreaking reflections on the universal, mutual, and common priesthood of believers did not really take hold? Peter Cornehl speaks of a "pedagogizing" of Lutheran worship: "All the initiative came from the clergy, and that forced the *congregation* into a *structural passivity*."[6] There are certainly a number of factors at work in all that. But in the context of a critical presentation of Luther's theology we must raise the question of the extent to which the theological switches were wrongly laid within the process of the Reformation itself. Can we dismiss Luther's obvious weaknesses, perhaps even including his dreadful writings on the Jews, as attributable to "the spirit of the times"?[7] How was it that his theology did not prevent him from offering such a massive tribute? This question becomes more intense in view of what we have to call Luther's superstition, his ideas about witches, and his incessant talk about the devil.

The answer, it seems to me, lies in an inconsistent way of dealing with Sacred Scripture. Luther was aware of what the center of Scripture is, and he gave it a recognition such as few theologians of Christianity have achieved. It furnished him with all he needed to combat the concentrated power of the Roman church of his time. He could coolly say that if "the opponents play off the Scripture against Christ, we will play Christ against the Scripture." But Luther played Christ within Scripture too little against Scripture. He probably succeeded in dealing with the "works righteousness" extolled in the Letter of James.[8] But there was also much to be read in Scripture about an ethos that scarcely surpassed contemporary morals, about demons and possession as imagined in the late Middle Ages, about the Jews and their father, the devil (John 8:44). Luther abandoned his christologically grounded critique of Scripture too soon.

Religious Intolerance

If there is anything that makes reading Luther's texts painful, it is the almost constant polemic. Therefore people like to go back to his works in which the polemic is softened or not yet fully developed: the early sermons or the writings whose whole purpose was edification. But many of Luther's writings and speeches are dominated by attacks on his opponents, the Pope and the "agitators," wrong forms of devotional expression, whether the "caps and tonsures" of the monks or the "grey robe" of the enthusiasts, against individual theologians such as Karlstadt or Thomas Müntzer, or against princes such as Count Georg of Saxony, to say nothing of Jews and Turks. One could almost ask: whom did Luther *not* call a "devil"? This can be explained psychologically, up to a point; the Reformer found himself under pressure and had to defend himself and his cause; his opponents were not squeamish, either. Against the background of what seems unquestionably negative he was able to develop his message with special clarity. Besides, polemic apparently gave him intellectual satisfaction; he was a master of his craft. Behind it all was certainly a need for clarity and specificity. The polemic seems to have been supported by his way of referring to Sacred Scripture. He knows a biblical saying that is "a thunderbolt on the head of Dr. Karlstadt,"[9] and then there are the arguments with Zwingli and his friends in Marburg: "All this is here . . ." written.[10]

It is obvious that Luther, after a certain phase of liberality in matters of tolerance, changed his mind in the course of his life, though not without some hesitation. Ideas from traditional medieval law regarding heretics regained their place. While he insists in his document on authority that God "cannot and will not permit anyone but himself to rule over the soul,"[11] two years later he asserted that the authorities were obligated to suppress the "abomination of the secret mass" because it represented a public blasphemy.[12] In interpreting the parable about the weeds in the wheat, which pleads against the uprooting of the weeds, he at first advocates that heretics should not be rooted out because if one of them is to be converted, he or she has to be alive; who knows "when the word of God will touch his heart?"[13] But in the reports Luther also signed calling for capital punishment of Anabaptists it is asserted that the parable does not apply to the actions of authority. Here again there is a biblical saying available, one that is in no way read through the lens of Christ as the center of Scripture, namely Leviticus 24:16: "One who blasphemes the name of the Lord shall be put to death."[14] What was called *ius emigrandi* and must be regarded as a step in the direction of tolerance was nevertheless banishment from our point of view; it was, naturally, then practiced also by Catholics during the Counter-Reformation, and even more decisively. It continues in the twenty-first century under the label "ethnic cleansing." It is certainly an "advance" over sword and pyre; it was a "right in law" for those concerned, but for the authorities it was a method of violent expulsion.[15] Joseph Lecler, SJ, who describes the lamentable situation, concludes that, looked at from today's concept of religious freedom, "the situation created by the Lutheran Reformation in Germany did not represent any progress worthy of the name."[16]

At the same time, Luther at times did reveal a certain openness to plurality and freedom of conscience. In the preface to the "German Mass" he wrote that he did not think the Wittenberg Order for Mass should be adopted throughout Germany.[17] That is, of course, a comparatively harmless area. In a letter to Georg Spalatin, Luther writes soothingly that princes need only punish public crimes, but in doing so they would not exercise any compulsion on persons since they would leave them the freedom "to believe or not."[18] So here he is still distinguishing between freedom of worship, which he rejects, and public freedom of expression, which he affirms. We certainly cannot speak of freedom of conscience in the modern sense, because for him such a thing only exists when the conscience knows itself to be bound by God's word; that is how he experienced his own conscience as both bound and free. In his "Letter to the Princes of Saxony" he urges the authorities to intervene when there is unrest and violence, but they are not to concern themselves with doctrine: "Let them preach as confidently and boldly as they are able and against whomever they wish . . . Let the spirits collide and fight it out."[19] In the early period of the Reformation he quite calmly recommended that those who would not follow should be let alone: "whoever deceives, let him deceive; whoever stinks, let him go on stinking . . . God will take care of it."[20]

There were a number of political and psychological reasons why Luther was unable to sustain this calm attitude. But it was also based on a fundamental theological choice: love bears everything, but faith bears nothing! The word must be perfectly pure.[21] That is certainly a fundamentalistic idea that essentially makes religion a dangerous thing. Here it is just barely tolerable as it is formulated, because "the word" is named as the critical authority. But if the word is fully identified with one's own opinion and conviction there is no stopping point left.

Tendencies to Dualistic Thinking

It is understandable for various reasons that the Reformer would have been drawn to dualistic thinking. In reading the Bible he noticed that he perceived something different than did those around him, that he seemed to be "different," and that he had to distance himself from a good deal of what he was accustomed to. He discovered his identity less in agreement with what had been received than in resistance to it. The more he had to contend with his opponents, the more strongly the tendency to a dualistic sense of the world entrenched itself in him. However, he may from the beginning have found it appealing to think in terms of oppositions. He was sensitive to the tensions in which life and faith revealed themselves to him, and in that he was in some sense a modern person. The *distinguo* of the Scholastics, existing peacefully under a vast unifying heaven, no longer satisfied him. He had to articulate his theology dialectically, indicating complementarities and polarities that seemed to match the contradictions in life and his experience in faith. We can readily find that approach in his interpretation of the Our Father. A Christian always prays the Our Father against herself or himself by acknowledging that she or he does not hallow the name of God or let the reign of God rule within. But Christians also pray against "whoever teaches and lives otherwise than as the Word of God teaches," and that "God curbs and destroys every evil counsel and purpose of the devil, of the world, and of our flesh which would hinder us from hallowing his name and prevent the coming of his kingdom."[22] In his exposition of the Sermon on the Mount he finds that a time is coming when one must curse or do injustice if one omits it. Christians should pray regarding the pope, bishops, and possibly some princes (!): "Dear Lord, curse and destroy and throw all their schemes to the abyss of hell." Then follows what I find so horrible: "Therefore no one can pray the Lord's Prayer correctly without cursing." For whoever speaks the first three petitions must "put all the opposition to this on one pile and say: 'Curses, maledictions, and disgrace upon every other name and every other kingdom! May they be ruined and torn apart. . . .'"[23]

Thus the Reformer took a step beyond mere dialectic. He saw himself faced with a clear alternative: Satan or Jesus Christ. God fights in Jesus Christ, through the word and with the aid of the true church, against the kingdom of the devil. On the basis of his strongly christocentric theology, Luther concentrates the struggle in the conflict between Jesus Christ and the devil. This is not about a dualism between God and the devil. God maintains the upper hand in any case, and God's reign will have overcome by the end of days. But on earth the battle between Jesus Christ and Satan rages. "The Gospel calls forth Satan."[24] When Christ's word comes, "he makes a racket."[25] When Christ is in the ship, the storm begins.[26] If the Gospel is preached and everything remains peaceful, something is wrong.[27] If I believe in Christ and have him in me, the devil will be "at my throat"; "simply begin to be a Christian," and you'll find out![28] For Luther, not only the present but also the history of the church, both past and future, are interpreted in terms of the alternative "Satan or Christ."[29]

The Reformer's christocentric, indeed primarily soteriological approach unlocked for him the heart of the Gospel, and for Christianity it recalled and shed new light on the message of the justification of the sinner. But it needs to be asked whether a price did not have to be paid for it. A stronger emphasis on trinitarian thought would probably have preserved him from drifting into the realms of dualism. It is true that he adopted the traditional trinitarian dogma, and not only formally, but he neither recognized nor made use of its integrative power. Lutheran theologians love to praise theology as the art of making distinctions. But what we need today, despite the enduring necessity to make distinctions, is the ability to establish links and, beyond that, to make connections and strive to integrate what can be integrated.

NOTES

[1] Cf. von Loewenich 1963, 110.

[2] Cf. Bornkamm, Heinrich 1970, 107–10, at 110.

[3] Junghans 1983 has made a significant contribution here.

[4] Cf. von Loewenich 1963, 129.

[5] Ulrich Becke, *Die Welt voll Teufel. Martin Luther als Gegenstand psychohistorischer Betrachtung* (Marburg: Görich & Weiershäuser, 1981), gives an overview.

[6] Peter Cornehl, "Gottesdienst VIII. Evangelischer Gottesdienst von der Reformation bis zur Gegenwart," *TRE* 14: 54–85, at 58.

[7] Cf. Gerhard Müller, "Tribut an den Geist der Zeit. Martin Luthers Stellung zu den Juden," 38–44 in idem, *Zwischen Reformation und Gegenwart II. Vorträge und Aufsätze* (Hannover: Luther Verlagshaus, 1988).

[8] Bernhard Brons has pointed me to more recent studies on James in which the confrontation with Paul has declined in importance; cf. Rudolf Hoppe, "Jakobusbrief," *RGG4* 4: 361–63, with bibliography.

[9] LW 40, 178 (WA 18, 166, 34).

[10] See "The text of the words of institution" in chapter 10.

[11] LW 45, 105 (WA 11, 262, 9-10).

[12] LW 36, 328 (WA 18, 36, 18-25).

[13] WA 17/2, 125, 5-6.

[14] WA 50, 12, 6-7. Gury Schneider Ludorff, *Der fürstliche Reformator. Theologische Aspekte im Wirken Philipps von Hessen von der Homberger Synode bis zum Interim* (Leipzig: Evangelische Verlagsanstalt, 2006), 126–66, places this report in the context of the discussions about how to deal with Anabaptists and Jews in Hesse; cf. esp. 136–44.

[15] Bernhard Brons has pointed out to me that the *ius emigrandi* even found its way into the Declaration of Human Rights (Article 13 §2). Happily, in contrast to the situation in the sixteenth century, this article cannot be used to legitimate banishment!

[16] Joseph Lecler, *Geschichte der Religionsfreiheit im Zeitalter der Reformation*, vol. 1 (Stuttgart: Schwabenverlag, 1965), 231–52, at 251.

[17] LW 53 62 (WA 19, 73, 1-10).

[18]". . . interim nihil cogentes, sive credant, sive non, qui prohibentur, neque si clam maledicant, sive non," WA.Br 3, 616, 32-33.

[19]LW 40, 57 (WA 15, 218, 19-20; 219, 1 [1524]).

[20]WA 10/2, 167, 12-15 (1522).

[21]"For love bears all, endures all. Faith bears nothing, and the Word endures nothing; the Word must be perfectly pure (charitas omnia suffert, omnia tolerat, fides nihil suffert et verbum nihil tolerat, sed perfecte purum esse debet verbum)," LW 9, 166 (WA 14, 669, 14-16).

[22]*The Book of Concord*, 346–47.

[23]LW 21, 101 (WA 32, 384, 1-8).

[24]WA 15, 459, 15; cf. LW 12, 215 (WA 40/2, 496, 1-2).

[25]WA 45, 405, 30-32.

[26]". . . quando Christus, so gehts an," WA 32, 14, 15-16.

[27]LW 27, 43 (WA 40/2, 53, 12).

[28]WA 37, 183, 22-23; LW 21, 20 (WA 32, 313, 31-32).

[29]For this whole subject cf. Barth, Hans-Martin 1967, esp. 18–82. The title of Heiko Oberman's book (1981a), *Luther. Mensch zwischen Gott und Teufel* [Luther: Between God and the Devil], falls short.

19

What Needs to Be Developed

The epoch of orthodoxy following Luther devoted itself not to development but to securing and defending the theological achievements of the Reformation. In the process many features of the Reformer's theology faded into the background, a development clearly visible in the fact that, for example, *De servo arbitrio*, which he himself called especially important,[1] was not included in the confessions.[2] In later phases of the history of Protestant theology individual aspects of his theology were favored: for example, the universal priesthood (Philipp Jakob Spener),[3] concentration on the redeeming work of Christ (Nikolaus Graf von Zinzendorff), or concentration on the literal sense of Sacred Scripture in historical-critical exegesis since the end of the eighteenth century. Luther's theology gave impetus to thought in non-Lutheran churches as well. Here we can think of the recovery of interest in Sacred Scripture, engagement on behalf of the lay apostolate and the "common priesthood" of the faithful after Vatican II, the growth of Latin American base communities,[4] or the concepts of community in congregationalist-leaning churches.

What are the aspects of Luther's theology that should be developed today? Possible themes extend from questions of lifestyle through hermeneutics, ecclesiology, and eschatology, to a further development of his doctrine of the Trinity. The goal must be discovery of the ability of his theology to connect with contemporary global processes in the ongoing history of churches and religions.

A Visibly Protestant Way of Life

Luther certainly worked toward a particular lifestyle for his congregations and their members. Characteristic of the congregations was worship, clerical office and the functions associated with it, the school, and the common purse. The daily lives of believers should be shaped by the catechism, with morning and evening prayer; children and servants were urged to come "reverently and with folded hands to the table" and say their table prayers.[5] But this should not deceive us into overlooking the fact that a great many forms that up to that time had been used as expressions of Christian faith fell victims to Luther's critique. Fasting, kneeling, crossing oneself, and even monasticism were not forbidden by Luther, but he did not value them for their possible spiritual significance.[6] So it is that, at the latest since the Enlightenment, these things have largely and ineradicably been regarded as "Catholic." Luther probably did not as a rule imagine that all these rituals and gestures could be carried out without latent thoughts of gaining merit. He did not reflect on the ways in which they could be helpful if one separated them from that intention and valued them for themselves. Today, however, we know from various insights, including anthropological studies, what significance rituals in general have for individuals and for communities. Islam shows Christians and non-Christians vividly what power is developed by ritual prayer and the common celebration of Ramadan. In addition, the intention to "earn" heaven through rituals and ascetic forms of life has long since become obsolete even within Catholicism, at least in central Europe; there is no danger of it in Protestantism in any case. In the meantime, therefore, a self-correction has been in process for some time within Protestant devotion: fasting is practiced in the form of "seven weeks without" (or vice versa, "with"); pilgrimages are made to annual church gatherings or to Santiago; the Eastern churches' "prayer of the heart" and even East Asian forms of meditation have found their way into Lutheran spirituality, and new Lutheran religious orders and communities have come into existence. Kneeling, which was still practiced for a long time at least in receiving Holy Communion, and the sign of the cross have returned to Lutheran congregations only in individual instances. But theologically there is no more objection to these than to holy water, understood as a remembrance of baptism, though it needs to be separated from the notion of "holiness" or "blessing." We need to consider, on the basis of Luther's theology, the extent to which these old forms can be made fruitful for believers and their congregations, but also what new forms can be discovered and tried. I find the "Servizio Cristiano" in Riesi in Sicily, in which a group of Christians come together for a period of time to engage in social service, to be a communitarian form that is not simply a copy of the Catholic monastery but represents an authentic way to live a Protestant Christianity. Luther rightly polemicized against the idea of a *habitus*, insofar as it was supposed to be the basis of staying power or approval before God,[7] but in doing so he overlooked the fact that people have their own need for a *habitus*, psychologically and sociologically. However, the creation of such a *habitus*, which is altogether legitimate theologically, requires a community and external aids for practicing and maintaining it. These, if they do not become ends in themselves and detached from diaconal service, can certainly serve as encouragement and assurance to believers.

SPIRITUAL HERMENEUTICS

PERSPECTIVES THAT GUIDE INSIGHT

According to Luther, God's word is like God's womb: "in it he conceives us, carries us, gives birth to us, as a woman conceives and carries a child in her womb and gives birth to it."[8] His reference to the literal meaning of Sacred Scripture is an act of spiritual hermeneutics. The Bible must be understood *proprio spiritu*, an interpretative principle that is regarded today as a matter of course for interpreting any literary document. Luther's spiritual goal is clearly evident in his criterion for interpretation: "what drives Christ." But the Reformer did not apply it consistently; he again and again allowed himself to be diverted into a scriptural positivism "for which every statement in the Bible is regarded as infallible and the work of the Holy Spirit, independent of any religious or christocentric content."[9] Walther von Loewenich points, for example, to the fact that the Reformer rejected Copernicus's theory by appealing to Joshua 10:12.[10] It is true that Luther's insistence on the christological center of the biblical witnesses should be brought to bear again to counter evangelical-fundamentalistic voices and ideas such as creationism. But at the same time that Christocentrism has proved itself too narrow; a christological interpretation of the Old Testament such as Luther practiced is unsustainable in any case. The Reformer himself gives an indication of how this constriction can be released when he says: "The Credo . . . is my Bible."[11] If that is really so, not only does the Bible explain the Credo, but the Credo also sheds light on the Bible. The Credo, however, can be summarized in the trinitarian confession. Biblical words and stories are then to be interpreted in terms of how they correspond to the saving work of the triune God. The Reformer rejected the so-called fourfold sense of Scripture because he saw it as a means to falsify the real statement of the scriptural words. But he himself clung to allegoresis when it was useful for articulating a christological or soteriological statement. In the same way we can say that even the traditional fourfold sense of Scripture can no longer be a danger if it is applied in a disciplined way in light of the trinitarian confession.

MULTIPLE SENSES OF SCRIPTURE

The literal sense addresses a particular level of awareness, namely the cognitive. But as a rule it does not lead to existential experience, for which a spiritual hermeneutics is necessary. The oft-lamented crisis of the scriptural principle is not at all the fault of historical-critical exegesis, but lies in the fact that the latter is not, as a rule, augmented by a spiritual hermeneutics, and that as a result it is no longer possible to have one's own experience of Sacred Scripture. The allegorical sense speaks of what I may believe, the moral of what the law demands of me; the anagogical sense, finally, shows me the goal of my life and where I therefore should direct my efforts and where they are actually headed.[12] There is no need to hold to this ancient late-medieval division; we could also inquire into the trinitarian sense of a scriptural passage: where is the work of the Creator found in it, where the reconciling act of the Redeemer, and where does the sanctifying and perfecting action of the Holy Spirit speak? How do these three guiding perspectives harmonize? This approach would at the same time make it clear that the Sacred Scriptures are not isolated but, seen also from the perspective of the aesthetics of reception, can only be appropriately understood in the context of believers. Such a hermeneutical procedure could certainly be applied also to extra-canonical writings, under the presumption that God's rule is also accomplished in a hidden way even in non-Christian religions. It could be used in reading the Old Testament apocrypha, the Gospel of Thomas, even non-Christian sacred scriptures without any need thus to make them compete with Sacred Scripture itself.[13]

PENTECOST LANGUAGE

But all that would not remove the difficulty today's believers have with religious language as such. They will not be satisfied by Luther's advice that, when faced with the doctrine of the Trinity, one should "boldly nail mathematics to the cross." Walther von Loewenich had already issued the challenge half a century ago: "Or is anyone seriously prepared to repeat Luther's statement that 'Mary nursed God, the Creator of heaven and earth'?"[14] In the meantime the problems of communication have only intensified. Even concepts like "Son of God" or "Father in heaven" often evoke only misunderstanding or head-shaking bafflement; they obscure the sense of what they are intended to express in the Christian creed. The Reformer scarcely had such difficulties; at the same time, in speaking of the *novae linguae*—a new, Pentecost language— he gave us some important hints for how to overcome them. The most recent attempts at this in Luther research are trying to proceed in terms of modern metaphor theory.[15] Simply put, that means, for example in the conflict over the real presence of Christ in the Eucharist: "We have the reality only in the image (against Luther); but the image is the reality (against Zwingli)."[16] "Real" is expressed by means of an image, something the Reformer would not have found satisfying. Eberhard Jüngel is more on the mark when he says that Luther used "the figure of metaphor metaphorically, not to make an improper way of speaking still less proper, but to show that thanks to ontological reduplication the christological-soteriological metaphor is a direct and accurate way of speaking, such that a transfer of being that has already occurred is definitively brought into speech in the transfer of word that is proper to it."[17] Undoubtedly, more work needs to be done on this question. In any case, it is clear even without a complicated metaphorology that the language of faith moves on a level different from that of common speech, which is rushing ever faster toward a materialistic-positivistic superficiality, and that it is one of the tasks of theology to make the difference clear and prevent any confusion.[18]

A More Intensive Ecclesiology

In view of the omnipresent power of the Roman church, which penetrated every sphere of life, it could not have been the Reformer's primary aim to conceive an ecclesiology. His task was to focus on individuals, their dignity and their mission in relation to the masses alienated from the Gospel by religious strictures. The vision of the church that Luther nevertheless proposed was grounded in the effective power of the Gospel as he experienced it, and therefore it was tailored to individual believers. What was lacking, however, was an ecclesiological dynamic, a missionary and ultimately— also necessarily—ecumenical ecclesiological consciousness. The eschatological side of ecclesiology was present in principle, but in fact it remained without influence.

Dynamic ecclesiology

The Reformation's discovery of the relevance of the Gospel for individuals resulted in a structural problem for ecclesiology. While in the late medieval church people were united in devout action and distinguishing themselves in service to one another, under the preaching of the Gospel the church broke apart into groups of those who "earnestly desired" to be Christians and the mass of those who had to be "driven" to hear preaching. Since Luther, with good reason, could not decide simply to gather the serious-minded and organize them by themselves, but tried to yoke them and hold them together by means of catechism and common worship with those who were essentially uninterested, the ground was taken out from under the universal, mutual, and common priesthood. The members of the community who, grasped by living faith in the Gospel, could have practiced it were fundamentally unaware of one another and so could not offer mutual support; at the same time, they were not in a position to offer any aid to those who were not serious or were less so. Both groups depended on the ministry, which nevertheless had to remain alien to the uninterested; ultimately the latter could only be kept in line by social controls or police action. This *crux* exists in the national Lutheran churches till today; in Germany the church tax is the last publicly-sanctioned tie that keeps many "in the church" although they are estranged from it. What does that mean ecclesiologically?

The doctrine of the church must, altogether in Luther's sense, begin with the preaching of the Gospel and state the gathering of believers as its goal. It must present the dynamic of the power of the Gospel from within outward by showing how, within the visible group of those gathered, the invisible and real finds its place. The Latin American liberation theologian Leonardo Boff has called this process "ecclesiogenesis."[19] It implies that the "real" church is invisible, so that what is visible in the church acquires a twofold task: on the one hand it must humbly admit that it "is not it," but that something greater will come after (cf. John the Baptizer); on the other hand, however, it must insist, with a graced self-confidence, that the eschatological community is organizing itself within it: here are the living gifts of grace that can be attributed only to the working of the Holy Spirit. Luther shamefully neglected Paul's writing about charisms (Romans 12; 1 Corinthians 12–14), even though he could have made a truly persuasive connection between them and his concept of the universal, mutual, and common priesthood of the faithful. A retrieval of awareness of the charisms has great significance for a fully developed ecclesiology.

Missionary ecclesiology

The missionary moment is, in Luther's view, entirely directed inward, toward the congregation that is to be expanded and maintained. That was appropriate in view of the situation of the church at the time and the fact that Christians always remain both sinners and justified. Nevertheless, the Reformer did consider something like a mission among the Jews and could always imagine that Christians captured by the Turks could give missionary witness. But he did not reflect on this matter in ecclesiological terms. It is not the whole community that has a missionary duty; it is individuals in particular situations, and the ministry. It cannot be the community because it does not exist as an empirical entity; all that is present is the corpus permixtum, the mixed heap within which mission is to be conducted.

For the same reasons a congregation, if it wanted to organize itself according to Reformation ideas, had a hard time establishing itself in the eyes of the princes or city government; it was scarcely in a position to articulate its protest against wrong developments within the church and injustice in the realm of God's rule with the "left hand." There was no question of adopting a path like that of the pre-Reformation Spiritual Franciscans or the Waldensians, or one of the ways attempted during the Reformation by Anabaptist groups. Here again, the ministry had to act.[20] Even in World War II it happened that the

Norwegian Bishop Eivind Berggrav interpreted Luther's doctrine of the two regimes as a manifesto against the church's conformity with the interests of the Nazis.[21] The problem still exists: how can the church as an institution that, so far as observable from without, belongs to the majority of the disinterested, lift up its voice believably and with authority on behalf of human needs, justice, and human rights? For a long time this has been pursued by way of delegations to particular commissions or by individual representatives. But can that be a satisfying solution in the sense of the Reformation? Is there not need for a community of those who are able to make it clear through their faithful witness and way of life that the church is not fighting for its own self-preservation but means to be the community of Jesus Christ, the church for others?

ECUMENICALLY-ORIENTED ECCLESIOLOGY

Since Luther had to distinguish himself polemically against pope, bishops, and the whole Roman church, it is easy to overlook that he was able at the same time to presume the existence of the Gospel and the true church even among his opponents. It is obvious that he regarded the Reformation as a whole as an ecumenical event. In addition, although just as critically, he had the "Greeks," that is, the Orthodox Church, as well as the Waldensians in view. He was familiar with some of the liturgical gestures from the Greek church,[22] and he knew that the "Greeks" had been threatened by the pope but had never been under his authority.[23] He had heard that the Waldensians supposedly did not have much regard for languages[24] and that they baptized children without believing in the power of baptism; he was aware of the extent to which they were persecuted by the Roman church.[25] He considered it a matter of course that the church would endure through and beyond all times and deformities.[26] This is the place to begin again today. Today's desire for ecumenical harmony, which we may be tempted to dissolve into "political correctness," cannot conceal the fact that mutual criticism among believers and churches can be fruitful and may represent an ecumenical enrichment. It is true that the Reformer perceived this altogether one-sidedly: he was ready to offer his services to the whole church, and indeed regarded it as inevitable. But he was not able to ask which insights could be present in other churches, even though they might be opaque to him. Today, however, it is evident that the different churches have been given different gifts that they should make available to one another: Protestantism the charism of binding to the word of God that testifies to itself in Sacred Scripture, Catholicism a sacramentally-oriented spirituality, the Orthodox churches the awareness of the comprehensive activity of the Holy Spirit. Hence we need to develop an ecclesiology based on Lutheran theology that allows us not only to affirm the different confessional profiles but to live and celebrate an ecumenism of charisms. In that way the Reformer's ecclesiology can be made available to the various non-Lutheran Protestant churches of the world, but also to the Roman Church and Orthodoxy.

A more difficult question is whether on the basis of Luther's theology there can be a "theology of religions," something that appears unavoidable today. The exclusive linking of salvation to Jesus Christ and the faith seems to make this impossible. But the Reformer saw even the "Turks" as being under God's rule, though exclusively in the regime of the "left hand." Had he taken seriously the thought that God can ultimately not desire to do anything with the "left hand" other than what God does with the "right hand," because the Creator's work is not in contradiction to the work of reconciliation in Jesus Christ and perfection in the Holy Spirit, he might have been able to advance to new insights in this connection as well. He did not see himself in a position to posit that Socrates and other representative figures of antiquity were in heaven, as Zwingli thought possible. But even he broke through the *sola fide* at one point, at least in thought. As described earlier, he maintained great admiration for Cicero and in his table talk once expressed the hope that our Lord God would "be gracious to him and those like him," even though of course we human beings are not entitled to judge. God could certainly act among other nations in unexpected ways, but we do not know the corresponding points in time and the means by which God accomplishes God's will. The new heaven and new earth would be in many ways broader and wider than we can imagine.[27] This opinion is certainly marginal to Luther's theology and conviction, but it has been handed down as historically authentic. Further theological work needs to be done at this point. The saying about *ecclesia semper reformanda*, which does not appear to match the self-awareness of the Lutheran confessional writings, was apparently created on the basis of the Lutheran concord.[28] In light of developments in church history and the overall process of globalization, this saying must be augmented today by adding an *ecclesiologia semper reformanda*.

AN ECCLESIOLOGY SHAPED BY ESCHATOLOGY

Luther's ecclesiology is thoroughly eschatological in its conception: it describes the tension between the true and false church and is aware of the "eschatological struggle of Christ with the adversary."[29] But the eschatology he presents is ordered to the present, even when it presents itself as forward-looking. We find ourselves "at the dawn of future life," so that we are now able to see the world anew.[30] The Holy Spirit is even now active in achieving his work, and he will do so until the last day; we must await it patiently, and possibly under heavy suffering. So it will be until the end of days, but within that time nothing will happen except that preaching and its rejection will go on, again and ever again. The Augsburg Confession grasps this mood exactly when it says laconically *quod una sancta ecclesia perpetua mansura sit,* "that one holy Christian church will be and remain forever. . . ." but within that time, until the last day, little will change in the church. The ability of Lutheran congregations to endure until the present day is amazing. The custom introduced in times of crisis of singing "Graciously grant us peace" at the end of worship lives on, decades after the end of the crisis. On the whole, tradition seems easier to legitimate than innovation. This may be connected to something Wilhelm Dilthey observed: "The 'central point' of early Christian piety, the expectation of the *parousia,* had no reality in the religious life of the Reformers."[31] It is true that Luther waited with longing for the "dear last day," but for him that was a matter of patience and not an inspired jubilation. He was unable to convey to his community that in it was revealed the goal of all creation and that it represented, so to speak, a bodily anticipation of the reign of God. Modern theologians of hope and liberation challenge Luther's ecclesiological approaches to further development.

Luther's eschatology is clearly subject to the expectation of judgment. Albrecht Peters in particular has emphasized this repeatedly in his writings. He occasionally uses, almost as a technical term, the horrible concept "decisive for salvation" and sees before him "the abyss of either-or, which God in Christ has set up over all humankind."[32] In fact, the Reformer shared Cyprian's conviction: *extra ecclesiam nulla salus,* even though he can refine the *extra ecclesiam* to *extra praedicationem Evangelii.*[33] In "this Christian Church, wherever it exists, is to be found the forgiveness of sins. . . . Outside this Christian Church there is no salvation or forgiveness of sins, but everlasting death and damnation. . . ."[34] It is true that Luther is not applying this statement to non-Christian religions, but to the old-church practice of merits and indulgences. The Reformer gave scarcely any thought to the salvation of members of non-Christian religions; that problem was not a question for him as it is for Christianity today in view of the processes of secularization and globalization. Christian theology needs to take a position on this question. If it cannot achieve a concept of universal reconciliation it should at least make it clear that it cannot present faith in the triune God as a condition to be fulfilled in order to attain salvation. If its preaching consists, even subliminally, of the notion that one must, or at least should "believe," it makes the Gospel into law that the human being does not want to follow and even with the best will in the world cannot follow. The device *extra ecclesiam nulla salus* must be transformed, in the sense of the Gospel and ultimately of Luther as well, into the message: "*intra* ecclesiam salus!" That certainty would change the mood within the church as well and allow it once again to be recognizable as a community of those filled with a great confidence.

An Integrative Doctrine of the Trinity

In recent years there has been increasing emphasis on the essential role of trinitarian faith for Luther.[35] This finding should indeed be underscored, but it also needs to be refined. The Reformer speaks of each of the three trinitarian Persons, reflectively in theological terms and emphatically in terms of soteriology. The work of the Holy Spirit is also given a thorough valuation:[36] The Spirit brings us to Christ,[37] incorporates us into the communion of believers, and "makes [us] holy,"[38] as "his name implies."[39] But "where Christ is not preached, there is no Holy Spirit to create, call, and gather the Christian church, and outside it no one can come to the Lord Christ."[40] The cooperation of the Holy Spirit with Christ, like that between God the Father and the Son, is more clearly articulated than that between God the Father and the Holy Spirit. To that degree Luther stands within the Western tradition, which places value on the doctrine that the Spirit proceeds also from God the Son.[41] The connection between the work of the Spirit and the crucified and risen Christ was especially important to Luther. At the same time he can write, summarizing: "These are the three persons and one God, who has given himself to us all wholly and completely, with all that he is and has."[42]

If we go through the Reformer's statements on soteriology we are immediately struck by the fact that they frequently refer to one or other of the trinitarian Persons and not to the "one" God. Father, Son, and Spirit work together for the salvation of lost humans, but as individual hypostases. Wolfgang A. Bienert has pointed out that the Reformer thus takes up the tradition of the ancient church, which emphasized "the hypostatic character and thus the uniqueness of the divine persons."[43] So in Luther's confession the divine Persons stand alongside one another: "I believe in God the Father, who created me, I believe in God the Son, who redeemed me, I believe in the Holy Spirit, who sanctifies me."[44] But in this way the doctrine of the Trinity in a certain way loses its integrative power (something that is not true of the Eastern church/Orthodox view inasmuch as it does not tie the work of the Spirit exclusively to proclamation). So for Luther there is a hiatus between the salvific work of the Trinity for believers and a governance of the Creator that can be made a separate theme from the salvific work of Christ and the Spirit. The formula traced to Augustine, that the "outward works of the Trinity are not separate from one another" (*opera trinitatis ad extra sunt indivisa*), which Luther mentions occasionally and even explicates at length in a late writing,[45] is not recognized and used for its integrative power. This prepares a basis that may nourish dualistic tendencies, religious intolerance, and a biting polemic. Other potential consequences are a narrowing of hermeneutics and an exclusivistic ecclesiology.

Probably Luther does not see a contradiction here because he thinks in "infralapsarian" terms, on the basis of "original sin." Heaven and earth and all living things in them are the work of the Creator, but in the fallen world Christ and the Spirit must act in order that at least a part of humanity may attain blessedness. But Luther was unable to see that the Father of Jesus Christ, and the Spirit with him, could be effecting their saving work in the world not reached by the Gospel. Hence a theology that follows the Reformer has the task of exploiting and using the integrative possibilities of the trinitarian confession. That could at the same time be the basis for this theology to become ecumenical, globally accessible, and able to exercise an inspirational service in many different contexts.

Notes

[1] LW 50, 172 (WA.Br 8, 99, 7-8).

[2] Bernhard Brons rightly points out that *De servo arbitrio* in fact does not represent a confession as such.

[3] Cf. Barth, Hans-Martin 1990, 54–78.

[4] Ibid., 104–60.

[5] Cf. *The Book of Concord*, 353.

[6] The same is true for the crossing of oneself that is recommended in the Small Catechism, *The Book of Concord*, 352.

[7] He opposed, among others, those "who invent for us a kind of common faith, a snoring, or rather dead *habitus*, that now and then produces an act of faith." Instead, it is faith that gives value to every deed and omission. WA 5, 396, 15-16 (trans.).

[8] LW 52, 79 (WA 10/1/1, 232, 12-15).

[9] Walther von Loewenich 1963, 342; see further examples and references there.

[10] WA.TR 1, 419, 16-23; 4, 412, 32-35 (no. 4638).

[11] WA 37, 55, 13.

[12] Augustine of Denmark: "Littera gesta docet, quid credas allegoria, moralis quid agas, quid speres [or, according to Nikolaus of Lyra, quo tendas] anagogia" = The literal sense teaches what happened, the allegorical what you believe, the moral what you should do, the anagogical what you may hope (or: where you are going)." Cf. Peter Walter, "Schriftsinne," *LTK3* 9: 268–69.

[13] Cf. Barth, Hans-Martin 2008, 216–21.

[14] Von Loewenich 1963, 409; WA 47, 705, 19.

[15] Cf. Streiff 1993; Goertz 1997, 33–69; Wolff 2006.

[16] Von Loewenich 1963, 434. Von Loewenich calls this an "apostolic relativism," whereby, however, he speaks more for Zwingli and against Luther. We would do better to call it an "apostolic realism!"

[17] Cf. Jüngel 1981, 40–49, at 48.

[18] On this cf. also Barth, Hans-Martin 2008c.

[19] Cf. Leonardo Boff, *Ecclesiogenesis: The Base Communities Reinvent the Church* (Maryknoll, NY: Orbis, 1986).

[20] One example is the (unpublished) letter Luther wrote in connection with the so-called Wurzen Feud, WA.Br 10, 31–37; cf. Brecht 1987, 288–89.

[21] Cf. Bayer 2003, 284, with bibliography at nn. 19–20.

[22] LW 28, 271 (WA 26, 43, 3-5).

[23] Cf., e.g., WA 50, 85, 30-34; WA 2, 225, 35-38.

[24] LW 45, 365 (WA 15, 42, 16-17).

[25] LW 40, 255 (WA 26, 167, 16-18); WA 38, 78, 3; 7, 734, 21.

[26]Cf. Wolfgang Höhne, *Luthers Anschauungen über die Kontinuität der Kirche* (Berlin: Lutherisches Verlagshaus, 1963).

[27]". . . quamvis non est nostrum illud dicere et definire, sondern sollen bey dem verbo revelato bleiben: 'Qui crediderit et baptizatus fuerit etc.' Quod autem Deus non possit cum aliis dispensare et discrimen habere inter alias gentes, hic non est nostrum scire tempora et modum. Erit enim novum coelum, nova terra multo amplior et latior. Bene potest singulis secundum sua merita retribuere," WA.TR 4, 14, 3-9 (no. 3925).

[28]Theodor Mahlmann makes this seem probable in his essay, "'Ecclesia semper reformanda.' Eine historische Aufklärung," 57–77 in Hermann Deuser, et al., eds., *Theologie und Kirchenleitung. FS für Peter Steinacker zum 60. Geburtstag* (Marburg: Elwert, 2003).

[29]Asendorf 1967, 234.

[30]WA.TR 1, 574, 8-10 (no. 1160).

[31]Quoted from von Loewenich 1963, 53.

[32]Peters 1991, 236.

[33]"Outside the church there is no salvation" to "outside the preaching of the Gospel there is no salvation." This is the interpretation of Peters 1991, 236.

[34]LW 37, 368 (WA 26, 507, 7-12).

[35]Cf. Markschies 1999; Müller, Gerhard 2004.

[36]Cf. Kärkkäinen 2005.

[37]*The Book of Concord*, 415.

[38]Ibid., 416.

[39]Ibid.

[40]Ibid.

[41]Cf. WA 49, 467, 16-20. For the significance of the *filioque* for Luther cf. Joachim Heubach, ed., *Luther und die trinitarische Tradition* (Erlangen: Martin-Luther-Verlag, 1994), as well as Peters 1991, 41, n. 194.

[42]LW 37, 366 (WA 26, 505, 38-39).

[43]Wolfgang A. Bienert, "Die Reformation als dogmengeschichtliches Ereignis—Ein Beitrag zur Geschichte des pneumatologischen Dogmas," 35–56 in Heubach 1996, esp. 56.

[44]*The Book of Concord*, 411.

[45]WA 49, 239, 21-25; cf. esp. LW 15, 302 (WA 54, 57, 35–58, 3): one should distinguish the Persons within the Godhead and yet "ascribe, externally, each work to all three without distinction." But Luther only does that in particular cases, e.g., in exegeting Luke 1:35: LW 15, 305 (WA 54, 60, 5-11). Cf. also "The Last Words of David" (1543), *passim*: LW 15, 265–352 (WA 54, 28–100); for the whole subject see "The Triune God" in chapter 6.

Martin Luther's Theology: Existentially Inspiring and Open for Global Integration

After this preliminary overview of Luther's theology, I want to ask myself how my engagement with it has done me good, where I found it inspiring, what points have left me dissatisfied, and where it presses beyond its historical form. Must one be socialized as a Lutheran, or at least as "evangelical" in a general sense, to understand Luther at all, let alone love him? It is certainly helpful to know the most important events from the Reformer's life and be familiar with the language of his translation of the Bible. That probably gives one a head start on comprehending his thought; on the other hand, it may be particularly his strangeness that provokes interest. But in religion one cannot remain content with a subjectively perceived meaning; the goal is an intersubjective communicability and ultimately the possibility of global integration.

But is it even permissible for Christian theology to be capable of socio-cultural integration?[1] Is Luther not necessarily the great contrarian whose ability to resist is something that Reformed Christians, Catholics, Hindus, Buddhists, and Muslims (and Jews!) simply have to endure? I would (though not as regards the Jews!) say a limited "yes" to that, under the precondition that they have really understood what Luther meant and what he was fighting for. Even those who do not share his views on Christian faith should at least understand what he was aiming at. Christian faith in its Reformation shape should be formulated and present in such a way that thoughtful and sensitive people of all religious and non-religious worldviews are put in a position to reject or accept it for good reasons. What is important is to make it clear that the Reformation, at least the Lutheran Reformation, is not an obsolete quarrel among theologians that happened centuries ago, but is a pastoral movement motivated by the most serious reasons; it is simply and ultimately about the success of human life and death, salvation and its absence. For the present that means that a faith oriented to Luther serves to strengthen the identity of the individual; it enables a person to encounter difficulties that could not have been anticipated and to master crises. Luther's theology, whatever else it may have been, is therapeutic theology! It is not the Gospel, but it witnesses to the Gospel in an original and inspiring way that touches many people in their hearts. Healing power emanates from it. It inquires about injury and how it can be relieved. It wounds the self-concept of today's people especially, and it presents then with answers that are hard to digest. But that is how it helps them to understand their lives more deeply and to react more ably to the challenges of existence. Formulating in the abstract, one could say that its utterly frank existential analysis serves the human ability to be what one is, by the very fact that it is aware of a transcendence of human existence and indefatigably points toward it.

EXISTENTIAL ANALYSIS

Luther's starting point is not a set of universal anthropological principles but the way he understands the Christian. Nevertheless, this yields points of view that are thoroughly capable of intersubjective communication. In my judgment this is true, for example, of the formulae in the Small Catechism: "I believe that God has created me and all that exists," "that Jesus Christ . . . is my Lord," and that I cannot come to faith on my own initiative, but "the Holy Spirit has called me. . . ." These statements are translatable! These three basic statements say to me that my life is taking place within a great and good creative context; it is subject to an authority that makes me independent of powers that are hostile to life; I am called to "something higher" than an existence that exhausts itself in the greyness of everyday and ultimately ends in nothingness. None of this is rationally demonstrable, but it is available for integration even by people of other religions or non-religious orientations, because it addresses the questions that are posed by personal reflection on human existence: how do I deal with the fact that I am not the source of my own being? What authorities are valid for me, and which are not? To what am I called, what constitutes the meaning of my life? One may suppress these questions, but probably no one can call them groundless.

Luther made the question of the authority that is valid for humanity more profound in three respects. Can I decide what it is on the basis of my own rational capacity? Can I bring my rational decision into effect through my own will? How can I be certain when I am making wrong decisions and when my will is subject to mistaken goals?

The Reformer attributed far more value to reason than is usually recognized. The negative cliché that he sketched a pessimistic image of human reason in particular is completely false. A person ought to use reason according to her or his best knowledge and conscience; it is competent in science, economy, and culture, and especially in the shaping of social life. Of course people today need no persuasion regarding the abilities of reason, and yet they are increasingly aware of the limitations and ambivalence of rational endeavors. This makes Luther's critique of reason globally accessible. In ultimate questions reason lets us down.

The case is similar with what Luther said about the bondage of the will. Of course, in the Reformer's view, human beings had ample opportunity to use and apply their freedom in earthly matters. But even here it has only a narrow field to work in. Modern brain research has done even more to relativize the freedom of the will,[2] and thus has gone beyond Luther's critical view. The Reformer, of course, was operating on a different level: human beings are not in a position to decide against their natural egocentricity, against themselves, and for the neighbor and for God. Hindu and Buddhist traditions are more clearly aware of this than are Judaism, Islam, and a number of groups within Christianity.

Those who are aware of the ambivalence of their reason and the limits of their ability to will cannot be ignorant of the state of their relationships to their fellow humans, their environment, and ultimately themselves. Luther may have been oversensitive in this matter; he saw himself as above all responsible to God, and guilty. He gives the impression that this is the basic component of human awareness. If we see things differently today, we are still aware that guilt and failure can create the greatest problems. In the West a horde of psychologists and psychotherapists are working to communicate a right way of dealing with guilt and guilt feelings. Hindu and Buddhist traditions speak of the law of evil begetting evil and the burden of karma. Luther's view should be realizable in that context. Islam and Judaism minimize the weight of sin in comparison to Reformation Christianity. Luther's analysis of existence can still provoke them to test their ideas. This is true also of secular people who are trying to explain evil as something natural, without being able to make its radical nature rationally comprehensible.

The Reformer invites people to use their ambivalent reason and relative freedom, not ignoring their limits, but allowing them to take an indication from those limits about what could lie beyond them. Luther's analysis of existence is, in my opinion, by no means lacking in plausibility.

Existential Transcendence

Luther's theology is articulated in a different language from that we are used to. To him, talking of transcendence was an abomination. In spite of that, I would call what he experienced an inbreaking of transcendence. I am not thinking primarily of the so-called "tower experience." He experienced the inbreaking of transcendence again and again in his encounters with the word of God, something he himself did not control. In approaching Sacred Scripture he knew himself to be touched by God. Law and Gospel unsettled him. It seems to me that this experience is Luther's heritage for Christianity, indeed, for humanity: the holy God encounters us in the word. In the word of God as attested in Sacred Scripture, Luther found the basis and perspective for his life, and confidence in the face of his death. Here he found liberation from everything that burdened him in view of the ambivalence of reason, the unfreedom of the will, and therefore his sinful existence. God's word transcends reality as we find it. For Christians this is an experience that happens again and again, especially because in this word they are encountered by a living partner: the triune God. It seems to me that this is comprehensible, at least in theory, even to nonbelievers or those of different belief, since the mere human word is capable of unlocking reality and transcending it.

In the word the Reformer was seized by an appeal from another dimension. The unconditional claim of God made demands on him, while the promise of God's grace consoled and mobilized him. The placing of Law and Gospel side by side or even against one another that we sometimes encounter in his preaching may seem somewhat schematic, but it is a reaction to two great and foundational human experiences: "I should" and "I may." Here again we see a possibility for global connection. It is not clear to the natural human being, at the outset, what one should and what one may. Luther was not concerned about details here. His experience of transcendence was an encounter with the unconditional will of God that on the one hand challenged him and on the other hand transferred him into a realm of freedom from any kind of demand.

For the Reformer all this was articulated in the language of the tradition he inherited, which is, as we would now say, highly theistic in nature. He speaks of a "wrathful God" and he has no difficulty calling Jesus of Nazareth "the Son of God." There are great difficulties in understanding this today. It tends rather to evoke misunderstanding and rejection. Here theology must work at translation if it wants to make comprehensible what moved Luther and what can still move us today. In his later years he himself talked of a "new language" that was by no means identical to everyday language and yet retained its relation to it. He, indeed, had the gift of speaking in "new tongues," precisely with the aid of everyday language.

There is no religion in which the word has such a central function as in the Christian churches that are heirs of the Reformation, but it is not completely absent anywhere. Beyond Luther, today anthropology and religious psychology raise the question of the relationship between word and silence, nonobjective meditation and reflection on the word, reading something external and sinking within oneself. How are the verbal and nonverbal communication of the Gospel related? To what extent can ritual and gesture, image and play, theoretical and practical ethos come to "speech"? Further clarification is necessary here in connection with the ability to forge links globally.

Others of the Reformer's experiences were unlocked and ordered for him by his experience of transcendence in the encounter with the word. He knew the experience of transcendence in a twofold form: as the human being's call to God and as God's call to him or her. He saw his life with an immediacy that can scarcely be exaggerated as existence "before God," *coram Deo*. The rustling of a leaf on a twig can frighten him; looking at a rose or a kernel of grain astonishes him. He is moved not so much by the logical question of why there is something and not nothing. He is amazed at creation, at particular events in history, at humanity; he is shaken by the self-centeredness he observes in himself and others. All that keeps him in an unsettled state. He experiences what Paul Tillich called "existential estrangement."[3] Luther experienced that estrangement primarily on the moral level. It may be that today such a polarization is more likely to be experienced in the context of the theodicy question. What explains all the horrors that people have to suffer or that they inflict on each other? Does not everything favor the idea that there is no God, and that even talk about an absence of God represents a euphemism? Luther's talk about the hidden God is not intended as an explanation but as a challenge to seek, behind even the worst experiences and events, the God who will show Godself gracious in Jesus Christ. Existential transcendence opens itself in faith. This answer will not satisfy those who believe differently or do not believe, but they will understand the questions behind it.

Humanity is aware of any number of indications of the inbreaking of transcendence. Experiences of transcendence are described in all religions. Luther was able to tell about his and to give an account of them, but they cannot be proven valid or even played off against other and possibly conflicting experiences. It is possible to dismiss them as projections or the product of a notorious fanaticism.[4] Luther's understanding of the Gospel is on the open market. But it should be on the market as something that invites and challenges to testing. For that purpose it must be appropriately presented and located in relation to other offers. An object whose use we do not know we simply pass by, unaware of it—when shopping, for example. I am not trying to accomplish a banal functionalization of Reformation theology, but I do want to plead earnestly that it be adequately articulated within the horizon of today's thoughts, feelings, and needs, and that it be presented in its healing offensiveness.

Existential Competence

In the bookstores one will not find Luther's works, or publications about him, in the "Self-Help" section. Nevertheless there are probably quite a few people, myself included, whom he has helped to better understand their lives and make them spiritually richer. The encounter with his theology awakens a desire for life: it demands an existential competence. In confronting God's word the human being gains her or his identity. Now one learns who one is: a human being with its contradictions that can live cheerfully with that contradictory nature. One knows oneself to be willed and valued by God. We need not produce our own dignity, and no one can take it from us. Christians guided by Luther's theology lose their fear of constantly making mistakes or neglecting what is important. They seek to free themselves from the compulsions of a self-realization falsely understood. On the other hand they will hazard their talents and use their sound human understanding and energy to get a grasp on urgent problems and find adequate solutions for them. They are responsible adults, independent of the standards of secular or even ecclesial authorities because they find their freedom and guidance in the authority of the word of God promised to them. They welcome good fortune, but even in bad times they do not lose the ground under their feet. A kind of "positive thinking of a higher order" fills them, something that rests not only on natural optimism or reversing the polarities of viewpoint and feeling. It is founded on a faith that knows its weaknesses and vulnerability and is able to entrust even doubt and despair to God.

Identity includes social existence. Luther gives this a specific profile: a Christian is for others and lays claim to others. Within the congregation one lives the universal, mutual, and common priesthood: believers are available to one another with their witness, with advice and action. Together they battle for a better world and live a solidary existence in the face of all fragmentation. Their ethos is situational and not governed by frozen norms.

Socially this corresponds to a consciously democratic life. This is a point that Luther, in the context of the sixteenth-century world, was unable to grasp adequately. Nevertheless, his approach offers a variety of impulses for constructive contributions within the framework of a free and democratic fundamental order. Democracy requires adult citizens willing to participate in it. Those who are guided by Luther's insights have no hesitation in accepting responsibility, an "office," and risk along with it, thus encountering difficulties and even entering into sinful contexts. Luther saw the individual's contribution to common life primarily in the context of class and calling: each, within the frame of his or her specialty, directs what is his or her own to the welfare of the whole. Although infinitely much has changed in the world of work, it seems to me that this idea is not obsolete. Even in shifting jobs and in phases of unemployment or in retirement one can attempt to bring about what is best for the common good.

The existential competence to be learned from Luther may not be viewed as an ideal that one could finally achieve by one's own efforts. It is broken and fragmentary, but it is open to expansion. It is not once and for all. It draws strength ever anew from the fountain of faith—in Luther's language, from the proclamation expressed in the form of Law and Gospel. From a psychological point of view it is a processual event in which trust grows firm and inner freedom expands.

A joyful awareness of one's own identity despite all brokenness and imperfection, a social nature ready to accept responsibility, and a perspective that comprehends the whole of life and even goes beyond it—that is the offering of competence in relation to existence that ultimately flows from the Gospel. Luther newly articulated and described it. His task within world history was and is to invite people to a realistic analysis of existence under the promise of the Gospel, to confront them with the existential transcendence communicated in the word of God, and so to open to them an existential competence that humanity needs if it is not to destroy itself.

Existential competence in this sense should characterize the churches, at least those that are the outgrowth of the Reformation. They ought to live their charism calmly and "non-exclusively," as "traditional orders within world Christianity,"[5] so to speak, but also as therapeutically competent working groups or, when necessary, as socially relevant "pressure groups" on behalf of the human beings for whom they exist.

Luther's theology needs to be thought through anew if its global openness to integration is to become visible. There must be a new battle over Luther and his heritage! Above all, a critical engagement with the Reformer will bring to light what in his insights is helpful for individuals and required by church and society. The ecumenical tug-of-war over his theology is inadequate; it conceals his real significance for the understanding of and responsible shaping of human existence. Even a new interest in Luther within the discipline of church history is not sufficient. Lutheran theology must ask what in his thought can be useful for the "world community now coming to be,"[6] and can also carry it further. It should steadily and ever anew allow itself to be aided by that theology, to make use of its insights and, when necessary, to go beyond them.

NOTES

[1] In what follows I am adapting material from Barth, Hans-Martin 2008b.

[2] Cf., e.g., Wolf Singer, *Ein neues Menschenbild? Gespräche über Hirnforschung*, stw 1596 (Frankfurt: Suhrkamp, 2003), esp. 24–34.

[3]Cf. Paul Tillich, *Systematic Theology* 1 (Chicago: University of Chicago Press, 1951), 44, 62, 172.

[4]"[R]eligious fanatics who sought the direct path to Alpha-being" have always existed, before and since Luther; thus Karl Eibl 2004, 189.

[5]Thus formulated in a letter from Bernhard Brons.

[6]A concept from *TRE* 33: 300 (subhead within the article). For a situational analysis cf. Peter Sloterdijk, *Im Weltinnenraum des Kapitals. Für eine philosophische Theorie der Globalisierung* (Frankfurt: Suhrkamp, 2005).

Appendix: Technical Notes

The author cites the Weimar Edition of Luther's works (WA) as well as the Lateinisch-Deutsche Studienausgabe (LDStA) and Studienausgabe (StA) by volume, page, and line(s). Where available, corresponding citations of the Concordia edition (LW) are given, with volume and page numbers.

In the notes, books and articles are cited in full if they are not included in the bibliography; otherwise the author-date system from the bibliography is used. There is a list of title abbreviations on p. 499–500. The secondary literature not listed in the bibliography can be found through the index of names, but this does not include the Foreword, Contents, and Bibliography, nor are editors' names indexed. The origin of the Latin translations is not given; most are by the author.

ABBREVIATIONS

BIBLICAL BOOKS

OLD TESTAMENT

Gen	Genesis
Exod	Exodus
Lev	Leviticus
Num	Numbers
Deut	Deuteronomy
Josh	Joshua
Judg	Judges
Ruth	Ruth
1–2 Sam	1–2 Samuel
1–2 Kgs	1–2 Kings
1–2 Chr	1–2 Chronicles
Ezra	Ezra
Neh	Nehemiah

Esth	Esther
Job	Job
Ps/Pss	Psalms
Prov	Proverbs
Qoh	Qoheleth (Ecclesiastes)
Song	Song of Songs
Isa	Isaiah
Jer	Jeremiah
Lam	Lamentations
Ezek	Ezekiel
Dan	Daniel
Hos	Hosea
Joel	Joel
Amos	Amos
Obad	Obadiah
Jonah	Jonah
Mic	Micah
Nah	Nahum
Hab	Habakkuk
Zeph	Zephaniah
Hag	Haggai
Zech	Zechariah
Mal	Malachi

New Testament

Matt	Matthew
Mark	Mark
Luke	Luke
John	John
Acts	Acts of the Apostles
Rom	Romans
1–2 Cor	1–2 Corinthians
Gal	Galatians
Eph	Ephesians
Phil	Philippians
Col	Colossians
1–2 Thess	1–2 Thessalonians
1–2 Tim	1–2 Timothy
Titus	Titus
Phlm	Philemon

Heb	Hebrews
Jas	James
1–2 Pet	1–2 Peter
1–2–3 John	1–2–3 John
Jude	Jude
Rev	Revelation
Sir	Sirach

TITLES

Apol	Apology of the Augsburg Confession, in *The Book of Concord*
AWA	Archiv zur Weimarer Ausgabe
CA	Augsburg Confession (Confessio Augustana)
CCC	*Catechism of the Catholic Church*
CIC	*Codex Iuris Canonici*
Clemen	*Luthers Werke in Auswahl*, ed. Otto Clemen. 8 vols. Berlin, 1929–.
DH	H. Denzinger,
DV	Dogmatic Constitution *Dei Verbum*
EG	*Evangelisches Gesangbuch*
EKG	*Evangelisches Kirchengesangbuch*
EKL	*Evangelisches Kirchenlexikon*
GER	Gemeinsame Erklärung zur Rechtfertigungslehre
HeidKat	*Der Heidelberger Katechismus*, ed. Otto Weber.
HST	Handbuch Systematischer Theologie, ed. C. H. Ratschow
HWP	*Historisches Wörterbuch der Philosophie*
Insel-Ausgabe	*Martin Luther. Ausgewählte Schriften*, ed. Karin Bornkamm and Gerhard Ebeling. 6 vols.
LDStA	Martin Luther, *Lateinisch-deutsche Studienausgabe*, ed. Wilfried Härle, et al.
LG	Dogmatic Constitution *Lumen Gentium*
LK	Leuenberger Konkordie
*LTK*²	*Lexikon für Theologie und Kirche*, 2d ed. (1957ff.)
*LTK*³	*Lexikon für Theologie und Kirche*, 3d ed. (1993ff.)
MdKI	*Materialdienst des Konfessionskundlichen Instituts in Bensheim*
*RGG*³	*Die Religion in Geschichte und Gegenwart*, 3d ed. (1956ff.)
*RGG*⁴	*Die Religion in Geschichte und Gegenwart*, 4th ed. (1993ff.)
StA	*Studienausgabe Martin Luther*, ed. Hans-Ulrich Delius, et al. 6 vols.
TRE	*Theologische Realenzyklopädie*

WA 1883ff.	Martin Luther, *Werke*. Kritische Gesamtausgabe. Weimar,
WA.BR	Ibid., Briefwechsel (Letters), Weimar, 1930ff.
WA.DB	Ibid., Deutsche Bibel (German Bible), Weimar, 1906ff.
WA.TR	Ibid., Tischreden (Table Talk), Weimar, 1912ff.

Selected Bibliography

Editions of Luther's Works

AE	*Luther's Works.* Jaroslav Pelikan and Halmut T. Lehmann, eds. 55 vols. Philadelphia: Muhlenberg Press, 1957–1986.
AWA	*Archiv zur Weimarer Ausgabe der Werke Martin Luthers. Texte und Untersuchungen.* Cologne and Vienna: Böhlau, 1981–1991.
Clemen	*Luthers Werke in Auswahl.* Ed. Otto Clemen. 8 vols. Berlin: de Gruyter, 1929–1935.
Insel-Ausgabe	Martin Luther. *Ausgewählte Schriften.* Ed. Karin Bornkamm and Gerhard Ebeling. 6 vols. Frankfurt: Insel, ²1983.
LDStA	Martin Luther. *Lateinisch-Deutsche Studienausgabe.* Ed. Wilfried Härle et al. 2 vols. Leipzig: Evangelische Verlagsanstalt, 2006.
StA	*Martin Luther: Studienausgabe.* Ed. Hans-Ulrich Delius et al. 6 vols. Leipzig and Berlin: Evangelische Verlagsanstalt, 1979–1999.
WA	Martin Luther. *Werke. Kritische Gesamtausgabe.* Weimar: H. Böhlau, 1883–.
WA.BR	Idem. *Briefwechsel.* Weimar: H. Böhlaus Nachfolger, 1930–.
WA.DB	Deut Idem. *Deutsche Bibel.* Weimar: H. Böhlaus Nachfolger, 1906–1961.
WA.TR	Idem. *Tischreden.* Weimar: H. Böhlaus Nachfolger, 1912–.

Secondary Literature

Althaus 1961:
Paul Althaus. "Die Rechtfertigung allein aus dem Glauben in den Thesen Martin Luthers," *LuJ* 28 (1961): 30–51.
Althaus 1962:
Paul Althaus. *Die Theologie Martin Luthers.* Gütersloh: Mohn, 1962 (⁶1983). English: *The Theology of Martin Luther.* Trans. Robert C. Schultz. Philadelphia: Fortress Press, 1981.
Althaus 1965:

Paul Althaus. *Die Ethik Martin Luthers*. Gütersloh: Mohn, 1965. English: *The Ethics of Martin Luther*. Trans. Robert C. Schultz. Philadelphia: Fortress Press, 1972.

Altmann 1992:
Walter Altmann. *Luther and Liberation. A Latin American Perspective*. Minneapolis: Fortress Press, 1992.

Asendorf 1967:
Ulrich Asendorf. *Eschatologie bei Luther*. Göttingen: Vandenhoeck & Ruprecht, 1967.

Asendorf 1988:
Ulrich Asendorf. *Die Theologie Martin Luthers nach seinen Predigten*. Göttingen: Vandenhoeck & Ruprecht, 1988.

Barth, Hans-Martin 1967a:
Hans-Martin Barth. *Der Teufel und Jesus Christus in der Theologie Martin Luthers*. Göttingen: Vandenhoeck & Ruprecht, 1967.

Barth, Hans-Martin 1967b:
Hans-Martin Barth. "Luthers Predigt von der Predigt," *PT* 56 (1967): 481–89.

Barth, Hans-Martin 1967c:
Hans-Martin Barth. "Zur inneren Entwicklung von Luthers Teufelsglauben," *KD* 13 (1967): 201–11.

Barth, Hans-Martin 1971:
Hans-Martin Barth. *Atheismus und Orthodoxie. Analysen und Modelle christlicher Apologetik im 17. Jahrhundert*. Göttingen: Vandenhoeck & Ruprecht, 1971.

Barth, Hans-Martin 1984:
Hans-Martin Barth. "'Pecca fortiter, sed fortius fide . . .' Martin Luther als Seelsorger," *EvT* 44 (1984): 12–25.

Barth, Hans-Martin 1989a:
Hans-Martin Barth, ed. *Martin Luther, Amen. Das Weitere findet sich. Gelebtes Vaterunser*. Freiburg: Herder, 1989.

Barth, Hans-Martin 1989b:
Hans-Martin Barth. "Wort und Bild. Ein Beitrag zum Gespräch zwischen Orthodoxie und Luthertum," *KD* 35 (1989): 34–53.

Barth, Hans-Martin 1990:
Hans-Martin Barth. *Einander Priester sein. Allgemeines Priestertum in ökumenischer Perspektive*. Göttingen: Vandenhoeck & Ruprecht, 1990.

Barth, Hans-Martin 1992:
Hans-Martin Barth. *Sehnsucht nach den Heiligen? Verborgene Quellen ökumenischer Spiritualität*. Stuttgart: Quell, 1992.

Barth, Hans-Martin 2008a:
Hans-Martin Barth. *Dogmatik. Evangelischer Glaube im Kontext der Weltreligionen*. 3d rev. ed. Gütersloh: Kaiser, 2008.

Barth, Hans-Martin 2008b:
Hans-Martin Barth. "Die Theologie Martin Luthers im globalen Kontext. Lutherforschung auf dem Weg zum Jahr 2017," *Materialdienst des Konfessionskundlichen Instituts Bensheim* 59 (2008): 3–8.

Barth, Hans-Martin 2008c:
Hans-Martin Barth. "Plausibilität statt überholter Metaphysik," 73–88 in Carl-Friedrich Geyer and Detlef Schneider-Stengel, eds., *Denken im offenen Raum. Prolegomena zu einer künftigen postmetaphysischen Theologie*. Darmstadt: Wissenschaftliche Buchgesellschaft, 2008.

Barth, Karl 1946:
Karl Barth. *Christengemeinde und Bürgergemeinde*. TS 20. Zollikon-Zürich: Evangelischer Verlag, 1946.

Barth, Karl KD:
Karl Barth. *Die kirchliche Dogmatik*. Vols. I/1–IV/4. Munich: Kaiser, 1932–1967. English: *Church Dogmatics*. Ed. G. W. Bromiley and T. F. Torrance. Edinburgh: T & T Clark, 1975–.

Bayer 1994:
Oswald Bayer. *Theologie*. HST 1. Gütersloh: Gütersloher Verlagshaus, 1994. English: *Martin Luther's Theology: A Contemporary Interpretation*. Trans. Thomas H. Trapp. Grand Rapids: Eerdmans, 2008.

Bayer 2003:
Oswald Bayer. *Martin Luthers Theologie. Eine Vergegenwärtigung*. Tübingen: Mohr Siebeck, 2003 (^{3}2007).

Beiner 2000:
Melanie Beiner. *Intentionalität und Geschöpflichkeit. Die Bedeutung von Martin Luthers Schrift "Vom unfreien Willen" für die theologische Anthropologie*. Marburg: N. G. Elwert, 2000.

Beintker 1989:
Michael Beintker. "Das Schöpfercredo in Luthers Kleinem Katechismus," *NZSThR* 31 (1989): 1–17.

Beutel 1991a:
Albrecht Beutel. *In dem Anfang war das Wort. Studien zu Luthers Sprachverständnis*. Tübingen: Mohr (Siebeck), 1991.

Beutel 1991b:
Albrecht Beutel. *Martin Luther*. Munich: Beck, 1991.

Beyer 2007:
Michael Beyer. "Theologische Grundlagen für Martin Luthers Sozialengagement," 53–72 in Stefan Oehmig, ed., *Medizin und Sozialwesen in Mitteldeutschland zur Reformationszeit*. Leipzig: Evangelische Verlagsanstalt, 2007.

Blaumeiser 1995:
Hubertus Blaumeiser. *Martin Luthers Kreuzestheologie: Schlüssel zu seiner Deutung von Mensch und Wirklichkeit*. Paderborn: Bonifatius, 1995.

Blöchle 1995:

Herbert Blöchle. *Luthers Stellung zum Heidentum im Spannungsfeld von Tradition, Humanismus und Reformation.* Frankfurt and New York: Peter Lang, 1995.

Bobzin 1995:
Hartmut Bobzin. *Der Koran im Zeitalter der Reformation. Studien zur Frühgeschichte der Arabistik und Islamkunde in Europa.* Beirut: In Kommission bei Franz Steiner Verlag, Stuttgart, 1995.

Bobzin 2004:
Hartmut Bobzin. "'Aber itzt . . . hab ich den Al Coran gesehen Latinisch. . . .' Gedanken Martin Luthers zum Islam," 260–76 in Hans Medick and Peer Schmidt, eds., *Luther zwischen den Kulturen. Zeitgenossenschaft—Weltwirkung.* Göttingen: Vandenhoeck & Ruprecht, 2004.

Bockmühl 1987:
Klaus Bockmühl. *Gesetz und Geist. Eine kritische Würdigung des Erbes protestantischer Ethik. I. Die Ethik der reformatorischen Bekenntnisschriften.* Giessen: Brunnen, 1987.

Bornkamm, Heinrich 1960:
Heinrich Bornkamm. *Luthers geistige Welt.* Gütersloh: Bertelsmann, [4]1960.

Bornkamm, Heinrich 1970:
Heinrich Bornkamm. *Luther im Spiegel der deutschen Geistesgeschichte.* Göttingen: Vandenhoeck & Ruprecht, [2]1970.

Bornkamm, Karin 1998:
Karin Bornkamm. *Christus: König und Priester. Das Amt Christi bei Luther im Verhältnis zur Vor- und Nachgeschichte.* Tübingen: Mohr Siebeck, 1998.

Brecht 1983:
Martin Brecht. *Martin Luther.* Vol. 1: *Sein Weg zur Reformation 1483–1521.* Stuttgart: Calwer, [2]1983. English: *Martin Luther: His Road to Reformation.* Trans. James L. Schaaf. Philadelphia: Fortress Press, 1985.

Brecht 1986:
Martin Brecht. *Martin Luther.* Vol. 2: *Ordnung und Abgrenzung der Reformation 1521–1532.* Stuttgart: Calwer, 1986. English: *Martin Luther: Shaping and Defining the Reformation, 1521–1532.* Trans. James L. Schaaf. Philadelphia: Fortress Press, 1985.

Brecht 1987:
Martin Brecht. *Martin Luther.* Vol. 3: *Die Erhaltung der Kirche 1532–1546.* Stuttgart: Calwer, 1987. English: *Martin Luther: The Preservation of the Church, 1532–1546.* Trans. James L. Schaaf. Philadelphia: Fortress Press, 1985.

Corsani 2001:
Bruno Corsani. *Lutero e la bibbia.* Brescia: Editrice Queriniana, 2001.

Dalferth 1996:
Silfredo Bernardo Dalferth. *Die Zweireichelehre Martin Luthers im Dialog mit der Befreiungstheologie Leonardo Boffs.* Freiburg: Herder, 1996.

Duchrow 1983:

Ulrich Duchrow. *Christenheit und Weltverantwortung. Traditionsgeschichte und systematische Struktur der Zweireichelehre.* Stuttgart: ²1983.

Ebeling 1964:
Gerhard Ebeling. *Luther. Einführung in sein Denken.* Tübingen: Mohr, 1964. English: *Luther: An Introduction to His Thought.* Trans. R. A. Wilson. Philadelphia: Fortress Press, 1970.

Ebeling 1983:
Gerhard Ebeling. *Martin Luthers Weg und Wort.* Frankfurt: Insel, 1989.

Ebeling 1989:
Gerhard Ebeling. *Lutherstudien.* Vol. 2: *Disputatio de homine. Part 3: Die theologische Definition des Menschen. Kommentar zu These 20–40.* Tübingen: Mohr (Siebeck), 1989.

Ehmann 2008:
Johannes Ehmann. *Luther, Türken und Islam. Eine Untersuchung zum Türken- und Islambild Martin Luthers (1515–1546).* Gütersloh: Gütersloher Verlagshaus, 2008.

Ferel 1969:
Martin Ferel. *Gepredigte Taufe. Eine homiletische Untersuchung zur Taufpredigt bei Luther.* Tübingen: Mohr, 1969.

Führer 1984:
Werner Führer. *Das Wort Gottes in Luthers Theologie.* Göttingen: Vandenhoeck & Ruprecht, 1984.

Gänssler 1983:
Hans-Joachim Gänssler. *Evangelium und weltliches Schwert. Hintergrund, Entstehungsgeschichte und Anlass von Luthers Scheidung zweier Reiche oder Regimente.* Wiesbaden: Steiner, 1983.

Glaser/Stahl 1983:
Hermann Glaser and Karl Heinz Stahl, eds. *Luther gestern und heute. Texte zu einer deutschen Gestalt.* Frankfurt: Fischer Taschenbuch Verlag, 1983.

Goertz 1997:
Harald Goertz. *Allgemeines Priestertum und ordiniertes Amt bei Luther.* Marburg: Elwert, 1997.

Gritsch 2006:
Eric W. Gritsch. *The Wit of Martin Luther.* Minneapolis: Fortress Press, 2006.

Grönvik 1968:
Lorenz Grönvik. *Die Taufe in der Theologie Martin Luthers.* Göttingen: Vandenhoeck & Ruprecht, 1968.

Hahn/Mügge 1996:
Udo Hahn and Marlies Mügge, eds. *Martin Luther: Vorbild im Glauben. Die Bedeutung des Reformators im ökumenischen Gespräch.* Neukirchen-Vluyn: Neukirchener Verlag, 1996.

Härle 2004:

Wilfried Härle. "Zweireichelehre II. Systematisch-theologisch," *TRE* 36: 784–89.

Hagemann 1983:
Lugwig Hagemann. *Martin Luther und der Islam.* Altenberge: Verlag für Christlich-Islamisches Schrifttum, 1983.

Hamm 1982:
Berndt Hamm. *Frömmigkeitstheologie am Anfang des 16. Jahrhunderts. Studien zu Johannes von Paltz und seinem Umkreis.* Tübingen: Mohr, 1982.

Hamm 1998:
Berndt Hamm. "Von der Gottesliebe des Mittelalters zum Glauben Luthers. Ein Beitrag zur Bussgeschichte," *LuJ* 65 (1998): 19–52.

Hamm 2004:
Berndt Hamm. "Die 'nahe Gnade'—innovative Züge der spätmittelalterlichen Theologie und Frömmigkeit," 541–47 in Jan A. Aertsen and Martin Pickavé, eds., *"Herbst des Mittelalters?" Fragen zur Bewertung des 14. und 15. Jahrhunderts.* Berlin and New York: de Gruyter, 2004.

Handbuch 2005:
Albrecht Beutel, ed. *Luther Handbuch.* Tübingen: Mohr Siebeck, 2005.

Hauschild 1995:
Wolf-Dieter Hauschild. *Lehrbuch der Kirchen- und Dogmengeschichte.* Vol. 1: *Alte Kirche und Mittelalter.* Gütersloh: Kaiser, 1995.

Hauschild 1999:
Wolf-Dieter Hauschild. *Lehrbuch der Kirchen- und Dogmengeschichte.* Vol. 2: *Reformation und Neuzeit.* Gütersloh: Kaiser, 1999.

Haustein 1990:
Jörg Haustein. *Martin Luthers Stellung zum Zauber- und Hexenwesen.* Stuttgart: Kohlhammer, 1990.

Heckel 1989:
Martin Heckel. "Die Menschenrechte im Spiegel der reformatorischen Theologie," 1122–63 in idem, *Gesammelte Schriften. Staat. Kirche. Recht. Geschichte.* Vol. 2, ed. Klaus Schlaich. Tübingen: Mohr (Siebeck), 1989.

Helmer 1999:
Christine Helmer. *The Trinity and Martin Luther. A Study on the Relationship between Genre, Language and the Trinity in Luther's Works (1523–1546).* Mainz: von Zabern, 1999.

Helmer 2002:
Christine Helmer. "Gott von Ewigkeit zu Ewigkeit. Luthers Trinitätsverständnis," *Neue Zeitschrift für Systematische Theologie und Religionsphilosophie* 44 (2002): 1–19. English: "God from eternity to eternity: Luther's trinitarian understanding," *HTR* 96 (2003): 127–46.

Herms 1987:
Eilert Herms. *Luthers Auslegung des Dritten Artikels.* Tübingen: Mohr, 1987.

Heubach 1989:

Joachim Heubach, ed. *Luther und Barth.* Veröffentlichungen der Luther-Akademie e.V. Ratzeburg 13. Erlangen: Martin-Luther-Verlag, 1989.

Heubach 1990:
Joachim Heubach, ed. *Luther und Theosis.* Veröffentlichungen der Luther-Akademie e.V. Ratzeburg 16. Erlangen: Martin-Luther-Verlag, 1990.

Heubach 1991:
Joachim Heubach, ed. *Luther als Seelsorger.* Veröffentlichungen der Luther-Akademie e.V. Ratzeburg 18. Erlangen: Martin-Luther-Verlag, 1991.

Heubach 1996:
Joachim Heubach, ed. *Der Heilige Geist: Ökumenische und reformatorische Untersuchungen.* Erlangen: Martin-Luther-Verlag, 1996.

Holm 2006:
Bo Kristian Holm. *Gabe und Geben bei Luther. Das Verhältnis zwischen Reziprozität und reformatorischer Rechtfertigungslehre.* Berlin and New York: de Gruyter, 2006.

Iwand 1983:
Hans Joachim Iwand. *Nachgelassene Werke.* Ed. Helmut Gollwitzer, et al. Vol. 5: *Luthers Theologie.* Ed. Johann Haar. Introduction by Karl Gerhard Steck. Munich: Kaiser, 1983.

Joest 1967:
Wilfried Joest. *Ontologie der Person bei Luther.* Göttingen: Vandenhoeck & Ruprecht, 1967.

Jüngel 1981:
Eberhard Jüngel. *Zur Freiheit eines Christenmenschen. Eine Erinnerung an Luthers Schrift.* Munich: Kaiser, ²1981. English: *The Freedom of a Christian: Luther's Significance for Contemporary Theology.* Trans. Roy A. Harrisville. Minneapolis: Augsburg, 1988.

Junghans 1983:
Helmar Junghans, ed. *Leben und Werk Martin Luthers von 1526 bis 1546.* 2 vols. Göttingen: Vandenhoeck & Ruprecht, 1983.

Kaennel 1999:
Lucie Kaennel. *Lutero era antisemita?* Introduction by Daniele Garrone. Turin: Claudiana, 1999.

Kärkkäinen 2005:
Pekka Kärkkäinen. *Luthers trinitarische Theologie des Heiligen Geistes.* Mainz: von Zabern, 2005.

Kasten 1970:
Horst Kasten. *Taufe und Rechtfertigung bei Thomas von Aquin und Martin Luther.* Munich: Kaiser, 1970.

Kastning 2008:
Wieland Kastning. *Morgenröte künftigen Lebens. Untersuchungen zu Martin Luthers Geschichts- und Wirklichkeitsverständnis.* Göttingen: Vandenhoeck & Ruprecht, 2008.

Kaufmann 2005:
Thomas Kaufmann. *Luthers "Judenschriften" in ihren historischen Kontexten.* Nachrichten der Akademie der Wissenschaften zu Göttingen aus dem Jahr 2005. Philologisch-Historische Klasse. Göttingen: Vandenhoeck & Ruprecht, 2005.

Kaufmann 2006:
Thomas Kaufmann. *Martin Luther.* Munich: Beck, 2006.

Korsch 2005:
Dietrich Korsch, ed. *Die Gegenwart Jesu Christi im Abendmahl.* Leipzig: Evangelische Verlagsanstalt, 2005.

Korsch 2007:
Dietrich Korsch. *Martin Luther. Eine Einführung.* Tübingen: Mohr Siebeck, 2d rev. ed. 2007.

Kühn 1980:
Ulrich Kühn. *Kirche.* HST 10. Gütersloh: Mohn, 1980.

Kühn 1985:
Ulrich Kühn. *Sakramente.* HST 11. Gütersloh: Mohn, 1985.

Leiner 2008:
Hans Leiner. *Luthers Theologie für Nichttheologen.* Nüremberg: Nürnberg VTR, 2007.

Leppin 2006:
Volker Leppin. *Martin Luther.* Darmstadt: Primus; Wissenschaftliche Buchgesellschaft, 2006.

Lexutt 2008:
Athina Lexutt. *Luther.* Cologne: Böhlau, 2008.

Lienemann 1995:
Wolfgang Lienemann. *Gerechtigkeit.* Göttingen: Vandenhoeck & Ruprecht, 1995.

Lienhard 1980:
Marc Lienhard. *Martin Luthers christologisches Zeugnis. Entwicklung und Grundzüge seiner Christologie.* Göttingen: Vandenhoeck & Ruprecht, 1980.

Locher 1969:
Gottfried W. Locher. *Huldrych Zwingli in neuer Sicht. Zehn Beiträge zur Theologie der Zürcher Reformation.* Zürich and Stuttgart: Zwingli-Verlag, 1969.

Löfgren 1960:
David Löfgren. *Die Theologie der Schöpfung bei Luther.* Göttingen: Vandenhoeck & Ruprecht, 1960.

Lohse 1981:
Bernhard Lohse. *Martin Luther. Eine Einführung in sein Leben und Werk.* Munich: Beck, 1981. English: *Martin Luther: An Introduction to His Life and Work.* Trans. Robert C. Schultz. Philadelphia: Fortress Press, 1986.

Lohse 1995:

Bernhard Lohse. *Luthers Theologie in ihrer historischen Entwicklung und in ihrem systematischen Zusammenhang.* Göttingen: Vandenhoeck & Ruprecht, 1995. English: *Martin Luther's Theology: Its Historical and Systematic Development.* Trans. and ed. Roy A. Harrisville. Minneapolis: Fortress Press, 1999.

Mantey 2005:
Volker Mantey. *Zwei Schwerter—Zwei Reiche. Martin Luthers Zwei-Reiche-Lehre vor ihrem spätmittelalterlichen Hintergrund.* Tübingen: Mohr Siebeck, 2005.

Markschies 1999:
Christoph Markschies. "Luther und die altkirchliche Trinitätstheologie," 37–85 in idem and Michael Trowitzsch, eds., *Luther: Zwischen den Zeiten.* Tübingen: Mohr Siebeck, 1999.

Maron 1993:
Gottfried Maron. *Die ganze Christenheit auf Erden. Martin Luther und seine ökumenische Bedeutung. Zum 65. Geburtstag des Verfassers.* Ed. Gerhard Müller und Gottfried Seebass. Göttingen: Vandenhoeck & Ruprecht, 1993.

Mau 2000:
Rudolf Mau. *Evangelische Bewegung und frühe Reformation 1521–1532.* Kirchengeschichte in Einzeldarstellungen II/5. Ed. Ulrich Gaebler, Gert Haendler, and Joachim Rogge. Leipzig: Evangelische Verlagsanstalt, 2000.

Maurer 1970:
Wilhelm Maurer. *Luthers Lehre von den drei Hierarchien und ihr mittelalterlicher Hintergrund.* Munich: Bayerische Akademie der Wissenschaften in Kommission bei C. H. Beck, 1970.

Maurer 1976, 1978:
Wilhelm Maurer. *Historischer Kommentar zur Confessio Augustana.* Vol. 1: *Einleitung und Ordnungsfragen.* Vol. 2: *Theologische Probleme.* Gütersloh: Mohn, 1976. 1978. English: *Historical Commentary on the Augsburg Confession.* Trans. H. George Anderson. Philadelphia: Fortress Press, 1986.

Medick/Schmidt 2004:
Hans Medick and Peer Schmidt, eds., *Luther zwischen den Kulturen. Zeitgenossenschaft—Weltwirkung.* Göttingen: Vandenhoeck & Ruprecht, 2004.

Meurer 1996:
Siegfried Meurer, ed. *"Was Christum treibet." Martin Luther und seine Bibelübersetzung.* Stuttgart: Deutsche Bibelgesellschaft, 1996.

Mikoteit 2004:
Matthias Mikoteit. *Theologie und Gebet bei Luther: Untersuchungen zur Psalmenvorlesung 1532–1535.* Berlin: de Gruyter, 2004.

Mostert 1998:
Walter Mostert. *Glaube und Hermeneutik. Gesammelte Aufsätze.* Ed. Pierre Bühler und Gerhard Ebeling, with Jan Bauke, et al. Tübingen: Mohr Siebeck, 1998.

Müller, Gerhard 1989:

Gerhard Müller, "Luthers Zwei-Reiche-Lehre in der deutschen Reformation," 417–37 in idem, *Causa Reformationis. Beiträge zur Reformationsgeschichte und zur Theologie Martin Luthers. Zum 60. Geburtstag des Autors.* Ed. Gottfried Maron and Gottfried Seebass. Gütersloh: Mohn, 1989.

Müller, Gerhard 2001:
Gerhard Müller, "Martin Luther über Kapital und Arbeit," in Reinhold Mokrosch and Helmut Merkel, eds., *Humanismus und Reformation. Historische, theologische und pädagogische Beiträge zu deren Wechselwirkung.* Münster: Lit, 2001.

Müller, Gerhard 2004:
Gerhard Müller, "Martin Luthers Theologie der Trinität heute," 538–56 in Friederike Schönemann and Thorsten Maassen, eds., *Prüft alles, und das Gute behaltet! Zum Wechselspiel von Kirchen, Religionen und säkularer Welt. Festschrift für Hans-Martin Barth zum 65. Geburtstag.* Frankfurt: Lembeck, 2004.

Neebe 1997:
Gudrun Neebe. *Apostolische Kirche. Grundunterscheidungen an Luthers Kirchenbegriff unter besonderer Berücksichtigung seiner Lehre von den notae ecclesiae.* Berlin and New York: de Gruyter, 1997.

Nicol 1984:
Martin Nicol. *Meditation bei Luther.* Göttingen: Vandenhoeck & Ruprecht, 1984.

Oberman 1981a:
Heiko A. Oberman. *Luther. Mensch zwischen Gott und Teufel.* Berlin: Severin und Siedler, 1981. English: *Luther: Man between God and the Devil.* Trans. Eileen Walliser-Schwarzbart. New Haven and London: Yale University Press, 1989.

Oberman 1981b:
Heiko A. Oberman. *Wurzeln des Antisemitismus. Christenangst und Judenplage im Zeitalter von Humanismus und Reformation.* Berlin: Severin und Siedler, 1981. English: *The Roots of Anti-Semitism in the Age of Renaissance and Reformation.* Trans. James I. Porter. Philadelphia: Fortress Press, 1984.

Pawlas 2000:
Andreas Pawlas. *Die lutherische Berufs- und Wirtschaftsethik. Eine Einführung.* Neukirchen-Vluyn: Neukirchener Verlag, 2000.

Pesch 1996:
Otto Hermann Pesch, "Was hat Luther den Katholiken (noch) zu sagen?—Eine Art Nachruf," 122–44 in Udo Hahn and Martin Mügge, eds., *Was bedeutet mir Martin Luther? Prominente aus Politik, Kirche und Gesellschaft antworten.* Neukirchen-Vluyn: Neukirchener Verlag, 1996.

Pesch 1994:
Otto Hermann Pesch. *Martin Luther, Thomas von Aquin und die reformatorische Kritik an der Scholastik. Zur Geschichte und Wirkungsgeschichte eines*

Missverständnisses mit weltgeschichtlichen Folgen. Göttingen: Vandenhoeck & Ruprecht, 1994.

Pesch 1982:
Otto Hermann Pesch. *Hinführung zu Luther.* Mainz: Matthias-Grünewald, 1982.

Peters 1981:
Albrecht Peters. *Gesetz und Evangelium.* HST 2. Gütersloh: Mohn, 1981.

Peters 1984:
Albrecht Peters. *Rechtfertigung.* HST 12. Gütersloh: Mohn, 1984.

Peters 1990:
Albrecht Peters. *Kommentar zu Luthers Katechismen.* Vol. 1: *Die Zehn Gebote. Luthers Vorreden.* Ed. Gottfried Seebass. Göttingen: Vandenhoeck & Ruprecht, 1990.

Peters 1991:
Albrecht Peters. *Kommentar zu Luthers Katechismen.* Vol. 2: *Der Glaube— Das Apostolikum.* Ed. Gottfried Seebass. Göttingen: Vandenhoeck & Ruprecht, 1991.

Peters 1992:
Albrecht Peters. *Kommentar zu Luthers Katechismen.* Vol. 3: *Das Vaterunser.* Ed. Gottfried Seebass. Göttingen: Vandenhoeck & Ruprecht, 1992.

Peters 1993:
Albrecht Peters. *Kommentar zu Luthers Katechismen.* Vol. 4: *Die Taufe. Das Abendmahl.* Ed. Gottfried Seebass. Göttingen: Vandenhoeck & Ruprecht, 1993.

Peters 1994:
Albrecht Peters. *Kommentar zu Luthers Katechismen.* Vol. 5: *Die Beichte. Die Haustafel. Das Traubüchlein. Das Taufbüchlein.* With contributions from Frieder Schulz and Rudolf Keller. Ed. Gottfried Seebass. Göttingen: Vandenhoeck & Ruprecht, 1994.

Prien 1992:
Hans-Jürgen Prien. *Luthers Wirtschaftsethik.* Göttingen: Vandenhoeck & Ruprecht, 1992.

Pinomaa 1977:
Lennart Pinomaa. *Die Heiligen bei Luther.* Schriften der Luther-Agricola-Gesellschaft A 16. Helsinki: s.n., 1977.

Reinhuber 2000:
Thomas Reinhuber. *Kämpfender Glaube. Studien zu Luthers Bekenntnis am Ende von De servo arbitrio.* Berlin and New York: de Gruyter, 2000.

Rieger 2007:
Reinhold Rieger. *Von der Freiheit eines Christenmenschen = De libertate christiana.* Tübingen: Mohr Siebeck, 2007.

Rieske-Braun 1999:
Uwe Rieske-Braun. *Duellum mirabile. Studien zum Kampfmotiv in Martin Luthers Theologie.* Göttingen: Vandenhoeck & Ruprecht, 1999.

Rolf 2008:
Sibylle Rolf. *Zum Herzen sprechen. Eine Studie zum imputativen Aspekt in Martin Luthers Rechtfertigungslehre und zu seinen Konsequenzen für die Predigt des Evangeliums.* Leipzig: Evangelische Verlagsanstalt, 2008.

Rothen 1990:
Bernhard Rothen. *Die Klarheit der Schrift 1: Martin Luther: Die wiederentdeckten Grundlagen.* Göttingen: Vandenhoeck & Ruprecht, 1990.

Scharffenorth 1982:
Gerta Scharffenorth. *Den Glauben ins Leben ziehen . . . . Studien zu Luthers Theologie.* Munich: Kaiser, 1982.

Schneider-Ludorff 2006:
Gury Schneider-Ludorff. *Der fürstliche Reformator: theologische Aspekte im Wirken Philipps von Hessen von der Homberger Synode bis zum Interim.* Leipzig: Evangelische Verlagsanstalt, 2006.

Schönemann/Maassen 2004:
Friederike Schönemann and Thorsten Maassen, eds., *Prüft alles, und das Gute behaltet! Zum Wechselspiel von Kirchen, Religionen und säkularer Welt. Festschrift für Hans-Martin Barth zum 65. Geburtstag.* Frankfurt: Lembeck, 2004.

Schulken 2006:
Christian Schulken. *Lex efficax. Studien zur Sprachwerdung des Gesetzes bei Luther im Anschluss an die Disputationen gegen die Antinomer.* Tübingen: Mohr Siebeck, 2006.

Schulz 1978:
Frieder Schulz, ed. *Heute mit Luther beten. Eine Sammlung von Luthergebeten für die Gegenwart.* Gütersloh: Mohn, 1978.

Schwambach 2004:
Claus Schwambach. *Rechtfertigungsgeschehen und Befreiungsprozess. Die Eschatologie von Martin Luther und Leonardo Boff im kritischen Gespräch.* Göttingen: Vandenhoeck & Ruprecht, 2004.

Schwanke 2004:
Johannes Schwanke. *Creatio ex nihilo. Luthers Lehre von der Schöpfung aus dem Nichts in der Grossen Genesisvorlesung (1535–1545).* Berlin and New York: de Gruyter, 2004.

Schwarz 1998:
Reinhard Schwarz. *Luther. Studienausgabe.* Göttingen: Vandenhoeck & Ruprecht, [2]1998.

Schwarz 2005:
Reinhard Schwarz, "Die Selbstvergegenwärtigung Christi. Der Hintergrund von Luthers Abendmahlsverständnis," 19–50 in Dietrich Korsch, ed., *Die Gegenwart Jesu Christi im Abendmahl.* Leipzig: Evangelische Verlagsanstalt, 2005.

Schwarzwäller 1970:

Klaus Schwarzwäller. *Theologia crucis. Luthers Lehre von Prädestination nach De servo arbitrio, 1525*. Munich: Kaiser, 1970.

Simon 2003:
Wolfgang Simon. *Die Messopfertheologie Martin Luthers: Voraussetzungen, Genese, Gestalt und Rezeption*. Tübingen: Mohr Siebeck, 2003.

Slenczka 2005:
Notger Slenczka, "Neubestimmte Wirklichkeit. Zum systematischen Zentrum der Lehre Luthers von der Gegenwart Christi unter Brot und Wein," 79–98 in Dietrich Korsch, ed., *Die Gegenwart Jesu Christi im Abendmahl*. Leipzig: Evangelische Verlagsanstalt, 2005.

Slomp 2004:
Jan Slomp, "Christianity and Lutheranism from the Perspective of Modern Islam," 227–45 in Medick/Schmidt (2004).

Stephens 1997:
W. Peter Stephens and Karin Gredull Gerschwiler. *Zwingli: Einführung in sein Denken*. Zürich: Theologischer Verlag, 1997. English original: W. Peter Stephens. *Zwingli: An Introduction to His Thought*. Oxford and New York: Oxford University Press, 1992.

Stolt 2000:
Birgit Stolt. *Martin Luthers Rhetorik des Herzens*. Tübingen: Mohr Siebeck, 2000.

Streiff 1993:
Stefan Streiff. *"Novis linguis loqui." Martin Luthers Disputation über Joh 1,14 "verbum caro factum est" aus dem Jahr 1539*. Göttingen: Vandenhoeck & Ruprecht, 1993.

Suda 2006:
Max Josef Suda. *Die Ethik Martin Luthers*. Göttingen: Vandenhoeck & Ruprecht, 2006.

***Unser Glaube*:**
Unser Glaube: Die Bekenntnisschriften der evangelisch-lutherischen Kirche. Ausgabe für die Gemeinde. Im Auftrag der Kirchenleitung der Vereinigten Evangelisch-Lutherischen Kirche Deutschlands (VELKD). Ed. Lutherischen Kirchenamt, by Horst Georg Pöhlmann. Gütersloh: Mohn, 1986.

von der Osten-Sacken 2002:
Peter von der Osten-Sacken. *Martin Luther und die Juden: neu untersucht anhand von Anton Margarithas "Der gantz Jüdisch glaub" (1530/31)*. Stuttgart: Kohlhammer, 2002.

von Loewenich 1963:
Walther von Loewenich. *Luther und der Neuprotestantismus*. Witten: Luther-Verlag, 1963.

von Loewenich 1982:
Walther von Loewenich. *Martin Luther. Der Mann und das Werk*. Munich: List, 1982.

von Soosten 2005:
Joachim von Soosten, "Präsenz und Präsentation, Die Marburger Unterscheidung," 99–122 in Dietrich Korsch, ed., *Die Gegenwart Jesu Christi im Abendmahl*. Leipzig: Evangelische Verlagsanstalt, 2005.

Weier 1967:
Reinhold Weier. *Das Thema vom verborgenen Gott von Nikolaus von Kues zu Martin Luther*. Münster: Aschendorff, 1967.

Wehr 1999:
Martin Luther—Der Mystiker. Ausgewählte Texte. Ed. Gerhard Wehr. Munich: Kösel, 1999.

Wertelius 1970:
Gunnar Wertelius. *Oratio continua. Das Verhältnis zwischen Glaube und Gebet in der Theologie Martin Luthers.* Lund: Gleerup, 1970.

Wiemer 2003:
Axel Wiemer. *"Mein Trost, Kampf und Sieg ist Christus." Martin Luthers eschatologische Theologie nach seinen Reihenpredigten über 1. Kor 15 (1532/33).* Berlin and New York: de Gruyter, 2003.

Wisselinck 1991:
Erika Wisselinck, "Hexen," 190–94 in Elisabeth Gössmann, et al., eds., *Wörterbuch der Feministischen Theologie*. Gütersloh: Mohn, 1991.

Wolff 2005:
Jens Wolff. *Metapher und Kreuz. Studien zu Luthers Christusbild.* Tübingen: Mohr Siebeck, 2005.

Zahrnt 1952:
Heinz Zahrnt. *Luther deutet Geschichte. Erfolg und Misserfolg im Licht des Evangeliums. Mit einem Geleitwort von Landesbischof D. Dr. Hanns Lilje.* Munich: P. Müller, 1952.

zur Mühlen 1972:
Karl-Heinz zur Mühlen. *Nos extra nos. Luthers Theologie zwischen Mystik und Scholastik.* Tübingen: Mohr, 1972.

zur Mühlen 1995:
Karl-Heinz zur Mühlen. *Reformatorisches Profil. Studien zum Weg Martin Luthers und der Reformation.* Ed. Johannes Brosseder und Athina Lexutt, with Wibke Janssen, Volkmar Ortmann, and Jochen Remy. Göttingen: Vandenhoeck & Ruprecht, 1995.

Indexes

515

New Testament

Index of Names

Index of Subjects